Law of International Trade in the Region of the Caucasus, Central Asia and Russia

Nijhoff International
Trade Law Series

VOLUME 20

The titles published in this series are listed at *brill.com/nint*

Law of International Trade in the Region of the Caucasus, Central Asia and Russia

Public International Law, Private Law, Dispute Settlement

Edited by

Alexander Trunk, Marina Trunk-Fedorova, and Azar Aliyev

BRILL
NIJHOFF

LEIDEN | BOSTON

Library of Congress Cataloging-in-Publication Data

Names: Trunk, Alexander, editor. | Trunk-Fedorova, M. P. (Marina Pavlovna), editor. | Aliyev, A. (Azar), editor.
Title: Law of international trade in the region of the Caucasus, Central Asia and Russia : public international law, private law, dispute settlement / edited by Alexander Trunk, Marina Trunk-Fedorova, and Azar Aliyev.
Description: Leiden ; Boston : Brill Nijhoff, [2023] | Series: Nijhoff international trade law series, 1877-7392 ; volume 20 | Includes bibliographical references and index. | Summary: "The region of the Caucasus and Central Asia is politically, economically and legally very diverse. However, the common legacy of the Soviet Union (and even the Russian Empire) is still present, with a considerable influence even on today's societies and legal regulation. Russian legal approaches to topics such as international trade, continue to influence or at least serve as a major model of reference in the legal systems of all countries of the region - even if political relations with Russia are strained"– Provided by publisher.
Identifiers: LCCN 2022034434 (print) | LCCN 2022034435 (ebook) | ISBN 9789004357822 (hardback) | ISBN 9789004357839 (ebook)
Subjects: LCSH: Foreign trade regulation–Asia, Central | Foreign trade regulation–Caucasus
Classification: LCC KL9842 .L39 2023 (print) | LCC KL9842 (ebook) | DDC 343.508/7–dc23/eng/20220924
LC record available at https://lccn.loc.gov/2022034434
LC ebook record available at https://lccn.loc.gov/2022034435

Typeface for the Latin, Greek, and Cyrillic scripts: "Brill". See and download: brill.com/brill-typeface.

ISSN 1877-7392
ISBN 978-90-04-35782-2 (hardback)
ISBN 978-90-04-35783-9 (e-book)

Contents

Notes on Contributors

Azar Aliyev
Dr. jur., LL.M. (Heidelberg), associate professor, University of Halle-Wittenberg

Elena Babkina
Dr. jur., professor, Belarus State University

Ekaterina Dmitrikova
Dr. jur., associate professor, St. Petersburg State University

Cyril R. Emery
Legal officer, UNCITRAL Secretariat

Eric Evtimov
Dr. jur., LL.M. Eur., Deputy Secretary General, International Rail Transport Committee (CIT), lecturer, Institute of European and International Economic Law, University of Bern

Michael Geistlinger
Dr. jur., professor, Salzburg University

Thomas Jürgensen
Dr.jur., senior counsellor, European Commission, DG Trade

Zhenis Kembayev†
Dr. jur, professor, KIMEP University (Almaty)

Vitaly Kim
Dr. jur., LL.M. (Univ. Potsdam), German Foreign Chamber of Commerce in Central Asia, Almaty

Irina Kireeva
NCTM O'Connor, Brussels

Andrey Kotelnikov
Dr. jur., LL.M. (Manchester), lecturer, Robert Gordon University, Aberdeen

Nicolas Lamp
Dr.jur., LL.M. (LSE), associate professor, Queen's University

Timothy Lemay
Principal Legal Officer and Head of the Legislative Branch, UNCITRAL Secretariat

Karsten Nowrot
Dr. jur., LL.M. (Indiana), professor, Hamburg University

Tetyana Payosova
Dr. jur., LL.M. (Bern), senior associate, Van Bael & Bellis

Ilia Rachkov
Dr. jur., LL.M. (Frankfurt), associate professor, Moscow State Institute of International Relations

Dagmar Richter
Dr. jur., professor, Heidelberg University

Philipp-Christian Scheel
CMS Hasche Sigle, Brussels

Vladislav Starzhenetsky
Dr. jur., associate professor, Higher School of Economics, Moscow

Peter-Tobias Stoll
Dr. jur., professor, University of Göttingen

Alexander Trunk
Dr. jur., professor, Director of the Institute of East European Law, Kiel University

Marina Trunk-Fedorova
Dr. jur., LL.M. (Connecticut), IELPO LL.M., associate professor, St. Petersburg State University, senior research fellow, Kiel University

Larysa Workewych
Dr. jur., research fellow, Institute of International Law, Wuhan University

Jia Xu
Dr. jur., research fellow, Institute of International Law, Wuhan University

Andreas R. Ziegler
Dr. jur., professor, Lausanne University

Introduction

Alexander Trunk, Marina Trunk-Fedorova, and Azar Aliyev

More than thirty years – a generation's time – have now passed since the self-caused dissolution of the Soviet Union in December 1991. The 12 "New Independent States",[1] which have emerged on the territory of the former USSR, have in the meantime established themselves as active players on the political scene and also in the economic and legal spheres. Starting with (new or derived) membership in the United Nations all post-Soviet countries have developed and are still developing their legislation and have concluded various international treaties. Concerning their international economic relations, most countries of the region have entered the World Trade Organization (WTO) or have concluded bilateral or regional agreements – among themselves or with outside partners such as the European Union. They have also set-up judicial systems with a continuously growing body of jurisprudence.

Nevertheless, the image of the countries of the post-Soviet region is still, at least from outside, rather vague and imbalanced. The largest attention is usually given Russia as the largest and most powerful successor state of the USSR.[2] Other countries are less known. . However, all countries in the region have their own specific economic strengths or are strategically important. It is not surprising that already in the 1990s, the European Union has concluded Partnership and Cooperation Agreements with nearly all post-Soviet countries, some of which have recently been upgraded to "Association Agreements" (with Georgia, Moldova and Ukraine) or "Comprehensive and Enhanced Partnership Agreements" (with Armenia and Kazakhstan). At the same time, various structures of cooperation between countries of the region have been established, starting with the Commonwealth of Independent States (CIS) and culminating, for the time being, in the Eurasian Economic Union (EAEU). These regional networks have their own political, economic and legal relevance – also for relations with outside countries. In any case, a solid knowledge

---

1   Armenia, Azerbaijan, Belarus, Georgia, Kazakhstan, Kyrgyzstan, Moldova, Russia, Tajikistan, Turkmenistan, Ukraine, and Uzbekistan. One might add the three Baltic States, which have however a particular self-understanding of historic continuity across the USSR period and are commonly not counted as successor States of the USSR.

2   The term "successor state" is used here in a broad, untechnical sense (not in the sense of legal successorship, which is controversial in all post-Soviet states).

© KONINKLIJKE BRILL NV, LEIDEN, 2023 | DOI:10.1163/9789004357839_002

and understanding of the developments in these countries is indispensable for any cooperation with States in this region.

The following collective monograph addresses a broad range of issues of international and comparative economic law relating to the post-Soviet region. The study is the result of a several-years research project, which was carried out between 2010 and 2015 by the Institute of East European Law of Kiel University in cooperation with the Academy of Public Administration under the President of the Republic of Azerbaijan, the Al'Farabi National University in Almaty, and the Ural State Law University in Ekaterinburg (main partners) and was financed by the VolkswagenStiftung (Germany).[3]

The regional focus of the study is on two subregions of the post-Soviet space: Caucasus and Central Asia. In addition, any study of these subregions (and the post-Soviet region in general) has to take into account Russia, as Russian law continues to serve at least as a tool of comparison in the region, sometimes even as a legislative model. Also Russia is the key partner of nearly all regional cooperation structures within the post-Soviet region, and remains relevant even for the study of countries, which are or were in political or even armedconflict with Russia such as at present Ukraine[4] and (still, though to a varying degree) Georgia. Thematically, the study addresses international law in the broad sense: public international law and (comparative) private law, with a particular part on (international and national) dispute resolution. Dimensions of public international law and private law are mutually complementary elements of both of economic foreign relations and domestic economic development, and must be seen in conjunction with each other. This is particularly visible in the field of dispute resolution, which is grounded on a mix of international and national regulations and practices and may offer parties a choice to use dispute resolution under public international law or under national instruments including ADR.

Most of the contributions for this book are based on oral presentations of the authors in the above-mentioned research project and were brought to a publication format after the finalization of the project. They have been updated as far as possible for the current publication, at least in the footnotes and, if it seemed necessary, also in the text. The final editorial deadline for this study was in November 2021.

Some of the chapters of this book relate to political developments which may be evaluated differently, and it should be mentioned that the editors did

---

3   Project "Law of International Trade in the Region of the Caucasus and Central Asia with Particular Regard to Azerbaijan, Kazakhstan and Russia".

4   Ukraine is, however, not in the regional focus of this study, neither are Belarus and Moldova.

not impose any particular view or terminology in this respect, which have been left to the authors' choice. For the purposes of the book, commonly used terminology has been used for the sake of convenience. For example, the book uses the traditional denomination of Kiev instead of the term Kyiv, all the more as the geographic focus of this book (Caucasus and Central Asia) does not include Ukraine. This is not to be understood as taking sides in disputes about language.

The *first part* of the study is devoted to *aspects of public international law* relating to economic matters. At first, several contributions deal with questions arising from the membership of countries of the region in the WTO. The second subpart deals with legal issues of regional cooperation in the post-Soviet space, including the topical issue of mutual economic sanctions between the EU and Russia due to the Ukraine conflict (before the escalation in 2022). A third subpart thematizes several other issues of international economic law relevant to the region, such as antidumping measures, customs, sanitary and technical regulation, and environmental governance

The *first subpart* of the book begins with a general analysis of regional economic integration processes in the Eurasian region both among the countries of the region and with third partners, including the topical issue of economic sanctions from the perspective of institutional and substantive law.[5]

Zhenis Kembayev[6] makes the start with a description and analysis of the legal structures of the *Eurasian Economic Union* (EAEU), which came into existence on 1 January 2015, stepping into the place of the Eurasian Economic Community (EurAsEC) created in 2000. As of today, members of the EAEU are – in alphabetical order – Armenia, Belarus, Kazakhstan, Kyrgyzstan, and Russia. Among the countries situated in the region of Caucasus and Central Asia, Azerbaijan, Georgia, Tajikistan, Turkmenistan, and Uzbekistan are not members of the EAEU, though most of them continue being members of the Commonwealth of Independent States (CIS) created in December 1991 in the context of the dissolution of the USSR. The author describes the objectives, institutional structures and competences of the EAEU, marking, among others, the lack of references in the EAEU Treaty to democracy, human rights and rule of law, the missing of a parliamentary body and the relatively limited competences of the EAEU court.[7] The author devotes particular attention to the instruments and policies of Eurasian integration (which include, e.g. "decisions" of

---

5   The procedural dimension of sanctions is dealt with in Part 3 of this book, see the contribution of Andrey Kotelnikov, 492 et seq.

6   Unfortunately, Professor Kembayev passed away prematurely in 2019.

7   A more detailed description of the Court is given by Elena Babkina (in this book), 336 et seq.

EAEU organs) as well as to the external competences of the EAEU, which has concluded, for example, a Free Trade Agreement with Vietnam.

The contribution by *Michael Geistlinger* is devoted to the legal evaluation of *trade agreements between countries of the Central Asian and Caucasus region and the European Union.* The article contains a critical analysis of the development of EU bilateral cooperation with individual countries of the region. The author conducts a thorough analysis of numerous trade agreements concluded by the European Union throughout the time after the dissolution of the Soviet Union, from partnership and cooperation agreements (PCAs) to Association Agreements with chapters on Deep and Comprehensive Free Trade Areas (DCFTAS).

The following contribution by *Karsten Nowrot* focuses, from a general trade law perspective, on the *relationship between different regional economic integration agreements.* Taking examples both from the post-Soviet region (including relations with the European Union) and other parts of the world, the author observes that there is a large practice of competing regional trade agreements between different countries. While such treaties are usually made compatible by rules of origin (in case of "basic", low level trade agreements), the situation gets significantly more complicated if a customs union or similar high level trade agreements concludes regional trade agreements with different partner countries, or – even more so – if only some member countries of a customs union conclude such treaties. Nevertheless, there exists a practice of such treaties even in such cases, e.g. with regard to the customs union between the EU and some "micro-states" such as Liechtenstein or Andorra, but also with regard to the customs union between the European Union and Turkey. Nowrot shows that – in contrast to some statements even on the high political level – there are some possible approaches on how to minimize incompatibilities between the rules of the customs union and regional trade agreements with third countries (e.g. a pactum de negotiando). This finding is extremely important as it could open the way to overcome political and economic tensions arising from a perceived necessary choice for countries such as Ukraine between two trading blocs such as the European Union and the Eurasian Economic Union.

Two contributions address the issue of *economic sanctions* relating to the Eurasian region.[8] First, *Vitaly Kim* gives an overview of the history and legal bases of economic sanctions under public international law in general including their compatibility with WTO law. The author then describes how the

---

8   See also the contribution of Andrey Kotelnikov (in this book), 492 eet seq.

economic sanctions passed by Western countries (including the European Union) against Russia and vice-versa in the context of the Ukrainian crisis affect other member states of the Eurasian Economic Union besides Russia. Thereafter he analyses in detail the provisions of the Treaty on the Eurasian Economic Union (EAEU) relating to such sanctions and counter-sanctions. In contrast with the European Union, the EAEU Treaty does not provide for a competence of the EAEU to pass economic sanctions against third countries, but it contains a security valve for sanctions or counter-sanctions passed by EAEU member states similar to the WTO model. *Philipp Scheel* turns to economic sanctions ("restrictive measures") passed by the European Union with particular regard to the possibilities of challenges of such sanctions in the Court of Justice of the European Union (CJEU). Based on provisions both in the Treaty on the European Union (Common Foreign and Security Policy, CFSP) and in the Treaty on the Functioning of the European Union (in particular Art.215 TFEU), EU sanctions regulations distinguish, roughly speaking, between sanctions against particular persons or entities and sanctions directed at particular economic sectors or goods and services. Legal protection in the CJEU is available by way of direct challenge of the sanctions directed against specific persons or entities, but not against sanctions directed at particular economic sectors or goods passed under the CSFP.

The *second subpart* of the book comprises two contributions dealing with more general aspects of international treaties (including WTO law) relating to the Caucasus and Central Asian region.

Zhenis Kembayev contributes a general analysis of the status, conclusion, and effects of international treaties from the perspective of the law of Kazakhstan, in particular according to the Constitution of Kazahkstan and the Law "On International Treaties of the Republic of Kazakhstan" (2005). The author also addresses the interpretation of this Law by the Constitutional Council of Kazakhstan, which approved ratification of the EAEU Treaty, but stated various caveats limiting any "supranational" effects of the EAEU Treaty or other EAEU law by the priority of Kazakhstan's Constitution.

The contribution by *Marina Trunk-Fedorova* is devoted to the question of whether *WTO norms* have direct effect *in the Russian legal system*, i.e. whether it is possible to refer to WTO norms in Russian domestic courts. The analysis of recent jurisprudence shows that there is no uniform approach as to the effect of WTO norms in the Russia. Courts generally affirm that WTO norms are part of the Russian legal system, but this does not automatically mean that WTO norms have a direct effect in Russia and can be relied upon in litigation before Russian courts. However, when issues within areas of competences of the Eurasian Economic Union, in which Russia's WTO obligations have become obligations of the EAEU, were analyzed by Russian national courts, WTO norms have been directly applied by national courts.

The third subpart of the book brings together several specific aspects of international trade: customs, SPS/TBT, environment, trade in energy, international transport.

To start with, *Ekaterina Dmitrikova* gives an analytical introduction into the Customs Code of the EAEU, which was passed in the form of an international treaty in 2017. The EAEU Customs Code is by now the most important uniform legislative text of "secondary" EAEU Law and is accompanied by numerous normative decisions of EAEU organs. The author also analyzes the jurisprudence of Russian courts, which apply the EAEU Customs Code directly and also give due deference to the decisions both of the EAEU Court and the (former) Court of the Eurasian Economic Community (EurAsEC).

Another highly important topic, primarily for public health and security, are legal requirements for *food safety, other health-related circumstances, and technical requirements* of different kinds. These matters are also dealt-with under a trade perspective by WTO law as well as regional agreements in the Eurasian context. *Irina Kireeva* gives a thorough analysis both of the relevant WTO agreements on these issues (SPS and TBT Agreements) and, on a comparative basis, of applicable legislation in Azerbaijan, Kazakhstan, and Russia. The author identifies various circumstances where application of this legislation encounters difficulties in these countries, involving international trade as well.

Andreas Ziegler deals with the *relationship between trade regulation and protection of the environment* by combining a general analysis with the specific issue of *trade in hazardous waste.*[9] He observes a very fragmented state of regulation on the international level, ranging from exceptions in the general WTO framework,[10] which apply also to environmental protection, to specific Environmental Agreements such as the Basel Convention on the Control of Transboundary Movements of Hazardous Wastes and Their Disposal, which has been ratified, among others, by Azerbaijan, Kazakhstan, and Russia (as well as by the European Union, but not the United States). Apart from cases of clearly illegal disposal of such waste, the author identifies various problems and conflicts concerning the application of the respective treaties, such as issues of incompatibility and regulatory loopholes.

Azar Aliyev touches upon *regulation of international trade in energy resources* and analyzes challenges to post-Soviet energy resources exporters

---

9   A further contribution on the linkage between trade law and environmental law (by Karsten Nowrot) is contained in Part 3 of this book, 353 et seq.

10   The author also draws attention to the parallel discussion in international investment law.

at the example of Azerbaijan, Kazakhstan, and Russia. All three countries are important energy exporters and therefore competitors on the regional and global energy markets. At the same time, they cooperate in the energy sector in the framework of global and regional organizations, such as the WTO, the Energy Charter Treaty, the Commonwealth of Independent States, the Eurasian Economic Union, as well as Cooperation Agreements with the European Union. These countries have concluded numerous oil and gas production sharing agreements with foreign investors containing international obligations of the states. In fact, trade in energy in the region is governed by very specific and fragmentary regulations, which hide substantive risks for the energy trade. The author structures the sources applicable to energy trade and identifies conflicts and specific risks. Special focus is made on possible conflicts between the attempt to create a single energy market in the framework of the Eurasian Economic Union and the energy trade regime provided in the European Union–Kazakhstan Enhanced Partnership and Cooperation Agreement.

International trade basically consists of two prongs: sales and transport. The next contribution in this part addresses issues of *international transport law*. *Erik Evtimov* and *Tetyana Payosova* blend in their chapter aspects of *public international law (international economic law) and private law (contract law)*. At first they determine the position of transport law in the framework of the WTO, in particular by way of the Trade Facilitation Agreement of 2013. From there they turn to the more particular issue of rail transport, which plays a central role in political projects such as the Chinese-inspired Belt and Road Initiative, economic integration in the Eurasian Economic Union or global projects such as the Transport Networks and Corridors put forward, in particular, by UNCTAD and UNESCAP. With regard to railroad transport there exist in the Eurasian space presently two competing international organizations, the International Organisation for International Carriage by Rail (OTIF) (Western and parts of Eastern Europe) and the Agreement on International Goods Transport by Rail (SMGS) (Asia and parts of Eastern Europe). Some countries are members of both organizations. Both organizations have developed uniform rules of (public and private) transport law. The article focuses on legal techniques to bridge differences in the transport regulations of both organizations, such as the common consignment note CIM/SMGS and the development of electronic versions of the respective consignment notes. Particular attention is also given to the transport of postal items from China to Europe through the Central Asia-Caucasus region.

The *second part* of the book addresses issues of *private (commercial) law in the region*. It mainly addresses comparative and international sales law as sales contracts are the basic type of contract in the economy and may be seen as a model for future regulation of other contracts. However, there is also a contribution (in the first part of the book) on international transport law bridging the gap between public and private law.[11] Some further oral presentations in the project on topics of private law did not lead to written contributions.

The contributions on sales law start with a short *comparative overview* by *Alexander Trunk*. The large majority of legal systems in the Caucasus-Central Asia region follow, though with variations, the Model Civil Code of the Commonwealth of Independent States (CIS), which contains very detailed provisions on the sales contract in general and numerous subcategories of sales. Georgia and, following the Georgian example, Turkmenistan have in their Civil Codes much shorter provisions on sales, which are inspired mainly by German law. Azerbaijan takes a position in between, having shortened-down the sales provisions of its CIS based Civil Code in direction of the German model. The contribution then addresses a number of specific provisions in sales law where some countries (or groups of countries) show peculiarities. The contribution also accentuates that the Soviet tradition still has an important influence on interpretation of the sales laws in the region, and that Russian law continues to have an interpretative impact as well. The on-going reform processes of civil law in the region have – with the exception of Azerbaijan – not yet touched sales law in a significant manner.

The second contribution in this part, also by *Alexander Trunk*, compares the provisions on *international sales law* in the countries of the region. Focusing on conflict of laws, the contribution analyses both international treaties and national legislation on private international law. All countries of the Caucasus-Central Asia region are contracting states of the Minsk Judicial Assistance Treaty of 1993, which contains also provisions on conflict of laws including sales. Most countries of the region, with the exception, most notably, Russia, have also ratified the 2002 Kishinev Judicial Assistance Treaty as successor treaty to the Minsk Convention. In addition, several bilateral judicial assistance treaties have been concluded between countries of the region and as well as other countries. Application of these treaties appears to be limited to citizens of the contracting States or established there. The treaties presently provide only for rudimentary provisions on international sales, most importantly the freedom of choice of law. The contribution then analyses the much more developed provisions on international sales in the respective national laws (Civil Codes, particular conflict of laws legislation or other).

---

11   Contribution of Erik Evtimov and Tetyana Payosova (in this book), 200 et seq.

The third contribution, by *Cyril Emery* (then a staff member of the secretariat of UNCITRAL) deals with the relevance of the *UN Convention on International Sales (CISG) of 1980* for the Caucasus-Central Asia region. Its starts with a general presentation of the CISG and its function to improve participation of States and their economic actors in global supply chains. This is highly relevant for the Caucasus-Central Asia region as it is situated between China and Europe and at the same time is engaged in regional economic integration. More specifically, the article addresses Kazakhkstan, Tajikistan, and Turkmenistan, which have not yet ratified the CISG, and Kyrgyzstan and Uzbekistan, which – according to the author – should be supported in using the CISG more actively, e.g. by seminars and other information.

The *third part* of the book deals with issues of *dispute resolution*, joining contributions on dispute resolution[12] under public international law and "private" law, including selected aspects of investment arbitration as a subject combining public and private elements. The term "dispute resolution under public international law" as used in this book refers to disputes between States or assimilated parties under public international law, while "private law dispute resolution" refers to disputes between private parties or even private parties against States or assimilated parties primarily under domestic (usually private) law, but possibly also under international law. The subpart on public international law disputes focuses on the dispute resolution mechanisms in the WTO (with particular regard to countries of the region) und regional Free Trade Agreements, addressing also issues of the mutual relationship of such regulations among themselves and with dispute resolution under private law. The private disputes subpart thematises the quality of dispute resolution in the State courts of the region and further addresses various issues of international civil procedure and arbitration.

Nicolas Lamp and *Larysa Workewych* start the subpart of the book on *dispute settlement under public international law* with a contribution on *Russia's experience in WTO* dispute settlement. From the beginning of its membership in the WTO, Russia has been an active user of the WTO system, both as complainant and respondent. The analysis of a number of selected cases brought to the WTO shows that some of them were purely trade disputes, whereas some of them appear to have a connection between the measure at issue in the dispute and the tensions between Russia and its trading partners due to the current political situation.

---

12   The term "dispute resolution" is used in this book synonymously with "dispute settlement", if no further distinction is made in a specific context.

Peter-Tobias Stoll and *Jia Xu* continue with a contribution on the relationship between dispute settlement mechanisms under the WTO system and under preferential trade agreements (PTAs, the term used by the authors for regional trade agreements).[13] They describe and analyze different approaches used or proposed in this context, such as a transfer of the concepts of res judicata or lis pendens from international civil procedure to WTO/PTA dispute settlement systems or a use of the concepts of comity, of estoppel (good faith), or of waiver in this context. Generally speaking, none of these arguments has been pleaded successfully in WTO/PTA dispute settlement so far. Another option, which has yet to be tested in practice, are fork-in-the-road clauses in PTAs, which are otherwise well-known in investment arbitration.

While the dispute settlement mechanism established in the framework of the WTO has developed successfully in the last decades, it may not suit all needs. Recent regional trade agreements (RTAs) therefore sometimes provide for specific dispute settlement models. *Thomas Jürgensen* describes in detail the dispute settlement rules which the European Union has developed for use in the EU's RTAs and which have been agreed in several agreements, e.g. in the RTAs with Korea or Kazakhstan or the Association Agreements with Georgia and other East European countries. The author explains the specifics of these mechanisms in comparison with the WTO DSU. Particular characteristics are, for example, more detailed provisions on mediation, more previsible and stable rosters of arbitrators, renouncement of an appeal procedure, shorter timeframes, and other elements of enhanced efficiency. DCFTAs as core elements of Association Agreements, but also other agreements with energy-supplying partner countries, contain in addition specifically-tailored rules for urgent energy-related disputes ("super fast-track procedures") and cases relating to regulatory approximation (preliminary ruling mechanism leading to the CJEU).

Elena Babkina contributes a detailed article on the *Court of the Eurasian Economic Union*.[14] She analyses the general structure of the Court, its jurisdiction, procedure before the Court, applicable law (standards of scrutiny), and issues of execution of decisions. Generally speaking, the Court's competences are more limited than the competences of the (former) Court of the Eurasian Economic Community and, even more so, than the Court of Justice of the European Union. Also, the decisions of the Court are not given binding effect for the Eurasian Economic Commission or the EAEU's member states,

---

13   Some aspects of this topic are also addressed in the contributions of Thomas Jürgensen
       and Ilya Rachkov (in this book), 323 et seq. and 372 et seq.
14   Some aspects of this topic are also addressed by Zhenis Kembayev (in this book), 19 et seq.

but there is tendency that both the Commission and courts in the EAEU member states give deference to the Court's jurisprudence.

Turning to the *environmental dimension* of trade disputes, *Karsten Nowrot* places the issue of dispute resolution in the general context of the relationship between trade law and environmental protection. Focusing on regional trade agreements (e.g. NAFTA or the EU–Georgia Association Agreement), the authors systemizes modern trends in this field both as to substantive and procedural matters.[15] With regard to substantive matters, he distinguishes a traditional "minimalistic" approach from significantly more detailed regulations in this field. With regard to dispute settlement, he distinguishes mere negotiation approaches to growingly "hard" quasi-judicial types of dispute settlement. However, the author remarks that these mechanisms have so far been little used, although this might change in the future.

Concluding the subpart on dispute settlement under public international law, *Ilya Rachkov* turns to the relationship between dispute settlement under public international law mechanisms and private dispute settlement, as well as giving a deepened analysis of the public law mechanisms particular relevant to the Eurasian region (dispute settlement under WTO, EurAsEC and EAEU rules). Particularly interesting are the concrete cases analyzed by the author in the respective fora. The author shows that the public mechanisms are usually used only after unsuccessful (from one party's perspective) exhaustion of private law dispute settlement, but are sometimes carried-through in conjunction with each other.

The *"private disputes resolution"* subpart of the monograph begins with an overview by *Alexander Trunk* on *issues of quality of State courts* in the region. Practically speaking, the vast majority of disputes relating to international trade are dealt with by State courts or different means of alternative dispute resolution, in particular international commercial arbitration. The quality of dispute resolution in a country is therefore not only of theoretical interest, but also has an impact on the economic attractiveness of the respective country. Trunk's contribution first defines central terms such as "quality" and "efficiency" of courts and court practice and endeavours to structure criteria of quality. Thereafter, it gives an overview of public and private institutions active in the field of measuring and comparing the work of courts in different countries and analyses their methods of work. Finally, some results of such research relating to countries of the Caucasus and Central Asia or Central Asia

---

15   The "substantive" part of this article should be read in conjunction with the contribution of Andreas Ziegler, (in this book), 223 et seq.

(e.g. reports of CEPEJ or rankings of the World Justice Project) are presented and commented.

The second contribution, by *Vladislav Starzhenetskij*, addresses *trends of recognition and enforcement of foreign judgments and arbitral awards in economic disputes in Russia*. The author, firstly, discusses the criterion of reciprocity as a prerequisite of recognition of foreign judgment. Generally, this criterion has been upheld in the Caucasus-Central Asia region, but some countries (e.g. Georgia) interpret it flexibly, while others, e.g. Russia, continue to require formal reciprocity. The author analyses the rather inconsistent and changing interpretation of this criterion by Russian courts. Secondly, the author deals with the rather extensive list of cases of exclusive jurisdiction in Russian law, which have caused numerous disputes. The third issue dealt with by the author are the standards of notification as a condition of recognition and enforcement. Finally, the issue of public policy is discussed, the author sees here a clear tendency of restrictive, i.e. recognition-friendly, interpretation by recent court practice.

Three other contributions are devoted to *international commercial arbitration*, even if they sometimes refer to State courts as well.

At first, *Alexander Trunk* presents a short *overview of international commercial arbitration in the Caucasus-Central Asia region*, summing-up applicable treaties and national legislation and then discussing some characteristic issues of international commercial arbitration in the region: the scope of the respective regulations, issues relating to the arbitration agreement, conduct of the arbitration proceeding and recognition and enforcement of foreign awards.

Thereafter, *Dagmar Richter* gives a fundamental analysis of the *impact of public international law on the enforcement of foreign arbitral awards*. The contribution is not limited to the Caucasus-Central Asia region, but analyses numerous cases relating to this region, e.g. the *Yukos* cases. The contribution is of particular interest also for the reason that the analysis is directed to international commercial arbitration from the perspective of a public international lawyer. Particular regard is also given to investment arbitration.

Timothy Lemay, also a staff member of UNCITRAL, contributes an overview of UNCITRAL's activities as to the *transparency of investment dispute resolution*. UNCITRAL has always devoted much of its work to international (commercial) arbitration, and the UNCITRAL Arbitration Rules are often applied in investment arbitration as well. In recent years UNCITRAL has started to deal more specifically with investment arbitration, developing Transparency Rules and an accompanying Transparency Convention (2014), both designed for investment arbitration. Information on the UNCITRAL website shows that there are a present two pending arbitrations under the Arbitration Rules concerning investors from or linked with the Eurasian region.[16]

Finally, *Andrey Kotelnikov*, deals with the issue of *international commercial arbitration and economic sanctions*. Although the focus of this contribution is on arbitration, the author addresses in this context many general aspects of economic sanctions (notion, types, legitimacy under public international law, legal bases, etc.) and issues of conflict of law. The article contains also a solid analysis of arbitration practice and case law on sanctions including the perspective, in particular, of Russian courts.

The editors would like to express their deep gratitude to the authors for the interesting, thought-provoking contributions on a large spectrum of topics, ranging from global topics (with particular regard to their relevance for the Caucasus and Central Asian region) to regional and country-specific issues. They would also like to thank all participants in the project "Law of International Trade in and with Countries of the Caucasus and Central Asia", particularly speakers from the European Commission, the UNCITRAL Secretariat and Unidroit, other international organizations and ministries and courts from several countries as well as legal practitioners, for their input and interest in this project and topic. We would also like to express our deep gratitude to the VolkswagenStiftung, which made this project possible by granting generous financial support. Particular thanks go to our copy editor Ms. Diana Steele and Ms. Kelley Baylis, Associate Editor, both from the Brill team for their excellent support during the preparation of this volume. Last but not least we would like to sincerely thank our publisher Brill N.V., in particular Ms. Marie Sheldon (now President of Brill USA), for accepting this book for print and for their patience in waiting for the manuscripts of the book.

Alexander Trunk
Marina Trunk-Fedorova
Azar Aliyev
Kiel, 10 August 2022

---

16   *Manolium Processing v Belarus* and *Nord Stream 2 AG v European Union*, see <https://www.uncitral.org/transparency-registry/registry/index.jspx> accessed 14 November 2021.

PART 1

The Perspective of Public International Law

∴

SECTION 1

Regional Economic Integration

∵

CHAPTER 1

The Eurasian Economic Union: An Overview and Evaluation

Zhenis Kembayev†

1 Establishment

Regional integration processes in Eurasia, which trace their roots to the Commonwealth of Independent States (CIS)[1] and subsequently continued in the framework of the Eurasian Economic Community (EurAsEC),[2] have culminated in the establishment of the Eurasian Economic Union (EAEU).[3] On 29 May 2014, three most advanced EurAsEC members, Belarus, Kazakhstan and Russia (the Three), which launched a Customs Union on 1 January 2010,[4] signed the Treaty on the EAEU.[5] On 10 October 2014, the EurAsEC Member States signed a Treaty dissolving the EurAsEC,[6] which then ceased to exist on

---

1 See eg Sergei Voitovich, 'The Commonwealth of Independent States: An Emerging Institutional Model' 4(3) European Journal of International Law (1993) 403–417; Zbigniew Brzezinski and Paige Sullivan, *Russia and the Commonwealth of Independent States: Documents, Data, and Analysis* (Sharpe1997); Richard Sakwa and Mark Webber, 'The Commonwealth of Independent States 1991–1998: Stagnation and Survival' 51(3) Europe-Asia Studies (1999) 379–415.

2 See eg Zhenis Kembayev, *Legal Aspects of the Regional Integration Processes in the Post-Soviet Area* (Springer Verlag 2009); Julian Cooper, 'The Development of Eurasian Economic Integration' in Rilka Dragneva and KatarynaWolczuk (eds), *Eurasian Economic Integration: Law, Policy and Politics* (Edward Elgar Publishing 2013) 15–33.

3 See eg Zhenis Kembayev, 'Regional Integration Processes in Eurasia: The Legal and Political Framework' 41(2) Review of Central and East European Law (2016) 157–194; Maksim Karliuk, 'The Eurasian Economic Union: An EU-Inspired Legal Order and Its Limits' 42(1) Review of Central and East European Law (2017) 50–72.

4 See eg Olga Shumylo-Tapiola, 'The Eurasian Customs Union: Friend or Foe of the EU?', The Carnegie Papers (Carnegie Endowment for International Peace, October 2012); Rilka Dragneva, 'The Legal and Institutional Dimensions of the Eurasian Customs Union' in Dragneva and Wolczuk (n 2) 34–60.

5 See Dogovor o Evraziiskom Ekonomicheskom Soiuze (29 May 2014) <http://www.consultant.ru/document/cons_doc_LAW_163855> accessed 12 July 2021 (hereinafter "TEAEU").

6 Dogovor o prekrashchenii deiatel'nosti Evraziiskogo ekonomicheskogo soobshchestva (10 October 2014) <http://www.consultant.ru/document/cons_doc_LAW_170016> accessed 12 July 2021.

1 January 2015. On the same day, the Three, on the one hand, and Armenia, on the other, signed a Treaty on the accession of Armenia to the EAEU.[7] On 23 December 2014, a Treaty on the accession of Kyrgyzstan was signed.[8] On 1 January 2015, the EAEU became operative with the Three as initial Member States. On 2 January 2015, the EAEU was formally joined by Armenia and on 12 August 2015 by Kyrgyzstan.

2   Principles and Objectives

The EAEU is defined as "an international organization of regional economic integration",[9] which is founded on the following principles: (a) respect for the universally recognized principles of international law, in particular the principles of sovereign equality of the Member States and their territorial integrity; (b) respect for specifics of the political structures of the Member States; (c) ensuring mutually beneficial cooperation, equality and respect for the national interests of the Member States; (d) compliance with the principles of market economy and fair competition; (e) ensuring the functioning of the Customs Union without exceptions and limitations; and (f) creating favorable conditions for the operation of the EAEU and refraining from any actions that may jeopardize the achievement of its objectives.[10] At the same time, however, the text of the Treaty on the EAEU is fully devoid of any mention of democracy, human rights or rule of law.

The EAEU's main objectives include: (a) creating proper conditions for sustainable economic development of the Member States and improving the living standards of their population; (b) promoting comprehensive modernization and global competitiveness of Member States' national economies; and (c) establishing a Eurasian Internal Market in which the free movement of goods, services, capital and labor is ensured.[11] While a Eurasian Internal Market

---

7   Dogovor o prisoedinenii Respubliki Armeniia k Dogovoru o Evraziiskom ekonomich-eskom soiuze ot 29 maia 2014 goda (10 October 2014) <http://www.consultant.ru/cons/cgi/online.cgi?req=doc&base=LAW&n=286812&fld=134&dst=1000000001,0&rnd=0.5705431718812413#0> accessed 12 July 2021.

8   Dogovor o prisoedinenii Kyrgyzskoi Respubliki k Dogovoru o Evraziiskom ekonomich-eskom soiuze ot 29 maia 2014 goda (2 January 2015) <http://www.consultant.ru/cons/cgi/online.cgi?req=doc&base=LAW&n=172976&fld=134&dst=1000000001,0&rnd=0.76506 44423978692#0> accessed 12 July 2021.

9   TEAEU (n 3) art 1(2).

10   ibid art 3.

11   ibid art 4.

is yet under construction (e.g. an Internal Gas Market and an Internal Market of Oil and Petroleum Products are planned to be established on the basis of separate international agreements by 1 January 2025), the Eurasian Customs Union is fully operational. Having established the EAEU's common customs tariff, the Member States have agreed on the following allocation of import customs duties: Armenia – 1.11 percent, Belarus – 4.56 percent, Kazakhstan – 7.11 percent, Kyrgyzstan – 1.9 percent, and Russia – 85.32 percent.[12] The same allocation principle is also applied with respect to the contribution shares to the EAEU budget, which in 2018 amounted to 8.1 billion Russian rubles.[13]

3 Policies

For the purpose of achieving its objectives the EAEU is endowed with competences conferred upon it in the Treaty on the EAEU and international treaties concluded within the EAEU[14] and conducts "coordinated", "concerted" or "common" policies in the areas determined by the Treaty on the EAEU and international treaties adopted within the EAEU.[15]

A coordinated policy means a course of actions based on "common approaches" approved by EAEU organs for the purpose of achieving EAEU objectives.[16] In particular, EAEU Member States agreed to conduct coordinated energy policy for the purpose of gradually creating (as an integral part of the Eurasian Internal Market) a Eurasian Internal Energy Market, which will include an Internal Electric Power Market, an Internal Gas Market, and an Internal Market of Oil and Petroleum Products.[17] The emerging Eurasian

---

12 Prilozhenie No 5 k Dogovoru o Evraziiskom ekonomicheskom soiuze: Protokol o poryadke zachisleniya i raspredeleniya summ vvoznykh tamozhennykh poshlin (inykh poshlin, nalogov i sborov, imeiushhikh ekvivalentnoe deistvie), ikh perechisleniia v dokhod biudzhetov gosudarstv-chlenov (29 May 2014), Par 12 <http://www.consultant.ru/document/cons_doc_LAW_163855> accessed 12 July 2021.

13 See "Biudzhet EAES v 2018 godu sostavit bolee 8,1 mlrd rossiiskikh rublei" <http://www.belta.by/economics/view/bjudzhet-eaes-v-2018-godu-sostavit-81-mlrd-rossijskih-rublej-270894-2017> accessed 12 July 2021. Information on the EAEU budget is not publicly available and this web link seems to be a news link. According to this link, Belarus contributed 370 million rubles to the EAEU budget (4.56 percent of the total). Thus, Russia provided 6.91 billion rubles, Kazakhstan – 576 million rubles, Kyrgyzstan – 154 million rubles, and Armenia – 90 million rubles.

14 TEAEU (n 3) arts 1(2), 5(1).

15 ibid art 1(1).

16 ibid art 2.

17 ibid arts 81, 82, 83.

Internal Energy Market will encompass an area which has a total installed capacity of 282,8 GW and generates more than 1219 kWh of electrical power, possesses oil deposits of 18,071 million ton and gas reserves of 34,109 bcm, produces 624.7 million ton of oil and 671.9 bcm of gas.[18]

A concerted policy implies a course of actions based on harmonization of national legislations of EAEU Member States, implemented inter alia by decisions of EAEU organs, to the extent required to achieve EAEU objectives.[19] Specifically, EAEU Member States agreed to conduct a concerted macroeconomic policy;[20] a concerted monetary policy;[21] a concerted regulation of financial markets;[22] and a concerted competition (anti-trust) policy with respect to economic entities of third countries.[23] A concerted policy will also be applied in the fields of developing informatization and information technologies;[24] ensuring uniformity of measurements within the Union;[25] applying sanitary, veterinary-sanitary and phytosanitary quarantine measures;[26] and securing consumer protection.[27]

A number of fields foresee conducting both coordinated and concerted courses of action, in particular transport policy[28] and agro-industrial policy.[29] The transport policy aims at the gradual formation of a single transport space and the creation of Eurasian transport corridors.[30] In this regard, of particular note are the following words of the Kazakh President Nazarbayev: "The Eurasian Union should emerge as a link connecting the Euro-Atlantic and Asian development areas ... and serve as a bridge between the dynamic economies of the European Union and East, South-East and South Asia".[31] The agro-industrial policy seeks to create a single agricultural market in particular with

---

18   See "Energeticheskaya statistika gosudarstv-chlenov EAES za 2016 god" <http://www
      .eurasiancommission.org/ru/act/energetikaiinfr/energ/energo_stat/Pages/default.aspx>
      accessed 12 July 2021.
19   TEAEU (n 3) art 2.
20   ibid art 62(1).
21   ibid art 64.
22   ibid art 70(1).
23   ibid art 74(4).
24   ibid art 23(3).
25   ibid art 51(15).
26   ibid art 56(2).
27   ibid art 61(1).
28   ibid art 86.
29   ibid art 94.
30   ibid art 86(3).
31   See Nursultan Nazarbaev, 'Evraziiskii soiuz: ot idei k istorii budushchego' Izvestiia (25
      October 2011) <https://iz.ru/news/504908> accessed 12 July 2021.

the purpose of increasing exports of agricultural products.[32] Here it is worth noting that in 2017 Russia and Kazakhstan planned to export 44 and 9 million tons of wheat respectively.[33]

A common policy means a course of actions based on the application by EAEU Member States of unified legal regulation, which in particular consists of decisions adopted by EAEU organs within their competences.[34] In this regard, of particular note is that EAEU Member States apply the common customs tariff, the common customs regulations and the common trade regime in relations with third parties.[35] Also, the EAEU may adopt mandatory and directly applicable technical regulations in order to protect the life and/or health of people, property, environment, life and/or the health of animals and plants, to prevent consumer misleading actions and to ensure energy efficiency and resource conservation.[36]

4   Institutions

The EAEU institutional framework is composed of: (a) the Supreme Eurasian Economic Council (Supreme Council); (b) the Eurasian Intergovernmental Council (Intergovernmental Council); (c) the Eurasian Economic Commission (Commission), which is composed of two chambers: the Council (*Sovet*) and the Board (*Kollegiia*); and (d) the EAEU Court.[37] The meetings of the Supreme Council, the Intergovernmental Council and the Commission's Council are presided by a Chairman, a position held by each Member State on a rotational basis in the Russian alphabetical order for a term of one year.[38] The working language of the EAEU organs is Russian.[39]

---

32   TEAEU (n 3) art 95(1).

33   See 'Rossiia vpervye zaimet vtoroe mesto sredi mirovykh eksporterov zerna' *Vedomosti* (22 January 2018) <https://www.vedomosti.ru/business/articles/2018/01/22/748561-rossiya -vpervie-stanet-eksporterom-n2>; 'Kazakhstan planiruet uvelichit' eksport zerna v 2017 do 9,1 mln ton *Forbes.kz* (12 December 2017) <https://forbes.kz/news/2017/12/12/newsid _161379> both accessed 12 July 2021.

34   TEAEU (n 3) art 2.

35   ibid art 25(1).

36   ibid art 52.

37   ibid art 8(1). Of the total EAEU budget, 7.7 billion Russian rubles were allocated to the Commission and 362 million rubles to the EAEU Court. See 'Biudzhet EAES v 2018 godu...' (n 13).

38   ibid art 8(4).

39   ibid art 110(1).

On the eve of the establishment of the EAEU, intensive discussions were held about the possibility of transforming the EurAsEC Parliamentary Assembly, which existed from 2000 to 2014 and in particular provided recommendations with respect to the approximation and harmonization of national economic laws, into a Eurasian Parliament and expanding its authority.[40] However, this idea met with fierce opposition from, in particular, the political leadership of Kazakhstan and Belarus. Being aware of the evolution of the European Parliament, which started as a consultative body but has developed a truly supranational character, and fearing that the creation of a Eurasian Parliament would undermine their national sovereignty, the leaders of Kazakhstan and Belarus were extremely reluctant to create bodies that could potentially challenge and undermine their authority.[41] As a result, the final text of the TEAEU fails to include any representative body in the EAEU institutional framework.

4.1   Supreme Council

The Supreme Council is the topmost EAEU organ, which consists of the heads of the Member States.[42] It meets at least once a year; in addition, extraordinary meetings may be called at the initiative of its Chairman or any Member State.[43] Meetings of the Supreme Council may, at the invitation of the Chairman, be attended by members of the Commission's Council, the Chairman of the Commission's Board and other invited persons.[44] The meetings' agenda is set by the Commission based on proposals of the Member States.[45] The Supreme Council adopts decisions (*reshenie*) and instructions (*rasporiazhenie*) by consensus.[46] Decisions are regulatory acts while instructions are acts containing "organizational and administrative" orders usually on operative issues.[47]

The Supreme Council considers fundamental issues of the EAEU's activity, defines its strategy and determines main directions of integration processes with the purpose of achieving EAEU objectives.[48] In particular, its numerous

---

40   See Sergei Naryshkin and Taliia Khabrieva, 'K novomu parlamentskomu izmereniiu' (2012) No 8 Zhurnal Rossiiskogo Prava 5–15, at 11.
41   See Alexei Podberezkin and Olga Podberezkina, 'Eurasianism as an Idea, Civilizational Concept and Integration Challenge' in Piotr Dutkiewicz and Richard Sakwa (eds), *Eurasian Integration – The View from Within* (Routledge 2015) 51–52.
42   TEAEU (n 3) art 10.
43   ibid art 11(1).
44   ibid art 11(3).
45   ibid.
46   ibid art 13(2).
47   ibid art 2.
48   ibid art 12(1).

competences include: (a) appointing the Chairman and other members of the Board of the Commission and releasing them from office, approving the composition of the Board and distributing responsibilities among its members; (b) issuing instructions to the Intergovernmental Council and the Commission; (c) considering issues related to the termination or amendment of decisions adopted by the Intergovernmental Council or the Commission on the proposal of a Member State; (d) considering issues on which no consensus was reached on the proposal of the Intergovernmental Council or the Commission; (e) determining the procedure for acquiring and termination of EAEU membership; (f) granting and revoking the observer status or the status of a candidate country for accession to the EAEU; (g) approving the procedure of international cooperation of the EAEU; deciding on negotiations and conclusion of international treaties with a third party on behalf of the EAEU as well as on termination, suspension or withdrawal from those treaties; (h) approving the EAEU budget; (i) approving the staff size of the EAEU organs and the scope of representation of the Member States in the EAEU organs; (j) approving the procedure for remuneration of the members of the Commission's Board, the judges of the EAEU Court, officials and employees of the EAEU organs; (k) approving the regulation on external audit in the EAEU organs and reviewing the results of this audit; (l) approving the EAEU symbols; and (m) establishing subsidiary bodies.[49] In addition, the Supreme Council may exercise any other powers provided for by the Treaty on the EAEU or international treaties adopted within the EAEU.[50]

4.2 *The Intergovernmental Council*

The Intergovernmental Council is the second highest EAEU organ, which consists of the heads of government of the Member States.[51] It regularly meets at least twice a year; extraordinary meetings may also be convened at the initiative of its Chairman or any Member State.[52] Meetings of the Intergovernmental Council may, at the invitation of the Chairman, also be attended by members of the Commission's Council, the Chairman of the Commission's Board and other invited persons.[53] The meetings' agenda is also set by the Commission based on proposals of the Member States.[54]

---

49   ibid art 12(2).
50   ibid.
51   ibid art 14.
52   ibid art 15(1).
53   ibid art 15(3).
54   ibid.

The Intergovernmental Council may adopt decisions and instructions by consensus.[55]

The Intergovernmental Council is responsible for overseeing and ensuring compliance with the Treaty on the EAEU, other international treaties concluded within the EAEU framework, and the decisions of the Supreme Council.[56] It may also: (a) issue instructions to the Commission; (b) consider issues on which no consensus was reached on the proposal of the Commission; (c) approve the draft EAEU budget and a report on the EAEU's budget implementation; (d) consider issues related to termination or amendment of a decision issued by the Commission on the proposal of a Member State, or submits those issues, in case no agreement is reached, for consideration of the Supreme Council; and (e) suspend decisions of the Commission's Council or Board.[57] The Intergovernmental Council may also exercise any other powers provided for by the Treaty on the EAEU or international treaties adopted within the EAEU.[58]

4.3   *The Commission*

The EAEU's executive body, the Eurasian Economic Commission was established as an executive body in the framework of the Three's Customs Union already in November 2011 and became operative in early 2012.[59] It is a "permanent regulatory body of the Union"[60] with the seat in Moscow.[61] The composition, functions and powers of the Commission are governed by its Regulation, which is annexed to the Treaty on the EAEU.[62] According to the Regulation, the Commission is responsible to "ensuring the operation and development of the Union" and to "developing proposals in the sphere of economic integration within the Union".[63] It is also required to ensure within its competences

---

55   ibid art 17.
56   ibid art 16.
57   ibid.
58   ibid.
59   See Dogovor o Evraziiskoi ekonomicheskoi komissii (18 November 2011) <http://www .consultant.ru/document/cons_doc_LAW_121990> accessed 12 July 2021. This Agreement entered into force on 2 February 2012 and was replaced by the TEAEU (however, most of its provisions remained the same).
60   TEAEU (n 3) art.18(1).
61   ibid art 18(4).
62   ibid art 18(3); Prilozhenie No 1 k Dogovoru o Evraziiskom ekonomicheskom soi-uze: Polozhenie o Evraziiskoi ekonomicheskoi komissii (29 May 2014) <http://www.con sultant.ru/document/cons_doc_LAW_163855/8e3543f8dc9861d6acfa6a0c6678b972da1d0 7d0/> accessed 12 July 2021 (hereinafter "Regulation on the EAEC").
63   Regulation on the Eurasian Economic Commission (n 62) para 1.

the performance of international treaties that constitute the EAEU law,[64] to compose the draft EAEU budget and to prepare a report on the EAEU budget's implementation.[65]

The Commission's upper chamber, the Council, consists of the deputy heads of government and adopts decisions by consensus.[66] The Council meets as and when needed but at least every quarter.[67] It performs "the general regulation of integration processes" within the EAEU and "the general management of the Commission's activities".[68] Meetings of the Council may be attended by the Chairman of the Commission's Board and, upon the invitation of the Council, by other members of the Board. Members of the Council may also invite representatives of Member States and other persons, including those from third States.[69] The Council may adopt within its competences decisions, instructions and recommendations by consensus. Where no consensus can be reached, the issue is referred for consideration to the Supreme Council or the Intergovernmental Council on the proposal of any member of the Council.[70] The Council's competences inter alia include: (a) issuing instructions to the Commission's Board; (b) improving legal regulation of EAEU activities; (c) elaborating main directions of integration within the EAEU and submitting them for the approval of the Supreme Council; (d) considering the termination of the decisions taken by the Commission's Board or their amendment; (e) evaluating the results of monitoring and overseeing the implementation of international treaties adopted within the EAEU and submitting an annual report to the Intergovernmental Council; (f) approving the draft EAEU budget; and (g) determining, on the proposal of the Chairman of the Board, the list of the Commission's departments, their structure and staffing, and their distribution among the members of the Board.[71]

The Commission's lower chamber, the Board, is made up of an equal number of representatives from each Member State, one of whom is the Board's Chairman.[72] The initial membership of the Board (from February 2012 to

---

64   ibid para 4.
65   ibid para 9.
66   ibid paras 23, 29.
67   See Reglament raboty Evraziiskoi ekonomicheskoi komissii (21 December 2012) <http://www.eurasiancommission.org/ru/act/trade/Documents/P_Reshenie_1.pdf> accessed 12 July 2021.
68   Regulation on the Eurasian Economic Commission (n 62) para 22.
69   ibid para 27.
70   ibid para 29.
71   ibid para 24.
72   ibid para 31.

February 2016) consisted of nine members, i.e. three members from each of the Three.[73] Starting from 1 February 2016, the Board consists of ten members, two each from Armenia, Belarus, Kazakhstan, Kyrgyzstan, and Russia.[74] The members of the Board have the rank of ministers,[75] have a specific portfolio of responsibilities and direct the activities of two, three or four departments.[76] Currently there are 25 departments employing 1071 full-time officials.[77] The members of the Board are nominated by their respective Member States and are appointed by the Supreme Council for a term of four years with a possibility

---

73   Reshenie Vysshego Evraziiskogo ekonomicheskogo soveta No 2 (19 December 2011) <http://www.tsouz.ru/eek/RVSEEK/MGS-17/Pages/default.aspx> accessed 12 July 2021ll.

74   Reshenie Vysshego Evraziiskogo ekonomicheskogo soveta No 23 (16 October 2015) <https://docs.eaeunion.org/docs/ru-ru/0148755/scd_19102015_23> accessed 12 July 2021.

75   Prilozhenie No 23 k Dogovoru o Evraziiskom ekonomicheskom soiuze: Polozhenie o sotsialnykh garantiyakh, privilegiyakh I immunitetakh v Evraziiskoi ekonomicheskom soiuze (29 May 2014) para 48 <http://www.consultant.ru/document/cons_doc_LAW_163855> accessed 12 July 2021.

76   Specifically, (1) the Chairman oversees the Department of Protocol and Organizational Support, the Department of Finance, the Legal Department, and the Administrative Department; (2) the Board's Member (Minister) of Integration and Macroeconomics – the Department of Macroeconomic Policy, the Department of Statistics, and the Department for the Development of Integration; (3) the Board's Member (Minister) of Economic and Financial Policy – the Department of Financial Policy, the Department of Business Development, and the Department of Labor Migration and Social Protection; (4) the Board's Member (Minister) of Industry and Agro-Industrial Complex – the Department of Industrial Policy, and the Department of Agro-Industrial Policy; (5) the Board's Member (Minister) of Trade – the Department of Customs, Tariff and Non-Tariff Regulation, the Department of Internal Market Protection, and the Department of Trade Policy; (6) the Board's Member (Minister) of Technical Regulation – the Department of Technical Regulation and Accreditation, and the Department of Sanitary, Phytosanitary and Veterinary Measures; (7) the Board's Member (Minister) of Customs Cooperation – the Department of Customs Legislation and Law Enforcement Practice, and the Department of Customs Infrastructure; (8) the Board's Member (Minister) of Energy and Infrastructure – the Department of Transport and Infrastructure; and the Department of Energy; (9) the Board's Member (Minister) of Competition and Antimonopoly Regulation – the Department of Antimonopoly Regulation, and the Department of Competition and Public Procurement Policy; and (10) the Board's Member (Minister) of Domestic Markets, Informational Support, Information and Communication Technologies – the Department of Information Technologies, and the Department for the Functioning of Internal Markets. The composition and structure of the Board see in "Struktura Kommissii", available at <http://www.eurasiancommission.org/ru/Pages/structure.aspx> accessed 12 July 2021.

77   Reshenie Soveta EEK No.1 Ob utverzhdenii perechnia, shtatnoi chislennosti departamentov Evraziiskoi ekonomicheskoi komissii i raspredelenii ikh mezhdu chlenami Kollegii Evraziiskoi ekonomicheskoi komissii (12 December 2016) <https://docs.eaeunion.org/docs/ru-ru/0149674/cncd_15022016_1> accessed 12 July 2021.

of reappointment.[78] One of the members is appointed by the Supreme Council as a Chairman. The chairmanship is held by representatives of each Member State for a term of four years on a rotational basis in the Russian alphabetical order, without the right of prolongation.[79] Members of the Board work on a permanent basis, are supposed to be independent from the Member States and may not request or receive instructions from government authorities or officials of the Member States.[80]

The Board is inter alia responsible for: (a) developing recommendations and evaluating proposals submitted by the Member States on issues related to the development of the EAEU; (b) implementing decisions and instructions adopted by the Supreme Council and the Intergovernmental Council and decisions adopted by the Council; (c) monitoring and overseeing the implementation of international treaties adopted within the EAEU and decisions of the Commission as well as notifying the Member States of their duty to implement them; (d) submitting an annual report on work performed to the Council; (e) assisting the Member States in the settlement of disputes within the EAEU before applying to the EAEU Court; (f) representing the interests of the Commission in judicial bodies, including the EAEU Court; (g) developing a draft budget of the EAEU and a draft report on its implementation; (h) drafting international treaties and decisions of the Council, as well as other documents required for the exercise of powers by the Commission; (i) monitoring and evaluating the impact of regulatory enforcement and preparing an annual report thereon; and (j) ensuring the holding of meetings of the Supreme Council, the Intergovernmental Council, the Council and subsidiary bodies.[81]

The Commission may adopt decisions, instructions and recommendations.[82] Decisions, instructions and recommendations of the Council are adopted by consensus.[83] Decisions, instructions and recommendations of the Board may be adopted by a two-thirds majority.[84] Yet the Supreme Council may determine a list of sensitive issues requiring the Board to take decisions on those issues by consensus.[85] Decisions of both the Council and the Board are binding for the Member States and directly applicable in their territories.[86] However,

---

78   Regulation on the Eurasian Economic Commission (n 62) paras 33, 40.
79   ibid.
80   ibid para 34.
81   ibid para 43.
82   TEAEU (n 3) art 18(2).
83   ibid.
84   ibid.
85   ibid.
86   Regulation on the Eurasian Economic Commission (n 62) para 13.

the Board's decisions may be revoked or changed at the initiative of any of the Council's members or a Member State.[87] Furthermore, should a Member State disagree with a decision of the Council, it may refer it to the Intergovernmental Council or the Supreme Council and thus make the adoption of the decision in question subject to consensus.[88] Accordingly, the Commission is designed to implement Eurasian integration law under the guidance and strict supervision of EAEU Member States.

4.4   The EAEU Court

The EAEU's institutional framework includes also a Court consisting of two judges from each Member State who are appointed by the Supreme Council upon the proposal of the Member States for a term of nine years.[89] The EAEU Court may rule on actions brought not only by the EAEU Member States, but also by business entities,[90] which include legal persons registered under the laws of a Member State or a third country or natural persons registered as an individual entrepreneur in accordance with the legislation of a Member State or a third country.[91] The Court is endowed with compulsory jurisdiction with respect to claims submitted to it, and the parties must execute the Court's decisions. Upon an application from a Member State or EAEU body, the Court may issue advisory opinions providing explanations of EAEU agreements.[92]

The Court is tasked with ensuring that the law of the EAEU is applied by its Member States in a uniform manner.[93] Even though Court's rulings and advisory opinions have no strict legal value and are not a part of the Eurasian Integration Law (see below), they are of crucial importance for the development of substantive law within the Eurasian integration grouping, as they clarify the substance of legal norms that are otherwise often ambiguous. Yet the rules governing the activities of the EAEU Court represent a significant setback in comparison with its predecessor, the EurAsEC Court,[94] mainly because

---

87   ibid paras 24(3) 30.
88   ibid para 30.
89   See Prilozhenie No.2 k Dogovoru o Evraziiskom ekonomicheskom soiuze: Statut Suda
        Evraziiskogo ekonomicheskogo soiuza (29 May 2014) <http://www.consultant.ru/docum
        ent/cons_doc_LAW_163855> paras 7, 8, accessed 12 July 2012 (hereinafter "Statute of the
        EAEU Court").
90   ibid para 39.
91   ibid para 39(2).
92   ibid para 46.
93   ibid para 2.
94   See eg Alexei Ispolinov, 'First Judgments of the Court of the Eurasian Economic
        Community: Reviewing Private Rights in a New Regional Agreement' (2013) 40 Legal
        Issues of Economic Integration 225–46.

the EAEU Court does not have a competence to render preliminary rulings.[95] Also, it is explicitly stated that the Court's decisions may not change or revoke the law of the Union or the legislation of Member States.[96] Thus, the EAEU Court may not create law, nor does it have the power to invalidate the laws of EAEU Member States when those laws conflict with Eurasian integration law. Moreover, it is explicitly stated that in case of non-performance of a decision of the Court, a Member State may ask the Supreme Council to adopt necessary measures for the implementation of the decision.[97] Accordingly, the role of the final arbiter of Eurasian integration law is performed by the Supreme Council.[98]

5   Eurasian Integration Law

The law of the EAEU is constituted by: (1) the Treaty on the EAEU; (2) international treaties concluded in the framework of the EAEU; (3) international treaties concluded by the EAEU with third parties; and (4) decisions and instructions of the Supreme Council, the Intergovernmental Council, and the Commission adopted within the limits of the authority provided by the Treaty on the EAEU and international treaties concluded in the framework of the EAEU.[99]

The Treaty on the EAEU forms the (quasi-)constitutional basis of the EAEU. It prevails in case of conflict between it and international treaties concluded in the framework of the EAEU.[100] Also, it is provided that decisions and instructions of the EAEU organs must be in compliance with the Treaty on the EAEU and international treaties concluded in the framework of the EAEU.[101] In the very same manner as EU law, the law of the EAEU can be divided into two parts: 1) institutional; and 2) substantive. The former deals with the legal nature, and constitutional and institutional order of the Eurasian integration grouping, while the latter focuses on the legal and regulatory framework of the internal market, examining in particular the legal rules related to the free

---

95   See Zhenis Kembayev, 'The Court of the Eurasian Economic Union: An Adequate Body for Facilitating Eurasian Integration?' (2016) 41(3–4) Review of Central and East European Law 342–67, at 359–60.
96   Statute of the EAEU Court, para 102.
97   ibid para 114.
98   See Kembayev (n 3) 365.
99   TEAEU (n 3) art 6(1).
100   ibid art 6(3).
101   ibid.

movement of goods, persons, services, and capital. The Treaty on the EAEU consists of four parts, 118 articles, and 33 annexes. The first part contains inter alia rules related to the legal personality, principles, objectives, competences, the institutional framework, and the budget of the EAEU. The second part deals with the operation of the Customs Union and includes rules related to customs regulations and duties, a common customs tariff, foreign trade policy, trade statistics, sanitary and phytosanitary measures, and consumer protection. The third part comprises rules related to the creations of a single economic space (or an internal market), in particular those governing macroeconomic policy, monetary policy, trade in services, right of establishment, investment, financial markets, taxation, competition, natural monopolies, internal energy market, transport policy, government procurement, intellectual property, industrial and agro-industrial policy, and labor migration. The fourth part encompasses concluding remarks. The Treaty on the EAEU explicitly stipulates that reservations are not permitted.[102] Yet the EAEU Member States may conclude bilateral international treaties envisaging deeper integration or providing additional benefits for their natural and/or juridical persons unless those treaties do not affect the performance of obligations of the Member States under the Treaty on the EAEU and other international treaties concluded in the framework of the EAEU.[103]

At the present there are over 240 international treaties in force that were concluded in the framework of the EAEU.[104] This category includes also those treaties that were adopted within the Three's Customs Union starting from 2010.[105] Among the recent treaties of particular importance is the Treaty on the Customs Code of the EAEU that was signed on 11 April 2017 and entered into force on 1 January 2018.[106] Also, the EAEU may conclude international treaties with third parties (discussed below). Those treaties may not contradict the main objectives, principles and rules of the functioning of the EAEU.[107] As to the legal acts of the EAEU organs, it is provided that in case of conflict between decisions of the Supreme Council, the Intergovernmental Council, or

---

102   TEAEU (n 3) art 117.

103   ibid art 114(2).

104   See "Pravovoi portal Evraziiskogo ekonomicheskogo soiuza" <https://docs.eaeunion.org/ru-ru/Pages/AllDocuments.aspx#npbdocumentbelongstaxId=%5B%5D> accessed 22 November 2021.

105   TEAEU (n 3) Art 99.

106   Dogovor o Tamozhennom kodekse Evraziiskogo ekonomicheskogo soiuza (11 April 2017) <https://docs.eaeunion.org/docs/ru-ru/01413569/itia_12042017> accessed 12 July 2021.

107   TEAEU (n 3) art 6(2).

the Commission, decisions of the Supreme Council prevail over decisions of both the Intergovernmental Council and the Commission, while decisions of the Intergovernmental Council prevail over decisions of the Commission.[108]

6   External Action

The EAEU is endowed with international legal personality.[109] It is entitled to perform, within its competences, international activities aimed at addressing the challenges faced by the Union. As part of such activities, the EAEU may engage in international cooperation not only with states and international organizations but also with "international integration associations".[110] This provision is in particular intended to become a basis for establishing relationship with the European Union. As put by Belarusian President Alexander Lukashenko already in 2011: "[T]he Eurasian Union is an integral part of pan-European integration. It should become a key regional player that will help build relations with the world's leading economic structures ... [in particular with] the European Union, thus ultimately creating a single economic space from Lisbon to Vladivostok ... [and] merging the two integration projects".[111]

International cooperation is exercised on the basis of a procedure approved by the Supreme Council and must aim at achieving the objectives of the EAEU and positioning the EAEU as a reliable, predictable partner in the international arena.[112] An important role in conducting international cooperation is played by the Commission, which elaborates the main directions of the EAEU's international activities based on proposals of the Member States and both chambers of the Commission.[113] The main directions of the EAEU's international activities are annually approved by the Supreme Council.[114] In 2017, the main directions of the EAEU's international activities foresaw inter alia continuing working on establishing direct contacts between the Commission and the

---

108   ibid art 6(4).
109   ibid art 1(2).
110   ibid art 7(1).
111   Alexander Lukashenko, 'O sud'bakh nashei integratsii' *Izvestiia* (17 October 2011) <https://iz.ru/news/504081> accessed 12 July 2021.
112   Reshenie Vysshego Evraziiskogo ekonomicheskogo soveta No.99 O Poryadke osushhestvleniia Evraziiskim ekonomicheskim soiuzom mezhdunarodnogo sotrudnichestva (23 December 2014), para 4 <https://docs.eaeunion.org/docs/ru-ru/0147032/scd_25122014_99> accessed 12 July 2021.
113   ibid para 5.
114   ibid.

European Commission; elaborating an Agreement on Trade and Economic Cooperation with China and interlinking the EAEU with the China-led Silk Road Economic Belt project; and examining practicability of concluding free trade agreements with India, Iran, Israel, and Singapore.[115]

The EAEU may conclude international treaties with "third states, their integration associations, and international organizations" on any matters within its jurisdiction independently or jointly with the Member States.[116] Negotiations and the signing of EAEU international treaties with a third party are conducted based on a respective decision of the Supreme Council.[117] Thus, on 19 December 2012, the Supreme Council charged the Commission's Board to start negotiations in cooperation with the Member States on the conclusion of a Free Trade Agreement with Vietnam.[118] On 8 May 2015, the Supreme Council took another decision authorizing the Chairman of the Board to sign the Agreement upon the completion of internal legal procedures by the Member States, i.e. the signature of the text by the presidents of the Member States;[119] and, on 29 May 2015, the Free Trade Agreement between the EAEU and its Member States, of the one part, and the Socialist Republic of Vietnam, of the other part, which was done in two originals in the English language, was signed by the presidents of the Member States and the Chairman of the Board.[120] Furthermore, the Supreme Council decides on giving consent to be bound by an EAEU international treaty with a third party, as well as on termination, suspension or withdrawal from such treaty upon the completion of internal legal procedures by the Member States.[121] Accordingly, on 31 May 2016,

---

115   Reshenie Vysshego Evraziiskogo ekonomicheskogo soveta No.18 Ob Osnovnykh napravleniyakh mezhdunarodnoi deiatel'nosti Evraziiskogo ekonomicheskogo soiuza na 2017 god (26 December 2016), Section II <https://docs.eaeunion.org/docs/ru-ru/01413605/scd_11042017_18> accessed 12 July 2021.

116   TEAEU (n 3) art 7(1).

117   ibid art 7(2).

118   Reshenie Vysshego Evraziiskogo ekonomicheskogo soveta No 27 O nachale provedeniia peregovorov s Sotsialisticheskoi Respublikoi V'etnam po zakliucheniyu Soglasheniia o zone svobodnoi torgovli (19 December 2012) <https://docs.eaeunion.org/docs/ru-ru/0044 672/scd_20122012_27> accessed 12 July 2021.

119   Reshenie Vysshego Evraziiskogo ekonomicheskogo soveta No.14 O Soglashenii o svobodnoi torgovle mezhdu Evraziiskim ekonomicheskim soiuzom i ego gosudarstvami-chlenami s odnoi storony i Sotsialisticheskoi Respublikoi V'etnam s drugoi (8 May 2015) <https://docs.eaeunion.org/docs/ru-ru/0147681/scd_12052015_14> accessed 12 July 2021.

120   The text of the Agreement is <https://docs.eaeunion.org/docs/ru-ru/0147849/itot_02062 015> accessed 12 July 2021.

121   TEAEU (n 3) art 7(3).

the Supreme Council recognized the Agreement as binding on the EAEU from the date of its entry into force,[122] which occurred on 5 October 2016.

7   Evaluation

Examining the objectives and the institutions of the EAEU, one can easily see a superficial resemblance of this Eurasian integration with the process of European integration, which led to the creation of today's European Union. However, the current legal and political nature of both integration groupings is completely different: While the European Union is in principle an association of (mostly) parliamentary states with a significant degree of decentralization, the EAEU is a union of highly centralized presidential republics.

Although Russian President Vladimir Putin noted that the Eurasian integration project is aimed at creating "a powerful supranational association capable of becoming one of the poles of the modern world",[123] the current EAEU cannot be qualified as a truly supranational organization. In fact, the decision-making powers are exercised by representatives of the Member States and the Member States cannot be bound against their will. While the Commission's Board may adopt binding and directly applicable decisions by a two-thirds majority, those decisions may be revoked or changed by any Member State. Also, the Commission may not enforce the Eurasian integration law by commencing proceedings before the EAEU Court against an infringing Member State. Even though the EAEU Court may rule on actions brought not only by the Member States, but also by business entities, it does not have the power to invalidate the laws of EAEU Member States when those laws conflict with the Eurasian integration law.

The EAEU institutional framework clearly reflects the constitutional structures of their Member States, which are republics with strong presidential authorities and (semi-)authoritarian political regimes. Replicating the lack of democratic traditions and an effective separation of powers in Eurasian

---

122   Reshenie Vysshego Evraziiskogo ekonomicheskogo soveta No 3 O vstuplenii v silu Soglasheniia o svobodnoi torgovle mezhdu Evraziiskim ekonomicheskim soiuzom i ego gosudarstvami-chlenami, s odnoi storony, i Sotsialisticheskoi Respublikoi V'etnam, s drugoi storony ot 29 maya 2015 goda (31 May 2016) <https://docs.eaeunion.org/docs/ru -ru/01410318/scd_01062016_3> accessed 12 July 2021.

123   See Vladimir Putin, 'Novyi integratsionnyi proekt dlia Evrazii: budushchee, kotoroe rozhdaetsia segodnia' *Izvestiia* (4 October 2011) <https://iz.ru/news/502761> accessed 12 July 2021.

countries, the EAEU institutional framework shows the preeminence of its supreme body and the complete domination of the presidents of its Member States, who make virtually all important decisions. This circumstance may significantly facilitate decision-making processes, which can be confirmed by the very speedy development of regional integration in recent years, as reflected in particular in the launch of the Customs Union in 2010 and the EAEU in 2015. Yet, at the same time, it represents a major flaw in the Eurasian alliance, which is clearly dependent on the will of only a few individuals and is completely detached from strong party-based movements and processes.

Legal Evaluation of Agreements on Trade between the Central Asian and Caucasus Region and the EU

Michael Geistlinger

1 Introduction

The following chapter gives an analysis of the Partnership and Cooperation Agreements concluded between the European Union and its Member States and most countries in the region of the Caucasus and Central Asia in the 1990s. It does not yet address the Enhanced Partnership and Cooperation Agreement between the EU and its Member States and Kazakhstan of 21 December 2015 and the Comprehensive and Enhanced Partnership Agreement between the EU and its Member States and Armenia of 24 November 2021, which were concluded after this contribution had been finalized.[1]

Partnership and cooperation agreements (PCA) between the Republic of Kazakhstan,[2] the Kyrgyz Republic,[3] the Republic of Uzbekistan,[4]

---

1 For an analysis of the EU-Kazakhstan Agreement of 2015 see Vitaliy Kim, Das Freihandelsabkommen zwischen der Eurasischen Wirtschaftsunion und der Sozialistischen Republik Vietnam und das Abkommen über eine Verstärkte Partnerschaft und Zusammenarbeit zwischen der Republi Kazakhstan und der Europäischen Union (2020, Berlin, BWV) Band 29 Schriftenreihe zum Osteuropäischen Recht. A short analysis of the EU-Armenia Agreement of 2017 is given by Anahit Shirinyan, 'What Armenia's new agreement with the EU means', <euobserver.com/opinion/140017> accessed 5 February 2022.

2 1999/490/EC, ECSC, Euratom: Council and Commission Decision of 12 May 1999 on the conclusion of the Partnership and Cooperation Agreement between the European Communities and their Member States, of the one part, and the Republic of Kazakhstan, of the other part, Official Journal (OJ) L 196, 28.7.1999, 0001–0002.

3 1999/491/EC, ECSC, Euratom: Council and Commission Decision of 12 May 1999 on the conclusion of the Partnership and Cooperation Agreement between the European Communities and their Member States, of the one part, and the Kyrgyz Republic, of the other part, OJ L 196, 28.7.1999, 0046–0047.

4 1999/593/EC, ECSC, Euratom: Council and Commission Decision of 31 May 1999 on the conclusion of the Partnership and Cooperation Agreement establishing a partnership between the European Communities and their Member States, of the one part, and the Republic of Uzbekistan, of the other part, OJ L 229, 31.8.1999, 0001–0002.

© KONINKLIJKE BRILL NV, LEIDEN, 2023 | DOI:10.1163/9789004357839_004

Armenia,[5] Azerbaijan,[6] and Georgia,[7] and the European Union (EU) (former European Communities [EC]) / European Atomic Energy Community (Euratom) / former European Coal and Steel Community (ECSC)[8] and their Member States have been in force since 1 July 1999. An agreement with Turkmenistan negotiated during the same period of time was signed in May 1998 but has not yet entered into force.[9] Turkmenistan is covered by an Interim Trade Agreement with the European Union and Euratom.[10] An agreement with Tajikistan entered into force on 1 January 2010.[11] At the same time, development of ever-growing economic integration with established and steadily reinforced organization structures can be witnessed in this area beginning with the Commonwealth of Independent States (CIS) customs union between Belarus, Russia and Kazakhstan in 1996,[12] the Common Economic Area, which

---

5   1999/602/EC, ECSC, Euratom: Council and Commission Decision of 31 May 1999 on the conclusion of the Partnership and Cooperation Agreement between the European Communities and their Member States, of the one part, and the Republic of Armenia, of the other part, OJ L 239, 9.9.1999, 0001–0002.

6   1999/614/EC, ECSC, Euratom: Council and Commission Decision of 31 May 1999 on the conclusion of the Partnership and Cooperation Agreement between the European Communities and their Member States, of the one part, and the Republic of Azerbaijan, of the other part, OJ L 246, 17.9.1999, 0001–0002.

7   1999/515/EC, ECSC, Euratom: Council and Commission Decision of 31 May 1999 on the conclusion of the Partnership and Cooperation Agreement between the European Communities and their Member States, of the one part, and Georgia, of the other part, OJ L 205, 4.8.1999, 0001–0002.

8   Except for Tajikistan, where the agreement was negotiated after the end of the ECSC.

9   The entry into force was blocked by the lack of ratification by some EU Member States, whereas Turkmenistan ratified the agreement in 2004. See also the Resolution of the European Parliament of 22.4.2009, which requires, *inter alia*, the inclusion of a suspensive human rights clause, see number 9, (2010/C 184 E/05).

10   Interim Agreement on trade and trade-related matters between the EC, ECSC, Euratom of the one part, and Turkmenistan, of the other part, Council, 22.1.1999 (OR.en), 5144/1999, in force since 1.8.2010.

11   2009/989/EC, Euratom: Decision of the Council and of the Commission of 17 November 2009 on the conclusion of a Partnership and Cooperation Agreement Establishing a Partnership between the European Communities and their Member States, of the one part, and the Republic of Tajikistan, of the other part, OJ L 350, 29.12.2009, 0001–0002.

12   The Customs Union had been originally set up between Russia and Belarus by agreement dating 6 January 1995. The Russian text can be found on the official archive site <www.tsouz.ru/Docs/IntAgrmnts/Pages/Dogovor_06011995.aspx> accessed 30 June 2021. The agreement was extended to Kazakhstan by agreement between Russia and Belarus, of the one part, and Kazakhstan, of the other, dating of 20 January 1995. The Russian text can be found on the same official archive site. <http://www.tsouz.ru/Docs/IntAgrmnts/Pages/Dogovor_20011995.aspx> accessed 30 June 2021.

also embraced the Kyrgyz Republic, in 1999,[13] culminating in the Eurasian Economic Community in 2000[14] and providing for a Common Economic Area in force since 1 January 2012.[15]

In parallel, negotiations between the European Union and Georgia and Armenia took place, aiming for the establishment of Deep and Comprehensive Free Trade Areas (DCFTAS) as part of Association Agreements. On 22 July 2013, the European Union reported on the successful completion of the negotiations with Georgia,[16] and on 24 July 2013 respectively with Armenia on the key elements of these areas, although Armenia later decided not to sign the Association Agreement.[17]

Belarus is still covered by the Trade and Cooperation Agreement entered into by the European Commission with the former Soviet Union in 1989 and Russia by the Partnership and Cooperation Agreement dating from 1994.[18] Negotiations with Russia opened on 26/27 June 2008 at the Khanty-Mansiysk

---

13   The agreement dates from 26 February 1999. See Russian text on the official archive site <www.tsouz.ru/Docs/IntAgrmnts/Pages/Dogovor_26021999.aspx> accessed 30 June 2021.

14   The Treaty on the Establishment of the Eurasian Economic Community dates from 10 October 2000 and entered into force also for the Republic of Tajikistan on 30 May 2001. It was amended on 25 January 2006 and on 6 October 2007. The Russian text of the treaty can be found on the official website <www.tsouz.ru/docs/intagrmnts/pages/dogovor_evra zes.aspx> accessed 30 June 2021. The Republic of Uzbekistan joined the Community by accession to the treaty on 28 August 2006. (It suspended its membership in 2008).

15   See art 2 of the treaty (n 13). The Common Economic Area originally had been agreed upon on 23 February 2003 by the presidents of Russia, Belarus, Kazakhstan, and Ukraine. Ukraine later left the process. It is in effect for Russia, Belarus and Kazakhstan since 1 January 2012 and resulted in the Eurasian Economic Union in 2015. On the Eurasian Economic Union see Zhenis Kembayev, 'The Eurasian Economic Union: An Overview and Evaluation' in this volume, 19 et seq.

16   See <http://europa.eu/rapid/press-release_IP-13-721_en.htm> accessed 30 June 2021. On Deep and Comprehensive Free Trade Areas see Karsten Nowrot, '"Competing Regionalism" vs. "Cooperative Regionalism": On the Possible Relations between Different Regional Economic Integration Agreements', 'The Eurasian Economic Union: An Overview and Evaluation' in this volume, 19 et seq.

17   See <www.politico.eu/article/armenia-chooses-russia-over-eu/> accessed 30 June 2021. On 24 November 2017 Armenia and the European Union signedthe Comprehensive and Enhanced Partnership Agreement, which has been provisionally applied since June 2018 and entered into force on 1 March 2021. The new agreement has replaced the Partnership and Cooperation Agreement of 1999. See: <https://ec.europa.eu/trade/policy/countries -and-regions/countries/armenia/> accessed 30 June 2021.

18   97/800/EC, ECSC, Euratom: Council and Commission Decision of 30 October 1997 on the conclusion of the Partnership and Cooperation Agreement between the European Communities and their Member States, of the one part, and the Russian Federation, of the other part, OJ L 327, 28.11.1997, 0001–0002.

summit[19] have not yet led to a new agreement. This paper analyses the legal problems regarding the functioning of these agreements and the deficits ensuing from an anachronistic parallelism between bilateral external treaty regimes and the emergence of collective bargaining power through regional economic integration that is not recognized or respected by the European Union.

2   Some Historical Reminiscences

2.1   *The Soviet Perception of the EEC and Euratom*

The recognition of the then European Economic Community (EEC) and Euratom as treaty partners with regard to trade relations happened, very close to the end of the Soviet Union. The Agreement between the EEC, the ECSC and the Euratom, of the one part, and the Union of Soviet Socialist Republics (USSR), of the other part, on Trade and Commercial and Economic Cooperation of 18 December 1989 was concluded by the EEC and Euratom in parallel to their Member States.[20] The agreement entered into force on a preliminary basis on 1 April 1990. It is still in force and covers trade and economic relations between Belarus and the EU/Euratom and their Member States.

The agreement was initiated by a verbal note conveyed by the Soviet ambassador in Belgium to the European Communities on 9 June 1988 following a substantial change in the relationship between the former Soviet Union and the European Communities (EC). This note announced the intent of the Soviet government to accredit a permanent mission at the EC headed by an ambassador and was followed by a Joint Declaration signed in Luxemburg on 25 July 1988, which opened official relationships between the USSR and the EC.[21] The revolutionary dimension of such a step can be seen from considering the fact that, only in 1987, did the Soviet Council of Ministers allow for the establishment and activity within the territory of the USSR of joint enterprises between Soviet organizations and companies from capitalist and developing countries.[22] The dimension of change in the evaluation of Western economic

---

19   The EU Council adopted the mandate for such negotiation on 28 May 2008. See for more details <http://europa.eu/rapid/press-release_IP-08-1008_en.htm?locale=en> accessed 30 June 2021.

20   English text in: OJ L 068, 15.03.1990, 0002–0017.

21   See <https://base.garant.ru/2562470/> accessed 30 June 2021.

22   See the Decree of the Soviet Council of Ministers of 30 January 1987, N 49, 'O poryadke sozdaniya na territorii SSSR I deyatel'nosti sovmestnykh predpriyatiy s uchastiem Sovetskikh organizaciy I firm kapitalisticheskikh I razvivayushchikhsya stran.', Sobranie Postanovleniy (SP) Pravitel'stva SSSR 1987/8/38, reprinted in Vneshne-ėkonomicheskie

integration can also be deduced from the fact that, since the beginning of this integration, the Soviet Union had expressed itself explicitly against it, primarily because of concerns regarding Euratom and the danger of cooperation of the Western European states in the field of nuclear energy use in line with their membership to the NATO.[23] The EC were understood as organizations set up by monopolies with the aim of jointly dominating markets, resources and investments and defending the interests of the exploiters.[24]

It took until 1972 for the Soviet government to no longer exclude the possibility that at some point in time relations between the Soviet Union and the EC might be established depending on Western recognition of the interests and achievements of the members of the Council for Mutual Economic Assistance (COMECON).[25] In this period, some Soviet authors started to recognize the historical need of economic integration as a higher form of cooperation.[26] Western European economic integration was, however, understood as a political and systemic danger for the Soviet Union.[27] During this time, the Soviet

svjazi. Sbornik normativnykh materialov [External economic relations. Collection of normative materials] (1991) I, 8–15; and the analysis of S. Heger, *Joint Ventures in der Sowjetunion. Rechtliche Voraussetzungen und wirtschaftliche Aspekte* (A. Orac 1989) 6ff as well as P. Smirnov, *The Legal regulation of Soviet Foreign Economic Relations* (Progress Publishers 1989) 107–124 and H. Clement, 'Reformansätze in der UdSSR' in M. Haendcke-Hoppe (ed), *Außenwirtschaftssysteme und Außenwirtschaftsreformen sozialistischer Länder* (Duncker & Humblot 1988) 105, 116–127.

23 See for others eg E. Schulz, *Moskau und die europäische Integration* (Oldenbourg 1975) 74ff with further references. See also I. N. Puzin, M. A. Balanchuk, *Mezhgosudarstvennye svyzi stran NATO* (1979) 162.

24 See Schulz (n 22), 76 und Yu. V. Shishkov, *Formirovanie integracionnogo kompleksa v Zapadnoy Evrope: tendencii i protivorechiya* (1979) 24–30; Kh. Fundulis, E. Popov, *Associaciya razvivayshchikhsya stran s Evropeyskim Èkonomicheskim Soobshchestvom* (1978) 117ff.

25 See Schulz (n 22), 83.

26 See M. M. Maximowa, *Kapitalistische Integration* (Berlin Staatsverlag 1975) 129ff. See also Schulz (n 22), 91–101; Shishkov (n 23), 263; and G. V. Chernyavskaya, *Obshchiy rynok: regulirovanie cen* (1985) 11.

27 See Schulz (n 22), 129. It fits to this understanding that the USSR in official statements in external economic matters persistently ignored the existence and role of the EC (see eg A. N. Manzhulo (ed), *SSSR i mezhdunarodnye èonomicheskie otnosheniya. Sbornik dokumentov i materialov* (1985)). At the same time Soviet authors paid much attention to the coming into being of the Lomé Convention and its functioning, see eg Z. I. Kuzina, *Evropeyskoe èonomicheskoe soobshchestvo i Afrika* (1976) 22–43 and M. Ja. Volkov, 'EÈC i tretiy mir: Novye peregovory o Lomeyskoy Konvencii' in Ju. A. Borko (ed), *Evropeyskoe soobshchestvo v seredine 80-kh godov* Moscow (1986) 204–217.

theory of public international law in general neither explicitly nor implicitly recognized the EC as international organization(s).[28]

In the 1980s the prominent theoretician on the Soviet view on international economic law, M. M. Boguslavskiy, who after the end of the Soviet Union was called to the University of Kiel, showed a significant change in the perception of the EEC. Not only did he assigned a chapter of his respective manual to the organization, but he also followed the scientific discussion in the EEC Member States and positioned the Soviet theory within the framework of this discussion.[29] Boguslavskiy understood European community law not as law sui generis, but as part of public international law and pointed to the fact that the EEC was partner to multilateral conventions as well as being bound by a treaty to the Association of Southeast Asian Nations (ASEAN).[30] Boguslavskiy favored the conclusion of a framework convention between the EEC and the COMECON.[31] He, thus, continued a position already laid down 10 years earlier by a study set up by an editorial team composed of specialists from the Member States of the COMECON.[32] In this study, V. Grabska pointed to the growth of trade between the Member States of the two organizations, as well as to its limits and problems at the time[33] and welcomed initiatives of the then Executive Secretary of the COMECON, addressed to the European Commission around the negotiations which led to the Helsinki Final Act, to come to an agreement

28   See J. Jacobs, *Die EWG und die sowjetische Völkerrechtsdoktrin* (Verlag Rüegger 1977) 74–81. The position of the theory in general was, however, not shared by all authors of that period. There exists, for example, a translation into Russian of the Polish author Zbigniew M. Klepacki, *Zachodnio-Europejskie organizacje międzynarodowe* (1969), where a broad chapter deals with the EEC and leaves no doubt that it was considered by the author to be an international organization under public international law. See 238–337. Also I. S. Shaban, *Imperialisticheskaya sushchnost' zapadno-evropeyskoy integracii* (1971) 19–25 implicitly recognized the international organization character of the EEC through arguing that "international organizations of capitalist countries have always been and continue to be organs of domination of the bourgeois" in the context of the Council of Europe, EEC and Euratom.

29   M. M. Boguslavskiy, *Mezhdunarodnoe èkonomicheskoe pravo* (1986) 157–166. Similarly, but limited to a description of treaties and bodies: V. Lisovskiy, P. Reyt, 'Mezhdunarodnye organizacii v oblasti vneshney torgovli' in V. Lisovskiy, *Mezhdunarodnoe torgovoe pravo* (1979) 72–120, 92–99. No doubt as to the character of the EC as regional international organizations had also M. L. Èntin, *Sud evropeyskikh soobshchestv* (1987) eg 25.

30   ibid 157, 162.

31   ibid 165ff.

32   Ch. Nokov (Bulgaria), T. Palankai (Hungary), R. Gündel (GDR), Z. Nowak (Poland), P. Khvoynik, Yu. Shishkov (USSR), S. Tikal (CzSSR) (eds), *Zapadno-Evropeyskaya integraciya I mirovaya èkonomika* (1979) 319ff.

33   ibid 319–336.

between the two organizations concerning the principles of their mutual relationships.[34] She described the contents of such a proposal submitted by the COMECON on 16 February 1976.[35] In her view, the reaction of the Council of the EEC, which proposed working relationships between the two organizations, thereby exchanging information and contacts concerning statistics, economic programming and protection of environment, together with insisting on the requirement that trade agreements were to be concluded by the EEC, of the one part, and the individual Member States of the COMECON, of the other part, led to a failure of this initiative.[36]

By means of the agreement of 1989, the Soviet Union finally submitted to the format offered by the EC and accepted negotiating and concluding an unbalanced treaty.[37] A state, even as large as the Soviet Union, stood on the one side, whereas the EC became the negotiation partner on the other side, representing a number of Member States which smoothly accepted to be bound by one and the same agreement negotiated by the European Commission on behalf of all of them.

2.2   The Contents of the Agreement of 1989

The Agreement between the USSR and the EEC and Euratom on Trade, Commercial and Economic Cooperation may be called revolutionary because of the fact that it was concluded at all. The contents of the agreement itself, however, were rather modest and technical, reflecting a typical trade agreement.

Apart from mentioning "the importance of giving full effect to the Final Act of the Conference on Security and Cooperation in Europe and the Concluding Documents of subsequent meetings of the CSCE participating States", the preamble of the agreement does not mention any general political reference document or purpose to be achieved which goes beyond trade and economy. There were to be created "favourable conditions for the harmonious development and diversification of trade and the promotion of commercial and economic cooperation in areas of mutual interest on the basis of equality, mutual benefit and reciprocity." The agreement intended to extend the volume and structure for trade and economic development to their actual potential given

---

34   ibid, 339.
35   ibid, 339ff.
36   (n 31) 340.
37   Other Member States of the COMECON had done so before, see eg the People's Republic of Hungary: EC Council decision of 21 November 1988 concerning the conclusion of an Agreement between the EEC and the Hungarian People's Republic on Trade and Commercial and Economic Cooperation, OJ L 327, 0001–0010.

the current levels of economic development and their future prospects. Last but not least, the parties took into account "the favourable implications for trade and economic relations between the Contracting Parties of the economic restructuring under way in the USSR".

The general purpose of the agreement, as laid down in Article 1, consisted in facilitating and promoting "the harmonious development and diversification of their trade," "and the development of various types of commercial and economic cooperation". The agreement provided for most-favored-nation treatment with regard to customs duties, customs clearance, transit, warehouses, transshipment, taxes, methods of payments, as well as rules concerning sale, etc. of goods on the domestic market (Article 3, paragraph 1). The parties allowed for relief from duties, taxes, etc., with regard to goods that remained temporarily in their territories for re-exportation (Article 4). As a rule, trade and commercial cooperation had to take place within the scope of the applicable parties' regulations (Article 6), thereby providing for the highest possible degree of liberalization (Article 7). The parties set up a schedule and timetable for progressive elimination of quantitative restrictions applied to the importation of goods from the other party respectively, with the exception of sensitive products (Articles 8–12). They promised to inform each other on changes in nomenclature, respective procedures or classification (Article 13). The agreement provided for treatment of goods between the parties at market-related prices (Article 14).

In case of conflict situations, consultations should take place. Only upon their failure, should restrictions on the importation of products become possible (Article 15), except for a general escape clause on grounds of "public morality, law and order or public security, the protection of life and health of humans, animals or plants, the production of industrial, commercial and intellectual property, or rules relating to gold or silver or imposed for the protection of national treasures of artistic, historic or archaeological value" (Article 16, paragraph 1) and grounds of protection of essential security interests (Article 16, paragraph 2).

Regarding commercial and economic cooperation promotion, expansion and diversification of the parties' trade should be achieved. The parties promised each other to facilitate useful exchange of commercial and economic information and publication of comprehensive relevant data (Article 17, paragraphs 1 – 2). Their respective customs services promised to cooperate on vocational training, simplification of customs documentation and procedures and administratively with regard to infringement of applicable rules (Article 17, paragraph 3). Trade promotion activities, mutual guarantees of property rights for individual and legal persons, including non-discriminatory access to courts and administrative bodies, and contacts between business associations of the parties were assured (Article 17, paragraph 4). Counter-trade practices were to be counter-acted on both sides (Article 17, paragraph 5) and favourable business regulations, facilities and practices for firms and companies of the sides were to be maintained and improved (Article 17, paragraph 6). The parties wanted to encourage and develop arbitration based on the UNCITRAL rules and recognized the New York Convention of 1958 for settlement of eventual disputes (Article 18). They committed themselves to ensure adequate protection and enforcement of industrial, commercial and intellectual property rights (Article 19).

The parties wanted to establish the broadest possible economic cooperation, in particular, in the areas of statistics, standardization, industry, raw materials and mining, agriculture, including the food-processing industries, environmental protection, management of natural resources, energy, science, technology, banking, monetary, insurance and financial services, transport, tourism, other service activities, management, and vocational training (Article 20, paragraphs 1 and 2). Furthermore, they agreed to facilitate exchanges and contacts between persons and delegations representing any kind of business organizations, market research and marketing activities, promotion activities, information and contacts on scientific subjects of mutual interest and, last but not least, to foster a favourable mutual investment climate (Article 20, paragraph 3). On the EC side, additional bilateral activities between the EC Member States and the USSR should remain possible, as far as they are not overruled by the agreement (Article 21, read together with Article 23).

The agreement provided for establishing a joint committee acting by mutual consent as a supervisory body as to the execution and implementation of the agreement by the parties (Article 22).

3   Features of the Contractual Approach of the European Union towards the Caucasus and Central Asian States after the End of the Soviet Union

3.1   *Individualization of Treaty Relationships*
When the Soviet Union collapsed, the EU identified regions to approach that had comparable problems to meet and solve which consisted of states that were more mutually dependent than states outside the respective region. As for the Caucasus and Central Asia, the driving force and key interest were

the oil goods. The Caspian Sea Basin[38] and its huge energy resources lay on the very ground and if the states, where these resources were mainly concentrated (Kazakhstan, Turkmenistan and Azerbaijan), could have been isolated from their neighbors this certainly would have happened. Since Georgia and Armenia were needed for the export of these goods, they were included, thus, forming the Caucasus region closely linked to the Central Asian region. Rosemarie Forsythe correctly points to the fact that this regional identification at the end of the Soviet Union did not happen for the first time in history, but had much in common with the so-called "Great Game" between Tsarist Russia and Victorian England in the 19th century and had its historical roots even many centuries before.[39] Thus, the perception of these regions as such also followed an old tradition and could reinforce historical, ethnic, and traditional arguments to the predominant economic and geographic factors and interests.[40]

Apart from that, the breakdown of the Soviet Union itself and the fragmentation of the nation-wide industry – which was followed by the interruption of formerly functioning business links involving technological supply, maintenance and capital investments, as well as purchase of products – contributed to the appearance of these regions, thereby leaving the states of the regions in a relatively poor economic condition with significant economic problems to overcome.[41] The struggle for filling the gap of political power in the transition phase led to military conflicts in the Caucasus (Georgia – Abkhazia, Georgia – South Ossetia, both involving Russia and finally ending up in a direct conflict between Georgia and Russia, it also had impacts on Azerbaijan and Armenia regarding the Nagorno-Karabakh issue) and contributed to an intensification of regional interdependencies and resulted in an ever growing weakness of the Caucasus region in terms of political, economic and legal maneuvering.

The poor state of politics, economy and the lack of any regional structure in the Caucasus and Central Asian regions at the end of the Soviet Union made it easy for the European Union to continue and extend the policy developed with

---

38   See R. Forsythe, *The Politics of Oil in the Caucasus and Central Asia. Prospects for oil exploitation and export in the Caspian basin.* Adelphi Paper 300 (OUP 1996) 6.

39   (n 37) 9–11.

40   As for the Caucasus region the concept and commons of the so-called "South-Caucasus region", which widely is the same as simply "Caucasus region" in the Western perception is discussed also by G. Lordkipanidze, 'What is the South Caucasus?' in M. Geistlinger and others (eds), *Security Identity and the Southern Caucasus. The Role of the EU, the US and Russia* (Neuer Wissenschaftlicher Verlag 2008), 17–25 and with regard to Azerbaijan by Y. Nasibli, 27–31.

41   See also Forsythe (n 37) 12, with further references.

the Member States of the COMECON with regard to the newly independent states in the territory of the former Soviet Union. Instead of urging the states of the regions to first agree among themselves to any kind of regional cooperation, the European Union and Euratom stuck to their practice that was established during Soviet times. They elaborated regional model treaties for certain groups of countries and negotiated them one after the other, thereby offering them little space or options for deviating from the model contents, which were vastly, and nearly exclusively, determined by the EU/Euratom and their bodies, in particular, the European Commission. The EU/Euratom defined its policy priorities for the respective region but negotiated and concluded treaties with these states on an individual basis. This is exactly the situation Armenia, Azerbaijan, Georgia, Kazakhstan, Kyrgyzstan, Tajikistan, Turkmenistan, and Uzbekistan were confronted with. As for Belarus, by means of organizational treaties linked to a part of the regions, nothing changed with regard to the Soviet Union except for the fact that Belarus itself instead of the former Soviet Union is considered to be the treaty partner now.

As has been shown in another study, the difference between the partnership and cooperation agreements (PCAs) is very small, even considering the analysis of, and proposed reaction to, conflicts that arose between the states of a region or on the territory of one of them, but also involving other states.[42]

3.2   The Difference between the PCAs and the EC/Euratom – USSR Agreement

Using the example of the PCA with Azerbaijan[43] it can be shown, focusing on titles 1 (General Principles) and 2 (Political Dialogue), how far the agreement deviates from its predecessor: the EC/Euratom – USSR Agreement 1989, which the EC and the Republic of Azerbaijan wished to widen (preamble). But also, the preamble itself includes many more political and general points and documents of reference than the predecessor, which was a pure trade agreement. Most of these requirements are addressed unilaterally to Azerbaijan and deviate quite considerably from a general appearance of equal relationships with regard to international commitments, which to a minor degree, is shown in the preamble of the Agreement.

In the preamble, the following commitments are addressed to Azerbaijan, as well as to the EU/Euratom and their Member States:

---

42   See M. Geistlinger, 'The European Union Acting in the Southern Caucasus – Legal Perspective' in Geistlinger and others (eds) (n 39) 149–167, 150–154.

43   See n 5.

- to strengthen "the political and economic freedoms which constitute the very basis of the partnership";
- to "promote international peace and security, as well as the peaceful settlement of disputes and to cooperate to this end" in the framework of the UN and OSCE;
- to adhere to the Final Act of the CSCE, the Concluding Documents of the Madrid and Vienna Follow-up Meetings, the Document of the CSCE Bonn Conference on Economic Cooperation, the Charter of Paris for a New Europe and the CSCE Helsinki Document 1992.

More or less on a neutral basis in the interests of both sides, it is possible to find encouragement of "the process of regional cooperation in the areas covered by this Agreement with neighboring countries in order to promote prosperity and stability in the region and, in particular, initiatives aimed at fostering: cooperation and mutual confidence among Independent States of the Transcaucasus region and other neighboring States", the desire "of establishing and developing regular political dialogue on bilateral, regional and international issues of mutual interest.", the desire "of establishing close cooperation in the area of environment protection taking into account the interdependence existing between the Parties in this field", and the desire "of establishing cultural cooperation and improving the flow of information". As can be seen from the trade statistics, the "commitment of the Parties to liberalize trade, in conformity with World Trade Organization (WTO) rules", turned out not to be truly neutral.

All other statements laid down in the preamble challenge the political system of Azerbaijan, even if formulated as assistance to development and legal status from the perspective of a generous outsider (EU/Euratom). The EU/Euratom exported its own values, political and economic ideas and concepts, in order to gain political, legal and economic influence. These convictions are:

- the "support of the independence, sovereignty and territorial integrity of the Republic of Azerbaijan", which, however, "will contribute to the safeguarding of peace and stability in Europe.";
- the conviction of the "paramount importance of the rule of law and respect for human rights, particularly those of persons belonging to minorities, the establishment of a multiparty system with free and democratic elections and economic liberalization aimed at setting up a market economy";
- the belief that full implementation of the PCA "will both depend on and contribute to continuation and accomplishment of the political, economic and legal reforms in the Republic of Azerbaijan, as well as the introduction of the factors necessary for cooperation, notably in light of the conclusions of the CSCE Bonn Conference";

- the "necessity of promoting investment in the Republic of Azerbaijan, including in the energy sector, and in this context the importance attached" by the European Union and its members "to equitable conditions for access to and transit for export of energy products; confirming the attachment" of both sides (including Azerbaijan) "to the European Energy Charter, and to the full implementation of the Energy Charter Treaty and the Energy Charter protocol on energy efficiency and related environmental aspects";
- the EU's willingness "to provide for economic cooperation and technical assistance as appropriate";
- the "utility of the Agreement in favoring a gradual rapprochement between the Republic of Azerbaijan and a wider area of cooperation in Europe and neighboring regions, and its progressive integration into the open international system;"
- the consciousness of the "need to improve conditions affecting business and investment, and conditions in areas such as establishment of companies, labor, provision of services and capital movements";
- the conviction that "this Agreement will create a new climate for economic relations between the Parties and, in particular, for the development of trade and investment, which are essential to economic restructuring and technological modernization";
- the recognition that "cooperation for the prevention and control of illegal immigration constitutes one of the primary objectives of this Agreement."

The first of the above considerations raises the question against whom the independence, sovereignty and territorial integrity of Azerbaijan shall be protected and why by the EU? The primary addressee, as can be understood from the parallel PCA with Armenia and the Country Strategy Papers 2007–2013[44] for Armenia[45] and Azerbaijan[46] is not Armenia, which could be one possible understanding, taking into consideration the Nagorno-Karabakh issue.[47] It is,

---

44   The Country Strategy Papers are based on the European Neighbourhood and Partnership Instrument (ENPI) (Regulation (EC) N° 1683/2006 of the European Parliament and the Council of 24 October 2006) and are complemented by the European Neighbourhood and Partnership Instrument Eastern Regional Programme Strategy Paper 2007 – 2013 <www.europarl.europa.eu/document/activities/cont/201306/20130603ATT67192/201 30603ATT67192EN.pdf> accessed 30 June 2021.

45   See <www.edrc.am/images/Partnership_Strategies/EU/enpi_country_strategy_paper_% 202007_2013_eng.pdf> accessed 30 June 2021.

46   See <www.informest.it/docs/post/enpi_csp_azerbaijan_en.pdf> accessed 30 June 2021.

47   The European Union does not recognize that the Republic of Nagorno-Karabakh historically came into being by assistance of armed forces of the Republic of Armenia, thereby violating the territorial integrity of the Republic of Azerbaijan in the borders of the former

moreover, Russia which is addressed between the lines, which means that the European Union set up the PCA, *inter alia*, in order to replace Russian influence with its own.[48]

In the second consideration it is, in particular, the establishment of a multiparty system with free and democratic elections and economic liberalization aimed at setting up a market economy, which intends to export inherent components of the political and economic system of the EU Member States to Azerbaijan and by identical preamble provisions in the other PCAs to the other countries of the Caucasus and Central Asian regions. The PCAs stick to a concept of predominance of a multiparty system. The EU experience serves as measure, both as to the political as well as to the economic system. The European Union sets the model and the parties to the PCAs on the other side have to implement the model, whether it fits or not. There is no space for discussion or tests of eventual alternatives. That economic, legal and political reforms in the Republic of Azerbaijan had to take place accordingly follows from the third consideration of the quoted part of the list of the preamble.

Through the fourth consideration in this list, the European Union imposes its interests in the access to and supply of energy, thereby referring to the Energy Charter,[49] which was negotiated at the Hague Conference on 16 and 17 December 1991 which immediately followed the end of the Soviet Union (8/ 26 December 1991). All states of the Central Asian and Caucasus regions had taken part in the negotiations of the declaration called the "European Energy Charter", which was followed by the signing of the Energy Charter Treaty on 17 December 1994 and then later the Decisions of the European Energy Charter Conference, as well as the Protocol on Energy Efficiency and Related Environmental Aspects, and certain Amendments to the Treaty adopted on

---

USSR Republic Azerbaijan, whose borders were protected by the uti-possidetis principle otherwise applied by the international community, including the Member States of the European Union, with regard to the dissolution of the Soviet Union. The quoted documents show that the position of the European Union comes closer to Armenia than to Azerbaijan, see for more details and explanation Geistlinger (n 41) 160ff. By mentioning the principle of self-determination of peoples just on the Armenian side, the European Union accepts an eventual interference with the territorial integrity of Azerbaijan as a possible result of the conflict, which means that in the given context it is primarily not Armenia, which is addressed by the PCA.

48   For more details see Geistlinger (n 41) 163ff.

49   See 98/181/EC, ECSC, Euratom: Council and Commission Decision of 23 September 1997 on the conclusion, by the European Communities, of the Energy Charter Treaty and the Energy Charter Protocol on Energy Efficiency and Related Environmental Aspects, OJ L 69, 9.3.1998, 1–116.

23/24 April 1998.[50] The treaty and related documents involved considerable amendments in the national laws of the states of the two regions and used the weak economic and political situation of the region, when the Soviet Union had just broken down, in order to create and safeguard a legal regime which was significantly in the favor of EU/Euratom interests. An analysis of the further extracts of the preamble could provide even more examples in addition to the results achieved through the Energy Charter Treaty.

But more than that, the objectives of the partnership established by the PCA and listed in Article 1 PCA with Azerbaijan underline a rather aggressive approach of the Community in order to influence the internal economic, political and legal system of the regions' states. The objectives 1 ("to provide an appropriate framework for the political dialogue between the Parties allowing the development of political relations") and 2 ("to support the Republic of Azerbaijan's efforts to consolidate its democracy and to develop its economy and to complete the transition into a market economy") clearly go beyond a trade agreement. Only objective 3 ("to promote trade and investment and harmonious economic relations between the Parties and so to foster their sustainable economic development") pays due respect to the character of an agreement providing for fostering trade and economic cooperation on an even playing field. Even objective 4 ("to provide a basis for legislative, economic, social, financial, civil scientific, technological and cultural cooperation") abandons this ground, however, without seeming to attempt to intervene into the internal affairs of one of the treaty partners.

Such an approach becomes visible from the principles enumerated in title 1 of the PCA with Azerbaijan serving as an example for the other PCAs concluded with states of the Central Asian and Caucasus regions. Each of them read in the light of the preamble and Article 1 PCA can be adduced in a way to show the imbalance in the distribution of obligations and the aim of influencing the political, economic and legal orders in the states of the region, whereas no influence in the opposite direction was calculated or expected. It is necessary to also mention Article 4 providing that the "Parties shall as appropriate review changing circumstances in the Republic of Azerbaijan, in particular regarding economic conditions there and implementation of market-oriented economic reforms. The Cooperation Council may make recommendations to

---

50   For the text of all these documents see: Energy Charter Secretariat (ed), The Energy Charter Treaty and Related Documents. See <https://energycharter.org/> accessed 30 June 2021. The legal role of this Charter in the energy dialogue EC – Russia has been analyzed by K. Hober, 'Energeticheskiy dialog EC – Rossiya: pravovaya sfera' in D. Rauschning, V. N. Rusinova (eds), *Rossiyskaya Federaciya v Evrope* (2008) 148–202.

the Parties concerning development of any part of this Agreement in the light of these circumstances."

Whereas the EEC/Euratom – USSR Agreement of 1989 had refrained from direct involvement in the economic process going on in the USSR at the time and instead positively watched the developments in the USSR in terms of economic reforms and a new economic structure, the PCA with Azerbaijan, even if only by "recommendations", directly addressed the economic conditions and the implementation of market-oriented economic reforms in the Republic of Azerbaijan, thereby making them part of the scope of application of the treaty.

Title II (Articles 5–8) of the PCA with Azerbaijan set up a regular political dialogue between the parties in order to "accompany and consolidate the rapprochement between the Community and the Republic of Azerbaijan." (Article 5, first part of second sentence). The further part of this sentence: "support the political and economic changes underway in that country and contribute to the establishment of new forms of cooperation", leaves no doubt that "rapprochement" is to be understood as the political system of Azerbaijan approaching the political system(s) of the Member States of the European Union and not vice versa or even trying to find a potential middle ground in between them. The Community and its Member States are called a "community of democratic nations as a whole". Economic convergence shall serve as a tool to achieve more intense political relations, and ever-growing convergence of positions on international issues of mutual concern.

A few examples from the PCA with Azerbaijan may serve to demonstrate the one-way-road concept of the EU/Euratom with respect to the implementation of objectives and principles of the PCA. Article 43, paragraph 1 of the PCA underlines "that an important condition for strengthening the economic links between the Republic of Azerbaijan and the Community is the approximation of the Republic of Azerbaijan's existing and future legislation to that of the Community." This provision under title V ("Legislative Cooperation") means, in fact, that Azerbaijan's legislation shall be "gradually made compatible with that of the Community". The list of which laws are to be approximated accordingly is comprehensive and extends from customs law even as far as the protection of health and life of humans, animals and plants (see Article 43, paragraph 2 PCA with Azerbaijan). The approximation is safeguarded by the exchange of experts, the provision of early information, organization of seminars, training activities and aid for translation of Community legislation in the relevant branches of law.[51]

---

51   See art 43 para 3 PCA with Azerbaijan (n 5).

Similarly, "economic cooperation" as laid down in title VI (Articles 44–70) of the PCA with Azerbaijan makes the EU/Euratom appear as directing the Republic of Azerbaijan where to go:

– The European Union participates in Azerbaijan's efforts to restructure its industry (Article 46, paragraph 1, 2nd line PCA);
– EU competition rules applicable to undertakings have to be enforced (Article 46, paragraph 2 PCA);
– the use of EU technical regulations has to be promoted and European standards and conformity assessment procedures have to be applied (Article 50, paragraph 2, 2nd line PCA);
– promotion of teaching in the field of European studies shall take place (Article 53, paragraph 2, 5th line PCA);
– EU languages shall be taught (Article 53, paragraph 2, 6th line PCA);
– Azerbaijan's standards shall be approximated to EU technical regulations related to industrial and agricultural food products (Article 54 PCA) etc.

In regard to democracy and human rights, Article 71 PCA with Azerbaijan shows that cooperation between the parties means technical assistance programs of the European Union with regard to the Republic of Azerbaijan, *inter alia*, "in drafting of relevant legislation and regulations; the implementation of such legislation; the functioning of judiciary; the role of the State in questions of justice; and the operation of the electoral system." Training, as well as contacts and exchanges between the respective bodies are envisaged.

Thus, the commitments that the states of the regions are burdened with in exchange for being granted temporary financial EU assistance by way of technical assistance in the form of grants[52] are essential and include a reform of their economic, political and legal systems which comes close to revolution.[53]

---

52   See eg title X (arts 77–80) PCA with Azerbaijan (n 5).

53   It is rather surprising that an evaluation of the PCAs, based on the example of the PCA Russia, which, however, is more balanced in comparison to the PCAs of the regions, in the Russian legal literature does not at all address the (remaining) lack of balance between the rights and obligations of the treaty partners. See P. A. Kalinichenko, S. Yu. Kashkin, 'Pravovye osnovy vzaimootnosheniy mezhdu Rossiey i Evropeyskim Soyuzom' in S. Yu. Kashkin (ed), *Pravo Evropeyskogo Soyuza* (2002) 886, 888–898. S. Yu. Kashkin, 'Kakovy perspektivy ukrepleniya sotrudnichestva mezhdu Rossiey i Evropeyskim Soyuzom' in S. Yu. Kashkin (ed), *Pravo Evropeyskogo Soyuza v voprosakh i otvetakh* (2005) 287–290 refers to the official Russian strategy for the period 2000–2010 and points, in particular, on the fundamental aim that the national interests of Russia and the strengthened authority of Russia need to be considered. These interests are not really well understood and conceived on the EU side, see eg V. Tchakarova, 'Die Europäische Union und Russland. Eine strategische Partnerschaft ohne strategische Bindung?' in *Wiener Blätter zur Friedensforschung* N°154, Vienna (March 2013) 36–46, 41. The renegotiations with

In order to better balance mutual rights and obligations in current and future negotiations, the general principle, laid down in Article 3 PCA with Azerbaijan, that the states in the territory of the former Soviet Union "should maintain and develop cooperation among themselves in compliance with the principles of the Helsinki Final Act and with international law and in the spirit of good neighborly relations", where, also, the EU/Euratom committed to "make every effort to encourage this process", could serve as a decisive tool for raising the bargaining power of the states of the regions to a standard, still far from EU/Euratom, but clearly above the one of individual states.

4   Options for Multilateralization on the Regions' Side

As the center of conflicting interests of the rival global players – US, Russia, EU, China, and others – and bearing the heritage of unresolved conflicts, in particular, in the Caucasus region, it is a difficult task to agree on formalized regional cooperation. Such cooperation would have relevance for the European Union only if all states of the regions were to be members and agreed on a common position for negotiations with the European Union prior to the start of such negotiations. Only under such preconditions could sufficient bargaining power be coalesced in order to make the EU shift from bilateral to regional negotiations. Recent history shows that five options have started; one of them, however, has already definitively failed since 2005:

- The CIS Free Trade Zone or CIS directly (CIS FTZ/CIS)
- The Eurasian Economic Community (EurAsEC)
- The Shanghai Cooperation Organization (SCO)
- The Eurasian Economic Union (EAEU, from 2015 onwards)
- The Central Asian Cooperation Organization (CACO).

---

regard to the PCA Russia tend to reduce the legislative challenges for Russia to more pragmatism. See eg P. W. Schulze, 'Russische Föderation'in W. Schneider-Deters, P. W. Schulze, H. Timmermann (eds), *Die Europäische Union, Russland und Eurasien* (Berliner Wissenschafts-Verlag 2008) 57, 138ff. Some (minor) critics at the consequences of the PCA Russia raises B. N. Topornin, *Evropeyskoe pravo* (2001) 263. Political literature, however, shows to be very critical, see eg T. Bordachev, 'A. Moshes, Is the Europeanization of Russia over?' (April – June 2004) Russia in Global Affairs, 90ff. Major aspects of Russian interest and concern in the ongoing negotiations are discussed by M. L. Ėntin, 'Budushchee bazovoe soglashenie mezhdu Rossiey i Evropeyskim Soyuzom glazami biznesa' in Rauschning, Rusinova (n 49) 111–129; P. A. Kalinichenko, 'Formirovanie strategic partnership acquis v kontekste razrabotki Dogovora o strategicheskom partnerstve mezhdu Rossiey i Evropeyskim Soyuzom' ibid 130–138; and V. V. Voynikov, 'Pravovye

The CACO[54] can be considered as no longer relevant. The Treaty on the Establishment of the CACO had been signed on 28 February 2002 by all Central Asian states with the exception of Turkmenistan and was joined by Russia in 2004. It succeeded to the Central Asian Economic Community which had been founded in 1994. On 6/7 October 2005, the CACO, by decision of its summit in St. Petersburg, merged with the EAEC.

As for the CIS, there is no doubt regarding its character as a regional international organization under public international law.[55] Due to the fact that Georgia, with legal effect as of 18 August 2009 and in accordance with the CIS Statutes, ended its membership within the CIS, neither the CIS, nor any agreement concluded in the framework of the CIS can fulfill the basic requirement of representing all states of the Central Asian and Caucasus regions in their relationships with the EU/Euratom. This goes, in particular, for the Treaty on a free trade zone in the CIS, which was originally signed by Belarus, Russia, Armenia, Kazakhstan, Kyrgyzstan, Moldova, Ukraine, and Tajikistan on 18 October 2011.[56] The treaty entered into force for Belarus, Russia, and Ukraine on 20 September 2012, for Armenia on 17 October 2012, for Kazakhstan on 8 December 2012, and for Moldova on 9 December 2012. Uzbekistan acceded to the treaty on 31 May 2013. Thus, besides Georgia, Azerbaijan, as well, in the Caucasus region is not a member of the treaty.

The SCO[57] was founded in Shanghai by China, Kazakhstan, Kyrgyzstan, Russia, Tajikistan, and Uzbekistan on 15 June 2001. The organization does not extend to the Caucasus region and, due to the fact that Turkmenistan is not

---

osnovy sotrudnichestva Rossii i Evropeyskogo Sojuza v oblasti obespecheniya svobody peredvizheniya' ibid 139–147.

54 See Zenis Kembayev, 'Legal Aspects of Regional Integration in Central Asia' (2006) 66 ZaöRV 967–983 <www.zaoerv.de/66_2006/66_2006_4_b_967_984.pdf> accessed 30 June 2021.

55 See eg the convincing analysis having been done already shortly after its establishment by V. V. Pustogarov, 'SNG – Mezhdunarodnaya regioanl'naya organizaciya' (1992) Rossiyskiy Ezhegodnik Mezhdunarodnogo Prava; in general: E. G. Moiseev, *Mezhdunarodno-pravovye osnovy sotrudnichestva stran SNG* (1997). With regard to the CIS' potential as to international trade law see A. Tynel, Ya. Funk, V. Khvaley, *Kurs Mezhdunarodnogo torgovogo prava* (2000) 35ff; as to international economic law see eg V. M. Shumilov, *Mezhdunarodnoe ėkonomicheskoe pravo* (2011) 204–206.

56 Russian text of the treaty available on the official CIS website <http://cis.minsk.by/reestr/ru/index.html#reestr/view/text?doc=3183> accessed 30 June 2021 and in Byulleten' mezhdunarodnykh dogovorov 2013/1/71.

57 See for more details the description on the official website <http://eng.sectsco.org/> accessed 30 June 2021.

a member, does not cover the full region of Central Asia either. Apart from this weakness of its territorial range, the SCO was more influential and visible in the field of settlement of longstanding border disputes along the former border between China and the Soviet Union. It was successful in implementing confidence- and security- building measures in the border areas and in addressing the issues of terrorism, extremism and separatism, in particular through the 2001 Shanghai Convention on Combating Terrorism, Extremism, and Separatism, which entered into force on 29 March 2003.[58] As for the field of economic cooperation, the major achievement of the SCO was the establishment of a Business Council on 14 June 2006. It established special working groups on healthcare and on education and launched joint projects. Apart from that and an Agreement on an Interbank Consortium, which was signed on 26 October 2005, Programs and Action Plans for multilateral trade and economic cooperation which were adopted and implemented,[59] the SCO has not yet effectively realized its main goals in the economic field, which are the promotion of effective cooperation, *inter alia*, in trade, economy, energy, transportation, and other fields to such an extent that it could effectively balance the organizational strength of the EU/Euratom. The membership of China and a clear Asian focus of the organization, which is also visible from the observer status of Afghanistan, India, Iran, Mongolia, and Pakistan, are another reason why the SCO will hardly be the organization to gain the necessary regional organizational force in order to serve as an instrument of the members of the regions in their relations with the EU/Euratom.

The founding treaty of the EurAsEC was signed in Astana on 10 October 2000 and entered into force for Belarus, Kazakhstan, Kyrgyzstan, Russia, and Tajikistan on 30 May 2001. Uzbekistan acceded to the treaty on 25 June 2006 but stopped its participation in the work of the EurAsEC bodies in October 2008.[60] Ukraine, Moldova and Armenia had observer status. Thus, neither the Central Asian, nor the Caucasus regions were (fully) covered by the EurAsEC. The EurAsEC certainly had a potential from the perspective of its

---

58   See, in particular, R. Maksutov, 'The Shanghai Cooperation Organisation: A Central
       Asian Perspective. SIPRI' (August 2006) 3, 10ff. An English translation of the Shanghai
       Convention on Terrorism, Extremism and Separatism, which has been set up in Russian
       and Chinese, is available at <www.refworld.org/docid/49f5d9f92.html> accessed 30 June
       2021.

59   See Maksutov (n 57), 19–23.

60   See the official description of the organization on the official website <www.evrazes
       .com> accessed 30 June 2021.

organizational structure to balance the EU/Euratom. This may also be true after the EurAsEC transformed into the EAEU on 1 January 2015. Already since 1 January 2012 between Belarus, Kazakhstan and Russia, the Common Economic Space started to work based on a relatively dense net of international treaties concluded between its members.[61]

On 5 July 2007, the Interstate Council of the EurAsEC adopted the concept for the international activity of the EurAsEC.[62] This concept declared that the EurAsEC felt committed to the world-wide framework of the UN and to the aims and principles of the UN Charter (Chapter1). The EurAsEC undertook to develop a partnership on the international level in order to cooperate for a more just international trading system, based on strict compliance with norms of public international law, equality, mutual confidence, and respect of mutual interests (Chapters 2–4). It aims to create regional stability and guarantee economic safety for its members (Chapter 2). The EurAsEC pleaded for agreed-upon conditions concerning the accession to the WTO. It considered the European Union as one of the key partners with widely the same interests as the ones of the EurAsEC (Chapter 5). Together, a sustainable economic development should be achieved. The Secretary General of the EurAsEC periodically provided information about the realization of implementation plans set up on the basis of this concept.[63]

The EurAsEC, moreover, now transformed into the EAEU, thus, demonstrates an organizational potential to balance the EU/Euratom. For the states of the Central Asian and Caucasus regions, profiting from this potential means cooperation with Russia within this organization. Once more, the Georgia–Russia conflict and the Nagorno-Karabakh conflict between Armenia and Azerbaijan need to be overcome in order to eliminate the key obstacles on such a road. The only other alternative to individualization and marginalization in relations with the European Union is regional cooperation without organizational framework. Austria, Switzerland, Norway, Finland and Sweden chose such an

---

61   For the period of the EurAsEC until 2010 see a list of the most important treaties eg at Shumilov (n 54) 206ff. All these and all later documents can be found in the document section of the official website (n 59).

62   Koncepciya mezhdunarodnoy deyatel'nosti EAEC. Prilozhenie k Resheniyu Mezhgosudarstvennogo Soveta EvrAzÈS, 5 July 2007, N° 344.

63   See eg Informaciya o khode vypolneniya Plana meropriyatiy po realizacii Koncepcii mezhdunarodnoy deyatel'nosti EvrAzÈS na 2008–2010 g (Information on the course of implementation of the Plan concerning measures as to the realization of the Concept for the international activity of EurAsEC).

approach when negotiating accession to the European Union. Prior exchange of information, prior consent on negotiation positions, and mutual assistance in achieving these positions are the minimum conditions for attaining a better result than the PCAs have in the past.

CHAPTER 3

"Competing Regionalism" vs. "Cooperative Regionalism"

On the Possible Relations between Different Regional Economic Integration Agreements

Karsten Nowrot

1   The Rise of Regionalism … and Its Consequences

When asked to name a number of current mega-trends in the progressive development of the international economic legal order, one of the first issues that probably comes to the mind of most scholars and practitioners is the perception that regionalism is on the rise.[1] And indeed, it is an almost incontrovertible fact and hardly needs to be emphasized that in particular since the beginning of the 1990s, for a variety of reasons numerous treaties establishing free trade zones as well as other bilateral and regional economic integration agreements have been successfully concluded or are currently under negotiation, among them more recently also emerging so-called "mega-regionals", occasionally also referred to as "super-RTAs";[2] a term and concept that mostly refers to economic agreements that are inter-regional in character in the sense of connecting different regions of the world and are concluded by a group of countries that together have a significant economic weight in current global trade and investment relations.[3] Among the respective preferential trade agreements frequently classified as mega-regionals are the

---

1   On this perception see, e.g., UNCTAD World Investment Report 2013, *Global Value Chains: Investment and Trade for Development* (*2013*), 103ff ("Regionalism on the rise"); Alschner Wolfgang, 'Regionalism and Overlap in Investment Treaty Law: Towards Consolidation or Contradiction?' [2014] 17(2) Journal of International Economic Law 271 (273); Marc Bungenberg, 'Preferential Trade and Investment Agreements and Regionalism' in Rainer Hofmann, Stephan Schill, and Christian Tams (eds.), *Preferential Trade and Investment Agreements – From Recalibration to Reintegration* (2013) 269, 270ff.

2   See for example Subhankar Karmakar, *Rulemaking in Super-RTAs: Implications for China and India, Bruegel Working Paper* (2014).

3   On these elements as well as for related characterizations of mega-regionals see, eg UNCTAD World Investment Report 2014, *Investing in the SDGs: An Action Plan* (2014) 118; Karsten Nowrot, 'Of "Plain" Analytical Approaches and "Savior" Perspectives – Measuring

– Trans-Pacific Partnership (TPP) originally signed by the United States as well as Australia, Brunei, Canada, Chile, Japan, Malaysia, Mexico, New Zealand, Peru, Singapore, and Vietnam on 4 February 2016 (whose fate, however, hung somewhat in the balance following the withdrawal by the United States in January 2017,[4] and led to the signature of the Comprehensive and Progressive Transpacific Partnership (CPTPP) by eleven signatory states without the United States[5]);

– the Comprehensive Economic and Trade Agreement (CETA) between Canada and the European Union (EU) which was signed by the parties on 30 October 2016 and has been provisionally applied since 21 September 2017;

– the Transatlantic Trade and Investment Partnership (TTIP) being negotiated between the United States and the EU since July 2013 (with the negotiations being currently on hold);

– the Regional Comprehensive Economic Partnership (RCEP) on which negotiations were launched in 2012 by the ten member states of the Association of Southeast Asian Nations (ASEAN) and six other countries including China, India, Japan and Australia,

– and the proposed free trade agreement (that at the time of writing still lacked a more or less fancy name and abbreviation) officially being negotiated between the EU and Japan since March 2013.[6]

Whereas within the time frame of close to fifty years under the former General Agreement on Tariffs and Trade 1947 (GATT 1947), from the beginning of 1948 until the end of 1994, only a total of 107 regional trade agreements and accessions thereto were notified by contracting parties under Article XXIV:7 GATT

---

the Structural Dialogues between Bilateral Investment Treaties and Investment Chapters in Mega-Regionals' (2017) 6; Opoku Awuku, 'Developing and Least-Developed Countries and Mega-Regional Trade and Investment Agreements' (2016) 7 European Yearbook of International Economic Law 615, 616; Joost Pauwelyn,Wolfgang Alschner, 'Forget about the WTO: The Network of Relations between PTAs and Double PTAs' in A. Dür, M.Elsig (eds), *Trade Cooperation – The Purpose, Design and Effects of Preferential Trade Agreements* (2015) 497, 512.

4   See, eg UNCTAD, Investment Policy Monitor (Issue 18, December 2017) 8–9.

5   Comprehensive and Progressive Agreement for Transpacific Partnership (CPTPP) (signed 8 March 2018) <https://www.mfat.govt.nz/en/trade/free-trade-agreements/free-trade-agreements-in-force/cptpp/> accessed 30 June 2021. The TPTPP entered into force on 30 December 2018.

6   Generally, on the phenomenon of mega-regionals see for examples the contributions in Rensmann Thilo (ed), *Mega-Regional Trade Agreements* (Springer International Publishing 2017).

1947.[7] By contrast, as of 1 December 2021, already some 786 respective notifications have been received by the WTO. These figures correspond to a total of 350 regional trade agreements that are presently in force.[8] As a result, the number of regional trade agreements has increased more than four-fold in the last two decades.[9] In order to illustrate the overall significance and consequences of these developments, let it initially suffice to draw attention to the fact that as of today the overwhelming majority of the current 164 WTO members – notable exceptions being for example Mauretania, the Democratic Republic of Congo and Mongolia – is party to at least one regional trade agreement. The most of them have concluded considerably more than one of these types of arrangements. Already towards the end of the previous decade, the average WTO member had concluded regional trade agreements with roughly fifteen other countries.[10] To mention just three more or less randomly chosen examples, according to respective information provided by the WTO, the EU, being a WTO member and itself based on an economic integration agreement, was, at the time of writing, party to some forty notified regional trade agreements in force and has made an early announcement[11] for thirteen more treaties currently under negotiation. Ukraine is currently negotiating three regional trade agreements and is party to roughly eighteen other respective arrangements. And the Russian Federation is at present bound by twelve agreements while having entered into notified negotiations on three more treaties aimed at a closer economic integration at the sub-multilateral level.[12]

---

7   See, WTO, *Turkey – Restrictions on the Imports of Textile and Clothing Products*, Panel Report (adopted on 19 November 1999) WT/DS34/R, para 2.3.

8   On these data as well as continuously updated information on this issue see the respective information provided by the WTO on its website available under: <www.wto.org/english/tratop_e/region_e/region_e.htm> accessed 1 December 2021.

9   See on this finding already WTO, 'The WTO and Preferential Trade Agreements: From Co-Existence to Coherence', World Trade Report 2011 (2011) 3.

10   Caroline Freund/Emanuel Ornelas, 'Regional Trade Agreements', World Bank Policy Research Working Paper 5314 (May 2010) 2.

11   Generally, on the procedure of early announcements see WTO, *Transparency Mechanism for Regional Trade Agreements* (WT/L/671 of 18 December 2006), paras. 1ff; as well as Jo-Ann Crawford, C.L. Lim, 'Cast Light and Evil Will Go Away: The Transparency Mechanism for Regulating Regional Trade Agreements Three Years After' (2011) 45 Journal of World Trade 375; Jürgen Bering and Karsten Nowrot, 'The 2010 WTO Transparency Mechanism for Preferential Trade Arrangements: As Good as it Currently Realistically Gets' (2012) 35 Policy Papers on Transnational Economic Law 7ff.

12   See the information provided by the WTO and available under: <https://www.wto.org/english/tratop_e/region_e/rta_participation_map_e.htm> accessed 30 June 2021.

In light of these findings, it appears hardly surprising that it is in particular the consequences arising from these structural developments in the international system that are of considerable practical importance and have thus – in principle already for quite some time – also attracted significant scholarly attention.[13] Thereby, the respective academic debates were until recently primarily concerned with the economic effects of regional integration agreements. Jagdish Bhagwati, for example, emphasized the – if compared to multilateral approaches aimed at trade liberalization – rising transaction costs for private economic operators as a result of the "spaghetti bowl" phenomenon created by the proliferation of bilateral and regional free trade agreements granting diverging trade preferences to the goods and services originating from a limited number of countries.[14] In addition, in order to mention but one further example, already in the beginning of the 1950s Jacob Viner identified, analyzed and contrasted the "trade-creating" and thus economic as well as social welfare-enhancing effects of regional trade agreements for the participating actors on the one side with the respective "trade-diverting" as well as welfare-reducing consequences for economic operators from third countries on the other side.[15]

Whereas it is increasingly recognized that any attempt to make unambiguous and generalizing determinations on the preponderance of the positive or negative consequences of regional integration agreements for the multilateral trading regime as a whole seems to be rather challenging and error-prone,[16]

---

13   See thereto as well as on the continuing need for additional research efforts for example the observations made by L. Alan Winter, 'Preferential Trade Agreements: Friend or Foe?' in Kyle W. Bagwell and Petros C. Mavroidis (eds.), *Preferential Trade Agreements – A Law and Economics Analysis*, (CUP 2011) 7 ("The literature on PTAs has proliferated even faster than the phenomenon itself, but not the set of convincing general results to which one can appeal for policy guidance.").

14   On the term "spaghetti bowl" phenomenon and its negative connotations in the present context see, eg Jagdish Bhagwati, 'U.S. Trade Policy: The Infatuation with Free Trade Areas' in J. Bhagwati and A. O. Krueger (eds), *The Dangerous Drift to Preferential Trade Agreements* (AEI Press 1995) 1, 2ff; Jagdisch Bhagwati, *Free Trade Today* (Princeton 2002) 112ff; see also for example Rafael Leal-Arcas, *International Trade and Investment Law – Multilateral, Regional and Bilateral Governance* (Edward Elgar 2010) 76.

15   Jacob Viner, *The Customs Union Issue* (OUP 1950) 41ff.

16   On this perception see already Viner (n 15) 52 ("Confident judgment as to what the overall balance between these conflicting considerations would be, it should be obvious, cannot be made for customs unions in general and in the abstract, but must be confined to particular projects and be based on economic surveys thorough enough to justify reasonable reliable estimates as to the weights to be given in the particular circumstances to the respective elements in the problem. Customs unions are, from the free-trade point of view, neither necessarily good nor necessarily bad; [...].''); see also more recently for example Markus Krajewski, *Wirtschaftsvölkerrecht* (4th edn, C.F. Müller 2017), para. 992;

the last mentioned aspect of potential "trade-diverting" effects with regard to non-participating countries already indicates one of the generally agreed "dark sides" of regionalism, the consequences of which are potentially not confined to the realm of economics: the exclusionary dimension of regional trade agreements. Although a sober evaluation of this aspect indeed reveals, first, that "nearly every country is excluded from nearly every PTA [preferential trade agreement]"[17] and, second, that this fact – at least under normal circumstances and in most situations – does not pose something even close to an insurmountable economic or normative challenge to the realization of regional integration projects, it should nevertheless be recalled that preferential trade agreements are rarely if ever concluded for economic reasons alone.[18] Just as transboundary economic relations never develop – and as a consequence should never be considered – in isolation from, and thus uninfluenced by, the respective political relationship between the states concerned, foreign trade policy measures and regulations have not infrequently been, and continue to be, used also as governmental means to promote and protect non-economic interests and objectives. This applies first and foremost also to the establishment of regional economic integration regimes, not infrequently also intended, *inter alia*, to promote peace and security, to foster democracy and stability in the region, to secure political influence as well as – in particular in the case of more advanced forms of regional trade agreements – to facilitate political integration among the contracting parties.[19] And it is precisely the frequent use of – and deliberate choice between – certain bilateral or regional

---

Mitsuo Matsushita and others, *The World Trade Organization – Law, Practice, and Policy* (3rd edn., OUP 2015) 513.

17 Winter (n 13), 17.

18 See, e.g., David A. Gantz, *Regional Trade Agreements – Law, Policy and Practice* (Carolina Academic Press 2009) 26 ("It would be naïve to assume that the United States and other nations busily concluding RTAs are doing so exclusively for economic and trade reasons."); Olivier Cattaneo, 'The Political Economy of PTAs' in S. Lester, and B. Mercurio (eds), *Bilateral and Regional Trade Agreements* (CUP 2009) 28, 50 ("It seems clear, however, that the political economy of bilateral/regional trade agreements revolves more around politics than economics."); Yoram Haftel, 'Trade Agreements, Violent Conflict and Security' in A. Dür and M. Elsig (eds.), *Trade Cooperation – The Purpose, Design and Effects of Preferential Trade Agreements* (CUP 2015) 295; Mosche Hirsch, 'The Sociology of International Economic Law – Sociological Analysis of the Regulation of Regional Agreements in the World Trading System' (2008) 19 European Journal of International Law 277, 293.

19 On these as well as other non-economic foreign policy goals often associated with the promotion of regional economic integration processes see for example Gantz (n 18), 26ff; Lorand Bartels, 'Regional Trade Agreements', para. 4 in R. Wolfrum (ed), *Max Planck Encyclopedia of Public International Law* (OUP 2013) available at:

economic integration projects as an instrument for the pursuit of broader foreign policy goals by individual states that occasionally results in this segregative or exclusionary dimension of respective trade agreements developing a notable and worrisome potential to contribute to the outbreak or deepening of a political crisis between the affected countries.[20]

A well-known recent example for such severe political consequences arising from – or at least also fueled by – the conclusion of and choice between different regional trade agreements is the Ukraine crisis that began towards the end of 2013. There is probably almost general agreement among academic observers that ever since the country gained independence in 1991, Ukraine has – from an overarching and to a certain extent simplifying perspective – more or less constantly oscillated, and is in fact somewhat torn, between two main different processes of regional economic integration.[21] On the one hand are the efforts of this country aimed at forming a closer alliance with, and even securing a perspective for membership in, the EU. Following the dissolution of the Union of Soviet Socialist Republics (USSR), Ukraine happened to be the first participant of the then newly-formed Commonwealth of Independent States (CIS) to sign a partnership and cooperation agreement (PCA) with the former European Communities on 14 June 1994 that entered into force on 1 May 1998.[22]

---

30 June 2021; UCTAD, Key Statistics and Trends in Trade Policy 2015, *Preferential Trade Agreements* (2015) 3.

20   See also generally thereto, e.g., Brad Kloewer, 'The Spaghetti Bowl of Preferential Trade Agreements and the Declining Relevance of the WTO' (2016) 44 Denver Journal of International Law and Policy 429, 435 ("PTAS [preferential trade agreements] between a selected number of nations can also serve another useful political purpose by pitting regions against one another in ideological battles.").

21   On this perception see for example Guillaume Van der Loo and Peter Van Elsuwege, 'Competing Paths of Regional Economic Integration in the Post-Soviet Space: Legal And Political Dilemmas for Ukraine' (2013) 37 Review of Central and East European Law 421, 422; Max Biedermann, 'Ukraine: Between Scylla and Charybdis' (2014) 40 North Carolina Journal of International Law and Commercial Regulation 219, 231; Boris N. Mamlyuk, 'Regionalizing Multilateralism: The Effect of Russia's Accession to the WTO on Existing Regional Integration Schemes in the Former Soviet Space' (2014) 18 UCLA Journal of International Law and Foreign Affairs 207, 232. More generally also, eg Christian Nitoiu, 'EU-Russia Relations: Between Conflict and Cooperation' (2014) 51 International Politics 234, 235 ("the distant prospect of EU membership and the influence of Russia have made the states of the Eastern Neighbourhood open to gamble between Moscow's short-term solutions and the EU's potential economic and democratic benefits").

22   Partnership and Cooperation Agreement between the European Communities and their Member States, and Ukraine of 14 June 1994, OJ EC L 49/3 of 19 February 1998. See thereto as well as generally on the political and historical background of EU-Ukraine relations since the beginning of the 1990s Guillaume Van der Loo, *The EU-Ukraine Association Agreement and Deep and Comprehensive Free Trade Area – A New Legal Instrument for EU*

In addition, Ukraine became, almost naturally, an important partner in the EU's European Neighborhood Policy (ENP), originally developed as a policy framework in 2003/2004[23] and subsequently, since the entry into force of the EU Lisbon Reform Treaty in December 2009, also enshrined in primary EU law on the basis of Article 8 of the Treaty on European Union (TEU).[24] The same applies to the eastern regional dimension of the ENP established in 2009 in the form of the so-called "Eastern Partnership", a policy regime that currently, in addition to Ukraine, comprises Armenia, Azerbaijan, Belarus, Georgia, and Moldova.[25] Last, but surely not least, it was under the umbrella of the ENP, that the negotiations between the EU and Ukraine on a successor agreement to the 1994 PCA were launched in March 2007;[26] a process that ultimately led to the conclusion of the EU-Ukraine Association Agreement in March/June 2014, that entered into force on 1 September 2017.[27]

    Integration without Membership (Brill 2016) 62ff; Rilka Dragneva and Kataryna Wolczuk, 'The EU-Ukraine Association Agreement and the Challenges of Inter-Regionalism' (2014) 39 Review of Central and East European Law 213, 214, each with further references.

23   For the creation of the ENP see originally in particular Commission of the European Communities, *Wider Europe – Neighbourhood: A New Framework for Relations with our Eastern and Southern Neighbours* (COM(2003) 104 final of 11 March 2003); Commission of the European Communities, *European Neighbourhood Policy – Strategy Paper* (COM(2004) 373 final of 12 May 2004).

24   Generally, on the ENP see, eg Rudolf Geiger, 'Article 8 TEU' in Rudolf Geiger, Daniel-Erasmus Khan and Markus Kotzur (eds), *European Union Treaties* (Hart 2015) paras 2ff; Peter Van Elsuwege and Roman Petrov, 'Article 8 TEU: Towards a New Generation of Agreements with the Neighbouring Countries of the European Union?' (2011) 36 European Law Review 688ff; Robert Schütze, *European Union Law*, (OUP 2015) 910ff; Markus Kotzur, 'Europäische Nachbarschaftspolitik' in Andreas von Arnauld (ed), *Europäische Außenbeziehungen* (Nomos 2014) § 7, paras 1ff; Michael Emerson, 'Just Good Friends? The European Union's Multiple Neighbourhood Policies' (2011) 46 The International Spectator – Italian Journal of International Affairs 45ff; as well as more recently European Commission/High Representative of the Union for Foreign Affairs and Security Policy, *Report on the Implementation of the European Neighbourhood Policy Review* (JOIN(2017) 18 final of 18 May 2017).

25   Generally on the Eastern Partnership see, eg Roman Petrov and Dominik Braun, 'Die Östliche Partnerschaft als besondere Ausprägung der Europäischen Nachbarschaftspolitik' in Armin Hatje and Peter-Christian Müller-Graff (eds), *Europäisches Organisations- und Verfassungsrecht* (Nomos 2014), § 2adop2, paras 1ff; as well as recently Joint Declaration of the Eastern Partnership Summit in Brussels on 24 November 2017, Council of the European Union Doc 14821/17 of 24 November 2017.

26   For a more detailed account of the negotiations see for example Van der Loo (n 22) 104ff.

27   Association Agreement between the European Union and its Member States, of the one part, and Ukraine, of the other part, OJ EU L161/3 of 29 May 2014. For a quite comprehensive description and analysis of this agreement see Van der Loo (n 22) 165ff; as well as for example Dragneva and Wolczuk (n 22) 222ff; Guillaume Van der Loo, Peter Van Elsuwege

On the other hand, in parallel with these efforts aimed at a closer integration into the EU realm, Ukraine was until more recently, also actively involved in various – albeit notably by far not all, in particular not the more ambitious[28] – processes of regional economic integration unfolding among a number of post-Soviet countries, frequently at the initiative of the Russian Federation.[29] Among the respective agreements also adopted by Ukraine are a free trade agreement (FTA) signed on 15 April 1994 by Armenia, Azerbaijan, Belarus, Georgia, Moldova, Kazakhstan, the Kyrgyz Republic, the Russian Federation, Tajikistan, Ukraine, and Uzbekistan,[30] a number of bilateral FTAs like the one concluded between Ukraine and Tajikistan on 6 June 2001,[31] as well as – in the form of a successor agreement to the 1994 FTA – the Treaty on a Free Trade Area signed by Armenia, Belarus, Kazakhstan, the Kyrgyz Republic, Moldova, the Russian Federation, Tajikistan, and Ukraine on 18 October 2011.[32] However, in the last two decades, Ukraine has for the most for the most part,[33]

---

and Roman Petrov, *The EU-Ukraine Association Agreement: Assessment of an Innovative Legal Instrument*, EUI Working Papers Law 2014/09 (2014) 7ff.

28 See thereto in particular Van der Loo (n 22) 131ff; European Parliament, *Study: When Choosing Means Losing – The Eastern Partners, the EU and the Eurasian Economic Union* (by Pasquale de Micco, DG EXPO/B/PolDep/Note/2015_108, March 2015) 44ff.

29 Generally on these processes see, eg European Parliament (n 28), 38ff; Azar Aliyev, 'Architektur der eurasischen Integration: Wirtschaftsgemeinschaft, Zollunion, Gemeinsamer Wirtschaftsraum, Wirtschaftsunion' (2013) 59 Osteuropa 378ff; Zhenis Kembayev, *Legal Aspects of the Regional Integration Processes in the Post-Soviet Area* (Springer 2009) 25ff; as well as the contributions in Rilka Dragneva and Kataryna Wolczuk (eds.), *Eurasian Economic Integration – Law, Policy and Politics* (Edward Elgar 2013).

30 The text of the agreement is for example available at: <https://wits.worldbank.org/ GPTAD/PDF/archive/CIS.pdf> 21 March 2019. The agreement was never ratified by the Russian Federation and consequently of only limited practical relevance, see thereto European Parliament (n 28), 41; Van der Loo (n 22), 132; Zhenis Kembayev, 'The (In-) Compatibility between Regional Integration Processes in the Post-Soviet Area and within the European Neighborhood Policy' (2013) 59 Osteuropa 369 (371); Rilka Dragneva and Joopde Kort, 'The Legal Regime for Free Trade in the Commonwealth of Independent States' (2007) 56 International and Comparative Law Quarterly 233, 238.

31 The text of the agreement is for example available at: <http://rtais.wto.org/UI/Public ShowMemberRTAIDCard.aspx?rtaid=576> 30 June 2021.

32 The text of the agreement is for example available at: <http://rtais.wto.org/UI/Public ShowMemberRTAIDCard.aspx?rtaid=762> 30 June 2021.

33 A temporary exception was the signing, by Belarus, Kazakhstan, the Russian Federation as well as Ukraine, of the Agreement on the Formation of a Single Economic Space on 19 September 2003, a project that was apparently primary initiated in order to induce Ukraine into a more advance regime of regional economic integration with the other three countries but was no longer pursued after the next Ukrainian President Yuschenko announced in August 2005 that his country does not intend to ratify those parts of the agreement that were related to the establishment of supranational organs and a customs

intentionally abstained from becoming involved in the process of regional economic integration among post-Soviet countries, which and has more recently even emerged as a serious competitor to the EU. The process began in January 1995 with the conclusion of a customs union agreement between Belarus, Kazakhstan and the Russian Federation, which subsequently lead, among others, to the following: the signing of the Treaty on the Customs Union and Single Economic Space by these three countries as well as the Kyrgyz Republic and Tajikistan in February 1999; the conclusion, by these five countries, of the Treaty on the Foundation of the Eurasian Economic Community (EurAsEC) in October 2000; the Treaty on the Establishment of the Common Customs Territory and Creation of the Customs Union agreed by the "core group" of Belarus, Kazakhstan and Russia in October 2007; the implementation of the EurAsEC Customs Union between these three countries on 1 January 2010[34] and the creation of Eurasian Economic Union as the successor to the Eurasian Economic Community on the basis of an agreement signed by Belarus, Kazakhstan and Russia on 29 May 2014, by Armenia on 10 October 2014 and by the Kyrgyz Republic on 23 December 2014 that entered into force for the first four members in January 2015 and for Kyrgyzstan in August 2015.[35]

Whereas in the two decades prior to the establishment and implementation of the EurAsEC Customs Union in 2010, the political and economic pressure exercised by the Russian Federation on Ukraine to participate in the

---

union. See thereto, e.g., Sherzod Shadikhodjaev, 'Trade Integration in the CIS Region: A Thorny Path towards a Customs Union' (2009) 12 Journal of International Economic Law 555, 564ff; Van der Loo and Van Elsuwege (n 21) 433ff; Dragneva and Wolczuk (n 22) 226ff; European Parliament (n 28), 44–45.

34   On the emergence and subsequent maturing of this regional economic integration regime see also for example European Parliament (n 27) 43ff; Alexei S. Ispolinov, 'First Judgments of the Court of the Eurasian Economic Community: Reviewing Private Rights in a New Regional Agreement' (2013) 40 Legal Issues of Economic Integration 225ff; Zhenis Kembayev, 'Eurasian Economic Community (EurAsEC)', paras 2ff in Wolfrum (n 19); Christoph Schewe and Azar Aliyev, 'The Customs Union and the Common Economic Space of the Eurasian Economic Community: Eurasian Counterpart to the EU or Russian Domination?' (2011) 54 German Yearbook of International Law 565ff; Hans-Michael Wolffgang, Gennadiy Brovka and Igor Belozerov, 'The Eurasian Customs Union in Transition' (2013) 7/2 World Customs Journal 93ff.

35   Concerning the founding of the Eurasian Economic Union and its institutional as well as substantive regulatory features see, eg Miguel Kühn, 'The Eurasian Economic Union' (2017) 20 Zeitschrift für Europarechtliche Studien 185, 197ff; European Parliament (n 28), 50ff; Marcus Schladebach and Vitaly Kim, "Die Eurasische Wirtschaftsunion: Grundlagen, Ziele, Chancen, Wirtschaft und Recht" [2015] Osteuropa 24 161ff. See also Zhenis Kembayev, 'The Eurasian Economic Union: An Overview and Evaluation' in this volume, 19 et seq.

post-Soviet regional integration processes "remained limited",[36] respective efforts clearly intensified from the beginning of 2011 onwards.[37] Particularly in the second half of 2013, these initiatives initially appeared to be successful. Not only did Armenia inform the EU in September 2013 about its decision not to sign the association agreement that it had negotiated with the EU between July 2010 and July 2013 but to join instead the Eurasian Customs Union,[38] but the Ukrainian government also famously announced on 21 November 2013 that the preparations for signing the respective agreement with the EU, scheduled to take place on the occasion of the third Eastern Partnership Summit in Vilnius on 28/29 November 2013, were suspended indefinitely. While it is incontrovertible that a number of different factors have contributed to the outbreak of the complex and ongoing Ukrainian crisis at the end of 2013,[39] there is by now probably almost general agreement among commentators that quite prominent among these causes was the decision by the Ukrainian government to halt the association process with the EU in favor of (potentially) acceding to the Eurasian Customs Union.[40] This choice between two different

---

36   Van der Loo (n 22), 135.

37   For respective Russian initiatives see for example Van der Loo (n 22), 135ff; in particular ibid 135 ("However, in 2011 – the same period when the negotiations on the EU-Ukraine AA and DCFTA were finalised –, Russia moved up a gear and tried to convince Ukraine to join the Eurasian Customs Union with several trade benefits and even threatened to retaliate with additional trade barriers if it would conclude the AA and DCFTA with the EU."); as well as Dragneva and Wolczuk (n 22) 229ff.

38   See thereto, eg Armen Grigoryan, 'Armenia's Membership in the Eurasian Economic Union: An Economic Challenge and Possible Consequences for Regional Security' (2015) 4 Polish Quarterly of International Affairs 7ff.

39   See for example the observation by Boris Mamlyuk, 'The Ukraine Crisis, Cold War II, and International Law' (2015) 16 German Law Journal 479, 482 ("Like any geopolitical phenomenon, the Ukraine crisis has multiple roots."); from a more overarching perspective see also, eg Nicholas Ross Smith, 'The Underpinning *Realpolitik* of the EU's Policies towards Ukraine: An Analysis of Interests and Norms in the EU-Ukraine Association Agreement' (2014) 19 European Foreign Affairs Review 581, 595 ("the Ukraine crisis appears to have been the product of structural forces in Europe, where two competing powers with overlapping spheres of influence have created a geopolitical 'pressure-cooker' in Ukraine").

40   On this perception see, eg Van der Loo (n 22) 131; Bernard Hoekman, Jesper Jensen and David Tarr, 'A Vision for Ukraine in the World Economy' (2014) 48 Journal of World Trade 795; Marten Breuer, 'Artikel 8: Nachbarschaftspolitik' para 32 in Matthias Pechstein, Carsten Nowak and Ulrich Häde (eds), *Frankfurter Kommentar zu EUV, GRC, und AEUV* (Mohr Siebeck 2017); Sarah Lain, 'Russia and EU Relations in Light of Ukraine' (2016) 3 Polish Quarterly of International Affairs 61; Kühn (n 35) 186ff; Christian Marxen, 'The Crimea Crisis – An International Law Perspective' (2014) 74 Zeitschrift für ausländisches öffentliches Recht und Völkerrecht 367, 368–369; Grigoryan (n 37) 25; Dragneva and Wolczuk (n 22) 214 ("It is not an understatement [sic] to say that this Agreement has

and apparently incompatible projects of regional economic integration sub-sequently resulted in the Euromaidan Revolution as well as, among others, the annexation of Crimea by Russia and the outbreak of an armed conflict between Ukrainian governmental forces and a separatist movement in the Donbas region of eastern Ukraine.

In light of this renewed[41] rise of "competing regionalism" in Europe[42] and the at times severe – and most certainly deplorable – consequences resulting from this phenomenon, the present contribution intends to present some systemizing thoughts, primarily from an international law perspective, on the apparently increasingly important issues concerning the relationship between different regional economic integration agreements in general and their mutual compatibility (or incompatibility) in particular. For this purpose, the following assessment is divided into three main parts. The first section illustrates the rising need for a broader analytical focus when evaluating the effects of regional trade agreements by not only taking into account the vertical relationship between these agreements and the multilateral trading regime but also a horizontal dimension and thus the interactions between different regional economic integration agreements (Section 2). Against this background, the following second part outlines and evaluates the compatibility of regional trade agreements in theory and current treaty practice from the perspective of international law (Section 3). Based on the findings made in this section, in the third and final section of this contribution an attempt will be made to provide some concluding thoughts on the issue of compatibility from a more policy-oriented perspective, thereby contrasting the phenomenon of "competing regionalism" with the generally more promising and desirable normative ordering idea of "cooperative regionalism" (Section 4).

---

fermented one of the most complex political, security and economic situations in Europe for many decades").

41 It seems appropriate to draw attention to the fact that "competing regionalism" is in principle also in the context of Europe not an entirely new phenomenon as illustrated – with, however, considerably less severe consequences – in particular by the political and historical circumstances that led to the almost parallel emergence and subsequent co-existence of the European Economic Community (EEC) and the European Free Trade Association (EFTA) since the end of the 1950s. See thereto, eg Luuk van Middelaar, *The Passage to Europe* (Yale University Press 2014) 166ff.

42 See, eg Kembayev (n 30) 376 ("we can clearly state that those processes are in principle of competitive character, Russia tries to create a Eurasian alliance consisting of former Soviet republics, while the EU attempts to establish a 'zone of friendly neighborhood' encompassing inter alia a number of post-Soviet countries").

2 · **Broadening the Analytical Focus: From Vertical to Horizontal Perspectives on the Effects of Regional Trade Agreements**

Academic discussions on the economic as well as the political effects of regional trade agreements have until recently primarily – not to say almost exclusively – adopted what might be labelled a vertical perspective by focusing on the respective consequences for the multilateral trading regime as legally manifested originally in the GATT 1947 and, following its entry into force in January 1995, the global legal order established by the WTO. Already for a number of decades we have found a quite intensive and controversial debate on whether regional economic integration agreements should more appropriately be perceived – to borrow from a distinction introduced by Jagdish Bhagwati – as "building blocks" or rather as "stumbling blocks" for the progressive development of the multilateral legal regime governing transboundary trade relations.[43] Furthermore, a truly notable amount of thought and ink has been devoted to an assessment of the interpretation as well as overall appropriateness and effectiveness of the provisions enshrined in the former GATT 1947 and the current WTO legal order – among them Article XXIV GATT, Articles V and V*bis* GATS as well as the "Enabling Clause"[44] – stipulating normative requirements for the legal compatibility of regional economic integration agreements

---

43   See for example Jagdish Bhagwati, *The World Trading System at Risk* (Princeton University Press 1991) 77 ("so that these arrangements more readily serve as building blocks of, rather than stumbling blocks to, GATT-wide free trade"); Bhagwati (n 14) 106ff; as well as in principle already Kenneth W. Dam, 'Regional Economic Arrangements and the GATT: The Legacy of a Misconception' (1963) 30 University of Chicago Law Review 615ff; and subsequently, eg Miroslav Jovanović, *The Economics of International Integration* (Edward Elgar 2006) 7ff; John H. Jackson, 'Regional Trade Blocks and the GATT' (1993) 16 The World Economy 121, 130; Sungjoon Cho, 'Breaking the Barrier between Regionalism and Multilateralism: A New Perspective on Trade Regionalism' (2001) 42 Harvard International Law Journal 419, 432ff; Richard Senti, 'Regional Trade Agreements: 'Stepping Stones' or 'Stumbling Blocks' of the WTO?' in Marise Cremona and others (eds), *Reflections on the Constitutionalisation of International Economic Law – Liber Amicorum for Ernst-Ulrich Petersmann* (Brill 2014) 441ff.

44   GATT, Decision on Differential and More Favourable Treatment, Reciprocity and Fuller Participation of Developing Countries, GATT Doc L/4903 of 3 December 1979; on the "Enabling Clause" see also, eg Won-Mog Choi and Yong-Shik Lee, 'Facilitating Preferential Trade Agreements between Developed and Developing Countries: A Case for 'Enabling' the Enabling Clause' (2012) 21 Minnesota Journal of International Law 1ff; Bartels (n 18) paras 42ff.

concluded by WTO members with their treaty obligations arising from the multilateral trading regime.[45]

While these as well as other issues related to the connection between regional trade agreements and the multilateral legal order established by the WTO have surely been – and most certainly remain – of outstanding importance and clearly merit continued intensive scientific evaluation,[46] it is equally incontrovertible that dealing with these questions can only illuminate one dimension of what is in fact a two-dimensional topic. As already indicated and quite vividly illustrated by the underlying developments leading to the Ukraine crisis,[47] the horizontal dimension of regional economic integration agreements is, from the perspective of practical relevance, surely no less important for the political and economic interactions in the international system than the respective vertical dimension. Against this background, the need arises to somewhat broaden and readjust the analytical focus when assessing the effects of these agreements by first and foremost taking into account and evaluating the interactions between, and compatibility of, the various regional economic integration regimes from a horizontal perspective. This is an analytical approach that has been until recently largely or – in light of the numerous contributions on the vertical relationship – at least comparatively neglected in the legal, economic and social science literature on regional integration.

3   Compatibility and Interactions between Regional Trade
       Agreements: Legal Implications

The institutional and substantive design of regional economic integration agreements does not follow something even close to a single model but, quite to the contrary, rather displays an almost infinite variety in treaty practice.[48]

---

45   From the numerous contributions on these issues see for example Van den Bossche and Zdouc (n 10) 671ff; Matsushita and others (n 16) 507ff; Kyle W. Bagwell and Petros C. Mavroidis (eds), *Preferential Trade Agreements – A Law and Economics Analysis* (CUP 2011); Karsten Nowrot, 'Steuerungssubjekte und -mechanismen im Internationalen Wirtschaftsrecht (einschließlich regionale Wirtschaftsintegration)' in Christian Tietje (ed), *Internationales Wirtschaftsrecht* (2nd edn, De Gruyter 2015) 67, 141ff, each with further references.

46   For a more critical perspective see, e.g., Pauwelyn and Alschner (n 3) 498 ("The vertical, top-down WTO-PTA relationship is, at least in legal terms, much overrated.").

47   See thereto supra under A.

48   See for example the observation made by Joel P. Trachtman, 'International Trade: Regionalism' in Andrew T. Guzman and Alan O. Sykes (eds), *Research Handbook in International Economic Law* (Edward Elgar 2007) 151, 153 ("regional integration defies

Nevertheless, in order to reduce the existing factual complexities by way of systemization,[49] it has become quite common among economists and legal scholars to distinguish between five different types of economic integration agreements according to the degree of economic integration, namely: preferential trade arrangements, free trade zones, customs unions, common markets, and economic unions.[50] For the purposes of the present analysis of the compatibility and interactions among regional trade agreements from the perspective of international law, however, it seems useful to reduce the given complexities even further by distinguishing between two forms of economic integration agreements: On the one hand, we find what might be referred to as "basic" or "shallow" integration regimes in the form of preferential trade arrangements and free trade agreements, both characterized by a comparatively low degree of economic integration between the contracting parties. On the other hand, there are regional trade agreements, among them customs unions, common markets and economic unions, that distinguish themselves by a higher degree of economic integration agreed upon by the participating countries and consequently, might be referred to as "advanced" or "deep" integration regimes.[51]

Taking this binary distinction as the overarching reference point of a systematic approach towards the mutual compatibility of regional trade agreements from a legal perspective, one can again basically distinguish between two main scenarios. First, there are those situations that exclusively involve

---

simple categorization"); Armand de Mestral, 'Economic Integration, Comparative Analysis' para 4 Wolfrum (n 19) ("the form and scope of RTAs can vary greatly"); Kembayev (n 30) 18 ("impressive variety of forms regional integration agreements can take").

49   Generally, on this underlying purpose pursued by approaches of systemization or categorization see, eg Niklas Luhmann, 'Soziologie als Theorie sozialer Systeme' (1967) 19 Kölner Zeitschrift für Soziologie und Sozialpsychologie 615, 618ff; and Jerome Bruner, Jacqueline Goodnow and George Austin, *A Study of Thinking* (Wiley 1956) 12 ("A first achievement of categorizing has already been discussed. By categorizing as equivalent discriminable different events, the organism *reduces the complexity of its environment.*") (emphasis in the original).

50   On the respective systemization of regional trade agreements see, eg Jovanović (n 43) 21ff; Gabrielle Marceau and Cornelis Reiman, 'When and How is a Regional Trade Agreement Compatible with the WTO?' (2001) 28 Legal Issues of Economic Integration 297, 302; Peter Hilpold, 'Regional Integration According to Article XXIV GATT – Between Law and Politics' (2003) 7 Max Planck Yearbook of United Nations Law 219, 224ff; Nowrot (n 44) 128ff; Bartels (n 18) para 2; de Mestral (n 47) para 4; Krajewski (n 15) paras 970ff; as well as in principle also for example already Bela A. Balassa, *The Theory of Economic Integration* (Routledge 1962) 2 (who distinguishes, however, only between four different categories of regional economic integration agreements).

51   On the distinction between "basic forms" and "advanced forms of regional integration agreements" see in principle also already for example Kembayev (n 30) 19ff.

countries not being a party to an "advanced" or "deep" regional economic integration agreement and therefore only concern the compatibility of multiple "basic" or "shallow" trade treaties concluded by these actors. It seems appropriate to recall that this first scenario actually reflects the normality in the international economic system by covering the most common relationship between regional trade agreements in current treaty practice, considering the fact that only about eight percent of all regional economic integration agreements belong to the category of what is here referred to as "advanced" or "deep" integration regimes[52] and that the overwhelming majority of countries is not a party to respective agreements. However, this first scenario is not only the most common one, rather, it is also the one that gives rise to comparatively few difficulties from the perspective of economics as well as international law.

The perception that countries not being party to a customs union or even more advanced forms of regional economic integration are in principle not inhibited from concluding multiple regional trade agreements with other states is confirmed by the quite extensive treaty practice in this regard. To mention but three examples, the United States has concluded numerous free trade agreements with countries like Australia, Israel, Jordan, Singapore as well as Canada and Mexico (North American Free Trade Agreement (NAFTA), now substituted by the United States-Mexico-Canada Agreement (USMCA), which entered into force on 1 July 2020).[53] Ukraine has entered into respective treaty arrangements with, among others, the members of the European Free Trade Association (EFTA), Macedonia, Georgia, and Uzbekistan.[54] Japan has free trade agreements in force with a variety of other states, among them Mexico, Thailand, Peru, and Malaysia.[55] Thereby, the legal "key" to the coordination and parallel implementation of the different and varying preferential regimes entered into by one country is – in the practically still most important realm of trade in goods – the stipulation of so-called "rules of origin": legal regimes that – in the absence of unconditional most-favoured-nation (MFN) obligations that

---

52   See thereto WTO, World Trade Report 2011, *The WTO and Preferential Trade Agreements: From Co-Existence to Coherence* (2011) 62; Christine Kaufmann, 'Customs Unions' para 34 in Wolfrum (19); Roberto Fiorentino, Luis Verdeja and Christelle Toqueboeuf, *The Changing Landscape of Regional Trade Agreements: 2006 Update* (WTO Discussion Paper 12,2007), 5ff; Nowrot (n 45) 132–133.

53   See the information provided at: <https://ustr.gov/trade-agreements/free-trade-agreeme nts> accessed 30 June 2021.

54   See the information provided at: <https://mfa.gov.ua/en/about-ukraine/economic-coop eration/free-trade-agreements-fta> accessed 30 June 2021.

55   See the respective information at: <http://www.mofa.go.jp/policy/economy/fta/index .html> accessed 30 June 2021.

are normally not included in free trade agreements[56] – provide the domestic customs authorities with the necessary normative tools to determine whether imported products at issue are manufactured in the respective treaty partner and thus benefit from the preferential tariff treatment stipulated in the specific free trade agreement in question.[57] Consequently, the design and more limited degree of economic integration of "basic" or "shallow" regional trade agreements allow countries that are not a party to an "advanced" or "deep" regional economic integration agreement to commit themselves to a variety of different – and often quite ambitious – preferential treaty regimes with numerous other countries at the same time, while nevertheless safeguarding their independence with regard to their own external commercial policy, since each contracting party to a free trade agreement retains the option of pursuing its own foreign trade policy vis-à-vis third states.[58]

In the second main scenario, the situation appears to be quite different once a country decides to be become a member of an "advanced" or "deep" regional economic integration agreement in the form of a customs union or even a more advanced type of integration regime like a common market or an economic union. Although still a comparatively rare phenomenon in the international economic system, respective examples for such a commitment are provided, among others, by France being a member of the EU, by the Russian Federation as one of the members of the Eurasian Economic Union, by Switzerland having entered into a customs union with the Principality of Liechtenstein based on a treaty concluded on 29 March 1923, and by Botswana,

---

56   Generally on MFN obligations in the realm of international economic treaty law see, eg Matsushita and others (n 16) 155ff; Van den Bossche and Zdouc (n 10) 305ff Specifically on the observation that regional free trade agreements usually do not provide for an unconditional MFN obligation see for example Joost Pauwelyn, 'Legal Avenues to 'Multilateralizing Regionalism': Beyond Article XXIV' in Richard Baldwin and Patrick Low (eds), *Multilateralizing Regionalism* (WTO 2009) 368, 393.

57   On functioning and design of rules of origin particularly in regional trade agreements see, eg Donner Abreu, 'Preferential Rules of Origin in Regional Trade Agreements' in Rohini Acharya (eds.), *Regional Trade Agreements and the Multilateral Trading System* (CUP 2016) 58ff; Brenton, 'Preferential Rules of Origin' in Jean-Pierre Chauffour and Jean-Christophe Maur (eds), *Preferential Trade Agreement Policies for Development* (World Bank 2011) 161ff; Moshe Hirsch, 'Rules of Origin' paras 19ff, Wolfrum (n 19); M Köbele, 'Free Trade Areas' paras 5ff, in Wolfrum (n 19); Matthias Herdegen, *Principles of International Economic Law* (2nd edn, OUP 2016) 319ff; Stefano Inama, *Rules of Origin in International Trade* (CUP 2009) 174ff.

58   On this finding see also for example Fiorentino and Verdeja and Toqueboeuf (n 52) 6.

one of the contracting parties of the Southern African Customs Union (SACU), apparently being the world`s oldest still existing customs union.[59]

Whereas in the case of "basic" or "shallow" regional trade agreements where each contracting party still retains the right to determine its own tariffs and other foreign economic policy measures in its relations with third countries,[60] an "advanced" or "deep" integration regime in the form of a customs union – as for example indicated by Article 28 (1) of the Treaty on the Functioning of the European Union (TFEU)[61] as well as Article XXIV:8 (a) GATT 1994[62] – requires the adoption of a common external tariff policy by all of its members applying to the imports of goods from all non-members as well as a considerable over-all harmonization of their external commercial policies vis-à-vis third states.[63] Customs unions thus do not only require a certain degree of economic and

---

59   Generally, on SACU see for example the information at: <http://www.sacu.int/> accessed 30 June 2021; as well as Gantz (n 18) 435ff; Mareike Meyn, *The Impact of EU Free Trade Agreements on Economic Development and Regional Integration in Southern Africa – The Example of EU-SACU Trade Relations* (P Lang 2006) 45ff.

60   Soamiely Andriamananjara, 'Customs Unions' in Chauffour and Maur (n 57) 111 ("They [free trade agreements] tend to achieve significant preferential and reciprocal trade liberalization within a short time while simultaneously preserving a member's sovereignty over its trade policy vis-à-vis the rest of the world, including its option of joining other preferential trade agreements (PTAs)."); Fiorentino and Verdeja and Toqueboeuf (n 52) 7 ("the parties to an FTA [free trade agreement] have, in principle, full flexibility with regards to their individual choices of future FTA partners").

61   Art28 (1) TFEU: "The Union shall comprise a customs union which shall cover all trade in goods and which shall involve the prohibition between Member States of customs duties on imports and exports and of all charges having equivalent effect, and the adoption of a common customs tariff in their relations with third countries."

62   Art XXIV:8 (a) GATT 1994: "For the purposes of this Agreement:
   (a)   A customs union shall be understood to mean the substitution of a single customs territory for two or more customs territories, so that
      (i)   duties and other restrictive regulations of commerce (except, where necessary, those permitted under Articles XI, XII, XIII, XIV, XV and XX) are eliminated with respect to substantially all the trade between the constituent territories of the union or at least with respect to substantially all the trade in products originating in such territories, and,
      (ii)   subject to the provisions of paragraph 9, substantially the same duties and other regulations of commerce are applied by each of the members of the union to the trade of territories not included in the union; [...]."

63   See thereto as well as generally on the characteristics of customs unions for example Andriamananjara (n 60) 111ff; Kaufmann (n 52) paras 1ff; Nowrot (n 44) 132ff; Jovanović (n 43) 28ff, each with further references.

political homogeneity of its members.[64] They first and foremost also entail the potential to considerably limit the participating countries' autonomy with regard to pursuing an individual foreign trade policy in their relations with non-member states;[65] and this applies also to their options to sign and ratify additional regional trade agreements with third countries. Thereby, it should be recalled that membership in a customs union does not *per se* prevent the conclusion of other economic integration agreements involving non-members. Compatibility is obtained if all members of the customs union are – jointly or/and in the form of the (supranational) economic integration organization being itself a treaty party – also a contracting party of the "basic" or "advanced" regional trade agreement with the third country in question.[66] Respective examples in current treaty practice are provided by:

- the free trade agreement between the Eurasian Economic Union and its member states, of the one part, and the Socialist Republic of Vietnam, of the other part, signed on 29 May 2015 and in force since 5 October 2016,[67]
- the free trade agreement between the member states of SACU and the EFTA states, signed on 26 June 2006 and in force since 1 May 2008,[68]
- the economic partnership agreement, establishing a free trade area, between the EU and its member states, of the one part, and the member states of SACU as well as Mozambique, of the other part, signed on 10 June 2016 and provisionally in force since 10 October 2016,[69]
- the free trade agreement between the EU and its member states, of the one part, and the Republic of Korea, of the other part, signed on 6 October 2010 and in force since 13 December 2015,[70]

---

64   See, eg Kaufmann (n 51) para 7; Giovanni Faccini, Peri Silva and Gerald Willmann, 'The Customs Union Issue: Why do We Observe so Few of Them?' (2013) 90 Journal of International Economics 136ff; Nowrot (n 44) 133.

65   Fiorentino and Verdeja and Toqueboeuf (n 52) 7 ("loss of autonomy over the parties' national commercial policies"); Andriamananjara (n 60) 111ff.

66   For a different perception that is, however, not supported by respective treaty practice see Kembayev (n 30) 369 ("membership in one of the [advanced] RIAS [regional integration agreements] precludes the membership in another").

67   The text of the agreement is for example available at: <http://www.eurasiancommission. org/ru/act/trade/dotp/sogl_torg/Documents/EAEU-VN_FTA.pdf> accessed 30 June 2021.

68   The text of the agreement is for example available at: <http://www.efta.int/free-trade/ free-trade-agreements/sacu> accessed 30 June 2021.

69   Economic Partnership Agreement between the European Union and its Member States, of the one part, and the SADC EPA States, of the other part, OJ EU L 250/3 of 16 September 2016.

70   OJ EU L 127/6 of 14 May 2011.

– as well as – in the realm of "advanced" economic integration agreements concluded with third countries – the agreement establishing a customs union between the former European Economic Community and the Principality of Andorra concluded in the form of an exchange of letters on 28 June 1990.[71]

Furthermore, the same positive finding of compatibility applies in principle to situations in which all members of an "advanced" economic integration agreement have concluded – preferably simultaneously, but potentially also successively – virtually identical bilateral "basic" regional trade agreements with the non-member state in question; an approach first and foremost taken recourse to by the EU with regard to Turkey as outlined below.

Against this background, the question remains as to the respective compatibility of regional trade agreements concluded by only some of the members to an "advanced" economic integration regime like a customs union. This issue is far from theoretical, as for example the Ukraine crisis illustrates. It is precisely this question that lies at the heart of Ukraine's apparently required choice between deepening the association process with the EU or becoming a member of the Eurasian Customs Union. The former European Commissioner for Enlargement and Neighbourhood Policy, Štefan Füle, has outlined the EU's position on the issue of (in)compatibility in his "Statement on the Pressure Exercised by Russia on Countries of the Eastern Partnership" given at the European Parliament on 11 September 2013:

> It is true that the Customs Union membership is not compatible with the DCFTAs which we have negotiated with Ukraine, the Republic of Moldova, Georgia, and Armenia. This is not because of ideological differences; this is not about a clash of economic blocs, or a zero-sum game. This is due to legal impossibilities: for instance, you cannot at the same time lower your customs tariffs as per the DCFTA and increase them as a result of the Customs Union membership. The new generation of Association Agreements will bring enormous transformative benefits through legal approximation, regulatory convergence, and market liberalisation. Independent studies indicate that a DCFTA will bring substantial benefits. Exports to the EU could double over time, leading to increase in GDP of up to approximately 12%. But in order to implement

---

71   Agreement in the form of an exchange of letters between the European Economic Community and the Principality of Andorra of 28 June 1990, OJ EC L 374/14 of 31 December 1990.

these, our partners must enjoy full sovereignty over their own trade policies, which members of the Customs Union will not.[72]

In addition, former European Commissioner for Trade, Karel De Gucht, highlighted in a statement of 28 February 2014, that "[t]echnically, the DCFTA is not compatible with Ukraine becoming a member of the customs union between Russia, Belarus and Kazakhstan, but Ukraine is not [a member]".[73]

And indeed, the clearly prevailing view in scholarly discussions on this issue, referring especially to the common external tariff policy as one of the primary characteristics of a customs union, assumes that the need for a proper functioning of such an integration regime prevents individual members of an "advanced" regional trade agreement to separately and autonomously sign and ratify additional economic treaties with third countries. To mention but two examples, Roberto V. Fiorentino, Luis Verdeja and Cristelle Toqueboeuf – drawing attention to the unacceptable economic consequences for the other members of the customs union at issue – have emphasized that

> [t]he requirement in a CU of a common external tariff and harmonization of the parties' commercial policies does not allow in principle a 'go alone' policy whereby one party alone negotiates a preferential agreement with a third party. Such a situation would disrupt the functioning of the CU since products from the third party could enter the union at a preferential rate through the bilateral RTA, implying a loss of tariff revenues for the other members to the union.[74]

Moreover, in an analysis by Guillaume Van der Loo we find the statement that "since the establishment of the Customs Union, Russia cannot conclude a FTA with a third country on its own, but only together with Belarus and Kazakhstan as one customs union entity".[75] This perception in academia also finds its

---

72   The full statement is for example available at: <http://europa.eu/rapid/press-release
      _SPEECH-13-687_en.htm> accessed 30 June 2021; see thereto also, eg Lain (n 40) 73ff; Van
      der Loo (n 22) 149ff.
73   The full statement is for example available at: <http://trade.ec.europa.eu/doclib/docs/
      2014/february/tradoc_152219.pdf> accessed 30 June 2021.
74   Fiorentino and Verdeja and Toqueboeuf (n 52) 7 fn 19.
75   Van der Loo (n 22) 158; see also for example Pauwelyn (n 56) 393 ("makes negotiating
      an FTA with only one member of a CU most difficult"); Lain (n 40) 73ff; Van der Loo and
      Van Elsuwege (n 21) 442; Hoekman and Jensen and Tarr (n 40) 797; Andriamananjara
      (n 60) 118 ("Indeed, membership in a CU [customs union], at least in principle, prevents
      an individual member from acting individually, since any agreement with a third party or
      any change to the CET [common external tariff] needs to be decided by the CU as a whole.

support in more recent state practice. The – currently stalled – negotiations on a free trade agreement between the United States and South Africa were, apparently at the insistence of the United States, expanded to also include the other members of SACU.[76] Moreover, although the EFTA states had originally envisioned negotiations on a free trade agreement with the Russian Federation only,[77] the respective – and currently suspended – discussions were subsequently expanded to also include Belarus and Kazakhstan, following the implementation of the Eurasian Customs Union.[78] Finally, the Comprehensive and Enhanced Partnership Agreement, recently signed on 24 November 2017 by the EU and the European Atomic Energy Community and their member states, of the one part, and Armenia, of the other part,[79] provides a vivid example in the present context. Compared to the association agreements concluded by the EU with Georgia, Moldova and Ukraine, the partnership agreement with Armenia – in the same way as the Enhanced Partnership and Cooperation Agreement signed by the EU and Kazakhstan on 21 December 2015 and provisionally applied since 1 May 2016[80] – stipulates rather modest regulations in the field of trade liberalization, thereby "taking full account of Armenia's obligations as a member of the Eurasian Economic Union".[81]

[...] In a world of criss-crossing and overlapping trade agreements, the issue of the loss of autonomy can severely constrain members of CUs in using trade agreements as an effective commercial instrument – cat least in theory. In the current wave of regionalism, in which flexibility and speed are valued, membership in a CU, if played by the rules, could constitute a straitjacket for some countries."). Andriamananjara subsequently mentions some examples of situations "in which a CU member alone negotiates an FTA with a third party" and thus has not "played by the rules".

76   See thereto Pauwelyn (n 56) 393.

77   See, eg Results of the Analysis Regarding the Perspective of Closer Trade and Investment Relations between the Russian Federation and the EFTA States, November 2008, available at: <http://www.efta.int/media/documents/free-trade/News/EFTA-Russia-Joint-Study -Group-Report-17-November-2008-Summary.pdf> accessed 21 March 2019.

78   Guillaume Van der Loo, 'EU-Russia Trade Relations: It Takes WTO to Tango?' (2013) 40 Legal Issues of Economic Integration 7, 30; Van der Loo (n 22) 158.

79   Comprehensive and Enhanced Partnership Agreement between the European Union and the European Atomic Energy Community and their Member States, of the one part, and the Republic of Armenia, of the other part, reprinted in: European Commission/High Representative of the Union for Foreign Affairs and Security Policy, Joint Proposal for a Council Decision, JOIN(2017) 37 final of 25 September 2017, Annex 1.

80   Enhanced Partnership and Cooperation Agreement between the European Union and its Member States, of the one part, and the Republic of Kazakhstan, of the other part, OJ EU L 29/3 of 4 February 2016.

81   Explanatory Memorandum, reprinted in European Commission/High Representative of the Union for Foreign Affairs and Security Policy, Joint Proposal for a Council Decision, JOIN(2017) 37 final of 25 September 2017.

Nevertheless, certain notable state practice also exists that indicates the compatibility – at least in principle and under certain circumstances – of regional trade agreements concluded by only some of the members of an "advanced" economic integration regime like a customs union. For example, the possibility for the Principality of Liechtenstein to become a contracting party to the Agreement on the European Economic Area (EEA), signed on 2 May 1992 and in force since 1 January 1994 (with Liechtenstein having joined in May 1995),[82] despite the fact that Switzerland – the other member of the 1923 Swiss-Liechtenstein Customs Union – has abstained from concluding the EEA Agreement, is ensured on the basis of Article 121 (b) of the EEA Agreement as well as with a bilateral treaty between Liechtenstein and Switzerland of 2 November 1994 complementing their customs union agreement.[83] Aside from this rather unique case, it also seems noteworthy that a considerable number of "basic" regional trade agreements include provisions allowing each contracting party to become a member of a customs union with third countries. Respective examples are provided by Article 1.3 (2) of the free trade agreement between the EFTA states and Ukraine, Article 39 (1) of the EU-Ukraine Association Agreement, Article 1.3 (2) of the Dominican Republic-Central America Free Trade Agreement (CAFTA-DR), Article 16 (1) of the free trade agreement between Macedonia and Ukraine, Article 157 of the EU-Moldova Free Trade Agreement, as well as Article 4 (1) of the free trade agreement concluded by Ukraine and Montenegro. However, a closer look at the wording of these treaty clauses quickly reveals the legal and political challenges also arising in connection with this regulatory approach. As stipulated in Article 39 (1) of the EU-Ukraine Association Agreement, this economic integration treaty does "not preclude the maintenance or establishment of customs unions, [...]" only insofar as they do not "conflict with trade arrangements provided for in this Agreement". The EU-Ukraine Association Agreement, in the same way as the other regional trade agreements mentioned above, thus in fact claims priority over "advanced" economic treaty regimes subsequently entered into by one of the contracting party.[84] Consequently, joining a customs union with third countries will, from a practical perspective, in all likelihood only be feasible for a contracting party at the price of, if possible, renegotiating or ultimately abandoning and thus terminating the "basic" regional trade agreement,

---

82   OJ EC L 1/3 of 3 January 1994.
83   See thereto, eg Pelkamsand Böhler, The EEA Review and Liechtenstein's Integration Strategy, 2013, 21 and *passim*.
84   See thereto generally also for example David Evans, 'Bilateral and Plurilateral PTAs' in Lester and Mercurio (n 18) 52, 71.

i.e. for example the EU-Ukraine Association Agreement, at issue – a finding that clearly illustrates the difficulties a country is potentially faced with when trying to unilaterally coordinate its treaty commitments arising from a combination of "advanced" and "basic" economic integration agreements.

Finally, the EU itself is also a notable case in point when assessing the issue of (in)compatibility in the present context. On the one hand, this supranational organization comprises a customs union of its member states in accordance with Article 28 (1) TFEU. On the other hand, however, the EU is also itself a member of a number of other customs unions, namely the ones with the Principality of Andorra concluded in the form of an exchange of letters on 28 June 1990,[85] with the Republic of San Marino by an agreement signed by the two parties on 16 December 1991 and in force since 1 April 2002,[86] as well as with Turkey on the basis of Decision No. 1/95 of the EC-Turkey Association Council,[87] a joint institution created as the central decision-making body within the framework of the EEC-Turkey Association Agreement of 12 September 1963.[88] Despite this quite impressive multiple membership in three separate customs unions, however, it is well-known that the EU and its member states continue to regularly negotiate and conclude free trade agreements with third countries alone. In order to ensure – or at least facilitate – the compatibility of these "basic" regional economic integration treaties with its membership in three customs unions, the EU currently adopts two main regulatory approaches. The first one addresses the concerns of Andorra and San Marino. In this regard, the EU acts on the basis of an approach that might be characterized as including modified rules of origin. This regulatory concept finds its manifestation, for example, in Annex 7 to the Comprehensive Economic and Trade Agreement (CETA) between Canada, of the one part, and the EU and its member states, of the other part, signed on 30 October 2016 and provisionally in force since 21 September 2017.[89] Annex 7 CETA contains joint declarations by the parties concerning Andorra and San Marino, stipulating, among others, that

---

85   Agreement in the form of an exchange of letters between the European Economic Community and the Principality of Andorra of 28 June 1990, OJ EC L 374/14 of 31 December 1990.

86   Agreement on Cooperation and Customs Union between the European Economic Community and the Republic of San Marino, OJ EC L 84/43 of 28 March 2002.

87   Decision No 1/95 of the EC-Turkey Association Council of 22 December 1995 on Implementing the Final Phase of the Customs Union (96/142/EC), OJ EC L 35/1 of 13 February 1996.

88   Agreement establishing an Association between the European Economic Community and Turkey, OJ EC L 361/1 of 31 December 1977.

89   OJ EU L 11/23 of 14 January 2017.

[p]roducts originating in the Republic of San Marino shall be accepted by Canada as originating in the European Union within the meaning of this Agreement, provided that these products are covered by the *Agreement on Cooperation and Customs Union between the European Economic Community and the Republic of San Marino*, done at Brussels on 16 December 1991, and that the later remains in force.[90]

As a result of this stipulation, as also enshrined in the EU-Ukraine Association Agreement,[91] the EU-Korea Free Trade Agreement,[92] the EU-Georgia Association Agreement[93] and the EU-Moldova Association Agreement,[94] – on the basis of similar joint declarations – San Marino and Andorra are, with regard to the realm of trade in goods, under the respective agreement entitled to the same preferential treatment as the member states of the EU. This incorporation into the regional economic integration regime at issue ensures the compatibility with Andorra's and San Marino's status as members of customs unions with the EU. While this legal approach undoubtedly provides an elegant solution to the compatibility challenge, it nevertheless should not be left unmentioned that this method has to be accepted by the other contracting party and, moreover, that such acceptance is surely easier to obtain in the present cases involving so-called "micro states"[95] than in situations concerned with larger economies.

This last-mentioned consideration is probably also one of the main reasons why the EU adopts – or is required to adopt due to the insistence of negotiating partners – in its respective treaty practice a different regulatory approach when trying to accommodate the interests of Turkey – an approach that might appropriately be qualified as including a *pactum de negotiando* in favor of Turkey. In this regard, Annex 30-D of CETA stipulates in the first paragraph of a "Joint Declaration of the Parties on Countries that have Established a Customs

---

90   Para 1 of the Joint Declaration concerning the Republic of San Marino, OJ EU L 11/566 of 14 January 2017 (emphasis in the original).

91   Joint Declaration concerning the Republic of San Marino, OJ EU L 161/2120 of 29 May 2014.

92   Joint Declaration concerning the Republic of San Marino, OJ EU L 127/1413 of 14 May 2011.

93   Joint Declaration concerning the Republic of San Marino, OJ EU L 261/734 of 30 August 2014.

94   Joint Declaration concerning the Republic of San Marino, OJ EU L 260/731 of 30 August 2014.

95   Generally, thereto as well as for the qualification of Andorra and San Marino as micro-states see, eg Thomas D. Grant, 'Micro States' para 1 Wolfrum (n 17); James Crawford, *Brownlie's Principles of Public International Law*, (8th edn, OUP 2012) 129; Jan Klabbers, *International Law* (2nd edn, CUP 2017) 75.

Union with the European Union" that the EU "recalls the obligations of the countries that have established a customs union with the European Union to align their trade regime to that of the European Union, and for certain of them, to conclude preferential agreements with countries that have preferential agreements with the European Union". Paragraph 2 of this Joint Declaration emphasizes that

> [i]n this context, Canada shall endeavour to start negotiations with the countries which, (a) have established a customs union with the European Union, and (b) whose goods do not benefit from the tariff concessions under this Agreement, with a view to conclude a comprehensive bilateral agreement establishing a free trade area in accordance with the relevant WTO Agreement provisions on goods and services, provided that those countries agree to negotiate an ambitious and comprehensive agreement comparable to this Agreement in scope and ambition. Canada shall endeavour to start negotiations as soon as possible with a view to have such an agreement enter into force as soon as possible after the entry into force of this Agreement.[96]

Annex 30-D CETA, as in comparable joint declarations attached to the trade agreement between the EU and its member states, of the one part, and Colombia and Peru, of the other part, signed on 26 June 2012 and provisionally applied with Peru since 1 March 2013 and with Colombia since 1 August 2013,[97] and to the EU-Ukraine Association Agreement,[98] arguably stipulates from a public international law perspective a *pactum de negotiando*, by which the other contracting party assumes an obligation to enter into future negotiations in good faith with the intention to conclude a similar free trade agreement with Turkey,[99] the country to which the – frequently quite generally phrased[100] – characterization included in the joint declarations applies. The

---

96   Joint Declaration of the Parties on Countries that have Established a Customs Union with the European Union, OJ EU L 11/464 of 14 January 2017.

97   Joint Declaration, OJ EU L 354/2607 of 21 December 2012.

98   Joint Declaration, OJ EU L 161/2129 of 29 May 2014.

99   On the *pactum de negotiando* as a normative concept under public international law see, eg Hisashi Owada, 'Pactum de contrahendo, pactum de negotiando' paras 5ff in Wolfrum (n 17); Ulrich Beyerlin, 'Pactum de contrahendo und pactum de negotiando im Völkerrecht?' (1976) 36 Zeitschrift für ausländisches öffentliches Recht und Völkerrecht 407ff, each with further references.

100   See, however, also for example the "Joint Declaration on Turkey", DSed in connection with the EU-Korea Free Trade Agreement and available at: <http://trade.ec.europa.eu/doclib/docs/2009/october/tradoc_145195.pdf> accessed 30 June 2021.

respective wording of these declarations is to be understood against the background of Turkey's obligations under Article 16 of the Decision No. 1/95 of the EC-Turkey Association Council, namely to "align itself progressively with the preferential customs regime" of the EU also as far as "preferential agreements with third countries" are concerned and, in this regard, to "take the necessary measures and negotiate agreements on mutually advantageous basis with the countries" at issue.

Compared to the solution regularly found in EU treaty practice concerning Andorra's and San Marino's position as members of customs unions of this supranational organization, the second approach as just outlined entails certain – not to say considerable – disadvantages for Turkey. Prominently among them is the fact that Turkey has no direct – and probably also a rather limited indirect – influence on the EU's choices and priorities with regard to potential negotiation partners, the timing, content and strategy of the respective trade talks, as well as the outcome of the treaty negotiations.[101] While this finding most certainly also applies to Andorra and San Marino, Turkey is – contrary to the two last-mentioned countries – in addition required to subsequently negotiate on its own with the individual treaty partners of the EU a regional economic integration agreement similar in terms to those concluded by the EU. Even more notable, not infrequently, Turkey faces, in this regard, considerable challenges due to a certain lack of enthusiasm and incentives for a successful conclusion of these treaty negotiations on the side of the respective countries. One of the main economic reasons for this occasional absence of motivation among the EU treaty partners is the consequence that once this supranational organization and its member states have concluded a free trade agreement, exporters of goods from the respective partner countries also enjoy – as a result of the EU-Turkey customs union – duty-free access to the Turkish market in case they enter it via the EU whereas Turkish products – contrary to EU products – do not benefit from a similar preferential treatment when being exported to the EU treaty partners' markets.[102] This leaves not only Turkish

---

101   On this observation see also already, eg Onur Bülbül and Asli Orhon, 'Beyond Turkey-EU Customs Union: Predictions for Key Regulatory Issues in a Potential Turkey-U.S. FTA Following TTIP' (2014) 9 Global Trade and Customs Journal 444, 446; Nanette Neuwahl, 'The EU-Turkey Customs Union: A Balance, but No Equilibrium' (1999) 4 European Foreign Affairs Review 37ff.

102   See thereto for example Bülbül and Orhon (n 101) 446 ("It is unquestionable that whenever the EU signs an FTA with a third country, it leads to disturbance in the CU due to the fact that Turkey has to indirectly open its markets to the goods traveling through the EU without benefitting in return from a similar preferential treatment."); World Bank, *Evaluation of the EU-Turkey Customs Union* (Report No. 85830-TR, 28 March 2014), para

companies at a competitive disadvantage to EU importers but first and fore-most undoubtedly weakens Turkey's negotiating position with the countries in question.[103]

Admittedly, when the EU-Turkey customs union was established in 1995, these – in fact foreseeable – complications for Turkey were meant to be merely temporary, as well as quantitatively speaking manageable, since, first, the legal scheme was intended to be transitional until Turkey becomes a member of the EU and, second, the EU did not have many free trade agreements in place with other countries in the middle of the 1990s. However, enduring these difficul-ties has more recently become increasingly burdensome for Turkey, bearing in mind the growing number of regional economic integration agreements con-cluded by the EU as well as the realization that Turkey's accession to the EU is for the time being obviously not at the doorstep.[104] Against this background, it is hardly surprising and understandable that there have been fervent calls for changes by Turkey – and respective suggestions by a World Bank team – aimed at remedying the "[a]symmetries in the FTA process"[105] by, among oth-ers, providing for joint or at least parallel and coordinated treaty negotiations of Turkey and the EU,[106] until now and probably for the time being to no avail. Viewed from an overarching perspective, this situation clearly indicates that this second approach currently adopted by the EU can only be implemented at the price of asymmetries in the treaty-making processes as well as inequality among the members of the EU-Turkey customs union. These considerations thus once more illustrate the considerable challenges arising in connection with regulatory strategies aimed at securing compatibility of "basic" regional

---

49 ("However, in those cases where the EU has concluded an FTA with a third country but Turkey has not, exporters have an incentive to transship goods via the EU resulting in trade deflection.").

103   Ceren Zeynep Pirim, 'The EU-Turkey Customs Union: From a Transitional to a Definitive Framework?' (2015) 42 Legal Issues of Economic Integration 31, 43 ("It is obvious that it is more advantageous for these countries not to conclude preferential agreements with Turkey because in the actual situation, they already have access to the Turkish market through the EC-Turkey customs union. However, the preferential agreements that the Community signs but that Turkey does not manage to conclude because of third coun-tries' objections, constitute a heavy burden for the Turkish economy: Turkey is obliged to apply reduced or zero rates for the imported products from these countries although these latter do not reduce the custom duties for the products that they import from Turkey."); World Bank (n 102), para 49.

104   On these challenges see, eg World Bank (n 102) para 51; Zeynep Pirim (n 103) 52 ("without a membership perspective, the EC-Turkey customs union risks failure").

105   World Bank (n 102) paras 48ff.

106   See thereto, eg World Bank (n 102) paras 53ff, 190; Bülbül and Orhon (n 101) 448.

trade agreements concluded only by some members of an "advanced" economic integration regime.

4   From Competing to Cooperative Regionalism: Some Concluding
thoughts from a Policy-Oriented Perspective

The analysis undertaken in the previous section has revealed that the relationship between different regional trade agreements concluded by one single
country and the need to ensure compatibility among them can give rise to considerable difficulties, in particular in situations where "basic" bilateral trade
agreements are entered into by only some of the members of an "advanced"
economic integration regime such as a customs union or a common market.
The constraints imposed on a political community as a result of membership in a customs union with regard to its more limited autonomy in pursuing an individual foreign trade policy in its relations with third states, make
it advisable for a country to carefully consider, first, whether to participate in
an "advanced" economic integration regime at all, as well as, second – in case
there is membership in more than one customs union available – which of
the respective regional trade agreements to align itself with. Bearing in mind,
however, that regional economic integration agreements are rarely concluded
on the basis of economic reasons alone, but not infrequently first and foremost
also in pursuit of broader foreign policy goals of a non-economic character,[107]
the just mentioned choices made by a country can – albeit admittedly only
under extreme and deplorable circumstances – give rise to political consequences that reach well beyond the realm of economics as, for example, sadly
illustrated by the case of Ukraine.

In order to avoid a situation that might give rise to such severe political consequences as the result of choices made by individual countries between different – and de facto competing – regional economic integration regimes, it is
submitted here that it seems potentially promising to prevent the emergence
and to remedy the continued existence of scenarios of competing regionalism
by taking recourse to the normative ordering idea of what might be appropriately qualified as "cooperative" regionalism or inter-regionalism. Based on such
a more accommodating approach, the exclusionary effects of regional trade
agreements and the potential rivalry arising between them could for example be mitigated by creating overarching (inter-)regional economic integration

---

107   See thereto already supra.

frameworks in the form of a free trade agreement between the competing regimes, preferably also providing for some kind of regulatory cooperation mechanism in order to facilitate compatibility between the two regime's regulatory standards.[108] In the realm of Europe, a respective example – among others also aimed at accommodating possible negative consequences of competing regionalism – is the Agreement on the European Economic Area (EEA), signed on 2 May 1992 and in force since 1 January 1994, between the EU and its member states on the one hand and three of the four EFTA states – Iceland, Norway and Liechtenstein – on the other hand.[109] And indeed, a quite comparable common legal framework, established between the EU and the Eurasian Economic Union and being also open to countries like Ukraine that are neither a member of the EU nor of the Eurasian Economic Union,[110] has most certainly also occasionally been suggested by politicians as well as in academia.[111] For the time being, and potentially for a long time to come, however, such an overarching inter-regional economic integration framework for the broader Eurasian realm – although in principle undoubtedly reflecting the normative ordering idea of cooperative regionalism – is for a variety of obvious and a number of less obvious reasons unfortunately quite unlikely to be agreed upon and successfully implemented in practice.

---

108   Generally on the approach of regulatory cooperation see, eg Karsten Nowrot, 'Regulatorische Zusammenarbeit als normatives Steuerungskonzept moderner Freihandelsabkommen: Betrachtungen zu einer umstrittenen Ordnungsidee der internationalen Gesetzgebungslehre' (2016) 31 Zeitschrift für Gesetzgebung 1ff, with numerous further references.

109   On the relations between the European Union and the fourth EFTA state, Switzerland, that are based on a comprehensive regime of bilateral treaties see for example Christine Kaddous, '§ 20: Die Zusammenarbeit zwischen der EU und der Schweiz' in Armin Hatje and Peter-Christian Müller-Graff (eds), Europäisches Organisations- und Verfassungsrecht (Nomos 2014) 937ff, with further references.

110   On the idea of "open regionalism" itself, see, e.g., UNCTAD World Investment Report 2014, Investing in the SDGs: An Action Plan (2014) 124.

111   See thereto for example European Parliament (n 27) 72ff; Alexander Libman and Evgeny Vinokurov, 'Eurasian Economic Union: Why Now? Will It Work? Is It Enough?' (2012) 13 Whitehead Journal of Diplomacy and International Relations 29, 39; Van der Loo (n 21) 153ff; Dragneva and Wolczuk (n 22) 241ff.

CHAPTER 4

Economic Sanctions as an Impediment to Trade in the Caucasus-Central Asian Region: A Legal View

Vitaliy Kim

On 13 September 2018, the Council of the European Union decided to extend its sectoral economic sanctions (technically called restrictive measures)[1] against the Russian Federation (RF) until 31 January 2020.[2] The Russian Federation answered by immediately extending its own counter-sanctions measures against the European Union (EU).[3]

The end of this war of sanctions, which started due to the Ukrainian conflict and now involves numerous countries on the one side, Russia on the other,[4] remains nowhere in sight. While some time ago politicians linked the means of lifting the economic sanctions with the Minsk II protocol, today however, the territorial restitution of the Crimean peninsula is declared to be the most important prerequisite to lifting EU sanctions.[5] The likelihood that these demands will be met in the foreseeable future, if at all, seems more than doubtful.

In general, economic sanctions encumber not only the directly-involved States, but also have negative effects on neutral third States, especially if there is a regional economic cooperation (e.g., free trade zone, customs union or economic union) between the respective third State and one of the States waging the sanctions war.[6]

---

1 On the legal basis of art 215, para 1, TFEU; see Burkhard Schöbener and others (eds), *Internationales Wirtschaftsvölkerrecht* (C.F. Müller 2010) 113, 115. More on EU economic sanctions see: Philipp Scheel, 'Challenge of EU Economic and Financial Sanctions before the European Court of Justice' in this volume, 103 et seq.

2 See <http://www.consilium.europa.eu/en/policies/sanctions/ukraine-crisis/> accessed 20 November 2021. The sanctions were prolonged and extended several times, currently until 31 July 2022.

3 See below at Part 4 of this article.

4 See <https://en.wikipedia.org/wiki/International_sanctions_during_the_Ukrainian_crisis> accessed 20 November 2021.

5 See the resolution of the European Parliament of 3 February 2016 on the human rights situation in Crimea, in particular of the Crimean Tatars, 2016/2556 (RSP).

6 cf Martin Gabriel Jürg, *Wirtschaftssanktionen als Mittel der internationalen Konfliktregelung* (1987), 24ff.

The ongoing war of sanctions between (mostly) "Western States" and the Russian Federation poses a multitude of questions regarding international economic law. On the forefront is the issue of compatibility of these sanctions and counter-sanctions with the law of the World Trade Organization (WTO).[7] As regards the compatibility of such sanctions with the EU Partnership and Cooperation Agreements (PCAs) with Eastern European and Central Asian States, the Courts of the EU (General Court and the Court of Justice of the EU) have affirmed the compatibility of such sanctions with the European Union–Russia PCA under the security clause (Article 99) of this Agreement,[8] deferring to the political decisions at the level of the Heads of State or Government of the EU Member States as well as of the Council.[9] Similar questions also arise in relation to the regulations of the Eurasian Economic Union (EAEU),[10] the current members of which are today – together with Russia – Armenia, Belarus, Kazakhstan, and Kyrgyzstan.[11] The following contribution

---

7   After the finalization of this article, a WTO Panel decided on 26 April 2019 on the compatibility of various restrictions of traffic passed by Russia against Ukraine in the context of the Ukraine crisis, affirming the compatibility of these measures with the security clause of Art XXI(b)(iii) of the GATT 1994, see <https://www.wto.org/english/tratop_e/dispu _e/cases_e/ds512_e.htm> accessed 20 November 2021. The Panel Report will not directly be analysed in this contribution, but the arguments given by the Panel are taken into account in Part 3 of this article.

8   See the ECJ judgment of 28 March 2017, C-72/15, Rosneft, ECLI:EU:C:2017:236 (preliminary proceeding at the request of the High Court of England and Wales) and the judgment of 17 September 2020, Case 732/18 P, *Rosneft and others v Council*, ECLI:EU:C:2020:727 (upholding a judgment of the General Court). These judgments will not be analysed in detail in this contribution.

9   It should be remarked that the sanctions, although directed against Russia, may also have an impact on PCAs with other East European countries including the new EU Association Agreements with Georgia, Moldova and Ukraine; for a first comparative analysis of these Association agreements, see Alexander Trunk, Nazar Panych and Susanne Rieckhof (eds), *Legal Aspects of the EU Association Agreements with Georgia, Moldova and Ukraine in the Context of the EU Eastern Partnership Initiative* (Joseph Eul Verlag 2016).

10   The Treaty on the EAEU was signed in Astana on 29 May 2014. On 1 January 2015, the treaty entered into force. The Treaty on the EAEU of 29 May 2014 (as amended on 8 May 2015) is available on the website of the Eurasian Economic Commission, <www.eurasiancommiss ion.org> accessed 11 September 2018.

11   See Tair Mansurov, *Evraziyskaya Ekonomicheskaya Integratsia: Opit i Perspektivi* (2014); Azar Aliyev, 'Architektur der eurasischen Integration: Wirtschaftsgemeinschaft, Zollunion, Gemeinsamer Wirtschaftsraum, Wirtschaftsunion' (2013) 4 Osteuropa-Recht 378–390; Zhenis Kembayev, 'The (In-)Compatibility between Regional Integration Processes in the Post-Soviet Area and within the European Neighborhood Policy' (2013) 4 Osteuropa-Recht 369–377; Marina Trunk-Fedorova, 'Der Gerichtshof der Eurasischen Wirtschaftsgemeinschaft' (2013) 4 Osteuropa-Recht 413–422; Marcus Schladebach and

will give an overview of legal aspects of economic sanctions in general (including WTO law) and will then analyze such sanctions from the perspective of the law of the Eurasian Economic Union.

1   Historical Background

Since the 18th century economic sanctions have been used from time to time as a conflict tool in the context of European wars – mostly between maritime powers (predominantly Great Britain) and continental powers (Napoleon's France and Tsarist Russia).[12] Contrary to trade wars, which were already known in the Middle Ages, economic wars have a primarily political goal (influence on internal politics, as well as foreign security policy). Trade wars, on the other hand, pursue mainly economic goals (including influence on internal economic policy, such as customs and tax policies).[13]

The concept of economic sanctions, as it is widely understood today in international law, was first codified by the League of Nations after the end of the First World War. Economic war, as a collective security measure of the League of Nations, was first codified in Article 16 of the Covenant of the League of Nations (hereinafter: Covenant) of 1919. From this article follows that 'neutral' States are no longer to be protected from the effects of economic wars. Furthermore, the modern concept of economic wars and measures was born, meaning that economic measures could be used either as accompanying measures or as a replacement for traditional conflict resolution mechanisms.[14] The radically wide definition of economic sanctions according to Article 16 of the Covenant englobes all financial, commercial and personal relations.

During the Second World War, the scope of economic conflict reached a new level. This includes pre-emptive buying of raw materials, strategic bombardment and freezing bank accounts.[15] This practice played a large role in the development of the modern concept of economic sanctions.

      Vitaliy Kim, 'Die Eurasische Wirtschaftsunion: Grundlagen, Ziele, Chancen' (2015) 6 WiRO 161–165.

12   cf Kenneth Rogoff, 'Economic Sanctions have a Long and Checkered History', *The Guardian* (5 January 2015) <https://www.theguardian.com/business/2015/jan/05/econo mic-sanctions-long-history-mixed-success> accessed 21 November 2021.

13   cf Jürg (n 6) 8.

14   ibid 13.

15   ibid 14.

During the Cold War, economic sanctions gained importance as an alternative method of leading a conflict; they practically replaced direct military conflict altogether. Otherwise, in the event that the situation should escalate, there would be the ever-present menace of nuclear weapons being used. Economic sanctions were an especially popular tool among NATO Member States against the Eastern Block.

2   Economic Sanctions in International Law

Today economic sanctions are in the repertoire of standard resolution tools of international conflicts.[16] Although Article 2 No. 3 and Article 33 No. 1 of the UN Charter obliges all UN Member States to seek peaceful methods of conflict resolution, economic sanctions are increasingly used without the authorization of the theoretically single international security organ – the UN Security Council. The pursuit of such unilateral or multilateral measures, in international law, from the side of States, but also from the side of international (or supranational) organizations such as the EU[17] without the authorization of the UN Security Council[18] is, at the very least, controversial.[19] Nevertheless, in practice States increasingly take recourse to economic means instead of applying force as a tool of political pressure in international law. Even after the end of the Cold War the number of economic sanctions between two or more states increased, not least with the accord of the United Nations. Over half of a century

---

16   See Security Council Committee Resolutions against the Democratic People's Republic of Korea ("the DPRK"), <https://www.un.org/sc/suborg/en/sanctions/1718/resolutions> accessed 21 November 2021.

17   Regarding the issue of the binding nature of sanctions decisions of the UN Security Council for all EU Member States as UN members see Christian Tietje (ed), *Internationales Wirtschaftsrecht* (De Gruyter 2015) 850.

18   According to ch VII, art 41 of the UN Charter, the Security Council may, in addition to military measures, invite the members of the UN to suspend economic relations in full or in part.

19   In juridical doctrine, the view is partly that economic sanctions are not contrary to international law even without the authorisation of the UN Security Council, see Maria Keshner and Gennadiy Kurdukov, 'Odnostoronii sankcii' (2013) Mejdunarodnoe Pravo 78, 89. At the same time, however, the ICJ's undisputed opinion is that there is no obligation to maintain economic relations between States, *Nicaraguav USA* [1986] ICJ Rep 9/138. It seems to be the opinion that the imposition of economic sanctions, taken as collective (for example in the context of the EU) or unilateral measures, does not need to be subject to a special permit under international law, nor does it require authorization by the Security Council, see Schöbener and others (eds) (n 1) 104ff.

the UN Security Council acted 26 times in accordance with Chapter 7 of the UN Charter creating programs of mandatory economic sanctions.[20] Since 11 September 2001, economic measures have gained even more popularity within the United Nations as a way to combat international terrorism (so-called war against Al-Qaeda). Only a couple years earlier, in 1999, the UN Security Council had established the 'Al-Qaeda Taliban Sanctions Committee' pursuant to its resolution 1267. Part of this Committee's role is to designate funds which are linked to the Taliban and which States are obliged to freeze.[21] It is important to note that neither the present Western sanctions against Russia nor the Russian counter-sanctions are based on a decision of the UN Security Council.

3   Economic Sanctions and WTO Law

Economic sanctions are not only a matter of economic policy, but also of international economic law under today's world trade law system (WTO).[22] Economic sanctions evidently contradict the basic idea of the GATT/WTO: global trade liberalization, which is made a legal concept in particular by the principles of the Most-Favoured-Nation (MFN) treatment and National Treatment (NT),[23] which themselves are based on reciprocity and the common principles of a substantial reduction in tariffs and other trade barriers and the elimination of discrimination in international trade.

It is remarkable that the WTO, which is the most influential international organization in trade matters today and has a much-acclaimed trade dispute resolution mechanism, has so far played almost no role in the present sanctions war. This is in line with the fact that after the founding of the WTO recourse to unilateral economic measures by member States, in particular the United States, has significantly increased.[24]

---

20   See <https://www.un.org/sc/suborg/en/sanctions/information> accessed 21 November 2021.

21   cf W. Michael Reisman, 'Sanctions and International Law', Yale Faculty Scholarship Series 3864 (2009) 12.

22   As of today the WTO comprises 164 members, notably the USA, China, the Russian Federation, all EU Member States and the EU itself as an international organization. One of the youngest members of the WTO is Kazakhstan (since November 2015), which is also a member of the EAEU.

23   See more: Henrik Horn and Petros Mavroidis (eds), *Legal and Economic Principles of World Trade Law* (CUP 2013) 1ff; 9ff, 205ff.

24   Thus, for example, the complete embargoes of the USA against Nicaragua in (Executive Order 12513 of 1 May 1985 Prohibiting Trade and Certain Other Transactions Involving

The main legal reason for this is that the commitments under WTO law do not apply without exceptions. Along with the "General exceptions" listed in Article XX of the GATT "General exceptions", "Security exceptions" listed in Article XXI of the GATT[25] are particularly relevant for this topic, as they might serve as a justification for WTO Members' measures restricting trade in particular situations.

For economic sanctions, Article XXI: (b) (iii) GATT seems particularly relevant.[26] This provision is often regarded as a pitfall in the successful legal solution of possible conflicts. De jure, this article provides all Member States of the WTO with the possibility of unilaterally restricting trade measures which they believe are necessary to protect their essential safety interests (so-called self-judging clause[27]): "Nothing in this Agreement shall be construed (…) to prevent any contracting party from taking any action which it considers necessary for the protection of its essential security interests taken in time of war or other emergency in international relations".[28] De facto, WTO Member States are thus offered a security valve, for the application of unilateral politically motivated (e.g. economic) or GATT-prohibited, protectively motivated trade-restrictive measures, which they can justify or even misuse.[29] Experience has shown that Article XXI: (b) (iii) GATT holds great potential for abuse. Currently, more than 90 states are under a sanctions regime from the United States alone.[30] It is possible to conclude from this that the present sanctions war between Russia and Western States may contradict the law of the WTO, which is, however, incapable of influencing the general course of developments. Thus, the WTO is hardly a feasible platform for resolving this conflict.

Nicaragua, 50 Fed. Reg. 18,629, implemented in the Nicaraguan Trade Control Regulations, 31 C.F.R. Pt. 540, 50 Fed. Reg. 19,890 of 10 May 1985), or the numerous economic embargoes of the USA since the 1960s against Cuba, such the Torricelli Act (1992), Cuban Liberty and Democratic Solidarity (so-called Helms-Burton Act) of 1996.

25   For more details see: Tim Stoberock, *Ausnahmebestimmungen im Warenhandel im WTO- und EU-Recht* (Duncker & Humblot 2013) 239ff.

26   This provision is also in the center of the WTO Panel Report of 26 April 2019 (supra n 7).

27   See Stephan Schill and Robyn Briese, 'Djibouti v. France: Self-Judging Clause in International Dispute Settlement' (2009) 13 Max Planck Yearbook of United Nations Law 61ff.

28   cf GATT art XXI: (b) (iii).

29   cf Alexey Petrenko, 'Ėkonomičeskije Sankcii i ih osparivanie s tochki zrenija prava WTO v kontekste iskluchenij po soobrajeniam nacionalnoy bezopasnosti (statja XXI:(b) (iii) GATT)', (2016) 2 Mejdunarodnoe Pravosudie 69ff.

30   cf <https://www.treasury.gov/resource-center/sanctions/Programs/Pages/Programs.aspx> accessed 20 November 2021.

4   The Russian Counter-Sanctions and the EAEU[31]

The Russian Federation has responded to the Western economic sanctions
with its own counter-sanctions (so-called retorsions)[32] following an executive
order of the Russian President on 6 August 2014,[33] which was later reinforced
by government resolutions[34] as a ban on the import of goods from the following 'sanctioned' States: the United States, the EU member countries, Canada,
Australia, Norway, Ukraine, furthermore Albania, Montenegro, Iceland, and
Liechtenstein. The Prime Minister of the Russian Federation, then D. Medvedev,
characterized this as a "forced reaction".[35] The following legislative texts were
named as a legal basis for these counter-sanctions: the Constitution of the
Russian Federation (in particular, Article 90, for the President's Executive
Orders),[36] Article 1194 of the Civil Code of the Russian Federation[37] and the

---

31   For a general analysis of this topic see also Vitaliy Kim, 'Wirtschaftssanktionen und
      Eurasische Wirtschaftsunion' (2017) 1 Zeitschrift für Internationales Wirtschaftsrecht 27.

32   See Barbara Roth and Alesia Wienold, 'Russische Gegensanktionen und ihre
      Auswirkungen – Ein Überblick' (2015) WiRO 32; Ilia Rachkov, 'Ėkonomičeskie sankziii s
      tochki zrenija prava GATT/WTO' (2014) 3 Mejdunarodnoe Pravosudie 101.

33   Executive Order of the president of the Russian Federation 'On the Implementation of
      Certain Special Economic Measures to Ensure the Security of the Russian Federation'
      of 6 August 2014, No 560, SZ RF of 2014 No 32 art 4470. Extended by the Executive Order
      of the President of the Russian Federation 'On the Extension of Certain Special Economic
      Measures to Ensure the Security of the Russian Federation' of 24.6.2015 pos. 320 and of
      29.6.2016 pos. 305, SZ of 2016 No 27, pos. 4458 (part III).

34   Government Resolution of the Russian Federation of 7.08.2014 pos. 778 on Measures to
      Implement the Russian President's Executive Orders of 6.8.2014 pos. 560, of 24.6.2015
      pos. 320 and of 29.6.2016 pos. 305, complemented through the Government Resolution
      of 21.12.2015 pos. 830, SZ RF of 25.8.2014 No 34 pos. 4685; of 25.6.2015 pos. 625 SZ RF of
      29.6.2015 No 26 pos. 3913; of 13.8.2015 pos. 842 SZ RF of 17.8.2015 No 33 pos. 4856; of 16.9.2015
      pos. 981 SZ RF of 28.9.2015 No 39 pos. 5402; of 21.12.2015 pos. 1397 SZ RF of 28.12.2015 No 52
      (Part i) pos. 7620; of 1.3.2016 No 157 SZ RF of 7.3.2016 No 10 pos. 1426; of 27.5.2016 pos. 472
      SZ RF of 6.6.2016 No 23 pos. 3320; of 30.6.2016 No 608 SZ RF of 11.7.2016 No 28, Pos. 4733;
      of 10.9.2016 No 987, SZ RF of 19.9.2016 pos. 5546; of 22.10.2016 No 1086 SZ RF of 31.10.2016
      No 44 pos. 6142; of 20.5.2017 No 604 SZ RF of 29.5.2017 No 22 pos. 3161; of 4.7.2017 pos. 790;
      of 25.10.2017 pos. 1292; of 12.7.2018 pos. 816.

35   See <http://government.ru/info/14200/> accessed 20 November 2021.

36   Constitution of the Russian Federation of 12.12.1993 (version of 30.12.2008), SZ of
      26.1.2009 No 4.

37   Civil Code of the Russian Federation (part III) of 26.11.2001 No 146-FZ (version of 3.7.2016),
      SZ RF of 3.12.2001 No 49 pos. 4552.

federal laws No. 281-FZ of 30.12.2006 "On Special Economic Measures"[38] and No. 390-FZ of 28.12.2010 "On Security".[39]

The content of the Russian sanctions rules against the "Western States" consists of a ban on imports of agricultural products, raw materials and foodstuffs.[40] Services and capital movements are not directly affected by the Russian sanctions regime. In the context of the 2015/2016 Russian-Turkish dispute (after the downing of a Russian military aircraft by a Turkish fighter-jet on the border between Turkey and Syria in November 2015), which has now largely been settled, the Russian Federation issued a trade embargo against Turkey, which consisted of an import ban on certain goods, but also affected the services sector.[41]

This sanctions war, which has now been ongoing for more than four years, between "Western States" and the Russian Federation, also affects trade within the Eurasian Economic Union (between Armenia, Kazakhstan, Kyrgyzstan, Russia, and Belarus)[42] as sanctions against Russia include the supply of goods via Kazakhstan or other Member States of the Eurasian Economic Union to Russia, and, conversely, the Russian countermeasures prohibit the import of foodstuffs from sanctioned countries even if these products are imported through other EAEU Member States. The sanctions thus fundamentally collide with the basic freedom of the free movement of goods within the EAEU internal market proclaimed in the Treaty on the Eurasian Economic Union (Treaty on the EAEU, in the following also termed EAEU Treaty).[43] This freedom has been restricted several times by the Russian Federation to protect its internal market from a systematic import of prohibited products across the

---

38   FG RF No 281-FZ "on Special Economic Measures" of 30.12.2006, SZ RF of 1.01.2007 No 1 (part i) pos. 44.

39   FG RF No 390-FZ "on National Security" of 28.12.2010 (version of 5.10.2015), SZ RF of 3.1.2011 No 1 pos. 2.

40   Annex to the Government Resolution of 7.8.2014 No 778 (version of 29.6.2016). cf also Roth and Wienold (n 32) 321ff.

41   These economic sanctions entered into force on 28 December 2015, see Roth and Wienold (n 32) 193ff.

42   Supra n 10.

43   The States sanctioning the Russian Federation are the most important trading partners for the other EAEU Member States. For example, trade in goods between the European Union and Kazakhstan in 2014 amounted to about USD 30 million, which means for Kazakhstan about 40% of its total foreign trade, see <http://ec.europa.eu/trade/policy/countries-and-regions/countries/kazakhstan/> accessed 21 November 2021. On 21 December 2015, the European Union and Kazakhstan signed the Enhanced Partnership and Cooperation Agreement in Astana, see <http://eeas.europa.eu/kazakhstan/index_en.htm> accessed 20 November 2021.

territory of other EAEU Member States, especially Belarus and Kazakhstan.[44] Subsequently, the substantive and procedural rules on trade-restrictive measures under the Treaty on the EAEU will be analyzed more in detail.

5   Trade-Restrictive Measures under the EAEU Framework

All Member States of the Eurasian Economic Union share the advantages of a common internal market with the neighboring countries, but they also have certain obligations. The Treaty on the Eurasian Economic Union, contrary e.g. to the Treaties on the European Union, contains no specific rules on the application of restrictive measures[45] by the Union against third countries.[46] The EAEU Member States may, however, under Articles 46 and 47 of the EAEU Treaty, unilaterally restrict the import of goods from third countries with so-called non-tariff barriers, under certain conditions. Can economic sanctions be defined as non-tariff trade barriers?

According to the usual terminology of international economic law, non-tariff trade barriers, such as classical import or export bans, import and export quotas of goods, licensing measures, etc.,[47] are negatively defined as all trade barriers other than customs duties.[48] The term "economic sanctions" contains very different forms, which can, nevertheless, be defined by common characteristics.[49] In any case, it is always a matter of the sovereign decision of individual states or, as the case may be, of international organizations (IO) which measures they intend to take in the area of foreign economic relations with the politically motivated goal of pressuring another subject of international law into a particular behavior.[50]

The motivation to use non-tariff trade barriers is usually a protectionist goal to shelter the domestic economy. However, the mechanism of non-tariff

---

44   See: <http://newskaz.ru/economy/20151202/10399039.html> accessed 20 November 2021.

45   TFEU, art 215, para 1. But see below at 5.b the competence of the EAEU Commission under a procedural perspective on the basis of the Protocol in Annex No.7.

46   See also, the rules on trade barriers between the Member States, art 28ff EAEU Treaty.

47   cf Frank Schorkopf, 'Nichttarifäre Handelshemmnisse' in Jan Bergmann (ed), *Handlexikon der Europäischen Union* (Nomos 2012) 5.

48   Christian Tietje, *Normative Grundstrukturen der Behandlung nichttarifärer Handelshemmnisse in der WTO/GATT-Rechtsordnung* (Nomos 1997) 42.

49   Schöbener and others (eds) (n 1) 99ff.

50   cf Christian Tietje, *Internationales Wirtschaftsrecht* (2 edn, De Gruyter 2015) §15 para 144; Schöbener and others (eds) (n 1) 99ff. In so doing, the sanctions, although intended to affect the conduct of a particular State, may be directly employed against natural or legal persons connected with that State. This is probably the situation in the case of Western sanctions as well as the Russian counter-sanctions in the situation around Ukraine.

trade barriers can also be used for political purposes, e.g. in response to political pressure from third countries or an international organization. Economic sanctions such as the ones taken in "Russia-Western conflict" have therefore effect equivalent to non-tariff trade barriers.

Non-tariff trade barriers are a legal area of tension between the legitimate national regulatory interest on the one hand and the interest in market access and non-discrimination on the other.[51] Under the law of the EAEU, as in other regulations of international public trade law, non-tariff barriers to trade are permitted only under certain conditions (justification grounds).[52] This mechanism will now be considered in more detail.

5.1 *Material Basis for Trade Restrictions in the Treaty on the EAEU*
In the EAEU, it is possible to justify non-tariff quantitative trade restrictions, both between the Member States (in the internal market), and between the EAEU or an EAEU Member State and a third country (in foreign trade).

5.1.1 Internal EAEU Trade Barriers
As under EU law (Article 34–35 TFEU with grounds for justification pursuant to Article 36 TFEU), likewise in the EAEU (Article 28 EAEU Treaty with grounds for justification pursuant to Article 29 EAEU Treaty) there are provisions on a general prohibition of discriminatory and quantitative restrictions on imports and exports between Member States. In contrast with EU law[53] the Eurasian Economic Union does not currently have clear rules or court decisions[54] to interpret the prerogative scope of Article 28 EAEU Treaty by the Member States. However, because of the negative effects on the free movement of goods, it can be assumed that Article 28 of the Treaty on the EAEU can also be narrowly interpreted, following the model of interpretation of Article 34 TFEU,[55] in particular with reference to the proportionality principle.

---

51   On the assessment of non-tariff barriers on the basis of the principles and rules of the WTO/GATT legal order, see: Tietje, (n 48) 189ff.

52   Winfried Bausback and Franziska Schuierer, 'Europarecht und Wirtschaftsvölkerrecht als Innovationsaccelerator, Steuerungsmedium und Motor globalen Fortschritts' in Wolfgang Baumann and others (eds) *Innovation und Internationalisierung* (Springer 2010) 426.

53   cf the case law of the CJEU: CJEU, Case 8/74 „*Dassonville*" [11 July 1974], 837/747; CJEU, Case 153/78 „*Fleischzubereitung*" [12 July 1979], Slg. 1979, 2555 para. 5; CJEU, Case 322/01 „*DocMorris*" [11 December 2003], Slg. 2003 I-14887 para. 102; CJEU, Case 113/80 „*Kommission/Irland*" [17 Juni 1981], Slg. 1981, 1625 para. 7.

54   The primary competence for this would lie with the Court of Justice of the EAEU, for an overview see: Schladebach and Kim (n 11) 161ff.

55   cf Stephan Hobe, *Europarecht* (Vahlen 2014) paras 713 and 725.

5.1.2   Barriers between the EAEU and Third States

Non-tariff trade restrictions of the EAEU in trade with third States are addressed in Section IX ("Foreign Policy") Article 46 of the Treaty on the EAEU. These trade restrictions must in turn be consistent with the principle of transparency and non-discrimination. Their adoption is regulated in more detail in the Annex No. 7 "On Non-Tariff Regulatory Measures in Relation to Third Countries" (hereinafter: Protocol), which is an integral part of the Treaty on EAEU.[56] This Protocol was adopted in accordance with Section IX of the EAEU Treaty and determines the procedure and cases for application of non-tariff regulatory measures only with respect to third countries.[57]

As regards the scope of the Protocol, it should be pointed out that the Protocol does not cover technical or sanitary and phytosanitary issues,[58] but it generally covers procedural rules for quantitative restrictions on imports and exports to third countries in exceptional circumstances (Chapter 3 of the Protocol).

In addition, there is a long list of exceptions for the application of non-tariff trade restrictions contained in Chapters 7 and 8 of the Protocol. These include trade restrictive measures with the purpose:

– to comply with public order;
– to protect human life and health;
– environmental, animal and plant health protection;
– protection of cultural values and heritage;
– ensuring national defense and security, etc.

Non-tariff measures by EAEU members against third States must not be used as an instrument for "arbitrary" discrimination or as a disguised restriction on foreign trade and can only be applied to the entire EAEU customs territory on the basis of an EAEU Commission (hereinafter: Commission) decision.[59]

5.2   *The Procedure for the Adoption of Non-tariff Trade Restrictions*

The legal basis for the application of non-tariff trade restrictions by the EAEU Member States with regard to third countries are contained in Articles 46 and 47 (for the application of unilateral trade restrictions) of the Treaty on the EAEU. The procedure has been laid down in the Protocol.

---

56   cf art 46 para 2 EAEU Treaty.
57   Structurally, the protocol is divided into ten chapters. It also contains a separate Annex, which provides for licenses and permits for the export and/or import of goods.
58   cf art 1 of the Protocol.
59   cf art 39 of the Protocol.

According to Chapter 2 of the Protocol, joint measures of non-tariff regulations (point 3 of the Protocol) apply to trade with third countries on the territory of the Union. The EAEU Member States and the Commission are entitled to apply quantitative restrictions and measures against goods from third countries (point 5 of the Protocol). The decision on the application, extension and abolition of such measures lies, in principle, in the competence of the Union's permanent executive organ, the Commission (point 4 of the Protocol). The procedure for application and abolition of non-tariff regulatory measures of the Eurasian Economic Union requires corresponding decisions[60] by the College of the Eurasian Economic Commission.

In Chapter 10 of the Protocol there is an express provision for the unilateral adoption of non-tariff trade restrictions by EAEU Member States. Chapter 10 point 50 of the Protocol gives EAEU Member States the right, in exceptional cases (formulated for the Union in Sections VII and VIII of the Protocol) to take unilateral preliminary commercial quantitative measures. To this end, the EAEU Member State concerned first notifies the Commission regarding the need for the application of such measures and submits a proposal to the Commission to introduce the measure on the whole customs territory of the EAEU. If the EAEU Commission does not reach a decision on the aforementioned proposal, the Member State may, according to Chapter 10 of the Protocol, apply the measure unilaterally on its territory. However, the Member State of the EAEU must ensure that, in such a case, the Commission is informed within a maximum period of three days (Section X point 51 of the Protocol). The Commission then examines this case and makes a decision on whether the unilateral measures taken by the EAEU Member State should be applied to the EAEU's entire customs territory (point 52 of the Protocol). In this case, the Commission shall determine the duration of the measures (point 53 of the Protocol). If the Commission does not take such a decision, it must inform the State concerned as well as the other EAEU Member States that the unilateral measures of the EAEU State are not to remain in force for more than six months from the date of their adoption (point 54 of the Protocol). The Commission shall forthwith inform the customs authorities of the EAEU Member States of the application of unilateral provisional non-tariff trade restrictions of the EAEU Member State on its territory, with the following instructions:

– Normative act of the EAEU Member State for the application of provisional measures,

60   Decision of the Board of the EAEU Commission of 31 March 2015 No 23, available on the website of the Eurasian Economic Commission, <www.eurasiancommission.org> accessed 21 November 2021.

– the name of the goods in accordance with their classification under the
  Common Customs Tariff of the EAEU,[61]
– date and duration of application.

Member States of the EAEU which have not applied provisional measures on
their territory may, in turn, prohibit the export of goods to a territory where
such goods are undesirable (Section X paragraph 56 of the Protocol).

5.3   *Analysis*

Pursuant to Article 47 EAEU Treaty the Member States may impose unilateral
non-tariff trade restrictions vis-à-vis third countries only in an exceptional
situation on their territory. From a substantive point of view, the conditions
for an exceptional situation in the Protocol are formulated in a very general
and broad sense. Moreover, there is currently no clear-cut interpretation by
supreme bodies, such as the EAEU Commission or the EAEU Court, on the
issue of such an exceptional situation in an EAEU Member State. Similarly to
the WTO, risks of an over-extensive use of this power by individual Member
States of the Union thus cannot be excluded.

From a procedural point of view, the EAEU Commission must be informed in
good time by an EAEU Member State of the planned measures. Also, according
to the transparency principle, the lack of publication of an existing document
leads to a violation of the Treaty on the EAEU.[62] In addition, unilateral trade
restrictive measures adopted by Member States must be limited to a period of
six months, without the Commission's approval. An extension of the unilateral
provisional non-tariff trade restrictive measures without the consent of the
Commission is not expressly provided for in the Treaty.

The basic principles of the Treaty on the EAEU oblige all Member States
to comply with its provisions, as well as to provide favorable conditions that
ensure the proper functioning of the Union.[63] Safeguarding the activities and
development of the Union is primarily, the task of the permanent EAEU executive body, the Commission. In addition, the Commission is responsible for

---

61   The Common Customs Tariff of the EAEU was approved by the decision of the EAEU
      Commission No 80 of 14 September 2021. Available at <www.eurasiancommission.org/ru/
      act/trade/catr/ett/Pages/default.aspx> accessed 21 November 2021.

62   cf Treaty on the EAEU, art 111; Decision of the Supreme Eurasian Economic Council
      "On the official publication of international treaties [...] decisions of the bodies of the
      Eurasian Economic Council" No 90 of 21 November 2014, supplemented by the decision
      of the Eurasian Intergovernmental Council No 3 of 13 April 2016.

63   cf art 3 Treaty on the EAEU.

developing proposals for further economic integration in the Union.[64] To this end, it issues decisions, dispositions and recommendations (Article 18 paragraph 2 EAEU Treaty). If the Commission infringes provisions of the EAEU Treaty, then Member States, the EAEU or economic operators[65] may bring an action before the EAEU Court (hereinafter: the Court).[66] The Court is competent to resolve disputes arising under the EAEU Treaty or through decisions taken by EAEU organs.[67] For example, if an EAEU Member State or one of its economic operators, which was significantly affected by a unilateral and unlawful trade-restrictive measure because of the violation of international obligations under the EAEU Treaty (or secondary legal acts of the EAEU) pursuant to Article 39 paragraph 1 of the Statute of the EAEU Court of Justice (hereinafter "the Statute") were to bring an action before the Court. The Court, however, does not have the power to decide on actions by an economic entity against an EAEU Member State or its organs.[68]

6   Conclusion

The ongoing war of economic sanctions between a number of Western States and the Russian Federation has a negative impact on the functioning of the newly founded Eurasian Economic Union (EAEU).[69] This could affect the whole Eurasian economic integration process if the EAEU does not find an approach compatible with the interest of all of its members.

Sanctions restrict the fundamental freedoms enshrined in the Treaty on the EAEU, in particular the right to free movement of goods within the common Eurasian customs territory. The imposition of counter-sanctions by the Russian Federation against the most important economic partners of the other EAEU

---

64   cf annex No 1 to the Treaty on the EAEU 'Regulation on the Eurasian Economic Commission' Chapter 1, pt 1.

65   A definition of EAEU-Economic Entities can be found in the Treaty on the EAEU, para 10, pt 30 of the Annex No 2.

66   For further details see Marina Trunk-Fedorova, 'Der Gerichtshof der Eurasischen Wirtschaftsgemeinschaft' (2013) Osteuropa Recht 413ff.

67   cf Annex No 2 to the Treaty on the EAEU 'Statute of the Court of the Eurasian Economic Union', Chapter 4, pt 39.

68   cf art 39, pt 2 of the Statute; see also the decision of the college of the EAEU Court in the case: IP Tarasik No CE-1-2/2-15-KC of 27 October 2015.

69   Regarding the implications of sanctions against Russia for the EAEU from an economic perspective, see: Larisa Grigorova-Berenda, *International Economic Sanctions against Russia and their Impact on the Integration Processes in the Countries of the EAEU*, available at: <www.economy.nayka.com.ua/?op=1&z=4313> accessed 21 November 2021.

Member States has already had a negative impact on the EAEU. For example, the systematic (re-)import of prohibited products through the territory of other EAEU Member States into the territory of the Russian Federation has led to the introduction of measures such as the search and non-admission of transit goods, which is painful for any integration process. Such measures do not correspond to the idea of a single internal market, with its four basic freedoms (free movement of goods, freedom to provide services, free movement of capital, free movement of workers). As the fore-going analysis of the non-tariff trade barrier mechanisms, from the perspective of both procedural and substantive law, has shown, the Treaty on the EAEU grants all Member States in exceptional situations, such as for the protection of national security, the right to pass unilateral non-tariff trade-restrictive measures towards third States or international organizations on the territory of the Union. In this case, the EAEU Member States must follow the principles of non-discrimination and transparency, but they have a wide margin of discretion with regard to the use of these exceptional powers.

The absence of judicial control increases the risk of overstretching of these powers by EAEU Member States. Arguably, this risk is, under the Treaty, limited by procedural rules requiring the participation of the EAEU Commission, but it remains to be seen to which degree the Commission will play a neutral and effective role in this field in the future. Furthermore, the Commission has a considerably significant competence for the protection of the national interests of Member States in such situations. Moreover, the possible hindering of the fundamental freedoms defined in the EAEU Treaty, particularly in the case of shortages, could lead in extreme cases to the failure of the entire integration process among the EAEU member states and indirectly also to the failure of the proposed idea of a common economic space between the European Union and the EAEU in the form of a free trade zone.

CHAPTER 5

Challenge of EU Economic and Financial Sanctions before the European Court of Justice

Philipp-Christian Scheel

1 Outline of Restrictive Measures on the EU Level[1]

1.1 *Basic Structure of (Mainly) Export Restrictions*

As a general rule, exports from the European Union (EU) to third countries are free and not subject to restrictions.[2] However, in certain cases the European Union and its Member States have restricted this freedom in their export control legislation.

Due to the allocation of competences within the legislative system of the European Union, export restrictions can be found in separate legal instruments at the EU level and at the level of EU Member States. Directly applicable restrictions in the legal form of Regulations on the EU level comprise, for example, restrictions on so called dual-use-goods (goods which can be used for civil as well as military purposes).[3] Furthermore, EU Member States may introduce directly applicable laws or regulations providing for export restrictions related to the protection of interests of national security and mostly focus on trade in military goods and weapons of war. Arms embargoes are mostly implemented at the national level. Further, EU Member States may also introduce their own additional restrictions on specific dual-use-goods.

Economic and financial sanctions, which will be the focus of the following chapter, have their basis in regulations on the EU level. They can be triggered by Resolutions of the United Nations (UN) Security Council, but might also go beyond these Resolutions or even be introduced without any Security Council Resolution.

The main restrictions provided for in EU economic and financial sanctions regimes are:

---

1   The chapter was written when the author was working as a lawyer in the Brussels office of a large international law firm. Later developments (since 2015) have only been taken account of in the footnotes.
2   cf Regulation (EU) 2015/479 of 11 March 2015, art 1.
3   Regulation (EC) No 428/2009 of 5 May 2009.

– outright prohibitions,
– obligations to apply for an export licence from the competent export control authority prior to a certain envisaged transaction,
– obligations to notify the competent export control authority of a certain envisaged transaction.

The above-mentioned restrictions are usually considered part of "export control" legislation. However, this term is somewhat misleading as the measures, usually, are not limited to the physical export of goods. Economic and financial sanctions also cover, inter alia, the provision of services, in particular where such services can be considered "technical assistance". Further, they not only relate to cross-border activities beyond the European Union, e.g., the prohibition of payments to designated persons or the prohibition to conclude certain contracts, but also cover intra-European Union and even intra-EU Member State cases.

When adopting economic and financial sanctions, the European Union has to bridge the intergovernmental realm of the Common Foreign and Security Policy ("CFSP") and the supranational realm of foreign trade (i.e. realm of EU legislation). This is laid down in the procedure of Article 215 of the Treaty on the Functioning of the European Union (TFEU), which is linked with Chapter 2 of Title V of the Treaty on European Union (TEU). Restrictive measures in the form of economic and financial sanctions based on Article 215 TFEU require, as a first step, an intergovernmental decision by the European Council within the CFSP framework. This decision is then the frame and basis for a regulation of the Council (then acting as Council of the European Union in the EU realm of foreign trade) providing for the restrictive measures and making them directly applicable in the EU Member States.

Enforcement and control of all restrictions – at the European Union and Member State level – is ensured exclusively by the competent national authorities of EU Member States. This can result in different authorities coming up with different interpretations of the applicable provisions. Sometimes, even the official language versions of an EU sanctions regulation can lead to uncertainties: For example, the German language version of the Iran-Sanctionsregulation[4] set out in one of its appendices „Zentrifugal- und/oder Kolbenkompressoren mit einer Nutzleistung von mehr als 2 mW nach API-Spezifikation 610“. By means of a "correction"[5] this was changed to „Zentrifugal- und/oder Kolbenkompressoren mit einer Nutzleistung von mehr als 2 MW nach

---

4   Regulation (EU) No 267/2012 of 23 March 2012.
5   Council Regulation (EU) No 961/2010 of 25 October 2010 on restrictive measures against Iran and repealing Regulation (EC) No 423/2007 [2012] OJ L332/31.

API-Spezifikationen 617 bzw. 618". Other language versions used the second wording from the beginning, which lead to considerable uncertainties.

1.2 Targets of Economic and Financial Sanctions
A very rough distinction can be made between economic and financial sanctions targeted at persons, organizations and entities and sanctions targeting specific economic sectors and goods.

1.2.1 Persons, Organizations and Entities
At the EU level, several sanctions regimes target specific groups of persons, organizations and entities ("POE"). These sanctions regimes regularly provide for lists of POE, which are subject to specific sanctions ("designated POE"). The designation of a POE usually has two consequences:

First, a freezing of assets: All funds or economic resources belonging to, owned, held, or controlled by designated POE, which are within the scope of application of the applicable EU sanctions regulation are frozen.

Second, a prohibition of making funds and economic resources available: No funds or other economic resources may be made available to designated POE. This results in a prohibition to make, inter alia, payments and deliveries to these designated persons. The particular difficulty with this restriction is that it also covers making assets available *indirectly*, i.e. to a POE which is not listed itself but which is owned or controlled by a listed POE. The typical example concerns a case, where a designated natural person controls a non-designated company. Providing goods to this non-designated company could constitute making economic resources available, indirectly, to the designated natural person. The European Union has issued guidelines on how these cases can be assessed.[6] Nonetheless, there still remains a great margin of uncertainty.

1.2.2 Economic Sectors and Goods
EU economic and financial restrictions often target business in specific economic sectors and specific classes of goods. This concerns, without being conclusive:
– equipment for internal repression (Belarus, Cote d'Ivoire, Libya, Myanmar, Syria, Zimbabwe,),
– oil (Iraq, Iran),
– cultural goods (Iraq, Syria),
– petrochemical products and certain ship-related services (Iran),

---

6   Document of the Council No 9068/13 of 30 April 2013.

– luxury goods (North Korea, Syria),
– infrastructure projects (Crimea/Sevastopol),
– the energy sector (Russian Federation).

These sanctions are tailored to the specific political aim of the sanctions regime.

2 Challenge before EU Courts

2.1 *Designated POE*

Each sanctions regime provides for abstract reasons, which can be invoked by the EU Council to designate a POE. These reasons are set out in the applicable sanctions regulation and tailored to the political aim of the restrictive measures. A POE fulfilling the criteria, e.g. providing financial support to a regime, runs the risk of finding itself on the blacklist and facing an asset freeze.

For the time being there is no kind of out-of-court judicial review system in place which would allow a designated POE to seek protection against an envisaged designation. A designated POE has to take recourse against the designation before the EU Courts, in first instance before the European Union General Court (formerly known as 'Court of First Instance') with a possible appeal to the Court of Justice of the European Union (ECJ). The defendant in such cases is the Council of the European Union, i.e. the EU institution which decides on the designation.

Recent years have seen an increasing number of cases being brought before the European Courts by designated POEs against their designation, quite a few of them with success. The European Courts have, over the past years, decided that fundamental principles of EU law must be complied with by the EU institutions when designating a POE. These fundamental principles, inter alia, entail the obligation of EU institutions to state reasons for the designation, the obligation to provide evidence as opposed to mere allegations and the obligation of the EU institutions not to commit a "manifest error of assessment" in deciding whether the evidence is sufficient to justify a designation.[7]

Even in cases where the designation by the EU institutions is based on a UN Security Council Resolution, the EU institutions cannot simply rely on this designation by the Security Council, but must assess the evidence themselves.[8]

---

7   cf WorldECR, *Lester* (May 2013).
8   Judgment of 18 July 2013, *Commission and Others v Kadi*, Joined cases C-584/10 P, C-593/10 P and C-595/10 P, EU:C:2013:518, paras 114, 115.

The outcome of a successful challenge, however, can be quite disappointing: The Court regularly upholds the designation for another two months even if the POE is successful.[9] This gives the Council enough time to find other or better reasons, respectively evidence, to back-up a re-listing of that POE.

A new variation of designation can be found in the Sanctions Regulation No. 833/2014 against Russia.[10] In its Annexes III, V and VI it designates several Russia-based companies in connection with a restriction on transferable securities and money-market instruments. These institutions are not designated in connection with an asset freeze and no individual reasons for their listing are stated (as opposed to the usual lists of designated POE). Whether this kind of designation calls for a different approach when applying the fundamental principles outlined above is for the EU Courts to decide. Several of these institutions have brought direct action before the EU General Court.[11]

2.2   Challenge of Restrictive Measures in General

Even if not designated, restrictive measures can have severe economic consequences for companies exporting to a country under economic and financial sanctions imposed by the European Union. This leads to the question, whether a company thus affected can take recourse against the general economic restrictions before the EU Courts.

In this context, it should be noted that the restrictive measures start from a decision of the European Council adopted in the context of the CFSP. As a basic rule, according to Article 275 (1) TFEU, the European Courts have no jurisdiction with respect to the provisions relating to the CFSP, nor with respect to acts adopted on the basis of those provisions. By exemption from this rule, the EU Courts shall have jurisdiction to rule on proceedings, brought in accordance with the conditions laid down in Article 263 (4) TFEU, reviewing the legality of decisions providing for restrictive measures *against natural or legal persons* adopted by the Council on the basis of Chapter 2 of Title V of the Treaty on European Union.

---

9   One rare exception: Judgement of 18 September 2015, *HTTS and Bateni v Council*, T-45/14, EU:T:2015:650.

10   Regulation (EU) No. 833/2014 concerning restrictive measures in view of Russia's actions destabilising the situation in Ukraine of 31 July 2014.

11   Particular mention should be made of the actions instituted (without success) by PJSC Rosneft both in English courts and in the EU courts, cf <https://curia.europa.eu/jcms/upl oad/docs/application/pdf/2020-09/cp200107en.pdf> accessed 30 July 2021.

This exemption basically allows for a designated POE to challenge the CFSP Decision and the Regulation leading to its designation.[12] The exemption, however, does not give the EU Courts jurisdiction to review the restrictive measure adopted under the CFSP in general, e.g. restrictions on the sale and export of goods. Even though natural and legal persons might be affected by these restrictive measures, they are not directed "against" these natural and legal persons. This prerequisite is not fulfilled where restrictions are of a general nature, their scope being determined by reference to objective criteria and not by reference to identified natural or legal persons.[13] A direct challenge (action for annulment) of economic and financial sanctions in general is therefore not admissible before the EU Courts. However, as the Court of Justice of the European Union has made clear in its judgment of 28 March 2017 (Rosneft),[14] this does not exclude preliminary rulings under Article 267 TFEU at the request of national courts on the validity and interpretation of CSFP decisions and ensuing regulations in so far as individual rights are involved. However, as to substantive scrutiny, the Court is not empowered to rule on general aspects of CSFP decisions and also takes a position of self-restraint with regard to aspects relating to individual parties.

3   Conclusion

Legal protection against economic and financial sanctions has seen a remarkable development over the past years resulting in a considerable case-load. After going through several phases of development[15] the legal framework for challenging the basic lines have now become clearer. And the cases brought forward in connection with economic and financial sanctions in the Russia-Ukraine-complex sound the bell for the next interesting phase.

---

12   On the difference between the wordings "natural and legal persons" and "persons, organization and entities (POE)" cf EuR, *Brauneck* (2015) 498.

13   Judgment of 25 April 2012, *Manufacturing Support & Procurement Kala Naft v Council*, T-509/10, EU:T:2012:201, para 37.

14   Case C-72/15, ECLI:EU:C:2017:236.

15   House of Lords, revised transcript of evidence taken before the select Committee on the European Union, witness Philip Moser, 6 February 2014, 5 <www.parliament.uk/docume nts/lords-committees/eu-sub-com-c/Restrictive%20Measures/cEUC060214ev1.pdf> accessed 30 July 2021.

SECTION 2

WTO Norms in the Context of the EAEU and Its Member States

∴

CHAPTER 6

Legal Regulation of International Treaties in the Republic of Kazakhstan

Zhenis Kembayev†

1 Introduction

According to the Constitution of the Republic of Kazakhstan of 30 August 1995, international treaties of the Republic constitute along with "the Constitution, the laws corresponding to it, and other regulatory legal acts" an integral part of the country's "functioning law".[1] The procedure for the conclusion, fulfillment, and termination of international treaties of Kazakhstan is determined by the Law of RK of 30 May 2005, "On International Treaties of the Republic of Kazakhstan".[2] Fully in line with international standards, this Law defines international treaties of the Republic as "international agreements concluded by the Republic of Kazakhstan with a foreign State(s) or with an international organization(s) in written form and regulated by international law, irrespective of whether such agreement is contained in one or in several related documents, and also irrespective of its specific name".[3] The Law explicitly prohibits the conclusion of international treaties that do not conform to Kazakhstan's national interests and may inflict damage to the national security or lead to the loss of the country's independence.[4]

---

1 See Konstitutsiia Respubliki Kazakhstan (30 August 1995), Art 4(1) <http://online.zakon .kz/Document/?doc_id=1005029> accessed 22 November 2021 (hereinafter "Constitution of Kazakhstan" or "Constitution").

2 See Zakon Respubliki Kazakhstan 'O mezhdunarodnykh dogovorakh Respubliki Kazakhstan' (30 May 2005) No 54-III, Preamble <https://online.zakon.kz/Document/?doc_id=30012 948#pos=0;0> accessed 22 November 2021. (hereinafter "Law on International Treaties" or "LIT").

3 ibid art 1.

4 ibid art 2(2).

© KONINKLIJKE BRILL NV, LEIDEN, 2023 | DOI:10.1163/9789004357839_008

2   Classification of Treaties

International treaties of Kazakhstan may be concluded in the name of: (1) the
Republic of Kazakhstan; (2) the Government of the Republic of Kazakhstan;
and (3) central state bodies of the Republic of Kazakhstan, i.e. state bodies
directly subordinated and accountable to the President[5] as well as central
executive bodies, within the competence established by Kazakhstan's legislation.[6] Treaties concluded in the name of the Republic of Kazakhstan are
designated as *inter-State* (*mezhgosudarstvennye*) treaties; those concluded in
the name of the Government as *intergovernmental* (*mezhpravitel'stvennye*);
and those concluded by empowered central state bodies as *interdepartmental*
(*mezhvedomstvennye*).[7]

Another important differentiation is that international treaties of
Kazakhstan may be divided into those subject to ratification and those capable
of entering into force without ratification. International treaties of Kazakhstan
are subject to ratification if: (1) their subject matter is the rights and freedoms
of man and citizen; (2) their performance requires changes of existing or the
adoption of new laws, and also the establishing of other rules than those provided for by laws of Kazakhstan; or they are related to (3) the territorial demarcation of Kazakhstan with other States, including treaties on the course of the
State boundary of Kazakhstan, and also the demarcation of the exclusive economic zone and continental shelf of Kazakhstan; (4) the basic principles of
inter-State relations, regarding questions disarmament or international control over armaments, ensuring international peace and security, and also peace
treaties and treaties on collective security; (5) participation of Kazakhstan
in inter-State unions and international organizations if such treaties foresee
the transfer of a part of the sovereign authorities of the Republic to them or
establish the binding power of decisions taken by their organs with respect to

---

5   State bodies of the Republic of Kazakhstan directly subordinated and accountable to the
    President of the Republic of Kazakhstan include inter alia the General Prosecutor's Office,
    the Committee of National Security, the National Bank, and the Presidential Administration.
    See Ukaz Prezidenta Respubliki Kazakhstan 'Ob utverzhdenii Polozheniya ob Administratsii
    Prezidenta Respubliki Kazakhstan' (11 March 2008) No 552, Annex 2 <https://online.zakon
    .kz/m/Document/?doc_id=30167498> accessed 22 November 2021.

6   See LIT (n 2) art 2(1).

7   See Postanovlenie Pravitel'stva Respubliki Kazakhstan 'Ob utverzhdenii Pravil razrabotki tek-
    ushhego i perspektivnogo planov zaklyucheniya mezhdunarodnykh dogovorov Respubliki
    Kazakhstan' (9 October 2014) No 1082 <https://tengrinews.kz/zakon/pravitelstvo_respubliki
    _kazakhstan_premer_ministr_rk/mejdunapodnyie_otnosheniya_respubliki_kazakhstan/id
    -P1400001082> accessed 22 November 2021.

the Republic; (6) state loans; or (7) rendering economic and other assistance except for the humanitarian and development aid.[8] Also, the ratification is mandatory if it is stipulated by the treaty itself.[9]

Ratified international treaties have priority over the laws of the Republic and may be directly implemented except in cases when the application of an international treaty requires the promulgation of a law.[10] However, international treaties that entered into force without ratification do not have priority over the laws of the Republic and may be implemented only if they do not contradict the national legislation.[11]

3 Preparation of Treaties

The treaty-making process in Kazakhstan must be planned. Accordingly, international treaties that Kazakhstan intends to conclude are to be included into either a current (drawn up for one year) or a perspective (elaborated for three years) plan. Drafts of both current and prospective plans are developed by the Ministry of Foreign Affairs, approved by a special Commission under the Government,[12] and subsequently endorsed by the President.[13]

Furthermore, draft international treaties of Kazakhstan are also subject, upon preliminary accord with the interested state bodies, to obligatory legal expert examination in the Ministry of Justice and subsequently to the agreement of the Ministry of Foreign Affairs.[14] Besides, draft international treaties may be subject to the scientific (legal, linguistic, environmental, financial or other) examination, which may be conducted under the instruction of the President, the Head of the Presidential Administration, the Prime Minister, and

---

8 See LIT (n 2) art11.
9 ibid.
10 Constitution of the Republic of Kazakhstan (n 1) art 4(2).
11 See Resolution of the Constitutional Council of the Republic of Kazakhstan, 11 October 2000, No 18/2, available in Russian at <http://egov.kz/wps/poc?uri=mjnpa:document& language=ru&documentId=S000000018> accessed 22 November 2021. An exception to this rule is constituted by treaties which were concluded before the adoption of the Constitution of 1995, provided that their priority is directly foreseen by the respective laws of the Republic. ibid.
12 See Postanovlenie Pravitel'stva Respubliki Kazakhstan 'O sozdanii Mezhvedomstvennoj komissii po voprosam mezhdunarodnykh dogovorov Respubliki Kazakhstan' (30 April 2013) No 436 <http://adilet.zan.kz/rus/docs/P1300000436> accessed 22 November 2021.
13 See LIT (n 2) art 2–1.
14 ibid art 3(1, 2).

the Head of the Prime Minister's Clerical Office.[15] The scientific examination may also be initiated by the deputies of the Parliament and interested central state bodies.[16] Furthermore, draft international treaties, which may affect the interests of private business entities, require obtaining an expert opinion of accredited associations of private business entities and Kazakhstan's National Chamber of Entrepreneurs.[17]

It is also provided that interdepartmental treaties must be elaborated by central state bodies in accordance with a special form,[18] which is approved by the Ministry of Foreign Affairs.[19] In addition, prior to their conclusion, inter-departmental treaties require a positive evaluation of the Ministry of Foreign Affairs with respect to their foreign policy expediency.[20]

4   Conclusion of Treaties

Proposals concerning the conclusion of inter-State treaties may be submitted for consideration of the President not later than 14 calendar days before the date of their signature by: (a) state bodies directly subordinated and accountable to the President (in this regard the Presidential Administration is certainly of particular importance); and (b) the Government.[21] Central executive bodies may submit proposals with respect to concluding inter-State treaties to the Government not later than 30 calendar days before the date of their signature.[22] As to proposals concerning the conclusion of intergovernmental treaties, they may be submitted to the Government not later than 14 calendar days before the date of their signature by: (a) state bodies directly subordinated and accountable to the President; and (b) central executive bodies.[23] All proposals concerning the conclusion of international treaties of Kazakhstan are to be

---

15   ibid art 4(4).
16   ibid.
17   ibid art 4–1.
18   ibid art 2–2(1).
19   Prikaz Ministra inostrannykh del Respubliki Kazakhstan 'Ob utverzhdenii formy kont-septsii zaklyucheniya mezhdunarodnogo dogovora Respubliki Kazakhstan' (11 March 2014) No 08-1-1-1/70 <https://tengrinews.kz/zakon/pravitelstvo_respubliki_kazahstan_pr emer_ministr_rk/mejdunapodnyie_otnosheniya_respubliki_kazahstan/id-V1400009318> accessed 22 November 2021.
20   See LIT (n 2) art 2–2(2).
21   ibid art 5(1, 3).
22   ibid art 5(2).
23   ibid art 5(1,2).

discussed with the respective central state bodies concerned and the Ministry of Foreign Affairs.[24] Notably, Kazakhstan's legislation does not foresee any role of the Parliament in the process of recommending or proposing the conclusion of international treaties, which points up the full dominance of the President and executive branch of power in Kazakhstan's political system.[25]

In his capacity of the Head of State and the highest official, the President represents Kazakhstan in international relations and determines the main directions of Kazakhstan's foreign policy.[26] The President may take all actions with respect to the conclusion of international treaties without special powers.[27] In particular, it is his competence to initial, adopt and sign inter-State treaties.[28] He may also delegate the latter competence to another official, also by word of mouth immediately prior to the signature of a treaty.[29] Decisions concerning initialing, adoption and signature of intergovernmental treaties are taken by the Government, which may also confer this power to heads of state bodies directly subordinated and accountable to the President, or their deputies.[30] Decisions concerning initialing, adoption and signature of inter-departmental treaties are taken by the heads of the respective central state bodies or their deputies.[31]

Along with the President, the Prime Minister and the Minister of Foreign Affairs also may represent the Republic of Kazakhstan without the need to present powers but taking into account the rules mentioned in the above paragraph.[32] Heads of diplomatic representations of Kazakhstan in foreign States and representatives of Kazakhstan attached to an international conference or an international organization may represent the country for the purposes of adopting the text of an international treaty between Kazakhstan and the receiving State or within the framework of the said international conference or organization without presenting powers.[33]

According to the Constitution, international treaties of Kazakhstan are ratified by the Parliament.[34] The Parliament implements this function only upon

---

24   ibid art 5(4).
25   See eg, Zhenis Kembayev, 'Recent Constitutional Reforms in Kazakhstan: A Move Towards Democratic Transition?' 42(4) Review of Central and East European Law (2016) 294–324.
26   Constitution of the Republic of Kazakhstan (n 1) art 40(1).
27   LIT (n 2) art 10(1).
28   ibid art 8.
29   ibid.
30   ibid.
31   ibid.
32   ibid art 10(2).
33   ibid.
34   Constitution of the Republic of Kazakhstan (n 1) art 54(1).

the proposal of the Government, which may, for its part, receive respective proposals from the central state bodies.[35] Consequently, those are the Government
and the central state bodies, which decide what treaties fall under the above
criteria and are subject to the ratification. After the Parliament, beginning
in its lower chamber, the Mazhilis, and then proceeding in the upper chamber, the Senate, adopts a law on the ratification of an international treaty, the
President signs and promulgates this law.[36] Given the full subordination of the
Government and the central state bodies to the President and the strong influence exerted by him on the Parliament,[37] it is evident that the President fully
dominates foreign policy decision making.

In line with international practice, international treaties of Kazakhstan,
which do not require ratification, may be subject to acceptance or approval.
The acceptance or approval of inter-State treaties is performed by the President
and of intergovernmental treaties by the Government.[38] Also, Kazakhstan may
accept the offer or the opportunity to become a party to a treaty already negotiated and signed by other states. Decisions concerning accession of Kazakhstan
to inter-State or intergovernmental treaties, which are subject to ratification,
are made by the Parliament through the adoption of a law on ratification.
Accession to inter-State or intergovernmental treaties, which are not subject
to ratification, is decided by the President or the Government respectively.[39]

A treaty subject to ratification may be applied provisionally, before its entry
into force, if this has been provided for in the treaty or if an arrangement was
reached concerning this with the parties who have signed the treaty. This
treaty is must be submitted to the Mazhilis within a period of not more than
six months from the date of the commencement of the provisional application
thereof. Unless provided otherwise in an international treaty or the respective
States agree otherwise, the provisional application by Kazakhstan of a treaty
or part thereof may terminate upon informing the other States which provisionally are applying the treaty of the intention of Kazakhstan not to become
a participant of the treaty. Such decisions may be taken either by the President
or the Government depending on what body signed the treaty.[40]

Should international treaties of Kazakhstan provide for the exchange
of instruments of ratification or the handing over of those instruments for
keeping by a depositary, the President, on the basis of the law concerning the

---

35   LIT (n 2) art 13.
36   Constitution of the Republic of Kazakhstan (n 1) arts 44(11), 54(1), 62(2).
37   See Kembayev (n 25).
38   LIT (n 2) art 15.
39   ibid art 17.
40   ibid art 18.

ratification of an international treaty of Kazakhstan, signs the instrument of ratification, which is affixed with his seal and the signature and the seal of the Minister of Foreign Affairs.[41]

5   Performance of Treaties

All international treaties of Kazakhstan are subject to mandatory and good-faith fulfillment.[42] Both the President and the Government may take measures directed towards ensuring the fulfillment of international treaties.[43] The central state bodies must monitor and warrant the fulfillment of obligations and the effectuation of the rights of the Republic of Kazakhstan arising from the treaties while the Ministry of Foreign Affairs is responsible to conduct a general observation over the fulfillment of international treaties.[44]

The central state bodies must provide an annual information statement to the Ministry of Foreign Affairs on the issued related to: 1) the fulfillment of international treaties; and 2) on the implementation of domestic procedures with respect to international treaties that were signed by the Republic of Kazakhstan and are expected to come into force.[45] The statement must include inter alia proposals for resolving existing problems.[46] The Ministry of Foreign Affairs must analyze and summarize the information statement provided by the central state bodies and within one month submit a consolidated report thereof including a foreign policy assessment to the Office of the Prime Minister.[47] The Office of the Prime Minister examines the report and submits it to the Presidential Administration with additional proposals (if any) with respect to the fulfillment of intergovernmental treaties within 15 days.[48] The

---

41   ibid art 31(1).

42   ibid art 20(1).

43   ibid art 20(3).

44   ibid art 20(4, 5).

45   Postanovlenie Pravitel'stva Respubliki Kazakhstan 'Ob utverzhdenii Pravil monitoringa za obespecheniem vypolneniya mezhdunarodnykh dogovorov Respubliki Kazakhstan' (30 October 2010) No 1141 <https://tengrinews.kz/zakon/pravitelstvo_respubliki_kaza hstan_premer_ministr_rk/mejdunapodnyie_otnosheniya_respubliki_kazahstan/id-P100 0001141> accessed 22 November 2021.

46   ibid.

47   ibid.

48   Ukaz Prezidenta Respubliki Kazakhstan 'O voprosakh podgotovki informatsii o vypol-nenii mezhdunarodnykh dogovorov Respubliki Kazakhstan ...' (12 August 2010) No 1037 <https://tengrinews.kz/zakon/prezident_respubliki_kazahstan/konstitutsionnyiy_stroy _i_osnovyi_gosudarstvennogo_upravleniya/id-U100001037_/#z18> accessed 22 November 2021.

Presidential Administration introduces the report to the President also within 15 days.[49]

6   Termination and Suspension of Treaties

The denunciation and suspension of the operation of international treaties of Kazakhstan are effectuated in accordance with the conditions of the treaty itself, norms of international law and rules established by Kazakhstan's Law on International Treaties.[50]

State bodies directly subordinated and accountable to the President in concert with the Ministry of Foreign Affairs may submit proposals concerning the denunciation and suspension of: (a) inter-State treaties to the President; and (b) intergovernmental treaties to the Government.[51] Central executive bodies in concert with the Ministry of Foreign Affairs may submit proposals with respect to the denunciation and suspension of both inter-State and intergovernmental treaties to the Government.[52] Upon examination of those proposals, the Government may propose: (a) the denunciation and suspension of inter-State treaties to the President; (b) the denunciation of ratified inter-State treaties to the Parliament by agreement of the President; and (c) the denunciation of ratified intergovernmental treaties to the Parliament.[53] Central state bodies may submit proposals concerning the denunciation and suspension of interdepartmental treaties in coordination with other interested central state bodies and the Ministry of Justice to the Ministry of Foreign Affairs, which provides its evaluation of those proposals with respect to their foreign policy expediency.[54]

Decisions on the denunciation and suspension of treaties of Kazakhstan are taken with respect to: (a) inter-State treaties by the President; (b) intergovernmental treaties by the Government; and (c) interdepartmental treaties by the heads of the respective central state bodies or their deputies.[55] The denunciation of ratified treaties requires the adoption of a law by the Parliament.[56]

---

49   ibid.
50   LIT (n 2) art 29(1).
51   ibid art 29(2).
52   ibid art 29(3).
53   ibid art 29(4).
54   ibid art 29(5).
55   ibid art 30.
56   ibid.

7   (Quasi-)judicial Review of Treaties

Before any international treaty is ratified, it may be reviewed with respect to its compliance with the Constitution by the Constitutional Council, a special body whose primary objective is to ensure the supremacy of the Constitution throughout the territory of Kazakhstan.[57] In the hierarchy of norms, resolutions of the Constitutional Council occupy a rank directly after the Constitution and no other regulatory acts of Kazakhstan may be in conflict with them.[58] Yet the activities of the Constitutional Council are also strongly influenced by the President, who appoints its Chairperson and two members,[59] and may (along only with (a) the Chairperson of the Senate; (b) the Chairperson of the Mazhilis; (c) a group of deputies of not less than one-fifth of the total number of parliamentarians; or (d) the Prime Minister) petition the Constitutional Council.[60] The latter rule, which allows the Constitutional Council to hold formal hearings only if mandated to do so by few officials, differentiates the Council from a truly judicial body and qualifies it as a quasi-judicial one.

Should the Constitutional Council consider an international treaty before its ratification and recognise it as contradictory to the Constitution, this international treaty may not be ratified.[61] The Constitutional Council may also review any international treaty that has already entered into force. Should an already ratified (or enacted without ratification) international treaty (or a part of it) be recognised as contradicting the Constitution, it (or its particular part) may not be implemented.[62]

8   Application of Treaties

On 11 October 2000, upon a petition of the Prime Minister, who requested an official interpretation of Article 4(3) of the Constitution providing that "ratified

---

57   Constitution of the Republic of Kazakhstan (n 1) art 72(1).

58   See Zakon Respubliki Kazakhstan 'O pravovykh aktakh' (6 April 2016) No 480-V <http://online.zakon.kz/Document/?doc_id=37312788> accessed 22 November 2021.

59   ibid art 71(2, 3). The Council also consists of four other members, who are appointed by the Senate and the Mazhilis, each selecting two members, ibid art 71(3).

60   ibid art 71(3).

61   LIT (n 2) art 12(3).

62   See Normativnoe postanovlenie Konstitutsionnogo Soveta Respubliki Kazakhstan 'Ob ofitsial'nom tolkovanii podpunkta 7) stat'i 54 Konstitutsii Respubliki Kazakhstan' (18 May 2006) No 2 <http://www.ksrk.gov.kz/rus/resheniya?cid=11&rid=791> accessed 22 November 2021.

international treaties shall have priority over the laws of the Republic", the Constitutional Council ruled that ratified international treaties have ad hoc superiority over national legislation in the case of conflict of their provisions.[63] This practically means that the international treaty provisions prevail over contradictory provisions of national law in a particular case without implying the invalidation or abolition of the latter.

The issue of application of ratified international treaties was also dealt with by the Supreme Court of the Republic of Kazakhstan that may issue regulatory resolutions, which contain "explanations on the issues of how to apply legislation" in judicial practice and are mandatory to all lower courts of the Republic. Thus, the Supreme Court ruled that "Kazakhstan's courts are obliged, where necessary, to be guided by the norms of international law" and that "ratified international treaties, which are directly applicable and do not require the promulgation of a law, may be used as material (except for criminal and administrative matters) or procedural law in adjudication in Kazakhstan".[64]

However, as international treaties have solely ad hoc superiority over national legislation and do not invalidate the conflicting national rules, Kazakhstan's courts apply international treaties only in very rare cases, usually related to disputes arising from bilateral agreements on avoidance of double taxation or protection of foreign direct investment.[65]

9   Towards Supranational Law?

Kazakhstan has been an active participant in the regional integration processes that have taken place in Eurasia since the collapse of the Soviet Union and is a founding member of the Eurasian Economic Union (EAEU), a regional integration grouping that aims at creating a Eurasian Internal Market. The EAEU institutional framework includes the Eurasian Economic Commission, which may adopt binding and directly applicable decisions. In this regard, it is important to note that, in October 2009, on the eve of launching a trilateral

---

63   See Normativnoe postanovlenie Konstitutsionnogo Soveta Respubliki Kazakhstan 'Ob ofitsial'nom tolkovanii punkta 3 stat'i 4 Konstitutsii Respubliki Kazakhstan' (11 October 2000) No 18/2 <http://www.ksrk.gov.kz/rus/resheniya?cid=11&rid=134> accessed 22 November 2021.

64   See Normativnoe postanovlenie Verkhovnogo Suda Respubliki Kazakhstan 'O primenenii norm mezhdunarodnykh dogovorov Respubliki Kazakhstan' (10 July 2008) No 1 <http://adilet.zan.kz/rus/docs/P08000001S_> accessed 22 November 2021.

65   See Z. Kembayev, 'Deistvie mezhdunarodnykh dogovorov v Respublike Kazakhstan' (2013) 4 Pravo i Gosudarstvo, 88–93.

Customs Union of Belarus, Kazakhstan and Russia, a forerunner of the EAEU, the Prime Minister requested that the Constitutional Council clarify the legal nature of the Commission's decisions.

Referring to the LIT's provision saying that Kazakhstan may ratify international treaties enabling its participation in international organizations that feature the transfer of a part of the sovereign powers of the Member States to those international organizations,[66] the Constitutional Council found that: (a) Kazakhstan may be a member of international organizations, whose organs are able to adopt mandatory decisions by majority voting; and (b) the decisions of the organs of those organizations may have priority over the laws of the Republic.[67]

At the same time, the Constitutional Council resolved that the Eurasian Economic Commission's decisions (like decisions of any other organs of international organizations) may not have priority over the laws of the Republic in the event that they infringe upon the constitutional rights and freedoms of individuals in Kazakhstan. Also, the Constitutional Council stipulated that the Commission's decisions may not contradict the Constitution. In particular, it was emphasized that the decisions of any international organizations may not violate the sovereignty of the Republic, its territorial integrity or its form of governance.[68]

10   Conclusion

Summing up this chapter, it may be argued that the legal regulation of international treaties in Kazakhstan is generally consistent with international practice. Moreover, Kazakhstan's legislation reflects one of the most important phenomena in modern international relations, i.e. the development of regional integration processes, and allows the creation of supranational organizations. At the same time, Kazakhstan's Law on International Treaties reveals the principles of the constitutional order of Kazakhstan, which is characterized by the high degree of centralization of political power in the hands of the President.

---

66   LIT (n 2) art 11(5).
67   See Normativnoe postanovlenie Konstitutsionnogo Soveta Respubliki Kazakhstan 'Ob ofitsial'nom tolkovanii norm stat'i 4 Konstitutsii Respubliki Kazakhstan primenitel'no k poriadku ispolneniia reshenii mezhdunarodnykh organizatsii i ikh organov' (5 November 2009) No 6 <http://www.ksrk.gov.kz/rus/resheniya?cid=11&rid=533> accessed 30 July 2021.
68   ibid.

Furthermore, even though the Constitution of Kazakhstan stipulates that ratified international treaties have priority over national laws and may be directly implemented, according to the official interpretation of the Constitutional Council, ratified international treaties have only ad hoc superiority. In the case of conflict the direct application of international treaties does not imply invalidation and abolition of the respective national laws. Also, any international treaty may be invalidated by the Constitutional Council, the activities of which may be strongly influenced by the President. In addition, in spite of the fact that the Constitutional Council ruled that the decisions of the Commission have priority over the laws of the Republic, it has also indicated a broad range of reasons (in particular, infringement upon the constitutional rights and freedoms of individuals) that may potentially lead to the invalidation of any of the Commission's decisions.

CHAPTER 7

WTO Norms in the Russian Legal System and the EAEU

Marina Trunk-Fedorova

1 Introduction

Russia signed its Protocol of Accession to the Marrakesh Agreement Establishing the World Trade Organization on 16 December 2011 at the Eighth Ministerial Conference in Geneva.[1] It became a WTO Member on 22 August 2012, after the completion of all necessary ratification procedures.[2] This means that Russia has undertaken, inter alia, the obligation stipulated in Article XVI:4 of the Marrakesh Agreement Establishing the World Trade Organization (hereinafter – "WTO Agreement"), which provides that each Member shall ensure the conformity of its laws, regulations and administrative procedures with its obligations as provided in the annexed Agreements.[3] But does this mean that WTO norms[4] have direct effect in the territory of the Russian Federation?

The WTO Agreement does not determine whether WTO norms shall have direct effect in the domestic legal systems of WTO Members. WTO case law follows this approach. The *United States – Section 301–310 of the Trade Act of 1974* panel stated that "[n]either the GATT nor the WTO has so far been interpreted by GATT/WTO institutions as a legal order producing direct effect. Following this approach, the GATT/WTO did not create a new legal order the subjects of which comprise both contracting parties or Members and their nationals."[5]

---

1   The WTO website <www.wto.org> accessed 30 June 2021.

2   Федеральный закон от 21 июля 2012 г. № 126-ФЗ «О ратификации Протокола о присоединении Российской Федерации к Марракешскому соглашению об учреждении Всемирной торговой организации от 15 апреля 1994 г» (Federal Law of 21 July 2012 N 126-FZ 'On Ratification of the Protocol of Accession of the Russian Federation to the Marrakesh Agreement on Establishing the World Trade Organization') <http://base.garant.ru/70204236/#ixzz3eXkxBWD3> accessed 20 June 2021.

3   Marrakesh Agreement on Establishing the World Trade Organization <www.wto.org> accessed 30 June 2021.

4   The author includes in the expression "WTO norms" both the WTO Agreement and DSB rulings.

5   WTO, *United States – Section 301–310 of the Trade Act of 1974*, Panel Report (adopted on 27 January 2000), WT/DS152/R, para 7.72.

Therefore, from the WTO perspective, WTO Members are free to regulate this issue within their territories, and it depends on their national regulation.

The present chapter addresses the question whether WTO norms have direct effect in the Russian legal system, i.e. whether it is possible to refer to WTO norms in Russian domestic courts.

Russian legislation and the Supreme Court of the Russian Federation have listed the requirements for direct effect of a treaty norm, which is possible if the following requirements are met: first, if the state in principle allows direct effect of treaty norms in its territory; second, if this treaty norm is formulated in a concrete way, so that it is not necessary to adopt a national act in order to enable the application of the treaty norm,[6] and, third if the treaty norm can create rights and obligations of subjects of national law.[7]

2   Direct Effect of International Legal Norms in the Russian Legal System: General Questions

The first question is thus whether Russia is following the concept of direct effect of international law norms in its national legal system. Article 15, part 4, of the Constitution of the Russian Federation stipulates that "generally re-cognized principles and norms of international law and international treaties of the Russian Federation shall be a component part of its legal system. If a treaty of the Russian Federation provides other rules than those stipulated by a law, the rules of the international agreement shall apply". This constitutional provision is rather open to international law and allows classifying Russia as a country that follows the monist approach.

This means that the Marrakesh Agreement and the whole package of WTO documents, including the Protocol of Accession of the Russian Federation to the WTO Agreement, are part of the Russian legal system. This was also stated

---

6 Федеральный закон от 15 июля 1995 г. № 101-ФЗ 'О международных договорах Российской Федерации' (Federal Law of 15 July 1995 N 101-FZ 'On International Treaties of the Russian Federation') art 5.3.

7 Постановление Пленума Верховного Суда РФ от 10 октября 2003 г. №5 "О применении судами общей юрисдикции общепризнанных принципов и норм международного права и международных договоров Российской Федерации" (Resolution of the Plenum of the Supreme Court of the Russian Federation of 10 October 2003 N 5 "On the Application of the Courts of General Jurisdiction of Generally Recognized Principles and Norms of International Law and Treaties of the Russian Federation") s 3.

in the ruling of the Constitutional Court of the Russian Federation N 2531-O of 6 November 2014.[8]

Having said this, we also note that the question whether WTO norms are part of the Russian legal system shall be distinguished from the question of whether the WTO Agreement (and, accordingly, the Protocol of Accession of the Russian Federation) have direct effect and can be applied by Russian national courts, because in order to be capable of this, the norms of treaties have to meet the criteria mentioned above.

Whereas the practice of Russian courts shows that there are numerous examples of application of treaty norms, e.g. of the European Convention on Human Rights or double taxation treaties,[9] Russian scholars and practitioners do not have a unanimous opinion whether this approach shall also apply to WTO norms.[10] One of the arguments against a direct effect of WTO norms is the lack of direct effect in many WTO Members (inter alia, the United States, the European Union, Japan).[11] These approaches are briefly summarized in the next section.

3   Approaches of Other WTO Members

States can be generally divided into two groups (with some modifications caused by specific national features) – those taking the monist position and those taking the dualist approach.[12] In countries with the monist approach

---

8   Определение от 6 ноября 2014 г. № 2531-O по запросу Пятнадцатого арбитражного апелляционного суда о проверке конституционности п. 3 ст. 1244 Гражданского кодекса Российской Федерации (Ruling of the Constitutional Court of the Russian Federation of 6 November 2014 N 2531-O on the Request of the Fifteenth Arbitrazh (Commercial) Appellate Court on the Reviewing the Constitutionality of Section 3 of art 1244 of the Civil Code of the Russian Federation) para 3.1.

9   See, eg <www.consultant.ru> accessed 30 June 2021.

10   See, eg, Ivan Gudkov, Nikolay Mizulin, 'WTO Rules: The Problems of Direct Application and the Effectiveness of Measures of Responsibility for Violations' ('Правила ВТО: проблемы прямого действия и эффективности мер ответственности за нарушения') (2012) (1) Pravo WTO (Право ВТО) 11–18; Alexey Ispolinov, 'Issues of Direct Application of WTO Law in the Legal Order of Russia' ('Вопросы прямого применения права ВТО в правопорядке России') (2014) (2) Zakonodatelstvo (Законодательство) 68–79.

11   See, eg, Peter van den Bossche and Werner Zdouc, *The Law and Policy of the World Trade Organization* (CUP 2013) 68.

12   See, eg Carolyn A. Dubay, 'General Principles of International Law: Monism and Dualism', International Judicial Monitor (Winter 2014) <http://www.judicialmonitor.org/archive _winter2014/generalprinciples.html> accessed 30 June 2021.

international law norms can have direct effect in the national legal systems. If a norm of international law corresponds to the requirements determining when an international law norm can have direct effect, national courts, as a general rule, can apply these norms. This is true, in any case, for norms of general public international law. Regarding WTO norms, however, many WTO Members take a more careful position. Indeed, while signing the WTO Agreement, a number of Members adopted documents stating that they do not regard WTO norms as having direct effect in their national legal systems. For example, the United States has adopted the Uruguay Round Agreements Act,[13] section 102 of which stipulates that norms of the WTO Agreement, which are in contradiction with US laws, are not to be applied.[14] The possibility to refer to WTO norms in US national courts is reserved only for the Federal Government in a limited number of cases.[15]

In the European Union, the issue of direct effect has been addressed in the EC Council Decision 94/800/EC of 22 December 1994 concerning the conclusion on behalf of the European Community, as regards matters within its competence, of the agreements reached in the Uruguay Round multilateral negotiations,[16] which states that these agreements do not have direct effect in the EU legal order. However, notwithstanding this Council Decision, there were quite a few attempts to refer to WTO norms in national courts and in EU Courts.[17] The Court of Justice of the European Union (CJEU) has consistently taken the position that provisions of WTO law are not norms, in the light of which EU law can be interpreted.[18] The argument was, inter alia, that if courts

---

13   Public Law no 103–465, 108 United States Statutes at Large (1994) 4809.

14   ibid art 102.

15   ibid.

16   Official Journal L 336, 23/12/1994, 2.

17   See, eg, Marina Trunk-Fedorova and Alexander Trunk, 'Application of WTO Norms in Law of the European Community' ('Применение норм ВТО в праве Европейского сообщества') in Sergey Bakhin (ed), *International Public and Private Law: Problems and Perspectives: Liber Amicorum in Honour of Professor L.N. Galenskaya* (*Международное публичное и частное право: проблемы и перспективы: Liber amicorum в честь профессора Л.Н. Галенской*) (St. Petersburg State University 2007) 335–344; Armin Steinbach, *EU Liability and International Economic Law* (Hart 2017); Jörg Philipp Terhechte, 'Common Commercial Policy and External Trade' in Herwig C H Hofmann, Gerard C Rowe, Alexander H Turk (eds), *Specialized Administrative Law of the European Union: A Sectoral Review* (OUP 2018) 94.

18   Two exceptions were formulated by the CJEU in cases *Nakajima* and *Fediol* (Judgment of 7 May 1991, *Nakajima All Precision Co. Ltd. v Council of the European Communities*, Case C-69/89 (1991) European Court Reports I-02069; Judgment of 22 June 1989, *Federation de l'industrie de l'huilerie de la CEE (Fediol) v Commission of the European Communities*, Case 70/87 (1989) European Court Reports 01781.) See also, eg Armin Steinbach, *EU Liability and*

in the European Union recognized a direct effect of WTO law, this would weaken the European Union's negotiating position in comparison with other WTO Members, which do not recognize such direct effect in their legal orders.[19]

Some WTO Members have not adopted particular acts on the absence of a direct effect of WTO norms, but when private parties tried to refer to WTO norms in national courts, the courts did not apply WTO norms, which was the case, for instance, in Japan.[20]

And finally, some WTO Members recognize a direct effect of WTO norms in their national legal systems, e.g. Mexico.[21]

It has to be noted that WTO Members denying a direct effect of WTO norms take this position not only in respect of the WTO Agreement but also with regard to rulings and recommendations of the Dispute Settlement Body (DSB). For example, when the claimant in *FIAMM* referred to the Appellate Body report, where a violation of WTO norms by the European Communities was found and which was not complied with by the European Communities (which caused considerable losses to FIAMM), the European Court of Justice (ECJ, now CJEU) confirmed that also in this case EC norms do not have to be interpreted in the light of WTO norms.[22]

4   Russian Approach: WTO Norms in the Russian Legal System

4.1   *The Working Party Report*[23]

Recalling that Article 15.4 of the Russian Constitution contains a provision that admits direct effect of treaty norms in Russia, it shall be also noted that Russia, while acceding to the Marrakesh Agreement (in contrast to the European Union and the United States) did not make any statement that would exclude

---

International Economic Law (Hart 2017) 29; Hélène Ruiz Fabri, 'Is there a Case – Legally and Politically – for Direct Effect of WTO *Obligations*?' (2014) 25 European Journal of International Law 1, 151–173.

19   See eg Order of the Court of 2 May 2001, in case C-307/99, para 24.

20   See Mitsuo Matsushita Thomas J Schoenbaum and Petros Mavroidis, *The World Trade Organization. Law, Practice and Policy* (OUP 2003) 109.

21   Stephen Clarkson, 'NAFTA and the WTO in the Transformation of Mexico's Economic System' in Joseph S Tulchin and Andrew D Selee (eds), *Mexico's Politics and Society in Transformation* (Boulder 2003) 219.

22   Judgment of 9 September 2008, Joined Cases C-120/06 P and C-121/06 P, ECLI:EU:C:2008:476, para 77.

23   Report of the Working Party on the Accession of the Russian Federation to the World Trade Organization (17 November 2011) WT/ACC/RUS/70 (hereinafter Working Party Report).

or limit direct effect of WTO norms in the territory of the Russian Federation. Moreover, Russia, to the contrary, included into the Working Party Report[24] a specific provision, paragraph 151, which states:

> The representative of the Russian Federation [...] explained that [...] once a treaty entered into force, through ratification or otherwise, it was binding and enforceable throughout the entire territory of the Russian Federation [...] [O]nce the Russian Federation ratified its Protocol of Accession, which included the WTO Agreement and other commitments undertaken by the Russian Federation as part of the terms of accession to the WTO, it became an integral part of the legal system of the Russian Federation. The judicial authorities of the Russian Federation would interpret and apply its provisions....

It might seem that Russia has confirmed by this that its national courts would apply WTO norms. However, the legal status of these statements is not completely clear. On the one hand, they are included into the Working Party Report, but on the other hand, they are not listed among the obligations, which Russia undertook upon joining the Marrakesh Agreement and which are contained in Paragraph 2 of the Protocol of Accession of the Russian Federation to the Marrakesh Agreement. Therefore, it can be concluded that these statements are not a part of Russia's legal obligations in the WTO framework. Paragraph 151 of the Working Party Report probably had only an information purpose, not amounting to an obligation taken by Russia that its courts would apply WTO norms. However, if Russia, indeed, did not intend to give direct effect to WTO norms, it would probably have been prudent not to include this statement in the Working Party Report, as this statement per se creates the impression as if Russia was intending to undertake an obligation regarding a direct effect of WTO norms. This formulation used in the Working Party Report was subjected to criticism by a number of scholars and practitioners.[25]

---

24   See <https://www.wto.org/english/thewto_e/acc_e/completeacc_e.htm#rus> accessed 30 June 2021.

25   See eg Alexey Ispoloinov, 'Issues of Direct Application of WTO Law in the Legal Order of Russia' ('Вопросы прямого применения права ВТО в правопорядке России') (2014) (2) Zakonodatelstvo (Законодательство) 77; Ivan Gudkov and Nikolay Mizulin, 'WTO Rules: the Problems of Direct Application and the Effectiveness of Measures of Responsibility for Violations' ('Правила ВТО: проблемы прямого действия и эффективности мер ответственности за нарушения') (2012) (1) Pravo WTO (Право ВТО) 12.

4.2   *Practice of Russian National Courts*

It is thus interesting to see how Russian judicial practice on the application of WTO norms has been developing. There were numerous attempts to refer to WTO norms in Russian national courts. The first remarkable group of claims concerned intellectual property rights.

It is worth noting that after the signature of its Accession Protocol to the Marrakesh Agreement by Russia (which took place on 16 December 2011, at the Eighth Ministerial Conference in Geneva) but still before the ratification of this document by Russia, the Russian Supreme Arbitrazh (Commercial) Court referred to the TRIPS Agreement. The Court briefly addressed this issue in its decision of 11 April 2012 on the complaint of a Czech national (a patent holder) concerning a provision of Russian Law, which provided for a higher patent prolongation fee for non-residents than for residents of the Russian Federation.[26] The Court, inter alia, stated that one of the main principles of the WTO is non-discrimination, referring to the provisions of the GATT 1994 (the Preamble and Article III:1), as well as of the TRIPS Agreement – regarding intellectual property. Article 3 of the TRIPS Agreement stipulates that a WTO Member "shall accord to the nationals of other Members treatment no less favorable than that it accords to its own nationals with regard to the protection of intellectual property".

Shortly after Russia became a WTO Member, the Russian Supreme Arbitrazh Court referred to the TRIPS Agreement in another dispute concerning the failure to provide national treatment to non-residents in respect of the possibility for non-residents to directly deal with the federal executive body on intellectual property.[27] The Court basically repeated the wording used in the previous decision of 11 April 2012, and also stated that "the provisions of the above-mentioned treaties of the Russian Federation provide for a non-discriminatory, national treatment for individuals permanently living outside the Russian Federation and foreign entities that are covered by the Russia–European Union Agreement[28] and by the TRIPS Agreement" in respect of

---

26 Решение Высшего Арбитражного Суда РФ от 11 апреля 2012 г № ВАС-308/12 (Decision of the High Arbitrazh (Commercial) Court of the Russian Federation of 11 April 2012 N VAS-308/12).

27 Решение Высшего Арбитражного Суда РФ от 1 октября 2012 г № ВАС-6474/12 (Decision of the High Arbirtazh (Commercial) Court of the Russian Federation of 1 October 2012 N VAS-6474/12).

28 The Court meant Agreement on partnership and cooperation establishing a partnership between the European Communities and their Member States, of one part, and the Russian Federation, of the other part (signed on 24 June 1994) <https://eur-lex.europa.eu/legal-content/EN/TXT/?uri=celex:21997A1128(01)> accessed 30 June 2021.

dealing with the federal executive body on intellectual property. This led the Court to a decision in favor of the claimant (foreign citizen).

This allows to conclude that in the first stage of Russia's WTO membership Russian courts had an open and favorable approach towards the application of WTO norms in the above-mentioned cases. Indeed, the review of judicial practice of the first years of Russia's WTO membership shows that judgments contained numerous references to WTO agreements, often in a general form, without specifying a concrete norm.[29] It seems that the courts did not deny the possibility of a direct application of WTO norms by Russian national courts. The situation, however, became more complicated in case of the following conflict between a WTO norm and a national provision: a considerable number of cases dealt with the so-called contract-free administration of exclusive rights on musical works by organizations, which had received state accreditation for such activities. Such a system of contract-free administration is not consistent with Russia's obligation under Paragraph 1218 of the Working Party Report to abolish this system within five years after the entry into force of Part Four of the Civil Code of the Russian Federation (this time period has passed). This obligation was included in the list of obligations of the Russian Federation by virtue of Paragraph 1450 of the Working Party Report and Paragraph 2 of the Accession Protocol.

It was only in one case that a court, resolving such a dispute, referred to Article 15.4 of the Russian Constitution and rendered a decision that the treaty (in this case – the Protocol of Accession of the Russian Federation to the Marrakesh Agreement) prevailed.[30] Moreover, this decision was later vacated by the appellate instance court.[31] In general, while resolving similar disputes on contract-free administration of exclusive rights, the courts applied the respective provisions of the Russian Civil Code and not that of the treaty, explaining that in the present case, there was no direct contradiction between the Civil Code and the respective treaty provision, but there was a non-fulfilled obligation of the Russian Federation to change its legislation: "The Russian Federation has undertaken an obligation before the parties to the international agreement

---

29   See <www.consultant.ru> accessed 30 June 2021.

30   Решение Арбитражного суда города Санкт-Петербурга и Ленинградской области Федерации от 23 мая 2013 г по делу   № А56-1753/2013 (Judgment of the Arbitrazh (Commercial) Court of St. Petersburg and Leningrad Region of 23 May 2013 in the Dispute N А56-1753/2013).

31   Постановление Тринадцатого арбитражного апелляционного суда от 6 сентября 2013 г. по делу № А56-1753/2013 (Ruling of the Thirteen Arbitrazh (Commercial) Court of 6 September 2013 in the Dispute N А56-1753/2013).

(the Protocol of Accession that is a part of the Marrakesh Agreement – M. T.-F.) to change the system of collective administration of rights and to revoke the system of contract-free administration of rights. The Treaty contains no precise provision on a specific date when the Russian Federation will have to denounce the contract-free representation of the holders of intellectual property rights. To implement provisions of the international treaty, it is necessary to make changes to national normative acts. However, at the moment of the hearings of the dispute, the aforementioned norms of Articles 1242, 1244 of the Civil Code of the Russian Federation were not yet repealed. Non-fulfillment of international obligations by the State may entail respective consequences in the sphere of public relations of WTO Members, which was, however, beyond the scope of analysis in the case before the Court".[32]

The Constitutional Court of the Russian Federation received in 2014 a request from a state arbitrazh (commercial) court in a dispute on the above-mentioned issue, in which the Constitutional Court was asked to pronounce itself on whether the respective Civil Code provision violated Article 15(4) of the Russian Constitution on the supremacy of treaties. The Constitutional Court came to the same conclusion as the dominant judicial practice mentioned before. The Constitutional Court stated that one of the indicators of an impossibility of direct effect of a treaty concluded by the Russian Federation is the obligation to change its domestic legislation contained in the treaty.[33]

The Constitutional Court affirmed that treaties of the Russian Federation prevail over national legislation, and if it is not necessary to pass a domestic act for their application, these norms have direct effect. The Court also affirmed that the Accession Protocol is "a ratified treaty of the Russian Federation, by virtue of Art. 15(4) of the Constitution of the Russian Federation, is part of its legal system".[34]

The Court, however, did not analyze the question of a direct effect of § 1218 of the Report of the Working Party on the Accession of the Russian Federation

---

32   See, eg, решение Арбитражного суда Нижегородской области от 9 апреля 2013 г. по делу.

       № A43-20091/2012 (Judgment of the Arbitrazh (Commercial) Court of Nizhegorodskaya Region of 9 April 2013 in the Dispute N A43-20091/2012) 25.

33   Определение от 6 ноября 2014 г. № 2531-О по запросу Пятнадцатого арбитражного апелляционного суда о проверке конституционности пункта 3 статьи 1244 Гражданского кодекса Российской Федерации (Ruling of the Constitutional Court of the Russian Federation of 6 November 2014 N 2531-О on the Request of the Fifteenth Arbitrazh (Commercial) Appellate Court on the Reviewing the Constitutionality of Section 3 of art 1244 of the Civil Code of the Russian Federation) para 3.

34   ibid para 3.1.

to the World Trade Organization stating that interpreting the respective treaty provision does not fall within the competences of the Constitutional Court under Article 125 of the Constitution and Article 3 of the Federal Constitutional Law "On the Constitutional Court of the Russian Federation". Therefore, the question of whether norms of the WTO Agreement (including those of the Protocol of Accession) have direct effect and can be applied by national courts was not resolved by the Constitutional Court.

The next category of disputes raising the issue of direct effect of WTO norms concerned customs duties levied on certain types of paper and palm oil at the importation of goods. The ground for complaints was the difference in bound tariff rates of the Russian Federation contained in its schedule of concessions within the WTO framework and the tariff rates applied by the Russian customs authorities. One should note that Russia is now a member of the Eurasian Economic Union (EAEU),[35] which is a customs union of Armenia, Belarus, Kazakhstan, Kyrgyzstan, and Russia, in which competencies in respect of the functioning of the customs union have been given to the EAEU. This means, inter alia, that customs duties for importation into the customs territory of the Eurasian Economic Union are determined by the EAEU,[36] and no longer by its Member States. For a certain period of time, the Common Customs Tariff of the Eurasian Economic Union contained higher duty rates, inter alia, for paper and palm oil than Russia's bound tariffs for these goods undertaken in the WTO. However, as Russia is a member of the EAEU, Russian customs authorities had to apply the EAEU customs duty rates. To illustrate the discrepancy in the bound tariffs and the EAEU Common Customs Tariff rates, one can give an example of a bound duty rate for certain types of paper that was 5% ad valorem, whereas the import customs duty rate for these tariff lines in the EAEU Customs Tariff was 10% ad valorem or 15% ad valorem.[37] In the case of palm oil, the Russian schedule of concessions foresaw an ad valorem bound duty rate, whereas the Common Customs Tariff contained a combined duty that could, under certain circumstances, be higher than the bound duty.[38]

It is worth noting that the application by the Russian customs authorities of the import tariff in excess of the bound duty rate on some manufacturing

---

35   For more on the Eurasian Economic Union see Zhenis Kembayev, 'The Eurasian Economic Union: An Overview and Evaluation' in this volume, 19 et seq.

36   Art 25 of the Treaty on the Eurasian Economic Union <www.consultant.ru/document/cons_doc_LAW_163855/> accessed 30 June 2021.

37   See, eg *Russia – Tariff Treatment of Certain Agricultural and Manufacturing Products*, Panel Report (adopted on 26 September 2016) WT/DS485/R, paras 7.41, 7.60.

38   ibid para 7.230.

and agricultural products, including paper and palm oil, was challenged by the European Union in the dispute *Russia – Tariff Treatment*.[39] The panel came there to the conclusion that Russia' regulation was not WTO-consistent. However, already in course of proceedings the majority of EAEU import duty rates challenged in this case were adjusted and became consistent with the Russian bound rates, therefore the panel did not make recommendations to Russia to bring its measures into conformity regarding tariffs on the majority of challenged measures.[40] Russia reported compliance on 15 June 2017.[41]

Therefore, compliance was achieved at the WTO level (as mentioned above, partly even before the panel report was adopted), which, however, does not usually help economic operators that have suffered before from non-compliance with WTO rules by a WTO Member. In the case under consideration, economic operators wanted to recover the difference between the bound rate and the rate applied at the time of importation and decided to try to reach this through the national judicial system. A number of importers of paper thus challenged the duties applied by the customs bodies, claiming back the duties paid in excess of those contained in the Russian schedule of concessions. The claimants referred in national arbitrazh (commercial) courts to the Protocol of Accession and the Russian Schedule of concessions.

Several courts decided in favor of the claimants, and when some identical cases came to the Supreme Court, it consistently supported the position of the importers. For example, in its judgment of 31 January 2018 the Russian Supreme Court[42] first has pointed out that treaties of the Russian Federation prevail over its national legislation. Then it turned to the analysis of the Treaty on the Functioning of the [Eurasian] Customs Union in the Framework of the Multilateral Trading System,[43] which provides that obligations of a EAEU Member undertaken in the WTO become part of the EAEU law. As the treaties concluded within the EAEU framework are mandatory for the EAEU Member States, the Russian Supreme Court concluded that WTO obligations (within the areas of EAEU competence) were part of the legal system of the EAEU. Therefore, Russian obligations regarding import duty rates on paper under

---

39   WTO, *Russia – Tariff Treatment of Certain Agricultural and Manufacturing Products*, Panel Report (adopted on 26 August 2016) WT/DS485/R.

40   ibid para 8.1.

41   WTO, *Russia – Tariff Treatment of Certain Agricultural and Manufacturing Products*, Communication from the Russian Federation (15 June 2017) WT/DS485/11.

42   Определение Верховного Суда Российской Федерации от 31 января 2018 г. N 307-КГ17-22096 (Judgment of the Supreme Court of 31 January 2018 N 307-KG17-22096).

43   <www.eurasiancommission.org/hy/act/trade/dotp/SiteAssets/wto/freddy-rus.pdf> accessed 30 June 2021.

consideration that are 5% ad valorem are part of the EAEU's legal system. The Court concluded that as treaties concluded within the EAEU were mandatory for its Member States, including Russia, the Treaty on the Functioning of the Customs Union in the Framework of the Multilateral Trading System was also mandatory, which meant that the import duty rate for paper of 5% ad valorem should apply. The Court thus supported the claim that the difference between 5% ad valorem (bound duty rate) and 15% ad valorem (applied duty) had to be paid back to the importers of paper.[44]

A similar approach was taken by the Supreme Court in respect of cases where a combined duty on palm oil was at issue: the customs applied the Common Customs Tariff of the Eurasian Economic Union, which stated "4%, but not less than 0,1 EUR/kg" instead of "4% ad valorem" in the bound tariff of the Russian Federation.[45] Although the reasoning of the Court in that case was rather short and did not address the specifics of the combined duty, it is based on the conclusion that a violation in such a situation takes place when the amount of duties paid under the applied tariff is higher than it would have been under the bound duty rate contained in the schedule of concessions. The comparison of the actually paid duties and the duties that had to be paid under the bound tariff was implied in this decision, as the Supreme Court supported the position of lowers courts, which had found that the amount of duties paid exceeded those that were to be paid if the bound duty rate had been applied. The lower courts decided that the customs duties paid in excess of bound duty rates under the Russian schedule of concessions had to be paid back to the claimants (importers).

5   Context of the Eurasian Economic Union

One further aspect might be the role of WTO law in the practice of the Court of the Eurasian Economic Union as its decisions influence the future practice of EAEU Member States. It is worth noting that the Court of the Eurasian Economic Community (EurAsEC, the predecessor of the EAEU) had referred to WTO norms in the context of a dispute regarding antidumping duties between

---

44   Определение Верховного Суда РФ от 31 января 2018 г. N 307-КГ17-22096 (Ruling of the Supreme Court of the Russian Federation of 31 January 2018 N 307-KG17-22096).

45   Определение Верховного Суда Российской Федерации № 307-КГ15-13054 от 28.12.2015 (Ruling of the Supreme Court of the Russian Federation of 28 December 2015 N 307-KG17-22096) 2.

a foreign economic operator and the Eurasian Economic Commission.[46] In that dispute the applicant claimed that acts of the Commission violated, inter alia, provisions of the WTO Agreement on Implementation of Article VI of the General Agreement on Tariffs and Trade 1994.[47] The Court confirmed that the GATT 1994 and the Agreement on Implementation of Article VI of the General Agreement on Tariffs and Trade 1994 were part of the legal system of the EurAsEC Customs Union but it did not find a contradiction between the norms of the Customs Union and norms of the WTO agreements and therefore did not apply WTO norms in the decided case.[48] The Appeal Chamber confirmed this reasoning.[49]

It seems that the Court of the Eurasian Economic Union shares this approach of its predecessor. Indeed, in a judgment of 27 April 2017, it confirmed that the provisions of the Marrakesh Agreement (relating to areas, in which EAEU member states delegated their competence to the Eurasian Economic Union) became part of the legal system of the EAEU and therefore, provisions of the General Agreement on Tariffs and Trade 1994 and the Agreement on Implementation of Article VI of GATT 1994 (Anti-Dumping Agreement) had to be taken into account in the case under consideration.[50]

One more potential issue is the status of WTO panel and Appellate Body reports in the Russian legal system. There are not yet any known precedents of Russian courts at the time of writing of this article. In this context, it may be worth mentioning that the EurAsEC Court made a reference[51] to the Appellate Body report in the dispute *Brazil – Measures Affecting Desiccated Coconut*.[52]

---

46 Решение Суда Евразийского экономического сообщества от 24 июня 2013 г. по заявлению публичного акционерного общества «Новокраматорский машино-строительный завод» (Judgment of the Collegium of the Court of the Eurasian Economic Community of 24 June 2013 on the application of the JSC 'Novokramatorsk Machine-Building Plant') 21–23.

47 ibid 15.

48 ibid 18–19.

49 Решение Апелляционной палаты Суда Евразийского экономического сообщества от 29 декабря 2014 г. (Decision of the Appellate Chamber of the Court of the Eurasian Economic Community of 29 December 2014) 5.

50 Решение Коллегии Суда Евразийского экономического союза от 27 апреля 2017 г. по заявлению публичного акционерного общества «АрселорМиттал Кривой Рог» (Judgment of the Collegium of the Court of the Eurasian Economic Union of 27 April 2017 on the application of the JSC 'ArselorMittal Krivoy Rog') 5–6, 22.

51 Решение Суда Евразийского экономического сообщества от (Decision of the Appellate Chamber of the Court of the Eurasian Economic Community) of 24 June 2013 (n 47) 21.

52 *Brazil – Measures affecting desiccated coconut* WT/DS22.

One can conclude that the Court of the Eurasian Economic Union follows this approach, an example being its above-mentioned judgment regarding an anti-dumping measure imposed by the Eurasian Economic Commission,[53] in which the Court referred to the WTO panel report in the dispute *Russia – Anti-dumping Duties on Light Commercial Vehicles from Germany and Italy.*[54]

6   Concluding Remarks

The analysis of recent jurisprudence shows that there is no one single, uniform approach as to the effect of WTO norms in the Russian legal system. The courts generally affirm that WTO norms are part of the Russian legal system, but this does not automatically mean that WTO norms have a direct effect in Russia and can be relied upon in litigation before Russian courts. Russian court practice shows that the obligation to change national legislation was not found to be concrete enough in disputes regarding the contract-free administration of exclusive rights. At the same time, when issues within areas of EAEU competences, in which Russia's WTO obligations have become obligations of the EAEU, were analyzed by Russian national courts, WTO norms have been directly applied by national courts.

It is worth noting that the Treaty on the Functioning of the [Eurasian] Customs Union in the Framework of the Multilateral Trading System is a rather unique example, as it incorporates WTO norms in those areas where the EAEU has competence, into the EAEU's legal system and thereby gives national courts the possibility to directly apply the corresponding WTO norms. This differs from the EU's approach, according to which the national courts of EU Member States and the Court of Justice of the European Union shall apply only norms of European law, without examining them in the light of WTO norms. In a situation when an EU importer pays customs duties in excess of the bound duty rates contained in the EU schedule of concessions, the importer is not able to receive the exceeding amount by the means of reference to WTO obligations, as it is only EU law that matters in such situations.[55]

---

53   Решение Коллегии Суда Евразийского экономического союза от 27 апреля 2017 г. по заявлению публичного акционерного общества "АрселорМиттал Кривой Рог" (Decision of the Collegium of the Court of the Eurasian Economic Union of 27 April 2017 on the application of the JSC 'ArselorMittal Krivoy Rog') 16.

54   *Russia – Anti-dumping Duties on Light Commercial Vehicles from Germany and Italy,* WT/DS479.

55   See, eg, Order of the Court of 2 May 2001, in case C-307/99 (n 19).

The practice of the Court of the Eurasian Economic Union reflects the provisions of the Treaty on the Functioning of the [Eurasian] Customs Union in the Framework of the Multilateral Trading System. The EAEU Court has already made references to WTO norms (to the GATT 1994 and the Anti-dumping agreement) in its judgment regarding a challenged anti-dumping measure, and it will be interesting to see how the Court's practice will develop in disputes relating to other issues that will be addressed.

SECTION 3

Selected Aspects of International Trade in the Region

∴

CHAPTER 8

Customs Regulation in the Eurasian Economic Union

Ekaterina Dmitrikova

1   The Customs Union of the Eurasian Economic Union

In the Declaration on Eurasian Economic Integration of 18 November 2011 (further referred to as the Declaration),[1] the Heads of State of the Republic of Belarus, the Republic of Kazakhstan and the Russian Federation noted the successful functioning of the Customs Union and reaffirmed the creation of a unified system for customs, tariff and non-tariff regulation of foreign trade. Later, based on this Declaration, Belarus, Kazakhstan and Russia established the Eurasian Economic Union (further – the EAEU).[2] The Eurasian Economic Union is an international organization of regional economic integration with international legal personality.[3]

The Treaty on the Eurasian Economic Union entered into force on 1 January 2015, creating an economic union, which ensures the freedom of movement of goods, services, capital, and labour, the establishment of a coordinated, concerted or common policy in economic sectors determined by the Treaty on the EAEU and treaties within the framework of the EAEU. A common policy presupposes the application by Member States of unified legal regulation, which may also be based on decisions of the bodies of the EAEU within their competences.[4] Part 2 of the Treaty on the EAEU establishes rules for the functioning of the Customs Union of the EAEU. Article 25 of the Treaty formulates

---

1   Official website of the Eurasian Economic Commission <www.eurasiancommission.org/docs/Download.aspx?IsDlg=0&ID=2738&print=1> accessed 10 July 2021.

2   In May 2014 in Astana (Kazakhstan) the Treaty on the Establishment of the Eurasian Economic Union was signed, Armenia joined the EAEU on 2 January 2015, Kyrgyzstan on 12 August 2015.

3   <www.eurasiancommission.org/ru/nae/news/Pages/01-01-2015-1.aspx> accessed 10 July 2021.

4   Customs regulation is carried out by the Eurasian Economic Commission on the basis of the provisions of the Agreement on the EAEU. Appendix No. 1 to the EAEU Agreement <www.eurasiancommission.org> accessed 10 July 2021.

principles of the functioning of the Customs Union of the EAEU, including single customs regulation.[5]

2   Uniform Customs Regulation

The Eurasian Economic Union has established a single customs regulation according to the Customs Code of the EAEU, regulating customs relations under international treaties as well as acts constituting the law of the Union, including the Treaty on the Eurasian Economic Union.[6] It should be noted that the Treaty on the Customs Code of the Eurasian Economic Union was signed only on 11 April 2017.[7]

Prior to the entry into force of the Customs Code of the Eurasian Economic Union, a single customs regulation was carried out in accordance with the Treaty on the Customs Code of the (EurAsEC) Customs Union of 27 November 2009[8] and other treaties of the Member States regulating customs relations, which were concluded within the legal framework of the Customs Union and of the Common Economic Space, themselves included in EAEU law.[9]

At present, the Customs Code stipulates that the customs legislation of the EAEU Customs Union consists of the Customs Code, treaties of the Member States of the Union regulating legal relations in the field of customs regulation, decisions of the Eurasian Economic Commission regulating legal customs relations in the Customs Union, and international treaties of the Member States of the Customs Union.[10]

The composition of the customs legislation mentioned above complies with Article 6 of the EAEU Treaty, which defines the constituent elements of EAEU law: the Treaty on the EAEU, treaties within the framework of the EAEU; international agreements of the Union with a third party; decisions and orders of the Supreme Eurasian Economic Council, the Eurasian Intergovernmental

---

5   Part 1 of art 25 of the Treaty on the Eurasian Economic Union <www.eurasiancommission. org> accessed 10 July 2021.

6   Art 32 of the EAEU Agreement <www.eurasiancommission.org> accessed 10 July 2021.

7   Official site of the Eurasian Economic Union <www.eaeunion.org> accessed 10 July 2021.

8   Decision of the EurAsEC Interstate Council on 27 November 2009, N 17 with changes from 11 April 2017 'On the Treaty on the Customs Code of the Customs Union'.

9   Arts 99, 101 of the EAEU Treaty <www.eurasiancommission.org> accessed 10 July 2021.

10   Art 3 of the Customs Code. Annex to the Treaty on the Customs Code of the Customs Union. Decision of the EurAsEC Interstate Council of 27 November 2009, N 17 <www.eur asiancommission.org/ru/docs> accessed 10 July 2021.

Council and the Eurasian Economic Commission adopted within their competencies under the Treaty on the EAEU and treaties within the framework of the Union.

Considering the significant multitude of acts regulating customs relations at the EAEU level, issues arising in connection with application of the legislation of the Customs Union by the national authorities of EAEU Member States are not out of the ordinary. In order to ensure the uniformity of judicial practice, the Supreme Court of the Russian Federation, explaining the application of customs legislation by the courts, noted that the legal regulation of customs relations is carried out in accordance with the Constitution of the Russian Federation and international treaties which are part of the national legal system in accordance with Article 15 (4) of the Constitution of the Russian Federation.[11]

In resolving customs disputes, courts of the Russian Federation often directly apply norms of the Customs Code of the Customs Union, for example, in cases where an interpretation of terms is necessary.[12] In Russian court practice there is also room for disputes in which provisions of the Customs Code are to be interpreted in a system with international conventions.[13]

In addition, the Supreme Court of the Russian Federation stressed the necessity for national courts to take into account the acts of the Court of the Union rendered under paragraph 39 of the Statute of the Court[14] following the consideration of disputes related to the implementation of the provisions of the Treaty, other international agreements within the Union and/or decisions by the Member States of the Union.[15]

The call for the application of the relevant norms of the EAEU law in the sphere of customs regulation, taking into account the acts of the EAEU Court, is oriented to the relevant experience in the practice of the EurAsEC Court.[16] For example, in the case of challenging the decision of the Commission of the

---

11   Resolution of the Plenum of the Supreme Court of the Russian Federation of 12 May 2016, N 18 "On some issues of the application by the courts of Customs legislation".

12   Judgment of the Arbitrazh Court of the Urals District of 19 March 2015, N F09-509/15 in case N A07 18456/2014.

13   Decision of the Arbitrazh Court of the Magadan Region of 27 February 2015 in case N A37-2164 / 2014; decision of the Sixth Arbitrazh Appeal Court of 06 June 2015, N 06AP-1757/ 2015; decision of the Judicial Panel on Economic Disputes of the RF Armed Forces dated 30 September 2015 in case N 305-KG15-1816.

14   Appendix N 2 to the EAEU Agreement <www.eurasiancommission.org> accessed 05 July 2021.

15   Resolution of the Plenum of the Supreme Court of the Russian Federation of 12 May 2016, N "On some issues of the application by the courts of Customs legislation".

16   The Court of the Eurasian Economic Community (EurAsEC), which existed between 2001 and 2014, ceased its activity together with the Eurasian Economic Community. The

Customs Union No. 335 of 17 August 2010, by the "Coal Company 'Southern Kuzbass'", the EurAsEC Court recognized the act of the supranational body as contradicting the Treaty on the Creation of a Single Customs Territory and the Formation of the Customs Union of 06 October 2007. As a result, the previous results of the applicant's dispute with customs authorities were reviewed and a basis for similar cases by national courts was provided.[17] We believe that this clarification is addressed not only to the courts, but also to the participants in foreign economic activity and potential participants in disputes with customs authorities. When choosing the proper procedure for protecting an infringed right, it should be borne in mind that in some cases it makes more sense to challenge the decision of the Eurasian Economic Commission (EEC), applied by the customs authority, at the Court of the EAEU than the decision of the customs authorities in the national court.[18]

3   Customs Regulations at the National Level

Article 1 of the (former: EurAsEC) Customs Code stipulated that customs regulation in the Customs Union was carried out in accordance with the Customs legislation of the Customs Union and, in a part not regulated by such legislation, prior to the establishment of appropriate legal relations at the level of the Customs legislation of the Customs Union and Members of the Customs Union.[19]

If, in accordance with the customs legislation of the Customs Union, the customs regulation in the Customs Union is carried out in accordance with the legislation of the Member State of the Customs Union, such legislation is valid on the territory of this Member State of the Customs Union. Taking into account the existing multi-level model of legal regulation of customs relations, the Supreme Court of the Russian Federation formulated an explanation of the procedure for resolving a conflict between norms of Russian legislation on

---

competencies of the EurAsEC court have been transferred to the Court of the Eurasian Economic Union on 1 January 2015.

17   Decision of the EurAsEC Court of 21 February 2013, N 1-7/2-2012.

18   See: para 39 of the Statute of the Court of the EAEU. Appendix N 2 to the EEA Agreement: <www.eurasiancommission.org> accessed 10 July 2021.

19   Customs Code of the Customs Union. Annex to the Treaty on the Customs Code of the Customs Union, adopted by the Decision of the EurAsEC Interstate Council at the level of the Heads of State of 27 November 2009, N 17 <www.eurasiancommission.org/ru/docs> accessed 10 July 2021.

customs matters and the norms of the Union's law in favour of the latter. The court pointed out that in the event of a conflict between the rules governing the customs relations of the Union (Article 6 of the EAEU Treaty) and legislation of the Russian Federation on customs matters, in accordance with Article 15 (4) of the Constitution of the Russian Federation, the Union's right is subject to application.[20]

At the same time, it should be noted that the Supreme Court of the Russian Federation did not recognize the absolute priority of the EAEU law. In the above explanation, an important reservation is formulated, guaranteeing the protection of the rights and freedoms of citizens and organizations. It is emphasized that the conflicts priority of the law of the Union cannot reduce the level of security guaranteed by the Constitution of the Russian Federation. This explanation is aimed at establishing a correlation between supranational regulation of customs relations and public policy. The main idea is to prevent the deterioration of the position of the participants in the relationship, if the "rules of the game" (customs rules established for participants in foreign economic activity) have changed. Given that reasonable expectations constitute the economic essence of customs relations, such a guarantee is especially important in the situation of cancellation of previously declared benefits and preferences.[21] An example is a dispute related to changing the procedure for exemption from payment of customs duties for goods imported as a contribution to the charter capital of companies. Changes were established at the supranational level, whereas the intention of the participants in the relations to take advantage of the tariff benefit was due to the rules fixed in the current national legislation during the investment period. The position of the Supreme Court of the Russian Federation is focused on the inadmissibility of giving retroactive force to the law, due to the deterioration of the position of the participant in the customs relationship. Previously, a similar position was formulated by the Constitutional Court of the Russian Federation.[22]

---

20   Resolution of the Plenum of the Supreme Court of the Russian Federation of 12 May 2016, N 18 'On some issues of the application of customs legislation by the courts'//Bulletin of the Supreme Court of the Russian Federation. N 7. 2016.

21   Ekaterina Dmitrikova and others, 'Impact of the Law of the WTO and the Eurasian Economic Union on the Formation of Russian Court Practice'//Bulletin of Economic Justice of the Russian Federation N 11/2016 <www.igzakon.ru/magazine458> accessed 10 July 2021.

22   Decision of the Constitutional Court of the Russian Federation of 03 March 2015, N 417-O.

4   Tariff Regulation in the Customs Union. Application of the
         Tariff Rate

Article 25 of the Treaty on the EAEU stipulates, within the framework of the
Customs Union, the levying of an import customs duty – a mandatory payment
charged by the customs authorities of Member States in connection with the
importation of goods into the customs territory of the Union. Paid (collected)
import customs duties are subject to enrollment and distribution between the
budgets of Member States.

The set of rates of customs duties applied to goods imported into the customs territory of the Union from third countries represents the Common
Customs Tariff of the Eurasian Economic Union (further referred to as the CCT
EAEU) systematized in accordance with the single Commodity Nomenclature
for Foreign Economic Activities of the EAEU.[23]

Concerning the issue of the application of customs duties, we note the
existence of a potential conflict within the framework of supranational regulation. Russian courts have already faced the need to determine the norms to
be applied.

In a dispute over the invalidation of the requirement to pay customs fees,
the court, relying on the Vienna Convention on the Law of Treaties, decided
that the Free Trade Area Treaty of 18 October 2011, effective from 20 September
2012 and stipulating the need for the Russian Federation to levy a customs duty
upon importation of the product "white sugar" from the territory of Ukraine,
ruled out the possibility of applying the Russia–Ukraine Free Trade Agreement
of 24 June 1993 and the protocols to the said Agreement of 14 November 1997,
04 October 2001 and 25 November 2005 in the part contradicting the terms
of the later concluded treaty (within the framework of which the Russian
Federation consolidated the right to apply customs duties when importing the
product "white sugar" from the territory of Ukraine).[24]

Other resonant examples of the determination by national courts of
norms to be applied for resolving the question of setting the rate of customs

---

23   The Common Customs Tariff of the EAEU was approved by the Decision of the Council of
       the Eurasian Economic Commission of 14 September 2021 No 80 <www.eurasiancommiss
       ion.org/ru/act/trade/catr/ett/Pages/default.aspx> accessed 30 November 2021.
24   Decisions of the Arbitrazh Court of the Kursk region of 26 March 2015 in case N A35-
       5354 / 2013 and of the Arbitration Court of the Kursk Region on 15 December 2014, of the
       Nineteenth Arbitration Appeal Court of 30 October 2014 in case N A35-6713/2013, upheld
       by the second appeal (cassation) instance, the Arbitrazh Court of the Central District of
       22 April 2015 N F10- 914/2015 in the case N A35-6713 / 2013.

payments are disputes over the application of a reduced duty rate for coated paper and palm oil. When determining the rate, the customs authorities proceeded from the provisions of the act of the supranational body,[25] whereas the declarants based their position on the obligations of the Russian Federation adopted in connection with the signing of the Protocol "On the Accession of the Russian Federation to the Marrakesh Agreement Establishing the World Trade Organization".

In resolving the dispute, the court stated that the rate of the import tariff should not exceed the level stipulated in the schedule of concessions and obligations on access to the goods market[26] and recognized that the decision of the customs body based on the act of supranational legislation violated the rights and legitimate interests of the applicant in the field of entrepreneurial and other economic activities.[27] One must keep in mind the fact that the national courts resolved the dispute without waiting for the relevant decision of the Eurasian Economic Commission or the supranational Court, being guided by a direct application of the law of the World Trade Organization (WTO).[28]

5 Tariff Regulation: Classification of Goods

Article 25 (2) of the EAEU Treaty provides for the establishment of a Single Commodity Nomenclature for Foreign Economic Activities of the EAEU based on the Harmonized System for Description and Coding of Goods of the World Customs Organization and the Common Commodity Nomenclature for Foreign Economic Activities of the Commonwealth of Independent States.

Classification of goods in accordance with the Commodity Nomenclature for Foreign Economic Activity is of fundamental importance. The Single

---

25 The EEC Decision on 16 July 2012 N 54, "On approval of the single Commodity Nomenclature for Foreign Economic Activities of the Eurasian Economic Union and the Single Customs Tariff of the Eurasian Economic Union".

26 This is stipulated by the decision of the Supreme Eurasian Economic Council of 19 December 2011, N 11 and the Treaty on the Functioning of the Customs Union within the Multilateral Trading System on 19 May 2011.

27 The conclusions of the Court of First Instance were supported by the courts of appeal and cassation, see the decision of the Arbitrazh Court of the Nizhny Novgorod Region of 18 November 2013; the decisions of the First Arbitrazh Court of Appeal of 26 February 2014 and the Federal Arbitrazh Court of the Volga-Vyatka region of 14 July 2014 in the case N A43-17771 / 2013.

28 As to further details on the application of WTO norms by Russian courts see Marina Trunk-Fedorova, 'WTO Norms in the Russian Legal System' in this volume, 123 et seq.

Commodity Nomenclature for Foreign Economic Activity of the Customs Union is applied for the examination of measures of customs and tariff and non-tariff regulation of foreign trade and other types of foreign economic activity as well as for the conduct of customs statistics.

The classification of goods to a certain classification code is carried out based on the results of an evaluation of the totality of information about the characteristics of the declared goods. In accordance with the rules of customs regulation of the EAEU, the examination of the correct classification of goods is carried out by the customs authorities.[29] The uniformity of practice in the classification of goods guarantees the protection of the rights of participants in foreign economic activity.

In this connection, the unity of the approaches of customs bodies and national courts, on the one hand, and the participants in foreign economic activity, on the other hand, to the assessment of information confirming the correct classification of goods is of high importance. As evidence, the listed entities usually present explanations of specialized organizations, expert opinions, explanations of experts from the chambers of commerce and industry, etc.

In this case, the Basic Rules for the Interpretation of Commodity Nomenclature should be taken into account for the purposes of classification of goods.[30] Along with the Basic Rules of Interpretation, explanations can be used for Commodity Nomenclature,[31] recommended as auxiliary materials, recommendations and clarifications on the classification of goods given by the World Customs Organization.

In one of its decisions the EurAsEC[32] Court pointed out that the recommendatory nature of the provisions of the Explanations to the Commodities

---

29   Art 52 of the Customs Code of the Customs Union. Customs Code of the Customs Union. Annex to the Treaty on the Customs Code of the Customs Union, adopted by the Decision of the EurAsEC Interstate Council at the level of the Heads of State of 27 November 2009, N 17 <www.eurasiancommission.org/ru/docs> accessed 10 July 2021.

30   Decision of the EEC of 16 July 2012 N 54, 'On the approval of the single Commodity Nomenclature for Foreign Economic Activity of the Eurasian Economic Union and the Uniform Customs Tariff of the Eurasian Economic Union'.

31   The explanations correspond to the WCO Harmonized System for Description and Coding of Goods, from which it is impossible to withdraw unilaterally.

32   As mentioned above, this was the judicial body of the Eurasian Economic Community. The competencies of the EurAsEC court have been transferred to the Court of the Eurasian Economic Union on 1 January 2015.

Nomenclature cannot be considered as the possibility of an unmotivated deviation from them.[33]

In favour of the admissibility of the Explanations, the fact that technological progress determines the appearance of new goods or new properties of existing goods also plays a part. Therefore, not all terms and concepts given in the commodity items and subheadings of the Commodity Nomenclature can be explained in detail and consistently by means of legal notes and explanations to the EAEU Commodity Nomenclature for Foreign Economic Activities, official decisions and explanations.[34]

In this regard, it is worth mentioning the decision of the Supreme Court of the Russian Federation in the "Apple Rus" case in connection with the implementation of the import of Apple Watch personal wireless receiving and transmitting portable devices to the Russian Federation. The Supreme Court of the Russian Federation pointed to the error f an ungrounded refusal by lower courts to take into account for the resolution of the dispute of the explanations of the World Customs Organization, on which the "Apple Rus" company relied when applying to the customs authority. The Court noted that, following the results of the 55th session of the Harmonized System Committee held in March 2015, a decision was made regarding the classification of "smart watches", according to which portable battery-powered devices capable of receiving and transmitting data and intended for wearing on the wrist are recommended to be classified in heading 8517.62 of the Harmonized System in accordance with the Basic Rules for Interpretation. At the level of the Eurasian Economic Union, a decision was not made to classify devices of the "smart clock" type according to one or another Commodity Nomenclature code. In this situation, the classification recommendations of the World Customs Organization are important for ensuring legal certainty in the classification of goods imported by economic operator for customs purposes.[35]

---

33   See the decision of the Collegium of the Court of the Eurasian Economic Community in the case on the applications of Private Limited Company 'Zabaikalresource' and Private Limited Company 'Nika' of 20 May 2014.

34   The relevant acts of the Eurasian Economic Commission or federal executive bodies are also not always able to provide clarification of all issues arising in the classification of goods, in the conditions of technical progress.

35   Decision of the Supreme Court of the Russian Federation of 20 September 2017 in the case N 305-KG17-3138, A40-32818/2016 <www.supcourt.ru/stor_pdf_ec.php?id=1579086> accessed 10 July 2021.

6   Responsibility for Violation of the Customs Legislation of the Customs Union

Article 4 of the Customs Code of the Customs Union stipulates that administrative offenses and crimes are acts for which, in accordance with the legislation of the Member States of the Customs Union, customs authorities carry-out proceedings in accordance with the legislation of the Member States of the Customs Union. Thus, the legislation of the EAEU Member States establishes types of unlawful acts, types and amounts of penalties for their commission, the procedure for bringing to criminal and administrative responsibility.

This approach is also reflected in the Treaty on the Specifics of Criminal and Administrative Liability for Violations of the Customs Legislation of the Customs Union and the Member States of the Customs Union, according to which the applicable law of a State is determined.[36] So, in the case of a person committing a crime on the territory of several States, the place of its commission is the territory of the country on which the last criminal act was committed; if the crimes are committed by a person on the territory of several States, then by agreement between authorized bodies in accordance with the law of the States, a criminal case may be investigated on the territory of the country where the majority of the crimes or the most serious crime is committed. Each State in accordance with its legislation can initiate and investigate criminal cases on crimes directed against its interests committed on the territory of other States.

A person who committed an administrative offense on the customs territory of the Customs Union shall be brought to administrative responsibility under the legislation of the State on the territory of which an administrative violation is found. If goods and documents are not delivered at the place of delivery established by the customs body of departure, a person shall be brought to administrative responsibility under the laws of that State whose customs authorities released the goods in accordance with the customs procedure for customs transit.

The administrative infringement procedure is carried out under the laws of the State in which a person is or has to be subject to administrative liability.

---

36   Treaty on the specifics of criminal and administrative liability for violations of the Customs legislation of the Customs Union and the Member States of the Customs Union (signed in Astana on 5 July 2010) <www.eurasiancommission.org/ru/docs> accessed 10 July 2021.

Undoubtedly, in solving the issue of bringing a person to liability for violation of customs legislation, administrative bodies and courts directly apply the provisions of the customs legislation of the Customs Union.[37]

7   The Customs Code of the Eurasian Economic Union

The further development of a single customs regulation in the Eurasian Economic Union is connected with the Customs Code of the Eurasian Economic Union. The Treaty on the Customs Code of the Eurasian Economic Union was signed only on 11 April 2017 and entered into force on 1 January 2018.[38]

Simultaneously with the Customs Code of the EAEU, more than 20 decisions of the Eurasian Economic Commission came into force, including those on the application of the customs transit procedure, customs operations with regard to temporarily imported vehicles of international customs transportation, and the status of a professional participant in customs relations.

The provisions of the Code are aimed at simplifying the interaction of participants in foreign economic activities with customs authorities (the terms of registration and release of the customs declaration have been shortened,[39] the obligation to submit documents simultaneously with the filing of the declaration has been removed).

The Customs Code of the EAEU is aimed at creating optimal conditions for electronic declaration and electronic document management, the introduction of the "one-stop-shop" system,[40] and other simplifications.

---

37   Qualification of unlawful acts taking into account the provisions of the Customs legislation of the Customs Union. See the decision of the Constitutional Court of the Russian Federation of 19 November 2015, N 2592-O, "On refusal to accept the complaint of citizen Sizov Mikhail Vladimirovich for violation of his constitutional rights by Article 229.1 of the Criminal Code of the Russian Federation" and Federal Law N 420-FZ of 7 December 2011 "On the Introduction of Amendments to the Criminal Code of the Russian Federation and Certain Legislative Acts of the Russian Federation"; Decision of the Constitutional Court of the Russian Federation of 29 September 2016, N 1924-O 'On refusal to accept a complaint of a citizen of the Republic of Kazakhstan Shelepova Tatyana Borisovna a violation of her constitutional rights in Articles 12, 226.1 and 234 of the Criminal Code of the Russian Federation'.

38   Official site of the Eurasian Economic Union <www.eaeunion.org> accessed 10 July 2021.

39   The release period will be four hours, registration – one hour (maximum).

40   State officials do not have the right to request documents if they were previously submitted to another government agency and the documents can be obtained through interdepartmental exchange.

In the process of preparation of the EAEU Customs Code, the drafters have tried to refrain as much as possible from referring to the legislation of the EAEU Member States, which corresponds to the formation of a common policy in the field of customs regulation, declared by the EAEU member states when they signed the EAEU Treaty.

CHAPTER 9

Major Difficulties of Some WTO Members in Complying with the SPS and TBT Agreements

Irina Kireeva

1   Introduction*

This chapter provides an overview of the major issues in relation to the Agreement on the Application of Sanitary and Phytosanitary Measures (SPS Agreement) and the Agreement on Technical Barriers to Trade (TBT Agreement) of the WTO for the Russian Federation, Kazakhstan and Azerbaijan. These three countries have a lot in common due to their past and share similar problems with the application of the SPS and TBT measures that often become trade barriers. Russia[1] and Kazakhstan[2] have recently joined the WTO after a lengthy period of accession; Azerbaijan[3] is not a member of the WTO yet, but has been in the process of accession since 1996.

Without doubt, Russia, Kazakhstan and Azerbaijan would benefit from the harmonisation of SPS and TBT measures. Moreover, all three countries still use the system of "GOST" (technical standards set by authorities of the USSR), and transition to international standards would facilitate trade and increase private sector participation.

---

*   A special word of thanks and appreciation for detailed comments and encouragement during the work on this chapter is due to my former colleague and friend, a practicing economist and Director General of the Technology Resource Center of the Philippines, Dr. Arthur Alvendia. The author is also thankful for general suggestions on the earlier draft to Dr. Robert Black and Bernard O'Connor, senior partner of the firm NCTM O'Connor. The opinions expressed in the article are those of the author.

1   Russia became a WTO Member on 22 August 2012 <www.wto.org/english/thewto_e/acc_e/a1_russie_e.htm> accessed 30 June 2021.

2   Kazakhstan's Working Party was established on 6 February 1996. Bilateral Kazakhstan became a WTO Member on 30 November 2015 <www.wto.org> accessed 30 June 2021.

3   Azerbaijan's Working Party was established on 16 July 1997 and the first meeting of the Working Party was held in June 2002. Bilateral negotiations on market access are underway on the basis of revised offers in goods and services. The fourteenth meeting of the Working Party took place in July 2017 <www.wto.org/english/thewto_e/acc_e/a1_azerbaidjan_e.htm> accessed 30 June 2021.

© KONINKLIJKE BRILL NV, LEIDEN, 2023 | DOI:10.1163/9789004357839_011

An impressive recovery of production and exports from the post-independence shock and from economic crises could be seen in each of the three countries,[4] however, further growth depends increasingly on product safety, quality and diversification of production. Major goods traded by the countries under review do not require application of the SPS or TBT Agreements per se; in addition, Azerbaijan has at most to consider future commitments in relation to these WTO agreements as it is not yet a WTO member. At the same time, it is evident that the traditional approach to risk management and GOST-based systems of these countries pose serious constraints to competitiveness of production, and issues regarding food safety and animal and plant health outcomes are not satisfactory.[5]

2   Normative Framework for Compliance with the WTO SPS and TBT
       Agreements

Logically, it is necessary to explain what norms should be followed and how compliance with the SPS and TBT Agreements should take place, i.e. what is the normative framework applicable.

The World Trade Organization emerged in 1995 from the GATT process as a new international organization devoted to the elimination of restrictions on trade, i.e. tariff and non-tariff trade barriers, reduction or elimination of governmental support measures and increase of market access.[6] One of the WTO

---

4 The particular aspects of the economic sanctions imposed on Russia by the United States, the European Union and other countries since 2014 as well as Russia's counter-sanctions are not considered here.

5 Perceived increase in zoonotic diseases from smallholder farms, although official databases show a strong decline in tuberculosis and brucellosis in Russia, Moldova and Ukraine. There is also a weak capacity to detect contaminants and pesticides residues, to deal with diseases and pest outbreaks, weak plant quarantine (UNIDO Report 'Managing SPS Measures in SPECA countries', 2010).

6 *Understanding the WTO,* Handbook at WTO official website, <www.wto.org/english/thewt o_e/whatis_e/tif_e/understanding_e.pdf> accessed 30 June 2021*21The GATT Years: from Havana to Marrakesh, World Trade Organization,* <www.wto.org/english/thewto_e/whatis _e/tif_e/fact4_e.htm> accessed 30 June 2021; Peter Malanczuk, 'World Trade Organization' in *Encyclopaedia Britannica* (1999) 442; Bernard Hoekman, 'The WTO: Functions and Basic Principles' (3rd edn, 2000) <http://documents.worldbank.org/curated/en/805981468763835 259/pdf/297990018213149971x.pdf> accessed 30 June 2021; Principles of the Trading System, WTO official site <www.wto.org> accessed 30 June 2021; Ignacio G. Bercero, 'Functioning of the WTO System: Elements for Possible Institutional Reform' (2000) 6 International Trade Law and Regulation 103; Frieder Roessler, 'The Institutional Balance between the Judicial and

Agreements applies specifically to trade in agricultural, food and health products and addresses the issues of minimum levels of quality, health and safety standards of these products regarding the way they are produced, packaged or transported, which may pose sanitary or phytosanitary hazards. This is the Agreement on the Application of Sanitary and Phytosanitary Measures.[7]

The SPS Agreement is the most important of the WTO Agreements addressing food safety. The idea of the SPS Agreement was to supplement Article XX(b) of the GATT 1994.[8] Unlike the rules governing the GATT, the SPS Agreement goes beyond the general principle of non-discrimination and provides a system that gives WTO Members specific rights and obligations related to SPS measures.

The SPS Agreement defines sanitary and phytosanitary standards broadly. It defines them generally as:

> ... all relevant laws, decrees, regulations, requirements and procedures including, inter alia, end product criteria; processes and production methods; testing, inspection, certification and approval procedures; quarantine treatments including relevant requirements associated with the transport of animals or plants, or with the materials necessary for their survival during transport; provisions on relevant statistical methods, sampling procedures and methods of risk assessment; and packaging and labelling requirements directly related to food safety. ...[9]

---

the Political Organs of the WTO', in: Marco C.E.J. Bronckers and Reinhard Quick (eds) *New Directions in International Economic Law: Essays in Honour of John H Jackson* (2000) 325–345.

7　The text of the SPS Agreement can be found in *The Results of the Uruguay Round of Multilateral Trade Negotiations - The Legal Texts* (reprint, Geneva, 1995), <www.wto.org/engl ish/tratop_e/sps_e/sps_e.htm> accessed 30 June 2021.

8　Under that Article, WTO Members may introduce measures that are necessary to protect human, animal or plant life and health so long as such measures are not applied in a manner that would constitute a means of arbitrary or unjustifiable discrimination between countries where the same conditions prevail. Therefore, art XX(b), while providing a general exception that allows WTO Members to take unilateral action to protect health, qualifies that exception by saying that measures adopted by national authorities must not discriminate arbitrarily or unjustifiably. General Agreement on Tariffs and Trade, 30 October 1947, 61 Stat. A-11, 55 U.N.T.S. 194 (GATT 1947), which has been incorporated into General Agreement on Tariffs and Trade 1994, 15 April 1994, WTO Agreement, Annex IA, 1867 U.N.T.S. 187, 33 I.L.M. 1153 (1994) [hereinafter GATT]. Major most-favoured-nations (MFN) clauses, in various forms, appear in GATT arts I:1, II:1, V:5, IX:1, and XIII:1. Major NT clauses appear in GATT arts III:2 and III:4.

9　SPS Agreement, Annex A, para 1.

and then provides in Article 1.1:

> This Agreement applies to all sanitary and phytosanitary measures which may, directly or indirectly, affect international trade. Such measures shall be developed and applied in accordance with the provisions of this Agreement.

Thus, as stated by the Panel in *EC – Hormones*, there are two requirements for the SPS Agreement to apply, namely that the measure in dispute is an SPS measure and that the measure, directly or indirectly, affects international trade.

The SPS Agreement has a two-fold objective. Firstly, it aims to recognize the sovereign right of WTO Members to provide the level of health protection they deem appropriate and, secondly, ensures that SPS measures do not represent unnecessary, arbitrary, scientifically unjustifiable, or disguised restrictions on international trade. Indeed, the SPS Agreement allows countries to set their own food safety and animal and plant health measures and administrative ways regarding how they are controlled.

However, this basic right of adopting SPS measures is further qualified by Article 2.3, which reiterates the non-discrimination requirement of the *chapeau* of GATT Article XX. The SPS Agreement requires that national SPS measures:
– be based on science,
– be applied only to the extent necessary to protect health, and
– not arbitrarily or unjustifiably discriminate between countries where identical or similar conditions prevail, or be applied in such a way as to constitute a disguised restriction on international trade.

In order to assist with the realisation of these objectives, the SPS Agreement encourages WTO Members to base their national measures on the international standards, guidelines and recommendations adopted in particular by the Codex Alimentarius Commission. This is the principle of harmonization established by Article 3 of the SPS Agreement. Harmonization is a trade facilitation tool for achieving uniformity. The idea of harmonization is to convert two differing standards or procedures into one or establish one new standard that applies in all WTO Member territories. Harmonization is a result of the acceptance of the same rules by all the international operators in a defined sector or activity. To achieve harmonization, all WTO Members agree to use international guidelines, recommendations and standards as a basis for their technical regulations or conformity assessment procedures. For animal and plant life and health, measures are to be based on those standards adopted and recommended by the Office International des Epizooties (OIE, the World

Organisation for Animal Health) and the International Plant Protection Convention (IPPC), respectively. Although the SPS Agreement acknowledges the limitation of means, it encourages the participation of all WTO Members, in particular, developing countries, in these international organizations, so that they may contribute to the formulation of sanitary and phytosanitary measures and have sufficient information to make decisions regarding the approval of international standards.

As long as a Member employs international standards in the formulation of the national measures, these are presumed to be consistent with the provisions of the Agreement. However, Members are allowed to adopt measures that establish a higher level of protection than that provided by the relevant international standard if there is a scientific justification, based on risk assessment.

In relation specifically to national administrative frameworks, Article 8 provides that WTO Members must follow certain specific rules (found in Annex C to the SPS Agreement) with respect to any procedures to check and ensure the fulfilment of SPS measures. Overall, SPS measures should not apply arbitrarily or unjustifiably discriminate between Members where identical or similar conditions prevail. Moreover, importing Members are obliged to accept the measures of other Members as equivalent if the exporting country objectively demonstrates to the importing country that its measures achieve the importing country's appropriate level of protection.

2.1 Better Understanding of the Difference between the SPS and TBT Measures

Often, there is confusion between measures in relation to food safety, given that some of them are within the scope of the SPS Agreement and others are clearly technical regulations subject to the TBT Agreement of the WTO.[10] The author would like to explain that the main differences of the SPS and TBT measures reside in the scope of application, the use of international standards and the reasons for application and maintenance of the measures.

---

10 The text of the Agreement on Technical Barriers to Trade can be found in *The Results of the Uruguay Round of Multilateral Trade Negotiations – The Legal Texts* (reprint, Geneva, 1995), <www.wto.org/english/tratop_e/tbt_e/tbt_e.htm> accessed 30 June 2021. More on the WTO TBT Agreement and its relevance to the food safety aspects can be found in Peter Van den Bossche, Denise Prévost and Mariëlle Matthee, 'WTO Rules on Technical Barriers to Trade' *Maastricht Working Paper, N° 2005/6; "Standards, Metrology, Conformity Assessment and the TBT Agreement"* (USAID Publication, 2010); Arthur E Appleton, 'Environmental Labelling Programmes: International Trade Law Implications' (Kluwer Law International 1997); Arthur E Appleton, 'Supermarket labels and the TBT Agreement' (2007) 4 Business Law Brief 10.

The SPS Agreement covers all measures whose purpose is to protect:
- human or animal health from so called food-borne risks;
- human health from animal or plant diseases; and
- plants and animals from pests or diseases.[11]

Therefore, distinguishing whether a measure is regulated by the SPS or the TBT Agreement becomes a subjective exercise. The type of the measure or institution adopting it is less important (so, it can be called a Technical Regulation, a Legal Notice or an Administrative Issuance, etc.) than figuring out the specific purpose of the measure itself.

The TBT Agreement covers all technical requirements and regulations, voluntary standards and the procedures to ensure that these are met (called conformity assessment procedures), except when these are SPS measures as defined by the SPS Agreement.[12]

The SPS Agreement and the TBT Agreement exclude each other from their scope. Article 1.4 of the SPS Agreement states "Nothing in this Agreement shall affect the rights of Members under the Agreement on Technical Barriers to Trade." Similarly, the TBT Agreement, in Article 1.5 excludes from its scope SPS measures. While the texts of the two agreements are similar, the most obvious difference is the test used to find non-compliance.

Unlike the SPS Agreement, which requires a scientific justification and a risk assessment, the TBT Agreement's test is one of non-discrimination. Discrimination is tolerated under the SPS Agreement (unless it is "arbitrary or unjustifiable") because protecting domestic human, plant and animal health, is by its very nature, a discriminatory task.

Both agreements instruct WTO Members to use international standards, but under the SPS Agreement, WTO Members are compelled to use these standards unless they can show a specific scientific justification based on an assessment of the possible risk.[13] WTO Members may set TBT measures that deviate from the international standards for other reasons, including technological difficulties or geographical issues.[14]

Furthermore, SPS measures may only be applied to "the extent necessary to protect human, animal or plant life or health, based on scientific principles and not maintained without sufficient scientific evidence", while TBT measures

11   See Annex A to the SPS Agreement with the definition of the SPS measures.
12   Art 1.5 of the TBT Agreement.
13   Art 5.1 of the SPS Agreement.
14   Art 2.4 of the TBT Agreement.

may be applied and maintained for other reasons, including national security or to prevent deceptive practices.[15]

Some examples of what measures fall under the TBT Agreement include the shape of food cartons, the labelling on cigarettes, pharmaceutical restrictions, specifications to ensure that farmers are protected from fertilizers, and food quality restrictions. Conversely, the SPS Agreement covers any measures which set acceptable levels of pesticide or veterinary drug residues, quarantine provisions, regulation of permitted levels of fertilizer residue in food and animal feed, regulations which prohibit or limit the types of acceptable food additives, and regulations mandating labelling on food or animal feed that gives health, use or dosage information.

It should be noted that both TBT and SPS measures can be used for ensuring food safety.[16] Although these measures are prepared and adopted by various competent authorities responsible for agriculture, human health, adoption of standards, etc., they contain basic SPS (veterinary, sanitary and hygiene norms) measures. Therefore, this research will focus on the analyses of multiple governmental bodies involved in ensuring food safety with uniform approach to the SPS measures in line with the SPS Agreement, as well as controls of the veterinary, phytosanitary and sanitary provisions by the responsible competent authorities in line with internationally developed norms.

2.2   *Use of the SPS and TBT Measures as Non-tariff Barriers to Trade*

WTO Member's right to employ protective measures in the veterinary, plant health/quarantine and human health areas, coincides with their obligation to comply with provisions of the SPS Agreement.[17] In practice, national protective measures known as sanitary and phytosanitary border controls, which include all official actions, decision or supporting laws, regulations or other documents, lead to restriction of trade. However, such restrictions are justified on condition that the objective is a legitimate purpose recognised by the SPS Agreement, such as protection of human life and health or plant and animal life and health. Often SPS or TBT measures or their administration and

---

15   Art 2.2 of the SPS Agreement and art 2.10 of the TBT Agreement.

16   The same idea, see in Denise Prevost, 'Private Sector Food-Safety Standards and the SPS Agreement: Challenges and Possibilities' (2008) 33 South African Yearbook of International Law 1–37.

17   Protective phytosanitary measures are examined using the example of the Russian Federation in the article by Irina Kireeva and Robert Black, 'International Trade and Plant Protection Issues: Example of Plant Quarantine Law of the Russian Federation' (June 2010) 44(3) Journal of World Trade 591–611.

application are not based on science or are not transparent (although per se appropriate) and that leads to a problem of non-compliance with the WTO obligations. This is exactly the case in the Russian Federation, Kazakhstan and Azerbaijan. For example, if the GOST system would be compared with the International Standards approach, the major shortcomings would be in the application of inconsistent, vague and non-transparent procedures, methodologies and criteria. Incompatible laboratory facilities, equipment and tests are often used and become impediments for trade.

It is true that compliance with the SPS Agreement poses difficulties for a number of countries. For the SPS Agreement's first phase of implementation (until the year 2000), some WTO Members were accorded special and differential treatment (given to all developing and least developed countries).[18] Still limited in technical, human and financial resources they did not have the ability to fully implement and enforce all SPS measures and regulations. In particular, they found it difficult to provide the necessary scientific and technical justification for their sanitary and phytosanitary measures and to conduct risk analysis – which is the process of evaluating biological or other scientific and economic evidence to determine whether a hazard should be regulated. This is also the problem for Russia, Kazakhstan and Azerbaijan, as the nature of GOST standards and mandatory regulations requirements is highly prescriptive and the focus of control is on the "end-of-pipe" and not in the process of production or "entire chain". Further, the responsibility for food safety is within the public sector, causing the private stakeholders to be subject to controls. In this way, the financial burden is not well-balanced and efficiency is low. However, the major problem of all countries is still in enforcing the existing provisions,

18   See also art 10 of the SPS Agreement on Special and Differential Treatment; see also Denise Prévost, '"Operationalising" Special and Differential Treatment to Developing Countries under the SPS Agreement', on-line publication of the University of Maastricht; Robert M Hamwey, 'Expanding National Policy Space for Development: Why the Multilateral Trading System Must Change', *Working Paper 25* (September 2005); Committee on Sanitary and Phytosanitary Measures, *Special and Differential Treatment: Note by the Secretariat*, G/SPS/W/105 (9 May 2000); CTD, *Information on the Utilisation of Special and Differential Treatment Provisions. Note by the Secretariat. Addendum* WT/COMTD/W/77/Rev 1/Add 4, (7 February 2002) at 21–22; *Recommended Notification Procedures for Implementing the Transparency Obligations of the SPS Agreement (Article 7). Revision* G/SPS/7/Rev 2 (2 April 2002); Committee on Sanitary and Phytosanitary Measures, *Notification of Determination of the Recognition of Equivalence of Sanitary and Phytosanitary Measures. Decision by the Committee. Addendum* G/SPS/7/Rev 2/Add 1 (25 July 2002).

effective controls and inspection services for any SPS or TBT measures including checks at the borders.[19]

The reasons for non-compliance are numerous and can be summarized as
following:

- a lack of infrastructure (e.g. sufficient number of accredited laboratories or
  other testing facilities);
- absence of a balanced and appropriate legal framework, a regulatory framework based not on risk assessment, but on mandatory compliance with
  setup requirements (often not justified or scientifically sound);
- a weak and insufficient institutional framework (e.g. multiple regulations
  and various agencies and bodies, without proper coordination and duplica-
  tion of work);
- scarcity of qualified human resources (this may not be the case for the
  Russian Federation, but in general the public sector has many vacant
  positions).

It should be noted that the SPS Agreement acknowledges the limitations of
means of developing and least developed countries, and at the same time
encourages the participation of all member states (especially developing countries) in the International Plant Protection Convention (IPPC), so that such
countries can contribute to the formulation of phytosanitary measures and
make informed decisions on the approval of international standards. However,
this is not directly applicable to the countries in question, because the root of
the problem is not in financial or budgetary constraints but rather in the con-
ceptual application of the existing norms. That can be well-illustrated with the
example of the Customs Union Regulations.[20]

To address these issues, it is necessary to understand the tradition and reasons for maintaining the system of mandatory standards, as well as answer the
question: why is it not possible to replace GOST standards with international
standards immediately.

---

19   See excellent work of Miss Mary Kenny, 'International Food Trade: Food Quality and
      Safety Considerations', FAO, <www.fao.org/docrep/W9474T/w9474t02.htm> accessed 30
      June 2021, the author was working with Miss Kenny on a number of projects together.
20   Since 1 January 2015 the Customs Union functions within the framework of the Eurasian
      Economic Union (EAEU). For more on the EAEU see Zhenis Kembayev, 'The Eurasian
      Economic Union: An Overview and Evaluation' in this volume, 19 et seq.

3   The General Food and Product Safety Situation in Russia,
       Kazakhstan and Azerbaijan

The problem of food safety and quality as well as controls is very relevant today
for the Russian Federation, Kazakhstan and Azerbaijan. According to various
publications, television and radio programmes, there are constant incidents
due to the poor quality / unsafe food that harmed or can harm the health of
consumers in these countries.

Taking Russia as an example, it can be found that the food safety situation
became worse in 2013 as a result of increasing food imports to the Russian
market (comparing with 2010), which was partly due to the bad harvest in
2011–2012. Products of foreign or domestic manufacturers in terms of safety
and quality did not always comply with the requirements to ensure safe
consumption.

Food safety is based on Hazard Analysis and Critical Control Points (HACCP)
principles (which are rather new to the Russian, Kazakh or Azeri producers)
and the requirements of the first international standard for food safety – ISO
22000:2005 (ISO 22000:2007). It is important to note that the safety aspect of
food supply has been raised at the World Summit on Food Security, held in
Rome in November 2009. Sixty heads of states and governments and 192 ministers from 182 countries and the European Union took part in that Summit.
The major purpose of the Summit was in stating the doctrine that *food security
exists when all people have physical, social and economic access to sufficient, safe
and nutritious food to meet their dietary needs and food preferences for an active
and healthy life.* It can be added that Russia, Kazakhstan and Azerbaijan pay a
lot of attention to the food safety and food security issues at present.

Again, looking at the national experience, the Food Security Doctrine of the
Russian Federation, approved by the Decree of the President of the Russian
Federation of January 30, 2010 № 120, pronounces one of the goals of food
security – overall food safety. It states that "in order to ensure food safety it is
necessary to control compliance with the legislation of the Russian Federation
in the field of agriculture, fisheries and food products, including imported
ones, at all stages of production, storage, transport, processing and sale".

The doctrine speaks of the need to avoid the uncontrolled spread of food
products derived from genetically modified plants, genetically modified organ-
isms and micro-organisms that are genetically modified analogues, and the
need for continued harmonization with international standards of safety of
food based on fundamental research in the field of nutrition science. It also
urges the improvement of management systems of food safety (for domesti-
cally produced foodstuffs), including the development of a modern technical

and methodological base (which is lacking). Similar political documents and directions can be found in Kazakhstan and Azerbaijan.

4   Legal Framework on Product and Food Safety of the Reviewed Countries

4.1   *Legislation of the Russian Federation*

The overall legal framework in relation to safety of food products in the Russian Federation can be characterised as fragmented and incomplete. It consists of the provisions of the following federal laws:

–   Federal Law N° 184-FZ "On Technical Regulation",[21] as last amended;
–   Federal Law N° 29-FZ "On Food Product Quality and Safety", as last amended;
–   Federal Law N° 4979-FZ "On Veterinary Medicine", as last amended;
–   Federal Law N° 206-FZ "On Plant Quarantine", as last amended, and
–   Federal Law N° 109-FZ "On Safe Use of Pesticides and Agrochemicals", as last amended.

The implementing provisions in relation to food safety can be found in the following legal documents:

–   Provisions on Federal Service of Veterinary and Phytosanitary Surveillance, established by the Russian Federation Government Decree № 327 from 30 June 2004;
–   Provisions on State Veterinary Service of the Russian Federation on Protection of the territory of Russia from contamination by infectious diseases of animals from foreign states, approved by the Russian Federation Government Decree № 830 from 29 October 1992;
–   Provisions on procedure and methods of control during entry of persons, transport vehicles, cargo, goods, live animals through the state border, approved by the Russian Federation Government Decree № 50 from 2 February 2005;
–   The Russian Government Federation Decree N° 883 from 22 November 2000 "About organization and monitoring of quality, safety of food products and health of population";
–   Administrative Rules of Procedure of the Federal Veterinary and Phytosanitary Control Service upon execution of state functions concerning

---

21   This and other laws of the Russian Federation are available at the commercial database Garant <base.garant.ru> accessed 30 June 2021.

import and export permits of the Russian Federation, as well as transit through the territory of the Russian Federation of live animals, products of animal origin, pharmaceuticals, feed and feed additives for animals, or other production under quarantine.

The major problems of the Russian legal framework can be outlined as follows. Chapter 1 of the Russian Federation Law on Food Product Quality and Safety introduces some basic concepts and administrative provisions but focuses on a poorly defined concept of 'food quality and safety' rather than appropriate basic food safety principles. Unlike in EU legislation or, more particularly, in EC Regulation 178/2002, there is no reference to risk analysis or risk assessment as the basis for determining food safety requirements under the law or as the basis of decision-making about whether food products may be placed on the market.

The comparison of definitions with similar or equivalent definitions in EC Regulation 178/2002 and other relevant European legislation suggests that serious amendments, and the addition of new terms and concepts, are required.

Chapter 2 of the law is dedicated to the competences of the Russian Federation in the field of safety, the central provisions of state regulation in the field of assurance of food product quality and safety, and the general requirements for the assurance of the foodstuffs quality and safety are presented in Chapters 3 and 4 respectively.

Consequent to the lack of true food safety principles in Chapter 1, the emphasis in these provisions is on registration and certification of products. The "hygiene package" in the EC Regulations 178/2002, 852/2004 and 853/2004 has a different approach. In relation to import controls on foodstuffs (Article 21), the provisions of the Russian law do not make it clear how exactly the authorities assess compliance with the Russian Federation's requirements for food product quality and safety in terms of the manner of certification. Therefore, it is not possible to make comparisons with EU food safety law or with the appropriate rules for international trade in the sanitary and phytosanitary areas provided by WTO.

The Russian Federation Law on Technical Regulation confirms inconsistencies in, and overlaps between, the key definitions of 'technical regulation' and 'veterinary-sanitary and phytosanitary measures'. These definitions are not consistent with the corresponding definitions in the WTO Agreement on Technical Barriers to Trade and the Agreement on the Application of Sanitary and Phytosanitary Measures (SPS). These two agreements clearly provide for an effective separation of the purpose and application of these two types of regulatory intervention, which is not maintained in the Russian Law on Technical Regulation. As a result, the application of these concepts in Chapter 3 (Articles

6–10) is problematic because it appears that there is an attempt to adopt the principles of the SPS Agreement directly through these provisions. In fact, consistency with the SPS Agreement should be achieved by adopting the norms, codes and conventions of the relevant international standard setting bodies in specific primary and secondary legislation in the veterinary, phytosanitary and food safety sectors. The remaining chapters of this law (Chapters 8–10, Articles 11–48) concern standardisation, conformity assurance and certification. These provisions are consistent with international norms for a 'Standards Law', apart from some relatively minor inconsistencies and redundancies in several concepts and their application.

4.2   Food Safety Law of Kazakhstan

In terms of legal framework, the situation in Kazakhstan is more advanced than in other countries, as the Law on Food Safety of the Republic of Kazakhstan was adopted in 2007, with amendments and additions made on 10 January 2011.[22] This law is almost fully compatible with the international and European legislation. That said, there are a number of issues that still have to be addressed and clarified, for example:

– The Kazakh Law on Food Safety does not explain in detail the purpose and aim of the law.
– It is not clear whether the procedures developed in accordance with the Kazakh legislation are based on HACCP and the second paragraph of Article 25, with reference to laboratories, suggests that only final products are controlled and not the process of production. Besides, Sanitary and Epidemiological Rules and Norms of production of food products also do not make reference to HACCP, so it can be concluded that, in reality, implementation of the risk analyses approach is problematic in the Republic of Kazakhstan.
– It is crucial to have a clear understanding of what is unsafe food and how to prevent unsafe food being placed on the market for the consumers. There are no criteria of food safety and food safety determination. It appears that food is safe if it complies with the Technical Regulations (mandatory standards) and if there is a certificate of compliance issued; this approach clearly differs from the EU and international one on assurance of food safety.
– None of the implementing measures or the Sanitary Rules and Norms (abbreviation SanPiNs) apply the rules of the Hazard Analysis and Critical

---

22   Law on Food Safety of 21 July 2007, № 301-III ЗРК (text available in Russian only).

Control Points (HACCP) to the primary production, as well as monitoring of CCP (as required by the Codex Alimentarius).

- There are no implementation programs or procedures for food safety, based on the rules of HACCP and Codex Alimentarius. In some plants, the food sector stands alone for the identification of critical control points, and in some cases, good hygiene practices can substitute for constant supervision of the critical control points. Development, dissemination and use of guidelines for good manufacturing practices can be encouraged but has not taken place.

- Issues of traceability and the concept of food business operators are not translated into practice and it is not clear how these provisions can be enforced in the future. Unspecified responsibility for food safety for the food business sector, which is based on HACCP, including the application of good hygienic practices. Registration, approval, and storing records for the control purposes are missing.

- No information is provided by the law for preventing the emergence and spread of infectious diseases that can pass to humans through food; or in the course of the acceptance of new animals; or in the notification of competent authorities of a suspected possible explosion of epidemics or such diseases.

To sum up all the findings in relation to the legal framework, it could be emphasised that, at present, the secondary legislation of Kazakhstan is not implementing the provisions of the primary legislation, i.e. the Law on Food Safety. So, de facto, the situation in relation to food safety is very similar to the issues highlighted for the Russian Federation and Azerbaijan.

4.3   Legal Framework of Azerbaijan
The food safety institutional framework in the Republic of Azerbaijan can be characterised by the following features:

- responsibilities on food safety issues are spread across a number of state agencies;
- state food safety agencies are funded from the national budget;
- within each agency, it is estimated that more than half or even three quarters of the professional personnel hold a relevant university degree.

The major role in food safety is played by the Ministry of Agriculture, which is responsible for the formulation and implementation of state policy in the field of agricultural production. The Ministry of Agriculture has two special agencies dealing with products of animal origin (the State Veterinary Service) and plant origin (the State Phytosanitary Service).

The Ministry of Health with its State Sanitary and Epidemiology Service is responsible for the strengthening of public health, formation of a healthy way of life and preventive healthcare. Within the Service structure, there is the Republic Centre for Hygiene and Epidemiology Control, Republic Centre against Black Death, Republic Sanitary Quarantine Inspection, and Hygiene and Epidemiology Centre of the Nakhchivan Autonomous Republic.

Surprisingly, the Ministry of Economic Development is also an active player in the national food safety system, as its State Office for Control of Consumer Market is responsible for control of consumer goods, including foodstuffs that are already presented in the stores, public markets or mass catering establishments.

The State Committee on Standardization, Metrology and Patents of the Republic of Azerbaijan is a government agency, which deals with standardization, conformity assessment (certification), metrology, protection of commercial property rights (patents, geographic indicators, etc.), and accreditation. This Committee controls safety and quality of products as well as compliance with obligatory technical requirements and standards.

Finally, the State Customs Committee is also involved in the food safety system, since it is responsible for veterinary and phytosanitary control of imported and exported food products at border inspection posts.

Since all these state agencies are involved in food safety assurance in the Republic of Azerbaijan, there are several laws and regulations pertaining to the food safety objectives, however, there is no one single legal act which provides the essential building blocks of an efficient food safety system in accordance with the National Food Safety and Control Strategy adopted by Azerbaijan in 2010, in particular:

– All food safety related activities of public authorities and food business operators in the Azerbaijan Republic should be based on a scientific approach that takes into account best international practices and rules, as well as considering national traditions.
– National food safety and control policy should be based on an integrated approach that considers all aspects of the food chain as a continuous and interconnected sequence of all product cycle steps.
– The main responsibility for ensuring the safety of foodstuffs should be placed on food processors and food business operators.
– Any activity performed by public authorities and food business operators should be directed to the advantage of consumer health and interests.
– Food safety management should be based on principles of hazard analysis and measures necessary to prevent, eliminate or reduce hazards to acceptable levels.

- While elaborating and implementing measures and actions targeted at ensuring the safety of food, preference should be given to measures and actions of a preventive nature.
- At all stages of the food chain, traceability of food, feed and ingredients, and transparency of processes, steps and operations should be ensured.
- All activities for the safety of food should be designed and implemented with consideration of international standards and practices.
- In planning and implementing food safety activities, the goals should be proportional to the realistically available resources.

For this reason, work on a Draft Law on Food Safety was initiated by the Working Group of the Ministry of Agriculture in 2009; however, no law has been adopted thus far.[23]

From the sections above it is clear that Russia, Kazakhstan and Azerbaijan are facing similar problems in relation to food safety.

5   Issues of Standardisation and Mandatory Certification of Goods Imported into Russia, Azerbaijan and Kazakhstan

Addressing the general product quality and safety, it is important to stress, for both consumers and producers, a need for producing harmless and environmentally friendly products.

In February 2010, Russia abolished the mandatory certification of industrial goods. Manufacturers can now offer their goods to consumers on the basis of their own pre-declaration of conformity with their own evidence for quality and safety. Before, manufacturers of food products had a choice to get a declaration of conformity or to issue a voluntary certificate. However, in relation to food products, the members of the Customs Union came to an agreement on compulsory certification, signed and ratified by all member states, which includes a unified list of products subject to mandatory certification and the application of a homogeneous display of certification forms (hence, in relation to agricultural products, there is mandatory certification of food).

---

23   However, a specialized Agency for Food Safety was established in 2018, see <https://en.wikipedia.org/wiki/Food_Safety_Agency_(Azerbaijan)> accessed 22 November 2021. For an overview of current Azeri legislation see <http://afsa.gov.az/en/legislation/law> accessed 22 November 2021.

At the same time, low-quality products continue to be produced. This is in accordance with the technical specifications, which are approved by the enterprises, because not many manufacturers make products in accordance with existing state standards. Quite a number of products produced today are produced in accordance with the specifications. Manufacturers strive to reduce the cost of production in order to sell their products at a lower price. Therefore, these products are increasing, especially in the economic crisis.

In accordance with the Federal Law "On Protection of legal entities", the planned state control over the enterprise may take place only three years after it was organized, and then, according to plan, every three years thereafter. Thus, the company will be "free swimming" for the first three years. The problem is aggravated by many "phantom" firms. These firms usually indicate non-existent addresses. As a result, production responsibility for the low-quality product is almost impossible to determine. Russia, Kazakhstan and Azerbaijan lack practice to review dangerous goods operating in Western countries. For example, in the United States, between 2009 and 2011, Toyota recalled 3.8 million vehicles because the floor mats sometimes blocked the gas pedal. The review cost the company USD 440 million. In Russia, Kazakhstan or Azerbaijan there has not been a single case of review of dangerous products so far.

A major international mark of quality is still the ISO standards. Conformity to these standards is checked by the International Organization for Standardization (Russia, Kazakhstan and Azerbaijan are members of the ISO[24]). As all three countries entered the path of convergence of national and international standards of quality and safety of products, it is appropriate to further develop this area and simultaneously to increase penalties for violations of the declarations.

Quality and usefulness of food products are often not visible characteristics, and therefore the consumer has to rely on information provided by the manufacturer. However, one of the major achievements of our time is the fact that in Western countries the relationship of trust between consumers and producers of food products is established. The national practice of the countries under review is far from that. Perhaps the solution is not only in transparent and clear system of controls, but also in the promotion of the development of regional systems that certify or establish a seal of quality endorsement for responsible manufacturers, producing high-quality and safe products.

---

24   <www.iso.org/iso/home.html> accessed 30 June 2021.

6   Specific sps and tbt Aspects of Importation of Goods into
         Azerbaijan, the Russian Federation and Kazakhstan

For the customs clearance of a wide range of products, the importer is required
to prove that those goods conform to the valid norms and standards. In
Azerbaijan, the State Agency for Standardization, Metrology and Patent is the
central executive body responsible for implementing the state policy in the
sphere of technical regulation, standardization, metrology, conformity assessment, accreditation, quality management, and protection of industrial property objects.[25]

In Russia and Kazakhstan, there are currently two standardisation systems
in force in these countries, the first is valid in the three member countries of
the Customs Union: Belarus, Kazakhstan and Russia, the other applies only
to the territory of the Russian Federation or Kazakhstan. On a national basis,
the conformity of the goods controlled by the Federal Customs Service is
to be proven either through a Certificate of Conformity or a Declaration of
Conformity, i.e. a self-declaration.

As regards the Customs Union, Kazakhstan and Russia have implemented
technical regulations (tr) to which certain goods must conform in all three
member states (in particular, these technical regulations concern food and agricultural products). In this context, the members of the Customs Union came to
an agreement on compulsory certification, signed and ratified by all member
states, which includes a unified list of products subject to mandatory certification and the application of a homogeneous display of certification forms.

The trs for pyrotechnic products, personal protective equipment, packaging, toys, cosmetic and perfume products, products for children and ado-
lescents, and light industry products entered into force in 2012. Later, other
regulation, e.g. the regulation regarding requirements of automotive and avia-
tion gasoline, diesel and marine fuel, jet fuel, and heating oil became valid as
well.

Those products that are not mentioned in the unified list of the Customs
Union may be subject to mandatory conformity confirmation in accordance
with the national legislation.

The Russian authority responsible for both the national certification
(gost-R certification) and the certification within the Customs Union is the
Federal Agency for Technical Regulation and Metrology, also referred to as
Rosstandart.[26]

---

25   <www.azstand.gov.az/index.php> accessed 30 June 2021.
26   <https://www.gost.ru/> accessed30 June 2021.

The Kazakh authority responsible for certification is the Committee of Technical Regulation and Metrology of the Ministry of Industry and New Technologies of the Republic of Kazakhstan (all given certificates are registered by the State Metrology Institute).[27]

Besides the required conformity certification, the member states of the Customs Union apply common sanitary, epidemiological and hygienic requirements to the goods. As a consequence, a wide range of goods is subject to state registration to determine if they are considered to be potentially dangerous to human health or are imported into the Customs Union for the first time.

The responsible authority in Russia is the Federal Service for Consumer Protection and National Welfare.[28] There is no similar authority in Kazakhstan. Until now, all consumer complaints were resolved by the courts or the Agency for Regulation of Natural Monopolies[29] (later – Committee for Regulation of Natural Monopolies, Protection of Competition and Consumers' Rights). On 25 February 2013 in Astana the Public Consumer Association "The National Consumers League" signed a Memorandum of Cooperation between the Agency and this public association.

Goods subject to the mandatory state registration will only be permitted for import into the Customs Union with a proof of registration. This state sanitary registration replaces the national hygiene certification. The Sanitary-Epidemiological Conclusion (Hygiene Certificate) will no longer be issued. Hygiene certificates that have already been issued may be used until their time of validity expires or until a TR, corresponding to the specific kind of product, enters into force.

The importation of goods subject to veterinary control requires a Veterinary Import Permit issued by the Federal Service for Veterinary and Phytosanitary Supervision that must be applied for 30 days prior to the actual importation.

In Russia, the Federal Service for Veterinary and Phytosanitary Supervision has implemented the "Argus", which enables importers to apply for the Veterinary Import Permit electronically. The importers must first be registered with said system.[30]

---

27   <http://memst.miid.gov.kz/> accessed 30 June 2021.
28   <www.rospotrebnadzor.ru> accessed 30 June 2021.
29   <http://www.kremzk.gov.kz/> accessed 30 June 2021.
30   Particular details on registration can be obtained from the Federal Service for Veterinary and Phytosanitary Supervision <www.fsvps.ru/fsvps/main.html?_language=en> accessed 30 June 2021.

6.1 *Veterinary Health Certificates*

All consignments of animals and products of animal origin into Russia, Kazakhstan or Azerbaijan must be accompanied by a Veterinary Health Certificate for Live Animals or a Veterinary Health Certificate for Animal Products issued in the country of origin. In Azerbaijan, import of goods subject to state veterinary surveillance, from a foreign country must pass through an official border inspection post under control of the State Committee for Veterinary Medicine of the Republic of Azerbaijan.

The certificates issued by the authorities of other Customs Union member states will be recognised in Russia and Kazakhstan. Moreover, the Russian and Kazakh authorities also accept veterinary health certificates issued by the appropriate authorities of the EU member states if all relevant information is provided.

Shipments of said goods are also subject to compulsory veterinary border inspection at the Customs Office of Entry and / or Destination. Besides the general documents listed under customs procedures and regulations, importers must present the following specific documents to the veterinary inspector:

– Veterinary Health Certificate for Live Animals (if applicable);
– Veterinary Health Certificate for Animal Products (if applicable);
– Veterinary Import Permit;
– Registration of Veterinary Medicines (if applicable);
– certificate of quality issued by the manufacturer (only required for goods of plant origin subject to veterinary control).

As a result of the successful veterinary inspection, foreign veterinary certificates will be exchanged for certificates of the Customs Union (for the Russian Federation and Kazakhstan) and certificates of Azerbaijan.

Importers should note that specific temporary protective measures may be imposed on the import of animals or products of animal origin, e.g. as a consequence of the outbreak of contagious diseases. It is advisable to contact the national veterinary or phytosanitary supervision in advance for information on the current status of the goods to be imported into the countries in question.

In order to import food of animal origin into the territory of the RF (Customs Union) a third country must appear on a list established by the Customs Union. These lists are established by the Russian Veterinary Authority (i.e. Federal Service for Veterinary and Phytosanitary Surveillance – ROSSELHOZNADZOR)[31] and the State Agricultural Inspection Committee for Kazakhstan.[32]

---

31 For more information, consult the official website of the Russian Federal Service for Veterinary and Phytosanitary Surveillance, <http://www.fsvps.ru/> accessed 30 June 2021. Lists can be checked - they are open to public.

32 <www.akimvko.gov.kz/> accessed 30 June 2021.

In accordance with the Russian, Kazakh and Azeri legislation, in order to import into the territory of the Russian Federation, Kazakhstan or Azerbaijan respectively live animals and products of animal origin, a number of requirements must be fulfilled. For clarity, these requirements can be divided into 4 steps:

1. Procedure of country approval (inclusion of the third countries on the list of countries eligible for import of particular products).
2. Approval or accreditation of the exporter establishment (particularly, for exports to the Customs Union).
3. Procedure of verification of conformity of a product, intended for import into the territory of the Customs Union.
4. Veterinary certificate (as well as certificate of public health for food of animal origin) from the country of origin given by the Veterinary Authority of the exporting country. This foreign certificate (in the EC – CVED – Common Veterinary Entrance Document) is exchanged at the border control post of the Russian Federation, Kazakhstan or Azerbaijan to internal veterinary certification, which permits admission of products.

This chapter only deals with the first two stages, i.e. procedure of country approval and accreditation of establishments.

6.2 Animal Health Situation as a Basis for Import Eligibility to the Customs Union and Azerbaijan

It is evident that all three states, the Russian Federation, Kazakhstan and Azerbaijan, share the same objectives and criteria concerning the animal health situations of the importing countries. This means that, as a rule, in order to import into the Customs Union or Azerbaijan the third country must be a member of the OIE and have systems in place for the rapid detection, reporting and confirmation of listed OIE diseases.[33]

In accordance with the OIE, an importing country also has a formal undertaking to notify the importing county of outbreaks of major serious diseases within 24 hours of confirmation or any change in the vaccination policy concerning such diseases. The third country must either have its own laboratory facilities that will allow this detection and confirmation to take place or have formal agreements in place with suitable laboratories in other countries.

In the Customs Union, the extent to which the animal disease situation will affect whether approval can be considered, or what conditions are linked to

---

33 Consult the list of countries Members of the OIE at <www.oie.int/eng/OIE/PM/en_PM.htm> accessed 30 June 2021.

the approval, varies according to the type of animal or product concerned. For example, imports of live domestic ungulate animals have not been authorised from countries which vaccinate against foot and mouth disease (FMD), or where the disease is present. On the other hand, for fully treated meat products and milk-based products, this would not cause a problem, because the causative pathogen is destroyed by appropriate heat or other specified treatments or by other risk-mitigating factors.

Further animal disease control systems must be in place. The operation and outcome of these systems must be recorded, including the registration of holdings, animal identification and movement controls (traceability) so that compliance with Customs Union health certification requirements can be confirmed. These certification requirements may provide, for example, that before slaughter an animal has spent a certain time on a farm and in a region which is free of certain diseases.

For live animal imports, a range of supplementary disease control/eradication programmes, as well as testing to demonstrate freedom from certain diseases, and reflecting the type of animals concerned, will have to be in place. The exporting country's import policy, including controls, and the animal health situation in neighboring countries, will be taken into account.

6.3   General National Veterinary Requirements for the Importation of Live Animals, Meat and Meat Products

In accordance with the national legislation, live animals from the third country intending to export to the territory of the Russian Federation, Kazakhstan or Azerbaijan must be free from a number of diseases. For example, Veterinary-Sanitary Requirements for Importation of Meat and Meat Products to the Russian Federation established by the Letter of the Ministry of Agriculture from 23 December 1999 N° 13-8-01/2-1, provide that meat and meat products eligible for import to Russia must originate from healthy animals (free from animal diseases and in general satisfactory in veterinary terms).

Cattle must be slaughtered and processed at meat processing establishments that are approved by the central state veterinary authority of the exporting country under its constant monitoring. Animals intended for human consumption must be subject to veterinary ante-mortem veterinary inspection. Their carcasses and internal organs have to pass post-mortem veterinary examination by the state veterinary authority of the exporting country. Meat intended for import to the Russian Federation must be acknowledged as suitable for human consumption.

Every carcass (half-carcass, etc.) must bear a clear identification mark of the state veterinary surveillance service providing the name and number of the meat processing establishment (slaughter, cold storage) where the slaughtering was executed. Jointed meat must bear a veterinary mark on the packaging material. A clearly marked label must appear on the packaging in a manner that makes its opening impossible without breaking the label integrity.

Meat and meat products must be derived from disease-free cattle, slaughtered at establishments and only in territories officially free of animal diseases including:

I. *For every kind of animal:*
   – of African pest of swine – for 3 previous years on territory of country;
   – of foot and mouth disease – for 12 previous months on territory of country.

II. *For bovine:*
   – bovine spongiform encephalopathy and Scrapie of sheep on territory of country in compliance with the demands of Terrestrial Code of OIE;
   – Pestis bovum, contagious Pleuropneumonia, Stomatitis vesicularis, Pestis ovium et caprum – for 12 previous months on territory of country;
   – Tuberculosis, Brucellosis, Leucosis – for 6 months on territory of establishment;
   – Anthrax, Gangraena emphysematosa – for previous 20 days on territory of establishment.

III. *For sheep and goats:*
   – bovine spongiform encephalopathy and Scrapie of sheep on territory of country in compliance with the demands of Terrestrial Code of OIE;
   – bluetongue, contagious Pleuropneumonia of bovine, Pestis ovium et caprum – for 12 previous months on territory of country;
   – Ovine pulmonary adenomatosis, maedi-visny, Arthritis-Encephalitis – for previous 3 years on territory of establishment;
   – Variola of sheep and goat – for previous 12 months on territory of establishment;
   – Tuberculosis, Brucellosis – for 6 months on territory of establishment;
   – Anthrax – for previous 20 days on territory of establishment.

IV.   *For swine:*

- Morbus vesicularis suum – for 12 previous months on territory of country;
- Pestis suum, Morbus Aujeczkyi, Enctphalomielitis enzootica suum – for 12 previous months on administrative territory of country (state, province, land, district etc.);
- Trichinellosis – for previous 3 years on territory of establishment;
- Porcine reproductive and respiratory syndrome (PRRS) – for previous 12 months on territory of establishment;
- Anthrax, Erysipelas suum – for previous 20 days on territory of establishment.

Each carcass (of any animal) must be tested for Trichinella spiralis with all consecutive results being negative.

Beef and mutton must originate from the slaughtering of animals that were not fed with feed of animal origin which had been manufactured with the use of internal organs and tissue of bovine.

Meat and meat products must derive from the slaughtering of animals that were not fed with feed containing raw materials manufactured using methods of genetic engineering or other genetically modified sources.

The following meat and meat products are not allowed for import into the Russian Federation:

- revealing, when subjected to post-mortem veterinary inspection, alterations specific to Foot and Mouth Disease, Pestis, anaerobic infections, Tuberculosis, Leucosis and other contagious diseases, helminth affection (Cysticercus bovis, Trichinellosis, Sarcosporydyoses, Onchocercoses, Echinoccosis and others), and intoxication of other nature,
- defrosted when stored,
- revealing signs of spoilage,
- having temperature in depth of muscle adjacent to bones over -8 Celsius for frozen meat and over 4 degrees for cooled meat,
- with traces of internal organs, hemorrhage in tissues, apostemes, larvas of botflies, skinning of serosal coating and removed lymphnodes, mechanical inclusion,
- with non-intrinsic colour and odour for meat and off-flavour for fish, medicine, grass and other,
- containing preservatives,
- contaminated by salmonella or agents of other bacterial infections,
- treated with colorants, ion radiation or ultraviolet rays,
- derived from slaughtered animals treated with synthetic estrogen, hormonal substances, thyreostatic preparations, antibiotics, pesticides and other

medical remedies applied ante-mortem later than dates recommended by their instruction of use.

Microbiological, chemical, toxicological and radiological measures of the exporting country should meet veterinary and sanitary rules and requirements in force in the Russian Federation at the time of import.

Containers and packaging material must be disposable and meet the Russian hygiene requirements.

Transport means must be treated and prepared for use in accordance with the exporting country's rules in force.

The fulfillment of terms provided by the national veterinary-sanitary requirements must be confirmed by veterinary certificate signed by an official (state) veterinarian of the exporting country in the language of the exporting country and in Russian.

The dispatch of meat and meat products on the territory of the countries in question is allowed only upon receipt by the importer of a corresponding permission by the Veterinary Department of the Ministry of Agriculture of Russia. The Veterinary Department of the Ministry of Agriculture of Russia reserves the right to carry out veterinary inspections and monitoring of animals (including veterinary–sanitary expertise of carcasses and internal organs at the exporter's establishments) as well as carrying out certification of meat processing establishments for the possibility to export its goods to the Russian Federation.[34]

Similar veterinary requirements can be found in the national legislation of Kazakhstan and Azerbaijan. Therefore, it can be concluded that from the veterinary point of view, general requirements for importation of meat and meat products into the territory of the Russian Federation, Kazakhstan and Azerbaijan appear to be sound and in line with the international and EU requirements. More detailed examinations of particular measures taken with respect to the OIE notifiable diseases can be subject to review conducted by a veterinarian.

6.4   Procedures of Country and Establishments Approval for Import of Products of Animal Origin

The procedure of approval of a third country for import of products of animal origin (inclusion of the third countries on the list of countries eligible for import of particular products) in Russia, Kazakhstan and Azerbaijan appears from a

---

34   Normative Act (Letter of the Ministry of Agriculture) from 23 December 1999, N° 13-8-01/ 2-1, Veterinary-Sanitary Requirements for Importation of Meat and Meat Products to the Russian Federation, <www.fsvps.ru/> accessed 30 June 2021.

legal point of view to be very similar to the procedure of the EU. However, it must be noted that in contrast with the EU system, Russian, Kazakh and Azeri requirements for approvals of importing countries and accreditation of establishments for import seem not to be so transparent and open for examination or evaluation. Moreover, information with veterinary and sanitary requirements for establishments is not readily available and accessible for foreign exporters (this also includes the language barrier, as most of the documents are not translated into other languages and provided only in Russian, Kazakh or Azeri).

In comparison, in the European Union, special guides for exporters are developed, such as "EU Import Conditions for Fresh Meat and Meat Products" and "General Guidance on EU Import and Transit Rules for Live Animals and Animal Products from Third Countries".[35] These documents provide guidance primarily to the national authorities in third countries who are interested in exporting live animals and/or their products to the European Union. They explain health and supervisory requirements of the European Union, designed to ensure that imported animals and products meet standards at least equivalent to those required for production in, and trade between Member States and list the main relevant legislation of the European Union.

Import of meat, all types of meat products, as well as by-products and milk products (except canned products) are completely prohibited from Africa and most of the countries of Asia and Latin America. While it may be true that the animal health situation or sanitary situation in general in most African countries (as well as transport and basic infrastructure) may not be up to the highest international standards, the approach of including certain regions on so-called "negative" lists may not be the best for the purposes of trade facilitation. Therefore, a "case by case" approach in the examination of possible importer countries from various regions should be adopted to allow trade with those that meet the established standards.

Permissions for import to the Russian Federation, Kazakhstan and Azerbaijan as well as conditions of release are given by the national veterinary authorities on the basis of the epizootic situation on the territory of the country in question and may be changed accordingly:
- to prohibit the import of the animal products or
- change the conditions of release applied earlier or
- revoke permissions given to the importers previously

---

35   <http://ec.europa.eu/food/international/trade/im_cond_meat_en.pdf> accessed 30 June 2021; <http://ec.europa.eu/food/international/trade/guide_thirdcountries2006_en.pdf> accessed 30 June 2021.

in cases of outbreaks of contagious diseases in exporting countries or for the purposes of prevention of import of deteriorated quality products into the territory of the Russian Federation, Kazakhstan or Azerbaijan.

Import of processed food products of animal origin (for final consumption) into the territory of the Russian Federation, Kazakhstan and Azerbaijan without permission of the veterinary authorities is allowed only from the countries with a satisfactory epizootic situation.

Various national restrictions and possibilities to revoke permissions granted for import is a normal practice intended for the protection of health and life of people, animals and the environment. However, it is not clear how often controls are conducted by the veterinary authorities of the Russian Federation, Kazakhstan and Azerbaijan. Considering the fact that for each consignment imported into the territory of the Russian Federation or Kazakhstan, a permit is required (which must be requested 45 days prior to the importation), for Azerbaijan it is 30 days, it could be logically concluded that monitoring and control are conducted *ad hoc*. In comparison, in the European Union, the monitoring and controls are the primary responsibility of the exporting country's national veterinary authority.

From the veterinary point of view, general requirements for the import of meat and meat products into the territory of the countries under review appear to be sound and in line with the international and EU requirements. However, it is not possible to conclude that the applicable national procedures for approval of countries and establishments are in full harmony with, e.g. the EU legislation or international guidelines. The major issue is transparency and availability of the information for the importers – this is clearly the problem for Russia, Kazakhstan and Azerbaijan.

7   Special Aspects of Import of Plants and Plant Products

In 2010, Kazakhstan, Belarus and Russia concluded an agreement concerning mutual phytosanitary measures.[36] In accordance with this agreement, all products subject to phytosanitary control are divided into two groups: products with a low and products with a high phytosanitary risk.

Consignments of both groups are subject to a mandatory phytosanitary border inspection at the customs office of entry or destination. The import of

---

36   The Treaty on the Eurasian Economic Union contains detailed provisions on the application of sanitary, veterinary and quarantine phytosanitary measures.

products with a high phytosanitary risk requires a Quarantine Import Permit. Moreover, all consignments of these products must be accompanied by a Plant Health Certificate. The Federal Service for Veterinary and Phytosanitary Supervision accepts phytosanitary certificates issued by a competent authority of any EU member state if all relevant information is provided. Importers must present the following documents to the phytosanitary inspector:
– Phytosanitary Certificate (if applicable);
– Quarantine Import Permit (if applicable);
– freight documents;
– Commercial Invoice;
– corresponding registration certificates (if applicable).
As a result of the successful phytosanitary inspection, foreign phytosanitary certificates will be exchanged for certificates of the Customs Union.

As there are import bans on certain plant products from designated countries of origin, the national competent authorities should be contacted prior to the intended importation.

The import of species that are subject to the Convention on International Trade in Endangered Species of Wild Fauna and Flora (CITES), also referred to as the Washington Convention, requires a permit from the Federal Service for Supervision of Natural Resources Management.[37] In addition, a Permit to Import Sturgeon Fish Species and Products Thereof must be obtained by the importer for the import of the goods in question.

The import of plants and products of plant origin into the Republic of Azerbaijan is regulated by the Law on Phytosanitary Control adopted in 2006. The provisions in relation to application of SPS measures are similar to the information on Russia and Kazakhstan presented above.

8   Import of Alimentary Products

Alimentary products to be imported into the Russian Federation, Kazakhstan and Azerbaijan must comply with the veterinary and phytosanitary requirements described in the related sections above. Furthermore, food additives or biologically active food supplements are usually subject to state registration (for more information, please refer to the section on standardisation, which also contains information on possible mandatory conformity certification).

---

37   For further information, please see the document entitled Permit to Import Endangered
       Species Covered by CITES.

9   Conclusion

The SPS and TBT Agreements do not contain sanitary and phytosanitary meas-ures or technical regulations and norms per se. They do not, in other words, give WTO Members a blueprint for their SPS or TBT laws and regulations. Rather, these WTO Agreements include rules by which national SPS and TBT measures are judged for consistency with the principles of free trade and elim-ination of trade barriers. SPS and TBT measures of Russia, Kazakhstan and Azerbaijan would require further harmonisation and transition of the system of GOST to international standards. It is evident that the traditional approach to risk management and GOST-based systems of these countries pose serious constraints on the competitiveness of production and issues of food safety; furthermore, animal and plant health outcomes are not satisfactory. The prob-lem of product and food safety and quality, as well as controls, is very relevant today for the Russian Federation, Kazakhstan and Azerbaijan. The major rea-sons for non-compliance with the basic provisions and principles of the SPS and TBT Agreements can be summarized as following:

– the lack of transparency in adoption of national SPS or TBT measures, insuf-ficient infrastructure to support scientific basis of the adopted provisions (e.g. accredited laboratories or other testing facilities);
– a fragmented and incomplete legal framework, regulatory framework based not on risk assessment, but on mandatory compliance with the set up requirements (often not justified or scientifically sound);
– a weak and insufficient institutional framework (e.g. multiple regulations and various agencies and bodies, without proper coordination and duplica-tion of work).

The traditional approach to risk management and the GOST-based systems of Russia, Kazakhstan and Azerbaijan is not economically advantageous and poses serious constraints on the competitiveness of production as well as issues of food safety and animal and plant health.

All countries have the right to employ protective measures in the veterinary, plant health/quarantine and human health areas, but for WTO Members this right comes together with an obligation to comply with provisions of the SPS Agreement. This means that national protective measures leading to restric-tion of trade should be justified by legitimate objectives recognised by the SPS and TBT Agreements. For example, regarding the substance of the SPS or TBT measures applied to the imported goods, from the veterinary, phytosanitary, sanitary, or technical points of view, general requirements for the import of goods into the territory of the Russian Federation, Kazakhstan and Azerbaijan, appear to be sound and in line with the international and EU requirements.

However, it must be noted that Russian, Kazakh and Azeri requirements for approvals of importing countries and accreditation of establishments for importation seem not to be so transparent and open for examination or evaluation. Moreover, information with veterinary and sanitary requirements for establishments is not readily available and accessible for foreign exporters. As a result, it can be concluded that SPS or TBT measures or their administration and application are not based on science or are not transparent (although per se appropriate) and that leads to a problem of non-compliance with the WTO obligations. This is exactly the case in the Russian Federation, Kazakhstan and Azerbaijan. Further, if the GOST system is to be compared with the International Standards approach, the major shortcomings would be in the application of inconsistent, vague and non-transparent procedures, methodology and criteria. Incompatible laboratory facilities, equipment and tests are often used and become impediments for trade.

It is true that compliance with the SPS and TBT Agreements poses difficulties for a number of countries including developed countries (the issue of hormones in the USA is a well-known illustration). Indeed, it is often difficult to provide the necessary scientific and technical justification for national sanitary and phytosanitary measures and to conduct risk analysis – which is the process of evaluating biological or other scientific and economic evidence to determine whether a hazard should be regulated. This problem is also apparent for Russia, Kazakhstan and Azerbaijan, because the nature of GOST standards and mandatory regulations requirements is highly prescriptive and the focus of control is on the process outcome and not the process of production or the "entire chain". One of the crucial issues and central parts of the primary legislation of the countries under review is in relation to responsibility for food safety within the public sector leaving the private stakeholders to be subject to these controls. This results in a financial burden that is not well-balanced and efficiency is very low. Finally, enforcement of the existing provisions, effective controls and inspection services for any SPS or TBT measures including checks at the borders also remains challenging for Russia, Kazakhstan and Azerbaijan.

CHAPTER 10

Regulation of International Trade in Energy Resources

Challenges for Post-Soviet Exporters of Energy Resources through the Example of Azerbaijan, Kazakhstan, and Russia

Azar Aliyev

1 Introduction

Trade in energy resources remains one of the least regulated aspects of international trade. Energy resource exporting countries closely monitor preservation of their sovereignty over those resources, including in the field of trade. However, the overall development of international trade law, the evolution of regional integration such as the Eurasian Economic Union (EAEU), the Energy Charter Treaty[1] (ECT) and the development of internationalized state contracts for the extraction and supply of hydrocarbons has led to trade in energy resources being regulated by a large number of international law norms.

The countries of the former Soviet Union are parties to numerous regional agreements and some of them recently negotiated Free Trade Agreements with the European Union,[2] they are Members of – or are negotiating their accession to – the World Trade Organization (WTO), and they have concluded a large number of production sharing agreements (PSAs),[3] which provide regulations on trade in energy resources. In addition, trade in energy resources of the post-Soviet states is increasingly influenced by the internal regulation of trade in energy resources of the European Union, which is the main importer of energy resources from the region.[4]

---

1   Energy Charter Treaty (signed in Lisbon on 17 December 1994), <www.energycharter.org/fileadmin/DocumentsMedia/Legal/ECT-ru.pdf>; English version <https://energycharter.org/fileadmin/DocumentsMedia/Legal/ECTC-en.pdf> both accessed 10 September 2021.

2   European Neighbourhood Policy <https://eeas.europa.eu/topics/european-neighbourhood-policy-enp_en> accessed 10 September 2021.

3   PSA between Azerbaijan and consortia of foreign investors, see <www.bp.com/en_az/caspian/aboutus/legalagreements.html> accessed 10 September 2021.

4   General information <https://ec.europa.eu/energy/en/topics/markets-and-consumers/market-legislation> accessed 10 September 2021.

This chapter will attempt to systematically present sources of law regulating the energy trade in the region and to show potential risks and opportunities for further development through the example of three energy resource exporting countries – Azerbaijan, Kazakhstan, and Russia.

2   Global Regulation of Energy Resource Trade

Regulation of trade in energy resources, as well as other commodities, is aimed at achieving a balance of two interests: stability of supplies to the market of importing countries and the sovereignty of exporting states over natural resources, including the opportunity to use the revenues thus acquired.[5] Hence, unlike trade in other goods, where countries exporting goods and services try to open as many markets for their producers as possible, in the trade in raw materials, especially energy resources, the initial interests are fundamentally different: importing countries compete with each other for the right to purchase limited resources, while exporters try to extract the greatest benefits from the limited resources available. The history of international trade regulation contains many attempts to resolve this conflict of interests. On the one hand, since the beginning of the twentieth century, cartels of producers were formed, the purpose of which was to prevent a fall in prices for raw materials due to crises of overproduction.[6] On the other hand, since as long ago as 1933, importers have attempted to completely liberalize commodity markets in order to provide themselves with the necessary raw materials.[7]

In general, attempts to create an effective cartel and attempts to fully liberalize the energy resource market in one form or another continue to this day, but neither of them has succeeded. The most successful cartel of oil-exporting countries – OPEC – currently has only limited potential, largely due to internal disagreements. However, attempts by importers of energy resources to liberalize markets have not been successful either. Thus, the norms on trade in raw materials were not reflected in the General Agreement on Tariffs and Trade (GATT) of 1947.[8] The Energy Charter Treaty also failed to liberalize the energy markets as importer countries imagined it would. Exporting countries include

---

5   Sebastian Pritzkow, *Das völkerrechtliche Verhältnis zwischen der EU und Russland im Energiesektor* (Springer 2011) 99; Friedl Weiss, 'Internationale Rohstoffmärkte' in Christian Tietje (ed), *Internationales Wirtschaftsrecht* (De Gruyter 2009) 268.
6   Weiss (n 5) 270.
7   ibid 270.
8   ibid 271.

norms on sovereignty over raw materials in all international agreements, thereby excluding resources not yet extracted from the scope of application of international agreements and thus retaining full control over them.

However, despite the apparent stalemate, processes are taking place that directly affect trade in energy resources.

2.1   Regulation of Trade in Energy Resources within the WTO

Relations between post-Soviet states and the WTO are developing in various ways. To date, only Turkmenistan has not applied to join the organization. Azerbaijan, Belarus and Uzbekistan are negotiating for accession. Azerbaijan has repeatedly stated at the highest level that accession to the WTO is not a priority for it and negotiations will be conducted until an acceptable compromise for Azerbaijan is reached.[9] Kazakhstan joined the WTO on 30 June 2015 after 19 years of negotiations.[10] Russia signed the Protocol of Accession to the Marrakesh Agreement on 16 December 2011.[11]

WTO rules contain practically no special provisions on trade in energy resources. Most of the WTO rules are created for the liberalization of imports, and in the case of trade in energy resources, unlike other goods and services, it is importers who are interested in deliveries.[12] As an exception to the general GATT regime, in Article XX (h) GATT common standards for interstate resource agreements were not adopted.[13] Attempts to include special rules governing the energy trade within the Doha Round[14] remain unsuccessful. Thus, a few rules on the restriction of exports play a decisive role. However, these few norms have already become the subject of lively discussions.

---

9   <http://cesd.az/new/?p=5864> accessed 10 September 2021.

10   <www.wto.org/english/thewto_e/acc_e/a1_kazakhstan_e.htm> accessed 10 September 2021.

11   <www.wto.org/english/thewto_e/acc_e/a1_russie_e.htm> accessed 10 September 2021.

12   For more detailed information on the application of WTO norms on energy trade Leal-Rafael Arcas, Andrew Filis and Ehab Abu-Gosh, *Energy Governance: Selected Legal Issues* (Edward Elgar 2014) 117–138; Anna Marhold, 'The World Trade Organization and Energy: Fuel for Debate' (2013) 2 (8) ESIL Insights; Alan Yanovich, 'WTO Rules and the Energy Sector' in Yulia Selivanova (ed), *Regulation of Energy in International Trade Law: WTO, NAFTA and Energy Charter Treaty* (Wolters Kluwer 2011); Gabrielle Marceau, 'The WTO in the Emerging Energy Governance Debate' (2010) 5(3) Global Trade and Customs Journal 83–93.

13   Weiss (n 5) 271–273.

14   Pascal Lamy, 'Towards a Strategic Approach for Energy at the World Trade Organisation' (2010) World Energy Insight 20–21.

To date, the legal literature identifies several major areas of application of WTO rules governing the energy trade.[15]

The most problematic question is that of admissibility of so-called dual pricing for energy resources. The essence of the discussion is the permissibility of setting lower prices for energy resources on the domestic market in comparison with the export price.[16]

Russia has already faced the issue of dual pricing. The European Union applies anti-dumping duties to a number of Russian products, the production of which is associated with high energy costs.[17] The European Union justifies these duties with the undervalued price of energy in Russia's domestic market. Russia is conducting several processes within the framework of the WTO dispute settlement mechanism. Thus, in 2013, Russia initiated procedures for duties on ammonium nitrate and metallurgical products, in particular for welded pipes.[18] After the European Commission (EC) imposed final anti-dumping duties on ammonium nitrates, welded pipes and certain cold-rolled flat steel products, as well as Ukraine's imposition of duties on Russian ammonium nitrate, Russia filed three more complaints against the European Union and Ukraine respectively.[19] Russia's position is based on the inadmissibility of comparing domestic prices, which are provided to all producers in Russia, with prices in third countries.

It is interesting to note that in the argument of its 2015 request, Russia refers not only to GATT 1994 and the Anti-Dumping Agreement, but also to the Agreement on Subsidies and Countervailing Measures. These arguments have

15   See Gabrielle Marceau (n 11) 83–93; Leal-Rafael Arcas. et al, (n 11) 134–136.
16   Vitaliy Pogoretskyy, 'The System of Energy Dual Pricing in Russia and Ukraine: The Consistency of the Energy Dual Pricing System with the WTO Agreement on Anti-Dumping' (2009) Global Trade and Customs Journal 313.
17   EU anti-dumping duties are based on EU Regulation 2016/1036 of 8 June 2016, OJ L 176/21–536. Based on this Regulation, special acts regulating the introduction of anti-dumping duties are issued, including the methodology for calculating dumping prices.
18   Dispute WT/DS474 [2014] *European Union – Cost Adjustment Methodologies and Certain Anti-dumping Measures on Imports from Russia*, Request for the establishment of a panel by the Russian Federation <www.wto.org/english/tratop_e/dispu_e/cases_e/ds474_e.htm> accessed 10 September 2021.
19   Dispute WT/DS494 [2016] *European Union – Cost Adjustment Methodologies and Certain Anti-Dumping Measures on Imports from Russia* (Second complaint) <www.wto.org/english/tratop_e/dispu_e/cases_e/ds494_e.htm> accessed 10 September 2021; Dispute WT/DS493 [2017] *Ukraine – Anti-Dumping Measures on Ammonium Nitrate* <www.wto.org/english/tratop_e/dispu_e/cases_e/ds493_e.htm> accessed 10 September 2021; Dispute WT/DS521 [2017] *European Union – Anti-Dumping Measures on Certain Cold-Rolled Flat Steel Products from Russia* <www.wto.org/english/tratop_e/dispu_e/cases_e/ds521_e.htm> accessed 10 September 2021.

already been analysed in the academic literature on issues of dual pricing[20] but a decision by the WTO dispute resolution bodies on these issues has not yet been reached. The relevance of the issues raised is confirmed by the accession of 14 states to the procedures as third parties.[21] If this dispute ends with a decision by the WTO Dispute Settlement Body,[22] this will play an important role in determining further interpretation of issues related to dual pricing.

Along with issues of dual pricing, the question of the conformity of regulation of the EU energy market with WTO rules is becoming increasingly important. The Third energy package has already caused problems for many large companies of energy exporters in the EU markets.

2.2   *The Energy Charter Treaty*

Immediately after the collapse of the Soviet Union, active work began on a new architecture for cooperation in the field of energy between the countries of the West and the post-Soviet states. The first result of this work was the Final Act of the Conference on the European Energy Charter of 16–17 December 1991,[23] in which the main principles of cooperation were fixed. The Treaty on the Energy Charter was prepared, guided by the basic principles of the Charter, and was signed on December 17, 1994. The ECT regulates a wide range of issues related to energy, including investment, trade, transit, and is a unique instrument of industry regulation.

All the post-Soviet states have signed the ECT. Even Turkmenistan, which has not signed many "standard" international agreements with less stringent obligations (for example, the New York Convention on the Recognition and Enforcement of Foreign Arbitral Awards)[24] and which has not even applied for WTO accession,[25] signed and ratified the ECT. Belarus and Russia signed – but

---

20   The possibility of such disputes was foreseen quite a while ago, see Vitaliy Pogoretskyy (n 15) 313–323; Julia Selivanova, 'World Trade Organization Rules and Energy Pricing: Russia's Case' (2004) 38 (4) Journal of World Trade 559–602.

21   Australia, Argentina, Brazil, Vietnam, Indonesia, Canada, China, Mexico, Norway, Saudi Arabia, USA, Turkey, and Ukraine.

22   The European Union and Russia have repeatedly stated their willingness to resolve existing disputes in the framework of negotiations; in particular, A V Ulyukaev declared the speedy settlement of disputes with the European Union in the WTO <www.rbc.ru/rbcf reenews/55ed7d659a7947fd5e6bea11> accessed 10 September 2021.

23   <www.energycharter.org/fileadmin/DocumentsMedia/Legal/ECTC-en.pdf> accessed 10 September 2021.

24   <https://uncitral.un.org/en/texts/arbitration/conventions/foreign_arbitral_awards/stat us2> accessed 10 September 2021.

25   <www.wto.org/english/thewto_e/acc_e/cbt_course_e/c1s1p1_e.htm> accessed 10 September 2021.

did not ratify – the ECT, and in 2009 Russia withdrew its signature.[26] Thus, among the countries under consideration, the ECT fully applies to Azerbaijan and Kazakhstan. Until 20 August 2009, the ECT applied to the Russian Federation on the basis of Article 45 ECT to the extent that it did not conflict with the Constitution and regulations of the Russian Federation. Temporary application does not apply to trade in energy resources.

Regarding regulation of the energy trade, the ECT contains a general reference to WTO law (Article 29) and thus includes countries that are not WTO members in the scope of application of WTO law. It should be noted that the ECT does not incorporate all WTO rules, but contains in Annex W a list of WTO rules that are not applicable.[27] In principle, the General Agreement on Trade in Services (GATS) and the Agreement on Trade-related Aspects of Intellectual Property Rights (TRIPS) are not applicable. However, the ECT rules on investment protection are applicable to many types of services and, in many respects, contain more effective legal instruments to protect investments. The GATT 1994 norms fully apply only to non-tariff measures. With regard to tariffs, Article 29 ECT, unlike the GATT standards, does not contain a strict obligation to limit tariffs, but obliges the member countries only to strive to reduce tariffs. This easing of tariff obligations is limited by the most-favoured-nation treatment principle. A country that has granted a privileged regime to any other country that is not even a party to the ECT and WTO is obliged to extend this regime to other ECT member countries.

Current regulation of the ECT is the result of the 1998 Amendments.[28] The initial version of the ECT was negotiated before the establishment of the WTO and referred to the GATT 1947. The 1998 Amendment also expanded the scope of the ECT. Trade regulations are now applied not only to energy materials and resources (EM list), but also to energy-related equipment (EQ List). The

---

26   <www.energycharter.org/who-we-are/members-observers/countries/russian-federat ion/> accessed 10 September 2021. See also Order of the Government of the Russian Federation No. 1055-r of 30 July 2009 on the intention of the Russian Federation not to become a party to the Energy Charter Treaty, as well as to the Protocol on the Energy Charter on Energy Efficiency and Related Environmental Aspects (together with the project "notes on the notification").

27   Appendix W contains an inconvenient negative list; a law enforcer had to compare the texts of the WTO agreements and Annex W each time. To facilitate application of Annex W, the Energy Charter Secretariat issued a document – Applicable trade provisions of the Energy Charter Treaty <www.energycharter.org/fileadmin/DocumentsMedia/Thematic/Trade_Provisions_of_the_ECT_2003_ru.pdf> accessed 10 September 2021.

28   <www.energycharter.org/process/energy-charter-treaty-1994/trade-amendment/> accessed 10 September 2021.

amendment also provides an opportunity to limit tariffs by the decision of the ECT Conference without introducing changes to the ECT.

Many ECT member countries, including Azerbaijan and Kazakhstan, have not ratified the 1998 Amendments, but are applying them temporarily. Some countries rejected provisional application of the 1998 Amendments. This means that in case of disputes related to trade in energy resources between countries that do not apply the amendments, on the one hand, and Azerbaijan or Kazakhstan on the other, the applicable references are the text of the ECT and, accordingly, the norms of GATT 1994.

In the event of a dispute over energy trade between ECT parties, if at least one of the parties to the dispute is not a WTO member, the dispute is resolved within the framework of the special mechanism for resolving ECT disputes for trade disputes involving non-WTO members (Annex D to the ECT).

Thus, Azerbaijan, even without being a WTO member, can use WTO norms to resolve energy disputes. However, not all energy disputes fall within the scope of the ECT. Thus, disputes concerning dual pricing for energy resources fall within the scope of the ECT only if the trade in products that are included in the EM List and the EQ List is affected.

Measures to regulate the energy market, adopted by the European Union in the framework of the Third Energy Package, belong to the scope of the ECT in part. In particular, in support of its claims the Russian Federation refers to the obligations undertaken by the European Union and EU member states in accordance with the GATS, which is not subject to application under the ECT. However, as already indicated, the ECT opens the possibility of challenging the EU's actions within the framework of the investment protection mechanism, which provides the possibility of resolving disputes not only in the state-state format, but also in the investor-state format. ECT norms on investment protection, unlike the GATS, do not provide the possibility of protecting investors at the stage of admission to the market, which significantly limits the ability of companies from Azerbaijan to challenge the legality of the Third Energy Package.

3   Regional Agreements

Azerbaijan, Kazakhstan and Russia have concluded a large number of bilateral and regional agreements that in some way regulate the trade in energy resources. The overwhelming majority of these agreements regulate the interstate level of issues concerning supply of energy resources, mainly gas. Contracts for the acquisition of energy resources are subsequently concluded on the basis of these agreements. The parties to these contracts are, as a rule, state-owned companies. Despite the fact that these agreements do not contain norms regulating the trade regime, in general their practical importance is very high. Notably, in these treaties negotiations and consultations are envisaged as a mechanism for resolving disputes. Arbitration clauses, however, are contained in contracts between economic entities concluded on the basis of these international agreements. Thus, the process of resolving disputes has been transferred to the level of economic entities.

Attempts to regulate the energy trade are also being made in the format of the Commonwealth of Independent States (CIS). The last example of such cooperation is the Concept of Cooperation of the CIS Member States in the Energy Sector,[29] to which, unlike Azerbaijan, Kazakhstan and Russia have acceded. The concept is the basis for signing international agreements that should regulate the energy sector. The developed plan of priority measures for implementation of the Concept does not contain obligations in the field of trade in energy resources. A common market is foreseen only for electricity, but even in this area, work is mainly based on bilateral agreements that do not create the prerequisites for creating a single market.[30]

The most ambitious project in the field of trade in energy resources in the region is being carried out within the framework of the Eurasian Economic Union (EAEU). Article 79 section 1 of the Agreement on the EAEU provides for the step-by-step creation of a single energy market. Among the goals defined in the Agreement are market pricing, a competitive market, and so on. Five articles and three annexes of the Agreement are devoted to the formation of a single energy market. In general, all regulation once again emphasizes the special situation of the energy market and represents an exception to the liberal regime envisaged for the commodity market. Interestingly, if regulation of other markets is, as a whole, based – with some differences – on the model used by the European Union, regulation of the single energy market differs significantly. Even though many policy documents will be adopted in the coming years, it is already possible to determine the main vector of development.

---

29   Approved by the Council of Heads of Government of the CIS on 20 November 2009 <www
      .consultant.ru/cons/cgi/online.cgi?req=doc;base=INT;n=47388#05448673884068906>
      (available in Russian) accessed 10 September 2021.

30   Item 3.1. Main results of implementation of the Plan of Priority Measures to Implement
      the Concept of Cooperation of the CIS Member States in the Energy Sector of 20 September 2013, approved by the CIS Economic Council at <www.consultant.ru/cons/cgi/onl
      ine.cgi?req=doc;base=INT;n=1355#06790353911733198> (available in Russian) accessed 10
      September 2021.

Concessions are far-reaching in the field of customs tariffs and standardization: Noteworthy are agreements on zero tariffs for oil and gas (paragraph 3.1 Protocol on Gas and paragraph 3.1 Protocol on Oil) and complete unification of standards for gas (paragraph 5 Protocol on Gas). However, the scope of these measures is limited only by trade between member countries, whereas transit and resale of gas to third countries are regulated by bilateral agreements.

The common market assumes equal competitive conditions for all market players. Unlike the EU, which, in the Third Energy Package, relies on unbundling and splitting up energy monopolies as the main tool for building a competitive market, the EAEU relies on market forecasting and so-called indicative planning (Article 81 of the Agreement on the EAEU). The agreement also provides for access to the transport infrastructure, but this access is limited. Thus, access to gas transmission networks is provided only in the presence of free capacity (Part 4, Article 83). For transportation of oil, participating states undertake to provide transit at prices not higher than those for national transit. The weakness of this seemingly attractive mechanism at first glance is the presence of monopolies that deal with extraction, transportation and trade in oil. In other words, companies can increase the cost of transit painlessly for themselves. Even more astonishing is the fact that all countries of the EAEU except the Russian Federation are contracting parties to the Energy Charter Treaty and are bound by Article 7 (1) and (3) ECT, which provides for freedom of transit. This means that transit obligations of all EAEU member states, except the Russian Federation, among and between each other and even towards third states are higher under the ECT than under the EAEU.

The EAEU faces a difficult task in terms of liberalizing the market with the preservation of very large companies which control extraction and transportation, as well as the sale of natural resources in individual member states.

4   Free Trade Agreements with the European Union

Despite projects on diversification of the energy trade, the European Union remains the most important energy trade partner for the region.[31] Only Turkmenistan exports its gas exclusively to China.[32]

---

31   Exports to the EU 27 average 40–50% of the total exports of Azerbaijan, Kazakhstan and Russia; trade statistics of the European Commission <http://ec.europa.eu/trade/policy/countries-and-regions/> accessed 10 September 2021.

32   Dmitry Shlapentokh, 'Turkmenistan's Gas Export Dilemma' <www.cacianalyst.org/publications/analytical-articles/item/13483-turkmenistans-gas-export-dilemma.html> accessed 10 September 2021.

The bases of cooperation between the European Union and the post-Soviet countries were Partnership and Cooperation Agreements (PCA) signed back at the end of the 1990s. With its Eastern Partnership Programme, which is embedded into the framework of the European Neighbourhood Policy (ENP), the European Union has been trying to establish a solid basis for cooperation with six post-Soviet countries: Armenia, Azerbaijan, Belarus, Georgia, Moldova, and Ukraine.[33] The initial idea – namely, to sign similar Deep and Comprehensive Free Trade Agreements (DCTFAS) with all six countries – failed. Only Georgia, Moldova and Ukraine signed DCFTAS with the European Union, which led to the deepest crisis between all these countries and the European Union on the one side and the Russian Federation on the other side. Under pressure from the Russian Federation, Armenia dropped negotiations with the European Union at the last moment and joined the EAEU.[34] Instead of an Association Agreement with a DCFTA, Armenia signed a Comprehensive and Enhanced Partnership Agreement (CEPA) in November 2017.[35] A CEPA is not a Free Trade Agreement, which is impossible between the European Union and Armenia, because Armenia as a member-state of the EAEU cannot conclude Free Trade Agreements by itself. It resembles more the European Union–Kazakhstan Comprehensive and Enhanced Cooperation Agreement than the Association Agreements concluded by Georgia, Moldova and Ukraine. Negotiations with Azerbaijan on an Association Agreement were not successful either. Azerbaijan requested special approaches with regard to a quite different structure of economic relations between Azerbaijan and the European Union, in particular trade in oil and gas as the main trade sectors.

The Russian Federation was not part of the ENP from the beginning. The political and economic weight of Russia demanded a special approach. Negotiations on a comprehensive cooperation framework based on four Common Spaces were launched in 2008 and suspended in 2014 due to the Ukraine crisis.[36]

---

33   More detail on the ENP <https://eeas.europa.eu/topics/european-neighbourhood-policy
      -enp_en> accessed 10 September 2021.

34   Armen Sahakyan, 'Armenia will join Russian Customs Union' <www.europeaninstitute
      .org/index.php/ei-blog/184-september-2013/1777-armenia-will-join-russian-customs
      -union> accessed 10 September 2021.

35   Comprehensive and Enhanced Partnership Agreement between the European Union and
      the European Atomic Energy Community and their Member States, of the one part and
      the Republic of Armenia, of the other part (25 September 2017) <https://eeas.europa.eu/
      sites/eeas/files/eu-armenia_comprehensive_and_enhanced_partnership_agreement_c
      epa.pdf> accessed 10 September 2021.

36   <https://eeas.europa.eu/headquarters/headquarters-homepage/35939/european-union
      -and-russian-federation_en> accessed 10 September 2021.

The European Union excluded post-Soviet states of Central Asia (Kazakhstan, Kyrgyzstan, Tadjikistan, Turkmenistan, and Uzbekistan) from the ENP. However, in 2007 the European Union adopted "The EU and Central Asia: Strategy for a New Partnership",[37] which was drafted as the basis for cooperation in some priority fields. Regular energy dialogue was declared as one of the priorities of cooperation. The media and NGOs criticized implementation of the Strategy.[38] In particular focus were problems in such areas as human rights and freedom of the media, but also mentioned was missing success in diversifying European gas supplies by acquiring access to Turkmen gas. The Council of the European Union adopted the EU and Central Asia: Strategy for a New Partnership on 17 June 2019.[39]

The first substantive step in the Central Asian Region on a bilateral level since the Partnership and Cooperation Agreements of the 1990s was the signing of the bilateral Agreement between the European Union and its member states on the one hand and the Republic of Kazakhstan on Enhanced Partnership and Cooperation (EPCA).[40]

The Agreement is a remarkable document: it is the first agreement the European Union has concluded with a Central Asian country after the PCAs of the 1990s and the first Partnership Agreement the European Union has concluded with a member state of the Eurasian Economic Union, which is, at least from an economic point of view, strongly dominated by the Russian Federation. The most interesting point is that the Russian Federation, in contrast to the DCFTA negotiations with the Eastern Partnership countries, never mentioned the EPCA in a negative way and the negotiations and initialization did not feature in the Russian media. One could think that such a "relaxed position" on the part of the Russian Federation is based on the fact that the EPCA is not a free trade agreement, since Kazakhstan is part of the Eurasian Economic Union and a free trade agreement is possible only with the involvement of the EAEU. However, even a cursory examination reveals numerous

---

37   <https://eeas.europa.eu/sites/eeas/files/the_european_union_and_central_asia_the_ne
      w_partnership_in_action.pdf> accessed 10 September 2021.

38   Sebastien Peyrouse, 'A Donor without Influence: The European Union in Central Asia'
      <www.ponarseurasia.org/memo/donor-without-influence-european-union-central
      -asia> accessed 10 September 2021.

39   <https://eeas.europa.eu/sites/eeas/files/st_10113_2007_init_en.pdf> accessed 10 September 2021.

40   Enhanced Partnership and Cooperation Agreement between the European Union and
      its Member States, of the one part, and the Republic of Kazakhstan, of the other part [21
      December 2015], OJ L29/1.

issues which will probably affect the development of the EAEU single market in a short or mid-term perspective.

Chapter 9 "Raw Materials and Energy" of Title III "Trade and Business" of the EPCA is a prime representative example in this regard. The very first substantive Article 139 "Price regulation" of the Chapter obliges the exporting Party (because of the trade structure, obviously this would be Kazakhstan) to provide information on price differences for raw materials and energy goods between the domestic and export markets. In fact, the European Union will receive important information for calculation of antidumping measures, which are often based on dual energy pricing. As mentioned above, the Russian Federation challenged these measures within the WTO dispute settlement procedures.[41] Today the information provided by Kazakhstan is not of any relevance for the Russian Federation, because there is no single energy market in the EAEU. However, the obligation on Kazakhstan could be a substantial burden for the future EAEU energy single market. In this case the information provided for Kazakhstan can be directly applied to all other member states of the EAEU, including the Russian Federation.

Another critical point could be access to transit capacities. For oil and gas pipelines, the EPCA (Article 143 section 1) simply refers to freedom of transit provided in the ECT (Article 7 (1) and (3)). Furthermore, the EPCA extends equal access to transmission infrastructure onto electric transmission grids and networks (Article 145). This means that the European Union exports the idea of unbundling by the EPCA and contributes to demonopolization of energy markets. The success of this policy in Kazakhstan means that the energy market of Kazakhstan is more open towards the European Union than the EAEU.

This situation is not limited just to trade and closely related transit issues. Access to the exploration market is also very liberal – Article 141 section 3 EPCA provides for non-discriminatory access to the market of hydrocarbons exploration. The provision is mandatory and covered by the dispute settlement instrument of the ECPA. This is an important difference to the market access rule of the ECT, which provides a non-binding rule.

5   Production Sharing Agreements between Foreign Investors
       and States

In the mid-1990s post-Soviet states were interested in attracting foreign investment in the energy sector. The most appropriate instrument for countries with

---

41   See (n 18); see (n 19).

considerable gaps in legislation and a very high level of insecurity were production sharing agreements (PSAs), which regulated the whole project in detail. Many of these treaties contain so-called grandfather clauses,[42] which freeze the law in relation to legal relations under the contract, in that changes in legislation do not apply to legal relations arising out of the PSA. In Azerbaijan, PSAs are ratified by the country's parliament and are equated with the country's international agreements and therefore have priority over the norms of national law.[43]

The attitude towards PSAs is far from unambiguous. In the Russian Federation, PSAs did not take root. To date, only three agreements are in force,[44] while numerous attempts to strengthen this tool have not been successful. In Kazakhstan, PSAs were initially the main tool of the extractive industry. However, since the beginning of the 2000s, much work has been done to change the concept of PSAs, especially regarding the transition from individual solutions to legislative settlement and the abandonment of "grandfather clauses" in PSAs.[45] Unlike Russia and Kazakhstan, Azerbaijan continues to actively use individualized PSAs.[46]

PSAs are discussed in the literature mainly in terms of contract and investment law. However, analysis of PSAs from the point of view of international trade law remains out of the debate.

Despite the fact that the terms of PSA agreements have not yet become the subject of international trade disputes, this cannot be excluded for the future. PSAs, especially Azerbaijani ones, contain a large number of conditions that directly affect trade in energy resources. For example, for PSA contractors, customs duties on the import of equipment are often zeroed. Due to the presence of a "grandfather clause", this condition remains in force throughout the whole period of the operation of PSAs, which are concluded for periods of decades.

---

42   Rainer Hausmann, 'Investment Contracts with Foreign Investors' and Maidan Suleimenov, '"Grandfather Clause" against the Reservation to Change the Terms of the Investment Agreement in order to Ensure the Property Interests of the Parties: New Trends in Kazakhstan's Legislation' in Alexander Trunk and others (eds), *Legal Aspects of Investment Contracts* (Eastlaw Press 2012) 34–35, 172–90.

43   Nurlan Mustafayev, 'Production-sharing Agreements in the Petroleum Industry of Azerbaijan' (2015) 8(4) Journal of World Energy Law and Busines 362, 367.

44   Johannes Rath, *Das Recht der Production Sharing Agreements in der Russischen Föderation* (Cuvillier Verlag 2006) 22–24.

45   See Suleymenov, (n 42) 172–190; Azar Aliyev, 'Der Staat als Vertragspartner: Ein Paradigmenwechsel in Aserbaidschan, Kasachstan und Russland im Vergleich' in Alexander Trunk and Azar Aliyev (eds), *Das Kaspische Meer als Wirtschaftsraum* (Josef Eul Verlag 2010) 89–106.

46   Mustafayev, (n 34) 362, 367.

Thus, the application of customs duties on the same equipment to other importers is potentially a violation of the MFN under the WTO regime, as well as the Agreement on Subsidies and Countervailing Measures. It should be noted that both the MFN and the Agreement on Subsidies apply to ECT parties.[47]

It is apparent that PSAs contain great potential for challenges within the framework of international trade law. The fact that these mechanisms are not used today does not provide any guarantees for the future. Signed in the middle and at the end of the twentieth century, agreements on protection of foreign investment have thus become the basis for challenging the actions of states towards investors only at the turn of the 21st century.[48]

6   The Impact of Normative Regulations of Third Countries on Energy
         Trade in the Region

It is clear that third countries can significantly influence trade in energy resources through their regulation. Most of the norms of international agreements, such as the WTO, ECT, and regional agreements are directed at protecting against this regulatory influence on trade. As already noted, states are as a rule interested in importing energy resources. In this regard, regulation of energy imports has been very limited. However, in recent years, one of the main energy buyers from Azerbaijan, Kazakhstan and Russia – the European Union – has conducted significant work on regulating the internal energy market. The European Union is developing a unified energy market in accordance with its energy strategy, one of the main objectives of which is the creation of a competitive energy market. The cornerstone of construction of a single competitive market has become the Third Energy Package, which consists of many EU legal acts.[49] The main objectives of the reforms are market liberalization and resolution of structural problems of the energy complex.[50]

---

47   See (n 27).
48   Rudolf Dolzer and Christoph Schreuer, *Principles of International Investment Law* (OUP
      2012) 11.
49   These are the EU Directives governing domestic electricity and gas markets EC Directive
      2009/73/EC of 13 July 2009, [14 September 2009] OJ L211/55; Directive 2009/73/EC of 13
      July 2009, [14 September 2009] OJ L211/94, as well as the Regulations governing the establishment of the Agency for the Cooperation of Energy Regulators, access to networks in
      the transborder exchange of electricity and access to gas networks: EC Regulation No 713/
      2009 of 13 July 2009, [14 September 2009] OJ L211/1; EC Regulation No 714/2009 of 13 July
      2009, [14 September 2009] OJ L211/15; EC Regulation No 715/2009 of 13 July 2009, [14
      September 2009] OJ L211/36.
50   <https://ec.europa.eu/energy/en/topics/markets-and-consumers/market-legislation>
      accessed 10 September 2021.

The Third Energy Package has had a significant impact on the activities of companies from energy exporting countries. The three most critical components of the Third Energy Package for gas suppliers – the separation of energy companies engaged in gas transportation from extractive and marketing companies (so-called unbundling), defining "projects of common interest", as well as admission to networks – were challenged by the Russian Federation under the WTO dispute settlement mechanism.

One of the main problems for gas suppliers is indeed unbundling – the separation of energy companies engaged in gas transportation from companies involved in the entire cycle – in extraction, transportation and marketing (Article 9 of Directive 2009/73/EC). Not only have Russian companies encountered problems in the European gas market, which was the main reason for the Russian Federation's challenge to the Third Energy Package. The State Oil Company of the Republic of Azerbaijan (SOCAR) failed to purchase 66% in DESFA, which is the owner of the only Greek high-pressure gas pipeline. The results of the EC investigation have not been published, because after very long investigation with several prolongations the case was ultimately withdrawn.[51] But from the information published on the EU website[52] it can be concluded that the main point of verification was the permissibility of the gas producer's acquisition of infrastructure in accordance with Directive 2009/73/EC, although SOCAR officials have repeatedly indicated that the deal was previously agreed with the European Union and SOCAR would own only 16% of the gas to be transported via the DESFA-owned gas pipeline.[53]

After the failure of negotiations SOCAR and Azerbaijan did not have resort to any legal remedies. Azerbaijan, which is not a WTO member, could not use the WTO mechanism; it could, however, use the mechanism for resolving investment disputes within the ECT and the Investment Protection Agreement between Azerbaijan and Greece[54] and the ECT's own trade dispute resolution mechanism. In this case, the mechanisms for resolving investment

---

51   <http://ec.europa.eu/competition/elojade/isef/case_details.cfm?proc_code=2_M_7095> accessed 10 September 2021.

52   Initiation of proceedings (case m.7095 – SOCAR/DESFA) (text with EEA relevance) (2014/ c 396/02), OJ EU of 11 November 2014; Commission opens in-depth investigation into proposed acquisition of Greek gas transmission system operator DESFA by SOCAR: <http://europa.eu/rapid/press-release_IP-14-1442_en.htm> accessed 10 September 2021.

53   <www.euractiv.com/sections/energy/minister-azerbaijan-concerned-commissions -desfa-investigation-312786> accessed 10 September 2021.

54   Agreement between the Government of the Hellenic Republic and the Government of the Republic of Azerbaijan on the Promotion and Reciprocal Protection of Investments, 26 November 2004 <https://investmentpolicy.unctad.org/international-investment-agr eements/treaty-files/234/download> accessed 10 September 2021.

disputes provided for in the ECT and the Agreement on the Protection and
Encouragement of Investments between Azerbaijan and Greece were not
applicable, since it is a question of admission to the market, and these agreements do not contain strict obligations to admit foreign investors to the market.[55] Azerbaijan could challenge both the legality of the Third Energy Package
and verification of the deal to acquire control over DESFA within the framework of the ECT's trade dispute resolution mechanism. At the same time,
unlike Russia, Azerbaijan could not refer to the obligations undertaken by the
European Union and Greece in the framework of the GATS, since GATS norms
are excluded from the scope of the ECT.

7   Conclusion

Energy trade continues to be one of the least regulated sectors of international
trade. The reason for this is not only the specificity of trade relations in which
importers, no less than exporters, are interested in obtaining goods and services, but also the specificity of energy resource generation and transportation.

   In recent years, various attempts have been made within the framework of
the WTO and the ECT to establish global rules for trade in energy resources.
However, these attempts remain unsuccessful. Despite this, the energy trade is
increasingly becoming the subject of regulation through various legal norms.
Thus, within the WTO questions are being raised about the admissibility of dual
pricing for resources and compliance with WTO norms of domestic rules for
regulation of energy markets. The ECT, in practice, extends the effect of many
WTO rules to countries that are not WTO members. The ECT thereby creates big
risks for countries like Azerbaijan and Turkmenistan that are not WTO members, but are members of the ECT. Today's absence of disputes on the basis of
the ECT can be deceptive. At the same time, WTO rules open up new opportunities for participating countries. In fact, Azerbaijan and Turkmenistan could
receive an effective mechanism for challenging the actions of other countries
and unions. This is becoming especially important in light of reforms to the

---

55   The agreement on the promotion and protection of investments between Azerbaijan and
      Greece applies only to investments made in the territory of the contracting parties in
      accordance with their legislation (art 2). Contained in art 10 (1) ECT, the norm on encour-
      aging investments and creating stable, equal, favorable, and transparent terms to inves-
      tors of other parties is not mandatory. Accordingly, it is not subject to the mechanism for
      resolving investment disputes provided for in art 29 ECT.

internal EU energy market, which are associated with significant restrictions on the energy companies of exporting countries.

This complex picture of international commitments undertaken by Azerbaijan, Kazakhstan and Russia is complemented by bilateral and regional agreements. Most of these agreements are framework agreements at the governmental level; on their basis contracts are concluded for the supply of energy carriers between business entities. A more ambitious approach is envisaged within the framework of the Eurasian Economic Union, but it still does not allow us to speak about the creation of a single and free market. In the interests of individual countries and even national companies, there are numerous exceptions. The EPCA between the European Union and Kazakhstan shows that hesitation within the EAEU allows the member states to develop their own energy policy, with far reaching consequences for the potential development of the single energy market of the EAEU.

Finally, production sharing agreements, signed between the state and foreign investors, provide foreign investors with a special regime that differs from national legislation. These internationalized contracts play a big practical role, especially for Azerbaijan and, in part, for Kazakhstan. The possibility of conflicts between these contracts – which to a certain extent have the force of international agreements and are ratified by parliaments – and the international obligations of states are real.

The need to minimise risks and conflicts suggests the necessity for a detailed "inventory" of the international legal obligations of states taken at the global, regional, and bilateral level, as well as contractual obligations. Systematization and analysis of these obligations in the light of current legal developments will minimize the risks that have arisen due to the disparity of sources of law governing international trade in energy resources.

CHAPTER 11

Trade Facilitation and International Rail Transport Law: The Eurasian Land Bridge Perspective

Erik Evtimov and Tetyana Payosova

The Trans-Siberian railroad will become one of the greatest trade routes in human history. It is destined to undermine the British seaborne trade.[1]

∴

1 International Trade Facilitation and Rail Transport in Eurasia – Connecting the Dots

Trade facilitation measures seek to deal with domestic procedures and requirements, which constrain efficiency of international trade, despite multilateral and regional trade liberalization efforts. Red tape, delays due to customs, transit and other procedures and formalities, as well as corruption can have significant prohibitive effects on imports and exports. Trade facilitation measures primarily aim at reducing costs related to importation and improving profitability of exports. Although they can be effectively pursued unilaterally, multilaterally concerted actions prove to be more efficient internationally in terms of engaging trading partners with different levels of development and boosting exports from developing countries.[2]

The successful negotiation of the Trade Facilitation Agreement (TFA) within the World Trade Organization (WTO) framework became the main breakthrough in the history of the WTO since the Uruguay Round.[3] Agreed upon as

---

1   Archibald R. Colquhoun, British administrator and economist, 1900.
2   See a detailed analysis of the Trade Facilitation Agreement by Bernard Hoekman, 'The Bali Trade Facilitation Agreement and Rulemaking in the WTO: Milestone, Mistake, or Mirage' in Jagdish N. Bhagwati, Pravin Krishna and Arvind Panagariya (eds), *The World Trade System: Trends and Challenges* (MIT Press 2016) 149.
3   See The Results of the Uruguay Round of Multilateral Trade Negotiations: The Legal Texts, World Trade Organization 1999.

a part of the "Bali package" in 2013,[4] the TFA entered into force on 22 February 2017 as soon as it has been ratified by two thirds of WTO Members.[5]

Before the adoption of the TFA, the WTO legal framework contained only some general provisions relevant tor trade facilitation, including WTO disciplines on freedom of transit for goods, on fees and formalities related to importation and exportation as well as transparency.[6] Despite trade liberalization reforms importers and exporters still often face red tape practices that have a significant negative effect on cross-border trade. Lack of transparency, cumbersome and duplicated documentation requirements, outdated paper-based customs and other administrative procedures are the most common "suspects".

According to some estimations, the implementation of the TFA could result in reduction of trade costs worldwide by up to 17.5% and boost global trade by up to 1 trillion dollars annually.[7] The full implementation of TFA provisions by a WTO Member would reduce its trade-related costs by up to 3.9% more in comparison to those WTO Members that would implement only the mandatory minimum required by the TFA.[8] The 2015 WTO Trade Report focusing specifically on potential benefits and challenges of TFA's implementation, concluded that trade facilitation measures eventually attract more foreign direct investment, contribute to improvement of government revenue collection and reduction in trade-related corruption.[9]

According to the WTO, in 2013 the value of business-to-business (B2B) e-commerce reached USD 15 trillion and business-to-customer (B2C) – USD 1 trillion both in international and domestic transactions. Development of new technologies, rapid growth of Internet access and new e-commerce business models help to reduce trade costs.[10] However, despite this rapid digitalization in all sectors of economy, most goods still retain their physical form, even if they are traded online, and require cross-border transportation by road, rail, sea or air. The efficient functioning of global value chains, but also the full

---

4   Agreement on Trade Facilitation, Ministerial Decision, WT/MIN(13)/36, WT/L/911. See also Bali Ministerial Declaration, WT/MIN(13)/DEC, adopted 7 December 2013.

5   WTO, 'WTO's Trade Facilitation Agreement Enters into Force', WTO 2017 News Items, 22 February 2017.

6   See (n 4) and arts V, VIII and X of the General Agreement on Tariffs and Trade (GATT).

7   WTO (n 5).

8   OECD, 'Implementation of the WTO Trade Facilitation Agreement: The Potential Impact on Trade Costs' (June 2015), <www.oecd.org/trade/WTO-TF-Implementation-Policy-Brief _EN_2015_06.pdf> accessed 15 November 2021.

9   WTO, World Trade Report 2015, Speeding up Trade: Benefits and Challenges of Implementing the WTO Trade Facilitation Agreement (WTO, 2016). See (n 3).

10   WTO, International Trade Statistics 2015 31.

enjoyment of benefits offered by e-commerce is impossible without reliable and timely delivery of goods both in B2B and B2C relations. The new legal relationship customer-to-customer (C2C), where sales contracts are concluded directly between single customers based on internet platforms like Zalando and Alibaba, raises new legal and logistical challenges in all transport modes. Whereas each transport mode is subject to its own set of international and regional rules on carriage of goods, the common denominator for all transport modes from the perspective of trade facilitation are customs formalities and transit procedures.

The new TFA establishes a number of obligations that shall contribute to a smoother and faster delivery of internationally traded goods. Among others, the TFA requires WTO Members to adopt and maintain procedures that allow pre-arrival processing of the necessary information and documentation, also in a digital form, on imported goods in order to expedite customs release of goods upon their arrival in addition to enhanced coordination with other governmental agencies, such as sanitary and phytosanitary authorities for the purpose of implementing the TFA and coordinating technical assistance for smoother capacity building.[11] The WTO Members will have to provide for additional trade facilitation measures related to import, export or transit formalities and procedures for the so-called authorized operators, provided that they meet the set qualification requirements. Such trade facilitation measures may among others include lower documentary and data requirements, lower rate of physical inspections and examinations, rapid release time, clearance of goods at the premises of the authorized operator.[12]

The TFA also went a step further in developing the existing disciplines on formalities and documentation requirements related to imports, exports and transit.[13] The WTO Members shall ensure that these requirements and formalities are applied in a manner to reduce time and cost of compliance for operators and are the least trade restrictive if several alternative measures are available. Among others this can be ensured by increasing acceptance of paper or electronic copies of supporting documents.[14] Moreover, WTO Members are encouraged to use relevant international standards when setting import, export or transit formalities and procedures.[15]

---

11   Art 7.1 of the TFA.
12   Art 7.7. of the TFA.
13   Art 10 of the TFA.
14   Art 10.2 of the TFA.
15   Art 10.3 of the TFA.

Finally, the transit disciplines in the General Agreement on Tariffs and Trade as further developed by the TFA have a direct impact on transport of goods. Transit-related regulations and formalities have to be proportionate to the objectives pursued and should not be applied in a manner to constitute a disguised restriction on trade.[16] The TFA requires WTO Members to apply only those formalities, requirements with respect to documents and customs controls in connection with traffic in transit that are necessary to identify goods and ensure fulfilment of transit requirements.[17]

This contribution focuses on the legal interface between trade facilitation measures and international rail transport law. Especially in the Eurasian region, rail transport offers a number of advantages in comparison to transportation of goods by air, road or sea. Rail outperforms other transport modes in terms of average time of delivery, costs of carriage and environmental externalities. At the same time, cross-continental transport of goods by rail traditionally faces some physical and regulatory constraints. Trains physically cross numerous borders on their way, travelling from the country of origin to the country of destination through several transit countries with separate customs and transit regimes. However, despite extreme distances, such constraints are limited in case of transportation of goods from China to Europe and in the reverse direction. Traders on both side of the continent benefit from the fact that there are only two customs borders to be crossed on most of the Eurasian Land Bridge between China and the Eurasian Economic Union (EAEU)[18] and between EAEU and the European Union (EU).[19] At least from the perspective of customs requirements and expenses related thereto, this makes the carriage of goods by rail in the Eurasia even more competitive. In this contribution we explore and explain the interlinkages between trade facilitation and implementation of international rail transport law in Eurasia and provide some examples of best practices that may eventually be implemented by other countries and regions, subject to availability of rail infrastructure.

---

16   Art 11(1) of the TFA.

17   Art 11(6) of the TFA.

18   The Eurasian Economic Union (EAEU) is an international organization for regional economic integration formed among the Republic of Armenia, Republic of Belarus, Republic of Kazakhstan, the Kyrgyz Republic, and the Russian Federation. <www.eaeunion.org/?lang=en> accessed 15 November 2021. For more on the EAEU see Zhenis Kembayev, 'The Eurasian Economic Union: An Overview and Evaluation' in this volume, 19 et seq.

19   The European Union (EU) is an economic and political union between 28 European countries. Further information is <https://europa.eu/european-union/about-eu_en> accessed 15 November 2021.

2   Legal Framework for Transportation of Freight by Rail in the Eurasian Region

International transportation of freight by rail in the Eurasian region, unlike by other means of transport, is subject to two separate international legal frameworks with distinct institutional structures, different approaches to the contract of carriage and liability regimes. The "construction" of an invisible legal border between Europe on the one hand, and Russia and Asia, on the other hand, dates back to the times of the Cold War. Despite significant geopolitical changes and the fall of the Soviet Union, the legal duality in the field of international rail transport law was preserved and its unification is a challenge for the years to come.

Currently, international carriage of goods is subject to a dual legal regime. The Convention on International Carriage by Rail (COTIF) 1999 and specifically its Appendix B containing Uniform Rules concerning the Contract of International Carriage of Goods by Rail (CIM UR) applies to a large extent in Europe.[20] It is administered by the Intergovernmental Organisation for International Carriage by Rail (OTIF), a successor of the Central Office for International Carriage by Rail founded in 1985.[21] Yet another regime – Agreement on International Goods Transport by Rail (SMGS) – applies to the international carriage of freight by rail in the countries of Eastern Europe and Asia.[22] The map below illustrates the geographical scope of application of international rail transport law in the framework of COTIF/CIM and SMGS (see Illustration 1).

Both the CIM UR and the SMGS provide for the use of a consignment note as a proof of the contract of carriage. Namely, Article 6 § 2 of the CIM UR requires that the contract of carriage be confirmed by a consignment note in line with a uniform model. The CIM UR vest the international associations of carriers with the task of establishing such a uniform model subject to a mandatory

---

20   Convention concerning International Carriage by Rail as amended by the Vilnius Protocol in force from 1 July 2006 (COTIF 1999) and with amendments adopted by the Revision Committee at its 24th session, amendments adopted by the RID Expert Committee at its 47th and 48th sessions, as well as amendments adopted by the Revision Committee at its 25th session in June 2014 and in a written procedure in May 2015.

21   See a more detailed information on the OTIF organisation, mission and legal regime <www.otif.org> accessed 15 November 2021.

22   See a detailed information on the OSJD, its mission and the applicable agreements <http://en.osjd.org/> accessed 15 November 2021. The SMGS entered into force in 1951 and has been revised on numerous occasions since. The most recent amendments entered into force on 1 July 2015.

Freight Traffic CIM/SMGS

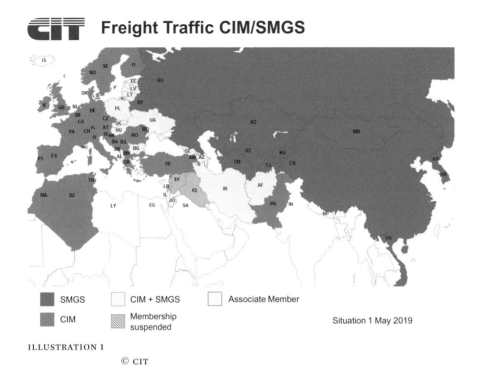

SMGS

CIM

CIM + SMGS

Membership
suspended

Associate Member

Situation 1 May 2019

ILLUSTRATION 1

© CIT

set of requirements in Article 7 of the CIM UR. Similar requirements are contained in Article 14 and 15 of the SMGS. Notably, both the CIM UR and the SMGS explicitly allow for the use of an electronic consignment note subject to the requirement of functional equivalence, i.e. the e-consignment note should meet the same requirements as the paper consignment note in terms of content to fulfil the same evidentiary function.[23]

Given the existence of the two separate transport documents for the parts of route in the SMGS and the CIM areas accordingly, the practical consequence of this dual legal regime is that goods transported from Russia and Asia to Europe and in the reverse direction have to be re-consigned at the legal 'border'. The procedure of re-consignment means that most of the information in the SMGS consignment note must be reentered as required into the CIM consignment note. This results not only in longer transit times, but also may lead to mistakes during manual re-consignment. These inherent problems with re-consignment create legal uncertainty for clients and rail carriers, due

---

23   See art 15 § 4 of the SMGS and art 6 § 9 of the CIM.

to potential liability problems at the customs or in case of damage to or loss of the goods. For customers and for carriers this also means the application of two different liability frameworks – under the CIM UR and under the SMGS. Although liability rules under both legal frameworks share some commonalities, they still retain quite important differences.[24]

Over the several last decades, freight traffic by rail between the countries of the European Union and their Eastern neighbours gained an enormous potential, which is still not being used to a full extent. The existence of two different legal regimes remained one of the main challenges for years, since it often led to interruption of liability in absence of a single transport contract, entailing delays, additional costs and administrative burdens for re-consignment of the carriage and edition of new consignment note CIM or SMGS. As governments need time to agree on unification of international rail transport law, railway sector associations, and in particular the International Rail Transport Committee (CIT), played a key role in a short-term prospective overcoming legal obstacles for a smooth and reliable carriage of goods by rail on the Eurasian Land Bridge.

The CIT as an international association of railway undertakings and shipping companies was created in 1902 and for many years has been active in the sphere of cross-border international transportation by rail. Although the main area of CIT's work is practical implementation of the COTIF – the Convention on International Rail Traffic, it has been also actively working towards the creation of a uniform international rail transport law. After more than 100 years a lot has been achieved and a lot more still can be done to ensure fast and reliable rail transportation of goods and passengers with clear-cut coherent rights and obligations for all participants of the transportation process.

Back in 2003, at the conference on International Rail Transport Law in Kyiv, the CIT took up a task of supporting the work of the railway sector towards the creation of uniform contractual solutions for international rail transport as a part of the newly launched project "Legal Interoperability CIM/SMGS".[25] Although CIT's activities have been always focused on the COTIF legal regime, rail transport business required new innovative solutions for the Eurasian transport. The CIM/SMGS project was conceptualized as a joint project together

---

24   For the comparison of the liability rules applicable under the CIM and the SMGS see: CIT and OSJD, Leitfaden zur Haftung CIM-SMGS (Guide to CIM-SMGS liability framework) (December 2006).

25   CIT is as an international association of rail transport undertakings is primarily vested with the task to ensure a smooth implementation of the international rail transport law by railway companies. On the history of the CIT, that was established in 1902 <http://cit-rail.org/en/objectives/> accessed 15 November 2021.

with the OSJD and involved railway companies that were doing business subject to the requirements of both legal regimes – the CIM and the SMGS. In the first phase the project aimed at creation of the common consignment note CIM/SMGS.

The work on the common consignment note CIM/SMGS was completed in 2006. The idea behind this new transport document was to physically merge the two existing consignment notes under the CIM and the SMGS legal regimes on the basis of the UNCTAD layout key for trade documents. Thus, the common consignment note CIM/SMGS is often referred to as a sum of the two consignment notes – with common fields, where the requirements of the CIM and the SMGS are the same and with separate fields to allocate the differences. This was in line with the main task of the common consignment note – to facilitate and simplify the transit procedure and re-consignment. At the same time, until harmonisation of the international rail transport law at the intergovernmental level is completed, each carriage of freight by rail in Eurasia, even when transported with the common consignment note CIM/SMGS, is still subject to the two separate contracts of carriage – the CIM and the SMGS. The existence of both contracts of carriage is simultaneously confirmed by the common consignment note CIM/SMGS. Thus, despite the absence of a harmonised international legal framework for Eurasian rail transport, the CIT managed to create a practical legal "bridge" between the two legal frameworks.

Since 2006, the CIM/SMGS consignment note gained broad international recognition, among others because it is based on the United Nations Layout Key for trade documents.[26] The right to use the common CIM/SMGS consignment note is also explicitly enshrined in Article 13 and Appendix 6 of the SMGS.[27] Since the introduction of the common CIM/SMGS consignment note it has been used on fifty traffic lines within the four Trans-European rail corridors. About 80% of the CIM/SMGS traffic is carried out using the common consignment note CIM/SMGS, which allows saving approximately 40 minutes on each wagon and 30 Euro on each consignment note. Since 2006 there has been a steady increase in the use of the common consignment note CIM/SMGS by 20–30% annually. Additional information on the background and use of the common consignment note CIM/SMGS is provided in Section 3 of this chapter.

---

26   Erik Evtimov, 'CIM/SMGS Project: Building a Bridge', (2014) 1(37) The RZD-Partner International 34–35.

27   Namely, art 13 of the SMGS refers to the Manual for the CIM/SMGS Consignment Note in Annex 6 to the SMGS, which is equivalent to the Manual for the CIM/SMGS Consignment Note (GLV-CIM/SMGS) of the CIT.

As outlined above, goods transported by rail between China and Europe on a distance of over 10,000 km will cross only two customs borders – that of the Eurasian Economic Union (EAEU) and the European Union (EU). From the perspective of trade facilitation, minimisation of documentary requirements for transit through different customs territories is an important pillar.[28] One of the easiest and most common ways to simplify customs requirements is to use commercial or transport documents as a transit declaration, since they usually contain all the necessary information to identify goods and also to comply with customs transit requirements. The common consignment note CIM/SMGS is a vivid example of a document that meets both the rail business and the customs transit requirements.[29] Within the framework of the EAEU, transit procedures are dealt with in the Agreement on the special conditions of customs transit of goods, carried by rail on the customs territory of the customs union of 21 May 2010 (hereinafter referred to as the EAEU Customs Transit Agreement). The EAEU Customs Transit Agreement explicitly mentions that a rail consignment note, including the CIM/SMGS consignment note, can be used as a transit declaration for the EAEU customs transit procedure. Similarly, in the European Union a rail consignment note can be also used as a transit declaration.[30]

Following the successful completion of the common consignment note project, in the recent years the CIT has been working on harmonised conditions of carriage for the through Eurasian transportation of freight by rail. Given that the processes within the UN institutional framework require significant amount of time to negotiate the draft texts of the new uniform international rail transport law and reach consensus on the most pertinent provisions, the CIT offers harmonised solutions on a contractual level. This initiative is strongly supported and promoted by the United National Economic Commission for Europe (UNECE).[31]

---

28 See arts 11 and 12 of the TFA.

29 WCO, Transit Guidelines: Route for Efficient Transit Regime (WCO, 2017) 62–63.

30 See with a specific reference to the CIM consignment note: European Commission, Transit Manual, Working Document, TAAXUD/A2/TRA/003/2016-EN, 27 April 2016. Note, that the CIM/SMGS consignment note on the territory subject to the CIM UR applies as a CIM consignment note.

31 Joint Declaration on the Promotion of Euro-Asian Rail Transport and Activities towards Unified Railway Law, Geneva, 26 February 2013 <www.unece.org/trans/main/sc2/sc2_ge url_itc_declaration.html> accessed 15 November 2021.

3   Best Practices: Trade Facilitation through Railway Lenses

For trade facilitation in the Eurasian region, two innovations in the railway sector are of crucial importance – the introduction of electronic data exchange in Eurasian rail freight transport, which can reduce the time spent at a border by 65%[32] and the use of the common CIM/SMGS consignment note. The CIT, as will be explained below, took the lead on both of these innovations which became the best practices of trade facilitation in the rail sector.

3.1   *Electronic Consignment Notes CIM and CIM/SMGS*

To ensure a fast and reliable exchange of data, which is contained in the transport documents, among all participating actors (sender, recipient, carrier, customs and other authorities), the CIT started working on the legal and functional specifications of the CIM electronic consignment note. This work is performed at the rail sector level and is based on the principle of functional equivalence (equal use of paper documents and data exchange), as provided in Article 6 § 9 of the CIM UR. The CIT is also actively supporting RailData and the UIC in the work involved in finalising the technical specifications required for the e-RailFreight project.

In connection with the practical implementation of the CIM electronic consignment note and the ongoing digitisation in the rail sector, the CIT is working on clarification of the legal issues relating to the recognition of the electronic consignment note by the national courts and other national authorities as evidence of the contract of carriage (Article 6 § 2 CIM). The preliminary results of the analysis conducted by the CIT shows that in light of the B2B relationship, the free appraisal of evidence by the national courts of the commercial transport documents is certainly possible (principle of freedom of contract). A contrario this means that an electronic signature (e-Signature) is not mandatory as a means of authentication of the consignment note. Thus, a unique consignment identification number, which has been suggested by the CIT as a security guarantee for the consignment note, can be used as an appropriate and cost-effective option by railway undertakings.[33]

---

32   Borna Abramovic, Vladislav Zitricky and Vedran Biskup, 'Organisation of Railway Freight Transport: Case Study CIM/SMGS between Slovakia and Ukraine' (2016) 8 European Transport Research Review 27.

33   Use of paperless exchange of date between two or more railway undertakings based on legal and functional specifications prepared by the CIT which can be understand as technical prove of single business approach for blockchain transfer of data in XML format.

To keep up with digitalization trends, the CIT and the RailData are trying to develop a coordinated "maximum dataset" for the electronic version of the CIM, SMGS and CIM/SMGS consignments notes. For this purpose, the dataset of the CIM/SMGS electronic consignment note, which contains the data of the two separate CIM and SMGS consignment notes, would be a suitable basis. For the other (electronic) consignment notes (CIM and SMGS, and possibly national), subsets/partial datasets can be defined in each case and then be made available as a variety of printed model paper consignment notes as required. Apart from working on the dataset, the CIT and the RailData are also trying to cope with additional technical constraints, including the differences between electronic data formats (EDIFACT and XML) that are currently being used for the exchange of information between and among the various actors in the transportation process. All these technical issues are reflected in the technical specifications (guidelines) for the electronic CIM-SMGS consignment note.[34]/[35]

The CIT has also successfully completed a project on modernisation the CIT documents for freight traffic and the use of wagons, following the trend of digitalisation and recognizing the changing needs of the railway sector and its clients.

3.2   *Common Consignment Note CIM/SMGS*

In transcontinental transportation of goods and passengers in the Eurasian region, rail transport offers significant advantages in terms of environmental externalities, time en route, reliability and safety. The CIT has long recognised an ever-growing potential of the Eurasian transport by rail and initiated in 2004 a project to enhance "legal interoperability" between the CIM and the SMGS legal regimes.

Up to 2006, all rail freight consignments have been re-consigned as they passed from the CIM to the SMGS legal regime – on their way from Europe to Asia and back. This re-consignment required time-consuming work and additional expenses with no value added and sometimes led to incorrect data

---

34   RAILDATA is international organization of European cargo Railway Undertakings <www.raildata.coop> accessed 15 November 2021. It is established as special group of the International Union of Railways (UIC). The main purpose of RAILDATA is to design, develop and run IT services to support the European freight railway business of its members.

35   See Technical Specifications for the Electronic CIM/SMGS Consignment Note: Recommendations to undertakings intending to use an electronic version of the CIM/ SMGS consignment note. Applicable with effect from 8 July 2009/Edition 1 October 2013 <www.cit-rail.org/en/freight-traffic/manuals> accessed 15 November 2021.

entered at the re-consignment points. In 2006 the common consignment note CIM/SMGS was created by the CIT. It forms an essential part of the joint CIT/OSJD project on the legal interoperability of the CIM and the SMGS. The CIM/SMGS consignment note significantly simplifies the transition procedure at the re-consignment points and is based on the United Nations Layout Key for trade documents. To some degree it represents the sum of the CIM and the SMGS consignment notes.

The CIT made available both the conventional and the paperless e-consignment note CIM/SMGS. In order to ensure flawless and easy implementation of the new common consignment note, the CIT prepared a "Manual for the CIM/SMGS consignment note", which is being regularly updated in cooperation with railway experts that deal with the use of consignment notes for the freight transport by rail on daily basis. The e-consignment note has been operationalized through technical, functional and legal specifications. Recently the CIT together with technical experts prepared the new updated version of these specifications for the e-consignment note, which are to be published in September 2013. It is an alternative to the classic system of consignment with re-transcription of a SMGS consignment note to a CIM consignment note or from a CIM consignment note to a SMGS consignment note at the re-consignment point. The common CIM/SMGS consignment note may be used as a CIM consignment note in the area in which the CIM applies and as an SMGS consignment note in the area in which the SMGS applies. The same principle also applies to the use of the CIM/SMGS consignment note as a customs document.

Thus, the common CIM/SMGS consignment note is building a bridge – between the different legal regimes of CIM and SMGS that eliminates the obstacles of language and borders. Behind each CIM/SMGS consignment note, there is a contractual link between those involved in the CIM or SMGS region: between the consignor of the goods, the carrier and the consignee. Thus, the common CIM/SMGS consignment note provides greater legal certainty:
- The route the goods take from the consignor throughout the carrier to the consignee is specified;
- The assumption of the transport costs between consigner and consignee is stipulated;
- In the event of loss of or damage to the goods, the procedure for providing compensation is laid down;
- System-based errors in the re-consignment of consignment notes are eliminated;

- The common CIM/SMGS consignment note is also recognized as a customs transit and bank document. It is used for block trains, wagon groups, single wagons or containers, in either paper or electronic format.[36]

As a result of the entry into force of the new Customs Code of the European Union,[37] the CIT recognized a need to update its documents for the common CIM/SMGS consignment note - the "CIM/SMGS Consignment Note Manual" (GLV-CIM/SMGS/ Appendix 6 to the SMGS) and the functional specifications for the electronic CIM/SMGS consignment note. These updates were approved by CIT working bodies in September 2016.

The development and simplification of Eurasian rail freight shipments gained support at the highest political levels in China, Russia, Poland and other origin, transit and destination states. The remarkable results achieved by Kazakhstan Railways (KZH) in the use of the CIM/SMGS consignment note for the pilot shipments speaks in favour of the regular use of this transport document for transport of goods by rail. Following these best practices, China opened the following three border crossing points for the use of the CIM/SMGS consignment note as of 1 May 2017:

- Alashankou-Dostyk, between the People's Republic of China and Kazakhstan;
- Erlian-Zamyn Uud, between the People's Republic of China and Mongolia;
- Manzhouli-Zabaikalsk, between the People's Republic of China and the Russian Federation.

The Russian Federation is actively using the common CIM/SMGS consignment note since its creation in 2006. It has recognized the important trade facilitation function of the CIM/SMGS consignment note by explicitly naming it as a customs transit document for the purposes of international freight traffic by rail in the Customs Code of the Customs Union between Russia, Belarus and Kazakhstan.

Furthermore, in accordance with Article 9 of the Annex 9 of the UNECE International Convention on the Harmonization of Frontier Controls of Goods

---

36   See a summary on the project development at Erik Evtimov, 'Rail Way to Uniform Law', CIT-Info 1/2017, 4.

37   The Union Customs Code (UCC) was adopted on 9 October 2013 as Regulation (EU) No 952/2013 of the European Parliament and of the Council. It entered into force on 30 October 2013 although most of its substantive provisions apply from 1 May 2016. The UCC has been amended once by Regulation 2016/2339, which modified Article 136 UCC on goods that have temporarily left the customs territory of the Union by sea or air.

of 1982,[38] the common CIM/SMGS consignment note is recognized internationally for the purposes of simplifying frontier procedures for international freight traffic by rail. Annex 9, including the common CIM/SMGS consignment note, was approved by the European Union on its own behalf and on behalf of the EU Member States.

The CIT has been also actively exploring a possibility of expanding the application of the CIM/SMGS consignment note to multimodal sea-rail transportation. Already the Kaliningrad Declaration of 7 November 2008 proposed the successive use of the common CIM/SMGS consignment note as a multimodal document for rail-ferry services on the Baltic Sea and the Black Sea.[39]

The economic growth of Baltic countries and the mutual trade with the Russian Federation – in addition to trade with Kazakhstan, China and others – allow to predict a substantial increase in demand for rail freight shipments in the Baltic region. Shipments of freight to Europe through the Port of Riga and its integration into the Trans-Siberian rail route provide an excellent opportunity to use the common CIM/SMGS consignment note for combined Eurasian shipments. However, a combined effort is necessary to ensure that favorable conditions are established for Kazakhstan, China and other Asian countries, so as to encourage them to select Baltic ports more frequently when they intend to use this rail-sea connection.

The Black Sea region has also witnessed significant developments during the last years. The new Samsun-Kavkaz rail ferry service was officially inaugurated at the end of February 2013 in the Turkish port of Samsun. It is now possible to transport goods from Russia by sea via the port of Kavkaz to Samsun in the eastern part of Turkey. The consignments are then forwarded by rail or road to their final destinations in Turkey or the Middle East. This new link will strengthen trade relations between the two countries, but also between all countries of the Black Sea basin. This will also enable a development of the combined transport system between Russia and Turkey, and beyond to the Middle East countries and the Caucasus.

To unlock the potential of the use of a single consignment note CIM/SMGS for such rail-ferry transport of freight, the CIT has already prepared the Special Transport Conditions for Sea-Rail Traffic to be applied on contractual basis. These transport conditions have an important potential of linking up the ports

---

38   UNECE International Convention on the Harmonization of Frontier Controls of Goods of 1982, ECE/TRANS/55/Rev.2 <www.unece.org/fileadmin/DAM/trans/conventn/harmone .pdf> accessed 15 November 2021.

39   See on the drafting and scope of the Kaliningrad Declaration, Erik Evtimov, CIT-Info 10/ 2008, 6–7.

to the key production and consumer centers in Europe, Russia and Asia. The CIT has called for the promotion and use of these Transport Conditions and the single consignment note as important means of trade facilitation.[40]

3.3   *Transportation of Postal Items by Rail from China to Europe*

Postal items transported by rail from the People's Republic of China to Western Europe are seen as a tremendous business opportunity for the member railways of the CIT, but also for the general development of global Internet trade (e-commerce). Goods can now be transported within 10 to 15 days at a competitive price from the People's Republic of China to Europe (the European Union and Switzerland) in transit on trans-Siberian corridors (Russian Federation) or on the Silk Road (Kazakhstan), and also in the opposite direction. According to the unimodal conventions of the 20th century for rail and road transport the carriage of postal items was within the exclusive powers of the postal authorities (Article 4(b) COTIF/CIM 1980 and SMGS 1951, as of 1 September 2011 Article 4(1)(2) in accordance with Appendix 1 or for carriage by road in accordance with CMR 1956 Article 1(4)(a)). Gradually, the prevalence of the Constitution of the Universal Postal Union (UPU) of 1964 was removed from the unimodal transport conventions. From the UPU's point of view, when rail transport is involved, the CN37 and CN34 or CP83[41] receptacle labels would enable the shipment to be recognized as surface mail and transported from origin to destination.[42] They could also enable the mail to be moved from the destination rail port to the destination office of exchange for postal customs clearance. The UPU Form CN37 Delivery bill for surface mails is the consignment document used in the transportation function, both for operational control and for accounting between the Post and the carrier. Operationally, the consignment moves the receptacles between an origin international mail processing centre (IMPC) and a destination IMPC, typically via a carrier such as an airline or

---

40   CIT Freight Documentation <www.cit-rail.org/en/freight-traffic/manuals> accessed 15 November 2021.

41   For more information regarding these labels see Convention Manual, Update 1 – June 2019, International Bureau of the Universal Postal Union, Berne 2019 <www.upu.int/ UPU/media/upu/files/UPU/aboutUpu/acts/manualsInThreeVolumes/actInThreeVolu mesManualOfConventionMaj1En.pdf> accessed 15 November 2021.

42   See the UPU Postal Transport Guide. The guide is maintained by the Transport Group of the UPU Postal Operations Council (POC), in conjunction with the International Air Transport Association (IATA) when airline issues are involved. The terms of reference of the Transport Group are outlined in document POC C1 TG 2013.1–Doc 2a, published in the UPU document database <www.upu.int/uploads/tx_sbdownloader/guidePostalTranspor tEn.pdf> accessed 15 November 2021.

shipping company. From an accounting perspective, the UPU CN37 Delivery bill for surface mail is the basis for payment from the post initiating the consignment to the carrier.

The international law for the carriage of goods by rail – including COTIF/CIM 1999 (in force since 1 July 2006) and the revised SMGS (in force since 1 July 2015) – in view of the booming e-commerce, legally enable cross-border transportation of goods, without any restrictions for postal items.[43] The monopoly of the postal authorities to transport postal items has been removed and now their cross-border carriage falls within scope of application of the CIM Uniform Rules (CIM UR – Appendix B to COTIF) and the SMGS.[44] Providing the consignor, consignee and carrier so agree, the CIM UR also allow to organize a cross-border carriage under the CIM UR, where either the place of handing over or the places of taking over of the goods is located in a COTIF Member State.

In the times of booming e-commerce and with the growing interest in alternatives to carriage of postal items by air and by sea, the UPU and the Coordinating Council on Trans-Siberian Transportation (CCTT) initiated a pilot project on carriage of postal items from China to Europe by rail. To this end, two workshops were held in collaboration between the UPU and the CCTT and with the participation of the CIT and the interested stakeholders, one in Bern (17 March 2016), and one in Moscow (24–25 May 2016). The CIT documents for freight transport, and in particular the CIM/SMGS common consignment note, were recognized as a perfect tool for the seamless handling of the transcontinental carriage of postal items both for the pilot project and on regular basis.

To ensure that the business model of carriage of postal items by rail succeeds, close cooperation between the states and the railway undertakings involved will be required. On 18 March 2016 at the UPU's headquarters in Bern, the three international organizations (UPU, CIT and CCTT) signed a Memorandum of Understanding (MoU) on the collaboration in providing support for the planned pilot projects of postal items' carriage from China to Europe. To facilitate the smooth operation of the pilot projects, the experts of the Universal Postal Union (UPU) and the CIT have prepared a document summarizing the necessary framework conditions from the perspective of the

---

43   According to the February 2015 issue of DVZ, the German newspaper for the transport and industry, the Chinese online commerce company Alibaba reported a 40% increase in revenue year on year 2013 – 2014 to USD4.2 billion. Online shoppers in Europe, on the other hand, triggered 3.7 billion parcel deliveries in 2013, see ITJ February 2015 issue, 16.

44   See also the article on the carriage of express parcels by H. Trolliet, CIT-Info 3/2012, 11.

rail transport law. Both the CIT and the CCTT will continue providing support to participating stakeholders on the questions of applicable international rail transport law.

The use of the CIM/SMGS consignment note for the transcontinental carriage of postal items was at the forefront of successful implementation of the pilot projects and its use shall be continued for such transport on regular basis. The CIM/SMGS Consignment Note Manual additionally offers railway companies CIT members and SMGS participants, which are enlisted in the Appendix 1 to the Manual, a possibility of using standard transport documents, provided such an arrangement has been agreed on between the customer and the carrier, and between the participating carriers themselves. The use of the CIM/SMGS consignment note is regarded as an agreement. In the SMGS area, the provisions of the Manual apply only to traffic axes determined by those SMGS participants who use this manual (Item 4 of the GLV-CIM/SMGS and Appendix 6 of the SMGS that came into force on 1 July 2015).[45]

Recent statistical data confirms that there is significant potential for transport of postal items between China and Europe by rail. According to the CCTT, the volume of postal traffic between the People's Republic of China and the Russian Federation came to 64,000 tonnes in 2013, equivalent to about 8,000 containers. Based on this data, the annual increase of carriage of freight is estimated at 10–15%, resulting in approximately 400,000 containers in transit from China to Europe.

An initial pilot transport of a container of postal consignments between Chongqing/China and Duisburg/Germany was launched by China Post and Deutsche Post (DHL DE) and was successfully carried out between 29th September and 13th October in the collaboration with the UPU and the CCTT. The main task of such pilot transports is to test compliance with and identify any hurdles related to customs formalities – in particular, at the external border of the EU. Table 1 provides a detailed information about this first pilot project. Finally, with the recent affiliation of La Poste (France) the project gained a truly pan-European dimension.

The use of CIM/SMGS consignment note, as indicated above, plays an important practical role for the compliance with the customs formalities. Currently, within the EU rail carriers can use the paper-based procedure for customs transit by rail through EU customs territory in the so-called 'co-operation mode'. In practice, this can be done by using the CIM or the CIM/SMGS consignment

---

45   Erik Evtimov, 'Mail by Rail from China to Western Europe: A New Business Model for Rail',
        CIT-Info 2/2017, 2–3.

TABLE 1   Initial pilot transport of a container of postal consignments between Chongqing/
China and Duisburg/Germany

Rail	Average speed	Distance	Travel time	Operators/ Freight forwarders	Route
CRCT	37km/h or 888 km/day.	3907 km	105 h 55 min	YuXinOu Logistics Company Ltd	*Chongqing (29.09)* - Alashankou (03.10)
KTZ	47 km/h or 1128 km/day.	2937 km	62 h 50 min	UTLC/ JSC RZD logistics/ KTZ Express	Dostyk (03.10) - Iletsk (06.10)
RZD	41 km/h or 984 km/day.	2058 km	50 h 15 min	UTLC/ JSC RZD logistics	Kanisai (06.10) – Krasnoe(08.10)
Bel Railway	17 km/h or 408 km/day.	609 km	35 h 10 min	UTLC/ JSC RZD logistics	Osinovka (08.10) – Brest (10.10)
PKP	Information requested	1160 km (Brest- Duisburg)	Information requested	DB CARGO POLSKA SA	Terespol (10.10) Malashevichi (11.10)-
DB AG	Information requested		Information requested	DB CARGO AG	*Duisburg (13.10) - Niederaula (13.10)*

SOURCE: CIT AND CCTT

note. Otherwise, the New Computerized Transit System (NCTS) will apply. For
the purpose of transportation of postal items, the EU customs territory forms
a single territory for the purpose of transit by post.[46] The use of the common
consignment note both as a transport document and as a customs transit document reduces administrative burden, saves costs and time and thus is at the
heart of trade facilitation in the rail transport sector.

---

46   Item 4.2.6 of the EU Transit Manual.

4   Conclusions

The TFA, similarly to some other WTO Agreements, including the Agreement on Technical Barriers to Trade and the Agreement on Sanitary and Phytosanitary Measures encourages WTO Members to use relevant international standards as a basis for their import, export, or transit formalities and procedures. Also the newly created Committee on Trade Facilitation is entrusted with a task to facilitate the sharing of information on such international standards. Given the fact that the common consignment note CIM/SMGS was prepared on the basis of the UN Layout Key, it arguably constitutes an international standard for the rail transport documents.

The common CIM/SMGS consignment note is a remarkable success story. Applied on more than 50 axis in 4 Trans-European Transport Network (TEN) corridors it ensures much more reliable and expedient international rail freight traffic that can easily compete with maritime transport. In recent years it was applied on long-distance transcontinental routes from China to Western Europe. In addition, the CIT is exploring together with its member railway companies further opportunities of utilizing the CIM/SMGS consignment note for multimodal (sea-rail) transport, mainly on the Baltic Sea and the Black Sea. To this end, the CIT Group of Experts on Multimodality prepared Special Transport Conditions for Sea-Rail Traffic that can be applied by rail and sea transport companies on contractual basis. Notwithstanding these very positive developments, freight traffic by rail between Europe, Russia and Asia still has a significant development potential, since only 1% of it has been captured so far. Thus, the long-term objective is a single regime for transport law from the Atlantic to the Pacific. A single framework of international rail transport law can contribute significantly to a further reduction in transport costs and the acceleration of traffic flows. It will contribute to the growth of traffic of goods along Eurasian corridors. This initiative, however, requires the involvement of states and the respective international organizations. In parallel the railway industry associations make their technical expertise available and in doing so they will help legislators to find appropriate technical solutions.

The creation of a harmonized international legal framework has been declared a long term legal and political goal for the next ten to fifteen years. The Political Declaration on Euroasian Rail Transport Law was signed in February 2013 by 37 representatives of the participating countries, which committed to officially start activities on harmonization of rail transport law within the UN framework. In addition, the Declaration invited all interested railway freight companies, other stakeholders and international railway organizations to develop interim standard rules for Euroasian rail transport contracts. Thus, whilst waiting for the states to create this new uniform legal framework the UNECE is encouraging railway companies and trade associations to agree on harmonised solutions that can be used on contractual basis. The third phase of the project "Legal Interoperability CIM/SMGS" is particularly aimed at the creation of standard rules for uniform rail transport law on contractual basis. Within this third phase, the CIT together with the CCTT and in close co-operation with other stakeholders prepared the General Terms and Conditions EurAsia (GTC EurAsia), which provide railway companies with an additional contractual legal basis, allowing them to transport freight between Europe and Asia with more legal certainty for the customers and the carriers. The use of the common CIM/SMGS consignment note still remains at the core of simplification and harmonization of transport formalities between Asia and Europe. With the adoption of the uniform rail transport law, the next step would be to move from the CIM/SMGS consignment not to a uniform consignment note, that will be prepared based on the new yet to be drafted legal framework. But until then, the CIM/SMGS consignment note remains the viable international standard.

Most recently, the WCO, in its updated version of the WCO Transit Guidelines, referred to the use of the CIM and CIM/SMGS consignment notes as transit documents as an example of best practice of the WCO Member States. With further growth of e-commerce and the development of a new railway infrastructure according to China's One Belt One Road initiative, the interest in existing ready-to-use well-functioning solutions will be even stronger.[47] The common consignment note CIM/SMGS will play a key role in facilitation of transport of goods by rail and thus trade facilitation on the Eurasian Land Bridge.

47 President Xi Jinping's speech at the 19th Party Congress in Beijing: 'China adheres to the fundamental national policy of opening up and pursues development with its doors open wide. China will actively promote international cooperation through the 'Belt and Road Initiative'. In doing so, we hope to achieve policy, infrastructure, trade, financial, and people-to-people connectivity and thus build a new platform for international cooperation to create new drivers of shared development.' Source: *Xinhua News* (English Translation).

SECTION 4

Environmental Issues

∴

Trade and Environment in the Region of the Caucasus and Central Asia: The Case of Hazardous Waste

Andreas R. Ziegler

1   Introduction

Despite temporary setbacks and a very uneven integration of various regions into the globalized economy, we speak today of global supply (or value) chains for the production of goods (and increasingly services).[1] They are based on the general concept that specialization leads to the possibility of producing larger quantities and thereby achieving economies of scale.[2] This specialization is thus considered to lead to a more efficient production and the possibility of achieving growth and increased welfare. This principle can be applied locally and within States (internal market) but also across political borders, which requires trans-border economic activities and leads to increased international trade flows, be it within a specific region or globally.[3]

Based on these very basic principles, States have tried to eliminate obstacles to international trade. The fight against protectionism is one aspect of this liberalization of international trade flows but other policy goals may also lead to the hindrance of international trade flows. Traditionally many States relied on the income from customs duties to finance government activities (and many developing states still do) and the elimination of such customs duties is a typical objective of trade negotiations. While the financing of government activities as such is not questioned, the use of customs duties shall be eliminated to reduce the negative effects on trade that they have. As a result,

---

1   See, for example, John Humphrey, 'Governance in global value chains' (2001) *IDS Bulletin* 32.3, 19–29.
2   See, for example, Peter K. Schott, 'Across-product versus Within-product Specialization in International Trade' (2004) 119.2 The Quarterly Journal of Economics 647–678.
3   See, for example, Geoffrey Garrett, 'International Cooperation and Institutional Choice: The European Community's Internal Market' (1992) International Organization 533–560.

States must usually find other ways to finance their activities, e.g. internal non-discriminatory taxation.[4]

The same consequences may result from border and domestic measures that States use to regulate certain policy areas. Governments have always been aware of the fact that, while it is absolutely indispensable for the authorities to take measures to protect the population from certain risks (e.g. sanitary and phytosanitary risk or fraud), the measures chosen may also impact trade flows. As a consequence, States typically try to reduce the trade effects of such regulatory measures in trade negotiations by promoting those measures that are least trade-restrictive or outlawing certain measures that are particularly distortive.[5] Of course this process can be difficult as there are fears that it may lead to the elimination of important regulatory measures that safeguard important policy goals for the sake of increased trade (race to the bottom).[6] On the other side, there is often a fear that a specific non-trade issue is invoked to take measures that in reality are intended to protect domestic industry (hidden or disguised protectionism).[7]

In particular, in the area of environment protection, this general tension has led to an extensive discussion – normally under the title "Trade and Environment".[8] Environmental policy, strictly speaking, has become a much more important part of most Governments' activities since the late 1960s and at the international level has become an area of international negotiations only since the 1970s. In the framework of multilateral negotiations, it is mostly since the 1980s that the potential risk of "green protectionism"[9] on one side and the dangers stemming from the negotiated elimination of certain environmental measures because of their trade effects on the other side, has crystallized in an

---

4   See, for example, David Greenaway and Chris Milner, 'Fiscal Dependence on Trade Taxes and Trade Policy Reform' (1991) 27.3 The Journal of Development Studies 95–132.

5   See, for example, Paul Krugman, 'What Should Trade Negotiators Negotiate about?' (1997) 35.1 Journal of Economic Literature 113–120.

6   See, for example, Gareth Porter, 'Trade Competition and Pollution Standards: "Race to the Bottom" or "Stuck at the Bottom"' (1999) 8.2 The Journal of Environment & Development 133–151.

7   See, for example, Thilo Glebe, EU Agri-Environmental Payments: Appropriate Policy or Protectionism in Disguise? (2005) available at <https://escholarship.org/uc/item/0719f4st> accessed 22 November 2021.

8   See Andreas R. Ziegler, Trade and Environmental Law in the European Community. (Clarendon Press 1996).

9   See, for example, Hugh R. Campbell and Brad L. Coombes, 'Green Protectionism and Organic Food Exporting from New Zealand: Crisis Experiments in the Breakdown of Fordist Trade and Agricultural Policies' (1999) 64.2 Rural Sociology 302–319.

intensive debate[10] and a number of known cases before international tribunals and dispute settlement bodies.[11]

This is mostly due to the increased awareness for environmental problems (locally and globally), e.g. in the case of hazardous waste that will be analysed in this Chapter, on one side and more ambitious trade liberalization measures once a substantive elimination of tariffs is achieved on the other side. A similar development has taken place in the area of investment negotiations where more recently the debate on "Investment and the Environment"[12] is also intensifying and cases before international arbitral tribunals highlight the potential tension between the "Right to regulate"[13] – as it is often referred to in the specific investment agreements – and environmental concerns of contracting parties to international agreements.

2   **The Peculiarities of Waste and the General Principles Underlying the Trade Liberalization in the Area of Goods**

The treatment of waste in general and of hazardous waste in particular, is a typical example where the protection of consumers, the environment and the public in general usually require government action. The associated risks generally lead, in developed States, to an extensive control of the handling, recycling and, in particular disposal of waste.[14] It is generally admitted that in this

---

10   See eg Rolf Weder and Andreas R. Ziegler, 'Economic Integration and the Choice of National Environmental Policies' (2002) 13:3 European Journal of Law and Economics 239–256; or Gene M. Grossman and Alan B. Krueger, 'Environmental Impacts of a North American Free Trade Agreement', No. w3914 (National Bureau of Economic Research, 1991).

11   See Andreas R Ziegler, 'The Environmental Provisions of the World Trade Organization (WTO)' in Friedl Weiss (ed), *International Economic Law with a Human Face*, (Kluwer 1998) 203–222; and more recently Philippe Sands and Jacqueline Peel, *Principles of International Environmental Law* (CUP 2012) 175ff; and James Watson, *The WTO and the Environment: Development of Competence beyond Trade* (Routledge, 2012).

12   See Ene Sebastian George, 'The Foreign Direct Investment-Investment Environment Relationship' (2012) 12.1 Ovidius University Annals, Economic Sciences Series 1414–1418 and Saverio Di Benedetto, *International Investment Law and the Environment* (Edward Elgar Publishing 2013).

13   See, for example, Caroline Henckels, 'Indirect Expropriation and the Right to Regulate: Revisiting Proportionality Analysis and the Standard of Review in Investor-State Arbitration' (2012) 15.1 Journal of International Economic Law 223–255.

14   See for example, R. G. P. Hawkins and H. S. Shaw, *The Practical Guide to Waste Management Law: With a List of Abbreviations and Acronyms, Useful Websites and Relevant Legislation* (Thomas Telford 2004).

area specific regulation is needed. Most often this is done through prohibitions of certain activities and the delivery of permits to approved agents. While such a regulation on the territory of a State (domestic regulation) may impact trade flows, it is usually not problematic if it is undertaken in a non-discriminatory and transparent way. This also corresponds to the regulations normally found in international, regional and bilateral trade agreements, when it comes to permits and the regulation of processes; in particular the most-favoured-nation (MFN) principle and the requirement of national treatment found in most agreements are usually interpreted as leaving enough policy discretion to justify non-discriminatory measures in this respect.[15] In recent years more and more agreements include stringent obligations to publish all information regarding such (environmental and other) regulations in a way that is easily accessible for importers and exporters worldwide.[16] This may constitute a certain bureaucratic burden.[17]

When it comes to specific import and export restrictions regarding goods, including environmentally sensitive ones like (hazardous) waste, most international trade agreements are much more specific. While the progressive elimination and non-discriminatory application of customs duties is normally not at stake, in particular the elimination of typical non-tariff obstacles like quotas can be seen as a stumbling block at first sight. Article XI GATT as well as Article 34 of the Treaty on the Functioning of the European Union (TFEU) are typical examples of provisions in international trade agreements, which have the general objective to totally eliminate quantitative restrictions (including total bans and quotas). Nevertheless, the outright prohibitions must be read in conjunction with the (general) exceptions normally provided for in these agreements, which leave room to maintain or even (re)introduce (new) trade restrictions in specific cases, such as to protect the health and life of human beings or the

---

15   Such as, for example, in the case of Articles I and III of the General Agreement on Tariffs and Trade (GATT). Other provisions in this Agreement and other multilateral trade agreements of the WTO contain these principles for more specific measures.

16   See for example the transparency obligations of the Agreement on Sanitary and Phytosanitary Measures (SPS-Agreement) of the WTO contained in art 5.8, art 7 and Annex B. In addition, the WTO's SPS Committee has elaborated recommended procedures for implementing the transparency obligations of the SPS Agreement (G/SPS/7/Rev.2). See also art X GATT which requires WTO Members to promptly publish laws, regulations, judicial decisions and administrative rulings of general application, including those pertaining to requirements on imports or exports and to administer them in a uniform, impartial and reasonable manner.

17   See Terry Collins-Williams and Robert Wolfe, 'Transparency as a Trade Policy Tool: The WTO's Cloudy Windows' (2010) 9.4 World Trade Review 551–581.

environment. Some observers regret the fact that only the application of an exception provision allows for the implementation of such measures, but that is basically due to the main rationale of these trade agreements and must not necessarily lead to an unsatisfactory balance between trade liberalization and environmental policy concerns. What must be noted, however, is that these expectations normally require an objective assessment of the risk at stake and a reasonable link between the risks and the quantitative measure taken.[18] In addition many modern trade agreements (including the WTO) include very specific conditions regarding all measures that have trade effects and whose rationale is the protection of human, animal and plant life and health (sanitary and phytosanitary [SPS] measures).[19] Even import permits (import licensing), which may be quasi-automatic or dependent on the fulfilment of specific conditions, are normally, these days, subject to specific disciplines in international trade agreements, and in particular within the WTO. For example, the WTO Agreement on Import Licensing Procedures says import licensing should be simple, transparent and predictable so as not to become an obstacle to trade.

3 The Use of Special Regimes Regarding Certain Goods: E.g. the Basel Convention

When it comes to the handling and trade of waste, one can trace the development of a special regime for hazardous waste back to the 1980s. During this time, a number of incidents led to concerns that certain regions might be used to dump waste from other regions in an inappropriate way and that thus the market-based specialisation referred to earlier in this chapter was not an adequate approach or at least needed some additional disciplines to avoid undesirable results and outcomes.

The famous Seveso disaster took off in 1976 in Italy when a fire broke out in a small chemical manufacturing plant north of Milan in the Lombardy region in Italy. Apart from the exposure of the local population to toxic substances, the waste from the clean-up of the plant was a mixture of protective clothing and chemical residues from the plant. Instead of being legally disposed of, as agreed among the companies involved, in 1983 the barrels containing the

---

18   See the abundant literature on art XX GATT.
19   See, for example, Lukasz Gruszczynski, *Regulating Health and Environmental Risks Under WTO Law: A Critical Analysis of the SPS Agreement* (OUP 2010).

waste disappeared for a while in Northern France before being incinerated in Switzerland.[20]

A second incident that started in 1986 is normally referred to as the Khian Sea Waste Disposal Incident 1986. The cargo ship Khian Sea, registered in Liberia, was loaded with more than 14,000 tons of non-toxic ash from waste incinerators in the United States and the company handling the waste struggled to find a place for disposal. After many States had refused to allow the landing of the waste, in January 1988, the crew finally dumped 4,000 tons of the waste in Haiti as "topsoil fertilizer".[21]

These and other incidents led to negotiations for an international treaty to better control transboundary movements of hazardous wastes and their disposal, resulting in the adoption of the Basel Convention on the Control of Transboundary Movements of Hazardous Wastes and Their Disposal (1989/1992) on 22 March 1989 by the Conference of Plenipotentiaries in Basel (Switzerland).[22] The main goals of this Convention were to reduce the movements of hazardous waste between Parties, and specifically to prevent the transfer of hazardous waste from developed to less developed countries (LDCs).[23] Contrary to the normal situation where specialization and the resulting trade are seen positively, the risk of shipping hazardous waste and disposing of it in an inappropriate way (especially in developing countries) were seen as justifying such an approach.

As of November 2020, 187 states and the European Union are parties to the Convention. The United States has signed the Convention but not ratified it. Also, most States in the Caucasus region and Central Asia have acceded to the treaty, e.g. Azerbaijan: 1st of June 2001 (Accession); Armenia: 1st of October 1999 (Accession), Georgia: 20 May 1999 (Accession); Kazakhstan: 3 June 2003 (Accession), and The Russian Federation: 31 January 1995 (Accession).

Technically the original Convention invited Member States to apply stringent requirements for notice, consent and tracking of the movement of wastes across national boundaries. Parties shall prohibit or shall not permit the export of hazardous wastes and other wastes to the Parties that have prohibited the

---

20   See Ivan Vince, *Major Accidents to the Environment: A Practical Guide to the Seveso II-Directive and COMAH Regulations* (Butterworth-Heinemann 2011).

21   See Marguerite M. Cusack, 'International Law and the Transboundary Shipment of Hazardous Waste to the Third World: Will the Basel Convention Make a Difference' (1989) 5 Am U J Intl L & Poly 393ff.

22   <www.basel.int/portals/4/basel%20convention/docs/text/baselconventiontext-e.pdf> accessed on 22 November 2021. See Katharina Kummer, *International Management of Hazardous Wastes* (Clarendon Press 1995).

23   It does not, however, address the movement of radioactive waste.

import of such wastes (Article 4 Paragraph 1 Letter b). Parties shall also prevent the import of hazardous wastes and other wastes if they have reason to believe that the wastes in question will not be managed in an environmentally sound manner (Article 4 Paragraph 2 Letter g).

In addition, the Convention places a general prohibition on the exportation or importation of wastes between Parties and non-Parties (Article 4 Paragraph 5). The exception to this rule is where the waste is subject to another treaty that does not take away from the Basel Convention. The United States is a notable non-Party to the Convention and has a number of such agreements (in particular with all OECD countries) for allowing the shipping of hazardous wastes to Basel Party countries.

These and other provisions of the Convention require States to adopt import and export licensing procedures that usually fall under the respective disciplines of trade agreements that a Party may have concluded, including the WTO. Normally, it should be possible to apply them in a non-discriminatory and transparent manner, as typically required, to reduce unnecessary obstacles to trade. Apart from the explicit reference to the possibility that Members introduce import restrictions, the outright prohibition to allow trade with non-parties to the Basel Convention (export restrictions) may be more problematic. The European Union fully implemented the Basel Ban in its Waste Shipment Regulation (EWSR),[24] making it legally binding in all EU member states.

Generally, the efficiency of the Basel Convention has not been too heavily criticized. Nevertheless, isolated incidents have come to the forefront. A particularly famous incident constituted the so-called 2006 Ivory Coast Toxic Waste Dump Incident. The unauthorized disposal of toxic hazardous waste led to a health crisis in Côte d'Ivoire. A ship registered in Panama, the *Probo Koala*, chartered by the Dutch-based oil and commodity shipping company Trafigura Beheer BV had offloaded the waste before the waste was then dumped by a local contractor at as many as 12 sites in and around the city of Abidjan in August 2006. In subsequent criminal and administrative proceedings Trafigura agreed on 13 February 2007 to pay the Ivorian government £100 million (USD 198m) for the clean-up of the waste. On 23 July 2010 Trafigura were fined €1 million by the Dutch authorities for the transit of the waste through Amsterdam before being taken to the Côte d'Ivoire to be dumped, plus later settlement. Trafigura's chairman, Claude Dauphin, accepted in 2012 a €67,000 fine. Furthermore, the settlement obliged Trafigura to pay an additional €300,000 – the money it

---

24   Regulation (EC) No 1013/2006 of the European Parliament and of the Council of 14 June
      2006 on shipments of waste. Norway and Switzerland have similarly fully implemented
      the Basel Ban in their legislation.

saved by dumping the toxic waste in Abidjan rather than having it properly disposed of in the Netherlands.[25]

4   Potential Conflicts

This problem of export restrictions to, and import restrictions from, certain States without their consent has been exacerbated by the negotiations of additional rules prohibiting exports to certain regions. The original Convention did not prohibit waste exports to any location other than Antarctica (Article 4 Paragraph 6: The Parties agree not to allow the export of hazardous wastes or other wastes for disposal within the area south of 60 South latitude, whether or not such wastes are subject to transboundary movement), except if States were non-parties to the Basel Convention or had themselves banned the imports. In 1995, however, the so-called (Basel) Ban Amendment (to the Basel Convention) was adopted. The amendment has been accepted by 73 countries and the European Union, but it has not entered into force (as this requires ratification by 3/4 of the member states to the Convention).[26] The Amendment prohibits the export of hazardous waste from a list of developed (mostly OECD) countries to developing countries. It should be noted that the Member States of what is now the Organisation of African Union (OAU; formerly Organisation of African States [OAS]), has itself adopted the so-called Bamako-Convention of 1991[27] which equally prohibits the import of certain types of hazardous waste.

The tensions that may exist between specific obligations not to import/ export certain goods from/to specific States, due to their legal or economic status (non-party, LDC etc.), have been recognized for a considerable time within the WTO. As a consequence, the WTO was, and still is, mandated under paragraph 31(i) of the WTO 2001 Doha Ministerial Declaration to consider the

---

25   See Liesbeth Enneking, 'The Common Denominator of the Trafigura Case, Foreign Direct Liability Cases and the Rome II Regulation' (2008) 16(2) European Review of Private Law 283–312; Laura AW Pratt, 'Decreasing Dirty Dumping – A Re-evaluation of Toxic Waste Colonialism and the Global Management of Transboundary Hazardous Waste' (2010) 35 Wm & Mary Envtl L & Poly Rev 581; Amnesty International, *The Toxic Truth* (London 2012).

26   A controversy exists regarding whether the calculation of ¾ of all members must be based on the number of parties at the time of the adoption of the amendment or the current number of parties.

27   Bamako Convention on the Ban on the Import into Africa and the Control of Transboundary Movement and Management of Hazardous Wastes within Africa, adopted on 30 January 1991. It also prohibits the import of radioactive waste and entered into force on 22 April 1998.

relationship between WTO rules and "specific trade obligations" set out in Multilateral Environmental Agreements (MEAs), such as the Basel Convention. The WTO Secretariat and various Secretariats of MEAs have undertaken activities to strengthen the information exchange and common reflection, but no conclusive analysis has been undertaken regarding the compatibility of the Basel Convention trade regime with the WTO.[28] In another situation, WTO Members have adopted a specific waiver to avoid any incompatibilities stemming from a system involving import/export permits and trade restrictions regarding non-parties. This is, for example, the case for the so-called Kimberley Process Certification Scheme (KPCS) to prevent the trade in "conflict or blood diamonds" to be used for the financing of civil wars and atrocities in Africa. The WTO waiver decision would exempt – from 1 January 2003 until 31 December 2006 – trade measures taken under the Kimberley Process by these 11 members and other members that would subsequently join from GATT provisions on most-favoured-nation treatment (Article I:1), elimination of quantitative restrictions (Article XI:1) and non-discriminatory administration of quantitative restrictions (Article XIII:1).[29] The waiver was extended in 2006, 2012 and then in 2018 (until 2024).[30]

Under paragraph 31(iii) of the 2001 WTO Doha Ministerial Declaration, the WTO is also mandated to negotiate "the reduction or, as appropriate, elimination of tariff and non-tariff barriers to environmental goods and services". A considerable debate has arisen as to which goods can be considered environmental goods. This is particularly interesting with regard to (hazardous waste) in light of the parallel debate on the controversial concept of "Green Economy".[31] This concept underlines that the recycling of (hazardous) waste

---

28   For a summary of the activities involving the WTO and the Basel Convention see the respective web page of the Basel Convention at: <http://archive.basel.int/trade/> accessed 22 November 2021; These questions are analysed in detail in Mirina Grosz, *Sustainable Waste Trade under WTO Law: Chances and Risks of the Legal Frameworks' Regulation of Transboundary Movements of Waste* (Nijhoff 2010).

29   WTO Council for Trade in Goods, *Waiver Concerning Kimberley Process Certification Scheme for Rough Diamonds, Communication from Canada, Japan and Sierra Leone,* G/C/W/431 (12 November 2002).

30   WTO, *Extension of Waiver Concerning Kimberley Process Certification Scheme for Rough Diamonds, Waiver Decision of 26 July 2018,* WT/L/1039 <https://docs.wto.org/dol2fe/Pages/SS/directdoc.aspx?filename=q:/WT/L/1039.pdf&Open=True> accessed 11 February 2021.

31   See Lakshmi Raghupathy and Ashish Chaturvedi 'Secondary Resources and Recycling in Developing Economies' (2013) Science of the Total Environment 830–834; Sean Connelly, Sean Markey and Mark Roseland, 'We Know Enough: Achieving Action Through the Convergence of Sustainable Community Development and the Social Economy' in Richard Simpson and Monika Zimmermann (eds) *The Economy of Green Cities: A World Compendium on the Green Urban Economy* (Springer 2013) 191–203.

can be a very ecological and economically attractive activity at the same time. Some authors argue, therefore, that the recycling of, and associated trade in waste should be revisited and that bans may not always be justified or may lead to sub-optimal results.[32]

5   Conclusions

The international trading regime is highly fragmented. This is not only due to the increasing number of bilateral and regional agreements and the perceived weaknesses of the WTO, but also due to the specific regimes that exist for various goods. Environmental concerns justify the existence of specific rules for (hazardous) waste, but the coordination with the multilateral rules is sub-optimal and leads to many controversies and uncertainties which, especially for developing countries, can become stumbling blocks in their internal reform projects and with regard to the optimal planning of their economic strategies. The fragmentation and the resulting uncertainties regarding the compatibility of various regimes may be less acute when the memberships in these instruments is large and more or less identical (as is the case with the WTO and the original Basel Convention), but it becomes highly problematic when important actors (like in this case the United States) are not involved in all regimes concerned or if new developments lead to further fragmentation (like the Ban Amendment).

32   European Environment Agency, EEA Report No 8/2011, *Earnings, Jobs and Innovation: The Role of Recycling in a Green Economy* (2011); Kummer, Katharina and Andreas R. Ziegler (eds), *Waste Management and the Green Economy: Law and Policy* (Edward Elgar 2016).

PART 2

The Perspective of Private Law

∴

Some Notes on the Law of Sales Contracts in the Region of the Caucasus and Central Asia

Alexander Trunk

Sales contracts are the most fundamental and most widely used types of contract and lie at the basis of national and international private trade law. Which characteristics can be seen in the field of sales contracts legislation in the Caucasus-Central Asia region? In view of the size of the subject, the following contribution can give only an initial overview and raise some issues for discussion. The contribution is limited to substantive law; it will not cover matters of conflict of laws.

1   **Legal Sources: Civil Codes and Special Legislation**

As the law in all countries of the region is based on the codification-type continental European model, sales law is primarily regulated in the respective Civil Codes.[1] Although the majority of these Civil Codes is based on the CIS Model Civil Code,[2] there are some differences even within this group of legislations. In the case of Azerbaijan, one can observe a gradual movement of the Civil Code of Azerbaijan away from the CIS Model Code towards Western European approaches with a certain inclination for German law. Completely independent from the CIS Model Code are the sales contracts provisions in the Georgian Civil Code of 26 June 1997, which closely follow the model of the German Civil Code (*Bürgerliches Gesetzbuch*). The Georgian model itself has been nearly literally followed by the Civil Code of Turkmenistan of 17 June 1998.[3]

---

1   In all countries of the region there is a considerable amount of jurisprudence interpreting the Civil Codes and other legislation. Due to limitation of space, jurisprudence cannot be analysed in this chapter.
2   The provisions on sales contracts are laid down in Part 2 of the Model Civil Code of 13 May 1995, Chapter 30, arts 449–535, <https://iacis.ru/upload/iblock/3df/model_gk_part2_g4.pdf> (in Russian) accessed 7 July 2021.
3   <www.minjust.gov.tm/ru/mmerkezi/doc_book_det.php?book_id=2> (in Russian) accessed 7 July 2021.

Besides the provisions in the Civil Codes, all countries (except to a smaller degree Georgia) have passed additional legislation on specific kinds of sales, supplementing the Civil Code provisions. Typical examples are particular Codes for certain economic areas such as Land Codes, Water Codes or Forest Codes, but also special legislation in the field of state contracts, consumer contracts, contracts for the sale of securities, energy contracts, and others.[4] The question of the relationship between such special legislation and the Civil Codes has to be answered in every specific case, which may cause problems of interpretation. A particular case is special legislation on international sales. Most countries of the Caucasus and Central Asia area – except Kazakhstan, Tajikistan and Turkmenistan[5] – have ratified the UN Convention on the International Sale of Goods of 1980.

While in several countries of the region there is currently a process of far-going modernization of the existing Civil Codes, this has not yet (or only to a small degree) reached the special part of the law of obligations. In particular, up to now, no proposals to fundamentally modify the existing provisions on sales contracts have been announced. "Europeanization" of sales law, for example along the lines of the 2008 Draft Common Frame of Reference [for European Private Law] (DCFR) is not a topic of discussion in the region at the moment, but this might change in the future as the DCFR has recently been published in Russian.[6]

2   Overview of Contents

2.1   CIS Model Civil Code Based Systems

The sales law provisions in the region, which are based on the CIS Model Code (Armenia, Kazakhstan, Kyrgyzstan, Russia, Tajikistan, Uzbekistan, and basically also Azerbaijan), are very detailed[7] and differentiate between a broad range of specific sales contracts. They all start with general provisions

---

4 The new Entrepreneurial Code of Kazakhstan of 29 October 2015 deals mostly with matters of administrative law; it is not a Commercial Code in the sense of the respective Codes in Germany and France, see <http://online.zakon.kz/m/Document/?doc_id=38259854#pos=3; -3&sel_link=1004794779_3> accessed 7 July 2021.

5 See <https://uncitral.un.org/en/texts/salegoods/conventions/sale_of_goods/cisg/status> accessed 7 July 2021. Azerbaijan acceded to the CISG on 1 June 2017.

6 Nataliya Rasskazova, *Model'nye pravila evropejskogo chastnogo prava* [Model Rules of European Private Law] (translated from English, Statut 2013).

7 The CIS Model Code contains 95 articles (arts 449–534), the Civil Code of Kazakhstan 94 articles (arts 406–500), the Civil Code of Uzbekistan 110 articles (arts 386–496).

on sales contracts (e.g. Articles 567–607 of the Civil Code of Azerbaijan) and add, typically, specific provisions on consumer sales (Articles 488–499 Model Civil Code), commercial sales (*postavka,* Articles 500 – 515 Model Civil Code), delivery of energy (Articles 516–526 Model Civil Code), and sales of enterprises (Articles 527–534 Model Civil Code). There are also specific provisions (often) in the Civil Codes and in the special Land Codes on sales of immovables (see e.g. Articles 646–658 Civil Code of Azerbaijan; Articles 561–570 Civil Code of Armenia; Articles 549–558 Civil Code of Russia). Some codes also provide special provisions for agricultural sales (*kontraktatsija,* e.g. Articles 535–538 Civil Code of Russia; Articles 478–481 Civil Code of Kazakhstan; Articles 465–567 Civil Code of Uzbekistan)[8] and state contracts[9] (Articles 525–534 Civil Code of Russia; Articles 457–461 Civil Code of Uzbekistan; Articles 562–568 Civil Code of Tajikistan). Azerbaijan has also passed particular provisions on sales of claims or other rights (Articles 651–654.2 Civil Code of Azerbaijan) with separate provisions on factoring (Articles 655–657.10 Civil Code of Azerbaijan[10]). All Civil Codes also provide specific provisions on exchange contracts, referring subsidiarily to sales contracts (see, e.g. Articles 662–665 Civil Code of Azerbaijan).[11]

2.2   *"German Model" Based Systems*

The "German model" based sales laws of Georgia and Turkmenistan are much shorter. The Georgian and the Turkmen Civil Codes essentially provide only provisions for sales contracts in general (Articles 477–504 Civil Code of Georgia; Articles 501–528 Civil Code of Turkmenistan) with minor particular provisions on installment purchases,[12] repurchases[13] and rights of preemption.[14] Azerbaijan has also adopted similar provisions of a seemingly German background as to purchases on approval (Articles 658–658.4 Civil Code of Azerbaijan) and rights of preemption (Articles 659–661 Civil Code of

---

8   Azerbaijan has a related specific sales type for "sales of livestock, birds and fish", arts 608–613 Civil Code of Azerbaijan.

9   State contracts are often additionally regulated in specific legislation.

10   The odd numbering shows that these are later amendments to the Code. In some other countries, factoring is regulated outside the sales law chapter in the credit relationships context, eg in Russia in arts 824–833 Russian Civil Code ("financing with assignment of money claims").

11   The "German model" based Codes of Georgia and Turkmenistan treat exchange contracts as a variant of sales contracts, cf. arts 521–523 Civil Code of Georgia.

12   Arts 505–508 Civil Code of Georgia; arts 529–532 Civil Code of Turkmenistan.

13   Arts 509–515 Civil Code of Georgia; arts 433–538 Civil Code of Turkmenistan.

14   Arts 516–520 Civil Code of Georgia; arts 540 – 544 Civil Code of Turkmenistan.

Azerbaijan). An interesting detail is that both the Georgian and the Turkmen Civil Code contain explicit provisions on contractual options (Article 515 Civil Code of Georgia; Article 539 Civil Code of Turkmenistan).[15] Specifics of sales of land, state contracts and other particular situations are sometimes governed by legislation outside the Civil Codes.[16]

3   Systematic Context

As the Civil Codes of all countries of the region are based on the pandectist tradition, the provisions on sales contracts must be read in conjunction with the general parts of the Codes and general provisions on the law of obligations, which are distinct (with some overlap) from property law (*Sachenrecht*). However, the spheres of these parts of the Codes are to a certain degree intertwined, for example when general provisions on contracts have to be applied in combination with specific provisions on sales contracts (e.g. as to the legal consequences of defects of the sold goods). This is also a common phenomenon in other pandectist systems. However, it should not be overlooked that some elements of the general parts of the Civil Codes or of the general parts of the law of obligations in post-Soviet legislations may differ from what observers from other civil law jurisdictions might expect.[17] For example, in Russia and some other countries of the region, the notion of "essential conditions" of a contract is interpreted quite extensively. This may lead to the consequence that contracts are regarded as "not concluded" only because a relatively minor aspect of the contract is not directly dealt with in the contract.[18] Another peculiar element is the limited effect of formal defects, which may in some cases – following the French tradition – leave the contract valid and exclude only proof by witnesses.[19] In contrast with this, sometimes formalities are accentuated more strictly than in Western countries, which may lead to an

---

15   In Russia, contractual options became expressly regulated in the Civil Code in 2015 (arts 429.2 and 429.3).

16   Eg in the Land Code of Turkmenistan (2004) or in the Georgian Law on State Procurement (2005).

17   See also Rolf Knieper, Lado Chant> and Hans-Joachim Schramm, *Das Privatrecht im Kaukasus und in Zentralasien – Bestandsaufnahme und Entwicklung* (Berliner Wissenschafts-Verlag 2010) 431ff.

18   See <https://rossovet.ru/articles/item/93/> accessed 7 July 2021.

19   See, eg art 153.1 of the Civil Code of Kazakhstan; in contrast, under art 68 of the Georgian Civil Code and art 93 of the Civil Code of Turkmenistan, which follow the German model, non-observation of the form requirement leads in principle to invalidity of the contract.

unexpected invalidity of the contract. One should not overstate, in this context, the distinction between the "CIS Model Civil Code-based" and "German model-based" systems in the region or even the sometimes differing wording of legislative provisions. There still remains a tendency in the region to follow the interpretational patterns and traditions of Soviet law and to use Russian legal doctrine and jurisprudence as a model for the interpretation of the laws of other countries of the region. This is even true for Georgia, though perhaps to a lesser extent than in other Caucasus and Central Asian countries. It should be added that this continuing habit still has the effect of keeping some degree of legal unity in the post-Soviet area beyond the growing differences in legal texts and even political conflicts.

4   Some Examples for Parallels and Differences

All countries define the *characteristics* of a sales contract – and at the same time rights and obligations of the parties – basically in the same way: the seller has to transfer property of the sold goods, the buyer has to pay for the goods (cf. Article 449 point 1 CIS Model Civil Code; Article 477 point 1 Civil Code of Georgia). The possible *objects of sales contracts* are, however, not described in the same way, which may lead to uncertainties. While it is clear that corporeal goods – movables and immovables – can be the objects of sales contracts, the applicability of the sales contracts provisions on contracts to transfer incorporeal goods, e.g. claims, other rights or even factual values (e.g. knowhow or other information) is not always clear. Article 477 of the Georgian Civil Code, for example, mentions only "things", i.e. probably corporeal goods,[20] but Article 498 of the Code declares the preceding provisions analogously applicable to sales of "rights and other property". Article 449 point 3 of the CIS Model Code states that the sales provisions apply to contracts to transfer "property rights" by analogy,[21] leaving open contracts on the transfer of incorporeal objects, which have some value, but do not qualify as "rights".

Although the *conclusion of sales contracts* is governed, in principle, by the general rules of the Civil Codes on legal transactions and contracts, the CIS Model Code-based Civil Codes contain a number of additional provisions on

---

20   In contrast, the equivalent provision of art 501 point 1 of the Civil Code of Turkmenistan refers to *imushchestvo* (property in a broad sense, which arguably includes also rights and factual assets).

21   Similar art 651 of the Civil Code of Azerbaijan, which extends, however, to all "claims" (not only for money) and all "rights" (not only property rights).

the conclusion of particular types of sales (consumer contracts, commercial contracts, energy delivery contracts). For example, they provide for particular information duties in the context of the conclusion of consumer sales contracts (see e.g. Article 490 CIS Model Civil Code), which are also characterized as "public contracts" (*publichnye dogovory*), the conclusion of which is obligatory for the commercial seller (see Article 489 CIS Model Civil Code). As to commercial sales, the CIS Model Civil Code provides for a special regime of contracting by exchange of offer and acceptance, which may lead to pre-contractual claims for damages (Article 502 CIS Model Civil Code). Contracts for the delivery of energy to consumers are deemed, under certain conditions, concluded by factual connection to the energy net (Article 517 point 2 CIS Model Civil Code).

As to the *form of contracts*, there are some interesting special provisions (and differences between the Codes) with regard to contracts for the sale of immovables. While the CIS Model Civil Code requires such sales to be concluded in notarial form (Article 450 point 1), in Kyrgyzstan the written form is sufficient (Article 415 point 1 Civil Code of Kyrgyzstan). Armenia requires both the written and notarial form (Article 562 Civil Code of Armenia).[22] Azerbaijan, on the other hand, does not state a form requirement in the sales chapter, but requires the notarial form in the General Part of the Civil Code (Article 144 Civil Code of Azerbaijan). Similar to Armenia, in Azerbaijan only the transfer of the property (not the sales contract) has to be entered into the public register (Article 139 Civil Code of Azerbaijan). In Russia the form requirements for sales of immovables have changed from the notarial form (until 1998) to written (see Article 550 part 1 Civil Code of Russia),[23] and the matter remains under discussion.

The sales chapters in all Civil Codes in the region contain detailed provisions on *factual and legal defects* of the sold goods (see e.g. Articles 466 – 479, 496 – 498, 512 – 515 CIS Model Civil Code; shorter and clearer Articles 487 – 497 Civil Code of Georgia; Articles 511 – 521 Civil Code of Turkmenistan) which correspond to international standards and also show influences of the UN Convention on the International Sale of Goods of 1980.[24]

---

22   Public registration is required in Armenia not for the sales contract, but only as to the transfer of property (art 563 Civil Code of Armenia).

23   Like in Armenia and Azerbaijan, in Russia (only) the transfer of the property needs to be publicly registered, art 551 Civil Code of Russia.

24   For a detailed analysis of this issue, taking the example of Russian law, see Andreas Steininger, *Das russische Kaufrecht* (Arno Spitz Verlag 2001), 290ff, 299ff.

The CIS Model Code-based Civil Codes contain in the sales chapters provisions allowing *retention of title agreements* (cf. Article 487 CIS Model Civil Code). Georgia and Turkmenistan also allow retention of title agreements but regulate them only in the context of the Property Law parts of the Codes (Article 188 Civil Code of Georgia; shorter Article 212 Civil Code of Turkmenistan). A particularly detailed provision on retention of title agreements is contained in Article 606 of the Civil Code of Azerbaijan, which also deals with the legal position of creditors and insolvency administrators. None of these provisions addresses the issue of "enlarged" or "prolonged" forms of retention of title agreements, which are common, for example, under German law.

5   Conclusion

Generally speaking, the sales laws in the region of the Caucasus and Central Asia can be classified into two groups: the large majority of the Civil Codes follow by and large the CIS Model Civil Code, while Georgia and Turkmenistan have taken their orientation from the German Civil Code. Outside the Civil Codes it is always necessary to look for special legislation, e.g. in the fields of consumer protection, sales of immovables or state contracts. In general, all legislation follows international standards, but the CIS Model Code-based systems are much more detailed and differentiated as to specific categories of sales contracts than the shorter sales provisions in Georgia and Turkmenistan. Practically, both approaches work, and it is probably a matter of legislative evaluation whether judicial practice and the legally interested population are better served by a clearer, but shorter regulation or the more detailed, but rather complicated CIS-based sales provisions. Discussion about important details will continue in any case.

CHAPTER 14

International Sales Law in the Region of the Caucasus and Central Asia – An Overview

Alexander Trunk

The term "international sales law" can be understood in the sense of substantive law or of conflict of laws: substantive law on international sales or conflict of laws with regard to sales contracts. The following contribution will focus on conflict of laws, but also includes some remarks on the substantive law of international sales in the region of the Caucasus and Central Asia.

1   Legal Sources

As regards *substantive law on international sales* the most important international treaty in this field is the Vienna (UN-)Convention on Contracts for the International Sale of Goods (CISG) of 1980.[1] Most countries of the Caucasus and Central Asia region – with the exception of Kazakhstan, Tajikistan and Turkmenistan – have ratified the CISG.[2] From an international trade perspective, it would certainly be desirable if these three countries, in particular Kazakhstan due to its economic importance, also acceded to the CISG. There is at present no regional treaty on substantive international sales law or other international contract law in the Eurasian region.[3] Also, the countries of this region have not passed specific autonomous legislation on international (transnational) sales. The existing legislation in some countries of the region

---

1   <https://uncitral.un.org/sites/uncitral.un.org/files/media-documents/uncitral/en/19 -09951_e_ebook.pdf> accessed 22 November 2021. In view of the 40th anniversary of the CISG in 2020, UNCITRAL has conducted various activities dedicated to the CISG, see <https://uncit ral.un.org/en/cisg40> accessed on 22 November 2021.

2   See <https://uncitral.un.org/en/texts/salegoods/conventions/sale_of_goods/cisg/status> accessed 22 November 2021. Azerbaijan acceded to the CISG on 1 June 2017.

3   By now, neither the Commonwealth of Independent States (CIS) nor the Eurasian Economic Union have developed treaties or model legislation on international sales contracts.

dealing with "foreign trade" is focussed on administrative law and does not directly address contract law.[4]

Turning to *conflict of laws*, the regulatory spectrum in the region is much broader. There is an important multilateral treaty in the region which covers both conflict of laws and judicial cooperation in a general manner: the Minsk Convention on Judicial Assistance and Legal Relationships in Civil, Family and Criminal Matters of 22 January 1993.[5] The Minsk Convention was developed under the auspices of the Commonwealth of Independent States (CIS) and entered into force between Azerbaijan, Armenia, Georgia, Kazakhstan, Kyrgyzstan, Russia, Tajikistan, and even Turkmenistan, i.e. between all countries of the region of the Caucasus and Central Asia.[6] However, on 7 October 2002 the CIS member countries signed a revised version of this Convention in Chişinău (Moldova).[7] This Convention (usually termed Kishinev Convention) has entered into force between Belarus, Armenia, Azerbaijan, Kazakhstan, Kyrgyzstan, and Tajikistan.[8] According to its Art.120 part 3, the Member Parties of the Kishinev Convention denounced the Minsk Convention and apply only the new Convention. The 2002 Kishinev Convention is more detailed than the 1993 Minsk Convention (124 articles instead of 87).

Both the Minsk Convention and the Kishinev Convention leave, in principle, other treaties between the Parties untouched,[9] i.e. they apply only subsidiarily.

One such treaty is the so-called Kiev Agreement on the Procedure of Resolving Disputes Linked with an Economic Activity of 20 March 1992.[10] The Kiev Agreement, which briefly preceded the Minsk Convention, was

---

4   See eg (without provisions on sales contracts) the Law of Kazakhstan of 12 April 2004 on the Regulation of Trade <https://online.zakon.kz/Document/?doc_id=1047488#pos= 1;-118>, the Russian Law of 8 December 2003 on Fundamentals of State Regulation of Foreign Trade Activity <www.consultant.ru/document/cons_doc_LAW_45397/> or the Law of Turkmenistan on Foreign Trade Activity of 16 Aug. 2014 <www.minjust.gov.tm/ru/ mmerkezi/doc_view.php?doc_id=15022> all accessed 22 November 2021.

5   See <http://legalacts.ru/doc/konventsija-o-pravovoi-pomoshchi-i-pravovykh-otnoshenij akh/> accessed 22 November 2021.

6   See <http://to76.minjust.ru/ru/print/76567> accessed 22 November 2021. Further parties to the Minsk Convention are Belarus, Moldova and Ukraine, see <www.consultant .ru/document/cons_doc_LAW_5942/5049b15ba00cdf0648a217d097c5513172fed9b4/> accessed 22 November 2021.

7   See <http://online.zakon.kz//Document/?doc_id=1034672#sub_id=1170000> accessed 22 November 2021.

8   See <http://online.zakon.kz/Document/?doc_id=1034672&show_di=1> accessed 22 November 2021.

9   See art 82 Minsk Convention, art 118 pt 3 Kishinev Convention.

10   See <www.arbitr.ru/_upimg/C97D53D6AFB4BAB50479oEAoo6AF2CBC_cogl.pdf> accessed 22 November 2021.

also concluded between the Member States of the CIS[11] and contains in its Article 11 a provision on conflict of laws which is largely, but not fully, identical to the respective provisions of the Minsk Convention. Technically, the Kiev Agreement prevails over the Minsk Convention, which would seem, however, to apply subsidiarily if this does not contradict the Kiev Agreement.

To complicate matters further, in 1992 Russia concluded, briefly before the Minsk Convention, bilateral judicial assistance treaties with Azerbaijan and Kyrgyzstan,[12] which – while being similar to the Minsk Convention – also prevail over the Minsk Convention. As to the relationship between the (multilateral) Kiev Agreement of 20 March 1992 and the later Russian-Azerbaijani and Russian-Kyrgyz (bilateral) agreements, the solution can be derived from Article 30 of the Vienna Convention on the Law of Treaties (VCLT) of 23 May 1969,[13] i.e. between Russia, Azerbaijan and Kyrgyzstan the bilateral treaties apply, but the Kiev Agreement remains applicable in a subsidiary function.[14] Following the example of Russia, some other countries of the region (e.g. Azerbaijan, Georgia, Kazakhstan and Uzbekistan) have also concluded bilateral judicial assistence treaties with each other which follow the model of the treaties with Russia.[15] They also prevail over the 1993 Minsk Convention and the 1992 Kiev Agreement.

As to relations with countries outside the Caucasus-Central Asia region, one can distinguish between other CIS countries, the Baltic countries, further countries sharing the common Socialist past, and other countries in the world. In relation to other CIS countries (Belarus, Moldova, Ukraine[16]), generally the 1993 Minsk Convention and also (with exception to relations with Georgia) the

---

11   The Kiev Agreement has been ratified by all CIS member states except Georgia (Georgia left the CIS in 2008, effective in 2009).

12   See <http://to76.minjust.ru/ru/print/76567> accessed 22 November 2021.

13   See <https://treaties.un.org/doc/publication/unts/volume%201155/volume-1155-i-18232 -english.pdf> accessed 22 November 2021.

14   This can easily become relevant as the Russian-Azerbaijani and the Russian-Kyrgyz treaty contain in the field of contracts law only one provision dealing with the form of legal transaction. In contrast, the Kiev Agreement and the Minsk Convention contain also conflicts provisions on the rights and duties under legal transactions, on powers of representation and on the applicable statute of limitations.

15   See eg the treaty between Kazakhstan and Azerbaijan of 10 June 1997 <https://zakon .uchet.kz/rus/docs/Z990000387> or the treaty between Uzbekistan and Georgia of 28 May 1996 <https://nrm.uz/contentf?doc=19142_&products=1_zakonodatelstvo_ruz> all accessed 22 November 2021. These two treaties are more modern than the Russian-Kyrgyz and Russian Azerbaijani treaties of 1992 and resemble the 1993 Minsk Convention.

16   Ukraine was never a member state of the CIS, though it participated as a quasi-member in the activities of the CIS. Due to the conflict with Russian, Ukraine withdrew its representatives from all CIS organs on 19 May 2018, see <https://en.wikipedia.org/wiki/Commonw ealth_of_Independent_States> accessed 22 November 2021. However, Ukraine is still a

1992 Kiev Agreement apply.[17] Also, there exist some bilateral judicial assistance treaties with other CIS countries similar to the treaties within the Caucaus-Central Asia region.[18] Corresponding bilateral treaties have been concluded between Russia and some other countries of the Caucasus-Central Asia region on the one hand and the Baltic countries on the other.[19] In relations with other East European or Asian[20] countries which formerly were part of the Socialist system, there exist also bilateral judicial assistance treaties, some of which contain provisions on conflict of laws.[21] With other third countries no bilateral treaties containing provisions on private international law seem to exist.[22]

A particular question is the destiny of Soviet treaties. Russia has declared to be the legal "continuer" of the USSR and this seems to have found recognition in the international community.[23] From this follows that Russia continues to apply treaties concluded by the USSR, including treaties on judicial assistance and conflict of laws. This also has been accepted by Russia's treaty partners. The answer to the question is less clear with regard to other countries, which have gained (or possibly: regained) their independence with the dissolution of the USSR in December 1992. The claim of the Baltic countries to have been illegally occupied by the USSR in 1940, from which was derived the consequence

---

    member of CIS conventions in so far as it has not denounced them. This has not been done as to the Minsk Convention.

17   See n 10.

18   Eg treaties between Georgia and Ukraine of 1995 (cf. <http://deafortis.com/en/zakony/dogovory-ukrainy-o-pravovoj-pomoshi.html> accessed 22 November 2021) or between Russia and Moldova of 1993.

19   Russian treaties with Estonia (1993), Latvia (1993) and Lithuania (1992); similar treaties between, eg Kazakhstan and Lithuania (1993), Uzbekistan and Latvia (1996), Uzbekistan and Lithuania (1997), cf <www.minjust.uz/ru/international_cooperation/explanation/> and <https://mfa.uz/ru/cooperation/legalrelations/> all accessed 22 November 2021.

20   Mongolia, North Korea and Vietnam, to a certain degree also China.

21   For example, a treaty between Uzbekistan and Czechia of 2002, between Russia and Poland of 1996, between Russia and Cuba of 2000, etc. Typically, these treaties are limited to procedural matters, excluding conflict of law. When they include provisions on conflict of laws, this is usually marked in their title [treaty on judicial assistance] "and legal relationships in civil matters".

22   Some multilateral treaties, which mainly deal with substantive law, contain sparse provisions on conflict of laws (eg the 1988 Unidroit Factoring Convention, which has been ratified, among others, by Russia). These treaties will not be addressed in this contribution. None of the states of the region has ratified the 1955 Hague Convention on the Law Applicable to International Sales of Goods or the newer Convention on the same subject of 1986.

23   See K A Bekjashev, in ibid (ed), *Mezhdunarodnoe publichnoe pravo*, (2nd edn 2003) 126ff, cf also William E Butler, *The Law of Treaties in Russia and the Commonwealth of Independent States* (CUP 2002) 15ff.

that they could not be regarded as successor states to the USSR, has been accepted by the international community. Other post-Soviet states have not taken a similarly explicit position. In terms of politics, Georgia, Moldova, possibly Azerbaijan and now also Ukraine have stated, too, that they were illegally occupied by the USSR and regard themselves as legal successors to the independent Republics on their territories, which came into existence after the First World War.[24] On the other side all CIS member states agreed in 1993 on a memorandum dealing with the legal destiny of Soviet treaties that they considered themselves in principle as legal successors of the USSR and each country should decide whether it would wish to continue to be bound (and entitled) by Soviet treaties.[25] Whether such a voluntaristic approach is in line with international law cannot be analyzed here.[26] None of the countries in the Caucasus-Central Asia region has taken a clear public position with regard to this question. This is also true with regard to the Soviet legal assistance treaties. For example, in contrast with the Russian Ministry of Justice, the Ministries of Justice of Kazakhstan and Uzbekistan do not mention in the lists of legal assistance treaties of their countries on their websites the treaties concluded by the USSR. On the other side, there is some arbitral and judicial practice both in post-Soviet countries and abroad that Soviet treaties also apply to the successor states of the USSR.[27]

For example, the Soviet judicial assistance treaties[28] with Bulgaria, Czechoslovakia, Hungary, Mongolia, Romania, Yugoslavia, and some others contain provisions on conflict of laws. As to contract law, however, these provisions are of little help, as they either do not address contractual matters at all or contain only a meager provision on the form of transactions.

In most countries of the Caucasus-Central Asia region the central regulation on conflict of laws is found in the Civil Codes. This can be seen as a part of the

---

24   cf <https://ru.wikipedia.org/wiki/Распад_СССР#Международное_право> accessed 22 November 2021.

25   Bekjashev (n 23) p 129ff, Shljantsev, *Mezhdunarodnoe pravo* (2006), ch 6.3 <https://lib .sale/mejdunarodnoe-pravo-besplatno/pravopreemstvo-svyazi-prekrascheniem.html> accessed 22 November 2021.

26   An important element of the analysis is the 1978 Vienna Convention on Succession of States in respect of Treaties of 1978 <http://legal.un.org/ilc/texts/instruments/english/ conventions/3_2_1978.pdf> accessed 22 November 2021.

27   See eg the arbitral decision of 19 October 2015 on jurisdiction in the investment dispute of World Wide Minerals Ltd v Kazakhstan, see <https://www.italaw.com/sites/default/files/ case-documents/italaw8945.pdf> accessed 22 November 2021.

28   cf <http://zags-15.ru/docs/Perechen-mezhdunarodnyh-dogovorov-Rossijskoj-Federatcii -po.pdf> accessed 22 November 2021.

Soviet tradition, but the same approach is used in some other civil law countries as well. The conflict of laws provisions in these Codes are based on the CIS Model Civil Code (Part 3) of 1996,[29] but show a number of particular features. Exceptions to the Civil Code approach are Azerbaijan and Georgia, which have passed separate Laws on Private International Law in 1998 (Georgia)[30] and 2000 (Azerbaijan).[31] Turkmenistan is the only country in the region which has not passed general legislation on conflict of laws. Its Civil Code of 17 July 1998[32] does not contain a chapter on conflict of laws. This is not to say that Turkmenistan has no conflict of laws legislation at all. Conflict of laws in family matters is codified in the Turkmen Family Code of 2012.[33] As to commercial matters, the Turkmen Law on International Commercial Arbitration of 16 August 2014[34] contains in Article 38 a provision on choice of law in arbitration proceedings, which is based on Article 28 of the UNCITRAL Model Law on International Commercial Arbitration. It can only be speculated how Turkmen courts would handle an international sales case outside the range of application of treaty law (Kiev Agreement, Minsk Convention, bilateral treaties).

2   Conflict of Laws Provisions – Structure and Contents

Following the Soviet approach, the judicial assistance treaties in the region try to create a theoretically comprehensive framework both for judicial cooperation (in civil and criminal matters) and for conflicts of laws (in civil matters). In so far as these treaties contain provisions on conflict of laws,[35] their focus is mainly on family law. They contain no "general part" of conflict of laws,[36] and the provisions on contracts are rudimentary. There are only two brief provisions on "legal transactions" (*sdelki*), one on the form of transactions, the other

---

29   The text of the CIS Model Civil Code Part 3 is available eg <http://iacis.ru/upload/iblock/938/018.pdf> accessed 22 November 2021.

30   See eg <https/pravo.hse.ru/intprilaw/doc/050301> accessed 22 November 2021.

31   See eg <https/pravo.hse.ru/intprilaw/doc/070801> accessed 22 November 2021.

32   See <www.minjust.gov.tm/ru/mmerkezi/doc_book_det.php?book_id=2> accessed 22 November 2021.

33   See <www.turkmenistan.gov.tm/?id=779> accessed 22 November 2021.

34   See <www.minjust.gov.tm/ru/mmerkezi/doc_view.php?doc_id=15025> accessed 22 November 2021.

35   Some treaties deal with procedural cooperation only, sometimes both in civil and criminal matters, sometimes only with one of these.

36   Some general aspects relevant to conflict of law can however be derived from the preambles and other general provisions of these treaties, see below at B.V.

on "rights and duties" arising from transactions.[37] Some treaties also include a provision on the law applicable to a power of representation.

In contrast the CIS Model Civil Code and the Civil Codes in the region following the Model Code have a fully developed regulation of conflict of laws, consisting of a general part and specific conflicts provisions on personal status, property, contracts, torts, unjust enrichment, and inheritance.[38] In particular, the conflicts provisions in the CIS Model Civil Code and the national Civil Codes on contractual matters are visibly inspired by the European Community's 1980 Rome Convention on the Law Applicable to Contracts.[39] It is surprising that the treaty law deviates so far from the much more modern and differentiated rules on conflict of laws established in the national legislation of the countries of the region. This raises general questions such as whether the treaties can be interpreted in the light of the CIS Model Code and whether national conflicts provisions may be applied subsidiarily even when a treaty is primarily applicable.[40]

2.1   *Basic Rule 1: Choice of Law*

The basic rule on conflict of laws in contractual matters, both under the treaties and national legislation in the region, is the freedom of the contracting parties to choose the law applicable to their contract. This rule is clearly expressed, for example, in Article 1224 part 1 of the CIS Model Civil Code, Article 27 part 1 in conjunction with Article 35 part 1 of the Georgian Private International Law (PIL) Act,[41] Article 24 of the Azerbaijani Private International Law (PIL) Act, etc. In the treaties, this rule is somewhat hidden in the formula that the "rights and duties of the parties to a transaction are governed by the law of the place of making of the transaction if the parties have not agreed otherwise" (cf. Article 11 lit.f Kiev Agreement; Article 41 Minsk Convention; Article 44 Kishinev Convention). Details with regard to such choice of law agreements are, however, completely left out in the treaties, while the CIS Model Civil Code and the

---

37   Such a provision was missing in some of the older treaties concluded by the USSR. It would seem these provisions relate also to the making and validity of the transaction.

38   Conflict of laws in family matters is usually regulated separartely in Family Codes.

39   See <http://eur-lex.europa.eu/legal-content/EN/TXT/HTML/?uri=CELEX:41980A0 934&from=EN> accessed 22 November 2021. The Rome Convention has in the meantime been been superseded by the Rome I Regulation of 2008.

40   See also n 9 and n 14.

41   The Georgian PIL Act takes a specific and solitary approach in that it distinguishes between conflicts rules on "transactions" (art 27–31) and "contracts" (art 35–38). As contracts are the main examples of (bilateral or plurilateral) legal transactions, in the case of contracts art 27 et seq. and 35ff have to be applied together.

respective national laws add a lot of specifics, often inspired by the EC's 1980 Rome Convention on the Law Applicable to Contracts.[42] It is submitted that at least the CIS treaties (Kiev Agreement, Minsk and Kishinev Conventions) should in this respect be interpreted in the light of the Model Civil Code as a tool for uniform application of these treaties. The same should be done for interpretation of the bilateral treaties between parties in the region to maintain, as far as possible, uniform legal standards between them.

2.2   *Basic Rule 2: Place of Transaction or Characteristic Performance*

If there is no choice of law agreement between the parties, the second basic rule (applicable to all types of contracts) comes into play. Here the treaties differ from the national laws: Under most of the treaties, the law of the country applies where the transaction was made ("sovershaetsja").[43] In the case of a contract as the most important type of legal transactions this would seem to refer to the place where the contract has been concluded. This raises the well-known problem of how to determine this place if both parties are physically present in different countries when they conclude the contract.[44] The question does not seem to have found a clear answer under the treaties for the time being. In contrast, the CIS Model Civil Code and most of the national laws in the region have chosen the more modern and adequate conflicts rule of the "place of characteristic performance" (see, e.g. Article 1225 part 2 and 3 CIS Model Civil Code; Article 36 part 1 sentence 2 Georgian PIL Act). The meaning of the term "place of characteristic performance" is made more explicit both in the CIS Model Civil Code and the respective national laws by lists of specific contracts (see Article 1225 part 1 and 2 Model Civil Code). Similar to the EU's Rome I Regulation, the place of domicile or main place of activities of

---

42   One aspect is, for example, the form of a choice of law agreement, see eg art 1248 part 4 of the Civil Code of Armenia, art 1112 part 2 of the Civil Code of Kazakhstan, art 1210 part 2 of the Russian Civil Code, art 1218 part 2 of the Civil Code of Tajikistan. The CIS Model Civil Code and the Civil Codes of Kyrgyzstan and Uzbekistan as well as the PIL Acts of Azerbaijan and Georgia do not specifically address this question.

43   Interesting, but rare exceptions are art 36 part 1 of the Russian-Polish treaty of 16 September 1996 <http://www.kdmid.ru/> and art 32 part 1 of the Russian-Cuba treaty of 14 December 2000 <http://to14.minjust.ru/ru/dogovor-mezhdu-rossiyskoy-federaciey -i-respublikoy-kuba-o-pravovoy-pomoshchi-i-pravovyh-otnosheniyah>, all accessed 22 November 2021, which establish the rule of the place of characteristic performance.

44   This factual situation is sometimes addressed in national regulation as to the law applicable to the form of a transaction, eg in art 17 part 2 of the PIL Act of Azerbaijan and art 29 pt 1 sentence 2 of the Georgian PIL Act, but it is not regulated as to the law applicable to the "rights and duties" of the contracting parties.

the seller is regarded as determinative for the application of a sales contract.[45] Interestingly, the Private International Law Act of Azerbaijan does not use the characteristic performance formula, but only the more general formula of the "closest connection" (Article 25.3 of the Act). Before coming to this general formula, however, the Azerbaijani Act defines the applicable law directly for a list of specific contracts (Article 25.1 and 25.2.), which is by and large identical with lists under the Model Civil Code and other national laws based on the characteristic performance rule.[46]

2.3   Basic Rule 3: Closest Connection

The principle that a legal relationship with a foreign element should be governed by the law to which it is most closely connected is, generally speaking, the basis of all modern conflicts law[47] More specifically, however, modern conflict of laws legislation often uses the principle of the closest connection as a concrete conflicts rule when other more specific rules either do not apply or do not seem to lead to an adequate solution. The treaties in the Caucasus-Central Asia region do not use the "closest connection" formula as a concrete conflicts provision, however the CIS Model Civil Code and national laws do, quite in line with EU legislation. Conflict of laws in contractual matters is one example. Article 25.3 of the PIL Act of Azerbaijan gives the "closest connection" test the most prominent place, leaving aside even the specific performance formula. However, the CIS Model Civil Code[48] and the Georgian PIL Act also use the closest connection test as a subsidiary formula, if the specific performance test cannot be used (cf. Article 1225 part 3 sentence 2 CIS Model Civil Code) or needs to be corrected (cf. Article 36 part 1 sentence 2 Georgian PIL Act).

2.4   Specific Conflicts Rules

In addition to the aforementioned basic rules, which apply to all contracts and, in principle, all aspects of contract law, both the treaties and national laws in the region contain some more specific conflicts rules applicable to contractual

---

45   Special rules apply to sales and other contracts relating to immovables: lex rei sitae, art 1225 pt 2 no 1 CIS Model Civil Code.

46   In contrast with the Civil Codes following the CIS Model Civil Code, the Georgian Act does not contain a detailed list of specific contract (only some few cases in art 36 parts 2–4). This was in line with the EC's 1980 Rome Convention, but the later Rome I Regulation of 2008 has also added a list of concrete contracts as an aid for better understanding the term "specific performance".

47   Developed by Friedrich Carl von Savigny in the mid 19th century, see <www.trans-lex.org/971000/_/law-applicable-to-international-contract/> accessed 22 November 2021.

48   And the Civil Codes based on the CIS Model Civil Code, with some differences in detail.

relationships. One can distinguish between specific aspects of contracts and specific contracts.

2.4.1   Specific Aspects of Contracts in General

Classic examples of specific conflicts rules dealing with particular aspects of (mainly) contract relations are provisions on the law applicable to the form of a transaction and to a power of representation. Such provisions already existed in the Soviet treaty practice and have found their way also into the modern judicial assistance treaties in the region (Kiev Agreement, Minsk and Kishinev Conventions, bilateral treaties).

2.4.1.1   *Form*

Under Article 11 lit. d) of the Kiev Agreement, Article 39 of the Minsk Convention and Article 42 of the Kishinev Convention, for example, the basic rule on the law applicable to the form of a transaction is the locus acti, with an exception for transactions relating to immovables where the lex rei sitae applies. This is more restrictive than, for example, Article 11 of the EU's Rome I Regulation, which also accepts formal validity under the lex causae and is less absolute with regard to contracts relating to immovables.[49]

Article 1216 of the CIS Model Civil Code is built upon similar principles as the aforementioned treaties, but is somewhat more liberal and differentiated. As a basic rule, formal validity is not exclusively governed by the lex loci acti, but the lex fori (more precisely: law of the legislator passing the respective Civil Code) is also held sufficient (Article 1216 part 1 CIS Model Civil Code). Application of the lex causae of the transaction is not foreseen. In Article 1216 part 2 the CIS Model Civil Code also provides for a special substantive rule with regard to "transactions of international commerce" (*vneshneekonomich-eskie sdelki*); such transactions must be in writing. Similar provisions were then introduced in the national Civil Codes,[50] but their restrictiveness became increasingly criticized even within the countries. In 2013 the Russian legislature reacted to this critique and passed far-reaching changes to the respective provision of Article 1209 of the Russian Civil Code. Article 1209 (new) now refers in the first place to the lex causae, but the lex loci actus is also held sufficient. Finally, observation of Russian law is also sufficient if one of the contracting parties is a Russian citizen or legal entity. Thus the relevance of

---

49   Art 11 pt 1 Rome I Regulation. The Rome I Regulation is also more differentiated in numerous other aspects.

50   Still today in this sense eg art 1104 Civil Code of Kazakhstan and art 1190 Civil Code of Kyrgyzstan.

Russian law in form issues has been kept, but only as an additional element of favor validatis and under the condition of a personal link to Russia. Also, the Russian legislature abolished the special writing requirement for transactions of international commerce (Article 1209 part 2 (old) and Article 165 (old) of the Russian Civil Code), trying to give international trade some support. It may be expected that other CIS countries will also liberalize their form provisions in a similar way in the coming years.

2.4.1.2   *Power of Representation*

The second classic example of special conflicts norms relating (mainly) to contractual relations concerns the power of representation. The treaty practice in the region typically contains a brief provision on the law applicable to the form and the duration of the effects of a power of representation (power of attorney)[51] referring to the law of the country where the power of attorney was issued. Article 1217 of the CIS Model Civil Code closely follows this traditional approach. In Russia, however, in the course of the recent broad reform of the Civil Code a new, detailed provision on conflict of laws relating to the power of representation was introduced (Article 1217.1 Russian Civil Code). It includes differentiated rules on the law applicable to the substance and form of powers of representation and tries to strike a balance between contractual flexibility (e.g. choice of law) and protection of third parties. It is a highly sophisticated provision which deserves a close analysis from the EU perspective where this topic is still widely excluded from the Rome I Regulation. A shorter, but also interesting provision on representation can be found in Article 28 of the Georgian Private International Law Act.

2.4.1.3   *Statute of Limitations*

The third classic example of special conflicts norms relating (also) to contractual relations concerns limitation of actions (more correctly: claims). Again, treaty practice in the region usually contains a short provision on this issue, referring to the lex causae (see, e.g. Article 12 lit.g Kiev Agreement; Article 43 Minsk Convention; Article 46 Kishinev Convention). The Model Civil Code follows this approach, but adds a unilateral provision on imprescriptibility (Article 1218 part 2 CIS Model Civil Code).

---

51   See eg art 11 lit e Kiev Agreement, art 40 Minsk Convention, art 43 Kishinev Convention (with some additions relating to proof).

2.4.1.4   *Others*

In particular, the Private International Law Act of Azerbaijan, the Georgian Private International Law Act and the Russian Civil Code in the revised version of 2013 contain some further specific conflicts rules relating to contracts in general. Article 16 of the PIL Act of Azerbaijan addresses the issue of participation of the State in private relationships with a foreign element clarifying that general rules of private international law apply if the State does not act iure imperii.[52] The Georgian Private International Law Act contains in Article 31 a conflicts norm protecting the contracting party under certain circumstances from limitations of representative powers of the other party.[53] Article 1216 and 1216.1 (revised) of the Russian Civil Code specifically address transfers of debts in a way similar to Articles 14 and 15 of the Rome I Regulation. A similar approximation to EU law is contained in art.1217.2 of the Russian Civil Code with regard to set-off. Other specific provisions are Article 1217 of the Russian Civil Code (unilateral transactions) and Article 1218 Russian Civil Code (claims for interest).

2.4.2   Specific Contracts

The EU's Rome I Regulation (formerly the 1980 Rome Convention) contains a number of special conflicts rules for specific contracts, which are characterized by particular balancing needs, often with a protective focus (consumer contracts, transport contracts, insurance contracts, labour contracts). The treaty practice in the Caucasus-Central Asia region does not address these specific contracts, which are therefore governed by the general provisions.[54] The CIS Model Civil Code and the national laws briefly mention transport and insurance contracts in the context of the general provisions.[55] Article 38 of the Georgian PIL Act gives priority to imperative norms with protective function even if they are not part of the lex contractus. Only the Russian Civil Code (as revised in 2013) contains in its Article 1212 an elaborate provision on consumer contracts, which is inspired by Article 6 of the Rome I Regulation.

---

52   The provision seems founded on art 1214 of the Model Civil Code but is more elaborated. See also art 1102 (revised in 2010) of the Civil Code of Kazakhstan.

53   The provision resembles art 13 Rome I Regulation but includes also corporate matters.

54   Labour law would seem not to be covered by the sphere of application of the legal assistance treaties and the Civil Codes, as "civil law" is in the Soviet tradition regarded as distinct from labour law.

55   Cf. arts 1225 pt 1 lit 6 and 12 Model Civil Code, art 36 pt 3 and 4 of the Georgian PIL Act.

2.5   *Supplementary Provisions*

In order to correctly apply the aforementioned conflicts rules, a number of supplementary questions have to be answered: Whether the conflicts provisions of the treaties apply only to parties domiciled in Contracting States; how the domicile of a party is to be determined; how terms used in the provisions are to be interpreted; whether the application of the conflicts provisions can be influenced by imperative norms or public policy considerations, etc.

2.5.1   Sphere of Application

The judicial assistance treaties in the region give only few clear answers to these questions. The preambles of the treaties and the introductory provisions on judicial protection can probably be interpreted in the sense that (in case of an international contract case) both contracting parties must be citizens or domiciliaries of the Contracting States.[56] From this follows that a contract between a party established in one of the Contracting States, e.g. Kazakhstan, and a party domiciled in a third State, e.g. Germany or the UK, would not be covered by the conflicts rules of the respective treaty. In contrast, national conflicts provisions are not limited to parties domiciled or established in specific countries. The conflicts rules in the Civil Codes or PIL Acts in the region therefore apply to any kind of contracts with a foreign element. Only some unilateral provisions may require citizenship, establishment or situation of an object in a specific country.

2.5.2   Interpretation

The treaties also do not specifically address issues of interpretation. It is, however, today generally recognized that uniform law should, if possible, be interpreted in a uniform manner in order to apply the treaties evenly and efficiently.[57] Arguably provisions in national laws which are based on the CIS Model Civil Code should also be interpreted as uniformly as possible.

2.5.3   Imperative Norms

The treaties do not address the topic of (internationally) imperative norms, which might limit or add to the application of the general conflicts provisions.

---

56   See eg the preamble and art 1 pt 1 of the Minsk Convention. Some older bilateral treaties refer only to "citizens" (of the Contracting Parties), not to domiciliaries. The preamble and arts 1–3 of the Kiev Agreement add the requirement of being a registered "economic subject" in a Contracting State.

57   See Marianne Roth and Richard Happ, 'Interpretation of Uniform Law Instruments According to Principles of International Law' (1997) 2(4) Uniform Law Review 700ff.

It could be argued that the public policy exception under these treaties could be used in such cases. In contrast, both the Model Civil Code and all national conflicts regulations include special provisions on internationally imperative norms. While Article 1201 of the Model Civil Code and Article 5 of the PIL Act of Azerbaijan provide both for the application of (internationally) imperative norm of the forum and, in a mitigated form, of third countries, the Georgian PIL Act addresses only imperative norms of Georgia.[58]

2.5.4   Public Policy

Most treaties in the region contain a public policy exception. A noteworthy counter-example is the 1992 Kiev Agreement. This has been confirmed (in a case on mutual execution of judgments) in a consultative opinion of the CIS Economic Court.[59] The same is true for all national conflicts regulations. A problem in this field seems to be the need for a uniform and limited application of the public policy exception.[60]

2.5.5   Others

Both the CIS Model Civil Code and the national regulations contain – sometimes even surprisingly – further supplementary provisions, such as on characterization (see Article 1195 CIS Model Civil Code), renvoi (Article 1197 CIS Model Civil Code), fraus legis (Article 1198 Model Civil Code), dealing with countries with several legal subsystems (Article 1202). They also contain clauses on reciprocity and retorsion (see Articles 1199 and 1203 CIS Model Civil Code), which have however – seemingly – not yet been used in practice.

3   Evaluation and Outlook

In general, the overview of the regulation of international sales contracts (in the context of conflict of laws in general) in the Caucasus-Central Asia region has shown a surprisingly colourful and changing scenery. The CIS Model Civil Code plays a considerable unifying role in the field of conflict of laws, but would need an overhaul. Russia has started such an overhaul on the level of its

---

58   See art 6 Georgian PIL Act.
59   Opinion of 20 June 2011 Nr 01-1/3-10 <www.sudsng.org/download_files/rh/2011/zk_01-1_3 -10_20062011.pdf> accessed 22 November 2021.
60   cf Afanas'ev, in S N Lebedev and E N Kabatova (ed), *Mezhdunarodnoe chastnoe pravo, tom 1* (2011) 315; George Vashakidze, *Das Internationale Privatrecht von Georgien* (Mohr Siebeck 2014) 72.

national Civil Code, and it can be expected that some other countries might follow in this direction. Georgia and, to a somewhat lesser degree, Azerbaijan have taken separate ways in regulating conflict of laws by passing particular PIL Acts. Nevertheless, the Azerbaijani Act has taken quite a bit of inspiration from the CIS Model Civil Code. The Georgian PIL Act is more independent and sometimes leaning towards EU law, but has not yet been approximated to the EU's Rome I Regulation. A problem in most countries (with the exception of Russia) seems to be a lack of published court practice and legal analysis in the field of private international law and, consequently, an atmosphere of legal uncertainty and instability.

Although all countries in the region of the Caucasus and Central Asia have concluded among themselves (and partly also with third countries) multilateral and bilateral judicial assistance treaties, these treaties have little relevance as to contract law. They are mainly focused on family law and, more generally, judicial cooperation. The sparse conflicts rules in these treaties dealing with contractual matters hinder international trade more than they encourage it. From the perspective of international contracts law these treaties would need a fundamental overhaul.

CHAPTER 15

Uniform Sales Law as a Tool to Facilitate Complex Global Supply Chains in Central Asia

Cyril R. Emery

1 Introduction*

As a tool for achieving greater economic development, many of the countries of Central Asia have, since the 1990s, pursued increased cross-border trade and greater integration in the world economy.[1] Today, participation by domestic enterprises in global supply chains can be an important factor in continuing that development.[2] Domestic enterprises, however, face many barriers to participation in cross-border trade and global supply chains. The United Nations Convention on Contracts for the International Sale of Goods (Vienna, 1980) (the "CISG" or the "Convention")[3] was created under the auspices of the United Nations Commission on International Trade Law (UNCITRAL) in order remove the legal barriers encountered by traders looking to deal internationally. The purpose of this chapter is to highlight how the CISG may be of particular use to countries in Central Asia in enabling domestic enterprises to participate in the world economy and global supply chains.

This chapter will introduce, in part two, one of the legal barriers that prevents traders from completing cross-border transactions or participating in global supply chains. In part three, it will lay out the CISG's role in removing this barrier. Finally, in part four, it will look specifically at the CISG and global supply chains in Central Asia before concluding with some recommendations for the region.

---

* The following chapter addresses only the region of Central Asia as the CISG has already been adopted by all countries of the Caucasus region.
1 See eg United Nations Conference on Trade and Development, *Investment Guide to the Silk Road* (2014) 3. For the purposes of this paper, Central Asia includes Kazakhstan, Kyrgyzstan, Tajikistan, Turkmenistan, and Uzbekistan.
2 OECD, *Interconnected Economies: Benefiting from Global Value Chains* (2013) 156.
3 United Nations, *Treaty Series*, vol 1489, No 25567, 3.

© KONINKLIJKE BRILL NV, LEIDEN, 2023 | DOI:10.1163/9789004357839_017

2   Legal Barriers to Cross-Border Trade and in Global Supply Chains

When an enterprise is considering concluding a transaction with a foreign business, there are a number of barriers that may prevent the transaction. Perhaps the most obvious are tariffs. Even where tariffs are minimal or have been eliminated, however, additional barriers can remain. These can include cultural and linguistic differences, delivery problems, and tax regulations or other formal requirements related to, for example, licensing, registration, or packaging.[4] While these issues certainly need to be addressed in order for the transaction to be completed, the object of this chapter is to consider a remaining obstacle, namely the question of which law will be applicable to the contract in question.

In a simple cross-border transaction for the sale of goods, the prospective buyer and seller will need to negotiate a contractual clause as to which law will apply, assuming that they consider the issue at all. The cost of this negotiation (most directly seen in the price of legal advice) will either need to be factored into the price of the goods or may cause the transaction to be abandoned altogether.[5] If the issue of applicable law is not considered or if the parties do not agree on a choice of law clause but finalize the contract in any case, the legal uncertainty will drive up costs of any resulting legal dispute as the parties' lawyers will need to spend time making arguments as to applicable law.[6] If the parties choose one of their domestic laws and a dispute occurs in a court or arbitration tribunal unfamiliar with that law, the resulting difficulty of applying the foreign law will also increase legal costs.[7] All of these transaction costs, both those that would be incurred during negotiation and the potential ones in the event of a dispute, pose a very real barrier to trade. This barrier can result either in transactions being abandoned[8] or, to satisfy incurred costs

---

4   Gallup Organization, Hungary, *European Contract Law Business-to-Business Transactions: Summary* (Flash Eurobarometer 320, 2011) 7.
5   See René David, 'Chapter 5: The International Unification of Private Law' in René David (ed), *International Encyclopedia of Comparative Law: Volume II, The Legal Systems of the World and their Comparison and Unification* (Mohr 1975) para 18.
6   William J. Woodward Jr., 'Legal Uncertainty and Aberrant Contracts: The Choice of Law Clause' (2014) 89 Chicago-Kent Law Review 197, 198.
7   Peter H. Schlechtriem, '25 Years of the CISG: An International lingua franca for Drafting Uniform Laws, Legal Principles, Domestic Legislation and Transnational Contracts' in Harry M. Flechtner, Ronald A. Brand, Mark S. Walter (eds), *Drafting Contracts Under the CISG* (OUP 2008) 170, n 6.
8   See Gallup Organization (n 4) at 5 (indicating that 64% of companies surveyed in the European Union "stated that contract-law barriers at least occasionally [] deterred them from doing such business").

and manage the economic risks of potential ones, in higher priced or lower quality goods.

To complicate matters, there is frequently a disparity of bargaining power in cross-border transactions, and stronger parties will inevitably insist upon their domestic law,[9] or, at best, the law of a third State that is perceived to be "neutral".[10] While this may reduce some of the transaction costs as there is no negotiation, there are still the costs of the weaker party familiarizing themselves with the chosen law and the problem of courts or tribunals applying the foreign law. In addition, this unilateral choice does not assure a legal regime particularly well-suited for international transactions.[11] By definition, small and medium enterprises (SMEs) often find themselves as the weaker party and are, thus, unable to insist on their domestic law, which may make them reluctant to participate in cross-border transactions, in particular given the lower likelihood that they will be able to tolerate the costs of foreign legal research.[12] From the perspective of developing countries, this is particularly problematic as SMEs are key drivers of economic development and can maximize this role through engagement in cross-border trade.[13]

While this situation is already complex, it is made much more so when one considers this problem in the context of a global supply chain. Global supply chains, also known as global value chains,[14] are playing a growing role in the global economy.[15] They are credited with providing a "fast track to development and industrialization."[16] Global supply chains are characterized by numerous transactions concluded across various borders. On the very simple end of the spectrum, a t-shirt might be produced from cotton grown in the United States, manufactured in China, imprinted with logos and graphics in the United States, sold in both the United States and Canada, and, finally, exported to Uganda for

---

9   See David (n 5) para 18; Schlechtriem (n 7) 170, n 6.

10   Ingeborg Schwenzer & Pascal Hachem, 'The CISG: Successes and Pitfalls' (2009) 57 American Journal of Comparative Law 457, 465.

11   David (n 5) para 20; Consider, also, Schwenzer and Hachem's analysis of the shortcomings of the domestic sales law of Switzerland, a commonly selected "neutral law." Schwenzer & Hachem (n 10) 465.

12   Schlechtriem (n 7) 170, n 6.

13   OECD, Promoting SMEs For Development (2004) 9–10.

14   For a discussion of the nomenclature related to global supply chains, see Albert Park, Gaurav Nayyar & Patrick Law, Supply Chain Perspectives and Issues: A Literature Review (2013) 41–53.

15   OECD (n 2) 14–16; Alessandro Nicita, Victor Ognivtsev & Miho Shirotori, Global Supply Chains: Trade and Economic Policies for Developing Countries (WTO 2013) 7.

16   OECD (n 2) 156.

resale.[17] This type of arrangement will require multiple contracts, in particular those for the sale of goods. A large global brand could try to control the contractual situation by imposing a single legal regime (likely its domestic sales law) on all the sales contracts in the chain. This approach, however, has limits to its effectiveness. First, negotiation costs will be multiplied, as each buyer or seller may wish to negotiate for an alternate legal regime. Secondly, the choice of a foreign law or, say, a soft-law instrument such as the Unidroit Principles of International Commercial Contracts (the "Unidroit Principles"),[18] while increasingly accepted, may not be recognized in the country of every supply chain partner.[19]

To further confound the situation, the large global brand will not only be concerned with its own contractual arrangements, but also with those of its subcontractors and other supply chain partners. Global supply chains are particularly sensitive to sudden changes in circumstances (most notably, natural disasters[20]) since they involve interconnected networks of firms with small margins of error built on "just-in-time models, lean supply structures, and a lack of redundancy," which together mean that a "breakdown in one part of the chain may quickly have effects throughout the value chain."[21] In order to properly account for and manage the potential consequences of this risk, a large global brand will want as good an idea as possible as to the legal rules governing changed circumstances in all of the contracts in the supply chain. This means it will have an interest in influencing and unifying the law chosen by subcontractors and other supply chain partners in their cross-border sales and other contracts. Since foreign subcontractors are unlikely to share a preference for the domestic law of the global brand, this will result either in higher negotiating costs, or, more likely, an independent or nonexistent choice of law by subcontractors. The costs and complexity of managing the applicable law of

---

17   Example is based on one presented in OECD (n 2) 16 (citing Pietra Rivoli, *The Travels of a T-Shirt in the Global Economy: An Economist Examines the Markets, Power, and Politics of World Trade* (2nd edn, Wiley 2009)).

18   International Institute for the Unification of Private Law, *Unidroit Principles of International Commercial Contracts* (2010).

19   Symeon C. Symeonides, *Codifying Choice of Law Around the World: An International Comparative Analysis* (OUP 2014) 109–147 (note, in particular, p 114 and n 26, indicating that the recognition of choice of law based on the concept of party autonomy is now standard but not universal, in particular with some limitations in Latin America, see the chapter in general for additional limitations on choice of law).

20   OECD (n 2) 245, figure 8.1 (citing World Economic Forum, *New Models for Addressing Supply Chain and Transport Risk* (2012)).

21   OECD (n 2) 244.

a supply chain could be great enough to dissuade participation by even a large global brand but surely pose even greater barriers to SMEs possessed of limited bargaining power. With this in mind, it is probably not a surprise to note that SMEs have not been as successful as large enterprises in joining global supply chains.[22] Thus, considering the key role played by both SMEs and global supply chains in economic development, removing barriers to supply chain participation, including the legal ones discussed here, should be a high priority for developing countries.

3 Role of the CISG in Reducing Legal Barriers to Cross-Border Trade and in Global Supply Chains

The States that drafted the CISG were motivated by the principle that the "adoption of uniform rules which govern contracts for the international sale of goods and take into account the different social, economic and legal systems would contribute to the removal of legal barriers in international trade".[23] The Convention does this by providing a uniform set of neutral contract rules for the settlement of disputes related to the commercial cross-border sale of goods.[24] The Convention applies to these transactions by default when contracting parties each have a place of business in a State that has adopted the CISG (Article 1(1)(a)). It also applies if only one party is in a CISG State, but, in a dispute, the rules of private international law lead to the application of the law of a CISG State (Article 1(1)(b)). Where adopted, it becomes part of the national law of the country in question.[25] In practice, the Convention has been a major success, and its reach is quite broad. The 95 States which have adopted the CISG[26] account for more than 75% of world trade.[27]

---

22   World Economic Forum, *Enabling Trade: Valuing Growth Opportunities* (2013) 20.
23   From the preamble to the CISG.
24   For a comprehensive introduction to the CISG, see Schwenzer & Hachem (n 10).
25   See Pilar Perales Viscasillas, 'Applicable Law, the CISG, and the Future Convention on International Commercial Contracts' (2013) 58 Villanova Law Review 733, 746.
26   The only major trade players that have not adopted the Convention are the United Kingdom and India. See UNCITRAL, *Status: United Nations Convention on Contracts for the International Sale of Goods (Vienna, 1980)* <https://uncitral.un.org/en/texts/salegoods/conventions/sale_of_goods/cisg/status> accessed 15 June 2022.
27   Based on statistics from European Commission, DG Trade CG/MP <https://trade.ec.eur opa.eu/doclib/docs/2006/september/tradoc_122530.pdf> accessed 15 June 2022; see also <https://uncitral.un.org/en/cisg40> accessed 15 June 2022.

It is the neutrality and legal certainty provided by the CISG that serves to remove barriers and lower transaction costs. When the CISG applies, contractual parties have the freedom to choose another applicable law (article 6), but there are many reasons not to do this. First, the CISG's broad adoption means that, in any given cross-border sales transaction, it will frequently be the national law of both buyer and seller and, thus, during contract negotiations can offer a mutually attractive alternative to the domestic sales law of either party. When proposed by the party with the weaker bargaining position, the Convention's international standing and acceptance may assist in overcoming a domestic law bias of the stronger party.[28] When it applies, neither party will be unfairly favored or harmed by application of the other's domestic law.[29] This obvious neutrality can eliminate the costs of a protracted negotiation. In addition, as the CISG is part of each party's national law and should be known by its lawyers and judges, research costs should be lower than in situations requiring analysis of domestic sales laws of other States or even soft law principles. Research is further facilitated by the Convention's translation into an array of languages and the wide availability of published case law and academic literature analyzing its provisions.[30] All of these things can particularly benefit SMEs, with their typically weaker bargaining positions and smaller bank accounts.

Even where the choice of law is not considered by contractual parties from CISG States, its default application means that they can still benefit from its neutral and uniform provisions in the case of a dispute or when analyzing legal risk exposure under existing contracts. In the event of a dispute, parties, courts, and tribunals will be spared the legal costs associated either with complex conflicts of law analysis (where parties made no choice of law) or foreign law analysis (where an alien domestic law has been chosen).[31] Furthermore, unlike domestic sales laws, the CISG was designed for cross-border transactions making it a better fit for the types of disputes likely to arise.[32]

---

28   See Lisa Spagnolo, *Treasure Trove or Skull and Bones: Is the CISG Worth Knowing?*, Conference paper delivered at NYSBA International Section, seasonal meeting 2011: Latin America as an Engine for Economic Recovery and Growth, 20–24 September 2011, Panama City, Panama, at n 44 (as cited in Cyril Emery & Julia Salasky, 'Arbitration and UNCITRAL's Sales Conventions' (2013) 2:1 Slovenska Arbitražna Praksa 28, 31, n 31).

29   ibid see also, Urs Peter Gruber, 'The Convention on the International Sale of Goods (CISG) in Arbitration' (2009) 1 International Business Law Journal 15, 16 (as cited in Emery & Salasky (n 28) 31, n 32).

30   ibid 15–17.

31   Nils Schmidt-Ahrendts, 'CISG and Arbitration' (2011) 59:3 Belgrade Law Review 211, 223 (as cited in Emery & Salasky (n 28) at 31, n 33).

32   David (n 5) para 20; See also Emery & Salasky (n 28) 31, n 34 (citing Gruber (n 29) 16–17).

For all its potential utility, the CISG is not above criticism. The most frequently expressed concern is that the Convention only covers certain areas of the contractual relationship (for example, contract formation, obligations of the buyer and seller, third-party claims, remedies, passing of risk, damages, etc.) but leaves others to domestic law (for example, validity, agency, fraud, etc.).[33] This is, of course, the result of the diplomatic process that led to the CISG,[34] and it means that domestic law must occasionally be used to fill these gaps as provided for in CISG Article 7. Nonetheless, in practice, the most common international sales disputes relate to the conformity of the goods with the contract,[35] something well covered by the CISG (Articles 35–44).[36]

While the CISG should, therefore, provide what is needed in most situations, parties seeking legal certainty in a one-time transaction could also achieve that goal through the choice of a specific domestic regime or a soft-law instrument with greater coverage, such as the Unidroit Principles (understanding, of course, that there are also gaps in the Unidroit Principles[37]). The parties would need to be informed as to whether all potential dispute fora would recognize their choice of law,[38] and they might face higher negotiating and dispute resolution costs as described above, but an end-goal of legal certainty could be served.

Such choices of domestic law or soft-law instruments, however, are unlikely to be as effective in a global supply chain or more complex international contracting scenarios. In these situations, the CISG's value is particularly visible. As described in part one of this chapter, global supply chains involve multiple contracts across multiple borders, frequently undertaken by subcontractors or other parties. While legal obligations may rest with individual supply-chain

---

33   *Возможная будущая работа по международным нормам в области договорного права: Предложение Швейцарии относительно возможной будущей работы ЮНСИТРАЛ по международным нормам в области договорного права*, A/CN.9/758, p 6, n 2 (2012) <https://uncitral.un.org/ru/commission#45> accessed 15 June 2022.

34   See eg Milena Djordjevic, 'Article 4' in Stefan Kröll, Loukas Mistelis, Pilar Perales Viscasillas (eds) *UN Convention on Contracts for the International Sale of Goods* (CISG) (CH Beck 2011) 67–68.

35   See John O. Honnold, *Uniform Law for International Sales under the 1980 United Nations Convention*, edited and updated by Harry M. Flechtner (Kluwer Law 2009) 328.

36   With detailed additional interpretation provided in *UNCITRAL Digest of Case Law on the United Nations Convention on Contracts for the International Sale of Goods*, arts 35–44 <https://uncitral.un.org/sites/uncitral.un.org/files/media-documents/uncitral/en/cisg _digest_2016.pdf> accessed 22 November 2021.

37   International Institute for the Unification of Private Law, *Model Clauses for the Use of the Unidroit Principles of International Commercial Contracts* (2013) 9.

38   See (n 19).

participants, the risks they incur affect the entire the chain. Thus, all participants, but particularly the global brand, will be motivated to research and
understand, to the extent possible, the legal consequences in the event that
risks are realized. In a complex supply chain, the cost of this research will be
astronomical unless parties can rely on conflicts being resolved, for the most
part, under a single legal regime. Domestic law and soft-law instruments are
problematic choices for providing that regime. First, to attain any certainty
under these instruments, all parties involved would need to actively include
choice-of-law clauses selecting them in all of their contracts, something that
is frequently over-looked.[39] Second, it is unlikely that all chain participants
will be familiar with either the domestic law in question or any given soft-
law instrument, resulting in research costs that may discourage participation.
Third, down-chain participants are particularly unlikely to agree to the selection of a domestic law of, say, the global brand, when they are subcontracting
with other parties that have little or no connection with that law. Finally, selection of soft-law instruments, such as the Unidroit Principles, may not even be
recognized by the courts in the country of every supply chain partner.[40]

The CISG addresses many of these problems. First, because of its wide adoption, it will be the default law under its article 1(1)(a) or (b) in a large number of cross-border sales contracts, meaning that it will apply even if it is not
specifically chosen by the parties. In the t-shirt example given in part one, it
would be the default sales law for each transaction.[41] Second, since it is part
of the national law in 95 countries, it is quite likely that all participants, even
those from non-CISG States, will have some familiarity with the Convention.[42]
Third, it will either be the national law of down-chain participants or a fairly
attractive choice as a neutral and balanced international treaty. Finally, even
in situations where it does not apply by default, it can be chosen by parties as
part of the national law of any CISG State, something now recognized in most
jurisdictions.[43]

---

39   See Gilles Cuniberti, 'Is the CISG Benefiting Anybody?' (2006) 39 Vanderbilt Journal of
      Transnational Law 1511, 1529.
40   Symeonides (n 19) 140–146.
41   The United States, China, Canada, and Uganda are all States parties to the Convention,
      see UNCITRAL (n 26).
42   For example, one survey concluded that the CISG is taught at 42% of British universities,
      even though it is not in force in that jurisdiction. Sarah Lake, 'An Empirical Study of the
      Unidroit Principles – International and British Responses' (2011) 16 Uniform Law Review
      669, 699, graph 11.
43   See Symeonides (n 19) 114–115.

As mentioned, the CISG does not cover every aspect of contract law. Once again, however, it is well-situated to deal with the main issue that tends to come up in the long-term contracts inherent to global supply chains. Unlike single transactions, where issues of agency, validity, or, in particular, conformity of the goods with the contract are likely to arise, in long-term contracts, because the parties have established ongoing relationships where the quality of goods is generally known, the main issues tend to be related to hardship as the result of a change in circumstances,[44] in particular due to natural disasters. Like the issue of conformity of the goods, the CISG's approach to hardship is well-defined, both in its text in article 79,[45] and in the interpretation of that article by implementing courts and tribunals.[46] Article 79 is supplemented by article 74, which limits damages to that which parties ought to have foreseen at the time of the conclusion of the contract. Between these two articles, parties will be well-informed about the legal regime covering natural disasters or other hardship-inducing events.

All of this is to say that use of the CISG as the legal regime in a global supply chain can be an effective way of breaking down legal barriers and ensuring legal certainty. Obviously, some uncertainty will remain, for example for disputes involving issues outside the scope of the CISG or in purely domestic subcontracting situations, which will frequently be dealt with under the relevant domestic law. That said, however, because of its wide adoption, it represents the best existing way of simplifying the legal analysis needed to undertake and participate in complex global supply chains.

4   Participation in the CISG and Global Supply Chains in Central Asia

Increasingly, engagement in global supply chains is seen as an important tool for fostering economic development.[47] As discussed above, however, there are an array of barriers that prevent enterprises from joining supply chains, including legal barriers. The removal of these barriers can facilitate entry into global supply chains, spurring economic development.

In South and Central Asia, it is estimated that reduction of non-tariff supply chain barriers could result in as much as an 8% increase in gross domestic

---

44   See Klaus Peter Berger, 'Power of Arbitrators to Fill Gaps and Revise Contracts to Make Sense' (2001) 17:1 Arbitration International 1, 1.

45   Schwenzer & Hachem (n 10) 474–475.

46   See *Сборник ЮНСИТРАЛ* (n 33) art 79.

47   See OECD (n 2) 156.

product (GDP), a 65.2% increase in exports, and a 49.3% increase in imports.[48] Among 15 global regions, South and Central Asia would thus rank third in terms of potential percentage increase to GDP, second in terms of potential percentage increase to exports, and third in terms of potential percentage increase to imports.[49] These potential increases are based on reduction of a variety of non-tariff barriers, not just the legal ones, but are indicative of the potential benefits of facilitating entry by any means into global supply chains.

The high potential gains are no doubt related to geographic proximity to a major supply chain player, China.[50] Currently, Chinese "trade with Central Asia only accounts for 1% of China's total imports and exports, which also suggests an enormous potential for intraregional trade that has yet to be tapped."[51] Similarly, there is the opportunity to further facilitate participation in supply chains with enterprises in the Russian Federation, which is already a major trade partner with the countries in Central Asia.[52] Kazakhstan and Kyrgyzstan have already taken some steps to further their economic integration in that direction, joining the Eurasian Economic Union, together with the Russian Federation, Armenia and Belarus.[53]

Thus, the countries of Central Asia have much to gain by removing barriers to trade and facilitating entry into global supply chains. As described above, implementation of the CISG is one method for removing certain of those barriers. As of yet, however, the countries of Central Asia have had limited interaction with the text. Kazakhstan and Turkmenistan have yet to accede to the Convention. Kyrgyzstan (entry into force in 2000), Uzbekistan (entry into force in 1997), and Turkmenistan (entry into force in 2023) are State parties to the CISG, but, as of yet, only Uzbekistan has reported case law (13 cases) applying the Convention.[54] While things are progressing in a positive direction, the low

---

48 World Economic Forum (n 22) 13–14 (read together with the online appendix, *The Benefits of Trade Facilitation: A Modelling Exercise* <http://reports.weforum.org/global-enabling-trade-2013/view/appendix/> accessed 15 June 2022). Note also that these values are for merchandise trade, to which the CISG is directly applicable.

49 ibid.

50 For more on China's role in global supply chains, see OECD (n 2) 44–148.

51 United Nations Conference on Trade and Development (n 1) 11.

52 ibid.

53 Евразийская экономическая комиссия (ЕЭК), <www.eurasiancommission.org/ru/Pages/about.aspx> accessed 15 June 2022.

54 See the major CISG case law databases: CLOUT <https://uncitral.un.org/en/case_law> accessed 15 June 2022; Albert H. Kritzer (Pace Law School) CISG Database <https://iicl.law.pace.edu/cisg/search/cases> accessed 15 June 2022 (account creation and login required), Unilex <http://www.unilex.info/cisg/cases/country/all> accessed 15 June 2022. A proactive study was also conducted in late 2004 and early 2005, when the non-existence

number of cases implies limited use of or familiarity with the CISG and may discourage parties from States with active implementation of the CISG from doing business there due to uncertainty as to potential judicial interpretation of the Convention. Furthermore, it can be distinguished from the high level of use in the major neighboring trade hubs: China, with 532 reported cases, and the Russian Federation, with 326 reported cases.[55] In fact, China and the Russian Federation trail only Germany in the total number of reported cases. Removal of trade barriers with those countries through the implementation of CISG in Central Asia should thus be a particularly effective method for further facilitating trade in the broader region.

5   Conclusions and Recommendations

To further foster economic development, the countries of Central Asia may have a high interest in facilitating entry by their traders into global supply chains. A large number of barriers, however, including those that are legal in nature, may discourage participation, in particular by SMEs. Implementation of the CISG is an effective way for a State to remove some of these legal barriers and is potentially a particularly useful tool for SME participants in cross-border trade. Thus, further implementation of the CISG in Central Asia may be warranted. Kazakhstan and Tajikistan, therefore, may wish to consider accession to the text. Where the text is already in force, in Kyrgyzstan and Uzbekistan, limited case law may indicate a low level of use or familiarity by traders and/or the judiciary. In these countries, as in Turkmenistan, where the CISG will enter into force in 2023, training of the judiciary and active lawyers could be of use, as would inclusion of an in-depth CISG curriculum in the domestic legal education. Overall, these efforts could serve as the next step to broad regional implementation of the CISG, creating a uniform legal regime that would overcome legal barriers related to the sale of goods, and could be an important part of a broader initiative to remove non-tariff trade barriers and encourage supply chain participation.

of case law was first examined. Rolf Knieper, 'Celebrating Success by Accession to CISG' (2005–2006) 25 Journal of Law and Commerce 477, 479.

55   Albert H. Kritzer (Pace Law School) CISG Database (n 54).

PART 3

Settlement of International Trade Disputes

∵

SECTION 1

Dispute Settlement under Public International Law

∴

CHAPTER 16

Russia's Experience in WTO Dispute Settlement

Nicolas Lamp and Larysa Workewych

1 Introduction

The Russian Federation joined the World Trade Organization (WTO) on 22 August 2012, after negotiating for accession for 18 years. It was a watershed moment both for the acceding country and for the WTO: neither the Soviet Union nor the Russian Federation had ever been a member of the multilateral trade regime established after the Second World War,[1] and, at the time of its accession, Russia was the largest trading nation remaining outside of the multilateral system.[2] Russia's accession brought the WTO a step closer to covering virtually all of world trade.[3] At the same time, Russia joined the WTO with less enthusiasm than most other acceding countries. Not only was Russia's accession internally contested; Russia's political leadership at times appeared lukewarm about the prospect of joining the WTO.[4] The accession negotiations provoked concerns that Russia might not be willing to undertake the deep reforms that are normally required of acceding countries, and that WTO Members, eager to get Russia on board, might acquiesce.[5]

Given that WTO negotiations on new rules are largely stalled, Russia's willingness to implement rulings by the WTO's Dispute Settlement Body (DSB) has become an important yardstick for Russia's commitment to the WTO since

---

1 Some other communist countries had negotiated for accession; see Francine McKenzie, 'GATT and the Cold War. Accession Debates, Institutional Development, and the Western Alliance, 1947–1959' (2008) 10(3) JCWS 78.

2 See Bogdan Lissovolik and Yaroslav Lissovolik, 'Russia and the WTO: The "Gravity" of Outsider Status' (2006) 53(1) IMF Staff Papers 1.

3 At the time of writing, the WTO has 164 members and covers 97% of world trade. The largest economy remaining outside the WTO is Iran. Iran applied for accession in July 1996, but its accession negotiations have been blocked for political reasons. See Christopher G. Terris, 'Iran at the WTO: The Future of the U.S. State Sponsor of Terrorism Sanctions' (2017) 49 NYUJILP 891.

4 Richard Connolly and Philip Hanson, 'Russia's Accession to the World Trade Organization: Commitments, Processes, and Prospects' (2012) 53(4) Eurasion Geography and Economics 479, 488–489.

5 David Christy, 'Foreign Policy: The Terms of Russia Joining the WTO' (28 June 2010) <www.npr.org/templates/story/story.php?storyId=128160125> accessed 30 July 2021.

its accession. It is with a view to the broader question of Russia's commitment to the WTO that this chapter undertakes a review of Russia's experience in WTO dispute settlement to date. While it is too early to come to firm conclusions, we will argue that Russia's willingness to invoke the national security exception in WTO dispute settlement proceedings, as well as, in one instance, to impose measures on national security grounds to evade its obligation to comply with DSB rulings, compounds the lingering questions about its commitment to the multilateral trade regime.

Russia's experience in WTO dispute settlement is remarkable in at least two respects. First, given how recently Russia joined the WTO, it has been extraordinarily active in dispute settlement. Several years into its membership, Russia has already been the addressee of eleven requests for consultations.[6] In eight of these disputes, the WTO Dispute Settlement Body (DSB) has established panels.[7] At the time of writing, five of these panels have circulated their reports, three of which were appealed; the Appellate Body Report circulated its first report in a dispute involving Russia in February 2017. Offensively, Russia has also been quite active, making eight consultations requests. This is an unusual level of engagement for a recently acceded country, even for a large trader such as Russia. By comparison, five years into its membership, China had only been involved in three disputes[8]: it had settled the first dispute at the consultations stage,[9] had participated in a challenge against the United States along with seven other WTO Members[10] and was only in the early stages of a dispute that would eventually result in the first ruling against it.[11] Instead of becoming embroiled in numerous simultaneous disputes, China used its early years in the WTO to learn about the system by joining disputes among other WTO Members as a third party. Russia enjoyed no such honeymoon.

---

6   Under art 4 of the Dispute Settlement Understanding (DSU), submitting a request for consultations is the first step of dispute settlement proceedings. For the consultation requests involving Russia, see DS462 (EU), DS463 (Japan), DS475 (EU), DS479 (EU), DS485 (EU), DS499 (Ukraine), DS512 (Ukraine), DS532 (Ukraine), DS566 (US), DS604 (EU), DS608 (EU). The challenge by the European Union in DS462 and Japan in DS463 concerned the same measure, a "recycling fee" imposed on motor vehicles. DS532 and DS608 are still at the consultations stage. [Here and in the following, we will be referring to WTO disputes by their DS number; further information about these disputes can be found by searching for them by DS number on the WTO website: <www.wto.org> accessed 30 January 2022.].

7   DS462, DS475, DS479, DS485, DS499, DS512, DS566, DS604.

8   For a review of China's early experience in WTO dispute settlement, see Henry Gao, 'Taming the Dragon: China's Experience in WTO Dispute Settlement' (2007) 34(4) LIEI 369.

9   DS309.

10   DS252.

11   DS339/DS340/DS342.

The second remarkable feature of Russia's experience in WTO dispute settlement is that it unfolded against a backdrop of profound political acrimony between Russia and some of its largest trading partners. The political turmoil was caused by the Ukraine crisis and, in particular, Russia's annexation of Crimea, in response to which several Western states, including Russia's largest trading partner, the European Union, imposed economic sanctions against Russian individuals and companies. Russia responded to these sanctions by imposing trade sanctions of its own.[12]

Is Russia's unusual activity in WTO dispute settlement due to the deterioration of its relationship with the West? Until recently, there appeared to be little connection between these two aspects of Russia's WTO experience. To be sure, Russia threatened to challenge the sanctions imposed by its trading partners, and in particular the United States, in WTO dispute settlement,[13] and there was some overlap among the products affected by Russian measures that had been challenged in WTO dispute settlement and the products that were targeted by Russian countersanctions. However, Russia and its Western trading partners appeared to be observing the (already crumbling[14]) taboo against challenging measures imposed on national security grounds in WTO dispute settlement. However, while Russia has not followed through on its threat to bring a case against US sanctions, Russia's trading partners' reluctance to challenge Russian measures purportedly imposed for reasons of national security appears to be coming to an end. As we explain below, Ukraine challenged a range of restrictions imposed by Russia on goods in transit, which Russia defended on national security grounds.[15] And the European Union included

---

12 For an overview of the sanctions and countersanctions imposed by Russia and its Western trading partners, see Rostam J. Neuwirth and Alexandr Svetlicinii, 'The current EU/US-Russia conflict over Ukraine and the WTO: A Preliminary Note on (trade) Restrictive Measures' (2016) 32(3) Post-Soviet Affairs 237.

13 Communication from the Russian Federation S/C/W/353 – G/C/W/697 (Council for Trade in Services - Council for Trade in Goods, 17 April 2014).

14 This taboo was tested in 1996, when the European Communities (as they then were) brought a challenge again the so-called Helms-Burton Act; see DS38. In that case, a Panel was established, but the European Communities let the Panel's authority lapsed and reached a negotiated solution with the United States; for background, see Klinton W. Alexander, 'The Helms-Burton Act and the WTO Challenge: Making a Case for the United States under the GATT National Security Exception' (1997) 11 Fla. J. Intl L 559. The taboo has is now crumbling due to Qatar's decision to challenge the embargo imposed by the United Arab Emirates, Bahrain and Saudi Arabia in WTO dispute settlement; see DS526, DS527 and DS528.

15 See DS512.

Russia's "national security" ban on pork products in the compliance proceedings of a dispute in which it had challenged a ban on such products imposed on sanitary grounds.

Given the political and commercial tensions between Russia and some of its most important trading partners, Russia's experience in WTO dispute settlement is of interest not only as a gauge of its commitment to the WTO; Russia's involvement in disputes against a backdrop of political turmoil also serves as a test case for the potential and limits of legalized dispute settlement in international relations more broadly. On the one hand, the WTO dispute settlement system has – at least until recently – allowed Russia and its Western counterparts to address discrete trade disputes in a relatively depoliticized manner even in the highly politically charged atmosphere following the Ukraine crisis. In this sense, the disputes between the EU and Russia could be seen as examples of how international economic law allows countries – in John Jackson's memorable formulation – to "'chip off' bits and pieces of the amorphous complex totality of commercial relationships and find solutions to those chipped-off pieces"[16] in relative isolation from broader political and economic conflicts between them.

On the other hand, these dispute also bring the dangers of high stakes political standoffs for the WTO dispute settlement system into sharp relief. Russia's attempt to evade its compliance obligations in a WTO dispute by resorting to measures imposed on national security grounds could deprive the complainant of the commercial benefits of its WTO "win" and thereby undermine the structure of economic incentives that ultimately sustains the WTO dispute settlement system. Russia's reliance on the national security exception to justify its measures targeting Ukraine, coupled with the argument that the national security exception is "non-justiciable", appears designed to remove its measures from judicial scrutiny entirely.[17] In the relationship between Russia and Ukraine, there is thus little prospect that the parties will be able, or even willing, to prevent their political conflict from spilling over into WTO dispute settlement.

---

16   John H Jackson, *World Trade and the Law of GATT* (Bobbs-Merrill Company 1969) 767.

17   Russia's arguments are referenced in the European Union's third-party submission in the dispute; see *Russia – Measures Concerning Traffic in Transit*, Third Party Written Submission by the European Union, available at <http://trade.ec.europa.eu/doclib/docs/2018/february/tradoc_156602.pdf> accessed 30 July 2021. See also *Russia – Measures Concerning Traffic in Transit*, Panel Report (adopted on 26 April 2019) WT/DS512, paras 7.27 – 7.30.

While the disputes between Russia and Ukraine are thus highly relevant to the subject of this chapter, at the time of writing none of the Panels in those disputes had released its report.[18] The chapter will therefore focus on Russia's disputes with the European Union, in which panel and, in one case, an Appellate Body Report, are available. We will briefly address the disputes with Ukraine in the conclusion.

2   The Political and Economic Context: The Ukraine Crisis and the Sanctioning of Russia

In August 2013, a year after Russia's accession to the World Trade Organization, the United States cancelled a trade summit scheduled between the two countries.[19] According to a spokeswoman from the Office of the United States Trade Representative, the cancellation was in part due to the United States' disappointment that Russia had not yet implemented some of its WTO commitments.[20] Despite this disappointment, the spokeswoman acknowledged Russia's active role in the WTO dispute system a year in, with dispute settlement consultations already emerging between Russia and the United States, the European Union, and Japan.[21]

A couple of months later, new tensions began to develop in Europe between Russia and neighboring Ukraine. In late November 2013, protests began in Ukraine's capital city after Ukrainian President Viktor Yanukovych decided to pursue integration into the Eurasian Economic Union (EAEU) with Russia, putting Ukraine's integration plans with the European Union on hold.[22] These growing protests, known as the Euromaidan, coupled with the resulting instability in Ukraine, eventually resulted in Yanukovych's removal from

18   Panel and Appellate Body Reports, which were adopted after the submission of this article, are WT/DS499/AB/R, WT/DS499/AB/R/ADD.1, WT/DS499/R, WT/DS499/R/ADD.1, WT/DS512/R, and WT/DS512/R/Add.1.

19   Adam Behsudi, 'White House Cancellation of Russia Summit Partly Due to Trade Irritants' (15 August 2013) 31(33) *Inside US Trade's World Trade Online* <www.insidetrade.com> accessed 30 July 2021.

20   ibid.

21   ibid.

22   D.T., 'Where Three is a Crowd – Introducing the Eurasian Economic Union' *The Economist* (Moscow, 20 May 2014) <www.economist.com/blogs/banyan/2014/05/introducing-euras ian-economic-union> accessed 30 July 2021.

government.[23] Less than a month later, Ukraine's autonomous region Crimea was annexed by Russia.[24]

In response to the annexation, viewed as an undermining of Ukrainian sovereignty, the United States and eventually the European Union chose to impose sanctions on Russia.[25] Russia threatened to challenge these sanctions, claiming they violated the General Agreement in Trade in Services (GATS).[26] While threats of a WTO challenge were made, no official challenge was ever brought by Russia. Instead, Russia imposed retaliatory sanctions against the United States, the European Union, and Canada that impacted prominent industries in these countries.[27]

As tensions between Russia, the European Union and the United States grew, Ukraine's new government once again turned its sights on integration with the European Union.[28] The Eurasian Economic Union was created in May 2014 without Ukraine as a member.[29] Instead, Ukraine and the European Union signed a trade deal in June 2014, the same deal that was rejected by Yanukovych in November 2013.[30]

---

23   Natalia Zinets and Alessandra Prentice, 'Ukraine sets European Course after Ouster of Yanukovich' *Reuters* (Kiev, 22 February 2014) <www.reuters.com/article/us-ukraine/ ukraine-sets-european-course-after-ouster-of-yanukovich-idUSBREA1GoOU20140223> accessed 30 July 2021.

24   A.O., 'Ukraine's Amputation – Crimea Votes to Secede' *The Economist* (Kiev, 17 March 2014) <www.economist.com/blogs/easternapproaches/2014/03/crimea-votes-secede> accessed 30 July 2021.

25   Adrian Croft and Arshad Mohammed, 'Russia Faces New U.S., EU Sanctions over Ukraine Crisis' *Reuters* (Brussels / Washington, 11 September 2014) <www.reuters.com/article/us -ukraine-crisis/russia-faces-new-u-s-eu-sanctions-over-ukraine-crisis-idUSKBN61O72 0140911?feedType=RSS> accessed 30 July 2021.

26   'Russia's WTO Claims Against U.S. Sanctions Unlikely to Prevail: Experts' (29 April 2014) *Inside US Trade's World Trade Online* <www.insidetrade.com> accessed 30 July 2021.

27   Barrie McKenna and David Hains, 'Canadian Businesses Brace for More Russian Import Bans' *The Globe and Mail* (Ottawa and Toronto, 7 August 2014) <www.theglobeandmail .com/report-on-business/canadian-food-exports-feel-brunt-of-new-wave-of-russian -sanctions/article19966813/> accessed 30 July 2021.

28   Natalia Zinets and Alessandra Prentice, 'Ukraine sets European Course after Ouster of Yanukovich' *Reuters* (Kiev, 22 February 2014) <www.reuters.com/article/us-ukraine/ ukraine-sets-european-course-after-ouster-of-yanukovich-idUSBREA1GoOU20140223> accessed 30 July 2021.

29   D.T. (n 22).

30   Michael Birnbaum, 'Ukraine Signs Landmark Agreement with E.U.' *The Washington Post* (Washington, 27 June 2014) <www.washingtonpost.com/world/ukraine-signs-landmark -agreement-with-eu/2014/06/27/8e6ca59a-fdd2-11e3-932c-0a55b81f48ce_story.html?utm _term=.11bff1446c8f> accessed 30 July 2021.

Over the course of 2014 and 2015 Russia's relationship with Ukraine, the European Union and the United States continued to deteriorate, affecting not only their political relationships but also their economic relationships.[31] Total trade between the European Union and Russia fell 36% between 2013 and 2015; however, Russia remains one of the European Union's largest trading partners.[32]

In the background of these ongoing political tensions between Russia, Ukraine and the European Union is Russia's unusually active involvement in the WTO dispute system.

3   An Analysis of Russia's Disputes with the European Union

The present section provides an analysis of the first three disputes involving Russia that have so far resulted in the circulation of panel reports and, in one case, in the circulation and adoption of an Appellate Body Report.

3.1   *Russia – Tariff Treatment of Certain Agricultural and Manufacturing Products (DS485)*

The first panel report published in a dispute involving Russia was circulated on 12 August 2016 in a dispute called *Russia – Tariff Treatment of Certain Agricultural and Manufacturing Products (Russia – Tariff Treatment* for short). This case marked the first time that a WTO panel found that Russia had acted inconsistently with its WTO obligations. The provision that Russia was alleged to have violated – GATT Article II – represents one of the most elemental obligations in WTO law, namely the obligation not to levy tariffs that exceed the 'binding' for the tariff line at issue that is inscribed in the WTO Member's GATT schedule.[33] In the convoluted language of GATT Article II:1(b), the products listed in a WTO Member's schedule "shall, on their importation into the territory to which the Schedule relates, ... be exempt from ordinary customs duties in excess of those set forth and provided therein." Essentially, all that

---

31   Tom Miles, 'EU Scrapes a Win in WTO Row over Russian Duties on Vans' *Reuters* (Geneva, 27 January 2017) <www.reuters.com/article/us-eu-russia-wto-idUSKBN15B1N6> accessed 30 July 2021.

32   'WTO Confirms Russian Pork ban is Illegal' European Commission Press Release, (Brussels, 23 February 2017) <http://trade.ec.europa.eu/doclib/press/index.cfm?id=1627> accessed 30 July 2021.

33   An indication of how fundamental this obligation was seen is that the entire GATT was designed with the objective of "safeguard[ing] the value of tariff concessions" set out in the schedules.

is required to assess whether a WTO Member has acted inconsistently with its obligations under GATT Article 11:1(b) is to compare the tariff rate applied by the WTO Member when a product is imported to the tariff rate set out in the WTO Member's schedule regarding that product. If the applied rate is higher than the bound rate, Article 11:1(b) is violated; if the applied rate is equal to or lower than the bound rate, the WTO Member is acting consistently with its obligations under Article 11:1(b).

Despite the apparent simplicity of the exercise, the Panel report runs to 100 pages. There are several reasons for the length. First, the Panel used the opportunity to address several interpretative questions regarding Article 11:1(b). Second, the Panel faced some complicating factors in its assessment of the duties levied by Russia. Thus, the measure setting out those duty rates was not adopted by Russia, but rather by the Eurasian Economic Union (EAEU).[34] Moreover, some of the duties that Russia was required to apply under the measure were not simple ad valorem duties,[35] but more complex "combined duty rates" consisting of an ad valorem rate and an alternative minimum rate expressed as a specific duty.[36] Finally, the European Union did not limit itself to challenging individual rates, but also challenged what it described as Russia's practice of "systemic duty variation", i.e. Russia's use, in the case of numerous tariff lines, of combined tariff rates that could exceed its bound rates under certain circumstances. In the following, we will first discuss the panel's analysis of each of these elements in turn. We will then present the panel's conclusion and discuss Russia's implementation of the panel's findings. We will conclude by situating the significance of this dispute as regards Russia's commitment to the WTO.

3.1.1 Interpretation of Article 11:1(b)

As noted above, Article 11:1(b) requires that WTO Members not apply tariffs to imported products originating in the territory of other Members that are "in excess" of the rates set out in the Member's schedule. The Panel in *Russia – Tariff Treatment* explained what type of evidence a complainant has to adduce in order to demonstrate a violation of this provision. Building on the well-established principle that the basic WTO obligations on market access and

---

34 *Russia – Tariff Treatment of Certain Agricultural and Manufacturing Products*, Panel Report (adopted on 26 September 2016) WT/DS485/R, para 7.42 (*Russia – Tariff Treatment*).

35 An ad valorem duty is a tariff rate that is expressed as a percentage of the customs value of the imported product.

36 A specific duty is a tariff rate that is expressed in relation to the weight, quantity, or volume of the imported product, rather than its customs value.

non-discrimination protect "competitive opportunities of imported products" rather than trade flows,[37] the Panel agreed with the European Union that a complainant does not have to show actual trade effects[38] to allow a panel to find that a measure is inconsistent with Article 11:1(b).[39] Instead, the Panel referred to previous jurisprudence in support of the proposition that a violation of Article 11:1(b) can be established "on the basis of the structure and design of an impugned duty"[40] and can hence be made out "based solely on the 'text' of the relevant measures".[41] While this finding of the Panel is not unexpected, it serves as a confirmation that evidence of trade effects is indeed "irrelevant" to the analysis of a measure's consistency with Article 11:1(b).[42]

The second interpretive issue addressed by the Panel was the question of "whether Article 11:1(b), first sentence, permits an applied duty rate to exceed the relevant bound duty rate up to a *de minimis* level."[43] Drawing on the dictionary definition of "excess", the context provided by Article III:2, where the prohibition to tax imported products "in excess of" like domestic products has been interpreted not to allow a *de minimis* difference in taxation, and the GATT's purpose "to preserve the value of tariff concessions", the Panel found that Article 11:1(b) "admits of no *de minimis* exception" and that a WTO Member hence "must not exceed a tariff binding, even if the extent of the excess is only minimal".[44] Again, this is not a surprising finding, in light of the well-established jurisprudence under Article III:2, but a helpful confirmation that the same standard as under Article III:2 applies under Article 11:1(b) as well. The Panel also found that, as a logical implication of this finding, WTO

---

37   See *Japan – Taxes on Alcoholic Beverages,* Appellate Body Report (adopted on 1 November 1996) WTDS8/AB/R, para 110 (*Japan – Alcoholic Beverages II*). It should be noted that, in the context of other WTO provisions, an effect on trade flows is a material element of proving an inconsistency of a measure with WTO law; see, for example, the analysis of "adverse effects" that is required to show that a subsidy is inconsistent with art 5 of the Agreement on Subsidies and Countervailing Measures.

38   Evidence of such effects could take the form of documentation relating to transactions on which the above-ceiling tariff was levied, or data showing a depression or suppression of the level of exports as a result of the measure.

39   *Russia – Tariff Treatment* (n 34) para 7.20.

40   ibid para 7.19 (referring to *Argentina – Measures Affecting Imports of Footwear, Textiles, Apparel and other Items* Appellate Body Report (adopted on 22 April 1998) WT/DS56/R, paras 53, 55, 62).

41   ibid (referring to *Colombia – Measures Relating to the Importation of Textiles, Apparel and Footwear* Panel Report (adopted on 22 June 2016) WT/DS461/R, para 7.123).

42   ibid [7.18] (citing the Appellate Body's finding in *Japan – Alcoholic Beverages II* (n 37) para 110 that trade effects are "irrelevant" in the context of Article III of the GATT 1994).

43   ibid para 7.19.

44   ibid para 7.28.

Members cannot balance out duties that exceed their tariff binding in some instances with duties that remain below the binding in other instances. In other words, it is not sufficient for the *average* level of duties levelled on a particular product over a certain time frame to remain at or below the bound level. Instead, the tariff binding is an absolute ceiling that may not be exceeded at any time, "even if these duties are balanced or offset (at the same time or later) by duties imposed on identical products that are below the bound duty."[45]

3.1.2   Attributability of the Measures at Issue to Russia

Apart from having to resolve a number of interpretative questions, the Panel also felt the need to establish that the measures at issue, which required Russia to impose duty rates in excess of its tariff bindings, were in fact attributable to Russia.[46] This was because the measures at issue in the case were duty rates set out in the Common Customs Tariff of the Eurasian Economic Union (CCT), which had been adopted by the Eurasian Economic Union (EAEU) composed of Belarus, Kazakhstan and Russia.[47] As Lorand Bartels has pointed out, the Panel did not adopt the "straightforward argument" that "under Russian constitutional law the CCT had the status of Russian law",[48] but instead found that "the relevant CCT requirement are attributable to Russia, insofar as, on the evidence before us, it can be presumed that the CCT requirements will lead to the relevant duty rates being applied by Russia".[49] The Panel suggested that Russia could rebut that presumption, but noted that Russia had not attempted to do so.[50] On the Panel's reading, then, the CCT can be attributed to Russia not on the basis of some clear legal link between the CCT and Russia, but rather on the basis of Russia's presumed (subsequent) actions. As Bartels has noted, this is "a rather slender basis" for attributing the CCT to Russia,[51] but given that Russia

45   ibid para 7.33.

46   While the European Union had presented arguments on this point, Russia apparently did not feel the need to comment on this issue. ibid para 7.44.

47   While the European Union classified the EAEU as a customs union, the Panel characterized it as "international organization", presumably because it did not want to prejudge the question (which was not at issue in the dispute) of whether the EAEU meets the criteria for a "customs union" set out in GATT Article XXIV:8. ibid para7.42.

48   Lorand Bartels, 'Attribution of the Measures of an International Organization to a Member in the Russia - Tariff Treatment Panel Report' International Economic Law and Policy Blog <http://worldtradelaw.typepad.com/ielpblog/2016/08/attribution-of-the-measures-of-an-international-organization-to-a-member-in-the-russia-tariff-treatm.html> accessed 30 July 2021.

49   *Russia – Tariff Treatment* (n 34) para 7.46.

50   ibid.

51   Bartels (n 48).

was apparently content to accept the CCT as its own, the Panel did not feel the need to belabor the point.

3.1.3 Ad Valorem and "Combined" Duty Rates

Once the Panel had established that the measures at issue could be attributed to Russia, it had no difficulty finding that the first five tariff rates at issue, which concerned various paper and paperboard products, were inconsistent with Russia's WTO obligations. The Panel simply compared the ad valorem rates that Russia was required to apply under the CCT to the ad valorem rates for the respective tariff lines contained in Russia's schedule to find that the applied rates were in excess of Russia's tariff bindings and hence inconsistent with Article II:1(b).[52]

The issues presented by measures seven to eleven were more complex, because the measures did not take the form of a simple ad valorem rate, but instead combined an ad valorem rate with an alternative minimum rate expressed as a specific duty in the form: "x%, but not less than y per unit of measurement".[53] In contrast to the first five measures, the ad valorem component did not exceed Russia's binding (apart from one measure, which was amended by Russia during the course of the proceedings to bring the ad valorem component down to the bound level[54]). Instead, the alleged inconsistency arose from the specific component of the combined duty, which required Russia to levy a minimum duty of 0.09 Euros per kg or 0.13 Euros per litre, respectively. The minimum duty would kick in if the duty calculated on the basis of the ad valorem component would result in a lower duty than the minimum, or, as the Panel explained it: "the customs authority, in respect of every import of the affected goods, calculates and chooses the higher of either an *ad valorem* duty or a specific duty".[55]

The use of such combined duty rates is not uncommon among WTO members: Canada, for example, has inscribed combined duty rates for numerous

---

52 *Russia – Tariff Treatment* (n 34) paras 7.61–7.62. The Panel reached the same conclusion with respect to a sixth measure which provided for an applied tariff rate in excess of the bound rate to take effect at a future date. Because the inconsistent rate was not being applied at the time of the establishment of the Panel and the measure had been amended in the course of the Panel proceedings, the arguments of the parties on the sixth measures differed from the arguments on the first five measures and were addressed separately by the Panel; see ibid paras 7.67–7.149.

53 ibid para 7.168.

54 ibid paras 7.164–7.172.

55 ibid para 7.174.

TABLE 1   Comparison of Russia's applied and bound rates

Measures	Applied rate	Bound rate
Seven and eight	3%; but not less than 0.09 EUR/kg	3%
Nine	15%, but not less than 0.13 EUR/l	15%
Ten	16%, but not less than 0.156 EUR/l[a]	16.7%; or 16%, but not less than 0.156 EUR/l; whichever is the lower
Eleven	13.3%, but not less than 0.12 EUR/l[b]	14.5%; or 13.3%, but not less than 0.12 EUR/l; whichever is the lower

COMPARISON OF RUSSIA'S APPLIED AND BOUND RATES; SOURCE: PANEL REPORT, PARAS. 7.157, 7.208, 7.209, 7.238, 7.256.
a   At the time of the Panel's establishment.
b   At the time of the Panel's establishment.

agricultural products in its schedule.[56] There is nothing in WTO law that prohibits the use of specific duties or combined duties per se. The alleged inconsistency in the case of Russia's duties arose from its use of a combined duty to calculate its *applied* tariff rate, while the *bound* rate set out in its schedule, and hence the limit on what it was allowed to charge, was, in the case of some measures, a simple ad valorem rate and, in the case of other measures, a combined duty rate with an ad valorem ceiling (see Table 1 below).[57]

The European Union argued that, when the price of imports fell below a certain level, the minimum duty that Russia was required to apply would result in tariff rates that, when converted into ad valorem rates, were higher than the ad valorem rates set out in Russia's schedule. In other words, the European Union argued that "there is a breakeven price or customs value ... below which the *ad valorem* equivalent of the specific element of the applied combined duty

---

56   See Schedule V – Canada, Part i – Most-Favoured-Nation Tariff, Section 1 – Agricultural Products. For example, Canada's out-of-quota tariff for turkeys (tariff item number 0105.99.12) is 182%, but not less than 188.2 c/kg.

57   ibid para 7.174.

will inevitably exceed Russia's bound *ad valorem* duty".[58] Russia could have avoided this outcome by implementing a ceiling or cap on the tariff rate to be charged; in fact, such a ceiling was inscribed in Russia's schedule for measures ten and eleven. The tariff binding for these measures instructed Russia to choose between (1) an ad valorem rate or (2) a combined duty (which itself consisted of an ad valorem rate – lower than the first – coupled with a minimum specific duty). Since Russia, as per its schedule, had to choose the option that resulted in the lower duty, option 1 effectively functioned as a ceiling on the combined duty. Russia thus had a ready model, inscribed in its own schedule, for implementing a ceiling on a combined duty rate.[59]

After extensive discussions regarding the status of the challenged measures, all of which had been amended during the course of the Panel proceedings, the Panel agreed with the European Union's argument that the ad valorem equivalents of the specific elements of the combined duties applied by Russia exceeded the bound rates in Russia's schedule "at or below specified break-even prices (customs values)", in violation of Article II:1(b) of the GATT 1994.[60]

3.1.4   The Existence of "Systematic Duty Variation"

Perhaps the most important claim in the dispute was the last: the European Union's challenge of what it called the "Systematic Duty Variation" (SDV) embodied in the CCT. The European Union argued that "the CCT systematically provides, in relation to a significant number of tariff lines, for a type or structure of duty that varies from the type or structure of duty recorded in Russia's Schedule, in a way that results in the application of duties in excess of those provided for in the Schedule."[61] The European Union's challenge of the practice of systematic duty variation was thus an attempt to go beyond the duties applied to specific tariff lines and bring a generalized challenge against Russia's practice of applying a particular *type* of duty – namely, a duty that varies depending on import prices and that will inevitably exceed Russia's tariff binding when prices fall below a certain level. It is easy to see why it would have been significant for the European Union to obtain a finding of inconsistency of this practice: Russia would have been required to amend not just the duties on tariff lines that the European Union had specifically challenged, but

---

58   *Russia – Tariff Treatment* (n 34) para 7.175.

59   For the Panel's discussion of the implications of the absence of a ceiling mechanism, see ibid para 7.229.

60   For measures seven, eight and nine, see ibid paras 7.230, 7.231; for measures ten and eleven, see ibid para 7.272.

61   ibid para 7.275.

other applied duties with a similar structure as well. The implications were potentially far-reaching: at the time of its accession to the WTO, Russia applied combined duties on 1,746 tariff lines.[62] Equally importantly, a finding that the practice of systematic duty variation is inconsistent would also have constrained Russia in applying tariffs with this structure in the future.[63] Before the Panel, the European Union explained that it was not practicable to challenge every individual tariff line that was subject to a combined duty – as it had done with respect to measures seven to eleven – given that Russia's duties were "subject to frequent changes", making individual tariff lines a "moving target".[64]

The European Union is not the only WTO Member that has been concerned about Russia's practice of applying "combined duties" of the type discussed above. During Russia's accession negotiations, a number of (unnamed) WTO members urged Russia to convert its combined and specific duties into ad valorem duties "in order to increase transparency and reduce distortions in trade".[65] In its recent report on Russia's compliance with its WTO commitments, the US Trade Representative also highlighted Russia's use of combined duties as a "source of concern".[66]

As the Panel saw it, the European Union had to prove three propositions in order to succeed with its challenge: first, that SDV is a "measure" for purposes of WTO dispute settlement, second, that SDV exists, and third, that SDV violates Article II:1 of the GATT 1994.[67] The Panel decided to start by analyzing the second question, namely, whether the European Union had successfully made out that Russia engages in a "general practice" of systematic duty variation.[68] Drawing on the European Union's description of the measure in its submissions to the Panel, the Panel found that, in order to establish the existence of the measure, the European Union had to demonstrate (1) the "systematic application" of (2) "certain types of tariff treatment ('duty variation')" in relation to (3) a "significant number of individual tariff lines in the CCT".[69] In

---

62   Report of the Working Party on the Accession of the Russian Federation to the World Trade Organization [17 November 2011] WT/ACC/RUS/70, para 311 (Working Party Report).
63   At the very least, it could have done so only in isolated instances, but not on a wide-spread basis, ie it could no longer have applied such tariff rates in a "systematic" fashion.
64   ibid para 7.277.
65   Working Party Report (n 64) para 312.
66   2017 Report on the Implementation and Enforcement of Russia's WTO Commitments (December 2017) United States Trade Representative 9.
67   ibid para 7.281.
68   ibid paras 7.281, 7.282.
69   ibid para 7.291.

addition, the Panel considered that the European Union had to demonstrate the "general" nature of the measure.[70]

Given that the seventh to eleventh measures, which the Panel had already analyzed, exemplified the "duty variation" alleged by the European Union, the Panel had no difficulty concluding that the European Union had shown this element of the twelfth measure to exist.[71] The Panel also found that the European Union had demonstrated that this tariff treatment affected a "significant number of tariff lines".[72] While the European Union had only provided evidence with respect to 23 tariff lines, out of the approximately 11,000 tariff lines contained in the CCT, the Panel found that the total number of tariff lines in the CCT was not a relevant comparator, given that the European Union had not asserted that a significant "proportion", but only a significant *number* of tariff lines was subject to SDV.[73] 23 tariff lines, the Panel found, was a significant number of tariff lines.[74]

What the European Union had failed to do, in the Panel's view, was to show that Russia's use of duty variation with respect to a significant number of tariff lines was the result of a "system, plan, or organized method or effort"[75] and hence amounted to the "systemic application" of the tariff treatment in question. While the Panel conceded that the instances of duty variation "did not, of course, appear spontaneously in the CCT" and where hence "not purely accidental",[76] the Panel found that the European Union had failed to "articulate" the "system" or "plan" that gave rise to those instances and had hence not demonstrated that those instances were "inter-connected".[77] For related reasons, the Panel also found that the European Union had not demonstrated that the duty variation at issue constituted a "general practice".[78] Since the European Union was unable to show that duty variation was applied in a "systematic fashion", the Panel concluded that the European Union had "failed to establish the existence of the SDV as a single, overarching measure."[79]

---

70   ibid para 7.293; the Panel explained this element ibid [7.332–7.335]; in particular, the Panel understood it to mean that "the SDV is not confined to particular parts of the CCT".

71   ibid para 7.354.

72   ibid para 7.369.

73   ibid para 7.366.

74   ibid para 7.369.

75   ibid para 7.370.

76   ibid para 7.389.

77   ibid para 7.389.

78   ibid paras 7.399–7.401.

79   ibid para 7.403.

There are two possible take-aways from the European Union's failure to prove the existence of systematic duty variation. The first is that the European Union had simply failed to do its homework: it could have provided evidence of more than merely 23 instances of duty variation (recall that the Working Party Report on Russia's accession mentions the existence of combined duties on 1,746 tariff lines), and it could have articulated a rationale for these duties that would have allowed the Panel to see the "system" or "plan" behind their application.

A second possible take-away is that one cannot blame the European Union for failing to identify the "system" or "plan" behind the use of combined duty rates in the CCT, since the use of these rates appears rather pointless. As noted above, the specific duty component of the combined duty rates in the CCT functions as a minimum rate which kicks in once the customs value of the imported product falls to a level at which the ad valorem component would result in a tariff that is lower than the alternative specific duty. It follows that the minimum specific rate only applies when its ad valorem equivalent is *higher* than the ad valorem component of the combined duty. However, given that the ad valorem component of the combined duties in the CCT is typically at, or just below, the level bound in Russia's WTO schedule, the scope for the WTO-consistent application of the minimum specific rate is either non-existent (in the case of measures seven, eight and nine) or minimal (in the case of measure ten and eleven, where it applies when its ad valorem equivalent (AVE) is $16.7\% > \text{AVE} > 16\%$ and $14.5\% > \text{AVE} > 13.3\%$, respectively). Unless the "plan" motivating the use of combined duties involves the systematic violation of Russia's WTO bindings, it is thus hard to see how the use of these duty rates accomplishes anything of commercial significance.

3.1.5   Adoption and Implementation

The Panel Report in *Russia – Tariff Treatment* was adopted by the DSB on 26 September 2016, since neither the European Union nor Russia had decided to appeal the report. On 8 June 2017, Russia circulated a communication to the DSB reporting full implementation of the DSB's rulings and recommendations.[80] Russia noted that it had already brought some of the tariff rates into compliance during the Panel proceedings, and that the other tariff rates had been amended by the Council of the Eurasian Economic Commission in line

---

80   WT/DS485/11.

with the Panel's recommendations. The European Union did not take issue with Russia's statement.[81]

3.1.6   Assessment

At first glance, Russia's swift implementation of the Panel Report in *Russia – Tariff Treatment* appears to be an encouraging sign in terms of Russia's commitment to the WTO. However, one could also argue that the case did not really test Russia's commitment: the violations were so clear that Russia defended them only half-heartedly; it brought several of its measures into compliance while the Panel proceedings were still ongoing. Moreover, Russia's implementation obligations – changing a few tariff rates – were not particularly burdensome. Apart from the European Union's challenge of a general practice of systematic duty variation, on which it did not prevail, the dispute has the feel of a (very resource-intensive) housekeeping exercise; indeed, one may wonder why the dispute was not resolved at the consultations stage.[82] We do not know whether the deteriorating political relationship between the European Union and Russia in the year preceding the EU's request for the establishment of a panel contributed to the parties' inability to resolve the dispute through consultations.

3.2   *Russian Federation – Measures on the Importation of Live Pigs, Pork and Other Pig Products from the European Union (DS475)*

Just a week after the Panel in *Russia – Tariff Treatment* had circulated its report on 12 August 2016, another Panel released a report finding that Russia had acted inconsistently with its obligations under the Agreement on the Application of Sanitary and Phytosanitary Measures (SPS Agreement). This dispute, known as *Russia – Pigs (EU)*, is more complex and commercially significant than *Russia – Tariff Treatment* (the Panel report runs to 381 pages). The proceedings were lengthy: The Panel in *Russia – Pigs (EU)* was established 10 months before the Panel in *Russia – Tariff Treatment*, and yet it circulated its report after the Panel in the latter case. Moreover, the Panel report was appealed by both the European Union and Russia, and at the time of writing the dispute remains unresolved, as the parties spar over whether Russia has implemented the DSB's rulings and recommendations.

---

81   The discussion at the May and June 2016 meetings of the DSB concerned the timeliness of Russia's status report; see WT/DSB/M/397, 4.1–4.8 and WT/DSB/M/398, 13.1–13.3.

82   Apparently, the EU had attempted to resolve the matter through consultations since Russia joined the WTO in 2012; WT/DSB/M/359, 6.2.

Russia – Pigs (EU) concerned a number of Russian measures that the European Union argued amounted to an import ban on certain pork products from the European Union. Specifically, the measures at issue were a "refusal by Russia to accept imports for the products at issue from the entire EU", as well as country-specific import bans introduced between January and April 2014 concerning "live pigs and their genetic material, pork, and certain other pig products" originating in Estonia, Latvia, Lithuania, and Poland.[83] The justification for the ban was an outbreak in Lithuania of African swine fever (ASF), a highly contagious hemorrhagic disease that can be found in pigs and can lead to death in 2-10 days on average.[84] At the time of the Panel proceedings, the ASF outbreak had spread to Estonia, Latvia and Poland.[85] According to the European Union, the disease had "spread into the EU" from Russia, "either directly or via Belarus".[86]

It is not hard to see why the European Union would pursue the dispute aggressively: Before Russia implemented the import bans, the Russian market had been the top destination for EU exports of pork.[87] According to the European Union, the trade affected by the Russian measures was "worth EUR 1.4 billion or 24% of the EU's total pork exports in 2013".[88] Moreover, from the European Union's perspective, the Russian response to the outbreak of ASF on EU territory was clearly excessive. As the European Union noted, "Russia had blocked trade not only from the affected EU Member States near Russia ... but from ... places thousands of kilometres away from the outbreaks and regions that were historically free from the disease."[89]

While Russia imposed the measures challenged by the European Union in January 2014 – when the Ukraine crisis was heating up, but before the annexation of Crimea – there initially appeared to be no direct relationship between the *Russia – Pigs (EU)* dispute and the political crisis over Ukraine. Instead, the European Union saw the measures as motivated by economic protectionism, rather geopolitics. Based on Russian "press statements", the European Union speculated in its DSB statements that the measures were part of "Russia's overall policy of substituting imports for its own production".[90] Academic observers

---

83   ibid para 7.37.
84   ibid para 2.1.
85   ibid para 2.22.
86   WTO, Dispute Settlement Body Minutes of Meeting (21 March 2017) WT/DSB/M/394, para 8.2.
87   ibid.
88   ibid.
89   ibid.
90   ibid para 8.3.

have noted that pork producers have been among the "poorly performing sub-sectors" of Russia's agricultural sector and were likely to be "most negatively affected" by the terms of Russia's WTO accession, which "were subject to con-siderable resistance from the agrarian lobby".[91] At the time of its accession to the WTO, Russia had a history of employing SPS measures in "rather elastic ways"[92] to protect domestic producers. In fact, Russia had banned the impor-tation of live animals from the European Union as recently as March 20, 2012, mere months before it was set to join the WTO.[93] That ban was mostly affect-ing imports of live pigs[94] and was reportedly imposed to protect Russian pig farmers.[95]

The relationship between the dispute and the political crisis over Ukraine became more complex when Russia imposed countersanctions against the European Union in August 2014. These countersanctions covered some, but not all, of the pork products that were also subject to the measures challenged by the European Union in *Russia – Pigs (EU)*. In October 2017 – at a time when Russia was supposed to bring its SPS measures into conformity with its WTO obligations – Russia extended the political ban imposed in August 2014 to all products that were the subject of the dispute, effectively depriving the European Union of the commercial benefits of a removal of the SPS measures. In the most recent development, the European Union has decided to challenge this extension of the political ban as part of the compliance proceedings in *Russia – Pigs (EU)*. As a result, the SPS dispute and the countersanctions have become intermingled. We discuss the potentially far-reaching implications of these developments below. In the following, we first provide an overview of the substance of the dispute, focusing on the findings of the Appellate Body. The key substantive questions contested before the Appellate Body were the attributability of the EU-wide ban to Russia and the interpretation and appli-cation of Article 6 of the SPS Agreement.

3.2.1 Measures at Issue and Attribution

As noted above, the European Union argued that certain measures imposed by Russia amounted to a ban on certain pork products from the entire European

91   Connolly and Hanson (n 4) 483.
92   ibid 487.
93   Dave Keating, 'Russia Bans Live Animal Imports from the EU' *Politico* (20 March 2012) <www.politico.eu/article/russia-bans-live-animal-imports-from-the-eu/> accessed 30 July 2021.
94   ibid.
95   Connolly and Hanson (n 4) 487.

Union, resulting in an "EU-wide ban". In addition, the European Union also challenged bans on imports from specific EU Member States, namely Estonia, Latvia, Lithuania, and Poland.[96] According to the European Union, these bans were implemented through a series of letters from the Russian Federal Service for Veterinary and Phytosanitary Surveillance to the European Union and Russia's territorial departments.[97] The stated reason for the bans was the occurrence in EU territory of cases of ASF.[98]

Before the Panel and on appeal, Russia argued that the EU-wide ban was not a measure attributable to Russia. Russia based this argument on the fact that, as a result of the instances of ASF on EU territory, the European Union was no longer able to meet the conditions of the bilateral veterinary certificates that had been negotiated between Russia and the European Union in 2006 and that had to accompany each shipment of pork products from the EU to Russia. Specifically, exporters from the European Union could no longer certify that the entire territory of the European Union (except Sardinia) had been free of ASF for the preceding three years, as required by the certificates. Russia told the European Union in January 2014 that, given the inability of EU exporters to comply with the conditions of the certificates, it would reject shipments of pork products accompanied by such certificates, and it proceeded to do so.[99]

In response to Russia's argument, the Appellate Body noted that neither the Panel nor the European Union had attempted to attribute the *content* of the bilateral veterinary certificates to Russia; rather, the act that was challenged by the European Union and that was attributed to Russia by the Panel was "Russia's decision to deny the importation of the products at issue" on the grounds that they did not meet the requirements of the certificates.[100] In the Appellate Body's view, the grounds on which a WTO Member takes a decision is "immaterial" to the question of whether that decision can be attributed to the WTO Member (although it is may of course be relevant to the analysis of the decision's consistency with WTO law).[101] The Appellate Body noted that "Russia does not dispute that it banned the importation of the products at

---

96   *Russian Federation – Measures on the Importation of Live Pigs, Pork and Other Pig Products from the European Union* Appellate Body Report (adopted on 21 March 2017) WT/DS475/AB/R, para 1.2.
97   ibid para 5.3.
98   ibid para 2.1.
99   ibid 5.3.
100   ABR paras 5.17, 5.18.
101   ibid para 5.20.

issue".[102] Accordingly, the Appellate Body upheld the Panel's finding that "the EU-wide ban is attributable to Russia".[103]

3.2.2   Unappealed Findings by the Panel[104]

The Panel concluded that the EU-wide ban was an SPS measure within the meaning of Annex A(1) of the SPS Agreement. It further found that the EU-wide ban and the country-specific bans were inconsistent with virtually all the basic obligations of the SPS Agreement, including the obligation to base SPS measures on international standards (Article 3.1), the obligation to base SPS measures on a risk assessment (Articles 5.1 and 5.2), the obligation to adapt SPS measures to regional conditions (Article 6.1, though the Panel found that Russia had acted consistently with Article 6.2, as discussed below), and the obligation to adopt SPS measures only to the extent necessary to protect human, animal or plant life of health and to do so based on scientific principles and evidence (Article 2.2). Only the Panel's findings on attribution (discussed above), on the implications of Russia's protocol of accession[105] and on Article 6 of the SPS Agreement were appealed.

3.2.3   The Interpretation of Article 6 of the SPS Agreement

Article 6 of the SPS Agreement requires WTO Members to adapt their SPS measures to regional conditions both in the exporting and the importing Member (Article 6.1) and, in particular, to recognize that there may be "pest- or disease-free areas and areas of low pest or disease prevalence" in an exporting Member in which a pest or disease is present (Article 6.2). Article 6.3, in turn, requires exporting Members who claim that parts of their territory should enjoy such status to "provide the necessary evidence" to "objectively demonstrate to the importing Member that such areas are, and are likely to remain, pest- or disease-free areas or areas of low pest or disease prevalence".

Russia's appeal centred on the Panel's interpretation and application of Article 6.3, as well as the Panel's conception of the relationship between Article

---

102   ibid para 5.22.

103   ibid para 5.23. The Appellate Body also upheld the Panel's finding that its obligations under Article 6 of the SPS Agreement were not affected by the terms of Russia's accession to the WTO and that these terms hence "did not limit the Panel's assessment of the European Union's claims regarding the EU-wide ban"; ibid paras 5.35, 5.36.

104   For an overview of the findings by the Panel and Appellate Body, see Maria Alcover, 'Russian Federation – Measures on the Importation of Live Pigs, Pork and Other Pig Products from the European Union (Russia – Pigs (EU)), DS475' (2017) World Trade Review 757.

105   We do not discuss these findings for reasons of space.

6.3 and Article 6.1. Specifically, Russia claimed that the Panel should have found that "the scientific and technical evidence relied upon by an importing Member, as well as that Member's assessment of the evidence submitted by an exporting Member" must form part of a panel's assessment of whether the exporting Member has met the requirements of Article 6.3. In Russia's view, the Panel's failure to consider Russia's evidence in its analysis under Article 6.3 led it to wrongly find that the evidence submitted by the European Union met the threshold set by Article 6.3 of "objectively demonstrat[ing]" that the respective areas in the European Union were "ASF-free" and (except in the case of Latvia) "were likely to remain so".[106] Moreover, Russia argued that, in determining the point in time at which an exporting Member can be said to have met the requirements of Article 6.3, a panel should factor in the time that the importing Member requires to "evaluate and verify" the exporting Member's evidence. Finally – and this was arguably Russia's claim of most consequence for the structure of Article 6 of the SPS Agreement – Russia argued that, in the circumstances of this case, its obligation to adapt its SPS measures to regional characteristics under Article 6.1 was *subject to* the European Union providing the "necessary evidence ... to objectively demonstrate" the existence of disease-free or low-prevalence areas pursuant to Article 6.3. Accordingly, Russia argued that the Panel erred when it found that Russia had violated Article 6.1 with respect to Latvia, even though it had also found that the European Union had not demonstrated that "ASF-free areas within Latvia's territory were likely to remain" free of the disease.[107]

The European Union, for its part, appealed the Panel's finding that Russia "recognizes the concepts of pest- or disease-free areas and areas of low pest or disease prevalence in respect of ASF", and that Russia's measures were hence not inconsistent with the first sentence of Article 6.2 of the SPS Agreement.

The Appellate Body disagreed with Russia's claim that a panel should consider the evidence used by the importing Member in assessing whether an exporting Member has provided the "necessary evidence ... to objectively demonstrate" the existence of disease-free or low prevalence areas as required by Article 6.3. According to the Appellate Body, a panel's task under Article 6.3 is *not* to conduct its *own* assessment of whether the respective areas are, and are likely to remain, disease-free or low-prevalence areas (if that was the task of the panel, it would arguably have to consider the evidence provided

---

106   *Russian Federation – Measures on the Importation of Live Pigs, Pork and Other Pig Products from the European Union* (n 98) para 5.40. The Panel found that the European Union had not met the requirements in respect of Latvia.
107   ibid 5.43.

by both parties). Instead, Article 6.3 asks a panel to evaluate whether the exporting Member's evidence is "of a nature, quantity, and quality sufficient to enable" the importing Member's authorities "ultimately to make a determination as to the pest or disease status of the relevant areas" within the exporting Member.[108] This determination by the importing Member, in turn, is subject to the disciplines of Articles 6.1 and 6.2.

The Appellate Body thus identified a clear division of labour between the paragraphs of Article 6: Articles 6.1 and 6.2 regulate the conduct of the importing Member, whereas Article 6.3 imposes requirements on the exporting Member.[109] This does not mean that the circumstances of the importing Member are immaterial to the "nature, quantity, and quality" of the evidence that an exporting Member must provide pursuant to Article 6.3. The Appellate Body acknowledged the "interlinkages between the various provisions of Article 6"; in particular, the Appellate Body recognized that the appropriate level of sanitary and phytosanitary protection chosen by the importing Member "may inform" the evidentiary requirements in a particular case.[110] However, in order to assess whether an exporting Member has met the requirements of Article 6.3, a panel does not need to consider the evidence already in possession of the importing Member.

The Appellate Body's conception of the division of labour between the paragraphs of Article 6 also provided it with a ready response to Russia's second claim on appeal, namely, that the Panel should have made an allowance for the time it takes an importing Member to examine the evidence provided by an exporting Member in deciding *when* an exporting Member has complied with its obligations under Article 6.3. While the Appellate Body agreed with Russia that the "importing Member's evaluation of the relevant evidence ... can hardly be performed instantly",[111] it found that the amount of time that the importing Member may take to assess this evidence is properly considered as part of a panel's analysis of the importing Member's compliance with its obligations under Articles 6.1 and 6.2, rather than the panel's examination of the exporting Member's fulfilment of the requirements of Article 6.3.[112] The Appellate Body highlighted that Russia was not "required to comply with its obligations under Article 6.1 and 6.2 *immediately* after the European Union had provided the necessary evidence under Article 6.3", but instead "enjoyed

---

108 ibid para 5.72.
109 ibid.
110 ibid para 5.65.
111 ibid para 5.80.
112 ibid para 5.82.

a certain period of time to conduct its evaluation".[113] The length of that period of time is informed by the obligations in Article 8 and Annex C(1)(a) to the SPS Agreement to complete SPS procedures "without undue delay".[114]

What, then, are the implications of an exporting Member's failure to supply the required evidence under Article 6.3 for the importing Member's duties under Article 6.1? While the Panel had found that the European Union had not met its burden of providing the "necessary evidence" to "demonstrate objectively" that certain areas in Latvia were likely to remain free of ASF, the Panel had not addressed the "potential implications" of this finding for the question of whether Russia had fulfilled its duty under Article 6.1 to adapt its SPS measures to the regional conditions in Latvia and Russia itself. Russia's appeal gave the Appellate Body the opportunity to revisit its jurisprudence on the relationship between Articles 6.1 and 6.3 of the SPS Agreement in *India – Agricultural Products*. In that case, the Appellate Body had found that, even in the absence of "*explicit* conditional language linking Article 6.1 and 6.3",[115] an exporting Member that requests an importing Member to recognize certain "disease-free" areas in its territory "will be able to establish that the importing Member's failure" to do so "is inconsistent with Article 6.1 and 6.2 *only if* that exporting Member can also establish that it took the steps prescribed in Article 6.3."[116]

The Appellate Body made it clear that this did not mean that an importing Member "can only be found to have breached" Article 6.1 where the exporting Member had complied with Article 6.3,[117] and it described certain circumstances in which an importing Member could act inconsistently with Article 6.1 "irrespective" of the exporting Member's compliance with the requirements of Article 6.3.[118] However, as the Appellate Body explained in *Russia – Pigs (EU)*, those are very specific situations, and the Panel had failed to explain whether it considered the circumstances of that dispute "to be akin to one of the situations" that the Appellate Body had described in *India – Agricultural Products*.[119] To the Appellate Body, the fact that, in *Russia – Pigs (EU)*, the European Union

---

113   ibid para 5.83. (original emphasis).
114   ibid paras 5.84 and 5.86.
115   ibid para 5.97, citing *India – Measures Concerning the Importation of Certain Agricultural Products*, Appellate Body Report (adopted on 19 June 2015) WT/DS430/AB/R, para 5.155 (*India – Agricultural Products*).
116   ibid para 5.97, citing *India – Agricultural Products*, Appellate Body Report, para 5.156 (emphasis added).
117   ibid para 5.98, citing *India – Agricultural Products*, Appellate Body Report, para 5.157 (original emphasis).
118   ibid para 5.98.
119   ibid para 5.103.

had asked Russia to recognize certain areas as "ASF-free and likely to remain so" meant that the European Union's failure to meet the requirements of Article 6.3 with respect to Latvia had "potential implications ... for the question of whether Russia had complied with its obligation under Article 6.1 to adapt the ban on imports of the products at issue from Latvia to the SPS characteristics of those areas."[120] The Appellate Body found that the Panel's failure to consider these implications constituted a reversible error.[121]

What is the role of Article 6.2 in the division of labour that the Appellate Body identified in Article 6 of the SPS Agreement? The European Union's appeal of the Panel's finding that Russia "recognizes the concepts of pest- or disease-free areas and areas of low pest or disease prevalence in respect of ASF",[122] as required by Article 6.2, gave the Appellate Body the opportunity to clarify how that paragraph interacts with the obligations of the exporting Member to provide the necessary evidence to demonstrate the existence of such areas, on the one hand, and with the obligation of the importing Member to adapt its SPS measures to regional conditions, on the other hand.

The Appellate Body disagreed with the Panel's interpretation that the "acknowledgment of certain 'abstract ideas' is sufficient for the purposes of Article 6.2".[123] The Panel had considered that the duty to "recognize the concept" of disease-free areas etc. in Article 6.2 could not refer to the recognition of such areas in "specific instances", since Article 6.2 would then duplicate the duty to ensure the adaption of SPS measures to regional conditions set out in Article 6.1. The Appellate Body disagreed. In its view, the Panel's concerns about duplication could be addressed by reading Article 6.2 as imposing a *procedural* obligation on importing Members

> to provide an effective opportunity for the exporting Member to make the claim, addressed to the importing Member, that areas within its territory are pest- or disease-free or of low pest or disease prevalence, by maintaining a practice of, or a process for, receiving such claims from an exporting Member affected by a specific SPS measure, and thus render operational the concept of regionalization.[124]

---

120   ibid para 5.102.
121   ibid para 5.103.
122   ibid para 5.119.
123   ibid para 5.134.
124   ibid para 5.135.

By interpreting Article 6.2 as imposing an obligation of *conduct* – to receive and process requests for recognition of disease-free areas – the Appellate Body was able to clearly differentiate it from the obligation of *result* imposed by Article 6.1 – to ensure that SPS measure are adapted to regional characteristics. The Appellate Body's interpretation of Article 6.2 also fits neatly into the division of labour that the Appellate Body had identified within Article 6, which works as follows: The "main and overarching obligation" imposed on importing Members by Article 6 is the duty to ensure that SPS measures are adapted to regional characteristics (Article 6.1, first sentence).[125] Where an exporting Member wants the importing Member to recognize certain areas as pest- or disease-free or as having low pest or disease prevalence, it has to provide the necessary evidence to the importing Member (Article 6.3). The importing Member has a duty to provide a mechanism to receive claims to this effect from exporting Members affected by the SPS measure in question (Article 6.2., first sentence). The importing Member then has to "make a 'determination' as to the pest or disease status" of the area in question (Article 6.1, second sentence, and Article 6.2, second sentence).[126]

3.2.4   Adoption and Implementation

The Appellate Body report and the Panel Report as modified by the Appellate Body Report in *Russia – Pigs (EU)* were adopted by the DSB on 21 March 2017. The European Union and Russia agreed on a reasonable period of time for Russia to implement the recommendations and rulings of the DSB. That period expired on December 6, 2017. On December 8, 2017, Russia informed the DSB that it had "taken appropriate steps to comply with the DSB's recommendations and rulings". In particular, Russia claimed that it "resumes importation of live pigs, pork meat and raw meat preparations from the entire territory of the EU and its Members States" with the exclusion of territories affected by ASF, which are set out in an annex to a directive issued by the Federal Service for Veterinary and Phytosanitary Surveillance.[127]

In fact, it appears that Russia's claim that it had "resume[d]" the importation of pork products from the European Union was not accurate. When Russia and the European Union agreed on a reasonable period of time for implementation after the adoption of the reports in early 2017, the European Union knew that even if Russia brought the measures at issue in the dispute into compliance, its pork exports to Russia would remain severely restricted by

125   ibid para 5.57.
126   ibid paras 5.59, 5.60.
127   WTO, Communication from the Russian Federation (13 December 2017) WT/DS475/16.

the countersanctions imposed by Russia in August 2014. In a press release following the publication of the Appellate Body Report in *Russia – Pigs (EU)*, the European Union had called on Russia to withdraw the SPS measures at issue in that dispute but had also acknowledged that "[f]or most of the products dealt with in this case, trade continue[d] to be restricted by a politically motivated ban Russia imposed on EU agri-food products in August 2014". The reason that only "most of the products" would remain restricted was that the product coverage of the political ban and of the SPS measures was not identical. Thus, "certain products such as pig fat, offal and live animals for breeding were covered by the sanitary ban addressed by the WTO and [were] outside the scope of the 2014 political ban."[128] While it is perilous to read too much into a press release, it appears that in February 2017 the European Union was content – at least for the time being – with the prospect of the limited market access that it would regain through the removal of the SPS measures. At least publicly the European Union did not give any indication that it was planning to challenge the political ban in the WTO.

This calculus changed on October 25, 2017, when the Russian government published its decision to extend the political ban to all the products that had been subject to the SPS measures but had been outside the scope of the political ban. The effect of the extension of the political ban was that Russia's modifications of its SPS measures to comply with the DSB's rulings and recommendations in the *Russia – Pigs (EU)* dispute would have no effect in practice, since all the products that were subject to those measure would remain subject to the political ban. The extension of the political ban in October 2017 thus deprived the European Union of any commercial benefit of its "win" in *Russia – Pigs (EU)*.

It did not come as a surprise, then, that the European Union did not accept Russia's contention – in its communication to the DSB of December 8, 2017 – that it had complied with the DSB's rulings and recommendations in *Russia – Pigs (EU)* by modifying the SPS measures at issue in that case. Instead, on December 19, 2017, the European Union requested the right to retaliate against Russian exports in the amount of 1.39 billion Euro (increasingly yearly by 15%), pursuant to Article 22.2 of the DSU.[129] On the following day, Russia objected to the European Union's assertion that it had not complied, as well as to the European Union's proposed level of retaliation. On January 25, 2018, Russia also requested consultations with the European Union under Article

---

128 Mission of the European Union to the WTO, Press Release.
129 WTO, Communication from the European Union (20 December 2017) WT/DS475/17.

21.5 of the DSU – the first step that Russia needed to take to initiate compliance proceedings, a process in which a panel and, potentially, the Appellate Body examine whether the measures that Russia had taken to comply were consistent with its obligations under WTO law. On February 2, 2018, the European Union, for its part, requested consultations with Russia for proceedings under Article 21.5 of the DSU.

There is a crucial difference between the measures which are the subject of the consultations requests submitted by Russia and the European Union. As one would expect, Russia seeks confirmation through the Article 21.5 proceedings that the modifications that it has made to the measures at issue in the original dispute indeed bring those measures into compliance with its obligations under the SPS Agreement. For Russia, these modifications are embodied in the above-mentioned directive issued by the Federal Service for Veterinary and Phytosanitary Surveillance, which is hence the subject of its request for consultations. While this directive is also a subject of the European Union's request for consultations (along with two newer SPS-related letters by the Russian authorities and all the measures at issue in the original dispute), the European Union's consultations request also includes the extension of the political ban on pork products that was announced in October 25.

The European Union explains the inclusion of the October 25 decision by noting that the decision "effectively replaces the measures at issue in the original dispute, thereby effectively maintaining them in force and effect, in whole or in part".[130] The European Union does not explicitly address the fact that what it describes as "the first measure at issue", i.e. the October 25 decision, was purportedly imposed on national security grounds. However, several aspects of the European Union's consultations request make it clear that the European Union sees Russia's actions as having taken the dispute outside the realm of a standard SPS dispute. First, the European Union submits that the "first measure" is not only inconsistent with the provisions of the SPS Agreement that were at issue in the original dispute, but also with several provisions of the GATT 1994, including Articles I:1, III:4 and XI:1. This is an admission by the European Union that it could be hard to convince a panel that the "first measure" is an SPS measure. Moreover, the European Union also alleges several violations of the provisions of the DSU on Russia's part, including a violation of Article 3(10). While the European Union does not spell it out in so many words, this is an allegation that Russia has failed to "engage in these procedures in good faith in an effort to resolve the dispute".[131]

---

130   WTO, Request for Consultations (7 February 2018) WT/DS475/20, 2.
131   DSU, art 3(10).

Apart from the discrepancies in the consultations requests of Russia and the European Union, it is worth noting that the sequence of events described above itself reflects a breakdown of what used to be a well-established practice in WTO dispute settlement. Because the DSU requires complainants to request the right to retaliate within 30 days after the expiry of the reasonable period of time to implement the rulings and recommendations of the DSB, while at the same time instructing the parties to a dispute to resort to renewed dispute settlement proceedings in the case of a disagreement about compliance (which cannot realistically be completed within 30 days), it had become customary among disputing parties to conclude so-called "sequencing agreements". Under such an agreement, to borrow a description used by the European Union in this dispute,

> the European Union would request authorization to suspend concessions or other obligations only after the DSB has ruled as a result of a proceeding under Article 21.5 of the DSU that a measure taken to comply does not exist or is inconsistent with a covered agreement, and on the other hand, the Russian Federation would not assert that the European Union is precluded from obtaining such authorization because its request was made outside the time period specified in the first sentence of Article 22.6 of the DSU.[132]

Russia refused to enter into such a sequencing agreement with the European Union in this dispute. While the refusal to enter sequencing agreements has become an increasingly common feature of dispute settlement proceedings in recent years, Russia's unwillingness to enter into such an agreement in the very first dispute in which its compliance was in dispute can nevertheless be interpreted as a confrontational step. In the absence of a sequencing agreement, the dispute between the European Union and Russia about the level of retaliation is now referred to arbitration under Article 22.6 of the DSU.[133] However, as a practical matter, it is likely that the arbitration will not get under way until the proceedings under Article 21.5, which were initiated by the consultation requests by Russia and the European Union, are concluded.

---

132   WTO, Communication from the European Union (20 December 2017) WT/DS475/17.
133   ibid.

3.2.5   Assessment

It is safe to say that Russia's decision to attempt to evade its implementation obligations in the *Russia – Pigs (EU)* dispute by imposing a measure with equivalent effect purportedly on national security grounds is without precedent in WTO dispute settlement. Russia's decision calls into question its commitment to the WTO in at least two respects: first, Russia's apparently opportunistic use of the national security exception to avoid the commercial implications of what is only its second loss in a WTO dispute will lead WTO Members to regard any future invocation of the national security exception by Russia with heightened suspicion. The fact that Russia was willing to risk losing the confidence of WTO Members on the sensitive topic of national security for no other benefit than not having to reopen its market to pig fat, offal and live pigs for breeding from the European Union indicates that Russia has little regard for the informal norms that sustain any system of legalized dispute settlement. Second, Russia's decision undermines the purpose of using WTO dispute settlement proceedings against Russia. By depriving the European Union of any commercial benefit of its "win" in *Russia – Pigs (EU)*, Russia undermines the structure of commercial incentives that underpins WTO dispute settlement. Moreover, by intermingling the discrete matter in dispute with the broader political and economic relationship between the parties, Russia prevents WTO Members from realizing the benefit of legalized dispute settlement in their relationship with Russia more broadly: these countries will no longer be able to "'chip off' bits and pieces of the amorphous complex totality" of their commercial relationship with Russia "and find solutions to those chipped-off pieces"[134] by using WTO dispute settlement; rather, they will face the prospect that any WTO dispute with Russia will drag them into the uncomfortable territory of the national security exception and will thus implicate their broader political and economic relationship with Russia.

3.3   *Russia – Anti-Dumping Duties on Light Commercial Vehicles from Germany and Italy (DS479)*

Less than five months after the *Russia – Tariff Treatment* panel report was circulated, the Panel in *Russia – Anti-Dumping Duties on Light Commercial Vehicles from Germany and Italy (Russia –Commercial Vehicles* for short) released its report on 27 January 2017.[135] In this dispute, the European Union challenged the Board of the Eurasian Economic Commission (EEC) Decision No. 113,

---

134   Jackson (n 16) 767.
135   *Russia – Anti-Dumping Duties on Light Commercial Vehicles from Germany and Italy*, Panel Report (adopted on 9 April 2018) WT/DS479/R, para 2.1 (*Russia –Commercial Vehicles*).

pursuant to which Russia levied anti-dumping duties on certain light commercial vehicles (LCVs) from Germany and Italy. The European Union challenged these measures under the Anti-Dumping Agreement,[136] an agreement that disciplines the imposition of anti-dumping duties by WTO Members. A majority of the claims made by the European Union in this dispute centered around whether or not the analysis conducted by the Department for Internal Market Defence of the Eurasian Economic Commission (DIMD) was objective or not.

3.3.1 Definition of Domestic Industry

The first and arguably most important issue dealt with by the Panel was the definition of 'domestic industry' used by the DIMD, which the European Union alleged rendered the measures inconsistent with Articles 3.1 and 4.1 of the Anti-Dumping Agreement.[137] Specifically, the European Union argued that the DIMD did not conduct an objective examination because the way in which it defined domestic industry incorporated only one producer, Sollers, and excluded another producer, GAZ, from the definition.[138]

Analyzing Article 4.1 of the Anti-Dumping Agreement, the Panel confirmed that the Agreement intended "domestic industry" to be interpreted as "*either* the domestic producers as a whole of the like products, *or* the domestic producers whose collective output constitutes a major proportion of the total domestic production of those products".[139] Article 4.1 imposes a substantive obligation on a WTO Member to define their industry in accordance with this interpretation, and if a Member fails to do so it acts inconsistently with its obligations under the Anti-Dumping Agreement.[140] The Panel further concluded that Article 4.1 involves both a quantitative and a qualitative aspect, and that meeting the quantitative threshold "is a necessary but not sufficient condition of fulfilling its requirements as a whole".[141] The qualitative assessment, at a minimum, ensures that the investigating authority's approach or methodology for selecting the domestic industry "does not create a risk of material distortion".[142]

---

136 Agreement on Implementation of Article VI of the General Agreement on Tariffs and Trade 1994 (Anti-Dumping Agreement), 1868 U.N.T.S. 201.

137 *Russia – Commercial Vehicles* (n 137) para7.4.

138 ibid.

139 ibid para 7.9.

140 ibid paras 7.10–7.11.

141 ibid para 7.15.

142 ibid.

In light of the above analysis of Article 4.1, the Panel found that the DIMD erred in its approach to defining the domestic industry because the DIMD declined to include in the definition a known producer of a like product that had sought to cooperate in the investigation, and it did so *after* having reviewed that producer's data. The Panel noted that, because the Russian Federation's reasons for why GAZ was not included in the definition were not included in the DIMD's Investigation Report, they constituted "impermissible *post hoc* rationalization", and because regardless of whether or not the reasons were DIMD's, they were not "such reasons as a reasonable and unbiased investigating authority could have relied upon" to exclude GAZ from the definition.[143]

While such a finding of inconsistency with Articles 4.1 and 3.1 would normally end the analysis, the Panel decided to nonetheless address the full range of arguments presented by the Russian Federation and considered two alternative arguments: that the DIMD initially defined domestic industry to include both Sollers and GAZ but only considered Sollers because of deficiencies in GAZ's data, and that the DIMD redefined domestic industry after the initial definition included both producers.[144] The Panel found that such arguments were not supported by the chronology of events set out in the Investigation Report, but that even if the chronology were accepted as a matter of fact the DIMD still acted inconsistently with Article 4.1.[145]

The Panel therefore concluded that the DIMD acted inconsistent with Article 4.1 in its definition of "domestic industry", and as a result of the improperly defined domestic industry the DIMD consequently acted inconsistently with Article 3.1, rejecting arguments made by Russia that the redefinition of "domestic industry" by the DIMD was valid.[146]

An investigating authority's investigation plays a critical role in determining whether or not anti-dumping measures can be appropriately applied, and a key part of this investigation is the domestic industry. The ability for a WTO Member to apply anti-dumping measures depends on a determination that the dumping in question has caused injury to the domestic industry in the importing country. If an investigating authority improperly defines the domestic industry, as the European Union alleges occurred in this case, the injury analysis can become distorted.

---

143   ibid.
144   ibid para 7.18.
145   ibid paras 7.22, 7.27.
146   ibid para 7.16.

3.3.2   Selection on "Non-consecutive Periods of Non-equal Duration" for
           the Injury and Causation Analysis

The European Union's second claim was that by selecting "non-consecutive
periods of non-equal duration" for the examination of the trends for the
domestic industry the DIMD's injury determination was not based on an objective examination of positive evidence, and therefore breached Articles 3.1, 3.2,
3.4 and 3.5 of the Anti-Dumping Agreement.

While discretion is given to an investigating authority when establishing the periods of investigation and data collection in an investigation, the
Panel confirmed that the investigating authority's selection of such periods
of investigation and data collection must enable the investigating authority
to "make an injury determination based on an objective examination of positive evidence".[147] Similar to the domestic industry analysis discussed above,
it is important that the investigating authority's determination of injury is
objective and takes into account relevant evidence concerning the volume of
dumped imports, the effect of these dumped imports on prices of like products
in the importing country, and their consequent impact on the domestic industry.[148] The time period used by the investigating authority for investigating
such data impacts the ultimate determination of whether an injury consistent
with Article 3.1 of the Anti-Dumping Agreement occurred.[149]

The European Union presented two main arguments in support of its
claim: first, that the DIMD compared half-year data with full calendar year
data, though no specific instance where such a comparison occurred is identified; and second, that the DIMD split the period of investigation into two half-
year periods which consequently "artificially show[ed] negative trends".[150] In
this instance, the Panel found that the DIMD did not make an injury determination by looking only at half-year snapshots of data nor did it conduct the
injury analysis on the basis of an incomplete set of data, thus distinguishing
the facts of this case from *Mexico – Anti-Dumping Measures on Beef and Rice*
and *Mexico – Steel Pipes and Tubes*.[151] Noting that Article 3.1 does not prohibit
an investigating authority from focusing on part of a period of investigating
for a more detailed analysis of developments, and that it is generally necessary
for an investigating authority to consider intervening trends during its period
of consideration,[152] the Panel concluded that the European Union had failed

---

147   ibid para 7.30.
148   ibid para 7.31.
149   ibid.
150   ibid paras 7.33–7.36.
151   ibid paras 7.38–7.39.
152   ibid para 7.41.

to establish a violation of Article 3.1 of the Anti-Dumping Agreement and, therefore, the European Union's consequential claims of inconsistency under Articles 3.2, 3.4 and 3.5 of the Anti-Dumping Agreement were also rejected.[153]

3.3.3   Price Suppression

The European Union's third claim focused on price suppression. Specifically, the European Union argued that the DIMD acted inconsistently with Articles 3.1 and 3.2 of the Anti-Dumping Agreement because it failed to make an objective examination of the price suppression effect of dumped imports based on positive evidence.[154]

While Article 3.2 requires an investigating authority to consider, inter alia, whether the effect of the dumped imports is to "prevent domestic price increases, which otherwise would have occurred, to a significant degree", the investigating authority does not need to make a definitive determination on whether the effect is significant price suppression in order to meet the requirements of Article 3.2.[155] This leaves discretion with the investigating authority as to how an investigation considers whether or not there has been significant price suppression, subject to the principles of Article 3.1 of the Anti-Dumping Agreement.[156]

The benchmark year used by the DIMD in its analysis was 2009, which the European Union claimed led to a price suppression analysis that was not objective due to the high rate of return in that year.[157] The selection of a benchmark year is important as it is used as the assumed domestic price "which otherwise would have occurred" if the dumped imports had not taken place.[158] The financial crisis that affected the 2009 data, which the DIMD acknowledged in its Investigation Report, ultimately led the Panel to conclude that the DIMD acted inconsistently with Articles 3.1 and 3.2 when it failed to take into account the impact of the financial crisis.[159] However, the Panel rejected the rest of the European Union's arguments relating to evidence or data that the European Union alleged the DIMD failed to consider in its price suppression analysis.[160]

153   ibid para 7.52.
154   ibid para 7.54.
155   ibid para 7.57.
156   ibid.
157   ibid para 7.59.
158   ibid para 7.61.
159   ibid para 7.67.
160   ibid para 7.108.

3.3.4 State of the Domestic Industry

Once again focusing on whether or not the DIMD's analysis was objective, the European Union claimed that the DIMD failed to objectively examine the impact of the dumped imports on the state of the domestic industry based on positive evidence.[161] The European Union made ten claims related to this challenge, nine of which were dismissed by the Panel because the European Union was not able to demonstrate the DIMD's inconsistency with Articles 3.1 and 3.4 of the Anti-Dumping Agreement.

The European Union's claim relating to the magnitude of the margin of dumping, however, was successful.[162] The magnitude of margin of dumping is one of required fifteen injury factors listed in Article 3.4 of the Anti-Dumping Agreement, and while Article 3.4 does not require that this factor be analyzed in a particular way or be given any particular weight, the DIMD's failure to conduct this evaluation at all led the Panel to conclude that the DIMD acted inconsistently with Article 3.4 of the Anti-Dumping Agreement.[163]

3.3.5 Causation

The European Union next claimed that the DIMD failed to properly establish a causal link between the dumped imports and the alleged injury and failed to conduct a "proper non-attribution analysis of factors other than the dumped imports that were known to the DIMD", thereby acting inconsistently with Articles 3.1 and 3.5 of the Anti-Dumping Agreement.[164]

Establishing a causal link between the dumped imports and the injury to the domestic industry is a significant part of the anti-dumping analysis. The causal analysis does not require the dumped imports to be the only cause of the injury, so long as they are a cause of the injury to the domestic market.[165] Inherent in Article 3.5 of the Anti-Dumping Agreement is the idea of non-attribution, which requires the investigating authority to not attribute to dumped imports injuries that are caused by other factors.[166]

Building on its previous findings that the DIMD acted inconsistently with Articles 3.1 and 3.2 of the Anti-Dumping Agreement when it failed to consider the impact of the financial crisis in the price suppression analysis, the Panel concluded that the DIMD therefore acted inconsistently with Articles

---

161 ibid para 7.109.
162 ibid para 7.162.
163 ibid paras 7.159–7.162.
164 ibid para 7.175.
165 ibid para 7.178.
166 ibid para 7.179.

3.1 and 3.5 because of its reliance on price suppression in the causation analy-sis.[167] While the Panel found the European Union did not establish most of its other claims under Articles 3.1 and 3.5, the Panel did find that the DIMD acted inconsistently with these Articles when it failed to examine whether or not the "alleged overly ambitious business plan of Sollers" was causing injury to the domestic industry, and if so whether or not these injurious effects could be sep-arated and distinguished from the injurious effects of the dumped imports.[168]

3.3.6   Remaining Claims of the European Union

The European Union also challenged a number of procedural steps taken by the DIMD when it conducted its investigation including treatment of confi-dential information and sharing of essential information with interested par-ties. On the former claim the Panel found no inconsistency with Article 6.5 of the Anti-Dumping Agreement, despite the fact that the DIMD accorded confidential treatment to informational items without showing good cause for doing so.[169]

On the latter claim, however, the Panel did find an inconsistency with Article 6.9 of the Anti-Dumping Agreement.[170] Article 6.9 imposes an obligation on an investigating authority to inform all interested parties, before a final determi-nation is made, of essential facts that are under consideration or that form the basis for the decision of whether to apply the definitive measures.[171] Each element of this obligation is broken down, and if any of these elements are not satisfied an investigating authority acts inconsistently with Article 6.9.[172]

The Panel found that the European Union did not successfully demonstrate that the three essential facts alleged at issue met the requirements of Article 6.9.[173] Nonetheless, the Panel considered other essential facts at issue and found that by not disclosing these essential facts, the DIMD acted inconsist-ently with Article 6.9 of the Anti-Dumping Agreement.[174]

The Panel therefore recommended that the Russian Federation bring any inconsistent measures into conformity with the Anti-Dumping Agreement and the GATT 1994.[175]

---

167   ibid para 7.182.
168   ibid para 7.237.
169   ibid para 7.249.
170   ibid para 7.278.
171   ibid para 7.253.
172   ibid para 7.253–7.254.
173   ibid para 7.257.
174   ibid para 7.278.
175   ibid para 8.4.

3.3.7   Conclusion

Both the European Union and the Russian Federation have appealed certain aspects of the Panel's decision in this dispute.[176] On 30 May 2017 the Appellate Body confirmed that due to a substantially increased workload in 2017 the Appellate Body report would not be circulated within the 90-day timeframe provided for in Article 17.5 of the Dispute Settlement Understanding.[177] The Appellate Body report was circulated on 22 March 2018. The Dispute Settlement Body adopted the Appellate Body report and the panel report, as modified by the Appellate Body report, at its meeting on 9 April 2018.[178]

4   Concluding Observations: The Ukraine Crisis, Sanctions and WTO Dispute Settlement – How Long Can They Be Kept Apart?

Of the three WTO disputes reviewed in this chapter, two have no apparent link to the deterioration of the relationship between Russia and its Western trading partners following the Ukraine crisis. After the Panel report in *Russia – Tariff Treatment* was circulated, EU officials explicitly stated that the dispute was not linked with the sanctions and countersanctions imposed in the course of the Ukraine crisis.[179] The same may well be true for the *Russia – Commercial Vehicles* dispute, as there appears to be no connection between that measure at issue in the dispute and the increasing tensions between Russia and the European Union.

The *Russia – Pigs (EU)* disputes similarly started out independently of the crisis; indeed, it appears that Russia used the outbreak of ASF on the territory of some EU Member States as a pretext to accommodate the protectionist pressure of its pig farmers. However, the Ukraine crisis started getting uncomfortably close to the dispute when Russia chose pork products, among other agricultural products, as the subject for its countersanctions against

---

176   WTO, DS479: *Russia – Anti-Dumping Duties on Light Commercial Vehicles from Germany and Italy*, Panel Report (n 137).

177   WTO, Communication from the Appellate Body *Russia – Anti-Dumping Duties on Light Commercial Vehicles from Germany and Italy* [2017] WT/DS479/8 1.

178   On 20 June 2018, the Russian Federation informed the DSB that following the expiration of the measures at issue, the Russian Federation had fully implemented the DSB's recommendations and rulings in this dispute. See <www.wto.org/english/tratop_e/dispu_e/case s_e/ds479_e.htm> accessed 30 July 2021.

179   Reuters Staff, 'Russia to Lower Tariffs on EU's Paper, Fridges after WTO Ruling' *Reuters* (Zurich, 12 August 2016) <www.reuters.com/article/us-wto-russia-eu-idUSKCN10N1Y3> accessed 30 July 2021.

the Western powers in August 2014, and the measures at issue in the dispute became hopelessly intermingled with the countersanctions when Russia decided to align the products scope of the countersanctions with the products scope of the SPS measures in October 2017 in an attempt to evade its compliance obligations in the dispute.

The link between the Ukraine crisis and the WTO dispute settlement activity between Russia and Ukraine appears to be much closer. There are a total of five disputes between Ukraine and the Russian Federation currently being resolved through the WTO.[180] All five of the disputes were initiated within just over two years of each other, and all of them relate to measures imposed in late 2013 and onwards. Panels have been established and composed in three of the five disputes, and the remaining two are currently in the consultation stage. The only explicit references to the conflict between Ukraine and the Russian Federation can be found in *Russia – Measures Concerning the Importation and Transit of Certain Ukrainian Products* (DS532), where the Ukrainian government argues that the measures at issue in that dispute were imposed in retaliation for Ukraine's decision not to pursue the Eurasian Economic Union (EAEU), and were an attempt to deter Ukraine's integration with the European Union.[181] While this is the only mention of the Ukraine crisis in the WTO disputes between Russia, the European Union and Ukraine, the fact that Ukraine has explicitly made reference to the crisis suggests that the lines between politics and trade are indeed beginning to blur. The resulting implication is that the measures at issue may be purely political, and that the WTO dispute settlement mechanism is being used as a means of taking the Ukraine-Russia dispute to another level.

Of interest, an examination of the exchanges between Russia and Ukraine during DSB meetings reveals noticeably different responses to each other's requests for panel establishment. In response to Russia's request for establishment of a panel in the *Ukraine – Anti-Dumping Measures on Ammonium Nitrate* dispute, the Ukrainian representative offered a legal defence for the measures at issue.[182] Contrastingly, in the two cases where panels have been established

---

180   The five disputes are, in order of initiation: *Ukraine – Anti-Dumping Measures on Ammonium Nitrate* (DS493); *Russia – Measures Affecting the Importation of Railway Equipment and Parts Thereof* (DS499); *Russia – Measures Concerning Traffic in Transit* (DS512); *Ukraine – Measures Relating to Trade in Goods and Services* (DSDS525); and *Russia – Measures Concerning the Importation and Transit of Certain Ukrainian Products* (DS532).

181   WTO, Request for Consultations by Ukraine, *Russia – Measures Concerning the Importation and Transit of Certain Ukrainian Products* (19 October 2017) WT/DS532/1, 1.

182   *Minutes of Meeting* [22 April 2016] WT/DSB/M/377 [6.3].

in response to Ukrainian challenges of Russian measures, the Russian representative has offered no substantial defence to the measures at issue. Rather, the only comments offered by the Russian representative at the DSB meetings have been expressions of "disappointment with Ukraine's decision to request the establishment of a panel".[183]

As Panels have only been established in three of the five disputes, the significance of Russia's commentary is difficult to examine at this time. Nonetheless, Russia's lack of a substantive legal justification for the measures at issue in DS499 and DS512 could further suggest that there is no legal justification for the measures being imposed by Russia, and that these measures are simply political, intended to be sanctions in disguise.

183 See *Minutes of Meeting* (23 November 2016) WT/DSB/M/389, para 10.3; *Minutes of Meeting* (16 December 2016) WT/DSB/M/390, para 5.3; *Minutes of Meeting* (20 February 2017) WT/DSB/M/392, para 7.3; *Minutes of Meeting* (21 March 2017) WT/DSB/M394 para 5.3.

CHAPTER 17

Conflict of Jurisdictions: WTO and PTAS

Peter-Tobias Stoll and Jia Xu

1   Introduction

In recent times, an increasing number of trade agreements have been concluded bilaterally or by small groups of States.[1] Such agreements are often called
"free trade agreements" or – in the parlance of the World Trade Organization
(WTO) – "regional trade agreements" and in this paper will be referred to as
"preferential trade agreements" (PTAs) to signify that the rights and duties,
that they define, exclusively apply among parties and are not subject to most-
favoured-nations treatment as is the general rule in the WTO.[2]

Some of those agreements are outstanding in view of trade, the complexity
of their rules and the inclusion of important supply chain hubs. This is true
e.g. for the Comprehensive and Progressive Transpacific Partnership (CPTPP),
which includes several countries on the coasts of the Pacific, but also applies
to agreements involving countries in the Eurasian region or the Eurasian
Economic Union in its relation with third countries.

While being negotiated and concluded outside the WTO, these agreements
hardly signify a departure from the WTO. On the contrary, the WTO allows
for such agreements under certain conditions with the understanding, that a

---

1   By 30 September 2021, WTO has received notification about 568 PTAs, of which 350 have
     been in force. See <www.wto.org/english/tratop_e/region_e/region_e.htm> accessed 30
     September 2021. For recent instances of the growing literature on these trade agreements,
     see Lorand Bartels and Federico Ortino (eds), *Regional Trade Agreements and the WTO
     Legal System* (OUP 2006); Simon Lester, Bryan Mercurio & Lorand Bartels (eds), *Bilateral
     and Regional Trade Agreements: Case Studies* (2nd edn, CUP 2016); Kyle W. Bagwell & Petros
     C. Mavroidis (eds), *Preferential Trade Agreements: A Law and Economics Analysis* (CUP 2011).
2   This article employs the term 'PTAs' when 'RTAs' applied merely for those agreements
     between geographically proximate trade partners and the term 'FTAs' excludes the customs
     unions. Further references to these terminologies, see, eg, *Global Economic Prospects 2005:
     Regional Trade and Preferential Trade Agreements: A Global Perspective* (Washington: World
     Bank 2005); see also <http:// openknowledge.worldbank.org/bitstream/handle/10986/14783/
     9780821357477.pdf?sequence=1&isAllowed=y> accessed 30 June 2021; *World Trade Report
     2011: The WTO and Preferential Trade Agreements: From Co-existence to Coherence* (Geneva,
     WTO, 2011), see also <www.wto.org/english/res_e/booksp_e/anrep_e/world_trade_report11
     _e.pdf> accessed 30 June 2021.

closer economic integration among some of its members is to be welcomed as is further detailed in Article XXIV GATT and Article V GATS. As a consequence, parties to PTAS remain members of the WTO and have to observe its rules in parallel to the rights and obligations agreed among themselves. The only exception to this rule is provided for by the aforementioned two provisions in view of the most-favoured-nation principle: in order for such smaller coalitions to establish more advanced forms of economic integration, they need not share certain concessions and privileges, as agreed upon among them, to the larger WTO membership.

The obvious increase in numbers of such PTAS, as well as their significance in economic and political terms, has caused a vivid debate concerning the interrelationship between the WTO and such agreements as well as in regard to the governance of the world trade system at large.[3] Evidently, the current inability to achieve progress in the WTO negotiations has persuaded its members to seek advances in trade liberalization in small "coalitions of the willing" and the question arises whether this will help the WTO to gain momentum again or whether it will eventually contribute to a further loss of relevance.

On a more detailed level, the coexistence of the WTO and such PTAS has been discussed. This does not only concern the application of WTO and PTA rules in parallel but also dispute settlement.[4] As far as can be seen, all the PTAS include a dispute settlement mechanism and such a mechanism is evidently necessary to effectively establish a system of economic integration. However, as a number of cases indicate, the coexistence of dispute settlement institutions and procedures may result in conflict. This raises the question of how PTA dispute settlement can be designed in a way to effectively promote the settlement of disputes within PTAS and to safeguard compliance with its rules.

---

3   For early works on this debate, see, eg, Panagiotis Delimatsis, 'The Fragmentation of International Trade Law' (2011) 45(1) Journal of World Trade 87; Colin B. Picker, 'Regional Trade Agreements v. The WTO: A Proposal for Reform of Article XXIV to Counter This Institutional Threat' (2005) 26(2) University of Pennsylvania Journal of International Economic Law 267; Bartels and Ortino (n 1).

4   For recent observations, see also: Gabrille Marceau and Julian Wyatt, 'Dispute Settlement Regimes Intermingled: Regional Trade Agreements and the WTO' (2010) 1(1) Journal of International Dispute Settlement 67; Armand C. M. Mestral, 'Dispute Settlement Under the WTO and RTAS: An Uneasy Relationship' (2013) 16 Journal of International Economic Law 777; Kyung Kwak & Gabrielle Marceau, 'Overlaps and Conflicts of Jurisdiction between the World Trade Organization and Regional Trade Agreements' (2003) 41 The Canadian Yearbook of International Law 83; Marc D. Froese, 'Regional Trade Agreements and the Paradox of Dispute Settlement' (2014) 11(3) Manchester Journal of International Economic Law 367; Felicity Hammond, 'A Balancing Act: Using WTO Dispute Settlement to Resolve Regional Trade Agreement Disputes' (2012) 4(2) Trade, Law and Development 421.

2   The Design and Structure of PTA Dispute Settlement Mechanisms

As far as can be seen, PTAs always contain some mechanisms for the settlement of disputes. Such mechanisms may be highly sophisticated, as is true
for the European Union – which, as may be recalled, is also a PTA – and the
application of its rules by courts of member states and by the courts of the
union itself. Other PTAs contain very simple dispute settlement systems as is
true for instance, for the early agreement of the European Union with Central
and Eastern European, Mediterranean and other states.[5] These agreements
envisage something like a diplomatic-type dispute settlement, which is very
much in line with the early beginnings of dispute settlement in the GATT.[6]
However, the bulk of recent PTAs contain a dispute settlement system which
can be roughly characterized as a WTO dispute settlement in miniature.[7] Such
systems envisage panels, to be established in case of a dispute, comprised of
three individuals, who are chosen from lists of potential panelists as provided
for by the parties on occasion of the establishment of the PTA. Normally, the
reports of such panels are binding and have to be implemented. In case of non-
implementation some sort of retaliation is envisaged.[8]

---

5   See, eg, EU PTAs with Mediterranean countries: <http://ec.europa.eu/trade/policy/
    countries-and-regions/agreements/#_mediterranean>; also, Stabilization and Association
    Agreements between EU and Albania, EU and the former Yugoslav Republic of Macedonia,
    EU and Montenegro: <http://ec.europa.eu/trade/policy/countries-and-regions/agreements/
    #_europe> both accessed 30 September 2021.
6   See for example: art 75 of Euro – Mediterranean Agreement Establishing an Association
    between the European Communities and their Member States, of the one Part, and the
    State of Israel, of the other part; art 82 of Euro – Mediterranean Agreement Establishing an
    Association between the European Communities and their Member States, of the one Part,
    and the Arab Republic of Egypt, of the Other Part; art 86 of Euro – Mediterranean Agreement
    Establishing an Association between the European Communities and their Member States,
    of the one part, and the Kingdom of Morocco, of the other part.
7   See, eg, art 22.9 of the Free Trade Agreement between The United States of America and
    The Republic of Korea; art 15.7 of the Free Trade Agreement between The Government of
    Australia and The Government of People's Republic of China; arts N-08, N-09, N-10, and N-11
    of the Free Trade Agreement between the Government of Canada and the Government of
    the Republic of Chile.
8   See also: art 22.13 of the Free Trade Agreement between the United States of America and the
    Republic of Korea; art N-18 of the Free Trade Agreement between the Government of Canada
    and the Government of the Republic of Chile.

3   The Potential for Conflict: Some Preliminary Thoughts and Relevant Cases

Dispute settlement in the WTO and in PTAs is designed in accordance with the general structure of dispute settlement in international law as a decentralized system. As such, any of these mechanisms in principle serves to apply, interpret and to enforce the rules of the treaty system and the agreement that they are attached to. At first glance, the potential for conflict might thus appear to be limited as the settlement of disputes concerns different sets of norms.

Indeed, to date, conflicts between the dispute settlement of the WTO and that of PTAs arose only in a small number of situations compared to the considerable number of PTAs. In part, this is due to the fact, that in a number of PTAs, dispute settlement mechanisms have scarcely ever been used. This is true for ASEAN, where the existing former dispute settlement mechanism has been never used.[9] It can be assumed, that the parties to ASEAN have preferred to settle their differences by diplomatic means. In a number of cases, parties to a PTA have obviously preferred to bring the case to WTO dispute settlement, an issue that will be seen later. Also, in many cases, dispute settlement activities within a PTA took place without any interference from WTO dispute settlement. This is obviously the case with the European Union, as its rules and the structure of its dispute settlement is quite different compared to the WTO. Furthermore, within the European Union, there is an effective prohibition for members to resort to other dispute settlement procedures.[10]

However, there have been disputes, where some sort of interference arose between PTAs and WTO dispute settlement. A number of those cases concern NAFTA and some occurred in regard to MERCOSUR.

3.1   *United States – Softwood Lumber*[11]

To start with, the *Softwood Lumber* cases must be mentioned, which are related to allegations by the United States against Canada in view of the subsidization

---

9   See Gonzalo Villalta Puig and Lee Tsun Tat, 'Problems with the ASEAN Free Trade Area Dispute Settlement Mechanism and Solutions for the ASEAN Economic Community' (2015) 49(2) Journal of World Trade 277.

10   Consolidated Version of the Treaty on European Union [2008] OJ C115/13, art 207, art 344.

11   See WTO, *US – Softwood Lumber III*, Panel Report (adopted on 27 September 2002); WTO, *US – Softwood Lumber IV*, Appellate Body Report (adopted on 19 January 2004) WT/DS257/AB/R; WTO, *US – Softwood Lumber V*, Appellate Body Report (adopted on 15 August 2006) WT/DS264/AB/RW; WTO, *US – Softwood Lumber VI*, Appellate Body Report (adopted on 13 April 2006) WT/DS277/AB/RW; and Notification of Mutually Agreed Solution – United States – Final Countervailing Duty Determination with Respect to

of the Canadian timber production. The dispute has been taken to NAFTA and
WTO dispute settlement more than once and resulted in contradictory decisions. As the various dispute settlement procedures were not considered to
have produced an acceptable result, the issue was finally addressed by the parties with a specific agreement.[12] This unfortunate parallelism of procedures
was caused by the fact that NAFTA contains provisions on subsidies which are
very close to the rules of the WTO on the same subject.[13] In addition, both rules
leave room for a dispute owing to divergence in interpretation depending on
the dispute settlement system used.

3.2   *Argentina – Poultry*[14]

Quite a similar situation occurred in a dispute between Brazil and Argentina
on anti-dumping concerning poultry. The case was originally brought to dispute settlement in MERCOSUR. However, as Brazil was unsatisfied with the
outcome, it brought the case to WTO settlement afterwards. In this case, the
WTO panel did not see any reason not to adjudicate the dispute and came to a
result, which contradicted the earlier MERCOSUR judgment.

3.3   *Mexico – Soft Drinks*[15]

However, the potential for conflict is not limited to cases with a similarity of
rules, as the *Mexico - Soft Drinks* case may demonstrate. In this case, the United
States complained to the WTO against a special tax imposed by Mexico on
soft drinks imported from the United States. Mexico took that measure as a
reaction against the alleged non-compliance of the United States with rules on
trade in sugar and sweeteners agreed within NAFTA and because of the lack of
cooperation on the side of the United States to have the dispute settled within
NAFTA dispute settlement. The WTO panel and Appellate Body both found the
Mexican taxes to be inconsistent with its WTO obligations. Furthermore and

---

       Certain Softwood Lumber from Canada, WT/DS257/26, G/L/539/Add.1, G/SCM/D45/2,
       notified 16 November 2006.
12   See Notification of Mutually Agreed Solution – *United States – Final Countervailing Duty
       Determination with Respect to Certain Softwood Lumber from Canada*, WT/DS257/26, G/L/
       539/Add.1, G/SCM/D45/2 notified 16 November 2006.
13   See Chapter 19 of NAFTA, see also: <www.sice.oas.org/trade/nafta/chap-191.asp> accessed
       30 September 2021.
14   See WTO, *Argentina – Poultry Anti-Dumping Duties*, Panel Report (adopted on 22 April
       2003) WT/DS241/R.
15   See WTO, *Mexico – Taxes on Soft Drinks*, Panel Report (adopted on 7 October 2005) WT/
       DS308/R; and WTO, *Mexico – Taxes on Soft Drinks*, Appellate Report (adopted on 6 March
       2006) WT/DS308/AB/R.

explicitly, the panel and the Appellate Body pointed out, that they saw no possibility to decline the exercise of jurisdiction in this case.

3.4   *Conclusion*

The *Softwood Lumber* cases and the *Argentina Poultry* case reveal a potential for conflict, which results from the similarity of norms in the two agreements. While certainly the norms are different from a formal point of view, as they belong to different agreements, they were quite similar in regard to substance.

In order to prevent such conflicts in dispute settlement, parties could abstain from including rules into PTAs which are similar to WTO rules. Also, they might exclude the applicability of their internal dispute settlement mechanism in such cases or defer related disputes to WTO dispute settlement.

4   A Coherent Relationship between Dispute Settlement in PTAs and the WTO

The potential interference between the jurisdiction of PTAs and WTO dispute settlement has been debated intensively.[16] With regard to the cases at hand, the main focus has been on how to exclude access to WTO dispute settlement in cases, which have been, could be or should be decided in PTA dispute settlement.

4.1   *Is Parallel or Subsequent WTO Adjudication Prevented by General Doctrines of Procedure?*

Often, general doctrines of procedural law have been discussed in order to understand, whether they would help to prevent conflicts.[17] The doctrine of *res iudicata* may be mentioned here, as it prevents a court from taking a case which has already been adjudicated. In a similar way, the *lis pendens* principle

---

16   See also, Kyung Kwak and Gabrielle Marceau, 'Overlaps and Conflicts of Jurisdiction between the World Trade Organization and Regional Trade Agreements' (2003) 41 The Canadian Yearbook of International Law 83; Caroline Henckels, 'Overcoming Jurisdictional Isolationism at the WTO – FTA Nexus: A Potential Approach for the WTO' (2008) 19(3) European Journal of International Law 571; Songling Yang, 'The Solution for Jurisdictional Conflicts Between The WTO and RTAs: The Forum Choice Clause' (2014) 23(1) Michigan State International Law Review 107.

17   See for instance, Son Tan Nguyen, 'The Applicability of Res Judicata and Lis Pendens in World Trade Organisation Dispute Settlement' (2013) 25(2) Bond Law Review 123; Joost Pauwelyn and Luiz Eduardo Salles, 'Forum Shopping Before International Tribunals: (Real) Concerns, (Im)Possible Solutions' (2009) 42(1) Cornell International Law Journal 77.

may prevent a court from hearing a case where the matter is already pending in another tribunal. However, both doctrines build on the identity of the subject matter at hand. When considering the disputes discussed above, the issues before NAFTA and WTO dispute settlement in the *Softwood Lumber* cases and in *Argentina - Poultry* look quite alike. However, for the two aforementioned doctrines to apply, the apparent similarity of facts and measures is not sufficient. In order to ascertain the identity of subject matters as a precondition for the application of the two doctrines, the cause of action has to be taken into account as well. From this perspective, the subject matter of the related disputes clearly differs, as the disputing parties relied on NAFTA rules in NAFTA dispute settlement and on WTO rules in WTO dispute settlement. The same holds true for the *forum non conveniens* doctrine, where a court may reject its own jurisdiction when another tribunal is more appropriate; nonetheless, a court could merely apply *forum non conveniens* when it has ensured that another tribunal could decide this dispute; neither WTO Dispute Settlement Body nor the NAFTA dispute settlement organ has this capability though.

4.2   *May WTO Dispute Institutions Refuse to Adjudicate a Case Concerning Relationships within a PTA?*

It has also been discussed whether parallel proceedings and potentially conflicting decisions in dispute settlement of the WTO and under a PTA can be prevented by a refusal of the WTO dispute settlement institutions to take up such case.

The doctrine of comity is sometimes put forward in this regard.[18] Indeed, on the basis of this doctrine, US courts used to deny hearing a case as a matter of courtesy where the jurisdiction of other or foreign courts is at stake. As is often and correctly observed, international tribunals, including WTO dispute settlement, enjoy a similar power in principle. It is voiced, that WTO panels and the Appellate Body may deny their jurisdiction as a matter of cooperation with PTA dispute settlement mechanisms in relevant cases. However, the dispute settlement understanding (DSU) in Article 23.1 uses quite strong language to make it clear that members shall exclusively use the WTO dispute settlement system to "seek the redress of a violation of obligations or other nullification or impairment of benefits under the current agreements". Also, that system

---

18   See also: Caroline Henckels, 'Overcoming Jurisdictional Isolationism at the WTO – FTA Nexus: A Potential Approach for the WTO' (2008) 19(3) European Journal of International Law 571; Andrew D. Mitchell and David Heaton, 'The Inherent Jurisdiction of WTO Tribunals: The Select Application of Public International Law Required by the Judicial Function' (2010) 31(3) Michigan Journal of International Law 561.

"Serves to preserve the rights and obligations of members under the covered agreements" (Article 3.2, 2nd sentence). In regard to these provisions, it is difficult to see a panel or the appellate body decline its jurisdiction in view of a complaint, which is based on rights and duties under the WTO, even though it may also relate to substantive provisions and dispute settlement in PTAs.

4.3   Can Parties to a PTA Be Prevented from Bringing a WTO Complaint?

The initiation of dispute settlement procedures in the WTO and in a PTA furthermore raises the question of whether members may exercise their rights in this way. Having agreed to a PTA with a proper dispute settlement mechanism in place, it might be considered unfair, if such a member turns to the WTO in parallel or subsequently. The principle of bona fide comes to mind in this context and indeed has been argued by Argentina as a defendant in the *Argentina – Poultry* case.[19] However, the panel rejected this argument by stating that Argentina failed to show that the criteria were met which had been defined by the Appellate Body in *U.S. – Offset Act (Byrd Amendment)* in this regard.[20] In that decision the Appellate Body determined that in order to argue a breach of good faith it must be shown that a member has 'violated a substantive provision of the WTO agreement' and that there has been something 'more than mere violation'.[21]

In addition, the panel rejected Argentina's assertion that Brazil was estopped from bringing the case to the WTO after having been adjudicated by the MERCOSUR tribunal. According to the panel, "the principle of estoppel applies in circumstances where (i) a statement of fact which is clear and unambiguous, and which (ii) is voluntary, unconditional, and authorized, is (iii) relied on in good faith."[22] The panel considered, however, that Brazil never did explicitly or implicitly make a statement to the effect that it would not bring the case to WTO dispute settlement after the decision of the MERCOSUR tribunal.[23] The panel explicitly referred to the fact that, at the time of the dispute, the Protocol of Brasilia was relevant since it did not contain any explicit provision in regard to the relationship between MERCOSUR and WTO dispute settlement. As the panel rightly pointed out, however, MERCOSUR members concluded a more comprehensive ruling by the Protocol of Olivos in 2002 – just at the time of the dispute. That protocol introduced a choice of forum clause, which requires

---

19   See WTO, *Argentina – Poultry Anti-Dumping Duties*, Panel Report, paras 7.18, 7.19.
20   ibid, paras 7.35, 7.36.
21   ibid, para 7.36.
22   ibid, para 7.37.
23   ibid, para 7.37.

members to make their choice between MERCOSUR and WTO dispute settlement and preempts parties from bringing a case to the other forum in parallel or subsequently. The panel concluded, that the very fact of the conclusion of the 2002 Protocol of Olivos indicates, that at the time of the dispute, the parties were aware of the lack of a meaningful rule on a choice of forum. As the Protocol of Olivos had not entered into force at the time of the proceedings, the panel concluded that there was, indeed, no "statement" which could be understood to estop Brazil from bringing the case to the WTO.[24] In drawing this conclusion, the panel did not take into consideration, however, that Brazil had signed the Protocol a few days before requesting the establishment of the panel. It is therefore an open question, whether in the light of Article 18 of the Vienna Convention on the Law of Treaties (VCLT) the signature may constitute a "statement" in view of the principle of estoppel.[25]

Yet another way to prevent PTA members from using the WTO to settle disputes among them could be argued by considering their participation in the PTA with its own proper dispute settlement to constitute an implicit waiver of rights to WTO dispute settlement.[26] However, it appears to be difficult to interpret the mere participation in a PTA in this way.

4.4   Are Forum Clauses in PTAs Helpful?

As the aforementioned Protocol of Brasilia and the Olivos Protocol indicate, PTAS may address the relationship between PTA dispute settlement mechanisms and the WTO dispute settlement with specific forum clauses. Not only the MERCOSUR Olivos Protocol, but also NAFTA contain such a choice of forum clause.[27] Moreover, in contrast to the *Argentina – Poultry* case, the NAFTA clauses were in force, when the *Softwood Lumber* and the *Mexico – Soft Drinks* cases were adjudicated in the WTO. While the forum clause was not at all

---

24   ibid, paras 7.38, 7.39.
25   See art 18 of Vienna Convention on the Law of the Treaties, in force 27 January 1980, 1155 UNTS 331. This article provides: "Obligation Not to Defeat the object and Purpose of A Treaty Prior to Its Entry into Force: A State is obliged to refrain from acts which would defeat the object and purpose of a treaty when: (a) *It has signed the treaty* or has exchanged instruments constituting the treaty subject to ratification, acceptance or approval, until it shall have made its intention clear not to become a party to the treaty; or (b) It has expressed its consent to be bound by the treaty, pending the entry into force of the treaty and provided that such entry into force is not unduly delayed."
26   See WTO, *Argentina – Poultry Anti-Dumping Duties*, Panel Report, para 7.38.
27   See art 2005.6 of the NAFTA, it provides: "Once dispute settlement procedures have been initiated under Article 2007 or dispute settlement proceedings have been initiated under the GATT, the forum selected shall be used to the exclusion of the other, unless a Party makes a request pursuant to paragraph 3 or 4."

mentioned in the *Softwood Lumber* dispute, the panel and the Appellate Body considered the clause in *Mexico – Soft Drinks*. Indeed, Mexico relied on the forum clause of NAFTA Article 2005(6), which is kind of an exclusive fork-in-the-road provision.[28] However, both the panel and the Appellate Body refused to decline their jurisdiction as they felt that this would be equal to "failure to perform the Panel's duties and have the effect of diminishing the rights of U.S., which is contrary to Articles 3.2 and 19.2 of DSU."[29] Clearly, this reasoning is much more far-reaching than *Argentina – Poultry*, where the panel simply – and possibly questionably – relied on the fact, that the Olivos Protocol did not yet enter into force. Indeed, the reasoning in *Mexico – Soft Drinks* indicated that the WTO dispute settlement institutions would hear disputes whenever the rights of a Member stand in question. As outlined before, this will be the case in those frequent situations where PTAs reiterate or refer to WTO rules or where a trade-related measure is adopted within a PTA, as was the case in *Mexico – Soft Drinks*. Thus, the many choice of forum clauses in PTAs may have an impact within the PTA itself, but are not likely to significantly limit the competence of the WTO dispute settlement institutions to hear related cases.

5   Conclusion: How to Achieve a Harmonious Coexistence between WTO and PTA Dispute Settlement

As has been seen, disputes, which arise within a PTA often can be, and indeed frequently are, taken to the WTO in parallel or after such disputes are litigated within the PTA. The resulting interferences can hardly be remedied with the help of general principles. Moreover, the considerable number of forum choice clauses, as contained in PTAs, will very likely fail to prevent WTO dispute settlement institutions from hearing a complaint brought by one PTA member against another PTA party which is a member of the WTO. As is sometimes overlooked, these interferences and the major role of WTO dispute settlement result from the substantial law at stake. In legal terms, PTAs hardly represent a departure from the WTO but build on it and spell out additional rules. Frequently, PTAs reiterate or refer to WTO rules and contain additional substantial or procedural elements. In order to prevent interferences, recent PTAs and drafts curtail the range of application of their proper dispute settlement mechanisms in these

---

28   See WTO, *Mexico – Soft Drinks*, Panel Report, para 4.407.

29   See WTO, *Mexico – Soft Drinks*, Panel Report, paras 7.8, 7.9; WTO, *Mexico – Soft Drinks*, Appellate Body report, para 54.

areas.[30] Furthermore, there is a clear trend to focus on dispute prevention and on non-formal dispute settlement procedures. For instance, many PTAs contain specific bodies and procedures for certain topics and rules, which aim to discuss related issues and to build a common understanding, which might prevent disputes from arising.[31] Furthermore, non-formal or non-controversial procedures for the settlement of disputes, for instance mediation, have been included in recent agreements.[32] Probably, these procedures and elements are promising, as they can make use of the special relationship, which may develop in an agreement with a small number of participants. However, the rather extensive range of application of WTO dispute settlement may well be considered a benefit in various regards. WTO dispute settlement may serve as a default arbiter in cases when dispute settlement within a PTA does not work properly, as has been the case more than once. Also, it may help to further explore and draw the line between PTAs and WTO rules. Lastly, it may provide security and predictability to the interpretation of general concepts of world trade law, on which PTAs build in various ways.

30   See for instance, ch 33 of Comprehensive Economic and Trade Agreement between The European Union and Canada (CETA).

31   For example: The establishment of 'Contact Points' in numerous PTAs, eg, art 15 of Agreement between Japan and the Republic of Peru for an Economic Partnership; likewise, institutions like secretariat and coordinator under PTAs, eg, Free Trade Agreement Between Canada and the Republic of Honduras, ie arts 21.2 and 21.3.

32   For instance, Free Trade Agreement between the European Union and its Member States, of the one part, and the Republic of Korea, of the other part contains a number of mediation provisions, especially a Mediation Mechanism for Non-Tariff Measures has been established in Annex 14-A; moreover, art 17.5 of the Singapore–Costa Rica Free Trade Agreement states: "mediation are procedures undertaken voluntarily if the Parties so agree", which mirrors art 28.6 of CPTPP; also, CETA draft envisaged an annex of Mediation Procedure, ie Annex III, ch 33, etc.

CHAPTER 18

Dispute Settlement Mechanisms in Free Trade Agreements with the European Union

Thomas Jürgensen[1]

1   Introduction[2]

In 2015, the European Commission published its Trade Strategy Communication *Trade for all*.[3] In this Communication, the Commission has put a strong emphasis on enforcing trade obligations, both at multilateral as well as bilateral level:

> The EU must ensure that its partners play by the rules and respect their commitments. […] The Commission will use dispute settlement procedures as necessary, including in FTAs; [and] use the mediation mechanism agreed in recent FTAs to tackle non-tariff barriers quickly.[4]

From 2009 to 2014, the European Union brought 15 cases under the WTO Dispute Settlement Understanding (DSU),[5] as many as the United States.[6] Yet, with increasing negotiations activity on the bilateral level, dispute settlement mechanisms under Free Trade Agreements (FTA) or other agreements with a significant trade component have become more important as they play a key role in enforcing international agreements. The more elaborate and efficient

---

1   European Commission, DG Trade. The views expressed in this article are purely personal and do not bind the institution.
2   The article is based on a lecture given at the conference "Settlement of International Trade Disputes in the Region of Central Asia and Caucasus: Public and Private Mechanisms" in Kiel on 28/29 November 2014. Some updates have been made in the footnotes.
3   European Commission, 'Trade for All' (2015) <http://trade.ec.europa.eu/doclib/docs/2015/october/tradoc_153846.pdf> accessed 30 July 2021.
4   ibid, 15ff.
5   Understanding on Rules and Procedures Governing the Settlement of Disputes <www.wto.org/english/tratop_e/dispu_e/dsu_e.htm> accessed 30 July 2021.
6   The United States is traditionally the heaviest user of the WTO DS system, at the time of writing, it has been involved in 451 cases, compared to the European Union in 413 cases <www.wto.org/english/tratop_e/dispu_e/dispu_by_country_e.htm> accessed 3 February 2022. By February 2022, the European Union has brought 108 cases, the United States – 124 cases under the WTO DSU.

these arbitration procedural rules are, the higher the rate of the compliance with the international obligations. At the same time, a credible enforcement system mirrors the scope of substantive commitments. A weak or best-endeavour obligation does not require a court-like judicial system. Conversely, a direct and unequivocal obligation would run empty if the only mechanism to enforce it would be by means of consultations.

Therefore, in its recent FTAs or other agreements with a significant trade component, the European Union has included elaborate dispute settlement systems to resolve state-to-state trade irritants. This concerns, e.g. the Association Agreements with Chile, Central America, Ukraine, Georgia, and Moldova, the FTAs with Korea, Singapore, Canada or the Partnership and Cooperation Agreement with Kazakhstan. Against the experience of the WTO Dispute Settlement system, the European Union considers that an efficient and sophisticated bilateral dispute settlement mechanism is the best guarantee to ensure the respect of the substantive trade obligations entered into by the parties.

In doing so, the European Union has not been content to simply mirror the WTO dispute settlement system. Rather, the European Union 's approach to the dispute settlement proceedings is characterized by distinct and innovative features with the aim to make the proceedings more efficient and effective compared to the DSU. The European Union aims, for instance, for shorter deadlines or to close gaps in the WTO dispute settlement system that exist with respect to the compliance phase. The European Union 's approach also strives to introduce innovations, e.g. by creating an elaborate mediation mechanism which provides more detailed guidance to the parties on the proceedings and the legal status of a possible outcome.

In the following two sections, we will explain the basic principles governing the European Union 's approach to the bilateral dispute settlement mechanism.

2   Basic Principles Governing the Bilateral Dispute Settlement Mechanism

2.1   *The Law Rules through Dispute Settlement*
Taking the WTO dispute settlement system as the universal benchmark, it expresses the importance of the dispute settlement system in Article 3(2) DSU in the following terms:

> The dispute settlement system of the WTO is a central element in providing security and predictability to the multilateral trading system.

In comparison, in the bilateral agreements, the function of the dispute settlement is formulated in different terms. For instance, the European Union–Korea FTA provides in Article 14.1:[7]

> The objective of this Chapter [the Dispute Settlement Chapter] is to avoid and settle any dispute between the Parties concerning the good faith application of this Agreement and to arrive at, where possible, a mutually agreed solution.

Similar formulations can be found in the European Union–Singapore FTA,[8] the European Union–Colombia and Peru FTA[9] or the Association Agreements with Ukraine,[10] Georgia[11] or Moldova.[12]

The formulation of this objective in the bilateral dispute settlement mechanism underlines the ambition and the purpose of the FTA system, namely to go beyond and to further develop the WTO dispute settlement mechanism. First, while the DSU is centred on the "security and predictability to the multilateral trading system" aiming at the integrity of the marketplace in the interest of WTO members, economic operators and other stakeholders; the bilateral approach is to inject a qualitative element which informs the procedural dispute settlement rules. In practical terms this means that arbitration procedures should be faster ("efficient") and more judicialized since decisions by panels are directly binding and not subject to a separate adoption by a Dispute Settlement Body ("effective"). Second, the bilateral dispute settlement mechanism formulates its objectives to "avoiding and settling any dispute". This means that the "success" of the bilateral system is not only measured by the number of cases that have been adjudicated by the system but also the "avoidance" of disputes is formulated as an objective of the bilateral dispute settlement chapter. Taking this thought a step further, it could be understood that an effective and efficient dispute settlement mechanism operates as a deterrent to non-compliance

---

7   European Union–Korea FTA [2011] OJ L127/65.

8   European Union–Singapore FTA [2014], art 15.1 <http://trade.ec.europa.eu/doclib/docs/2013/september/tradoc_151768.pdf> accessed 30 July 2021.

9   FTA Columbia Peru [2012] OJ L354/88, art 298 <http://trade.ec.europa.eu/doclib/docs/2011/march/tradoc_147704.pdf> accessed 30 July 2021.

10   European Union–Ukraine Association Agreement (hereinafter: Ukraine AA) [2014] OJ L161/126, art 303.

11   European Union–Georgia Association Agreement (hereinafter Georgia AA) [2014] OJ L261/96, art 244.

12   European Union–Moldova Association Agreement [2014] OJ L260/126, art 380.

with treaty obligations, or, if that happens, as a means to increase the political pressure to find an out-of-court solution to a dispute.

With respect to the scope of the bilateral dispute settlement chapter, it should be noted that an arbitration proceeding aiming to resolve a "dispute" is limited to violation complaints, excluding non-violation or situation complaints as they are foreseen under Article XXIII:1(b) and (c) GATT. The reason for this limitation is the experience for non-violation and situation complaints under the GATT. They have been hardly of any relevance in the WTO system and they have been extremely difficult to pursue.[13] Against the background of this limited relevance under the multilateral system, it was considered unnecessary to provide for a similar possibility in the bilateral context. Furthermore, certain chapters of a trade agreement may be excluded from the dispute settlement system. This typically concerns trade defence measures which are subject to adjudication under the WTO system, trade cooperation provisions or the trade and sustainable development chapter which establishes its own (softer) dispute settlement system.

2.2   More through Less: Improving on the WTO Dispute Settlement System

The DSU has, since its establishment in 1995, set the global benchmark against which any bilateral system should be assessed. The WTO dispute settlement system has established a quasi-monopoly for resolving trade irritants in accordance with Article 23 DSU, whereby the use of the WTO dispute settlement system is compulsory for matters falling under the WTO Agreement.[14] No WTO member shall resort to self-help or take unilateral retaliatory measures in case of a presumed violation of the WTO Agreements by another Member. This rule is a practical expression of the centrality of the WTO dispute settlement as enshrined in Article 3(2) DSU.

WTO dispute settlement procedures are very exceptional in international law due to their legalized nature, including deadlines and other formal procedural requirements. Proceedings cannot be blocked for political reasons so that the complainant knows that he will eventually receive a ruling. Yet, even under this elaborate and judicialized system panel and Appellate Body, decisions are not self-executing, but they are subject to the adoption by the Dispute Settlement Body (DSB), by way of negative consensus.[15] While in practice this

---

13   Peter van den Bossche and Werner Zdouc, *The Law and Policy of the World Trade Organization* (3rd edn, 2013) 175.

14   WTO, *US – Section 301 Trade Act*, Panel Report (adopted on 27 January 2000) WT/DS152/R, para 7.43.

15   For Panel reports: DSU art 16(4); for Appellate Body reports: DSU art 17(14).

ensures that panel and Appellate Body decisions are always adopted, it formally also means that it is a political committee established under the WTO and composed of the WTO membership that takes the final decisions, which become binding "recommendations and rulings" of the DSB.[16]

The bilateral system builds on these characteristics and further develops the WTO system, adapting to the needs of the FTA and where the DSU has proven deficient or less effective.

This includes the following:

First, in the bilateral dispute settlement rules there are fewer procedures. They do not foresee an appeal proceeding. Furthermore, the decision by a panel is final and binding and not subject to the adoption or confirmation by a political committee established under the agreement (like the DSB in the WTO system). Arguably, the non-existence of an appeal proceeding may raise eyebrows as decisions by a panel are not subject to any further judicial control. However, in a purely bilateral context the creation of an appeal mechanism could be seen as inflated for various reasons. One is that not many trade disputes may be expected to arise in a bilateral FTA context. The setting up of an appeal mechanism in these circumstances may be overly burdensome, heavy and costly. Related to this, one important aspect of an appeal system is to ensure the coherence and consistency of the jurisprudence in case different panels interpret the agreement in different ways. An appeal body can align such divergences and provide general guidance for the interpretation by panels. Yet, in the case that only very few disputes arise, this function of an appeal mechanism is not required. Finally, in the selection of members for a possible arbitration panel to be included in a pre-established list of arbitrators, the European Union aims for the highest standard, including former Appellate Body members.[17] Thereby, the European Union aims to ensure that despite the lack of an appeal, decisions by a single panel are of high quality and well-founded.

Second, bilateral dispute settlement proceedings involve fewer negotiations and enhance the automaticity of the panel process. This is, in particular, the case for the panel composition which in the European Union's FTAs is based on a binding roster system with a pre-established list of arbitrators. This list is, unlike under Article 8(4) DSU, not just indicative, but mandatory in case both parties do not succeed in a first phase to agree on the names of the arbitrators. The roster shall be agreed by the parties at the moment of entry into force

---

16   DSU art 21(1).
17   Eg Decision No 2 of the EU–Korea Trade Committee of 1 March 2013 [2013] OJ L58/13.

of the agreement. Arbitrators have thus been endorsed by both parties independently of a specific trade dispute. This system aims to enhance, on the one hand, the independency and credibility of the arbitrators. On the other hand, it also has the effect that the panel should be established in a shorter period of time since the pool of possible arbitrators is already known long before a dispute arises.

Third, a key distinctive difference between the DSU and a bilateral dispute settlement system is that the latter aims to come to a decision much faster. This is worth mentioning specifically at a time when the multilateral system is jammed and is facing severe backlogs. But even if a procedure was conducted in accordance with the rule book of the DSU, it would result in at least 590 days for a decision by a panel and 770/860 days[18] in case of an appeal counting from the request for consultations. In contrast, the bilateral proceedings should be concluded in 360/390 days or, in case of urgency, within 285/300 days.[19] And in case of Deep and Comprehensive Free Trade Area (DCFTAS) the procedure would be even faster for urgent energy disputes. This amounts to a time saving of around 50% for ordinary cases. They are mostly achieved by cutting on elements such as a shorter consultation phase, the lack of an appeal procedure and the involvement of a political committee such as the DSB. In addition, the compliance review has been shortened.

Fourth, an important innovation under the bilateral dispute settlement system is the inclusion of a full-fledged mediation mechanism. The first inclusion of such a mechanism was in the EU–Korea FTA, and it was limited to non-tariff measures.[20] In contrast, under the EU–Singapore FTA, it comprises a whole chapter on equal footing with Trade in Goods, Services or Intellectual property rights.[21] However, in most cases, the mediation mechanism is attached to the dispute settlement chapter, which means that the scope of this chapter,

---

18   This figure results from the following assumption: Consultations (60 days), Panel composition (20 days), Final Panel report (180 days plus 60 days for DSB), Appeal (60/90 days plus 30 days for the DSB), Determination of the reasonable period of time (90 days), Compliance review (90 days plus 60/90 days for appeal), Review of temporary remedies (60 days), Post-compliance review (90 days).

19   This figure is based on the Kazakhstan PCA. It should be noted that the time frame varies slightly from agreement to agreement. The calculation is made as follows: Consultations (30 days), Panel composition (20 days), Final Panel report (120/150 days), Determination of the reasonable period of time (70 days), Compliance review (45 days), Review of temporary remedies (30 days), Post-compliance review (45 days).

20   EU–Korea FTA [2011] OJ L127/1336, Annex 14-A.

21   EU–Singapore FTA ch 16 <http://trade.ec.europa.eu/doclib/docs/2013/september/tradoc _151771.pdf> accessed 30 July 2021.

also, in principle, defines the scope of the mediation mechanism.[22] While in the multilateral context Article 5 DSU provides for the possibility to engage in mediation procedures, this has hardly been used in the WTO.[23] The reason for this shortcoming may partly be that the DSU does not provide for clear rules on how the mediation is structured, e.g. with respect to the selection of a mediator, the procedures, the relevance of the outcome or the relationship with arbitration proceedings. Under the European Union's bilateral FTAs these deficiencies are addressed in order to provide greater guidance for the use of this alternative dispute resolution mechanism.

The underlying reasons for the European Union's inclusion of a mediation mechanism is that it should be a faster and less costly means to resolve trade irritants. While dispute settlement proceedings under the FTA can take around six months, the mediation proceeding is foreseen to last only two months.

In substance, the mediation mechanism is voluntary, and it can only be launched with the prior consent of both parties. If the parties do not succeed in agreeing on a mediator, he or she should be selected from the roster list for the chairpersons for arbitration panels. The procedures are very light and flexible, aiming in particular for the mediator to arrive at a proposal to resolve the irritant. Once both sides have found an agreement, it becomes binding and must be implemented. The mediation mechanism further specifies that any evidence relied on, or introduced, should not be used if, later, a formal dispute settlement procedure, either under the FTA, or under any other agreement, is launched.[24]

Fifth, a very important aspect of bilateral dispute settlement is the much greater emphasis on increasing transparency compared to the WTO dispute settlement. This becomes evident in particular in two areas: On the one hand, open hearings are established as a rule. This means that any person can follow the hearings held before the panel.[25] While this rule may be limited for confidentiality reasons, it is, unlike in the WTO, an established rule. On the other hand, in the bilateral FTAs, interested persons acquire for the first time a legal right to submit amicus curiae briefs. In the WTO context, this right has been handled – like open hearings – on a case-by-case basis.[26] Under the European Union's FTAs, individuals that are established in either party can put forward

---

22   Eg Georgia AA [2014] OJ L261/ 97, art 247 in conjunction with Annex XIX.

23   Van den Bossche and Zdouc (n 11) 181ff.

24   Eg Georgia AA [2014] OJ L261/97, art 7(4), Annex XIX.

25   Eg Georgia AA [2014] OJ L261/102, 562, art 263(2) in conjunction with Rule 22 Annex XX.

26   Van den Bossche and Zdouc (n 11) 263ff.

their views without depending on a separate decision by the parties or the panel.[27]

Sixth, without going further into details, two more particularities under the bilateral dispute settlement system should be noted, which deviate from the DSU.

The first point concerns cross-retaliation rules which in the DSU are subject to the principles set out in Article 22.3 DSU. In the FTA, the European Union does not foresee any specific provisions. There are two main reasons for this omission: the experience in the WTO has shown that the cross-retaliation rules are barely effective, rather they result in additional litigation.[28] Eventually, Article 22.3 DSU did not however limit cross-retaliation, if that ever was the intention of the original drafter of the DSU. Furthermore, in the specific EU context it could be difficult for certain cases, not to apply cross-retaliation, e.g. in the areas of services where commitments are often at Member States level and where it may be difficult for the European Union to adopt horizontal countermeasures. In view of the effectiveness of the dispute settlement system, including the application of temporary remedies, the European Union therefore has an interest not to be restricted by cross-retaliation rules, which either result in another litigation or, in the worst case, would limit the European Union's ability to take countermeasures in case of a persistent violation by the other side.

The second point where the bilateral dispute settlement mechanism goes beyond and deviates from the DSU is the inclusion of a provision on post-compliance review. Such a provision addresses the situation that arose in the case *United States – Continued Suspension* and *Canada – Continued Suspension.*[29] The European Union had adopted a second compliance measure after the United States and Canada had imposed sanctions against the European Union following the negative recommendation and ruling by the DSB on the EU's prohibition of import on hormone-treated beef. Since the United States and Canada did not lift their sanctions despite the EU's second compliance measure, the European Union challenged both at the WTO. The panel and the Appellate Body were confronted with two very difficult questions, namely whether the United States and Canada were obliged to initiate compliance proceedings or to lift the sanctions in accordance with Article 22.8 DSU and, second, what would be the fate of the sanctions in the case that a

---

27   Eg Georgia AA [2014] OJ L261/103, 564, art 264 in conjunction with Rules 37 to 39 Annex XX.
28   See for instance, EC – *Bananas III (Ecuador) (Article 22.6-EC)*, Decision by the Arbitrators (WT/DS27/ARB).
29   WT/DS320 and WT/DS321.

compliance review was indeed launched. In the WTO case, these issues were not decided in favour of the European Union. The Appellate Body ruled, first, that compliance proceedings could also have been launched by the defending party (in this case the European Union)[30] and that sanctions should remain in place until the DSB states that the implementing party has indeed achieved substantive compliance with its obligations.[31]

The post-compliance provision in the bilateral FTA addresses this issue directly and purports a solution that takes into account the interests of both sides, i.e. the party that has imposed sanctions and the party that makes efforts to comply with its obligations. Accordingly, the original complaining party would have to initiate a second compliance review or to end its sanctions. In return, the complaining party may maintain the sanctions even during the second compliance proceedings. Thus, while the complaining party bears the burden of initiating a new compliance review, it receives in return an extension of the right to retaliate. This could effectively result in a situation, in which a defending party would continue to suffer from sanctions even if the compliance panel were to find that the second compliance measure was consistent with the agreement.[32]

2.3   Dispute Settlement Plus: Specific Rules in Deep and Comprehensive Free Trade Area

In recent agreements the European Union has established a Deep and Comprehensive Free Trade Area (DCFTA) with some of its Eastern neighbours, i.e. Ukraine, Georgia and Moldova. These are agreements that contain a more political component as well as a dedicated chapter establishing a free trade area. In addition, the European Union has been negotiating a Partnership and Cooperation Agreement (PCA) with Kazakhstan which contains a non-preferential trade part. With respect to dispute settlement under the trade chapter, certain specificities apply concerning urgent energy disputes and regulatory approximation which will be set out below.

2.3.1   Urgent Energy Disputes

Against the background of the energy disputes between Russia and the Ukraine which occurred since 2005/6, the European Union has been very sensitive to its exposure to an energy conflict, from which it may indirectly suffer negative

---

30 WTO, *US/Canada – Continued Suspension*, Appellate Body Reports (adopted on 14 November 2008) WT/DS320 and WT/DS321, paras 346ff.

31 ibid para 306.

32 Eg Georgia AA [2014] OJ L261/102 art 259(2).

consequences. Therefore, in the Association Agreement with Ukraine as well as in the PCA with Kazakhstan, the European Union has included fast track dispute settlement procedures which would apply in the case of an urgent energy dispute. This situation is defined in the Association Agreement with Ukraine as an interruption, in full or in part, of any transport of natural gas, oil, electricity or a threat thereof, between Ukraine and the EU Party.[33]

The first element is a super fast-track procedure under which the proceeding from consultation until a final ruling would only last 52 days instead of the normal 120/150 days. To achieve such a short time limit the following measures are employed: the consultation time is, e.g. cut down from 30 to three days,[34] an immediate recourse to the roster system to compose the panel,[35] the possibility to dispense the interim report[36] and the notification of a final ruling within 40 days of the date of the establishment of the panel.[37]

The second novelty for urgent energy disputes is the recourse to specific compliance proceedings and the possibility to have particular remedies. This includes the dispensation of a reasonable period of time and a compliance review in case of non-compliance. Instead, the complaining party may immediately have recourse to countermeasures if it considers that the responding party is not in compliance with the panel ruling within 15 days. Proceedings against the countermeasures which may be initiated by the responding party have no suspensive effect.[38]

The third element different from normal dispute settlement proceedings is the possibility of a conciliation procedure. While this resembles the mediation mechanism it has a very different effect, as the conciliator shall recommend a resolution of the dispute or a procedure to achieve such a resolution and he/she shall decide on the terms and conditions to be observed. The parties as well as the entities under the control or jurisdiction of the Parties shall respect these recommendations for three months following the conciliator's decision or until the resolution of the dispute, whichever is earlier.[39] By this mechanism, a conciliator can bind the parties without a normal disputes settlement procedure and it can also create a direct effect of a decision to private

---

33   Eg Ukraine AA [2014] OJ L161/126ff arts 305 (5), 309(1), 314.
34   Ukraine AA [2014] OJ L161/126, art 305(5).
35   Ukraine AA [2014] OJ L161/128, art 307(8).
36   ibid art 308(4).
37   Ukraine AA [2014] OJ L161/129, art 310(3).
38   Ukraine AA [2014] OJ L161/130, art 314.
39   Ukraine AA [2014] OJ L161/128, art 309.

entities – something that is normally excluded in the EU's dispute settlement proceedings.

2.3.2   Regulatory Approximation

DCFTAs aim to establish a particularly close relationship between the European Union and a third country. In terms of trade it is apparent that when the regulatory provisions on both ends are aligned, trade can flow much more easily. Therefore, individual chapters of the DCFTA provide for rules on how the third partner should approximate its legislation to the European Union's for which it will receive, in return, further market opening concessions.[40]

With respect to dispute settlement, the most interesting provision relates to the interpretation of a provision of EU law. When such a question arises, it should not be decided by an arbitration panel, but the European Court of Justice (ECJ) shall have the final say on matters of EU law. Therefore, the arbitration panel shall request the ECJ to give a ruling on this issue.[41] In doing so, the agreements create a new preliminary ruling mechanism for an international tribunal outside Article 267 TFEU (Treaty on the Functioning of the European Union).

2.4   *Relationship with WTO Dispute Settlement Proceedings*

One important question in bilateral dispute settlement proceedings is the general relationship with the WTO dispute settlement system in case a measure might be in violation of a substantially equivalent obligation under the FTA and the WTO Agreement.[42] If both proceedings were allowed without any limitation it could result in forum shopping by either party until it has received an outcome that it considers satisfactory. In the worst cases, it could lead to conflicting rulings, one by the bilateral panel and the other one by a panel or the Appellate Body under the WTO.

Against this background, the European Union includes in its FTAs a choice of forum clause. While this provision departs from the principle that a party is free to choose its forum, it stipulates that once a choice has been made, the complaining party shall not have recourse to the other forum. There are only two exceptions to this rule which concern cases where a panel does not come to substantive findings for procedural or jurisdictional reasons and, therefore,

---

40   Eg Ukraine AA [2014] OJ L161, arts 64, 114, 124, 133, 138, 474, 475 and Annex XVII.

41   Ukraine AA [2014] OJ L161/132, art 322(2).

42   For a more general discussion about the relationship between the WTO and an FTA see the decision by the Appellate Body, *Peru – Additional Duty on Imports of Certain Agricultural Products*, Appellate Body Report (adopted on 31 July 2015) WT/DS457/AB/R, para 5.81ff.

there exists no risk of conflicting rulings. These cases may be, for instance, if a panel dismisses a case because the panel request is deficient or when the Appellate Body adopts a different legal interpretation as a panel but is then unable to conclude the legal analysis because it lacks the necessary factual elements.

The choice of forum clause is also remarkable in another aspect, namely that it draws a line in between the bilateral and the multilateral system with respect to the suspension of obligations. It provides that a party shall not be precluded from imposing countermeasures under the DSU by the FTA and vice versa.[43] In doing so, it considerably reinforces the suspension of obligations under the FTA because countermeasures may then not only apply to the additional FTA concessions, but also to WTO obligations. For instance, if the most-favoured-nations (MFN) tariff for a particular good is 10% and the preferential tariff under the FTA is 5%, the suspension of the tariff preference under the FTA may not only go up to the limit of 10% but beyond.

3   Conclusion

The bilateral dispute settlement system in the EU's FTAs is an innovative mechanism based on the experience gained under the WTO dispute settlement understanding. Yet, despite the improvements and innovations brought by bilateral dispute settlement systems it is remarkable that these mechanisms have not or have hardly been used in bilateral FTAs, not only those concluded by the European Union, but more generally. Rather, it appears that states continue to prefer the WTO dispute settlement avenue.[44] Various reasons have been invoked to explain this phenomenon. They stem from the fact that the WTO DSU is more familiar, the possibility to form alliances, the experience and legitimacy of the WTO, the predictability of its jurisprudence or the existence of an appellate review or experienced secretarial staff. Other explanations go in the direction of the higher reputational costs in case of non-compliance

---

43   Eg Georgia AA [2014] OJ L261/104, art 269(4). See in this context also the decision Appellate Body, *Peru – Additional Duty on Imports of Certain Agricultural Products*, WT/DS457/AB/R.

44   A recent example of a dispute decided under an FTA is *Restrictions applied by Ukraine on exports of certain wood products to the European Union*, Final Report of the Arbitration Panel established pursuant to Article 307 of the Association Agreement between Ukraine, of the one part, and the European Union and its Member States, of the other part. Lugano (Switzerland), 11 December 2020 <trade.ec.europa.eu/doclib/docs/2020/december/tra doc_159181.pdf> accessed 30 July 2021.

with WTO rulings or the broader effect on other non-disputing parties, which may be prevented for adopting a similar measure that has been found in violation of the WTO Agreement.[45]

From an executive point of view, the most straightforward explanation would be to assess where the chances are higher to win a case: under the bilateral agreement or under the WTO? This is not to say the elements put forward to explain the bias towards the WTO DSU system are without merits. However, confronted with a specific dispute, the first question will most likely be where the chances are higher to prevail.

Whatever the reasons for the limited use of the bilateral dispute settlement system may be, it remains that in trade relations the very existence of a fully operational dispute settlement mechanism, and the threat to use it, is key to ensure the proper operation of the agreement and ensures compliance with the commitments by each side. As it has been stated in the EU's bilateral FTAs the objective of the bilateral dispute settlement system is to establish an effective and efficient mechanism for *avoiding* and settling any dispute between the parties. This objective has been fully achieved by the EU's bilateral dispute settlement mechanism in its FTAs or in its agreements with a significant trade component.

---

45   See for more detail WTO Staff Working Paper ERSD-2013-07 of 10 June 2013, 48 <www.wto .org/english/res_e/reser_e/ersd201307_e.pdf> accessed 30 July 2021.

CHAPTER 19

The Court of the Eurasian Economic Union

Elena Babkina

Internationalization of economic relations in the contemporary world necessitates the identification of preferable forms for mutually beneficial cooperation among States in political, economic and cultural fields. The practice of the past five decades indicated that the collaboration of States in the economic field, particularly in such matters as common customs tariffs and technical regulation, competition policy and foreign trade is most effective in the form of regional economic integration, rather than cooperation at the international level, when any State may be involved irrespective of territoriality criteria. The drivers of these processes are evident: a similar level of economic development of the Contracting States, unity of historical and cultural traditions, related mentality, and similar legal consciousness of citizens.

Classic intergovernmental organizations occasionally apply outdated approaches of international law, which imply that decisions, as a rule, are of a non-binding character, shall be taken solely by consensus or there is a veto power that significantly delays or even renders such cooperation impossible. Such organizations are not always able to demonstrate their efficiency, strength and ability to rise to the current challenges of our time. With the aim to resolve these issues, States establish international organizations of a new type – supranational – and voluntary, through the conclusion of a founding treaty, devolve some of their sovereign powers thereto, including even core powers of territorial and population management.

Voluntary devolution of powers by States to supranational organizations has a number of legal implications. Firstly, the bodies of supranational organizations receive the authority to establish rules of conduct in certain spheres that are mandatory for state bodies, natural persons and legal entities of the Member States. Secondly, a new body is established in the structure of the regional integration organization with the authority to control the compliance of Member States and their bodies with the community law of this organization. The primary objective of such judicial authority is to ensure a uniform application by the Member States and the organization's bodies of acts that constitute the law of this organization. Consequently, economic entities are entitled to appeal to a judicial body the regulations of supranational bodies, their actions and failures to act. States may resolve their dispute by civilized legal means, or they may request an advisory opinion of the Court on the interpretation of the provisions in the law of the organization.

1 The Eurasian Economic Union: General Overview

The abovementioned is also applicable to the Eurasian Economic Union (EAEU).

The EAEU's forerunner, the former Eurasian Economic Community (EurAsEC),[1] was established on 10 October 2000. Its Member States included the Republic of Belarus, the Republic of Kazakhstan, the Kyrgyz Republic, the Russian Federation and the Republic of Tajikistan. International treaties concluded within this period were mostly of a declarative nature and did not establish a single or coherent policy in certain areas. For this reason, it was decided to strengthen integration and move onto the next level: the establishment of a Customs Union and a Single Economic Space of three States within the EurAsEC (the Republic of Belarus, the Republic of Kazakhstan and the Russian Federation).

On 29 May 2014, the Presidents of the Republic of Belarus, the Republic of Kazakhstan and the Russian Federation signed the Treaty on the Eurasian Economic Union (hereinafter referred to as the "Treaty on the EAEU" or "Treaty"),[2] which is now the legal basis of the Customs Union and the Single Economic Space.

The Treaty on the EAEU represents a complex international treaty with a rather complicated scope and structure.

Codification of international treaties that constitute the legal basis of the Customs Union and the Single Economic Space occurred not only with respect

---

1 See also: Konstantin Branovitsky, 'Sravnitel'noe issledovanie statusa Suda Evropeiskogo soyuza i Suda Evraziiskogo ekonomicheskogo soobshchestva v kontekste mekhanizma ureg-ulirovaniya konfliktov' [Comparative analysis of legal status of the European Court of Justice and the Court of the Eurasian Economic Community in the context of dispute resolution] (2014) 1 Kieler Ostrechts – Notizen 19; Christoph J Schewe and Azar Aliyev, 'The Customs Union and the Single Economic Space of the Eurasian Economic Community: Eurasian Counterpart of the EU or Russian Domination' (2011) 54 German YB of Intl L 565; Marina Trunk-Fedorova, 'Der Gerichtshof der Eurasischen Wirtschaftsgemeinschaft' (2013) 4 Osteuropa-Recht 413–422. See also Zhenis Kembayev, 'The Eurasian Economic Union: An Overview and Evaluation' in this volume, 19 et seq.

2 Treaty on Eurasian Economic Union (signed in Astana 29 May 2014) <https://docs.eaeunion .org/Pages/DisplayDocument.aspx?s=bef9c798-3978-42f3-9ef2-d0fb3d53b75f&w=632c7868 -4ee2-4b21-bc64-1995328e6ef3&l=540294ae-c3c9-4511-9bf8-aaf5d6e0d169&EntityID=3610> accessed 18 November 2021.

to the Treaty itself, but it also resulted in 33 annexes, supplementing its text. It is obvious that the constitutive acts of the European Union guided the drafters of the EAEU Treaty as a model.

The Treaty on EAEU entered into force on 1 January 2015. The Republic of Armenia signed the Treaty of Accession to the EAEU on 10 October 2014. The Kyrgyz Republic signed the Treaty of Accession to the EAEU on 23 December 2014. With the establishment of the EAEU, the EurAsEC ceased to exist. On 10 October 2014, the Presidents of the EurAsEC Member States signed the Treaty on Termination of the Activities of the EurAsEC.

The devolution of powers from States to the EAEU is exercised by the States' free will through signing the founding treaty of an international organization – in the present case the Treaty on the EAEU. The States clearly define in the Treaty the spheres, where common, joint and coordinated policies apply, as well as the scope of powers for the supranational bodies. As the constitutions of the EAEU Member States envisage the supremacy of the principles and/or provisions of international treaties (for example, paragraph 4 article 15 of the Constitution of the Russian Federation,[3] article 8 of the Constitution of the Republic of Belarus,[4] paragraph 3 article 4 of the Constitution of the Republic of Kazakhstan,[5] article 5 of Armenian Constitution[6]) due to the general principle of international law pacta sunt servanda the law of EAEU is implemented from the perspective of its supremacy. Understanding the principle of direct applicability (directly to entities and individuals) of the EAEU law in national legal systems, its supremacy over national legislation does not require States to assess the compliance of this law with the national interest in an economic perspective – the principles of direct applicability and supremacy of the rule of EAEU law are axiomatic.

The EAEU is an international organization of regional economic integration with full international legal personality, which implies the existence of international rights and obligations independent from the Member States. The EAEU is entitled to carry out international activities within its jurisdiction with the aim to fulfil the tasks of the EAEU.

---

3   <www.consultant.ru/cons/cgi/online.cgi?req=doc&ts=16611179300654107876oo85414&cach
     eid=229EC88E7E4F65DBDoABDD469E26685C&mode=splus&base=LAW&n=2875&rnd=
     0.41732271252624087#1g38y8gxbhe> accessed 18 November 2021.
4   <http://pravo.by/pravovaya-informatsiya/normativnye-dokumenty/konstitutsiya-respubl
     iki-belarus/> accessed 18 November 2021.
5   <www.akorda.kz/ru/official_documents/constitution> accessed 18 November 2021.
6   <www.president.am/ru/constitution-2015/> accessed 18 November 2021.

The EAEU may be distinguished from the EurAsEC in the following perspectives:

1) the *participants*: the EurAsEC united the Republic of Belarus, the Republic of Kazakhstan, the Kyrgyz Republic, the Russian Federation, and the Republic of Tajikistan, while the Republic of Tajikistan does not participate in the EAEU, but the Republic of Armenia is an EAEU Member State;

2) the *competence*: the EAEU provides conditions for ensuring four freedoms – movement of goods, services, capital and labour, ensuring joint, concerted or common policy in the key sectors of the economy;

3) the *system of bodies* of these regional organizations; the EAEU has no parliamentary body.

2   The Court of the EAEU

2.1   *Structure of the Court*

Along with the Supreme Eurasian Economic Council, the Eurasian Intergovernmental Council and the Eurasian Economic Commission (hereinafter referred to as the "Commission"), the Court of the Eurasian Economic Union is a EAEU judicial body, the main objective of which is to ensure the uniform application by the Member States and bodies of the EAEU of the EAEU Treaty, international treaties within the EAEU, international treaties of the EAEU with third parties and decisions of the bodies of the EAEU.

The Court commenced its functioning on 1 January 2015 and is located in Minsk. Its activity is regulated by the Statute of the Court of the Eurasian Economic Union.[7] Judges are appointed and dismissed by the Supreme Eurasian Economic Council on the proposal of the Member States. The judges' terms of office last 9 years. The Court includes two judges from each Member State. Consequently, the judiciary is formed in compliance with the principle of equal representation of all Member States. Currently, the EAEU Court is functioning with 10 judges.[8]

Two panels were established for the purpose of resolving disputes at the request of economic operators and include one judge from each Member State. At the same time, each of the panels simultaneously acts as an appellate instance, which investigates the lawfulness and validity of the other panel's

---

7   Annex 2 to the Treaty on the Eurasian Economic Union.
8   <http://courteurasian.org/page-24321> accessed 18 November 2021. https://courteurasian .org/about_the_court/judges/

decisions. The absence of a separate appellate instance is a disadvantage, in our opinion.

The Grand Panel of the Court, composed of all judges of the Court, resolves disputes at the request of Member States and conducts advisory proceedings. Apart from that, the Grand Panel may examine procedural matters prescribed by the Rules of Procedure.

Issues of an administrative character of the Court's functioning are resolved at plenary sessions of the Court with the participation of all judges. Other issues may as well be put forward for determination at the plenary sessions.

Apart from the judiciary, the structure of the Court also includes the Administration of the Court, composed of secretariats of judges (an advisor and a judicial assistant) and the Secretariat of the Court (expert-analytical department and the department of financial, organizational and personnel management). Officials and employees of the Secretariat are selected on a competitive basis. Candidates for the position of high-ranking officials – the Head of the Court's Secretariat and two of its deputies – heads of the departments – are presented for a competition by the Member States following the principle of equal representation (also considering Armenia's and Kyrgyzstan's accession to the EAEU and the functioning of EAEU consisting of five States while, de facto, the Secretariat of the Court consisted of three officials. In this part a relevant adjustment to the EAEU law is required). Employees of the Secretariat file the documents to the Competition Commission on their own behalf, however, in the course of selection the principle of proportionality is also considered, which means that vacancies are filled taking into account the amount of contributions by the Member States to the budget of the EAEU.

2.2   *Jurisdiction of the Court*

The jurisdiction of the EAEU Court is envisaged in Articles 39, 40, 46 of the Court's Statute.[9]

The Court has jurisdiction to resolve disputes and interpret the provisions of the Treaty on the EAEU, international treaties within the EAEU and decisions of the EAEU bodies and, at the request of employees and officials of the bodies of the EAEU and the Court, provisions of the Treaty, international treaties within the EAEU and decisions of the bodies of the EAEU regarding labour relations.

Both the Member States of the EAEU as well as economic operators may be claimants.

---

9   Annex 2 to the Treaty on EAEU.

The Court has jurisdiction to resolve disputes:

a)   at the request of a Member State:
1)   on compliance of an international treaty within the EAEU or its certain provisions with the Treaty on EAEU;
2)   on observance by another Member State (other Member States) of the Treaty, international treaties within the EAEU and/or decisions of the bodies of the EAEU;
3)   on compliance of a decision of the Commission or its certain provisions with the Treaty, international treaties within the EAEU and/or decisions of the bodies of the EAEU;
4)   on challenging actions (omissions) of the Commission;
b)   at the request of an economic entity:
1)   on compliance of a decision of the Commission with the Treaty and/or international treaties within the EAEU;
2)   on challenging actions (omissions) of the Commission.

It should be emphasized that the Court admits the dispute for resolution at the request of an economic entity (legal person or individual entrepreneur, registered in compliance with the legislation of Member States or third States) as to decisions, actions (omissions) of the Commission which directly affect the rights and legitimate interests of the economic operator in the sphere of business and other economic activities, if such actions (omissions) entail a violation of any rights and legitimate interests of the economic operator envisaged by the Treaty or international treaties within the EAEU. It should be highlighted that economic operators of third States may also apply to the Court for the protection of their rights (for example, to challenge the introduction by the Commission of anti-dumping duties with respect to the type of goods which they produce).

Natural persons who are not engaged in an economic activity are not entitled to apply to the Court as to decisions, actions (omissions) of the Commission which intervene with their interests. In our opinion, this gap should be eliminated at further stages of integration.

The fee to apply to the Court currently constitutes 47,846.00 rubles,[10] which is subject to annual indexation considering the growth of the consumer price index.

Decisions rendered by the Court Panel at the request of an economic entity may be appealed to the Appeals Chamber. The decision of the Appeals Chamber is final. All decisions of the Court with respect to disputes are binding.

---

10   This is approximately 500 Euros in 2021.

In comparison with the Statute of the EurAsEC Court, the Statute of the
EAEU Court provides for the establishment of specialized groups for specific
types of disputes, namely disputes concerning the provision of industrial subsidies, agricultural state support measures and the application of safeguard,
anti-dumping and countervailing measures.

The EAEU Member States introduce candidacies of experts to the Court (no
less than three for each type of dispute).

The objective of the specialized group is to prepare a report containing an
unbiased assessment of the facts of the case together with a statement on the
existence or absence of a violation. In this part, the report is of a non-binding
character. In case of the establishment of a violation, the report of the specialized group for disputes concerning the provision of industrial subsidies or
agricultural state support measures is completed by a conclusion on the application of appropriate compensatory measures which is binding for the Court
(paragraphs 90 – 92 of the Court's Statute).

Definitely, the very idea of involving experts in disputes concerning the
assessment of facts, such as agriculture or industrial production, where it is
required to conduct an economic analysis or accounting estimation should be
positively perceived. The participation of experts is intended to discharge the
judges from an initial assessment of facts and provide them with the opportunity to focus on legal issues. At the same time, the binding nature of the
specialized group's report in part of an imposition of corresponding compensatory measures to certain extent deprives the Court of its independence in
delivering justice.[11] In our opinion, only the Court should render the final decision on the issues of law and facts.

The Court has jurisdiction to provide an advisory opinion:
– at the request of a Member State or a body of the EAEU, the Court shall provide clarifications to provisions of the Treaty, international treaties within
  the EAEU and decisions of the bodies of the EAEU;
– at the request of employees and officials of the bodies of the EAEU and the
  Court, to provisions of the Treaty, international treaties within the EAEU
  and decisions of the bodies of the EAEU regarding labour relations.

For example, at the request of the Commission's employees, the Court estimated the level of implementation of the rights of the EAEU bodies' employees
for the purposes of attestation, in the Advisory Opinion dated 3 June 2016 on
clarifications of provisions of the Regulation on Attestation of Commission's

---

11   See also: Zhenis Kembaev, 'Sravnitel'no-pravovoj analiz funkcionirovanija Suda
        Evrazijskogo jekonomicheskogo sojuza' (2016) 2 Mezhdunarodnoe pravosudie 30.

Employees, approved by the Decision of the Commission's Council No. 98 dated 12 November 2014.[12] The Court underlined that the legislation of an international organization which regulates relations concerning international civil service is designated to exclude the effect of domestic law on the employee. This allows ensuring the employees independence when making their decisions. Therefore, it is necessary to amend the law of the international organization with the norms, covering the maximum range of relations concerning performance of duties, including the issues of attestation. In the Court's opinion, in general, EAEU acts comply with the abovementioned principles, however, some issues are of a general character and may be specified by a body that issued the act as well as the Court may interpret them.

The analysis of the Court's jurisdiction, its comparison with the jurisdiction of EurAsEC Court and one other authoritative judicial body – the Court of Justice of the European Union – allow one to draw the following conclusions and proposals, which, in our opinion, fully correspond to the idea of further Eurasian integration.

The Court of the EAEU has a favourable advantage in comparison with the Court of the EurAsEC in that it may consider applications at the request of natural persons concerning the clarification in the employment sphere of the EAEU bodies. Additionally, in our opinion, having solely an interpretative function is insufficient in this sphere. The example of the Court of Justice of the European Union necessitates to authorize the EAEU Court to resolve disputes between the EAEU bodies (which are immune from the jurisdiction of domestic courts) and its employees.

Apart from that, the integrational effect of Advisory Opinions (both at the request of Member States or EAEU bodies and at the request of employees and officials) is degraded, given that the Court's Advisory Opinion do not deprive the Member States of the right to make a distinct joint interpretation of international treaties (paragraph 47 of the Court's Statute).

The Commission has no authority to act as a claimant in disputes with Member States, which is a step back that does not allow the Court to achieve its main objective – to ensure the uniform application of EAEU law by its Member States.

The non-existence in the EAEU of such an important legal instrument as a preliminary ruling does not facilitate the development of Eurasian integration. It should be remarked that in the practice of the courts of international organization of regional economic integration requests for preliminary rulings on

---

12   See < https://courteurasian.org/court_cases/eaeu/P-1.16/ > accessed 22 November 2021.

the application of international treaties within the organization is the right of domestic courts, and in case of rendering final decisions, national courts may even be obliged to request a preliminary ruling.

At the same time, the consideration of preliminary requests is one of the main activities of courts in international organization of regional economic integration. For example, the Court of Justice of the European Union renders about 60% of its decisions as preliminary rulings. Acting within this jurisdiction, the court of such organization exercises supranational authority and, de facto, executes a regulatory function through lawmaking in addition to the function of judicial review of acts and actions of a supranational executive body. For example, within the competence of the EU Court in such decisions as *Van Gend & Loos,*[13] *Costa,*[14] *Simmenthal,*[15] *Francovich,*[16] the Court of Justice of the European Union (formerly EEC) formulated such basic principles of European (community) law which were not envisaged in the EU founding treaties – the supremacy of European (supranational) law and its direct applicability, the availability of the rights and conditions for the recovery of damage caused by a Member State's failure to comply with the deadline for the implementation of directives, etc.

It cannot be denied that the theoretical possibility of applying to the Court, even without amending the founding treatis of the EAEU, is still available to domestic courts through the bodies authorized by the respective Member State to apply to the Court on its behalf. However, given the indirect and non-binding nature of this duty, hardly any domestic court would use this opportunity. The other option for Member States is to endow its domestic courts with the right of direct request to the EAEU Court for an Advisory Opinion on behalf of the State. Currently, EAEU Member States mainly authorize their ministries of justice and do not provide their domestic courts with this authority.

The limitation of the Court's jurisdiction is also manifested in the peculiarities of rendering decisions in certain type of disputes. For example, when

---

13   Case 26/62 *NV Algemene Transporten Expeditie Onderneming van Gend & Loos v Netherlands* [1963] ECR 1. Reference to a preliminary ruling: <http://eur-lex.europa.eu/legal-content/EN/TXT/?uri=CELEX%3A61962CJ0026> accessed 18 November 2021.

14   Case 6/64 *Flaminio Costa v ENEL* [1964] ECR 587. Reference to a preliminary ruling: <http://eur-lex.europa.eu/legal-content/EN/TXT/?uri=CELEX:61964CJ0006> accessed 18 November 2021.

15   Case 106/77 *Amministrazione delle Finanze dello Stato v Simmenthal SpA* [1978] ECR 630; Reference to a preliminary ruling: <http://eur-lex.europa.eu/legal-content/EN/TXT/?uri=CELEX%3A61977CJ0106> accessed 18 November 2021.

16   Case C-6/90 and C-9/90 *Andrea Francovich and Danila Bonifaci and others v Italian Republic* [1991] ECR I-5357. References for a preliminary ruling: <http://eur-lex.europa.eu/legal-content/EN/TXT/?uri=CELEX:61990CJ0006> accessed 18 November 2021.

it comes to the jurisdiction of the Court with respect to disputes concerning the violation of competition rules in transboundary markets, it is possible to distinguish the approach in the EAEU from the jurisdiction of the EU Court of Justice in similar disputes. The EU Court of Justice has *unlimited jurisdiction,* which means that the EU Court may alter the content of the decision of European Commission concerning the violation of competition rules, cancel, reduce, or increase the fine or other sanction imposed should it be considered excessively high or insufficient (Article 31 of the Council Regulation (EC) No. 1/ 2003). The EAEU Court renders decisions only about the compliance or non-compliance of the Commission's decisions to the Treaty on the EAEU, international treaties within the EAEU and decisions of the EAEU bodies. The task of the Commission when executing the decision is to bring its decision in line with the law of the EAEU.

Another limitation of the Court's jurisdiction (its right for judicial lawmaking) is the indication in the Court's Statute that decisions of the Court do not amend and abrogate the existing rules of the law of the EAEU, the legislation of Member States, and cannot create new rules. At the same time, rendering the decision in certain disputes, the EAEU Court forms its case law, which, we believe, will be duly regarded by the EAEU bodies as well as Member States and domestic courts.

Obviously, the development of integration processes in the EAEU will lead to an extension of the Court's jurisdiction, including in the abovementioned areas.

2.3 *Procedural Aspects*

Procedural aspects of the Court's functioning are regulated by the Rules of Procedure of the Court of the Eurasian Economic Union, which have been approved by the decision of the Supreme Eurasian Economic Council No. 101 dated 23 December 2014.

A rather controversial issue is the continuity of the two international courts, the precedent nature of decisions, which were rendered by the EurAsEC Court, for the EAEU Court. From a formal point of view, one cannot speak of the precedent character of decisions of the EurAsEC Court for the EAEU Court in the absence of a special regulation at the integration level (in the transitional provisions of the EAEU Treaty, which establish the continuity in the decisions of the Supreme Eurasian Economic Council and the Commission in force as of the date of the entry into force of the EAEU Treaty, a mention of the decisions of the EurAsEC Court is omitted). Nonetheless, in the practice of other international judicial bodies (International Court of Justice, WTO Dispute Settlement Body, European Court of Human Rights, Court of Justice of the European

Union, the EurAsEC Court itself) the *stare decisis* principle plays a significant role. The principle points to the high probability of the continuity of legal positions expressed by the EurAsEC Court for the EAEU Court.

Paragraph 3 Article 3 of the Treaty on Termination of Activities of the EurAsEC dated 10 October 2014 envisages that the decisions of the EurAsEC Court continue to have their existing status. However, this statutory concept raises another issue: whether the provision of a ceased international organization of regional economic integration with a certain pool of participants would apply to the other newly established organization with different Member States.

Additionally, the absence of any indicated precedent nature of the EAEU Court's decisions does not preclude the application of its practice on an equal basis with the position of international courts as a *"persuasive precedent"*, which, though of a non-binding character, has still a significant effect.[17] International judicial proceedings, including within the framework of the EAEU, require to achieve a uniform application of the law of the integrated association. For example, in the decision at the request of General Freight CJSC dated 4 April 2016 the Panel of the Court referred to decisions of the EU Court of Justice in the cases *C-183/06 RUMA*, *C-339/09 SkomaLux*, *C-173/08 Kloosterboer Services BV*, the decision of the EurAsEC Court in the dispute at the request of Zabaikalresurs LLC and Nika LLC dated 20 May 2014. The Court then stated that following established international case law the objective criterion for classification of goods is its intended purpose, which is subject to an evaluation based on objective characteristics and features of goods.

This point of view is supported by the Statute of the International Court of Justice, which defines judicial decisions with respect to the parties of the dispute as a subsidiary means for determination of the rules of law. Those are generally recognized rules of international law, which the EAEU Court applies while rendering justice in accordance with paragraph 50 of the Court's Statute. Application in the subsequent decisions of legal concepts, and the content of rules of international law that originated from prior legal positions forms a single consistent and authoritative system of decisions of international courts.

---

17   On the precedent effect of the EAEU decisions, see also Ekaterina D'jachenko and Kirill Entin 'Kompetencija Suda Evrazijskogo jekonomicheskogo sojuza: mify i real'nost" (2017) 3 Mezhdunarodnoe pravosudie 76; T N Neshataeva 'Sud Evrazijskogo jekonomicheskogo sojuza: ot pravovoj pozicii k dejstvujushhemu pravu' (2017) 2 Mezhdunarodnoe pravosudie 64.

2.4 *Period for Case Consideration*

According to Article 96 of the Court's Statute, the period for consideration of cases constitutes 90 days, both for cases with the participation of economic entities and for interstate disputes. The Court's Rules of Procedure provide an extended period that may not exceed 135 calendar days for disputes concerning the provision of industrial subsidies, agricultural state support measures and the application of safeguard, anti-dumping and countervailing measures. As has been mentioned above, this relates to the special procedure (forming specialized groups) designed for these types of disputes.

It should be admitted that these timeframes do not always meet the needs of international justice, which has its own peculiarities. For example, by the end of 2016, the EU Court reported on reducing average length proceedings till 15.4 months.[18]

Obviously, the current caseload of the EU Court is incomparable with the caseload of the EAEU Court. Nonetheless, these numbers may give pause for thought in the future about the compatibility of the existing time-limits for proceed (especially in interstate disputes) with the principle of their full, comprehensive and objective consideration.

2.5 *Enforcement of the Court's Decisions*

The current mechanism of enforcement of the Court's decisions is far from ideal. Earlier, the Statute of the EurAsEC Court did not precisely fix the time when the act of the Commission shall be recognized as invalid. For this reason, the EurAsEC Court attempted to liquidate this gap in the decision of 8 April 2013 by clarifying the decision in the *Yuzhnyi Kuzbass* case. The Grand Panel of EurAsEC Court, having considered the issue of the validity of this decision in space and time, found that the legal consequence of recognizing the act of the Customs Union Commission as not in line with international treaties concluded within the Customs Union, is its legal nullity, i.e. invalidity from the moment of adoption, or from the time it began to contradict international treaties concluded within the Customs Union. Furthermore, the EurAsEC Court concluded that its decisions do not require a confirmation. They operate not only with respect to the parties of the dispute but with regard to an unlimited number of persons (*erga omnes*). With the purpose to fulfil the international legal principle of full compensation for harm, it became possible to review the

---

18   Court of Justice of the European Union, *Annual Report 2020 The Year in Review* (2020) <https://curia.europa.eu/panorama/2020/en/at-a-glance.html#the-year-in-figures> accessed 18 November 2021.

decisions of national courts in order to protect rights and legitimate interests of economic entities in the field of business and other economic activities provided by international treaties concluded within the Customs Union and the Single Economic Space.

It should be noted that national courts similarly assessed the legal consequences of the decisions of the EurAsEC Court to recognize an act of the Commission of the Customs Union as contradictory to international treaties within the Customs Union and the Single Economic Space. For example, referring to the purpose of justice, which is not only to prevent possible offenses, but also to restore the violated rights of citizens and economic entities, the decision of the Arbitrazh Court of the Kemerovo Region of the Russian Federation dated 15 February 2013 assessed the decision of the Commission of the Customs Union No. 335 dated 17 August 2010. The Commission's decision contradicted international treaties in force within the Customs Union and the Single Economic Space. In the opinion of the Arbitrazh Court, this meant that the Commission's decision lost its legal force from the time of its adoption. It became the basis for a revision of a previously considered dispute on newly discovered circumstances.

Other arbitrazh courts of Russian Federation took the same position, including in cases with the participation of other economic entities.

Thus, the established practice of EAEU Member States on this issue is indicative of the extension of the legal force of the Court's decisions both to the parties of the case and indefinite number of persons.

It should be noted, however, that in the course of the establishment of the EAEU, its Member States have more than cautiously approached the issue of the legal force of the Court's decisions. Paragraph 102 of the Court's Statute envisages that the decisions of the Court cannot amend and override the existing rules of the EAEU law or the legislation of the Member States, and cannot create new ones. Following paragraph 111 of the Court's Statute, the operation of the Commission's decision continues after the entry into force of the decision of the Court until the enforcement of this judicial act by the Commission.

The Commission, in its turn, within a reasonable time-limit not exceeding 60 calendar days from the date of entry into force of the Court's decision, unless a different term is established in the decision of the Court, shall adjust its decision to comply with the EAEU Treaty and/or international treaties within the EAEU.

Apart from that, paragraph 112 of the Court's Statute specifies that upon a duly substantiated petition of a party to the dispute the decision of the

Commission may be suspended by a judgment of the Court from the date of entry into force of such Court's decision.

From this problem stems the inadequacy of the enforcement controlling mechanism. According to paragraph 115 of the Court's Statute, should the Commission fail to execute the Court's decision, the economic entity may file a petition to the Court for taking measures required for its execution. In this instance, the Court shall apply to the Supreme Eurasian Economic Council for a decision on the indicated matter within 15 calendar days from the date of its receipt.

2.6   *Applicable Law*

Following paragraph 50 of the Court's Statute, the law, which is to be applied by the Court includes:

1)   generally recognized principles and rules of international law;
2)   the EAEU Treaty, international treaties within the EAEU and other international treaties to which the States that are parties to the dispute are participants;
3)   acts of the EAEU bodies (decisions and directions of the Supreme Eurasian Economic Council, the Eurasian Intergovernmental Council and the Commission);
4)   international custom as evidence of the general practice accepted as law.

In this context it is relevant to note that the decision of the Appeals Chamber of the Court at the request of General Freight CJSC dated 21 June 2016 made the important conclusion that an international treaty, which is not an international treaty within the EAEU or an international treaty of the EAEU with a third party, is subject to application within the EAEU if two cumulative criteria are present:

1)   all EAEU Member States are the parties to this international treaty;
2)   the scope of its application concerns a common policy within the EAEU.

In support of its point of view, the Court referred to the established international case law of recognizing such an international treaty as binding for international organization of regional economic integration.

Since its establishment, the EAEU Court has itself drafted local statutory acts. At the time, the Court developed and adopted Rules for the Organization and Functioning of the Court, the Procedure for Holding a Tender, an Instruction for Documents' Control, a Procedure for Holding Plenary Sessions and other acts.

3   Concluding Remarks

In just over seven years of the functioning of the EAEU Court, economic entities submitted 33 applications to the Court (24 applications were considered
on the merits) and 15 appeals (14 were considered), as well as 22 requests for
an advisory opinion (20 reviewed with the issuance of advisory opinion, 2
withdrawn) and one interstate dispute. The overwhelming majority of applications of economic entities has the subject of challenging decisions of the
Commission on the classification of goods under the Single Commodity
Nomenclature for Foreign Economic Activity of the Eurasian Economic Union.

These statistics are impressive for an international court at the initial stage
of its establishment. For example, the Court of Justice of the European Union,
which was a model for the EAEU Court, considered only two cases in the first
two years of its functioning, but after more than half a century, it has now rendered about 30,000 decisions in total.

The above statistics reflects the general trends in the development of judicial bodies of regional economic integrations: a fairly low number of cases considered in the first years of existence with the challenge of customs and tariff
regulation as the main subject of the proceedings.

The first cases reviewed by the EAEU Court demonstrate its ability to
develop integration ideas and allow to express assurance in its authority and
the demand for the protection of the interests of economic entities.

CHAPTER 20

Environmental Governance as a Subject of Dispute Settlement Mechanisms in Regional Trade Agreements

Karsten Nowrot

1 From Global to Regional: Genesis of the Relationship between Environmental Considerations and International Trade Agreements

From the perspective of public international law, so-called "trade and ..." issues or linkages[1] gained importance and received increasing attention among legal scholars and practitioners alike since the middle of the 1990s. These overarching themes primarily address questions of whether and, in the affirmative, how to incorporate non-economic concerns – like the protection of human rights and consumer interests, the promotion of sustainable development and cultural diversity as well as the enforcement of core labor and social standards – into the normative structure of the international economic system and thereby establish linkages between different policy fields and corresponding areas of law that have previously largely existed and progressively developed in "splendid isolation" of each other.[2]

A quite prominent position among these "trade and ..." topics has been, from the very beginning, – and continues to be – occupied by the intensive and controversial debates on potential suitable connections between trade and investment agreements and the effective promotion of environmental

---

1   On this labelling see, eg, Joel P. Trachtman, 'Trade and ... Problems, Cost-Benefit Analysis and Subsidiarity' (1998) 9 European Journal of International Law 32; Joel P. Trachtman, 'Institutional Linkage: Transcending "Trade and ..."' (2002) 96 American Journal of International Law 77; Bernhard Kluttig, *Welthandel und Umweltschutz – Kohärenz statt Konkurrenz* (2003) 5; David W. Leebron, 'Linkages' (2002) 96 American Journal of International Law 5.

2   Thomas Cottier, 'Trade and Human Rights: A Relationship to Discover' (2002) 5 Journal of International Economic Law 111 (112); on this perception see also for example Daniel C. Esty and Damien Geradin, 'Market Access, Competitiveness, and Harmonization: Environmental Protection in Regional Trade Agreements' (1997) 21 Harvard Environmental Law Review 265, 266 ("For most of the last century, trade liberalization and environmental protection initiatives have moved along separate tracks.").

objectives. These discussions frequently take place against the background of two main underlying perceptions. On the one side, the field of international environmental law itself is often regarded as being characterized by comparatively weak enforcement structures[3] with the consequence that those seeking to create more effective and robust implementation mechanisms are attempting to link environmental objectives, such as those stipulated in respective international conventions, to other areas and sources of public international law like trade and investment agreements "where the sticks are bigger and the carrots are tastier".[4] On the other side, it is more and more generally recognized today that both at the level of drafting agreements in the field of international economic law and dispute settlement one of the central challenges for lawmakers, judges and arbitrators alike is to provide an acceptable balance between the liberalization of transboundary trade and investment and protection of the environment. This includes the legal protection of economic interests of private business operators as well as the domestic steering capacity or "policy space"[5] of states and other governmental actors, allowing them to pursue the promotion and protection of public interest concerns such as environmental objectives.[6]

Although clearly belonging to the class of issues that are relevant for the global economic system and its legal structures as a whole, the rather complex relationship between the regulatory tasks of environmental protection and governance on the one side and the normative framework of international

---

3   Generally, on the main enforcement mechanisms in international environmental law see, eg Rüdiger Wolfrum, 'Means of Ensuring Compliance with and Enforcement of International Environmental Law' (1998) 272 Recueil des Cours 9; Ulrich Beyerlin and Thilo Marauhn, *International Environmental Law* (Bloomsbury 2011) 317ff, each with further references.

4   Sikina Jinnah and Elisa Morgera, 'Environmental Provisions in American and EU Free Trade Agreements: A Preliminary Comparison and Research Agenda' (2013) 22 Review of European Community & International Environmental Law 324.

5   See thereto, eg, Christian Tietje, 'The Future of International Investment Protection: Stress in the System?' (2009) 24 ICSID Review 457, 461 ("The need for a 'policy space' for governments, i.e. autonomy in national policy-making without constraints by international law and particularly international investment protection law, is one of the most significant consequences of the proliferation of investment law and the fragmentation of international law in general. We are currently witnessing discussions about the necessary policy space in the area of foreign investment, on both the national and international levels.").

6   On this perception see for example Karsten Nowrot, 'How to Include Environmental Protection, Human Rights and Sustainability in International Investment Law?' (2014) 15 Journal of World Investment & Trade 612; Aikaterini Titi, *The Right to Regulate in International Investment Law* (Nomos 2014) 53ff; Jorge E. Vinuales, 'Investment Law and Sustainable Development: The Environment Breaks into Investment Disputes' in Marc Bungenberg and others (eds), *International Investment Law* (C.H. Beck 2015) 1714, each with further references.

economic law on the other side has been initially – and indeed until more recently –discussed and analyzed with a focus on respective developments taking place in, and opportunities arising from, the multilateral regime established by the General Agreement on Tariffs and Trade (GATT 1947) and subsequently the World Trade Organization (WTO) which came into force in 1995.[7]

In the course of this first phase of scholarly debates on trade-environment linkages dominated by a multilateral perspective – with their global focus since the beginning of the 1990s admittedly first and foremost also fueled by respective well-known trade disputes like *US-Tuna* and *US-Shrimp* addressing the legality under the GATT/WTO legal regime of governmental measures aimed at the protection of dolphins and sea turtles[8] –, frequently insufficient attention had been drawn to the fact that these interfaces between environmental governance and trade agreements do not only materialize at the universal level. In particular, as a result of the ever-growing importance of treaties aimed at regional economic integration in the international system, comparable legal challenges and opportunities most certainly also arise, for example, in the realm of bilateral and other sub-multilateral free trade agreements.[9] In light of these findings, it is thus hardly surprising that, especially since the

---

7   On this perception see also, eg, Jinnah/Morgera (n 4) 326 ("most scholarship in this area has focused on the WTO"). From the numerous respective contributions see for example Daniel C. Esty, *Greening the GATT – Trade Environment and the Future* (Institute for International Economics 1994) 9ff; John H. Jackson, 'World Trade Rules and Environmental Policies: Congruence or Conflict?' (1992) 49 Washington & Lee Law Review 1227; Thomas J. Schoenbaum, 'International Trade and the Protection of the Environment: The Continuing Search for Reconciliation' (1997) 91 American Journal of International Law 268; Kluttig (n 1) 5ff; Mitsuo Matsushita and others, *The World Trade Organization – Law, Practice, and Policy* (2nd edn, OUP 2006) 785ff; Howard F. Chang, 'Towards a Greener GATT: Environmental Trade Measures and the Shrimp-Turtle Case' (2000) 74 Southern California Law Review 31; Dukgeun Ahn, 'Environmental Disputes in the GATT/WTO: Before and after US-Shrimp Case' (1999) 20 Michigan Journal of International Law 819; Ilona Cheyne, 'Environmental Unilateralism and the WTO/GATT System' (1995) 24 Georgia Journal of International and Comparative Law 433.

8   See for example GATT, *United States – Restrictions on Imports of Tuna*, Report of the GATT Panel of 3 September 1991, DS21/R - 39S/155 (unadopted); GATT, *United States – Restrictions on Imports of Tuna*, Report of the GATT Panel of 16 June 1994, DS29/R (unadopted); WTO, *United States – Import Prohibition of Certain Shrimp and Shrimp Products*, Appellate Body Report (adopted on 6 November 1998), WT/DS58/AB/R; as well as more recently WTO, *United States – Measures Concerning the Importation, Marketing and Sale of Tuna and Tuna Products*, Appellate Body Report (adopted on 13 June 2012), WT/DS381/AB/R.

9   See thereto, eg Jinnah and Morgera (n 4) 324 ("Despite a strong scholarly focus on trade-environment linkages in the context of the World Trade Organization (WTO), the growing importance of these linkages is currently nowhere better illustrated than in recent bilateral free trade agreements (FTAs).").

end of the previous decade, the current second phase of academic discourses and research dealing with the relationship between trade and environment is characterized by an increasing emphasis on respective developments in treaty practice at the bilateral and regional level.[10]

Against this background, the present contribution is intended to describe and evaluate some of the main aspects of how environmental governance is addressed in regional economic integration agreements. These are based on what types of regulatory approaches respective environmental provisions are incorporated as well as enforced. Thereby, it hardly needs to be recalled that "environmental governance and regional trade agreements" is far too broad a topic to be discussed in the course of this comparatively short contribution in something even close to a comprehensive way. Rather, this chapter largely confines itself to present some systemizing thoughts on this practically important issue, from the implementation perspective of dispute settlement mechanisms, thereby taking recourse in the notable regulatory schemes established under the EU Association Agreement with Georgia signed on 27 June 2014, provisionally applied since 1 September 2014, and entered into force on 1 July 2016.[11]

---

10   For the respective reports, analyses and scholarly contributions see for example OECD, *Environment and Regional Trade Agreements* (2007) 23ff; Gracia Marin Duran, 'The Role of the EU in Shaping the Trade and Environment Regulatory Nexus: Multilateral and Regional Approaches' in Bart Van Vooren and others (eds), *The EU's Role in Global Governance – The Legal Dimension* (OUP 2013) 224; Michele Potestà, 'From Mutual Supportiveness to Mutual Enforcement? The Contribution of US Preferential Trade and Investment Agreements to the Effectiveness of Environmental Norms' in Rainer Hofmann, Stephan W. Schill and Christian J. Tams (eds), *Preferential Trade and Investment Agreements – From Recalibration to Reintegration* (Nomos 2013) 167; Jinnah and Morgera (n 4) 324ff; Rok Zvelc, 'Environmental Integration in EU Trade Policy: The Generalised System of Preferences, Trade Sustainability Impact Assessments and Free Trade Agreements' in Elisa Morgera (ed), *The External Environmental Policy of the European Union* (CUP 2012) 174, 193ff; Chang-fa Lo, 'Environmental Protection through FTAs: Paradigm Shifting from Multilateral to Multi-Bilateral Approach' (2009) 4 Asian Journal of WTO and International Health Law and Policy 309; Chris Wold, 'Taking Stock: Trade's Environmental Scorecard after Twenty Years of "Trade and Environment"' (2010) 45 Wake Forest Law Review 319; Dale Colyer, 'Environmental Provisions in Recent Regional Trade Agreements (2008 & 2009)' (2010) 11 Estey Centre Journal of International Law and Trade Policy 321; David A. Gantz, 'Labor Rights and Environmental Protection under NAFTA and other U.S. Free Trade Agreements' (2011) 42 University of Miami Inter-American Law Review 297.

11   Association Agreement between the European Union and the European Atomic Energy Community and their Member States, of the one part, and Georgia, of the other part [30 August 2014] OJ L261/4.

For this purpose, the following analysis is divided into three main sections. The first part addresses the underlying reasons for the increasing importance attached to regional trade and investment agreements in the more recent debates on trade-environment linkages (Section 2). Based on the findings made in this section, the subsequent two parts are devoted to a description and evaluation of what is qualified here as the two main dimensions of regulatory approaches to environmental governance in regional trade agreements. In this regard, the second part provides some thoughts on the scope and depth of respective environment-related stipulations from a substantive law perspective (Section 3). In the third and final section an assessment will be given of the different types of environmental dispute settlement mechanisms in regional economic integration agreements (Section 4).

2 Underlying Reasons for the Broadening of the Perspective on the Issue of Environmental Governance and International Economic Treaty Law

The individual reasons for the growing importance attached to bilateral and regional trade agreements in the recent discussions on trade-environment linkages and the resulting broadening of the analytical focus on the relationship between environmental governance and international economic law are surely manifold. Prominent among them, however, is the rise of regionalism in the international economic legal order as a whole.[12] In particular, since the middle of the 1990s, for a variety of reasons, numerous treaties establishing free trade zones and other regional economic integration agreements have been successfully concluded or are currently under negotiation.[13]

In addition to the ever-growing importance of regionalism, as manifested by the conclusion of respective trade and investment agreements in the global economic legal system, albeit closely connected to this phenomenon, another notable factor contributing to the increasing prominence of regional cooperation projects in the discussions on the relationship between trade regulations

---

12 On this perception see, eg UNCTAD, 'Global Value Chains: Investment and Trade for Development', World Investment Report 2013 (2013) 103ff ("Regionalism on the rise"); Wolfgang Alschner, 'Regionalism and Overlap in Investment Treaty Law: Towards Consolidation or Contradiction?' (2014) 17 Journal of International Economic Law 271 (273); Marc Bungenberg, 'Preferential Trade and Investment Agreements and Regionalism' in Rainer Hofmann, Schill and Tam (n 10) 269, 270ff.

13 For the general trade context of this topic see Karsten Nowrot, '"Competing Regionalism" vs. "Cooperative Regionalism": On the Possible Relations between Different Regional Economic Integration Agreements', in this volume, 59 et ff.

and environmental governance is the current lack of substantial progress with regard to the multilateral trade negotiations in the ongoing Doha Development Round of the WTO in general and the debates on trade-environment linkages therein[14] in particular. As a consequence of these very slowly advancing trade negotiations at the global level, an ever-growing number of states have not only turned their attention to regional economic integration plans but they are, based on a variety of motives, also increasingly committed to coherently pursuing high levels of environmental protection in all policy fields, including foreign trade policies.[15] Finally, an additional reason for this paradigmatic shift – compared to the multilateral realm of the WTO – might very well also be seen in the apparently more expedient conditions for negotiating and reaching a consensus on the incorporation of environmental governance provisions into trade agreements at the bilateral and regional level.

3   Environmental Governance as a Regulatory Issue of Regional Trade Agreements: Two Main Dimensions

When attempting to map and systemize environmental governance as an increasingly important regulatory subject of regional trade agreements, it seems useful to broadly distinguish between two main dimensions or perspectives that might be appropriately termed the 'substantive law perspective' on the one side and the 'enforcement-oriented perspective' on the other side. The substantive law perspective is concerned with the scope and depth of environment-related provisions stipulating respective rules of behavior of the treaty parties, while the enforcement-oriented perspective addresses the different approaches towards environmental dispute settlement in regional economic integration agreements.

3.1   *Substantive Law Perspective: Scope and Depth of Environmental Provisions in Regional Trade Agreements*
Approaching the subject of environmental-related provisions in regional trade agreements from the perspective of substantive law, we can initially observe the existence of something like a minimalist substantive approach to

---

14   See WTO, 'Doha Ministerial Declaration', WTO Doc. WT/MIN(01)/DEC/1 (20 November 2001) paras 31ff.

15   On the different motives of states to include environmental concerns in their negotiations on regional trade agreements see, eg, OECD, *Environment and Regional Trade Agreements* (2007) 40ff.

environmental governance in many of the respective treaty regimes. In particular, this regulatory approach manifests itself in those regional trade agreements whose only reference to certain environmental issues is stipulated in exception or justification clauses, modelled after or even explicitly incorporating Article XX GATT 1994, and in addressing certain environmentally related concerns such as the protection of human, animal and plant life or health as well as the conservation of exhaustible natural resources.[16] Respective stipulations are a characteristic feature of those economic integration agreements that have already been concluded a number of decades ago.[17] A telling example is provided by the free trade agreement between Israel and the United States of 26 April 1985 stipulating in its Article 7 that "Article XX and XXI of the GATT are hereby incorporated into, and made a part of this Agreement".[18] However, such a minimalist regulatory approach to environmental governance can also be found in a considerable number of more recent economic integration treaties, among them – to mention but a few examples – Article IX of the revised Treaty of Trade between India and Nepal signed on 27 October 2009[19] as well as Article XIX of the Preferential Trade Agreement between Chile and India of 8 March 2006.[20]

While many of the numerous regional trade agreements currently in force are displaying what can be qualified as a kind of minimalist substantive approach to issues of environmental protection, today there is a clear trend in the relevant treaty-making practice towards the inclusion of considerably more comprehensive environmental provisions.[21] An important or even something

---

16 Generally, on the normative functions, regulatory structure and content of Article XX GATT 1994 see, eg Peter Van den Bossche and Werner Zdouc, *The Law and Policy of the World Trade Organization* (3rd edn, CUP 2013) 545ff.

17 Jinnah and Morgera (n 4) 325 ("early agreements only linked trade and the environment through a general exception clause, allowing parties to pursue environmental protection objectives through trade measures").

18 For the text of this agreement see the information available under: <http://tcc.export.gov/ Trade_Agreements/All_Trade_Agreements/exp_005439.asp> accessed 20 November 2021.

19 The text of the agreement is available under: <http://commerce.nic.in/trade/nepal.pdf> accessed 20 November 2021.

20 The text of the treaty can be found under: <www.sice.oas.org/trade/chl_ind/ptatext _e.pdf> accessed 20 November 2021. Generally, on this regulatory approach in regional trade agreements and its relevance for the realm of environmental governance see also for example OECD, *Environment and Regional Trade Agreements* (2007) 134ff.

21 Concerning the existence of such a trend see also, eg Clive George, 'Environment and Regional Trade Agreements: Emerging Trends and Policy Drivers', OECD Trade and Environment Working Papers 2014/02 (2014) 2 ("Analysis of the environmental provisions in RTAs reveals an encouraging upward trend. While basic provisions remain the most

like a pioneering example in this regard[22] was the North American Free Trade Agreement (NAFTA) that entered into force between Canada, Mexico and the United States on 1 January 1994.[23] In addition to stipulating respective environmental governance clauses in the text of the free trade agreement itself – attention might be drawn in this regard, for example, to the preamble emphasizing, *inter alia*, the desire of the parties to strengthen the development and enforcement of environmental laws and regulations, as well as Article 104 NAFTA including a list of multilateral environmental agreements whose provisions would supersede those of NAFTA in case of a conflict – NAFTA was first and foremost also accompanied by an environmental side agreement, the North American Agreement on Environmental Cooperation (NAAEC) that entered into force on 1 January 1994 and provided for a number of institutional and procedural features aimed at establishing an appropriate and acceptable balance between the promotion of international trade and the realization of environmental objectives.[24]

---

common types found in RTAs, the incidence of more substantive provisions has increased significantly in recent years."); ibid 4 ("However, the incidence of all the more substantive provisions covered by the analysis has increased significantly in recent years, from around 30% of those entering into force up to 2010, rising to over 50% in 2011 and close to 70% in 2012."); Sikina Jinnah, 'Strategic Linkages: The Evolving Role of Trade Agreements in Global Environmental Governance' (2011) 20 Journal of Environment and Development 191 ("Environmental provisions in trade agreements have evolved from weak statements of nonderogation (...) to strong mechanisms of transnational policy influence."); Clive George and Ysé Serret, 'Regional Trade Agreements and the Environment: Developments in 2010', OECD Trade and Environment Working Papers 2011/01 (2011) 4; Potestà (n 10) 167 ("In a number of PTIA [preferential trade and investment agreements] regimes, however, one can witness a growing attention towards non-economic concerns, such as labor, environmental and health issues.").

22   On this perception see also for example John H. Knox, 'The Neglected Lessons of the NAFTA Environmental Regime' (2010) 45 Wake Forest Law Review 391 (392); Potestà (n 10) 169 ("The NAFTA represents the initial milestone of a treaty regime addressing environmental issues within the context of an economic treaty."); Lo (n 10) 313; Gantz (n 10) 308.

23   North American Free Trade Agreement, reprinted for example in: (1993) 32 International Legal Materials 296ff, 612ff.

24   The text of this agreement is available under: <www.cec.org/about/agreement-on-enviro nmental-cooperation/> accessed 20 November 2021. For a more detailed account of the NAAEC see David L. Markell, 'North American Agreement on Environmental Cooperation' paras 1ff in Rüdiger Wolfrum (ed), *Max Planck Encyclopedia of Public International Law* (August 2009), available at <www.mpepil.com/> accessed 20 November 2021; Knox (n 25) 391ff; Gantz (n 10) 310ff.

Intended to provide for a uniform conduct of trade relations by European Union (EU) member states with third countries,[25] the free trade agreement signed by the European Union and its member states with the Republic of Korea in 2010 that entered into force on 1 July 2011[26] appears to be the first treaty of a kind of "new generation" of EU regional trade agreements[27] that distinguish themselves, *inter alia*, through the inclusion of an entire separate chapter on trade and sustainable development (Articles 13.1ff, EU–Korea FTA), that first and foremost, addresses issues of environmental governance.[28] This novel and considerably more comprehensive regulatory approach towards environmental issues adopted by the EU with regard to its external trade relations is also mirrored in the Association Agreement between the EU and Georgia. In accordance with its Article 22, the parties to this agreement establish a free trade area in conformity with the requirements enshrined at the multilateral level in Article XXIV GATT 1994.[29] In the same way as other economic integration agreements more recently concluded by the EU, the 2014 EU–Georgia Association Agreement not only emphasizes, as early as in its preamble, the importance of effective environmental governance in the economic relations between the parties[30] and provides for the incorporation of Article XX GATT

---

25 Generally thereto, for example, Daniel-Erasmus Khan, 'TFEU', art 207 in Rudolf Geiger and others (eds), *European Union Treaties – A Commentary* (Beck/Hart 2015) paras 1ff; Pieter Jan Kuijper and others, *The Law of EU External Relations* (OUP 2013) 373ff.

26 Free Trade Agreement between the European Union and its Member States, of the one part, and the Republic of Korea, of the other part [14 May 2011] OJ L127/6.

27 Generally, on the regional trade agreements concluded by the European Union see for example Alessandro Antimiani and Luca Salvatici, 'Regionalism versus Multilateralism: The Case of the European Union Trade Policy' (2015) 49 Journal of World Trade 253; Billy A. Melo Araujo, 'The EU's Deep Trade Agenda: Stumbling Block or Stepping Stone Towards Multilateral Liberalisation?' (2014) 5 European Yearbook of International Economic Law 263.

28 On the environmentally related provisions of the EU–Korea Free Trade Agreement see also, eg Garcia Marin Duran and Elisa Morgera, *Environmental Integration in the EU's External Relations – Beyond Multilateral Dimensions* (2012) 117ff; Zvelc (n 10) 195ff.

29 For a general account of these requirements under art XXIV GATT 1994 see, eg Matsushita and Schoenbaum and Mavroidis (n 7) 547ff; Karsten Nowrot, 'Steuerungssubjekte und –mechanismen im Internationalen Wirtschaftsrecht (einschließlich regionale Wirtschaftsintegration)' in Christian Tietje (ed), *Internationales Wirtschaftsrecht* (De Gruyter 2009) 61, 129ff.

30 See the respective stipulation in the preamble: "Committed to respecting the principles of sustainable development, to protecting the environment and mitigating climate change, to continuous improvement of environmental governance and meeting environmental needs, including cross-border cooperation and implementation of multilateral environmental agreements".

1994 (Article 33 2014 EU–Georgia Association Agreement) as well as for a general exception clause concerning the realm of trade in services in its Article 134, but also includes in its Articles 227 to 243 a chapter on trade and sustainable development (Chapter 13), thereby recognizing economic development, social development and environmental protection as the "interdependent and mutually reinforcing pillars" of this overarching steering concept (Article 227 (2) 2014 EU–Georgia Association Agreement).

Chapter 13 of the EU–Georgia Association Agreement contains a number of notable provisions from the perspective of environmental governance. Among them are substantive stipulations like the obligation of each party to ensure that its domestic laws provide for high levels of environmental protection in accordance with Article 228 (2) as well as the prohibition to encourage trade or investment by means of lowering the level of protection afforded in domestic environmental law or by way of failing to effectively enforce the respective environmental legal framework under Article 235 (1) and (3), thereby transforming the expectation of effectively implementing existing domestic laws aimed at environmental protection into an international legal obligation of the parties.[31] In addition, and as a kind of complementary means to the obligations just referred to, the parties explicitly recognize the importance of multilateral environmental governance (Article 230 (1) 2014 EU–Georgia Association Agreement) and, against this background, not only commit themselves to consult and cooperate with respect to multilateral negotiations on trade-related environmental matters (Article 230 (1)), but also stipulate an obligation to effectively implement the provisions of multilateral environmental agreements to which they are a party in their respective domestic legal orders in accordance with Article 230 (2). Finally, to mention but one further example, the EU, its member states and Georgia have under Article 239 of the agreement identified certain areas of environmental concerns as potential fields for cooperative efforts, among them the promotion of sustainable fishing practices, sustainable forest management and corporate social responsibility in general (lit. g, l and m), the development of private as well as public certification, traceability and labelling schemes (lit. f), and the identification of suitable trade-related measures aimed at promoting the conservation of biological diversity (lit. k).[32]

---

31   Generally, on this regulatory technique in the realm of regional trade agreements see for example Potestà (n 10) 177ff; OECD, *Environment and Regional Trade Agreements* (2007) 108ff; Lo (n 10) 325ff.

32   Generally, on these types of environmental cooperation provisions in regional trade agreements see also OECD, *Environment and Regional Trade Agreements* (2007) 76ff; Lo (n 10) 324ff; Peter Gallagher and Ysé Serret, 'Implementing Regional Trade Agreements with

These and numerous other substantive stipulations are complemented by provisions establishing an institutional framework intended to serve as oversight bodies as well as to facilitate the realization of the normative steering ideas and guiding principles enshrined in the 2014 EU–Georgia Association Agreement.[33] Article 240 (1) stipulates, in this regard, that each party to the agreement is required to designate a specific unit within its administration that shall serve as an institutional contact point for purposes of implementing the chapter on trade and sustainable development. Furthermore, in accordance with its Article 240 (2) the treaty regime establishes the Trade and Sustainable Development Sub-Committee comprised of senior administrative officials and entrusted with the task to oversee the implementation of the substantive and procedural provisions stipulated in Chapter 13 of the association agreement. Finally, and reflecting the participatory and inclusive approach adopted by the parties in order to promote an environmentally sound regional economic integration regime, a joint civil society dialogue forum is created on the basis of Article 241 that shall be convened once a year in order to conduct a dialogue between the parties and relevant non-state actors on sustainability aspects including environmental concerns.[34] With regard to the composition of the forum, the parties have committed themselves to promote – in the words of Article 241 (1) – "a balanced representation of relevant interests" and stakeholders by inviting, inter alia, representative organizations of employers, workers, environmental interests, and business groups to participate in the dialogue forum.

3.2   Enforcement Perspective: Environmental Dispute Settlement in Regional Trade Agreements

Turning to the enforcement-oriented perspective and thus assessing the different approaches towards environmental dispute settlement in regional trade agreements, it seems appropriate to start the evaluation by recalling that most – albeit not all[35] – economic integration treaties also contain provisions

---

Environmental Provisions – A Framework for Evaluation', OECD Trade and Environment Working Papers 2011/06 (2011) 8ff.

33   Generally, on this institutional dimension in the context of environmental provisions of regional trade agreements more recently concluded by the EU see, eg Zvelc (n 10) 199ff.

34   For a general account of this regulatory approach in economic integration agreements see, eg OECD, *Environment and Regional Trade Agreements* (2007) 149ff.

35   A respective example of a free trade agreement that does not contain a dispute settlement provision is the Agreement of the Government of Iceland, of the one part, and the Government of Denmark and the Home Government of the Faroe Islands, of the other part of 31 August 2005 ("Hoyvík Agreement"), available under: <www.government.fo/en/foreign-relations/foreign-trade/hoyvik-agreement/> accessed 20 November 2021.

that establish procedures for resolving disputes among the contracting parties.[36] Thereby, in previous decades until roughly the end of the 1990s, the
majority of regional trade agreements stipulated in this regard only a "negotiation model" of dispute settlement[37] by providing exclusively for the possibility of negotiated settlements between the disputing parties through informal
consultations or in the more formal and institutionalized context of political
bodies established under the treaty regime in question.[38] Nevertheless, more
recently these types of pragmatic, negotiations-based dispute settlement procedures are in relative decline since the respective treaty-making practice in
the realm of regional trade agreements shows a clear trend towards establishing and implementing a more "rule-oriented" model of dispute settlement, in
particular involving a right of access to third-party adjudication at some stage
of the dispute settlement process.[39]

The design of these more legalistic mechanisms in regional trade agreements frequently follows a structure that is quite similar to the WTO dispute
settlement process,[40] albeit in most cases without an institution exercising an

---

36   Generally, on this issue see, eg Victoria Donaldson and Simon Lester, 'Dispute Settlement'
      in Simon Lester and Bryan Mercurio (eds), *Bilateral and Regional Trade Agreements –
      Commentary and Analysis* (CUP 2009) 367; Claude Chase and others, 'Mapping of Dispute
      Settlement Mechanisms in Regional Trade Agreements – Innovative or Variations on a
      Theme?', WTO Staff Working Paper ERSD-2013-07 (June 2013) with further references.

37   On the distinction between "negotiation models" and "adjudication models" of dis-
      pute settlement in the context of dispute settlement mechanisms in the international
      economic system see William J. Davey, 'Dispute Settlement in GATT' (1987) 11 Fordham
      International Law Journal 51, 69ff. For a related systemizing approach distinguishing
      between "pragmatism" and "legalism" in the design of international dispute settlement
      mechanisms see already Robert E. Hudec, 'GATT or GABB? The Future Design of the
      General Agreement on Tariffs and Trade' (1971) 80 Yale Law Journal 1299, 1304ff; Kenneth
      W. Dam, *The GATT: Law and International Economic Organization* (University of Chicago
      Press 1970) 3ff. Generally on these approaches also Karsten Nowrot, 'NAFTA Dispute
      Resolution – Zwischen Diplomatie und Recht' in Dirk Ehlers and others (eds), *Aktuelle
      Entwicklungen des Rechtsschutzes und der Streitbeilegung im Außenwirtschaftsrecht*
      (Deutscher Fachverlag, Fachmedien Recht und Wirtschaft 2013) 81, 83ff with further
      references.

38   Chase and others (n 39) 13.

39   Chase and others (n 39) 11ff. Generally, on the differentiation between "rule-oriented"
      and "power-oriented" structures in the international economic system see already John
      H. Jackson, 'The Birth of the GATT-MTN System: A Constitutional Appraisal' (1980) 12 Law
      and Policy in International Business 21 (27ff); John H. Jackson, *The World Trading System*
      (MIT Press 1989) 85ff.

40   Chase and others (n 39) 13ff.

appellate review function.[41] With regard to a respective example from treaty-practice, attention can be drawn to the dispute settlement mechanism established on the basis of the Articles 244ff of the 2014 EU–Georgia Association Agreement. In addition, most of these more sophisticated, rule-oriented forms of dispute settlement in economic integration agreements – in principle in the same way as the WTO dispute settlement mechanism itself[42] – offer access to trade sanctions to be temporarily adopted by the complaining party against the respondent in cases of non-compliance with arbitration panel rulings as, again, for example, illustrated by the measures foreseen under Article 257 (2) of the 2014 EU–Georgia Association Agreement.

Although these findings undoubtedly serve as an indication that the legal regimes aimed at regional economic integration have more recently, from an enforcement perspective, in general, become considerably more rule-oriented in character on the basis of quasi-judicial or even judicial dispute settlement mechanisms, it needs to be emphasized that the respective situation and assessment is not as straightforward when turning specifically to the implementation dimension of environmental governance provisions stipulated therein. Rather, concerning the design and applicability of dispute settlement mechanisms, we often find in the regulatory framework of regional trade agreements a clear distinction being made between disputes over what might be qualified as "environmentally-related" provisions on the one side and traditional "trade-related" obligations of the contracting parties on the other side.

In order to establish a systemizing typology of the various respective dispute settlement procedures, it seems useful to broadly distinguish between three main approaches identifiable in current treaty practice of those regional trade agreements that include more comprehensive stipulations or even separate chapters devoted to environmental governance. Initially, we can find something like a minimalist procedural approach towards the enforcement of environmentally-related provisions that, strictly adhering to the above-mentioned "negotiation model", relies, in case of a dispute, exclusively on a settlement through consultations between the parties. A more recent example for such a minimalist approach is provided by the Canada–Peru Free Trade Agreement and its accompanying Agreement on the Environment that both entered into force on 1 August 2009.[43] While the stipulations enshrined in

---

41   For a number of notable exceptions in the realm of economic integration agreements see Chase and others (n 39) 30ff.

42   See thereto, eg, Van den Bossche and Zdouc (n 19) 291ff; Matsushita and others (n 7) 165ff.

43   See <www.international.gc.ca/trade-commerce/trade-agreements-accords-commerciaux/agr-acc/peru-perou/fta-ale/background-contexte.aspx?lang=eng> accessed 20 November 2021.

Chapter 17 on environmental matters in the free trade agreement itself are, in accordance with Article 2102 (1) of the treaty, excluded from the scope of application of the general dispute settlement mechanism established under Chapter 21, any disputes arising between the parties with regard to the interpretation and application of the Canada–Peru Agreement on the Environment are to be solved exclusively through consultations as laid down in Article 12 of the agreement.[44] The same applies for example to the Framework Agreement Establishing a Free Trade Area concluded between the Republic of Korea and Turkey that entered into force on 1 May 2013.[45] Article 5.12 (3) of the agreement explicitly proscribes that "[n]either Party shall have recourse to Chapter 6 (Dispute Settlement) for any matter arising under this Chapter [Trade and Sustainable Development]".[46]

The normative framework established by the Articles 242 and 243 of the 2014 EU–Georgia Association Agreement provides an example of the second main type of environmentally-related dispute settlement mechanisms in current regional trade agreements: a regulatory approach that might appropriately labelled as "soft" quasi-judicial dispute settlement.[47] In order to illustrate this qualification, it seems useful to draw attention to the fact that the procedure itself can again be subdivided into three principle phases of dispute settlement. The first phase – following the "negotiation model" – requires the disputing parties to make every attempt to arrive at a mutually satisfactory resolution of the matter on the basis of consultations, either on an informal basis or within the institutional framework of the Trade and Sustainable Development Sub-Committee (Article 242 (2) to (4) 2014 EU–Georgia Association Agreement). In this connection, Article 242 (3) and (5) foresees that the parties may seek advice from relevant multilateral environmental organizations and bodies as well as from their domestic advisory groups or other experts. In case the parties

---

44   See in this context also specifically Canada-Peru Agreement on the Environment, art 12 (6): "Neither Party may provide for a right of action under its law against the other Party on the ground that the other Party has acted in a manner inconsistent with this Agreement."

45   The text of the agreement is available under: <www.fta.go.kr/webmodule/_PSD_FTA/tr/1/02_tr_Hyeopjeongmun_eg.pdf> accessed 20 November 2021.

46   See thereto also, eg Clive George, 'Developments in Regional Trade Agreements and the Environment: 2013 Update', OECD Trade and Environment Working Papers 2014/01 (2014) 10ff.

47   In accordance with art 242 (1) of the 2014 EU-Georgia Association Agreement, for any dispute arising under ch 13 (Trade and Sustainable Development) "the Parties shall only have recourse to the procedure established under this Article and Article 243 of this Agreement", thus excluding the applicability of the general dispute settlement mechanism provided for in ch 14.

are unable to reach a satisfactory solution within a timeframe of 90 days after the first formal request for consultations in accordance with Article 242 (2) has been made, the dispute settlement procedure enters into its second phase that is designed on the basis of an "adjudication model". Article 243 (1) provides that each party may request that a panel of experts be convened, comprising of three experts selected from a list of at least fifteen individuals with specialized knowledge in legal or environmental issues as established by the Trade and Sustainable Development Sub-Committee in accordance with Article 243 (2) to (5) and Article 249, in order to examine the matter at issue. The panel of experts issues a report to the parties under Article 243 (7), thereby – in the words of this provision – "setting out the findings of facts, the applicability of the relevant provisions and the basic rationale behind any findings and recommendations that it makes".

While this second phase is clearly rule-oriented and justifies the qualification of this mechanism as a quasi-judicial dispute settlement procedure, the design of the subsequent third (implementation) phase indicates the "soft" character of this mechanism. Once the report of the panel of experts has been issued and published, the parties are, under Article 243 (8) of the 2014 EU–Georgia Association Agreement, in the enforcement phase of the dispute settlement procedure asked to "discuss appropriate measures to be implemented, taking into account the Panel of Experts' report and recommendations". In contrast to the general dispute settlement mechanism under Chapter 14, however, Article 243 (8) does not stipulate a right of the complaining party to adopt trade sanctions against the respondent in cases of non-compliance with the recommendations included in the panel report. The enforcement phase is thus, again, strictly adhering to the pragmatic "negotiation model" of dispute settlement.

It is precisely these "soft" implementation features that distinguish this second type of environmental dispute settlement mechanisms from the "hard" quasi-judicial dispute settlement procedures that constitute the third notable approach that can already occasionally be found in the current treaty-making practice of economic integration agreements. This most far-reaching approach in fact largely eliminates the above-mentioned procedural differences between disputes dealing with traditional trade-related obligations of the contracting parties on the one side and those addressing the more recently introduced environmental provisions in regional trade agreements on the other side. A respective example is provided by the free trade agreement concluded between Nicaragua and Taiwan on 16 June 2006.[48] This agreement includes in

---

48   The text of the agreement is available under: <www.sice.oas.org/Trade/nic_twn/nic_twn
      _e/TWN_NIC_full_text_06_16_09.pdf> accessed 20 November 2021.

its Chapter 19 (Environment) quite comprehensive stipulations, among them, for example, the obligation to effectively enforce the domestic environmental laws in accordance with Article 19.02 (1) (a). However, contrary to many other regional trade agreements, the obligations accepted by the parties under this chapter are not explicitly excluded from the scope of application of the general dispute settlement mechanism established under Chapter 22 of the agreement.[49] Consequently, in case a dispute arises between the parties concerning the interpretation and application of their environmentally-related obligations under Chapter 19, non-compliance with the recommendations made in the report of an arbitral group also gives the complaining party the right to suspend benefits to the respondent in accordance with Article 22.16.

Such a "hard" quasi-judicial dispute settlement procedure also finds its manifestation for example in the most recent generation of regional trade agreements concluded by the United States.[50] Article 20.9 (4) of the free trade agreement between the Republic of Korea and the United States that entered into force on 15 March 2012[51] explicitly stipulates that the parties, in case of a dispute arising in connection with the interpretation and application of provisions enshrined in Chapter 20 (Environment) may also have recourse to the general dispute settlement mechanism established under Chapter 22 (Institutional Provisions and Dispute Settlement), including the right to adopt trade sanctions in the event of non-compliance under Article 22.13.[52] Quite

---

49   See thereto also for example Clive George and Ysé Serret, 'Regional Trade Agreements and the Environment: Developments in 2010', OECD Trade and Environment Working Papers 2011/01 (2011) 6ff.

50   On the constitutional law background of this more recent innovation in the respective US treaty practice see for example David A. Gantz, 'The "Bipartisan Trade Deal", Trade Promotion Authority and the Future of U.S. Free Trade Agreements' (2008) 28 Saint Louis University Public Law Review 115, 135ff; Gantz (n 10) 340ff; Madison Condon, 'The Integration of Environmental Law into International Investment Treaties and Trade Agreements: Negotiation Process and the Legalization of Commitments' (2015) 33 Virginia Environmental Law Journal 102, 110ff.

51   The text of the agreement is available under: <https://ustr.gov/trade-agreements/free -trade-agreements/korus-fta/final-text> accessed 20 November 2021.

52   See thereto also already Jinnah (n 24) 208 ("The environmental provisions in the U.S.-Peru TPA are unprecedented. Most notably, the opening of the TPA's Dispute Settlement Chapter's procedures to environmental disputes not resolvable via environmental consultations means that implementation of covered agreements, including CITES, is for the first time subject to the full economic gravitas of FTA enforcement power."); Potestà (n 10) 181 ("these PTIA mechanisms effectively provide for potentially powerful cross-regime enforcement tools"); Christina Tébar Less and Simone Gigli, 'Update on Environment and Regional Trade Agreements: Developments in 2007', OECD Trade and Environment Working Paper No. 2008–02 (18 February 2008) 7 ("In the more recent agreements (eg, the

similar provisions can already be found, for example, in Article 18.12 (6) of the Peru–US Free Trade Agreement that entered into force on 1 February 2009,[53] as well as subsequently in Article 18.12 (6) of the Trade Promotion Agreement between Colombia and the United States that entered into force on 15 May 2012,[54] and in Article 17.11 (6) of the Trade Promotion Agreement between the United States and Panama and effective since 31 October 2012.[55]

4 Outlook

The necessarily selective assessment undertaken in the present contribution has revealed a number of indications in the relevant treaty-making practice that there is not only a trend towards the incorporation of more substantive and comprehensive environmental provisions into the legal frameworks of regional trade agreements, but also, as we can more recently observe, particularly in the realm these economic integration agreements, the emergence of more robust dispute settlement mechanisms designed to provide for a potentially quite effective enforcement of these substantive environmental stipulations in cases of non-compliance; a regulatory approach that results in the elimination of the traditional procedural differences between disputes relating to trade-related obligations of the treaty parties on the one side and those being concerned with environmental stipulations on the other side. It is first and foremost this last-mentioned that has been rightly considered in the

---

FTA with Korea) [signed by the United States], the whole Environment chapter is subject to formal dispute settlement."); Jinnah and Morgera (n 4) 331; Simone Gigli, 'Update on Environment and Regional Trade Agreements: Developments in 2008', OECD Trade and Environment Working Paper No. 2009–01 (24 March 2009) 11ff.

53   The text of the free trade agreement can be found under: <https://ustr.gov/trade-agreeme nts/free-trade-agreements/peru-tpa/final-text> accessed 20 November 2021. See also, eg, Gallagher and Ysé Serret, 'Environment and Regional Trade Agreements: Developments in 2009', OECD Trade and Environment Working Papers 2010/01 (2010) 12ff.

54   For the final text of this agreement see the respective information under: <https://ustr.gov/ trade-agreements/free-trade-agreements/colombia-fta/final-text> accessed 20 November 2020. See thereto also for example Clive George, 'Developments in Regional Trade Agreements and the Environment: 2012 Update', OECD Trade and Environment Working Papers 2013/04 (2013) 9ff.

55   The text of the treaty is available at: <https://ustr.gov/trade-agreements/free-trade-agr eements/panama-tpa/final-text> accessed 20 November 2021. See also, eg, Clive George, 'Developments in Regional Trade Agreements and the Environment: 2013 Update', OECD Trade and Environment Working Papers 2014/01 (2014) 11ff.

literature as one of the most notable normative innovations in recent years in the realm of regional economic integration agreements as a whole.[56]

Nevertheless, it should not be left unmentioned that the practical impact of these innovations in the realm of dispute settlement has been until now rather limited, to say the least. Already from a general quantitative perspective, it has frequently been emphasized that although most regional trade agreements now included dispute settlement mechanisms, the number of actual party-to-party disputes formally initiated by taking recourse to these mechanisms has remained very small.[57] This finding holds particularly true for respective disputes involving environmental provisions in economic integration agreements since no known dispute proceedings have been initiated yet, and some authors have expressed their skepticism as to future recourses to these mechanisms in dispute settlement practice.[58] However, while the future most certainly continues to be difficult to predict, in light of the unprecedented step recently taken by the United States to initiate dispute settlement proceedings against Guatemala based on an alleged failure to effectively enforce domestic labor laws under Article 16.2 (1) lit. a and Article 16.6 of the Dominican Republic–Central America Free Trade Agreement (CAFTA–DR),[59] it seems not entirely unrealistic that this new generation of respective dispute settlement mechanisms, created in more recently

---

56   On this perception see, eg Jinnah (n 24) 208; Potestà (n 10) 182ff; Jinnah and Morgera (n 4) 331.

57   See for example Chase and others (n 39) 6.

58   See thereto, eg Jinnah and Morgera (n 4) 335 ("Utilization of the dispute settlement provisions, however, is unlikely to occur in practice"); Jinnah (n 24) 208 ("Nevertheless, it is unclear whether the U.S. government would actually use its ability to file a dispute under the FTA for failure to implement the CITES-relevant provisions of the annex. Indeed, NGO representatives interviewed for this study did not see this as a likely option. U.S. government officials also expressed resistance to using this provision").

59   See on this labor rights dispute for example 'US, Guatemala Square Off as FTA Labour Dispute Advances, Bridges' (12 February 2015) vol 19, No 5, available at <www.ictsd.org/bridges-news/bridges/news/us-guatemala-square-off-as-fta-labour-dispute-advances> accessed 20 November 2021; Arbitral Panel of the Dominican Republic-Central America-Free Trade Agreement (CAFTA-DR), *Guatemala – Issues relating to the obligations under Article 16.2.1(a) of CAFTA-DR*, Initial Written Submission of Guatemala of 2 February 2015, available at <https://ustr.gov/sites/default/files/enforcement/labor/NON-CONFIDENT IAL%20-%20Guatemala%20-%20Initial%20written%20communication%20%202-02 -2015.pdf> accessed 20 November 2021. The text of the CAFTA-DR itself is for example available at <https://ustr.gov/trade-agreements/free-trade-agreements/cafta-dr-domini can-republic-central-america-fta/final-text> accessed 20 November 2021.

concluded regional trade agreements for the purpose of enforcing the implementation of certain non-economic concerns, might even in the foreseeable future also be taken occasionally to recourse in the context of environmental governance.

CHAPTER 21

Parallel Use of Public and Private Law Mechanisms in Resolution of International Trade Disputes

Ilia Rachkov

1 Introduction

A successful settlement of international trade disputes based on agreed upon rules and fair procedures is a common goal of both national and international law. Such disputes may be resolved at the private law or public law levels.[1] By the private law mechanism of resolution of international trade disputes I mean a direct challenging, by a private person (as a rule – by a legal entity), of measures which hinder international trade and are applied to such a person abroad. Usually, such lawsuits are filed with the courts of the State (or an economic integration community of States) which introduced such measures. Such economic integration communities are free trade zones, customs unions and economic unions (e.g. the European Union – the EU and – since 2015 – the Eurasian Economic Union – the EAEU).

The public law mechanism of international trade dispute resolution comes into play under the following circumstances: a State (alternatively: an economic integration community of States) files a claim against the measures of another State (or an economic integration community of States) which hinder international trade.

The choice of the mechanism (private or public law one) which is more suitable for the resolution of a specific international trade dispute depends on a number of factors. Out of them, the most important is this: Which mechanism allows for protecting the rights and legitimate interests most efficiently? Often companies use public and private law mechanisms in conjunction, i.e. simultaneously or consecutively.

Public law mechanisms of resolution of international trade disputes are set forth by universal, multilateral and regional international treaties. For Russia and former Soviet republics (except for the three Baltic States: Estonia, Latvia

---

1 Ernst-Ulrich Petersmann, 'Justice as Conflict Resolution: Proliferation, Fragmentation, and Decentralization of Dispute Settlement in International Trade' (2006) University of Pennsylvania Journal of International Economic Law 27(2) 273.

and Lithuania), these are the special mechanisms within the World Trade Organization (WTO), the Commonwealth of Independent States (CIS)[2] and its free trade zone, formerly the Eurasian Economic Community[3] (EurAsEC, which existed until 1 January 2015) and now the Eurasian Economic Union (EAEU, since 1 January 2015).

2 Dispute Resolution Mechanism within the WTO

The majority of CIS Member States/former Soviet republics are also members of the WTO (alphabetically listed):[4]
- Armenia (since 5 February 2003),
- Georgia (since 15 June 2000),
- Kazakhstan (since 30 November 2015),
- Kyrgyz Republic (since 20 December 1998),
- Moldova (since 26 July 2001),
- Russia (since 22 August 2012),
- Tajikistan (since 2 March 2013) and
- Ukraine (since 16 May 2008).[5]

The following CIS Member States have the status of observers within the WTO:
- Azerbaijan (the Working Group on its accession was established on 16 July 1997; on 3 December 2013, it submitted its Draft Working Party Report);[6] on 28 July 2017, Azerbaijan was urged to step up bilateral talks with WTO

---

2 At the CIS, the dedicated dispute resolution forum is the Economic Court of the CIS, see <www.sudsng.org/> accessed 22 November 2021. Between1 January 1994 and 31 December 2017 it rendered 135 judicial acts. This demonstrates that this Court is relatively high in demand and enjoys the trust of both the CIS Member States and the CIS bodies (L.E. Kamenkova, Ye.V. Babkina, 'Ekonomicheskiy Sud SNG i sud EvrAzES: skhodstvo i razlichiya' (2012) Rossiyskaya yustitsiya (8) 24–28). However, none of these judicial acts concerns the interaction between the public law and the private law mechanisms when deciding international trade disputes. That is why the activity of the Economic Court of the CIS is not dealt with in detail in this article.

3 On 10 October 2014, at its meeting in Minsk, the Inter-State Council of the EurAsEC adopted the resolution to liquidate the EurAsEC due to the entry into force, on 1 January 2015, of the Treaty on the EAEU (signed in Astana on 29 May 2014).

4 <www.wto.org/english/thewto_e/whatis_e/tif_e/org6_e.htm> accessed 22 November 2021.

5 On 19 May 2018, Ukraine declared that it called back the representatives of Ukraine in the CIS bodies <https://news.rambler.ru/world/39914797-ukraina-ofitsialno-vyshla-iz-sng/> accessed 22 November 2021.

6 <www.wto.org/english/thewto_e/acc_e/a1_azerbaidjan_e.htm> accessed 22 November 2021.

members on market access commitments for goods and services in order to accelerate its efforts to secure WTO membership;

- Belarus (the Working Group was established on 27 October 1993); however, before 2017 the last meeting of the Working Group took place in May 2005; in July 2019, Belarus reaffirmed its intention to complete WTO accession negotiations by the next WTO Ministerial Conference[7]; and
- Uzbekistan (the Working Group on its accession was established on 21 December 1994, but the negotiation process has become stuck at the stage of market access negotiations since 2005).[8]

Thus, the only post-Soviet republic which does not enjoy the status of a member or observer at the WTO is Turkmenistan.

According to the Marrakesh Agreement establishing the WTO dated 15 April 1994[9] the disputes between Member States of the WTO concerning alleged violations of the provisions of international treaties of the WTO system (so-called *covered agreements*) shall be resolved by the Dispute Settlement Body (DSB) of the WTO. Only WTO members (164) can be parties to the disputes which are resolved by the DSB; these are 160 States and 4 independent customs territories: the European Union, Taiwan (called "Chinese Taipei" at the WTO), Hong Kong, and Macao (called "Hong Kong, China" and "Macao, China" at the WTO). However, States often initiate disputes at the WTO on behalf of private persons who influence in the most crucial way the course and the outcome of the dispute resolution: collection of documents, elaboration of the strategy and tactics, etc. For instance, this was the case with the dispute between the United States and Japan regarding measures of Japan which distorted competition: actually, this was rather a dispute between Kodak (a US company) and Fuji (a Japanese company). The same is true for so-called Havana Club case, when the United States and the European Union submitted to the DSB their dispute on trademarks of two competing producers of hard alcoholic drinks.[10]

Since its accession to the WTO and as of 30 January 2022, Russia has initiated eight complaints before the DSB. In turn, Russia was/is being sued in eleven cases.[11]

---

7   <www.wto.org/english/thewto_e/acc_e/a1_belarus_e.htm> accessed 22 November 2021.

8   <www.wto.org/english/thewto_e/acc_e/a1_ouzbekistan_e.htm> accessed 22 November 2021.

9   The text of the Agreement in Russian has been published in Sobraniye Zakonodatelstva Rossiyskoy Federatsii, 10 September 2012, No 37 (Annex, Part VI) 2514–2523.

10   Ernst-Ulrich Petersmann, 'Justice as Conflict Resolution: Proliferation, Fragmentation, and Decentralization of Dispute Settlement in International Trade' (2006) University of Pennsylvania Journal of International Economic Law 27(2) 286.

11   See <www.wto.org/english/tratop_e/dispu_e/dispu_by_country_e.htm> accessed 30 January 2022.

In particular, as to the complaints brought by Russia, on 23 December 2013, Russia filed its first request for consultations with the European Union (dispute DS474) regarding the alleged violation of the Agreement on Implementation of Article VI of the General Agreement on Tariffs and Trade (GATT) 1994 (Anti-Dumping Agreement),[12] the Agreement on Subsidies and Countervailing Measures,[13] Articles I and VI of the GATT and Article XVI:4 of the Marrakesh Agreement establishing the WTO. The request concerned the measures set forth by Council Regulation (EC) No. 1225/2009 of the EU Council dated 30 November 2009 on protection against dumped imports from countries not members of the European Community, with regard to the following goods originating in Russia:
– ammonium nitrate,
– certain welded tubes and pipes of iron or non-alloy steel, as well as
– certain seamless steel pipes, of iron or steel.
This dispute (which is still pending) is related to the mechanism of adjustment of prices for calculation of the dumping margin when conducting anti-dumping investigations into these goods in the European Union. According to Russia's statement, this mechanism does not take into account the information on actual expenses of foreign producers or exporters that:

1) are recorded in the records of the foreign producers or exporters in accordance with generally accepted accounting principles of the country of exportation and

2) reasonably reflect the costs associated with the production and sale of the product under consideration.

Russia believes that this mechanism replaces the producers' and exporters' actual cost data with purported "market" cost data, including prices outside of the country of origin and exportation. Such information is being used to determine whether sales were made in the ordinary course of trade and subsequently to construct the normal value of such products. Russia requested that the European Union discontinue using energy cost adjustment methodologies when conducting anti-dumping investigations with regard to Russian goods. According to statements of representatives of the Russian Federation, these methodologies presume the calculation of the actual value of the goods based on European and not on Russian prices for energy resources; this allows the European Union to detect "dumping" even if the latter is not present.[14]

---

12 Sobraniye Zakonodatelstva Rossiyskoy Federatsii, 10 September 2012, No 37 (Annex, Part VI) 2654–2678.

13 ibid 2733–2775.

14 <www.kommersant.ru/doc/2324690> accessed 22 November 2021.

In its request for consultations Russia pointed out that the EU General Court confirmed these methodologies as a principle of law in its judgments dated 7 February 2013 on cases Nos.:

- T-235/08: *Acron OAO and Dorogobuzh OAO v Council of the EU*; and
- T-459/08: *EuroChem MCC v Council of the EU*.

In other words, long before Russia as a State of nationality of Acron and EuroChem filed its complaint with the WTO requesting to conduct consultations with the European Union on the legality of using energy cost adjustment in anti-dumping investigations against Russian producers of ammonium nitrate, Russian companies themselves tried to challenge these measures of the European Union using the private law mechanism – filing their lawsuits with the EU General Court. However, the above judgments of the General Court[15] confirmed and declared lawful the practice of the European Commission and of the Council – using cost adjustment for price of Russian gas (i.e. increasing that price) for the purposes of anti-dumping investigations with regard to Russian goods the production of which requires using Russian gas. The EU Court has also declared lawful the practice of application of energy cost adjustment to export prices of Russian producers of ammonium nitrate which export their goods into the EU market via their affiliated entities (e.g. EuroChem was exporting its products through a company registered in Luxembourg – Eurochem Trading).[16] Using these mechanisms by the EU Council and the European Commission – i.e. increase the normal value by using energy cost adjustment and lowering the export price by way of deducting the margin generated by affiliated persons – secures, according to the Court's opinion, a lawful increase of the dumping margin and allows the European Union to introduce increased anti-dumping import customs duties.

---

15   Technically, the EU Court rendered four judgments (two per each claimant: OAO Acron and OAO Dorogobuzh; OAO EuroChem). However, each judgment treats the same basic questions. I refer to the judgment on case No T-459/08 (*EuroChem v EU Council*): see Yu. Rudyuk, 'Resheniya Obschego Suda Evropeyskogo Soyuza otnositelno primeneniya popravok k raschyotu normalnoy stoimosti i exportnoy tseny dlya tseley raschyota dempingovoy marzhi v antidempingovykh rassledovaniyakh protiv exporta otdelnykh tovarov iz Rossiyskoy Federatsii' <www.traderemedies.ru/files/energokorrektirovka1.pdf> accessed 22 November 2021.

16   The Court declared that gaining certain profit by an affiliated company – Eurochem Trading – from the resale of ammonium nitrate to the EU market makes that company a trade agent of OAO EuroChem, ie de facto a commissioner of the claimant. Such profit (or – in other words – commission fee) generated by the affiliated company shall be deducted from the export price in order to compare it with the normal value. ibid.

This dispute was certainly aimed at the protection of rights of Russian companies. However, this dispute has a procedural drawback: according to Article 18:3 of the Anti-Dumping Agreement, its provisions apply to anti-dumping investigations and reviews of existing measures, initiated pursuant to applications which have been made on or after the date of entry into force for Russia of the WTO Agreement (i.e. on or after 22 August 2012). Thus, the DSB can decline Russia's claims, since the anti-dumping duties at stake have been introduced with regard to ammonium nitrate and other goods prior to Russia's accession to the WTO.[17] Apparently, Russia did not select the best moment to file its complaint with the WTO: on 23 September 2014, Commission Implementing Regulation (EU) No. 999/2014 imposing a definitive anti-dumping duty on imports of ammonium nitrate originating in Russia following an expiry review pursuant to Article 11(2) of Council Regulation (EC) No. 1225/2009 was adopted. It imposes certain anti-dumping duties on nitrate ammonium originating in Russia. This Regulation has been adopted upon review of earlier anti-dumping measures in accordance with Article 11(2) of Regulation No. 1225/2009 of the EU Council. By the Regulation of 2014, the European Commission extended the application of anti-dumping duties with regard to Russian ammonium nitrate; however, it did not refer to the energy cost adjustment.[18] It looked like challenging this later Regulation of 2014 (which was adopted after Russia's accession to the WTO) and not Regulation No. 1225/2009 of 30 November 2009 would allow Russia to comply with Article 18:3 of the Anti-Dumping Agreement.

Taking into consideration the above, on 7 May 2015 Russia filed a new request with the DSB for consultations with the European Union (dispute No. DS494), challenging the abovementioned legal acts of the European Union which were adopted after Russia's accession to the WTO. At the time of writing, panels to resolve the disputes were established (on 22 July 2014 and on 16 December 2016 respectively). Since that, dispute DS474 (initiated in 2013), has not been going forward. In dispute DS494, the panel was composed on 17 December 2018, the panel report was circulated on 24 July 2020 and is now under appeal.[19]

---

17 Initially, anti-dumping import customs duties on exports on ammonium nitrate from Russia into the European Union have been introduced by the European Union in 1995 by Council Regulation No 2022/95 dated 16 August 1995. See <https://eur-lex.europa.eu/legal-content/EN/ALL/?uri=CELEX%3A31995R2022> accessed 22 November 2021.

18 See <https://eur-lex.europa.eu/legal-content/EN/TXT/?uri=CELEX%3A32014R0999> accessed 22 November 2021.

19 <www.wto.org/english/tratop_e/dispu_e/cases_e/ds494_e.htm> accessed 22 November 2021.

Another dispute initiated by Russia at the DSB (DS476) – concerning the so-called Third Energy Package – may potentially protect the interests of Gazprom.[20] Having lost its hope to challenge the Third Energy Package[21] in the bodies (including courts) of the European Union or to secure substantial exemptions from those rules, Gazprom apparently suggested that the Russian Government launch this dispute within the DSB. In principle, this is an appropriate strategy as the EU Court itself will probably never declare the Third Energy Package to be not in line with the European Union's obligations arising out of the WTO agreements. The panel report was circulated on 10 August 2018 and is now under appeal.[22]

As to other States of Central Asia and the Caucasus who are members of the WTO (Armenia, Georgia, Kazakhstan, Kyrgyzstan, and Tajikistan), they also sometimes get involved in dispute settlement procedures at the WTO. For instance, Armenia is the respondent State in two cases[23] (both times complainant Ukraine); however, there has been no progress in the first case since autumn 2010, and the second case is also still pending. On 19 September 2017, Ukraine filed a complaint with the DSB against Kazakhstan in connection with anti-dumping import customs duties on steel pipes.[24] In November 2017, Kyrgyzstan announced that on 10 November 2017 it planned to file its first complaint – against Kazakhstan in connection with the latter's delays in clearing the cargo from Kyrgyzstan on the border between these two States. Kazakhstan's Prime Minister Bakytzhan Sagintaev answered that Kyrgyzstan did not comply with the requirements of phytosanitary and veterinary control

---

20   This is why the Romans used to ask: cui prodest?

21   The "third energy package" is a flash title for a number of EU documents: Directive 2009/72/EC of the European Parliament and of the Council of 13 July 2009 concerning common rules for the internal market in electricity and repealing Directive 2003/54/EC, Directive 2009/73/EC concerning common rules for the internal market in natural gas and repealing Directive 2003/55/EC and 3 Regulations (EC), all dated 13 July 2009: Nos 713/2009 (establishing an Agency for the Cooperation of Energy Regulators), 714/2009 (on conditions for access to the network for cross-border exchanges in electricity and repealing Regulation (EC) No 1228/2003) and 715/2009 (on conditions for access to the natural gas transmission networks and repealing Regulation (EC) No 1775/2005).

22   See <www.wto.org/english/tratop_e/dispu_e/cases_e/ds476_e.htm> accessed 22 November 2021.

23   *Armenia – Measures Affecting the Importation and Internal Sale of Cigarettes and Alcoholic Beverages*, DS411, see: <www.wto.org/english/tratop_e/dispu_e/cases_e/ds411_e.htm> accessed 22 November 2021, and *Armenia - Anti-Dumping Measures on Steel Pipes*, DS569, see <www.wto.org/english/tratop_e/dispu_e/cases_e/ds569_e.htm> accessed 22 November 2021.

24   *Kazakhstan – Anti-Dumping Measures on Steel Pipes*, DS530, see: <www.wto.org/english/tratop_e/dispu_e/cases_e/ds530_e.htm> accessed 22 November 2021.

and did not prevent smuggling from China, which is why Kazakhstan felt itself forced to strengthen its border control.[25] It is noteworthy that at the end of the day Kyrgyzstan did not file its complaint with the WTO as the parties reportedly settled their dispute amicably.[26]

Armenia is also an interesting example from another perspective: initially (in November 2013), using the private law mechanism, a company from that country – Rusal Armenal Closed Joint Stock Company (Russian acronym: ZAO)[27] that belongs to UC Rusal – did manage to get EU anti-dumping import customs duties set aside by the EU General Court.[28] This lawsuit was brought in December 2009. Although the European Union set import duties for Brazilian foil producing plants at 30% and for the Armenian plant of UC Rusal at only 13%, this made sales of the foil produced by Armenal non-profitable. On 16 January 2014, the European Commission filed its appeal against the above judgment of the General Court. On 16 July 2015 the Grand Chamber of the Court of Justice of the European Union rendered its decision (case No. in the appeal: C-21/14 P-R): the judgment of the first instance Court was set aside, and the case was transferred back to the General Court for re-examination of those questions on which the Court had not expressed its opinion at the outset. On 25 January 2017 the EU General Court (i.e. the first instance court) re-examined the case and declined Rusal Armenal's claims (case No. T-512/09 RENV).

3   Dispute Resolution Mechanism within EurAsEC and the Customs Union

The Treaty on Establishment of EurAsEC had been signed in October 2000 by the heads of five States: Belarus, Kazakhstan, Kyrgyz Republic, Russian

---

25   Tatyana Yedovina, 'Torgovle v SNG ne khvataet svobody' (3 November 2017) Kommersant.

26   Sergey Strokan', Kirill Krivosheyev, Kabay Karabekov, 'Kazakhstan i Kirgiziya ratamozhili otnosheniya' (18 December 2017) Kommersant.

27   This plant has been founded in Yerevan in May 2000 on the basis of Kanaker Aluminium Plant and is one of the largest industrial enterprises in Armenia and the only producer of aluminium foil in Caucasus and Central Asia. Jointly with plans Sayanal, Uralskaya Fol'ga and Sayanskaya Fol'ga this plant belongs to the business unit "Packaging" of UC Rusal. The production capacity of the plant is 25,000 mt/year.

28   Judgment of the General Court of the European Union in Case T-512/09 *Rusal Armenal v Council* EU:T:2013:571 annulling Council Regulation (EC) No 925/2009 of 24 September 2009 imposing a definitive anti-dumping duty and collecting definitively the provisional duty imposed on imports of certain aluminum foil originating in Armenia, Brazil and the People's Republic of China (OJ 2009 L 262, 1).

Federation, and Tajikistan. It entered into force on 30 May 2001. In 2005, Uzbekistan joined the EurAsEC (however, in 2008 its membership was suspended). Observers were Armenia, Moldova and Ukraine.

In 2008, Belarus, Kazakhstan and Russia created the Customs Union on the basis of the EurAsEC. The EurAsEC continued to exist in pursuing its treaty goals (enhancing economic integration), uniting the same five Member States.

In 2010, three Member States of the EurAsEC – Belarus, Kazakhstan and Russia – signed documents on the creation of a Common Economic Space.

Finally, on 18 November 2011 in Moscow the Presidents of Russia, Belarus and Kazakhstan signed a set of documents to move to a new stage of economic integration within the EurAsEC: the Declaration on Eurasian Economic Integration, the Treaty on the Eurasian Economic Commission (EEC) and Rules of its procedures. The aim of the Declaration on Eurasian Economic Integration is to secure the transfer to a new stage of integrational development – a Common Economic Area founded on the norms and principles of the WTO and open at any stage of its creation for accession of other countries. The ultimate goal of such integration was to create by 2015 the Eurasian Economic Union (EAEU), the treaty which was signed in Astana on 29 May 2014 by and between Russia, Belarus and Kazakhstan and which entered into force on 1 January 2015. Armenia and the Kyrgyz Republic also acceded to that treaty. In 2017, Moldova became an observer at the EAEU.[29]

Although the Court of the (former) EurAsEC was already mentioned in Article 8 of the Treaty on Establishment of the EurAsEC (2000), that Court started its operation only on 1 January 2012. Prior to that date, the functions of that Court were performed by the Economic Court of the CIS – based on an Agreement between the CIS and the EurAsEC on the performance of functions of the Court of the EurAsEC by the Economic Court of the CIS (2004). However, during that period (2000 – 31 December 2011) the Economic Court of the CIS admitted only one case within the EurAsEC to trial, but the claimant waived its claim.[30]

On 9 December 2010, the Member States of the Customs Union concluded the Treaty on Petitions by Business Entities in Disputes within the Customs Union to the Court of the EurAsEC and Particularities of Court Proceedings

---

29   'My ne stanem riskovat' tysychami zhizney nashikh ukrainskikh sosedey' ("We will not put thousands of lives of our Ukrainian neighbors at risk") (interview by Grigory Karasin, deputy minister of foreign affairs of Russia), (27 December 2017) Kommersant.

30   T. Neshataeva, P. Myslivskiy, 'Pervyi god suschestvovaniya Suda Evraziyskogo ekonomicheskogo soobschestva: itogi i perspektivy' (2013) Mezhdunarodnoye pravosudiye 2(6) 88–100.

with Respect to Such Disputes. According to that Treaty, business entities registered on the territory of the Customs Union were entitled to submit their claims to the Court of the EurAsEC. In 2012, the same right was also granted to business entities which were registered outside Member States of the Customs Union (Protocol to the Statute of the Court of the EurAsEC of 2012).

Thus, until the moment when the Treaty on the Eurasian Economic Union entered into force (1 January 2015) the Court of the EurAsEC served as the court of the Customs Union and of the Common Economic Space. The competence of the Court of the EurAsEC covered two categories of cases: direct competence to resolve disputes and indirect competence (to control the compliance of secondary law of the Customs Union and of the Common Economic Space with the primary law of these structures, i.e. with the international treaties on the establishment of the Customs Union and of the Common Economic Space). According to Article 13 paragraph 5 of the Statute of the Court of the EurAsEC (2010), its jurisdiction could also encompass other disputes, the resolution of which could be set forth by international treaties within the EurAsEC and the Customs Union. Article 14 of the same Statute determined the persons who were entitled to file their submissions with that Court:

1. Unless otherwise provided by international treaties within the EurAsEC, the disputes had to be examined by the Court upon application of:
   a) High Contracting Parties;
   b) bodies of the EurAsEC.
2. The Court considered cases within the Customs Union upon application of:
   a) Member States of the Customs Union;
   b) bodies of the Customs Union;
   c) business entities.
3. Business entities could have recourse to the Court in accordance with the Treaty on Recourse of Business Entities on Disputes within the Customs Union to the Court of the EurAsEC and the Particularities of Court Proceedings With Respect to Such Disputes dated 9 December 2010.

Thus, unlike the Economic Court of the CIS, the Court of the EurAsEC could also be used by legal entities, and not only by those which were registered on the territory of the Members of the Customs Union, but also outside in third countries. This gave foreign companies, which delivered goods and services to the territory of the Customs Union, standing to challenge actions and legal acts of the Commission of the Customs Union (later - the EEC) at the Court of the EurAsEC. In other words, contrary to the previous international treaties within the CIS, within the EurAsEC a private law mechanism of resolution of international trade disputes was created.

During the three years of its activity (2012–2014), the Court of the EurAsEC dealt with several cases connected with international trade. Due to the topic of this chapter, it makes sense to pay attention to the case of challenging certain provisions of decision No. 113 of the EEC Collegium dated 14 May 2013 "On the Application of the Antidumping Measure by Way of Introduction of an Antidumping Duty With Regard to Light Commercial Vehicles Originating in the Federal Republic of Germany, Republic of Italy and Turkish Republic Which are Being Imported into the Territory of the Customs Union".[31] This case had been instituted at the Court of the EurAsEC upon application of Volkswagen AG (Germany) dated 18 August 2014.

The applicant was of the opinion that clause 1 of the above decision of the EEC Collegium violated the applicant's rights and legitimate interests in the sphere of entrepreneurial and other economic activity, which were protected by the international treaties entered into within the Customs Union. In particular, the applicant attacked the anti-dumping duty (29.6%) introduced in the Customs Union for 5 years for the importation of certain light commercial vehicles (LCVs): those with full weight from 2.8 to 3.5 tonnes (inclusive) with diesel engines with cylinder capacity of no more than 3,000 cm³, with the type of body "van" and modification "all-metal cargo van" (destined for transportation of cargo up to 2 tonnes inclusive) or modification "combi – cargo and passenger van" (destined for a combined transportation of cargo and passengers), originating in Germany, Italy and Turkey and classified under codes 8704 21 310 0 and 8704 21 910 0 of the Good Nomenclature of External Economic Activity (Russian acronym: TN VED) of the Customs Union.

On 4 September 2014, the EEC submitted its objections to the Court of the EurAsEC, stating that Volkswagen AG had not complied with the procedure for a preliminary (out-of-court) settlement of disputes as set forth in Article 4 of the Treaty on Petitions by Business Entities in Disputes within the Customs Union to the Court of the EurAsEC and the Particularities of Court Proceedings with Respect to Such Disputes dated 9 December 2010. According to that Article, the Court of the EurAsEC could admit an application of a business entity for trial only after the latter had tried in vain to settle the dispute with the EEC. If within two months from such application to the EEC the latter did not undertake appropriate measures, the business entity was entitled to seek support from the Court of the EurAsEC.

---

31   See <http://tsouz.ru/eek/RSEEK/RKEEK/2013/14z/Pages/R_113.aspx> accessed 22 November 2021.

In addition, the EEC referred to the fact that the application of Volkswagen AG filed with the Court of the EurAsEC contained a number of new arguments and claims, including the following: those LCVs which Volkswagen imports into the Customs Union, are not analogous to those LCVs which are being produced by OOO Sollers-Yelabuga – a full-fledged production utility based on the territory of special economic zone Alabuga (Republic of Tatarstan, Russia). In that zone, OOO Sollers-Yelabuga used to produce LCVs of such brands as Fiat (model "Ducato"), but currently produces LCVs of brand Ford (model "Transit"). Volkswagen AG denied that its import supplies of LCVs influenced the production and the overall economic situation of OOO Sollers-Yelabuga. The EEC was of the opinion that these new arguments were not contained in the preliminary application of Volkswagen AG to the EEC. The EEC argued that this fact did not permit the EEC to take into account all circumstances and arguments of that applicant in the course of out-of-court settlement attempt.

The Court of the EurAsEC agreed with these objections of the EEC and declared that the new claims and arguments raised by Volkswagen AG were essential for the settlement of the dispute at the pre-trial stage. In other words, the Court of the EurAsEC came to the conclusion that Volkswagen AG did not exhaust the possibility of the pre-trial settlement of its dispute with the EEC (judgment of a panel of the EurAsEC Court dated 7 October 2014). In the reasoning of that judgment, the Court of the EurAsEC stressed that

> in accordance with Article 28 para. 2 of the Rules of the Court of the EurAsEC for Consideration of Applications of Business Entities, the refusal to admit the application does not prevent from a repeated filing of the same application with the Court in accordance with the procedure set forth by the Rules, after elimination of the errors which served as the ground to refuse to admit the application.

However, judge Tatiana Neshataeva gave a dissenting opinion to the above judgment: she did not agree with the conclusion of the panel of the EurAsEC Court; instead, she concluded that – having refused to admit the application of Volkswagen AG for trial – the EurAsEC Court violated basic principles of justice: access to justice, adversariality, *res judicata*, estoppel, and others. According to judge Neshataeva's opinion, Volkswagen did apply to the EEC as a pre-condition for the trial,[32] although this did not result in the settlement of the dispute. Thus, the requirement of Article 4 of the Treaty on Petitions by

---

32   Vladimir Shtanov, 'EEK otkazala Volkswagen' (19 August 2013) Vedomosti.

Business Entities in Disputes within the Customs Union to the Court of the
EurAsEC and the Particularities of Court Proceedings with Respect to Such
Disputes was complied with.

Judge Neshataeva believes that nothing prevented the applicant from
changing his arguments after filing his application with the EEC and prior to
approaching the EurAsEC Court. The Treaty of 2010 "does not contain a peremptory norm to the effect that all arguments of the business entity have to
be reflected in the application to the EEC". Besides, judge Neshataeva referred
to the case law of other international courts which developed a more sophisticated and softer approach to the exhaustion of remedies prior to recurring
to the court. She also stressed the specifics of disputes arising out of anti-
dumping investigations: their substance is always an attempt to challenge the
analogous nature of goods, the dumping margin and the anti-dumping import
customs duties. In its applications filed with the EEC (Volkswagen filed two of
them: in 2013 and 2014) that company referred to all these factors.

Judge Neshataeva did not agree with the idea expressed in the judgment of
the panel of the EurAsEC Court that prior to filing its lawsuit with that Court
Volkswagen should have approached the EEC for a third time in a row within
two years and would then be entitled to file its lawsuit with the Court only after
that! She opined that this constituted a violation of the *res judicata* principle.

However, Volkswagen AG's defeat at the EurAsEC Court does not rule out
that the company's rights cannot be successfully protected, this time – by
using a public law mechanism, namely dispute resolution at the WTO. On 21
May 2014, the European Union filed its request with the DSB for consultations with Russia regarding anti-dumping duties on light commercial vehicles
from Germany and Italy.[33] The European Union referred to the violation, by
Decision No. 113 of 14 May 2013, of Article VI GATT and a number of provisions
of the Anti-Dumping Agreement. On 18 June 2014, the parties to the dispute
held consultations but were not able to settle the dispute at that stage. That
is why on 15 September 2014 the European Union requested that a panel be
established, and this was done on 20 October 2014, and the panel was composed on 18 December 2014. This dispute was of interest for a number of third
parties: Brazil, China, India, Japan, Korea, Turkey, Ukraine, and the United
States reserved their right to join the proceedings at a later stage.

On 27 January 2017, the panel report was circulated to all members of
the WTO. In its report the panel came to the conclusion that Russia violated

---

33   WTO, *Russia – Anti-Dumping Duties on Light Commercial Vehicles from Germany and Italy*,
      DS479, see <www.wto.org/english/tratop_e/dispu_e/cases_e/ds479_e.htm> accessed 22
      November 2021.

a number of provisions of the Anti-Dumping Agreement. However, on 20 February 2017, Russia notified the DSB of its decision to appeal to the Appellate Body on certain issues of law and legal interpretations in the panel report. On 27 February 2017, the European Union also notified the DSB of its decision to cross-appeal. The Appellate Body report was circulated on 22 March 2018 and both reports were adopted on 9 April 2018.

Meanwhile, the anti-dumping measures at stake expired on 14 May 2018, so technically Russia (and the Eurasian Economic Union) fully implemented the DSB's rulings and recommendations in this dispute.

4 Mechanism of Dispute Resolution within the Eurasian Economic Union

Member States of the Eurasian Economic Union are Russia, Armenia, Belarus, Kazakhstan, and Kyrgyzstan. According to the Treaty on the Eurasian Economic Union, the Court of the Union has been established.[34] This is a permanent dispute resolution forum which has to consider lawsuits brought by the Member States of the Eurasian Economic Union and by business entities incorporated in those countries and in third countries. The EAEU Court has replaced the Court of the EurAsEC.[35] However, the jurisdiction of the EAEU Court is narrower than that of the EurAsEC Court. Basically, the jurisdiction of the EAEU Court consists of direct jurisdiction (resolution of the disputes on the merits) and indirect jurisdiction (control of compliance of secondary law provisions with the primary law of the EAEU).[36] However, many treaties within the EAEU provide for the possibility of enlarging the jurisdiction of the EAEU Court – by way of putting disputes set forth in other treaties of the EAEU under such jurisdiction. For instance, the EAEU Treaty mentions the interpretation of questions of public service at EAEU's bodies.

The first case which the EAEU Court considered on the merits was initiated by a claimant using the private law mechanism. This was an application of the sole entrepreneur Mr. Tarasik (a citizen of Kazakhstan) on challenging

---

34 See <http://courteurasian.org/en/> accessed 22 November 2021.
35 According to the Treaty on Discontinuation of the Activity of EurAsEC, adopted by decision No. 652 of the Inter-State Council of EurAsEC (at the level of heads of states) dated 10 October 2014 'On discontinuation of the activity of EurAsEC', the activity of the EurAsEC Court ceased from 1 January 2015.
36 T.N. Neshataeva, 'Yedinoobraznoye pravoprimeneniye – tssel Suda Evraziyskogo economicheskogo soyuza' (2015) Mezhdunarodnoye pravosudie (2) 115–125.

the Eurasian Economic Commission's failure to act in his case.[37] Mr. Tarasik was of the opinion that the failure to act consisted in the passive attitude of the EEC towards a dispute between the claimant and the customs authorities of Kazakhstan. Mr. Tarasik believed that the EEC's failure to act specifically resulted in a lack of monitoring and control over Kazakhstan's compliance with a number of international treaties by which that country was bound:

– Agreement on Turnover of Products Which Are Subject to Compulsory Assessment (Confirmation) of Conformity on the Territory of the Customs Union (dated 11 December 2009) – as regards the creation of a Uniform Register of certification bodies and testing laboratories of the Customs Union;
– the Geneva Agreement (dated 20 March 1958) Concerning the Adoption of Uniform Technical Prescriptions for Wheeled Vehicles, Equipment and Parts which can be fitted and/or be used on Wheeled Vehicles and the Conditions for Reciprocal Recognition of Approvals granted on the basis of these pre-scriptions – as regards the recognition of official approvals of the type of construction of vehicles granted by the state on the territory of which such vehicles were produced;
– the Treaty on the Customs Union and the Common Economic Space dated 26 February 1999 – as regards the application of a uniform system of collec-tion of indirect taxes in the trade with third parties.

In 2012–2014, Mr. Tarasik was importing cars – Nissan Titan, Toyota Tundra and Ford-F150 – from the United States into Kazakhstan. He was of the opinion that these cars were trucks since they had the frames of cargo vehicles. When declaring these cars at their importation, Mr. Tarasik classified these vehicles under code 8704 according to TN VED of the Customs Union ("motor vehicles for transportation of cargo"). However, the customs authorities of Kazakhstan requested him to pay the excise tax since they qualified these vehicles as "cars built on passenger car frames with a platform for cargo and a cabin for the driver separated from the cargo division by a stationary hard membrane". According to Article 279 paragraph 6 of the Tax Code of Kazakhstan such cars are subject to excise tax payment. Mr. Tarasik tried in vain to challenge this decision of the customs authorities of Kazakhstan in courts of the first appeal, final appeal and supervision instances of that country. Upon an internal check the customs authorities of Kazakhstan imposed on Mr. Tarasik the duty to pay the excise tax, VAT and a penalty, the total amount of which exceeded 8 million

---

37   The judgment of the EAEU Court in this dispute has been published at <http://courteuras ian.org/page-24161> accessed 22 November 2021.

tenge. Interestingly, at that time, in Russia these vehicles were classified as heavy-duty cars and were not subject to excise tax.[38]

In October 2014, Mr. Tarasik filed his complaint with the EEC challenging the decisions of the customs authorities and courts of Kazakhstan. In his complaint, he stated that these authorities and courts of Kazakhstan violated the principles of a uniform application and implementation of international treaties which form the legal basis of the Customs Union. On 27 November 2014, the EEC informed Mr. Tarasik that the legal assessment of lawfulness of the above decisions of Kazakhstani customs authorities and courts exceeded the powers of the EEC. Since the payment of excise taxes falls within the competence of the state bodies of Kazakhstan, the EEC forwarded Mr. Tarasik's complaint to the Committee of state income of the Ministry of Finance of Kazakhstan.

On 28 December 2015, a panel of the EAEU Court (4 judges) dismissed the application of Mr. Tarasik and declared that the EEC's failure to act was in line with the Treaty on the EAEU and international treaties within the EAEU and did not violate Mr. Tarasik's rights and legitimate interests in the entrepreneurial and other economic activity. The EAEU Court explained its position as follows: proceedings based on a lawsuit against failure to act can aim at a negative answer of the EEC, if the performance of an action which the claimant requests to undertake is the EEC's direct duty which cannot be delegated to other persons (so-called specific duty).

The duty to carry out an action, which a claimant requests, shall result from general principles and rules of international law, resolutions of bodies of the integration community. In the case at hand the applicable law did not impose on the EEC such a specific duty.[39] In particular, the EEC does not bear a direct duty to monitor and control, on the basis of individual applications of business entities, the implementation of international treaties within the Customs Union and the Common Economic Space and resolutions of the EEC. That is why the Court stated that it could not agree with Mr. Tarasik's argument that the respondent's connivance resulted in non-compliance with international treaties.[40] The EAEU Court also pointed out that the approval of a list of goods which are subject to the excise tax did not fall within the competence of the

---

38   On page 18 of the judgment of the EAEU Court dated 28 December 2015 it is indicated that when substantiating this argument Mr Tarasik referred to a judgment of the *Arbitrazh* court of Primorye region (Russia) dated 3 August 2012, case No A51-6609/2012: *OOO NTK v Nakhodka Customs Office*, claim on declaring unlawful its decision dated 6 February 2012 on refusal to clear the goods.

39   Page 15 of the judgment dated 28 December 2015.

40   ibid 17.

Customs Union, does not currently fall within the competence of the EAEU, but is an exclusive right of the Member State of the EAEU.[41]

The uniform procedure of regulating foreign trade and adoption of agreed upon decisions on synchronized introduction of amendments and additions to it also encompasses indirect taxation of operations with third countries. A unified approach to indirect taxation also presumes a uniform list of goods which are subject to excise tax payment and uniform rates of indirect taxes. However, such a uniform approach was not established by the Member States of the EAEU – neither within the Customs Union and the Common Economic Area nor later on within the EAEU.[42]

Both Mr. Tarasik and the EEC filed appeals against that judgment. On 3 March 2016, the Appeal Chamber of the EAEU Court left the judgment without any amendments and declined Mr. Tarasik's appeal. Only judge Neshataeva expressed her dissenting opinion, disagreeing with the opinion of the majority of three other judges. Already when being a judge of the EurAsEC Court, Ms. Neshataeva actively used teleological and systematic interpretation of international treaties at stake.[43]

It would appear that Mr. Tarasik's appeal should have had good prospects of success, if the Appeal Chamber had agreed to construe the applicable provisions of international law not literally but from the point of view of their object and purpose. Such an interpretation of international treaties is not only permitted, but explicitly prescribed by Article 31 of the 1969 Vienna Convention on the Law of Treaties: the treaty shall be construed in good faith in accordance with the usual meaning which shall be ascribed to the terms of the treaty in their context, as well as in light of the object and the purpose of the treaty;

– according to Article 9(b) of the Treaty on the Customs Union and the Common Economic Space dated 26 February 1999 one of the goals of the regime of free trade in goods is the application of a uniform system of collection of indirect taxes;

– the uniform procedure for external trade regulation and for adoption of coordinated decisions for a synchronic introduction of amendments and additions to it includes indirect taxation of external trade operations with third countries (Article 12 paragraph 4 of the same Treaty);

---

41   ibid 22.

42   ibid 23–24.

43   Joint dissenting opinion of judges T.N. Neshataeva and K.L. Chayka to resolution of the EurAsEC Court dated 8 April 2014 on the request of Ministry of Economics and Budget Planning of the Republic of Kazakhstan to render an advisory opinion on the Agreement on State (Municipal) Procurement dated 9 December 2010.

– these provisions were specified in greater detail on the Agreement on Principles of Collection of Indirect Taxes at Exportation and Importation of Goods, Performance of Works, Provision of Services in the Customs Union dated 25 January 2008 (which entered into force on 1 January 2015).

Taking this into account, it is very regrettable that the EAEU Court (both its first and its appeal instances) took such a conservative position when deciding this case.

In general, from 2016–2020, the EAEU Court has reached a substantial workload. Most often it had to do with lawsuits brought by private persons; so far there was only one decision on an application brought by a Member State of the EAEU against another Member State of the EAEU.

5   Conclusion

In the light of the above, the following conclusions can be made:

1)   Apparently, the private law mechanism is the main means to settle trade disputes. States should have recourse to public law mechanisms of dispute resolution only in exceptional cases – when a private law mechanism does not result in an efficient resolution of the dispute, i.e. does not allow to find a solution which would be acceptable for both parties.

2)   The most substantial disadvantage of the public law mechanism of resolution of trade disputes is that this mechanism unnecessarily politicizes an economic dispute. Due to that, it makes sense to consider whether – as a precondition to start using a public law mechanism – private law mechanisms should have been exhausted beforehand, provided that the applicant was not satisfied with the outcome of the private law mechanism.

3)   The public law mechanism constitutes a kind of appeal instance vis-à-vis the private law mechanism. Let us assume the EU Courts would refuse to set aside anti-dumping measures imposed by the European Commission, but the DSB of the WTO would find these measures inconsistent with the European Union's obligations under WTO law. Of course, such situation would seriously undermine the credibility of the fora which consider trade disputes under private law mechanisms. That is why States should refrain to the extent possible from escalating such disputes bringing them to a supranational or international dispute settlement body under the public law mechanism.

4)   The public law mechanism may allow to reach phenomenal and paradox conclusions. For instance, as a result of using this mechanism, Russia

may bear responsibility under public international law for the actions of another subject of international law – the Customs Union (or – since 2015 – the EAEU). This is due to the fact that neither the Customs Union nor the EAEU are members of the WTO. That is why Russia should endeavor to push the EAEU to accede to the WTO. Apparently, to achieve this goal, Belarus (being a Member State of the EAEU as well) should join the WTO either concurrently with the EAEU or before it.

5)   For Russia, the public law mechanism may also be dangerous for the following reason: it might potentially allow to impose on Russia international law responsibility for the trade policy of de-facto regimes (such as Abkhazia, South Ossetia, Transnistria, the Donetsk and Lugansk People's Republics). For instance, one of the obstacles to Russia's accession to the WTO was Georgia's request that Russia fulfill the agreements (reached in 2004) on legalization of customs checkpoints at the Abkhazian and South Ossetian parts of the Russian-Georgian border (the agreement was that Georgian customs officers should be admitted to such checkpoints).

6)   Generally, it seems preferable to solve state-to-state disputes within a regional economic integration community rather than recurring to dispute settlement bodies at the multilateral or universal level (such as the DSB of the WTO). For this purpose, it should be reflected in international treaties which create economic integration communities with Russia's participation that trade disputes between members of such a community shall be settled exclusively by the courts of such a community. This is precisely the approach followed within the European Union. Of course, this requires that within such economic integration communities dispute settlement bodies be created which fully rely on the principles of the rule of law.

SECTION 2

Dispute Resolution under Private Law

∵

Private Trade Disputes in State Courts in the Region of the Caucasus and Central Asia – Issues of Quality

Alexander Trunk

In order to bring justice to the parties in an efficient manner, proceedings in state courts must fulfil numerous criteria. This chapter will give an overview of approaches and some results of evaluation of national court systems, with particular regard to countries in the region of the Caucasus and Central Asia. One example of the quantitative measuring of national court systems and their functioning, as a basis for comparison, is the regular reports of the Council of Europe's European Commission for the Efficiency of Justice (CEPEJ).[1] The purpose of this chapter is to open a discussion on reasonable standards (or even minimal standards), best practices and possible approaches to improve proceedings in state courts in this region with regard to commercial disputes.

1 What is the Meaning of "Quality" of Dispute Resolution?

Generally speaking, the term "quality" refers to the features of a considered object allowing for the evaluation of the object positively or negatively in relation to other objects or to certain standards.[2]

1.1 Quality of Dispute Resolution System and the Concepts of "Efficiency", "Judicial Independence" and "Protection of Human Rights"

As regards the quality of dispute resolution systems, often the term "efficiency" is used as a descriptor of the quality of the dispute resolution system.[3]

---

1 cf <www.coe.int/T/dghl/cooperation/cepej/default_en.asp> accessed 22 November 2021. "Measuring justice" was also the special topic of the International Conference on Judicial Independence, Jerusalem, 2022, organized by the International Association of Judicial Independence and World Peace, <https://independence-en.forms-wizard.biz/> accessed 4 February 2022.

2 cf <www.oxforddictionaries.com/de/definition/englisch/quality> accessed 22 November 2021.

3 See eg the denomination of the European Commission for the *Efficiency* of Justice.

© KONINKLIJKE BRILL NV, LEIDEN, 2023 | DOI:10.1163/9789004357839_024

"Efficiency" itself is usually defined as a relationship between the degree of time and work needed to accomplish certain results.[4] Referring to dispute resolution systems, efficiency is an important element of the quality of such systems, but it does not describe all possibly relevant qualities of the system. In particular, the term "efficiency" relates more to the technical aspects of a dispute resolution system (how fast does it work? what are its costs? etc.) than to the contents of the dispute and its resolution. Theoretically, a dispute resolution system might be termed efficient (in terms of costs etc.), even if it leads to a high degree of "wrong" or "unjust" outcomes. If, however, the term efficiency is defined broadly, including elements of substantive or procedural justice, it is nearly identical to a general characterization of a dispute resolution system. Other terms (or concepts) which are often used in describing the quality of a dispute resolution system, in particular with regard to dispute resolution in state courts, are the degree of judicial independence, protection of human rights in the system and, more generally, the degree to which the system is characterized by "the rule of law".[5] Again, these are only specific, though highly important, elements of the general "quality" of the system. Overall, the quality of a dispute resolution system consists of numerous factors, which have to be seen as a whole and may lead to different evaluations – depending on which factors are regarded as (maybe) more important than others. There is no general objective standard of evaluating the quality of a dispute resolution system, but a quantitative comparison of factors on the basis of a broadly acceptable common understanding of which factors are most important, can lead to an informed opinion on strengths and weaknesses of some concrete dispute resolution system (e.g. the court system in one country or a more specific dispute resolution system within one country) in comparison with other systems.

1.2   *Relationship with "Goals of Procedure" and "Procedural Maxims"*
In the Continental legal doctrine of civil procedure, it is common to analyse procedural law from the perspective of "procedural maxims"[6] or of "goals of

---

4   cf <http://dictionary.reference.com/browse/efficiency> accessed 22 November 2021.

5   The term "rule of law" is very broad and includes both procedural and substantive elements, see eg <https://en.wikipedia.org/wiki/Rule_of_law> or <http://worldjusticeproject.org/what -rule-law> both accessed 22 November 2021. It may be understood to describe minimal standards, but it may also be understood to include more demanding, even sometimes controversial standards. The term "rule of law" puts together some basic legal standards, but it does not per se address issues of efficiency or the substantive quality of the outcome of the dispute resolution proceeding.

6   cf Ansay/Basedow (eds), *Structures of Civil and Procedural Law in South Eastern European Countries* (2008) 95 et seq.

the proceeding".[7] In some jurisdictions, the legislators have expressly laid-down such goals of the procedure or procedural maxims in the texts of the Procedural Codes or laws.[8] Definitions of the goals of the procedure and procedural maxims are without doubt useful tools, both for an analysis of existing legislation and for interpretation of the laws. They can also be used as a measure for the comparison of different systems of dispute resolution, and they may even be helpful for developing proposals for legislative reform. However, they are not structured as quantitative measures, and they are mainly focused on the "formal side" of the law – legislative texts, jurisprudence and other legal practice. They basically do not take into account or evaluate informal practices or economic effects of dispute resolution systems. In the context of a general evaluation of the quality of a dispute resolution system, the goals of the procedure and procedural maxims can be used as one of the factors determining the quality.

2 Criteria of Quality of Dispute Resolution

In order to measure and evaluate the quality of a dispute resolution system it is necessary to determine sets of criteria and, if possible, some kind of ranking between them.

2.1 *Formal Criteria*

Formal criteria are, in the first place, legal provisions (constitutional guarantees, legislation and subordinate legislation) or even soft law,[9] then jurisprudence by state courts, which may be supplemented or contrasted with available arbitral practice or even other documents of alternative dispute resolution, and finally even examples of contractual practice including general contract terms. The selection of criteria requires, itself, an analysis and evaluation of the relative importance and specificity of the different criteria. Legal texts should never be the exclusive focus of analysis, at least leading jurisprudence must be included.

---

7   See Alan Uzelac (ed), *Goals of Civil Justice and Civil Procedure in Contemporary Judicial Systems* (Springer 2014) passim.

8   See, for example, the Code of Civil Procedure of the Republic of Kazakhstan of 1999, arts 5–23, unofficial English translation available at <http://adilet.zan.kz/eng/docs/K990000411_> accessed 22 November 2021.

9   For the term "soft law" see <https://en.wikipedia.org/wiki/Soft_law> accessed 22 November 2021.

2.2   *Informal Elements and Criteria*

Apart from formal criteria, there are numerous "informal" elements, which determine the course and outcome of dispute resolution in different systems.[10] Some informal elements may be evaluated positively, others negatively (for example if they have a criminal character). They may be grounded in history or specifics of society in a certain context. There may be local specifics or informal practices on the level of a sub-group of the population or of a whole country or region. The informal elements may be specific to a certain legal context (e.g. in court proceedings) or they may be of a general nature, being applied, also, in the dispute resolution context. Taking into account and analysing informal structures (and structural elements) in legal contexts is usually not the area of experience of legal scholars or practitioners, but of sociologists or similar professions. A good analysis of the quality of dispute resolution requires solid interdisciplinary work. Changing informal practices is more difficult than changing legislation and requires different approaches and tools.

3   Measuring the Quality of Dispute Resolution

There are presently quite a number of public institutions or private organizations working in the field of measuring and evaluating dispute resolution in different parts of the world, including the region of the Caucasus and Central Asia.

3.1   *Institutions/Organizations*

3.1.1   International Institutions

In general, one can state that more attention is given today to the region of the Caucasus, as the three South Caucasian States are members of the Council of Europe, whose Commission for the Efficiency of Justice (CEPEJ) is today probably the lead institution in analysing the quality of national justice systems.[11]

---

10   cf Christian Giordano and Nicolas Hayoz (eds), *Informality in Eastern Europe – Structures, Political Cultures and Social Practices* (Peter Lang AG 2014) passim; see also <www.idlo .int/what-we-do/rule-law/informal-justice> accessed 22 November 2021, and the contributions on "law and informality" in (2020) Kieler Ostrechts-Notizen/Kiel Journal of East European Law, issue 1–2, pp. 4–42. More recently, the relationship between law and informality with a focus on judicial matters was dealt with in a panel organized by the author at the 10th World Congress of the International Congress for Central and East European Studies in Montreal, 2021, <https://sites.events.concordia.ca/sites/iccees/en/iccees2020> accessed 04 February 2022.

11   See supra n 1.

Besides, Armenia, Azerbaijan and Georgia are members of the European Union's Eastern Partnership Initiative, which has given an additional impetus on research and consultation in the field of the justice system.[12] The functioning of justice systems in the region of Central Asia is partly addressed by the Council of Europe in special agreements,[13] partly by the European Union's "Rule of Law Initiative for Central Asia".[14] Both the Caucasus region and the Central Asian region are addressed by international institutions such as the World Bank[15] or (partly) other UN suborganizations (in particular UNCITRAL, UNDP and UNCTAD). Depending on their areas of interest, other international organizations sometimes also develop programs with countries of the Caucasus and Central Asian region (for example, the European Bank for Reconstruction and Development [EBRD][16] or the Hague Conference on Private International Law[17]). One may also distinguish between global and regional institutions, in which some countries of the Caucasus and Central Asian region may have the status of a member, an observer or other cooperating partner. Some institutions have a particular focus on the post-Soviet region, notably the CIS[18] and the Eurasian Economic Union.[19] Some institutions address countries of the post-Soviet region in the broader context of transition economies (e.g. the Economic Cooperation Organization [ECO],[20] or the EBRD[21]) or of developing countries (e.g. UNDP[22] or the International Development Law Organisation

---

12   Both within the Eastern Partnership initiative and the more general European Neighbourhood Policy, the EU publishes regular "Progress Reports" on (to a large degree: legal) developments in the relations between partner States and the European Union, which also address issues of procedural law, see <http://eeas.europa.eu/enp/documents/progress-reports/index_en.htm> accessed 22 November 2020. For a general analysis of legal aspects of the European Neighbourhood Policy see Nariné Ghazaryan, *The European Neighbourhood Policy and the Democratic Values of the EU* (Hart 2014) passim.

13   See <www.coe.int/en/web/programmes/central-asia> accessed 22 November 2021.

14   See <https://eeas.europa.eu/regions/central-asia/4936/eu-rule-law-initiative-central-asia_en> accessed 22 November 2021.

15   See <http://web.worldbank.org/WBSITE/EXTERNAL/TOPICS/EXTLAWJUSTINST/0,,contentMDK:23138640~menuPK:1974078~pagePK:210058~piPK:210062~theSitePK:1974062,00.html> accessed 22 November 2021.

16   See, eg <www.ebrd.com/law-in-transition> accessed 22 November 2021.

17   cf <www.hcch.net/en/home> accessed 22 November 2021.

18   cf <www.cis.minsk.by/> accessed 22 November 2020; see also <https://en.wikipedia.org/wiki/Commonwealth_of_Independent_States> accessed 22 November 2021.

19   cf <www.eaeunion.org/?lang=en> accessed 22 November 20211.

20   cf <www.eco.int/> accessed 22 November 2020. Members of this organization are several West, Central and South Asian countries such as Azerbaijan (Caucasus region).

21   <www.ebrd.com/home> accessed 22 November 2021.

22   <www.undp.org/> accessed 22 November 2021.

[IDLO]²³). Rule of law issues play a role in the work of all abovementioned institutions. Although this necessarily requires a certain degree of comparing and measuring the quality of legal systems (including dispute resolution), the number of institutions which have put an express focus on comparing and measuring dispute resolution systems is more limited. Interesting examples can be found in the work of the World Bank, the UNDP, the EBRD and IDLO. The CIS and the Eurasian Economic Union have not yet chosen this as a specific work focus.

3.1.2   Private Organizations with International Focus

Among non-governmental organizations, particular mention must be made of the World Justice Project [WJP], a US-based NGO engaged in multidisciplinary research and practical work with the purpose to improve the rule of law in the world. It regularly publishes the WJP Rule of Law Index, which tries to benchmark the quality of judicial systems all over the world.²⁴ Some other NGOs or businesses deal, to a certain degree, with statistical evaluations of dispute resolutions systems of different countries or regions, for example the Davos World Economic Forum²⁵ or Transparency International.²⁶ Another kind of NGOs are scholarly or legal practitioners' associations, which sometimes lay a particular focus on (comparative) dispute resolution. One example is the International Association of Procedural Law,²⁷ others are the International Judicial Academy,²⁸ the International Association of Judges,²⁹ the World Jurist Association³⁰ or the International Bar Association.³¹ Similar associations can be found on different regional levels including the countries of the Caucasus and Central Asian region. Another approach is NGOs specialising on various legal subjects including procedural issues. For example, INSOL International³² has a particular focus on comparative insolvency law and practice, including

---

23   <www.idlo.int/> accessed 22 November 2021.

24   See <http://worldjusticeproject.org/rule-of-law-index> accessed 22 November 2021.

25   See eg The Global Competitiveness Report 2018, accessible at <http://reports.weforum
       .org/global-competitiveness-report-2018/> accessed 22 November 2021.

26   In general <www.transparency.org/> accessed 22 November 2020; more specifically The
       Global Corruption Perceptions Index, see <https://www.transparency.org/research/cpi/
       overview> accessed 22 November 2021.

27   <www.iaplaw.org/> accessed 22 November 2021.

28   <www.ijaworld.org/> accessed 22 November 2021.

29   <www.iaj-uim.org/> accessed 22 November 2021.

30   <http://worldjurist.org/> accessed 22 November 2021.

31   <www.ibanet.org/> accessed 22 November 2021.

32   <www.insol.org/> accessed 22 November 2021.

an Academics group and a Judicial Group. Some of these groupings have been established within public institutions, such as the International Hague Network of Judges[33] or the European Judicial Network in civil and commercial matters.[34]

3.1.3 State Institutions and Private Organizations

Moving from the international level to the States, evaluation of the quality of dispute resolution is of course to a large degree done in and by the respective States themselves, for example by the structures of ministries of justice or by State statistical organs.[35] These endeavours are sometimes carried through in cooperation with foreign partners. On the German side, for example, the Deutsche Stiftung für internationale rechtliche Zusammenarbeit[36] or the Deutsche Gesellschaft für Internationale Zusammenarbeit [GIZ][37] often function as partners. Such cooperation typically includes comparative approaches. Besides, there are numerous NGOs, academic institutions or even businesses in the countries doing analytical work on the quality of their justice systems.

3.2 *Methods*

There are various methods of analysing the quality of dispute resolution systems. Some of them may give a first impression (but may be misleading or even wrong), others may be very specific and concrete, but may be difficult to compare with other systems in the region. In order to come to sensible results, it is necessary to combine different methods and try to minimize errors. An analysis which should serve as a tool for legislative or administrative recommendations must in any case use the methods of several sciences – in particular legal analysis must be combined with sociological approaches. Some examples for such methods may be mentioned:

a) *Comparative studies of legislation and practice:* This is the classic approach of comparative law. It goes beyond a mere comparison of legislation, but also includes jurisprudence and, if accessible, other legal practices. It does not

---

33 cf <www.hcch.net/en/news-archive/details/?varevent=648> accessed 22 November 2021.

34 <https://e-justice.europa.eu/content_ejn_in_civil_and_commercial_matters-21-en.do> accessed 22 November 2021.

35 For the example of Kazakhstan see <www.kazakhstan-bern.ch/en/?page_id=355>; for Georgia see <http://hcoj.gov.ge/en/reforms/judicial-reform> both accessed 22 November 2021; or Lado Chanturia, *Judicial Reform – The Georgian Experience* (Bakur Sulakauri 2002).

36 <www.irz.de/> accessed 22 November 2021.

37 See, for example, <www.giz.de/de/weltweit/14355.html> accessed 22 November 2021 (project for improving the rule of law in Central Asia); and <www.giz.de/de/weltweit/20313.html> accessed 22 November 2021 (rule of law in the Southern Caucasus).

merely state parallels and differences but endeavors to find underlying values and can make suggestions for future reform in the sense of "minimum standards" or "best practices". In modern comparative law doctrine, it is recognized that comparative law also has to draw on research made in "neighbouring disciplines" such as sociology, history or economics.[38] There are numerous comparative studies (articles, Ph.D. theses, publications on the Internet, etc.) relating to the countries of the region of the Caucasus and Central Asia, some written in Western languages,[39] but also many of them in Russian and to a smaller degree in other languages.

b) *Statistical analyses:* Statistical analyses are very valuable for comparisons, even if they do not propose "rankings". The quality of these analyses depends both on "juridical" and "sociological" aspects. The analyses must be based on solid legal research defining, for example, which issues are particularly important for an analysis. Secondly, the used sociological methods must be very carefully used in order to avoid oversimplified or even wrong conclusions. Presently the best sociological comparative analyses are the biannual "Reports on European Judicial Systems: Efficiency and Quality of Justice" of the Council of Europe's European Commission for the Efficiency of Justice (CEPEJ),[40] The reports are very detailed and become continuously more elaborate. They are published, together with additional materials, on the website of the Council of Europe. The CEPEJ reports deliberately do not establish rankings in order to avoid misunderstandings or, perhaps, political discontent. However, the reader is well enabled to make one's own conclusions. The strength, but at the same time also a certain weakness of the CEPEJ reports, consists in that the data are based exclusively on information given by the national governments, which may sometimes contrast with findings of non-governmental analysts. As the three South Caucasus states are members of the Council of Europe, their legal systems are covered, but the Central Asian States are not.

---

38   cf Mathias Reimann and Reinhard Zimmermann (eds), *The Oxford Handbook of Comparative Law* (OUP 2008) passim.

39   In the first place, mention should be made of law journals or series of monographs specialising on Eastern Europe (for example the series *"Law in Eastern Europe"* (edited by Joseph Marko)), the *Review of Central and East European Law*, the *Journal of Eurasian Law*, in Germany the journals *Wirtschaft und Recht in Osteuropa* [WiRO]; *Osteuropa Recht*; *Kiel Journal of East European Law*; but also more general comparative law journals or journals devoted to procedural law (in English, eg the *International Journal of Procedural Law*; or *the International Judicial Monitor*; in German, eg the *Zeitschrift für Zivilprozess International*).

40   See <www.coe.int/t/dghl/cooperation/cepej/evaluation/default_en.asp> accessed 22 November 2021.

Based on an agreement with CEPEJ, the European Union has gone an important step further and publishes annual "EU Justice Scoreboards",[41] which use, on the one side CEPEJ data, but add other data as well (from internal EU sources, but also from the World Bank, the World Economic Forum and others) and create statistical scoreboards using these data. Thus, the results of the statistical analyses become considerably more conspicuous than the CEPEJ studies. However, the EU scoreboard is limited to EU Member States.

In comparison with the CEPEJ reports and the EU justice scoreboards, other international statistical analyses (or rankings) dealing with the region of the Caucasus and Central Asia are of a more limited quality, although they do have an indicative value. This is true for studies made by the World Bank,[42] but also by private organizations such as the World Justice Project, the World Economic Forum or Transparency International.

c) *Case studies, interviews:* As particular categories of quality analysis, case studies and interviews are worth mentioning. Although they do not necessarily meet scientific standards, they often give fresh and specific information, which can be used to counter-check the more abstract purely legal analyses or statistical analyses.

4   Quality of Dispute Resolution in the Caucasus and Central Asia Region: Some Results from Analyses

As a statistical starter, it is always helpful, at first, to look at ranking lists, published by organizations such as the World Justice Project or the World Economic Forum. It is important to differentiate between the general ranking and the ranking in more specific categories. Also, it is important to scrutinize on which kind of data the ranking is based: on surveys (among which kind and number of persons?) or on objective data, such as length of proceedings, etc.

If one takes as an example the WJP Rule of Law Index,[43] which has a strong focus on procedure, the select overall ranking positions of some countries of the Caucasus-Central Asia region are as follows (numbers of the Index 2019 given first, numbers of the index 2015 following in bracket for comparison): Georgia has position 41 of 126 (2015: 29 of 102; no relative change of

---

41   <https://ec.europa.eu/info/policies/justice-and-fundamental-rights/effective-justice/eu-justice-scoreboard_en> accessed 22 November 2021.

42   For example, in the Doing Business guides or other studies, cf <www.doingbusiness.org/> accessed 22 November 2021.

43   <http://worldjusticeproject.org/rule-of-law-index> accessed 22 November 2021.

ranking), Kazakhstan position 65 of 126 (2015: 65 of 102; relative improvement by two positions), Russia position 88 (2015: 75, relative improvement by six positions), Uzbekistan position 94 (2015: 81, relative improvement by two positions). For comparison: Sweden has position 4 (2015: 3, no relative change of position), Romania position 31 (2015: 32, relative downgrading of two positions), the US position 20 (2015: 18, relative downgrading of 1 position). It shows on the one hand "Western" countries like Sweden or the United States clearly in front, but some "new" EU member States like Romania are not much different in ranking from, e.g. Georgia. On the other hand, Russia and Central Asian countries take positions that are clearly behind. The more specific "civil justice" part of the survey shows similar, but sometimes slightly better results than the general ranking.[44] The WJP index is based on large surveys worldwide of households and experts.[45] The ranking shows that some countries of the Caucasus region come close to some new EU Member States, while Russia and Central Asia lag behind. Another finding is that the position of the civil justice system in the countries of the region is generally somewhat better than the general ranking, which indicates that these countries rank lower in the more "political" parts of the WJP Index.

Similar results are shown in the World Economic Forum's "Global Competitiveness Reports",[46] which are also based on surveys (among executives). Although the focus of these reports is on economics, they include several questions relating to legal matters such as "the efficiency of the legal framework in settling disputes" (1st pillar: Institutions, Question 1.10). Again, the ranking related to this question is interesting: in the 2015–2016 Report, for example, among the Caucasus States, Georgia ranks first at position 54 (of 102), Azerbaijan follows at position 63 and Armenia comes last at position 89. Interestingly, Kazakhstan is given position 48 in this ranking, which is clearly ahead of Azerbaijan and Armenia, but Russia and Kyrgyzstan are again seen

---

44   According to the explanations given in the Index, the topic "civil justice" was split into several questions: 7.1 People can access and afford civil justice; 7.2 Civil justice is free of discrimination; 7.3 Civil justice is free of corruption; 7.4 Civil justice is free of improper government influence; 7.5 Civil justice is not subject to unreasonable delays; 7.6 Civil justice is effectively enforced; 7.7 ADRs are accessible, impartial, and effective.

45   The WJP website states that the Index is based on over 100,000 household and 2,400 expert surveys, <http://worldjusticeproject.org/rule-of-law-index> accessed 22 November 2021. Although these are large numbers, they narrow considerably when one looks at individual countries.

46   Report 2018, <http://reports.weforum.org/global-competitiveness-report-2018/>, for comparison see also the Report 2015–2015, <http://reports.weforum.org/global-competitiveness-report-2015-2016/> both accessed 22 November 2021.

behind (Russia at position 102, Kyrgyzstan at 113). For comparison: France ranks here at position 28. This index shows that some Central Asian States are ahead of some Caucasus countries, and Georgia is again seen at the best place in this context.

Although the CEPEJ reports are less easily "readable" than the aforementioned rankings, they give more "objective" information, which can be used directly for legal reforms. The same is true for some other specific reports on the legal situation and reforms in some countries of the region, for example various studies of the World Bank.[47] Particularly interesting is the joint EU-Council of Europe programme "Enhancing Judicial Reform of the Eastern Partnership Countries", which focuses on the Eastern Partnership region as a whole, moving away from bilateral projects (with individual countries) to a subregional approach.[48] This approach is very reasonable as challenges to the justice systems, e.g. in the three countries of the Caucasus region, share many similarities, which can sometimes be efficiently addressed together. However, this does not mean that civil justice systems in the Central Asian countries and in Russia are fundamentally different from the Caucasus subregion. Depending on the specific topic and political will, it can be advisable to analyse and compare dispute resolution systems, not only in the subregional context (Caucasus or Central Asia), but in a broader post-Soviet perspective.

5 Conclusion: Which Steps Forward?

In summation, one can state that the dispute resolution system in civil and commercial matters in Georgia has received, in several surveys, the best grades, while Azerbaijan and (even more so) Armenia are seen behind but still in front of Russia and the Central Asian countries. In general, more attention is given, and more support is granted, by European institutions to the Caucasus countries (as parties to the EU Eastern Partnership initiative and members of the Council of Europe) than to the Central Asian countries[49]. This is apparently based on the political considerations of a "close neighbourhood", but it should not lead to neglect of relations with the Central Asian countries. From

---

47 cf <www.worldbank.org/en/region/eca/brief/justice> accessed 22 November 2021.
48 See <https://rm.coe.int/eastern-partnership-enhancing-judicial-reform-in-the-eastern-partnersh/1680788f3e> and <www.coe.int/en/web/cepej/cooperation-programmes/enhancing-judicial-reform-in-the-republic-of-moldova> both accessed 22 November 2021.
49 The particular case of Russia, which exited and was excluded from the Council of Europe in 2022, after the finalization of this chapter, cannot be dealt with here.

the perspective of dispute resolution in civil and commercial matters, the challenges in the Caucasus countries, the Central Asian countries and Russia are very similar and should, at least in some projects, be addressed together.

One possible step is certainly *legislative improvements* on the basis of comparative studies, also using experience gained in global or European fora such as the World Justice Project, the International Association of Procedural Law, the International Judicial Academy and, in particular, the Council of Europe's CEPEJ in cooperation with the European Union. Legislative reforms are a long-lasting journey; in order to make them a success, a combination of long-term vision and step-by-step approaches is necessary. In this context, mutual information and discussion about reform steps in the region should be encouraged.

A second important part of future improvement is *strengthening professional and civic education* in the field of dispute resolution. This relates, both to university education and to advanced vocational training for judges and other justice-related personnel.

A third important element of a reform policy in this field would be steps to influence *informal practices* in the dispute resolution system. This area has received considerably less attention than reforms of "formal" law texts and requires systematic cooperation between lawyers and other disciplines. Not all informal practices are negative, but some are, and they must be addressed, if legal reforms are expected to be successful.

CHAPTER 23

Emerging Trends of Recognition and Enforcement of Foreign Judgments and Arbitral Awards Issued in Economic Disputes in the Russian Federation

Vladislav Starzhenetskiy

An analysis of the practice of Russian commercial (arbitrazh) courts in economic disputes shows that in recent years the number of applications for recognition and enforcement of foreign judgments and arbitral awards has significantly increased.[1] This can be explained by the intensification of cross-border relations with participation of Russian companies, the proliferation of various offshore business schemes and the efforts of Russian companies to enter international markets. All of this inevitably entails an expansion of dispute resolution between businesses beyond the territory of the Russian Federation, and such disputes are now more frequently decided in foreign courts or international arbitration.

One may also observe that the Russian commercial courts have by now acquired sufficient experience to make it possible to state that they are developing or even have developed established approaches, which will define the resolution of analogous cases in the future, creating a reasonable level of legal certainty.

Contrary to a view, which can often be heard, that the Russian legal system is opposed to and biased against the recognition and enforcement of foreign judgments and that Russian judges are "favouring" Russian businesses, a closer look at court practice in this category of cases reveals a different picture. According to official statistics the majority of applications for recognition and enforcement of foreign judgements and arbitral awards are granted by Russian commercial (arbitrazh) courts. The success rate amounted to 70.7% in 2014, 66% in 2015 and 67.9% in 2016.[2] With regard to recognition and enforcement

---

1   The number of applications for recognition and enforcement of foreign judgments and arbitral awards amounted to 88 in 2009, 179 in 2012, 158 in 2013, 181 in 2014, 212 in 2015 and 231 in 2016 <www.consultant.ru/> accessed 20 November 2021.

2   See <www.consultant.ru/> accessed 20 November 2021. Judicial statistics are also available on the website of the Judicial Department at the Supreme Court of the Russian Federation <www.cdep.ru/index.php?id=79> accessed 20 November 2021.

© KONINKLIJKE BRILL NV, LEIDEN, 2023 | DOI:10.1163/9789004357839_025

of foreign arbitral awards, the success rate is even higher (95% in 2016, 80% in 2017)[3]

Given that the Russian legal system lacks the vast and longstanding experience of most Western European countries with regard to regulating relations and resolving disputes with foreign companies – only since the late 1990s have Russian courts begun to face a growing amount of such disputes with applicable foreign law, foreign judgments and arbitral awards –, it is understandable that the approach of Russian courts to such cases can be characterized as rather "cautious". Judges deciding such disputes are often still in the situation to be the first ones in Russian jurisprudence who have to formulate an approach to the application and interpretation of the relevant provisions of Russian law and international law in specific cases. Therefore, a cautious approach appears to be quite natural. The challenges and risks associated with the recognition and enforcement of foreign judgments in Russia need to be comprehended, discussed and balanced with the benefits and advantages of the regime of reciprocal recognition and enforcement of foreign judgments in various jurisdictions, and must also be compatible with the fundamentals of the Russian legal framework. One may expect that with the accumulation of relevant experience, the further development of the Russian legal system and the continuing growth of cross-border relations involving Russian companies, the approach of the Russian courts towards the recognition and enforcement of foreign judgments and arbitral awards will gradually become uniform with the approaches common in the Member States of the European Union as well as with general international practices.

Several issues can be mentioned as provoking the most heated discussions in Russian academia and creating the majority of difficulties in court practice. These are the following: 1) the applicability of the principle of reciprocity in the absence of an international treaty regulating the reciprocal recognition and enforcement of foreign judgments; 2) the assessment of whether the exclusive jurisdiction of Russian courts is violated by foreign courts deciding certain disputes; 3) the standards of due notification of Russian parties about litigation pending abroad; and 4) the interpretation of the public policy clause by Russian courts.

All these issues directly affect the possibility of recognition and subsequent enforcement of a foreign judgment in Russia under the Russian procedural

---

3   See <https://arbitration.ru/upload/medialibrary/91b/RAA-STUDY-RECOGNITION-ENFO RCEMENT-AWARDS-NY-CONVENTION-2018_eng.pdf> accessed 20 November 2021.

codes (Chapter 31 of the Russian Code of Commercial [Arbitrazh] Procedure[4] and Chapter 45 of the Russian Code of Civil Procedure[5]), and the decision in the case depends on how they are answered. It is not infrequent that defendants rely on these arguments as grounds for refusal of recognition and enforcement. In the following the evolving Russian court practice on these issues will be analysed.

1   The Principle of Reciprocity

There are no treaties on reciprocal recognition and enforcement of foreign judgments between the Russian Federation and a significant number of its key trade partners (including Germany, the Netherlands, the United Kingdom, Japan, South Korea, Finland, and others).[6] At the same time, the Russian procedural codes provide that the existence of such treaties is the key factor that makes the recognition and enforcement of a foreign judgment possible.

1.2   *Legislative Provisions*
Thus, Article 241 of the Russian Code of Commercial [Arbitrazh] Procedure reads:

> Decisions of foreign courts, rendered in disputes and other cases arising in the course of entrepreneurial and other economic activity (foreign courts), awards of arbitral tribunals international commercial arbitration courts, adopted in the territory of foreign states in disputes and other cases arising in the course of entrepreneurial and other economic activity (foreign arbitral awards), are recognized and enforced in the Russian Federation by commercial courts, *if the recognition and enforcement of such judgments is stipulated in an international treaty of the Russian Federation* and in a federal law.

---

4 The text of the Arbitrazh Procedure Code (of 2002 with later amendments) is available at <www.consultant.ru/document/cons_doc_LAW_37800/> accessed 20 November 2021.
5 The text of the Civil Procedure Code (of 2002 with later amendments) is available at <www .consultant.ru/document/cons_doc_LAW_39570/> accessed 20 November 2021.
6 This issue is primarily relevant for the judgments rendered by state courts. Awards in international commercial arbitration can be recognized and enforced in Russia under the 1958 New York Convention.

An analogous rule can be found in Article 409 of the Russian Code of Civil Procedure:

> The decisions of foreign courts, including decisions on the approval of amicable settlement agreements, shall be recognized and enforced in the Russian Federation, *if this is stipulated in an international treaty of the Russian Federation.*

The wording of these provisions provides no clear answer to the question of what should be done when there is no international treaty with the foreign State. Is the absence of a specific international treaty on recognition and enforcement of foreign judgments fatal? Or can its absence be compensated by the principle of reciprocity or comity?

Such discussions are rooted in the express provision of Article 1 point 6 of the Law "On Insolvency (Bankruptcy)",[7] which states that in the absence of international treaties of the Russian Federation, foreign judgments in insolvency (bankruptcy) cases shall be recognized in the territory of the Russian Federation based on the principle of reciprocity. Russian scholars have long debated on whether foreign judgments may be recognized in Russia based on the principle of reciprocity or comity.[8]

1.3 Court Practice

In this situation the practice of the Russian commercial (arbitrazh) courts, which suggested their own interpretation of the above-cited provisions of Russian procedural law, achieves particular importance.

---

7 The text of the law is available at <www.consultant.ru/document/cons_doc_LAW_39331/> accessed 20 November 2021.

8 T.N. Neshatayeva, 'The Court and General Principles and Rules of International Law' (in Russian) (2004) Bulletin of the Supreme Arbitrazh (Commercial) Court of the Russian Federation, Issue 3; A.I. Muranov, *International Treaty and Reciprocity as Grounds for the Recognition and Enforcement of Foreign Judgments in Russia* (in Russian) (2003) passim; N.I. Marysheva, 'Certain Matters of Recognition and Enforcement of Foreign Judgments in Russia' (in Russian) (2006) Journal of Russian Law 12; N.G. Yeliseev, 'International Comity as the Premise for Enforcement of Foreign Judgments' (in Russian) (2006) Russian Law 2006 77; V.V. Yarkov, 'Proceedings in Cases on the Recognition and Enforcement of Foreign Judgments and Arbitral Awards: A Brief Commentary to Chapter 31 of the Russian Arbitrazh Procedure Code' (in Russian) (2003) Commercial and Civil Procedure 9; R.V. Zaitsev (ed), *Recognition and Enforcement of Foreign Judicial Acts* (in Russian), (2007) passim.

1.3.1   Dominant Practice of Arbitrazh Courts

The approach of the arbitrazh (commercial) courts can be summarized as follows:

First, the provisions of Article 241 of the Russian Code of Arbitrazh Procedure do not contain an absolute prohibition of recognizing and enforcing a foreign judgment in the absence of a respective international treaty between the Russian Federation and a foreign jurisdiction. In such cases it is necessary to take into account the principles of comity and reciprocity, which are an integral part of the Russian legal system.

Second, when assessing whether a foreign judgment may be recognized and enforced, Article 241 of the Russian Code of Arbitrazh Procedure should be interpreted broadly: any international agreement between the Russian Federation and the foreign State governing cooperation in the legal and judicial spheres, reciprocal respect for the right to fair trial may serve as such a treaty.

Third, in the absence of specific provisions of an international treaty regulating the conditions for recognition and enforcement and the grounds for refusal of recognition and enforcement of a foreign judgment, the provisions of Chapter 31 of the Russian Code of Arbitrazh Procedure shall apply.

Below are several examples illustrating this approach.[9]

The most famous and frequently cited case on reciprocity (Case No. A40-56571/12-141-521, judgment of the Supreme Arbitrazh Court of the Russian Federation No. 6004/13 of 8 October 2013[10]) concerned the recognition in the territory of the Russian Federation of a judgment of the High Court of Justice in Northern Ireland invalidating a chain of transactions (assignment agreements and addenda thereto) made between foreign companies – Demesne and Galfis – since they were aimed at siphoning assets from the reach of the creditors and were detrimental to the interests of such creditors. The aforesaid judgment then needed to be recognized in Russia due to pending proceedings regarding the assets in dispute.

The Presidium of the Supreme Arbitrazh Court of the Russian Federation affirmatively answered the question of whether a Northern Irish judgment may in principle be recognised in Russia. The Court noted that the Russian Federation and the United Kingdom were both parties to the 2003 UN

9   All judgments mentioned below can be found in the database "Consultant Plus" <www .consultant.ru/> accessed 20 November 2021.

10   See <www.consultant.ru/cons/cgi/online.cgi?req=doc&base=ARB&n=371592#066590 22225763012> accessed 20 November 2021.

Convention against Corruption,[11] which obliged them to assist each other in implementing measures aimed at a more efficient prevention and combatting of corruption in the private sector (Article 12 of the Convention). This includes declaring contracts made under the influence of corruption-related factors invalid (Article 34 of the Convention). Accordingly, recognizing in Russia a foreign judicial act invalidating a transaction that was knowingly disadvantageous for one of the parties and was made in violation of the rules on conflict of interest, would be regarded as Russia's performance of its international obligations, in particular the principle of cooperation between judicial and enforcement authorities as well as financial regulators for the purposes of combatting money laundering envisaged in Article 14 (5) of the Convention against Corruption.

Other international treaties that set out the basic conditions for cooperation of States in the legal and judicial spheres, as well as guaranteeing the right to have judicial acts enforced within a reasonable time, were also listed by the Supreme Arbitrazh Court among the legal grounds for recognition of the aforementioned foreign judgment. These included

- the 1994 Agreement on Partnership and Cooperation Establishing a Partnership between the Russian Federation, the European Communities and their Member States,[12] obliging the Contracting Parties to ensure that natural and legal persons of the other party have access free of discrimination in relation to their own nationals to the competent courts and administrative organs of the parties to defend their individual rights and their property rights (Article 98 (1));
- Article 11 of the 1992 Agreement between the Government of the Russian Federation and the Government of the United Kingdom of Great Britain and Northern Ireland on economic cooperation,[13] that extends national treatment to individuals and legal entities of each of the countries as regards access to and procedure of all courts and administrative bodies in the territory of the other country as plaintiffs, defendants or otherwise in connection with commercial deals;

---

11   <www.unodc.org/documents/brussels/UN_CONVENTION_AGAINST_CORRUPTION.pdf> accessed 20 November 2021.
12   The text of this Agreement is available at <https://eur-lex.europa.eu/legal-content/EN/TXT/?uri=celex:21997A1128(01)> accessed 20 November 2021.
13   The text of this Agreement is available at <www.rusemb.org.uk/relations/12> accessed 20 November 20211.

– Article 6 of the 1950 European Convention on Human Rights,[14] which guarantees individuals the right to fair trial comprising the right to have a judgment enforced as one of its integral elements.

A similar logic was employed by commercial (arbitrazh) courts in other cases on recognition and enforcement of foreign judgments. For instance, a judgment of the Federal Arbitrazh Court of the Moscow District of 2 March 2006 in the Case No. A40-53839/05-8-388 recognized and enforced (like the first instance court) a decision of the High Court of England and Wales in one of the Yukos disputes. Another judgment (Case No. A56-68674/2012) recognized and enforced a court order issued on 7 May 2012 by the commercial division of the Supreme Court of the British Virgin Islands (part of the Eastern Caribbean Supreme Court). The judgment in Case No. A40-59094/2013 recognized and enforced in Russia judicial acts of the Court of first instance of Antwerp (Belgium). The judgment in Case No. A40-153603/13 recognized and enforced in Russia a summary judgment of the High Court of England and Whales – Queen's Bench Division dated 30 April 2013. Other examples of such jurisprudence might be quoted.

1.3.2   Present Situation and Future

Can one consider the court practice on this matter definitively formed? Alas, an affirmative answer to this question cannot be given at present for a number of reasons.

First of all, the practice of the commercial courts themselves is not entirely homogenous. Thus, there have been cases where courts refused to recognize and enforce foreign judgments in the absence of international treaties. Examples are the decisions of the Federal Commercial Court of the Moscow District in Case No. A40-73830/06-25-349 dated 14 February 2008 and in Case No. A40-7480/08-68-127 dated 17 February 2009, where the court refused to enforce judicial acts of Israel and the U.S.

Second, after the merger of the two Russian Supreme Courts – the Supreme Commercial [Arbitrazh] Court of the Russian Federation and the Supreme Court of the Russian Federation, which was carried out in 2014[15] – it is the now the view of the united Supreme Court of the Russian Federation that will be decisive. However, neither the Plenum nor the Presidium of the Court have as yet spoken on the matter. In the long run, the Court may eventually support the rather progressive approach of the commercial courts, but it might equally

---

14   See <www.echr.coe.int/Documents/Convention_ENG.pdf> accessed 20 November 2021.

15   See <https://ru.wikipedia.org/wiki/Высший_арбитражный_суд_Российской _Федерации> accessed 20 November 2021.

take the more conservative and prudent approach of the courts of general jurisdiction. Another possibility would be a procedural dualism retaining the progressive approach for business and commercial cases and the conservative one for all other cases.[16]

Prior to the reform of the two Supreme Courts both approaches could be found in the Supreme Court's practice. Thus, in its 7 June 2002 Ruling in Case No. 5-Go2-64 on the recognition and enforcement of a judgment of the Supreme Court of the United Kingdom, the panel of judges of the Supreme Court of the Russian Federation formulated a legal approach, pursuant to which the application for recognition and enforcement of a foreign judgment may be granted by the competent Russian court even without a relevant international treaty, if the courts of the foreign State reciprocally recognize judgments of Russian courts. Another approach that can, however, be regarded as dominant in the practice of the courts of general jurisdiction conversely attests to the impossibility of recognition and enforcement of foreign judgments in the absence of an international treaty (see, in particular, Ruling of the Supreme Court of the Russian Federation No. 4-Go9-27 dated 1 December 2009 on the refusal to recognize and enforce a judgment of a German court, as well as the Overview of Court Practice of the Supreme Court of the Russian Federation for the first quarter of 2013 on the refusal to recognize a Swiss court judgment).

Third, another important factor may also be seen in the position of the Constitutional Court of the Russian Federation, which has found in its Ruling No. 890-O of 17 June 2013 "On the Refusal to Admit the Complaint of Mr. Sergey Mikhailovich Nazarov Concerning the Violation of His Constitutional Rights by Article 409 Part 1of the Civil Procedure Code of the Russian Federation",[17] that the refusal to recognize and enforce a foreign judgment (in casu the judgment of a Finnish court) due to the absence of a respective international treaty was not to be viewed as a violation of the applicant's constitutional rights and was fully in compliance with Article 6 (3) of the Federal Constitutional Law of 31 December 1996 "On the Judicial System of the Russian Federation".

---

16   Evidence of that may be found in the case law of the Russian courts in 2014–2017. For example, in the case A40-34719/14-69-300 arbitrazh (commercial) courts and the commercial bench of the Supreme Court (decision of 1 February 2016, N.305-C15-18289) ruled in favour of recognition and enforcement of a judgment of the High Court of England and Wales relying on reciprocity principle. However, the Moscow City Court denied such a possibility in a case concerning the recognition of a Swiss judgement in a family dispute (Appeals Decision of 27 July 2016, N.33-24441).

17   See <https://base.garant.ru/70407300/> accessed 20 November 2021.

2 Exclusive Competence of Russian Courts

Another legal issue that has increasingly appeared in Russian court practice concerns the interpretation of exclusive competences of Russian courts. According to Article 244 of the Russian Code of Arbitrazh Procedure, a commercial (arbitrazh) court shall refuse to recognize and enforce a foreign judgment if the dispute falls within the exclusive competence of Russian courts.

Article 248 of the Russian Code of Arbitrazh Procedure provides for a rather impressive list of cases within the exclusive competence of commercial courts in the Russian Federation:

1) cases concerning state property of the Russian Federation, including disputes concerning the privatisation of state property and eminent domain;

2) cases concerning real property or the rights thereto as their subject matter, if such property is located in the territory of the Russian Federation;

3) cases concerning the registration or issuance of patents, certificates to trademarks, industrial designs and utility models, or the registration of other rights to intellectual property, which require registration or issuance of a patent or a certificate in the Russian Federation;

4) cases concerning the invalidation of entries in public registers (books of records, cadastres), made by a competent body of the Russian Federation keeping such the respective register (book of records, cadastre);

5) cases concerning the creation, liquidation or registration of legal entities and individual entrepreneurs in the territory of the Russian Federation, as well as challenges of the decisions of the bodies of such legal entities;

6) cases arising out of administrative or other public law disputes (tax, customs cases, cases on the challenging of normative legal acts, etc.);

7) under Article 249 of the Russian Code of Arbitrazh Procedure, cases with respect to which the parties have entered into a choice of court agreement providing for the trial of the case in a commercial (arbitrazh) court.

Due to such a broad list, the assessment of risks – which may emerge at the stage of recognition and enforcement of foreign judgments – is not an easy task. One must admit that there is no absolute legal certainty in this matter.

2.1 *Relationship between Exclusive Competence and Arbitrability*
A first question is whether the provisions of Article 248 of the Russian Arbitrazh (Commercial) Procedure Code on exclusive international competence should be interpreted as mandatory for international commercial arbitration as well. The fact that Article 248 of the Russian Arbitrazh (Commercial) Procedure Code applies to the recognition and enforcement of judgments by foreign

State courts does not give rise to disputes. However, it is controversial whether this provision also applies to international arbitral awards. In its Resolution No. 10-P of 26 May 2011 'In the Case Concerning the Verification of Consistency with the Constitution Article 11 point 1 of the Russian Civil Code, Article 1 point 2 of the Federal Law "On Arbitration Tribunals in the Russian Federation", Article 28 of the Federal Law "On State Registration of Rights to Real Property and Transactions Therewith", Article 33 point 1 and Article 51 of the Federal Law "On Mortgage (Charge of Real Property)"' the Constitutional Court of the Russian Federation has noted that Article 248 of the Russian Arbitrazh Procedure Code is aimed at delimiting the competence of state courts of various countries to examine cross-border disputes. Construing it as establishing an exclusive competence of state courts versus arbitration, i.e. precluding the possibility of referring such disputes to arbitration, is not justified as the institute of exclusive jurisdiction between state courts and is not meant to prevent parties from using methods of alternative dispute resolution under the general rules of law applicable to such methods.

This interpretation of Article 248 of the Russian Arbitrazh Procedure Code by the Constitutional Court of the Russian Federation may be viewed as narrowing the scope of application of rules of exclusive international competence. Nevertheless, the discussion of whether disputes listed in Article 248 of the Russian Code of Arbitrazh Procedure may be referred to international commercial arbitration, with subsequent recognition and enforcement of the respective awards in Russia, is continuing.[18] Within the 2015 reform of Russian arbitration legislation[19] certain disputes were expressly made arbitrable (e.g. disputes concerning real property, some corporate disputes) and parties now may refer them to arbitration. However, this does not yet mean that parties are free to conclude choice of court agreements concerning such cases.[20]

2.2   *Specific Aspects of Article 248 of the Arbitrazh Procedure Code*
The second question concerns the scope of issues falling under Article 248 of the Arbitrazh (Commercial) Procedure Code. At present, the key difficulties are focused on cases concerning rights to real property. The Russian Supreme

---

18   See for more details Ye. A. Kudelich, 'Arbitrability: Searching for Balance between Private Autonomy and Public Order' (in Russian), (2014) Zakon 94–111.

19   See eg <https://journal.arbitration.ru/upload/iblock/ddb/Arbitration.ru_2_2_October_2 018.pdf> accessed 20 November 2021.

20   The Russian Supreme Court seems to preclude such a possibility. See para 7 of the Order of the Plenum of the Supreme Court N.23, of 27 June 2017 "On Resolution of Economic Disputes with Foreign Element by Commercial Courts".

Court clarified the scope of *in rem* disputes in paragraph 5 of its Plenary Order No.23 of June 27, 2017 "On the Resolution of Economic Disputes with a Foreign Element by Arbitrazh Courts". In the long run, given the current tendencies in the sphere of international civil procedure, problems may also arise with respect to corporate disputes,[21] disputes concerning the validity of Russian patents, trademarks, disputes concerning state property (state procurement, the effects of privatisation, cultural property and displaced art), and private law disputes arising out of public law relations (antimonopoly laws, combatting of corruption, fraud, etc.).

3 Due Notification Standards

Almost in every second case related to the recognition and enforcement of foreign judgments in Russia the debtor argues that he has not been duly notified of the litigation or arbitration. It is well known that a failure of due notification undermines the judicial act and serves as one of the main grounds for a refusal of recognition and enforcement of foreign judgments under Russian law.

What is meant by "due notification" of a Russian natural person or entity and how it should be effected? This exact question was analysed by the Presidium of the Supreme Arbitrazh Court of the Russian Federation in its Resolution No. 3366/13 of 28 January 2014 in Case No. A40-88300/11-141-741. The case concerned an action for the recovery of debts and interest arising out of a default under a distributor agreement, initiated against a Russian company in an English court. The English court issued an order granting the claimants the right to ensure that the debtor is notified of the action and delivered the claim form. Subsequently, the claim form (the notification) was sent to the

---

21 Russian courts have received some guidance for interpretation of art 248 of the Arbitrazh Procedure Code as to corporate disputes eg by the Resolution of the Presidium of the Supreme Arbitrazh Court No 7805/12 of 23 October 2012. This case concerned the recognition and enforcement in Russia of a decision of the District Court of Limassol (Cyprus) of 7 July 2011 where the Cyprus court invalidated a permit (in the form of a resolution of an extraordinary general participants' meeting) issued by a Russian company to its Russian subsidiary for the sale of a share in the capital of another Russian company. The Presidium concluded that the Cyprus court examined an issue related to the challenging of a decision of the management body of a Russian legal entity that falls within the exclusive competence of Russian commercial courts and therefore refused to recognize such a judgment in Russia. It seems that this approach of the supreme judicial instance was aimed against "long arm statutes" and shows that all disputes related to the challenging or invalidation of decisions made by bodies of Russian legal entities, shall be tried in Russian courts.

defendant by registered mail with declared value and a list of enclosures by the
DHL courier service at the address of registration of the acting executive body
of the company and was received by an employee of the company. Deeming
the notification of the Russian entity to have been made, the English court
issued a summary judgment. The claimants then filed an application in a
Russian court for the recognition and enforcement of the judgment in Russia.

Objecting to the recognition and enforcement of the English judgment
in the territory of the Russian Federation, the defendant did not deny that it
received the documents from the claimants and agreed that it was aware of
the proceedings pending against it, but believed that the notification of the
litigation sent to it was undue, since it did not conform to the requirements of
the Hague Convention of 15 November 1965, given the declarations made at the
time when the Russian Federation acceded thereto. The Presidium was faced
with the choice between two potential notification standards – effective notification (where it is sufficient to make sure that the foreign court took measures
required by the procedural rules of its country to notify the litigating party, and
where the litigating party de facto knew or could not have not known about
the litigation pending against it) or formal notification (where it is necessary
to comply with the formal requirements of due notification under the international treaties on mutual legal assistance in effect). The Court chose the second option. Given that both the United Kingdom and Russia are parties to the
Hague Convention of 15 November 1965 on the Service Abroad of Judicial and
Extrajudicial Documents,[22] under Articles 2 and 3 of that Convention the service of judicial documents had to be carried out by forwarding by the authority
or judicial officer of the State of origin of a request to serve the documents to
the Central Authority of the addressee State, which is authorized to receive
such requests. Further service of the judicial documents to an addressee in
Russia had to be then to be carried out by the Russian judicial authorities.

Thus, the notification of the litigation sent to the defendant was declared
undue, since it did not conform to the 1965 Hague Convention, the Russian
Federation having declared that documents meant to be served in its territory
could be accepted only if made in Russian or accompanied by a translation
into Russian and only if the annexed forms of request and confirmation of service were complied with. Service of documents by means specified in Article
10 of the Convention, including direct posting of the documents, is thus prohibited in the Russian Federation. The Court also noted that the operation of

---

22   See <www.hcch.net/en/instruments/conventions/full-text/?cid=17> accessed 20 November 2021.

such a notification procedure could not be excluded by virtue of the fact that the Russian entity had concluded a foreign economic contract referring to foreign law and the jurisdiction of the courts of another country.

Thus the Court has formulated a legal approach, pursuant to which the notifications of litigation sent in violation of the rules of an international treaty of the Russian Federation, which provides for sovereign guarantees of protection to persons under its jurisdiction and in its territory, cannot be regarded as due notification and shall not create any adverse legal consequences for the recipients related to their failure to take part in the proceedings. Exceptions include cases where the party receiving an undue notification still takes part in the proceedings, including by pleading before the foreign court. In this case, such a party loses the right to rely on the defence of not being duly notified of the litigation.[23]

It should be noted that Russian courts have been at all times careful when assessing whether the formal notification requirements have been complied with or not. Thus, there was a case (Ruling of the Supreme Court of the Russian Federation No. 46-G09-14 of 18 August 2009) where a Lithuanian court notified a Russian party of the time and venue of a hearing by way of serving procedural documents via a public announcement in the press. However, at the stage of recognition and enforcement of the Lithuanian judgment in Russia such a notification was found to be improper since the plaintiff failed to provide the Russian court with evidence confirming, beyond reasonable doubt, that the debtor was at least once delivered the summons to the Lithuanian court at his residence, against his signature and in a timely manner.

The legal approach of the Presidium in Resolution No. 3366/13 of 28 January 2014 has been further elaborated in subsequent court practice.

In the Case No. A07-16859/2013 on recognition and enforcement of a judgment of the High Court of England and Wales, the commercial (arbitrazh) courts clarified that where a person unreasonably evades receiving the notification sent in accordance with the procedure envisaged in the 1965 Hague Convention and when there is proof that other means of notifying the defendant of the proceedings (courier service, email) with a translation into Russian have been used, the notification will be deemed proper. This finding was upheld by the Supreme Court of the Russian Federation (Ruling No. 309-ES14-69 dated 18 August 2014).

---

23   See, for example, the judgment of the Moscow Circuit Arbitrazh Court of 25 January 2017, Case No. A40-140062/16; para 36 of the Order of the Plenum of the Supreme Court No. 23 of 27 June 2017 "On Resolution of Economic Disputes with Foreign Element by Arbitrazh Courts".

In another Case No. A40-153603/13 the courts pointed out that the debtor's failure to provide the counterparty with information on its residence entails the debtor's assuming all the risks related to non-receipt or untimely receipt of legally relevant correspondence. In such a case, the notification of the debtor at its last known residence address will be deemed due. This conclusion was supported by the Supreme Court of the Russian Federation (Ruling No. 305-ES14-3869 dated 29 October 2014).

Apart from the violation of requirements to the procedure of sending judicial notices, the undue nature of the notification can also follow from the untimeliness of notification, insufficient time to present the defence, as well as the violation of requirements to document translations.[24] One should make the reservation, however, that the form of due notification in arbitration is less formalized than in state courts and should be analysed subject to the rules and procedures which the parties have consented to when they signed the arbitration agreement (in particular, subject to the rules of the respective permanent arbitration tribunal).

4   Public Policy

The issue of application of the public policy clause by Russian courts has long been the subject of a fierce debate in Russian doctrine and jurisprudence.[25] Scholars have often opined that the Russian courts engaged in an exceedingly broad interpretation of this protective clause of Russian law and unreasonably refused to recognize and enforce foreign judgments.[26] However, since the Presidium of the Supreme Arbitrazh (Commercial) Court of the Russian Federation has adopted the Information Letter No. 156 of 26 February 2013 "Overview of Practice of Examination by Commercial Courts of Cases on the Application of the Public Policy Clause as a Ground for the Refusal to Recognize and Enforce Foreign Judgments and Arbitral Awards", it has become

---

24   See eg, the Ruling of the Supreme Arbitrazh Court of the Russian Federation No. VAS-11330-12 of 28 August 2012 in the Case No. A67-487/2012, the Ruling of the Supreme Arbitrazh Court of the Russian Federation No. VAS-5137/12 of 4 June 2012 in the Case No. A40-62226/11-50-520, and the Resolution of the Federal Arbitrazh Court of the Urals District dated 3 June 2013 in the Case No. A07-19251/2012.

25   For an overview of the evolution of the Russian doctrine and jurisprudence on this matter, see Yu.G. Bogatina, *The Public Policy Clause in Private International Law: Issues of Theory and Modern Practice* (in Russian), (Statut 2010), passim.

26   See, specifically, B.R. Karabel'nikov, *International Commercial Arbitration* (in Russian), (2012) 352–401.

possible to form a uniform approach to the definition of public policy and to demonstrate which particular situations can trigger the clause.

The first paragraph of the Court's "Overview" contains the definition of the public policy clause to be applied in cases on recognition and enforcement of foreign judgments and arbitral awards:

> Public policy... means the fundamental legal bases (principles) of the highest mandatory and universal nature, as well as of special importance for the society and the public, which make the foundation of the economic, political and legal system of the State. These fundamentals include, in particular, the prohibition of actions expressly excluded by super-imperative[27] rules of the Russian legislation (Article 1192 of the Russian Civil Code), if such actions are detrimental to the State's sovereignty or security, affect the interests of large social groups or violate constitutional rights and freedoms of private individuals.

As we can see, this definition sets quite a high threshold for what can be regarded as a violation of public policy. Not just any breach of an imperative rule of Russian law may constitute such a violation, but only a violation which by virtue of its special social importance strikes at the very legal foundations of the Russian State. In addition, the violation should not be abstract, but has to have consequences (real or potential) in the form of detriment to the sovereignty or security of the State, damage to the interests of large social groups or constitutional rights and freedoms.

Which violations can fall under this definition? The "Overview" supplies an answer to this question as well. Paragraph 2 of the Overview discusses the example of an arbitral award legalizing acts of corruption. The rules on combating corruption, fraud or other criminal offenses may belong to the category of the public policy. Paragraph 6 of the Overview implies that public policy is also violated by an award of punitive damages subject to the following conditions: if the amount of such damages is so abnormally high that it exceeds the amount the parties could have reasonably anticipated when they concluded the contract; if the negotiations concerning the amount of such damages in the contract showed clear signs of abuse of the freedom of contract (by way of exploiting the weak bargaining power of the debtor, violation of public interests or the interests of third parties, etc.). Another example, which might

---

27   In the terminology of art 9 of the EU's Rome 1 Regulation: "overriding mandatory provisions".

involve a potential violation of the public policy, is mentioned in paragraphs 11 to 12 of the Overview and relates to fundamental procedural violations (in particular, the arbitral tribunal's incapability to ensure compliance with the guarantees of independence and impartiality of the arbitrators, or the award having been issued by an arbitrator who, in view of his office or powers, was capable of influencing the actions of one of the parties).

Perhaps even more valuable are the provisions of the Overview, which describe examples of erroneous references by the parties and courts to public policy violations. According to the Overview, the examples include cases where:

– Russian law lacks rules analogous to the rules of the foreign law that had been applied (paragraph 5 of the Overview), a fact that in itself simply cannot violate the public policy;
– the damages awarded under the foreign judgment exceed the amount of the real losses or lost gain of the debtor, provided that such excess does not constitute punitive damages (paragraph 6 of the Overview);
– the foreign court obliges Russian persons and entities as parties to the litigation to post a security for costs as a condition for the appeal (paragraph 7 of the Overview);
– there is evidence of incompliance by the foreign legal entity with the procedure for the approval of major transactions provided for in its national laws (paragraph 8 of the Overview);
– the spouse of the debtor, who subsequently asserts a violation of the joint ownership regime of the spouses, is not called to take part in the judicial or arbitral proceedings (paragraph 9 of the Overview);
– the foreign judgment contains typographical errors that do not affect its content and meaning (paragraph 10 of the Overview).

The Overview also sets out a mechanism of assessment by courts of potential violations of public policy: the public policy clause shall not be used for a revision of already issued judgments on the merits (paragraph 1 of the Overview); the court shall on its own initiative verify whether the foreign judgment complies with Russian public policy (paragraph 2 of the Overview); the party asserting a violation of the public policy must substantiate its arguments and present the necessary evidence in support of its case (paragraph 3 of the Overview); and in that case the arguments shall not substitute other special grounds (e.g. undue notification) for the refusal to recognize and enforce foreign judgments (paragraph 4 of the Overview). In general, it can be concluded that the Overview is aimed at a restrictive interpretation of the notion of public policy, and that the approaches set out therein are consistent with international standards.

CHAPTER 24

Some Remarks on International Commercial Arbitration in the Region of the Caucasus and Central Asia

Alexander Trunk

Generally speaking, it can be stated that international commercial arbitration has experienced an enormous upswing in many – though not all – countries of the Eurasian region since the dissolution of the USSR. This is partly due to the change of the economic model, involving a large increase in the number of business entities and in international trade, partly also to perceived or real weaknesses of the state court systems in the region, in particular with regard to complicated international commercial disputes.

Today, the International Commercial Arbitration Courts at the Chamber of Industry and Commerce of the Russian Federation in Moscow (MKAS/ICAC) counts among the world's leading arbitration centers with 522 (Moscow)[1] cases in 2019, and arbitration institutions in other countries of the region, e.g. in Kazakhstan and Georgia, are also developing their strategies of growth.[2]

However, the picture is not uniform. Despite the wide-spread use of the UNCITRAL Model Law on International Commercial Arbitration as a basis, legislation on arbitration in the region has kept significant differences. Not all countries of the region are members of the New York Convention of 1958.[3] The approach of state courts towards arbitral proceedings or awards is rather mixed, and in particular, recognition and enforcement of foreign arbitral awards is burdened with a high degree of uncertainty. The following chapter will try to give an overview of the relevant legal sources of the law of international commercial arbitration in the region and address some questions of their interpretation and application.[4]

---

1 See <http://mkas.tpprf.ru/ru/Stat/page.php> accessed 20 November 2021.
2 One should also not neglect the role of other arbitration institutions in the Eurasian (post-Soviet) region, eg in Ukraine. They are not included into this chapter, which is limited to the region of the Caucasus and Central Asia.
3 See <www.newyorkconvention.org/countries> 20 November 2020 (Turkmenistan missing).
4 For a detailed analysis see Kaj Hober and Yarik Kryvoi (eds), *Law and Practice of International Arbitration in the CIS Region* (Wolters Kluwer 2017).

1   Legal Sources

1.1   *International Sources*

Starting with the New York Convention on the Recognition and Enforcement of Foreign Arbitral Awards of 1958, in the region of the Caucasus and Central Asia, Turkmenistan is the only country which has not (yet) ratified this Convention. In the investment field,[5] the ICSID Convention of 1965 has not been ratified by Kyrgyzstan, Tajikistan and, most importantly, Russia, which means that ICSID arbitral awards can be recognized and enforced in these countries only under more general rules, in particular the New York Convention. In the energy sector, most countries of the region – even Turkmenistan – are members of the Energy Charter Treaty of 1994 (including its provisions on arbitration),[6] with the exception of Russia, which withdrew its signature in 2009, but remains bound by provisional application of the ECT for investments made until 18 October 2009. This has led to the exorbitant USD 50 billion damages award(s) against Russia in the Yukos case, which was rendered by the Permanent Court of Arbitration in The Hague on 18 July 2014.[7] The award was, however, quashed by the District Court of The Hague on 20 April 2016 because of lack of jurisdiction. Turning the matter around, the Court of Appeal in The Hague set aside the decision of the District Court on 18 February 2020 reinstating the arbitral awards, but on further appeal the Dutch Supreme Court rescinded the judgment of the Court of Appeal, accepting one argument made by the Russian Federation and referring the case back to the Court of Appeal.[8]

On a regional level, the Commonwealth of Independent States (CIS) legal assistance treaties of Kiev (1992), Minsk (1993) and Kishinev (2002) do not formally exclude arbitration, but they do not deal with arbitration specifically and can be left out of consideration here. The European Convention on International Commercial Arbitration of 1961 has found a limited following in the region – without the participation of Armenia, Georgia, Kyrgyzstan,

---

5 See <https://icsid.worldbank.org/en/Pages/about/Database-of-Member-States.aspx> accessed 22 November 2020.

6 See <www.energycharter.org/process/energy-charter-treaty-1994/energy-charter-treaty/> accessed 22 November 2020.

7 See <https://www.italaw.com/cases/544> accessed 22 November 2021.

8 See <https://jusmundi.com/en/document/decision/nl-yukos-universal-limited-isle-of-man -v-the-russian-federation-arrest-van-de-hoge-raad-der-nederlanden-friday-5th-november -2021#decision_18192> accessed 04 February 2022; <www.peacepalacelibrary.nl/blog/2021/ yukos-legal-saga-continues> accessed 04 February 2022. General overview of Yukos related litigation at <https://en.wikipedia.org/wiki/Yukos_shareholders_vs._Russia> accessed 4 February 2022.

Tajikistan, Turkmenistan, and Uzbekistan, but including, notably, Azerbaijan, Kazakhstan and Russia.[9] An interesting role is played by the bilateral legal assistance treaties, which have been concluded between countries of the region with other Eurasian countries or third countries. Although they usually do not address arbitration specifically, they may be applicable, subsidiarily, on the basis of the New York Convention's "most favourable approach".

A highly relevant international instrument in the region, though not a treaty, is the UNCITRAL Model Law on International Commercial Arbitration of 1985 (partly amended in 2006). The Model Law has been adopted nearly literally in some countries of the region (Russia 1993[10] and Azerbaijan 1999[11]) and has to a significant degree inspired the legislation of the other countries of the region (Armenia 1998,[12] Kazakhstan 2016,[13] Kyrgyzstan 2002,[14] Mongolia 2003,[15] Tajikistan 2015,[16] Turkmenistan 2014,[17] and Uzbekistan 2006[18]). Probably most independent from the Model Law was the Georgian Arbitration Act of 1997,[19] which has however been superseded by a new Arbitration Act in 2009, much more in line with the Model Law.[20]

---

9   See <https://treaties.un.org/Pages/ViewDetails.aspx?src=TREATY&mtdsg_no=XXII -2&chapter=22&clang=_en> accessed 22 November 2021.

10 <www.jus.uio.no/lm/russia.international.commercial.arbitration.1993/doc.html> accessed 20 November 2021.

11 <http://republic.preslib.az/ru_d4-65.html> (in Russian), accessed 20 November 2021.

12 <www.parliament.am/law_docs/040698HO219eng.pdf?lang=eng> accessed 20 November 2021.

13 <http://cis-legislation.com/document.fwx?rgn=84417> accessed 20 November 2021. The law of 2016 has superseded the Law on International Commercial Arbitration of 2004 <www.arbitrations.ru/userfiles/file/Law/Arbitration acts/Law of the Republic of Kazakhstan on international Commercial Arbitration.pdf> accessed 20 November 2021. For a brief analysis of the new law see <www.pwc.kz/en/PwC%20News/tax-alerts/spec ial-edition-2016-21-eng.pdf> (accessed 20 November 2021).

14 <www.arbitr.kg/web/index.php?act=view_material&id=146> (in Russian), accessed 20 November 2021.

15 <www.wipo.int/edocs/lexdocs/laws/en/mn/mn025en.pdf> accessed 20 November 2021, see also Altanststseg Dashdorj, *Arbitration in Mongolia* (2003) Journal of International Arbitration 421–428, available at <https://heinonline.org/HOL/LandingPage?handle= hein.kluwer/jiao020&div=49&id=&page> accessed 20 November 2021.

16 <www.base.spinform.ru/show_doc.fwx?rgn=74321> (in Russian) accessed 20 November 2021.

17 <www.turkmenistan.gov.tm/?id=7116> (in Russian) accessed 20 November 2021.

18 <https://regulation.gov.uz/ru/document/1301> accessed 20 November 2021.

19 <www.lexadin.nl/wlg/legis/nofr/oeur/arch/geo/LAWONPRIVATEARBITRATION.pdf> accessed 20 November 2021.

20 <https://matsne.gov.ge/en/document/download/89284/4/en/pdf> accessed 20 November 2021.

1.2   *National (Domestic) Sources*

The most important sources of arbitration law on the national level in the region of the Caucasus and Central Asia are specific arbitration laws.[21] Most countries in the region have passed separate laws on international commercial arbitration and arbitration in general,[22] the relationship of which is sometimes open to discussion. While the dominating view is that these laws have distinct spheres of application – international and domestic arbitration – a closer analysis sometimes shows that there may be overlaps.[23] The contents of the general arbitration acts in these countries are usually inspired by the international commercial arbitration acts, but differences remain. While the regulatory distinction between international commercial arbitration and domestic (private) arbitration is closely related to the approach of the UNCITRAL Model Law, there is a growing tendency in the region to pass "unitary" arbitration laws covering both domestic and international commercial arbitration.[24] One of the earliest examples for such an approach was the Georgian Arbitration Act of 1997, which was, however, criticized for numerous gaps and weaknesses, in particular with regard to international arbitration.[25] The new Georgian Arbitration Act of 2009[26] has aligned Georgian arbitration law much closer with the UNCITRAL Model Law (in its revised version of 2006), while keeping the unified approach. An interesting development in the opposite direction can be remarked in Uzbekistan, where there was a legislative proposal in 2013 to pass a specific law on international commercial arbitration besides the pre-existing general arbitration law.[27] Turkmenistan, on the other hand, has for the time being only passed an Act on International Commercial Arbitration (2014)[28]; a general Arbitration Act does not exist. In some countries with two

---

21   See already supra at (n 1).

22   Eg Azerbaijan, Russia.

23   See, for example, Cornelia S Iffland, *Börsenschiedsgerichtsbarkeit in Deutschland und Russland – Zugleich eine Untersuchung zum Recht der internationalen Handelsschiedsgerichtsbarkeit* (Dunker & Humblot 2008) 56–59.

24   Armenia, Georgia, Kyrgyzstan, Mongolia, Uzbekistan and, most recently, Kazakhstan (new unitary arbitration law of 2016).

25   See Michael Wietzorek, *New Arbitration Law in the Republic of Georgia* (September 2010) <http://kluwerarbitrationblog.com/2010/09/01/new-arbitration-law-in-the-republic-of-georgia/> accessed 20 November 2021.

26   <https://matsne.gov.ge/en/document/download/89284/4/en/pdf> accessed 20 November 2021.

27   cf <http://gazeta.norma.uz/publish/doc/text96072_vektor_razvitiya_zadast_mejdunaro dnyy_kommercheskiy_arbitraj> accessed 20 November 2021.

28   <www.turkmenistan.gov.tm/?id=7116> accessed 20 November 2021.

separate arbitration laws there is an ongoing discussion about modernizing these acts and making them more compatible.[29]

Apart from the specific arbitration acts, in many countries of the Eurasian region, the Codes of Civil Procedure, or (if existing) Codes of Economic Procedure, contain provisions on domestic and/or international arbitration overlapping with the arbitration acts.[30]

Another peculiar phenomenon of arbitration law and practice in the region of the Caucasus and Central Asia – or, more generally, in many East European countries – is a strong focus on institutional arbitration linked with national Chambers of Commerce and Industry. Sometimes the status of such institutional arbitration has been anchored in legislation, giving such "Courts of Arbitration" a semi-official status, although their independence is guaranteed by law.[31] These arbitration institutions, some of which had direct predecessors in Soviet times,[32] have given themselves arbitration rules, similar to arbitration institutions in other parts of the world.[33] Today, in most countries of the region these arbitration institutions no longer have a monopoly on arbitration[34] and ad hoc arbitration is also admitted. In some countries this has led, however, to the creation of sometimes questionable arbitration institutions ("pocket arbitrations" dominated by some businesses or otherwise dependent), with legislators now trying to limit such mis-developments.[35]

In the following, some characteristic elements of arbitration legislation in the region of the Caucasus and Central Asia will be looked at more closely.

---

29   See for example the recent reform of Russian arbitration law in 2017, cf <https://minjust .ru/ru/reforma-arbitrazha> accessed 20 November 2021.

30   See, eg chs 30 and 31 of the Russian Arbitrazh Procedure Code of 2002, <www.consultant .ru/document/cons_doc_LAW_37800/> accessed 20 November 2021.

31   This is true, eg in Belarus, Russia, Ukraine.

32   In particular the ICAC (MKAS) and the Maritime Arbitration Commission in Moscow.

33   See, eg a commentary (in German language) of the new 2017 rules of international commercial arbitration of the ICAC at the TTP of the Russian Federation by Alexander Trunk, in Rolf A Schütze (ed), *Institutionelle Schiedsgerichtsbarkeit* (3rd edn, Wolters Kluwer 2018), 549ff. (English edition forthcoming).A fundamental prerequisite for long-term success and international competitiveness of arbitration institutions is the trust of the business community in the quality of arbitral practice at these institutions, which includes the impartiality of the arbitrators.

34   Under art 6 of the Law on International Commercial Arbitration of Tajikistan of 2015 this seems to be the only legally accepted institutional arbitration in Tajikistan.

35   cf Margarita Govortsova, 'The Reform of Arbitral Courts: 7 Basic Tendencies' (in Russian) <www.garant.ru/article/555286/> accessed 20 November 2021 (at the example of Russia).

2   Scope of Application

The UNCITRAL Model Law defines the basic term "international commercial arbitration" only partially. The meaning of the component "commercial" is described mainly by a list of non-exclusive examples in a footnote to Article 1 of the Model Law. Much more precise is the definition of the component "international" (Article 1 (3) ML). In so far as arbitration laws in the region apply only to international commercial arbitration, they usually[36] contain definitions similar, but not identical to the Model Law. The arbitration laws in the region usually take the abstract term of "commercial" from the Model Law (see, e.g. Article 1 point 2 of the Act of Turkmenistan, Article 1 point 1 in conjunction with Article 7 point 1 of the Azerbaijan Act). Sometimes it is stated that (only) disputes of a civil law character are covered (see, e.g. Article 1 point 2 of the Russian Act, similar Article 1 point 2 of the Georgian Act).[37] However, investment disputes are sometimes expressly termed arbitrable as if independent from the "civil law" criterion.[38] It should be mentioned that the sphere of civil law is understood quite broadly in some countries of the region and may extend into areas, which would probably be categorized as "public" in Western countries (e.g. contracts under administrative law). Often, disputes "arising between enterprises with foreign investment" are expressly included, which goes beyond the Model Law (cf. e.g. Article 2 point 2 subpoint 2 of the Russian Act, Article 1 point 2 of the Act of Turkmenistan). Conversely, some countries define non-arbitrable matters quite broadly, e.g. referring to matters for which state courts of the respective country have an exclusive competence under civil procedure law (cf. Article 7 of the Mongolian Act).

3   Arbitration Agreement

Like the UNCITRAL Model Law, arbitration laws in the region of the Caucasus and Central Asia say little about the substantive requirements of arbitration agreements. There seems to be a tendency in the region to interpret arbitration

---

36   The (general) Arbitration Act of Mongolia, for example, does not contain any limitation to commercial matters.

37   Art 5 of the general Arbitration Act of Armenia provides for a negative list of non-arbitrable disputes.

38   For example, according to § 1 point 1 of the 2017 international commercial arbitration rules of the ICAC (MKAS) at the TPP of the Russian Federation. For an express legislative provision on investment disputes see, eg the Arbitration Act of Kyrgyzstan, art 21.

agreements rather literally and also to show some cautiousness against upholding unclear clauses. Also, there are no express provisions on the law applicable
to arbitration agreements with an international dimension (e.g. applicability
of the law governing the subject of the dispute – lex causae – or the law governing the arbitration procedure – lex arbitri).[39] However, the form of arbitration agreements is dealt with extensively in the various Acts, often deviating
in details from the Model Law. Writing is generally required, but mostly understood liberally, including the use of electronic communications.

4   (Domestic) Arbitral Proceeding

Compared with the sparse provisions on the conduct of arbitral proceedings in
Articles 18–27 of the Model Law, many Arbitration Acts in the Eurasian region
contain numerous additional, specific rules, for example on the contents of
statements of claim and defense (e.g. Article 18 Arbitration Act of Armenia,
Article 30 International Arbitration Act of Tajikistan, Article 29 Arbitration
Act of Uzbekistan), on counterclaims and set-off (Article 40 Arbitration Act
of Kazakhstan, see also Article 21 Arbitration Act of Kyrgyzstan and Article
31 Arbitration Act of Uzbekistan), on settlements (Article 27 International
Arbitration Act of Kazakhstan, Article 46 International Arbitration Act of
Tajikistan), and on the burden of proof (Article 25 Armenian Arbitration Act).
An interesting provision in the Georgian Arbitration Act of 2009 deals with
legal succession of parties, death and liquidation (Article 5 Georgian Act),
another with the calculation of time-limits (Article 7 Georgian Act). Some
Acts also state a number of general principles of procedure going beyond the
equal treatment provision of Article 18 Model Law, for example Article 5 of the
Arbitration Act of Kazakhstan (autonomy of parties, legality, adversarial principle, equal treatment of parties, good faith principle, confidentiality). Also,
the principle of independence of the arbitral tribunal is sometimes expressly
mentioned (e.g. in Article 6 of the Georgian Act). In general, these provisions
are in line with established practices of arbitration. The challenge is less the
law in books, but rather its application in practice.

---

39   Regarding this question see, for example, Gary B Born, 'The Law Governing International
      Arbitration Agreements: An International Perspective' (2014) 26 SAcLJ 814–48 <https://
      journalsonline.academypublishing.org.sg/Journals/Singapore-Academy-of-Law-Journal
      -Special-Issue/e-Archive/ctl/eFirstSALPDFJournalView/mid/513/ArticleId/343/Citation/
      JournalsOnlinePDF> 20 November 2021.

5   Setting-Aside, Recognition and Enforcement of Arbitral Awards

Most states of the Eurasian region closely follow in their arbitration acts the systematic approach of the Model Law distinguishing between the setting-aside
and recognition and enforcement of arbitral awards (domestic and foreign),
while at the same time aligning and limiting the grounds for setting-aside and
non-recognition. Some countries seem to have a somewhat extended approach
regarding grounds for setting-aside and non-recognition (cf. Article 47 of the
Arbitration Act of Uzbekistan). Following the Model Law, most Arbitration
Acts state that an (implicitly: foreign) arbitral award is not recognized and
enforced if it has been set-aside or suspended in its country of origin (see, e.g.
Article 36 point 1 Russian International Commercial Arbitration Act, Article 54
point 1 International Commercial Arbitration Act of Tajikistan, Article 57 point
1 Arbitration Act of Kazakhstan). Some provisions are, however, unclear on
the details in this respect, for example Article 43.1.2. Mongolian Act (must the
award already be set-aside or is it sufficient that the setting-aside proceeding
is still pending?). An interesting particular rule on this issue contains Article
45 of the Georgian Arbitration Act 2009, which grants the court in the recognition context a discretionary power of temporarily suspending its decision.
As most countries[40] are also member states of the New York Convention, the
above-mentioned provisions are usually superimposed by the Convention, but
may remain subsidiarily applicable under the principle of favor recognition
(Article VII point 1 of the Convention). As there are mixed views on whether
the New York Convention allows (or even commands under certain circumstances) the recognition of foreign awards even if they have been set-aside in
their country of origin,[41] this issue may also come up in the courts of States
of the Eurasian region. Probably the greatest uncertainty with regard to recognition and enforcement of foreign arbitral awards in the Eurasian region
lies in the, sometimes quite extensive, reference to public policy as a ground
for non-recognition, but it is evident – on the other side – that foreign arbitral awards, which are regarded as influenced by political considerations will

---

40   Except Turkmenistan, for which recognition of foreign arbitral awards is governed only by
       national law (Arbitration Act and Code of civil or economic procedure).
41   One such case was the enforcement of a Russian award by Dutch courts (Yukos context),
       although the award had been set-aside in Russia, see Yearbook Commercial Arbitration
       (Netherlands, 2010) 423–425. See also Albert Jan van den Berg, 'Should the Setting-Aside
       of the Arbitral Award be Abolished?' (2014) ICSID Review 263–88 <www.arbitration-icca
       .org/media/4/92247683911386/media21398254806727ovan_den_berg_setting_aside_ic
       sid_review_2014.pdf> accessed 20 November 2021.

hardly be recognized in countries, which see these awards as directed against their own interests. It may in such cases be possible to enforce such awards in third countries, but this embroils all participants in long-lasting legal battles and will not solve the typically larger political tensions at stake. In the long run, such conflicts must be solved either in a settlement or by political agreement.

CHAPTER 25

Transparency in Settlement of Investment Disputes – Public Interest and Transparency

The Work of UNCITRAL and Its Relevance for the Eurasian Region

Timothy Lemay

This chapter aims to give an overview of recent work in UNCITRAL (United Nations Commission on International Trade Law) in the area of transparency in treaty-based investor-State arbitration, and a brief review of both the UNCITRAL Rules in that regard and the Convention on Transparency. As countries of the Eurasian region often include in their bilateral investment treaties a reference to the UNCITRAL Arbitration Rules, and also private actors from the region make regular use of these rules in their arbitration agreements, it is important to follow the recent developments in this sphere, inter alia, those regarding transparency in investor-State arbitration.

1 Background and Context

UNCITRAL was created in 1966 with the mandate to further the progressive harmonization, unification and modernization of the law of international trade (to be understood as the law regulating commercial transactions between individual parties). Since then, UNCITRAL has become the core legal body within the United Nations system in the commercial law field. It is known worldwide for establishing modern legal rules regulating international commerce in a neutral and balanced manner and assisting States and other relevant stakeholders with the understanding, enactment, implementation, and interpretation of those standards.

UNCITRAL has a solid basis for its work in this area. It is the custodian of the Convention on the Recognition and Enforcement of Foreign Arbitral Awards (the "New York Convention 1958"), which now has 166 parties, and has produced model laws and procedural rules for both arbitration and conciliation which have been in worldwide use for several decades. The Rules and Convention on Transparency are a natural outgrowth of UNCITRAL's leading role in setting standards in international arbitration.

© KONINKLIJKE BRILL NV, LEIDEN, 2023 | DOI:10.1163/9789004357839_027

The UNCITRAL Arbitration Rules (initially adopted in 1976)[1] did not themselves address transparency and public access, as they were conceived primarily with international commercial arbitration in mind. There is of course a provision in the Rules, Article 34(5), by which parties can agree to make public an arbitral award and permitting disclosure where required of a party by a legal duty. The default rule regarding hearings, per Article 28(3), is that they are held in camera unless the parties agree otherwise.

It will be helpful to look at some of the context in which the work on transparency was undertaken. Over the past decades there has been a substantial increase in the cumulative number of international investment treaties, including BITs (bilateral investment treaties), although the number of new treaties has fallen off somewhat since its high point in the late 1990s and the early years of the 21st century. There was a concomitant rise in investor-State disputes arising from the treaties, with an overall total of 568 known treaty-based arbitrations by the end of 2013,[2] and 1104 by the end of 2021.[3] The UNCITRAL Arbitration Rules, last revised in 2010, were used in a substantial number of investor-State arbitrations – some 351 of the 1104 known cases.

There were many reasons for preparing a legal standard on transparency. It is clear that transparency is for the benefit of the public. It is also widely regarded as beneficial for States as it promotes good governance, and it may also serve as a means to counter corruption. The overall purpose is to enhance confidence in the system of investor-State arbitration. Also noteworthy is a trend in recent years in favour of transparency generally: in arbitration rules, in case law, in legislation, and investment treaties.

---

1 <https://uncitral.un.org/en/texts/arbitration/contractualtexts/arbitration> accessed 22 November 2021.

2 "As of January 2013, Central Asian states had been or were a party to 38 international arbitration disputes" (at least those that are publicly known) UNCTAD, *World Investment Report 2014: Investing in the SDGs: An Action Plan, at 124, cited in* B Sabahi and others, 'Investor State Arbitration in Central Asia' (2013) 4 *Transnational Dispute Management* 7. In 2013 itself, nine of the 14 cases involving Asia were against transition economies in Central Asia (namely Kazakhstan, Kyrgyz Republic, Turkmenistan, and Uzbekistan) in UNCTAD Issues Note, April 2014. By January 2022, Armenia has been respondent in four disputes; Azerbaijan - in five; Belarus – in three; Georgia – in 16; Kazakhstan 19 disputes; Kyrgyzstan – 17; Moldova – in 12; Russia – 26; Tajikistan – in two; Turkmenistan – in 14; Ukraine – in 26 <investmentpolicy.unctad.org/investment-dispute-settlement> accessed 30 January 2022.

3 See <investmentpolicy.unctad.org/investment-dispute-settlement> accessed 30 January 2022.

The Office of the United Nations High Commissioner for Human Rights, taking part in the UNCITRAL session which endorsed the Convention on Transparency, noted the importance of transparency for the protection of human rights and its close link to issues of business and human rights:

> The work of UNCITRAL in promoting the rule of law in commercial relations, in particular through its standards in the areas of transparency in investor-State arbitration and public procurement, was seen by the Working Group to be of high relevance to the effective protection of human rights and thus to the work of the [United Nations] Working Group on Business and Human Rights.[4]

In the context of development, it was said in UNCITRAL's Working Group II – made up of sixty States from all regions of the world – that ensuring transparency in investor-State arbitration "should be considered in the context of foreign direct investment as a tool for the long-term sustainable growth of developing countries", since foreign direct investment contributes to building productive capacity and improving infrastructure, enhancing access to essential services such as water, education and health care for the poor and marginalized, and it can generate spill-over effects by increasing demand and encouraging domestic entrepreneurship. This can form part of "a virtuous cycle of an increase in domestic employment, in domestic demand and, ultimately, sustained economic growth".[5]

Drafting of the Transparency Rules reflected the concern to balance two interests: that of the public in being informed, and the interest of the parties in having an efficient procedure. The arbitral tribunal is tasked with balancing those interests.

2   The Transparency Rules

Herewith is an overview of the main provisions of the UNCITRAL Transparency Rules (which focus on so-called 'future' investment treaties), which will be followed by a review of the Transparency Convention (which deals with arbitrations under 'existing' treaties). To begin with, note that Article 1 of the UNCITRAL Arbitration Rules is amended to include, by reference, the

---

4   Report of the United Nations Commission on International Trade Law (2014) UN Doc A/69/17, para 200.
5   Report of Working Group II (2010) UN Doc A/CN.9/712, para 16.

Transparency Rules in cases of investor-State arbitrations. The main areas dealt with by the Rules, which became effective on 1 April 2014, include: publication of information; submissions by amicus curiae and treaty parties; open hearings; exceptions to transparency; and the repository of published information.

The Rules apply to investor-State arbitrations initiated under the UNCITRAL Arbitration Rules pursuant to a treaty (e.g. an international investment agreement) concluded on or after 1 April 2014 (which is the date when the Rules came into effect) unless the Parties to the treaty have agreed otherwise. And so they were conceived as forward-looking. Since that date, dozens of treaties have been concluded, some of which already apply the Rules on Transparency (Georgia – Switzerland BIT,[6] the Treaty on the Eurasian Economic Union[7]; or the Armenia – United Arab Emirates BIT[8]). For treaties concluded before that date, the Rules apply only when the parties to the arbitration agree or the Parties to the treaty agree (after 1 April 2014) to their application.

This brief review does not purport to provide an article-by-article examination of each of the Rules, but an explanation of some of the key points will be helpful. The Rules on Transparency are a short text, consisting of eight articles.[9]

At the commencement of the arbitration, and so before the arbitral tribunal is constituted, the information to be published includes the names of the disputing parties, the economic sector involved and the treaty under which the claim is made. The Rules then provide for publication of documents and for open hearings, subject to some exceptions. Publication takes place through an online repository or 'registry' – the UNCITRAL Secretariat has been tasked with maintaining the registry.

Article 7 contains two categories of exceptions to transparency: first, confidential or protected information shall not be made public. A determination as to whether information is confidential is to be made by the arbitral tribunal after consultation with the parties. Article 7 contains a definition of

---

6   Agreement between the Swiss Confederation and Georgia on the Promotion and Reciprocal Protection of Investments of 3 June 2014 <uncitral.un.org/en/texts/arbitration/conventions/foreign_arbitral_awards/status> accessed 30 January 2022.

7   Treaty on the Eurasian Economic Union of 29 May 2014 <uncitral.un.org/en/texts/arbitration/conventions/foreign_arbitral_awards/status> accessed 30 January 2022.

8   Agreement between the Slovak Republic and the United Arab Emirates for the promotion and reciprocal protection of investments of 22 July 2016 <uncitral.un.org/en/texts/arbitration/conventions/foreign_arbitral_awards/status> accessed 30 January 2022.

9   The articles cover: 1 Scope of Application; 2 Publication of information at the commencement of arbitral proceedings; 3 Publication of documents; 4 Submission by a third person; 5 Submission by a non-disputing Party to the treaty; 6 Hearings; 7 Exceptions to transparency; 8 Repository of published information.

"confidential information" which is the first time that UNCITRAL defines such a concept in the field of arbitration. Another ground for limiting transparency is the need to protect the integrity of the arbitral process. For example, hearings could be closed if there were a risk of threats to witnesses or legal counsel.

Documents which are to be made available to the public, pursuant to Article 3, include the notice of arbitration, response, statements of claim and defence, lists of exhibits and witness statements, transcripts of hearings (where available), and orders, decisions and awards of the tribunal. The tribunal also has a discretion, per Article 3(3) – either on its own initiative or upon request by "any person" – to make exhibits and other material public after consultation with the parties.

Under Article 4, non-disputing "third persons" may file written submissions if the tribunal agrees after consulting the parties. Such third persons must have a significant interest in the proceedings, must disclose their funding sources and any relationship to a party, and be able to assist in the determination of factual or legal issues before the tribunal without unduly disrupting or burdening the proceedings.

The general rule is that hearings are to be public insofar as is feasible (including by video links or other means) except where parts of the hearing may need to be held in camera to protect confidential information. Exceptions to transparency, found in Article 7, include: confidential business information; information protected under the treaty; information protected under the law of the respondent State or another law determined by the tribunal to be applicable; information the disclosure of which would impede law enforcement. Information is not to be made public which would jeopardize the integrity of the arbitral process (because it could hamper the collection or production of evidence, lead to the intimidation of witnesses, lawyers acting for disputing parties or members of the arbitral tribunal, or in comparably exceptional circumstances).

Article 8 of the Rules provides for a publicly accessible repository of published information. Having in mind the importance of neutrality in administering these matters, the Commission (UNCITRAL) unanimously decided to recommend entrusting its Secretariat with the operation of the repository.[10]

---

10   The website address is <www.uncitral.org/transparency-registry/registry/index.jspx> accessed 22 November 2021.

3   The Transparency Convention

Having established the Rules applying transparency to arbitrations under (what were at that time) 'future' investment treaties (i.e. those concluded after the coming into force of the Rules), the next question for the Commission was how to encourage States to agree on the application of the Rules to arbitrations under their 'existing' treaties, namely those concluded before 1 April 2014, of which there were in excess of three thousand.

Firstly, of course, States could take action through unilateral or bilateral declarations. But to go a step further, UNCITRAL prepared a convention, the United Nations Convention on Transparency in Treaty-based Investor-State Arbitration (the "Transparency Convention") which was finalised by the Commission at its 47th session in July 2014 and adopted by the General Assembly at its 69th session in December 2014. The Convention opened for signature in Port Louis, Mauritius, on 17 March 2015, and thereafter at the United Nations Headquarters in New York. It entered into force on 18 October 2017, six months after the deposit of the third instrument of ratification, acceptance, approval, or accession. To date, twenty-three States have signed the Convention,[11] of which nine are parties. It is known as the Mauritius Convention on Transparency.

The Convention makes the Transparency Rules applicable to any investor-State arbitration under an investment treaty, whether or not conducted under the UNCITRAL Arbitration Rules. Again, the Convention is a brief document because it is a mechanism for applying the Rules. The Convention does not contain provisions on transparency; those substantive provisions are in the Rules. Essential areas covered include the scope of application, application of the Transparency Rules, as well as reservations and their formulation. The Convention permits a limited number of reservations. It is possible, pursuant to Article 3, to exclude its application to a specific investment treaty, a specific set of arbitration rules, or to exclude the possibility of unilaterally applying the Transparency Rules. Any reservation made after the entry into force of the Convention will be effective one year after its deposit. Any withdrawal of a reservation will have immediate effect.

The remaining articles of the Convention concern administrative matters such as signature and ratification, entry into force (requires three parties), effect on territorial units in federal states, and related matters.

---

11   See <https://uncitral.un.org/en/texts/arbitration/conventions/transparency/status> accessed 22 November 2021. So far there are signatory states from the Eurasian region.

4   Conclusion

What can we expect in the future from these instruments? First, that transparency enhances confidence in the dispute resolution system which is currently adopted under thousands of treaties. Next, that it modernizes investor-State disputes by permitting the public to be better informed about the process. And finally, these texts show that it is indeed possible to reform this area of practice, so it may be a first step for wider reforms in the field.

CHAPTER 26

The Impacts of Public International Law on the Enforcement of Foreign Arbitral Awards

Dagmar Richter

1   Introduction

The continuing importance of arbitration relies on the enforceability of arbitral awards.[1] However, enforceability is subject to a plenitude of sources and impacts comprising specific treaty provisions on recognition and enforcement, general international law principles, domestic law, but also the "special political embarrassment factor"[2] in the case of a state party being involved. This chapter deals with the impacts of international law of an unspecific character on the enforcement and execution of foreign arbitral awards. It will concentrate on the two most influential international treaties: the Convention on the Recognition and Enforcement of Foreign Arbitral Awards ("New York Convention")[3] and the ICSID Convention of the Settlement of Investment Disputes Between States and Nationals of Other States ("ICSID Convention").[4]

Particularly in international investment law, dispute settlement bodies have always acknowledged that investment law cannot be interpreted in isolation from public international law and its general principles.[5] No international treaty can exist in isolation from international law.[6] On the one hand, the treaties mentioned explicitly refer to some international law principles such

---

1   Loukas A. Mistelis, 'Award as an Investment: The Value of an Arbitral Award or the Cost of Non-Enforcement' (2013) 28 ICSID Review 64, 84; Stefan Kröll, 'Enforcement of Awards', in Marc Bungenberg and others (eds), *International Investment Law* (Bloomsbury 2015) 1482–1504, mn 1 (at 1483).

2   Kröll, in: Bungenberg and others (n 1).

3   Convention of 10 June 1958, United Nations Treaty Series (UNTS), vol 330, 3, available at UN Treaty Collection (Chapter 22: Commercial Arbitration): <https://treaties.un.org> accessed 20 November 2021.

4   Convention of 14 October 1966. Available at ICSID: <https://icsid.worldbank.org> accessed 20 November 2021.

5   *Phoenix Action Ltd. v Czech Republic*, ICSID Case No ARB/06/5, Award (15 April 2009) para 78; *Asian Agricultural Products Ltd. v Sri Lanka*, ICSID Case No ARB/87/3, Award (27 June 1990).

6   Campbell McLachlan, 'Investment Treaties and General International Law' (2008) 57 ICLQ 361, at 372.

as diplomatic protection or sovereign immunity.[7] On the other hand, international law from external (non-investment law) sources may be employed in order to complement specific treaty law where it shows *lacunae* or even fails to ensure the recognition and enforcement of foreign awards ("supplemental and corrective effect of international law").[8] A specific problem, relating to the standards of treatment of investments, lies in the possibility that, because of the huge rise in bilateral investment treaties (BITs), customary international law rules might not have developed, as they would have done if practice were to be produced independently from any BITs.[9]

With special regard to human rights,[10] an ambitious position holds that such rights as well as sustainable development issues "must be factors that condition the nature and extent of the investor's responsibilities, and the balance of rights and obligations between the investor and host state".[11] More extreme statements even call for an end to investor-State arbitration in its existing form: as investment treaty arbitration were to be considered a form of *public law adjudication*, private arbitration should be replaced by public courts, namely by an international investment court which alone would be capable of adequately addressing the relevant matters of public law.[12] Statements like these reveal the existence of a tension between investment protection on the one hand and human rights and other public policy concerns on the other hand, or even of a legitimacy crisis of investment law.[13] In numerous investment disputes, property rights of investors were opposed to public goods or public policy grounds such as public health, environmental protection, protection of indigenous peoples, energy supply, labor law, or even the reversal of Apartheid in South Africa.[14] However, arbitral tribunals decide quite

---

7   See s 3.3. regarding art 55 ICSID Convention, also IV.1.

8   See, with special regard to art 42 (1) ICSID Convention, Christoph H. Schreuer and others (eds), *The ICSID Convention: A Commentary* (2nd edn, CUP 2009) art 42, mn 205, 214–235.

9   cf McLachlan (n 6) 367.

10   See, comprehensively, Pierre-Marie Dupuy and others (eds), *Human Rights in International Investment Law and Arbitration* (OUP 2009).

11   The Lawyers' Environmental Action Team and others, Amicus curiae submission of 26 March 2007 relating to Case No ARB/05/22, *Biwater Gauff (Tanzania) Ltd. v United Republic of Tanzania*, para 51. Commenting on this Susan L. Karamanian, 'The Place of Human Rights in Investor-State Arbitration' (2013) 17 Lewis & Clark Law Review 423, 429–430.

12   Gus van Harten, *Investment Treaty Arbitration and Public Law* (OUP 2007).

13   See Bruno Simma, 'Foreign Investment Arbitration: A Place for Human Rights?' (2011) 60 ICLQ 573, 575.

14   *Piero Foresti and others v The Republic of South Africa*, ICSID Case No ARB(AF)/07/1 (4 August 2010) (discontinued).

disparately and in most of the cases evasively: even if public welfare objectives are included in investment agreements or contracts and despite the fact that NGOs increasingly may present public and human rights concerns to arbitral tribunals, investment law is not really prepared to take the challenge of balancing private and public values.[15] Some authors even speak of a "reluctance" by arbitral tribunals to refer to international human rights.[16] Accordingly, investment law is being described as a cluster of more or less depoliticized self-contained regimes, splendidly isolated from the rest of the legal universe[17] and perceived by the public opinion to be biased towards the interests of investors at the expense of the public interest.[18] If that is so, the question arises, whether such "unresolved issues" in the context of the making of awards could have similar impacts on decisions to be made in the stage of enforcement.

This article will show whether, and to what extent, the New York Convention and the ICSID Convention are receptive to general international law impacts when it comes to the enforcement of arbitral awards (receptivity towards international law). Additionally, some practices relating to enforcement will be assessed from an international law perspective (compatibility with international law). Last but not least, it will be discussed whether, and to what extent, resorts outside of the specific treaties on the recognition and enforcement of foreign arbitral awards may be taken, if such awards cannot be enforced (remedial effects of international law mechanisms).

The article was submitted in February 2016 and is based on the legal sources and state of discussion at that time.

2 Enforcement of Foreign Arbitral Awards under Multilateral Treaties

2.1 The Systemic Function of General International Law

This relationship between specific treaty law and general international law has been rightly described as "symbiotic": Whilst custom informs the content of the treaty rights, state practice under investment treaties contributes to

---

15   See Karamanian (n 11) with many references to arbitral practice; also, Simma (n 13) 576: 'Berührungsangst, vis-à-vis human rights within the foreign investment/arbitration profession', and 579.

16   McLachlan (n 6) 376.

17   Description by Simma (n 13) 576.

18   See Simma (n 13) 575; also, Filip Balcerzak, 'Jurisdiction and Tribunals in Investor-State Arbitration and the Issue of Human Rights' (2014) 29 ICSID Review 216–217.

the development of general international law, both working in a "structured process of treaty interpretation".[19] In this manner, general international law provides for a "systemic interpretation", necessary in order to avoid further fragmentation of the law, which usually goes along with the proliferation of international treaties.[20] As general international law, with regard to its general character and universal recognition, has a potential of *"systemic integration"*,[21] it may foster harmonization not only with respect to a diversified treaty situation but also with respect to divergent approaches of various arbitral tribunals applying the same treaties without any supervisory instance of appeal.

The most essential form of relationship between multilateral international treaties such as the New York Convention (NYC) and the ICSID Convention and general international law relates to the rules on the interpretation and application. Such treaties as well as the relevant BITs are subject to the rules of the Vienna Convention on the Law of Treaties (VCLT),[22] which mostly reflect customary international law.[23] Interpretation on grounds of the Vienna Convention can be described as a "process of progressive encirclement". Articles 31 and 32 VCLT, thereby, suggest an "orderly method" of interpretation putting the text of the treaty in the centre of the enquiry.[24] The interpreter starts under the general rule with the ordinary meaning of the terms of the treaty, considers their context, assesses the text in light of the treaty's object and purpose, and by cycling through this three-step inquiry iteratively closes in upon the proper interpretation.[25]

However, interpretation of the provisions of an international treaty (e.g. NYC, ICSID Convention or BIT) shall take into account, together with the

---

19   McLachlan (n 6). Quotation from ibid, 361 (abstract).

20   Martti Koskenniemi, Report of the Study Group of the International Law Commission, 'Fragmentation of International Law: Difficulties Arising from the Diversification and Expansion of International Law' (13 April 2006) UN Doc A/CN.4/L.682, paras 410–423.

21   Koskenniemi (n 20) para 413; also see part 1.

22   Convention of 23 May 1969, UNTS, vol. 1155, 331. For further details see August Reinisch, 'The Interpretation of International Investment Treaties' in Marc Bungenberg and others (eds), *International Investment Law* (Bloomsbury 2015) 372–410.

23   More restrictive Malcolm N. Shaw, *International Law*, (6th ed, CUP 2008) at 903: VCLT "partly reflects customary law". See on the requirements for the recognition of customary international law art 38 (1) (b) of the Statute of the International Court of Justice. Whenever a rule has become part of international customary law, it applies independently from the ratification by a state of the UN Convention on State Immunity or similar instruments.

24   McLachlan (n 6) 390.

25   *Aguas del Tunari S.A. v Republic of Bolivia*, ICSID Case No ARB/02/3, Decision (21 October 2005) para 91.

context, not only subsequent agreement and practice by the parties but also "any relevant rules of international law applicable in the relations between the parties" (Article 31 [3] [c] VCLT). However, the application of international law must always be considered "through the lens of the rules of treaty interpretation" in order to avoid subverting the very purposes for which states negotiated specific treaties.[26] As international treaty law takes priority over customary international law and general principles of international law,[27] the crucial question will always be whether the matter concerned is covered by the pertinent treaty (speciality rule) or rather leaves room for the employment of general international law.[28]

2.2   Guiding Principles of Treaty-Based Enforcement

There are two basic tenets of enforcement: First, that a claimant should be able to "follow the money", and, second, that when it finds some money, the enforcement procedure should be quick and easy, rather than presenting needless opportunities for procedural objections.[29] Accordingly, foreign arbitral awards can be executed much more easily than foreign court decisions. Other than judgments they do not require an order of exequatur prior to enforcement,[30] because they are made by a body being staffed on equal terms and acting in a more objective attitude than state courts. Provisions like Articles IV and V NYC or Article 54 ICSID Convention thus provide that any award, after being presented in due form, must be recognized and enforced. They thus establish a presumption of validity of foreign arbitral awards. Accordingly, domestic courts should apply a "deferential standard" when reviewing the existence of defenses, and thus should refuse enforcement only in exceptional cases.[31] To ensure this, standard domestic law often clarifies that enforcement shall be the rule and refusal of enforcement shall be exceptional.[32]

---

26   cf McLachlan (n 6) 383.

27   This priority rule is reflected by the descending order of international law sources mentioned in art 38(1) ICJ Statute, where treaty law comes first.

28   See s 2.4. (c) (bb).

29   See Joseph E. Neuhaus, 'Current Issues in the Enforcement of International Arbitration Awards' (2004) 36 Inter-American Law Review 23ff (31).

30   Eg, Richard H. Kreindler and Rita Heinemann, 'Commercial Arbitration, International', in: Max Planck Encyclopedia of Public International Law (May 2009) para 7 (f), available at: Oxford Public International Law, <http://opil.ouplaw.com/home/EPIL> accessed 20 November 2021.

31   Kröll, in Bungenberg and others (n 1) mn 16 (1488).

32   Eg, US Code, Title 9 (Arbitration), ch 2 (Convention of Recognition and Enforcement of Foreign Arbitral Awards), 9 US Code § 207: "The court shall confirm the award unless it

2.3   *The New York Convention*

2.3.1   The Enforcement Mechanism – Overview

The Convention on the Recognition and Enforcement of Foreign Arbitral Awards ("New York Convention"; "NYC") of 1958[33] must be considered a core instrument establishing the prevailing standard of regulation of the enforcement of foreign awards. As 156 states had ratified this international treaty by the end of 2015,[34] its provisions can be held to mostly reflect customary international law. This is also confirmed by the fact that the UNCITRAL Model Law has copied its provisions on recognition and enforcement.[35] The NYC deals with the recognition and enforcement of foreign arbitral awards,[36] arising out of differences between persons, whether physical or legal (Article I NYC).

According to Article III, section 1 NYC "[e]ach Contracting State shall recognize arbitral awards as binding and enforce them in accordance with the rules of procedure of the territory where the award is relied upon, under the conditions laid down in the following articles." In addition, the NYC establishes a couple of requirements that must be fulfilled prior to recognition and enforcement, namely that the award must have become "binding" (not "final"). It becomes binding as soon as it is made (cf. Article III NYC). Additionally, some requirements relating to certification and translation must be met (Article IV [1] [a] [b], [2] NYC). Rules applicable to enforcement are the rules of procedure of the lex fori as modified by the NYC. As this may open the door for an unfettered influence of domestic law and jurisprudence, Article III, section 2 NYC establishes as a general rule that with regard to recognition and enforcement foreign arbitral awards shall not be treated less favourably than domestic arbitral awards.

The crucial question is whether a state may refuse to recognise and/or enforce a foreign arbitral award. As this phenomenon occurs quite often,

---

finds one of the grounds for refusal or deferral of recognition or enforcement of the award specified in the said Convention."

33   See, generally, Herbert Kronke and others (eds), *Recognition and Enforcement of Foreign Arbitral Awards: A Global Commentary on the New York Convention* (Wolters Kluwer 2010); Reinmar Wolff (ed), *New York Convention on the Recognition and Enforcement of Foreign Arbitral Awards, Commentary* (2012).

34   See UN Treaty Collection, Status of Treaties, Chapter 22: Commercial Arbitration, available at: <https://treaties.un.org/> accessed 20 November 2021.

35   See Jan Kleinheisterkamp, 'Recognition and Enforcement of Foreign Arbitral Awards', in *Max Planck Encyclopedia* (n 30) (May 2008) para 21: The UNCITRAL Model Law thereby promotes "a single regime for the enforcement of 'international' awards".

36   The award must be issued by an arbitral body. Consequently, a decision by a court such as, eg the "St. Petersburg Court of Arbitration", cannot be enforced under the NYC. See Hanseatisches Oberlandesgericht Hamburg, Decision of 28 October 2004, N 6 U 89/ 04.

the NYC contains a clause on the presumption of validity (Article IV NYC). According to this presumption the opposing party must show evidence of specific grounds for refusal. Article V (1) NYC contains an exhaustive list[37] of legitimate grounds for refusal, the existence of which must be proven by the opposing party. The grounds mentioned in Article V(1) NYC relate to serious failures of the award threatening the fundaments of its legitimacy.[38] Special attention should be drawn to Article V (1) (e) NYC according to which recognition and enforcement may be refused if the award has been set aside or suspended by a competent authority of the country where the award was made. Even more relevant is Article V (2) NYC, according to which recognition and enforcement may be refused if the subject matter of the difference cannot be settled by arbitration under the law of the country where enforcement is sought, or if the recognition or enforcement of the award would be contrary to the public policy of that country. From this perspective, refusal of enforcement has only a territorial effect, which is limited to the country where enforcement is sought. The same award can still be enforced in other countries.

Article III NYC, in conjunction with Articles IV and V NYC, seeks to limit the grounds of refusing enforcement and to "allow for the free circulation of arbitral awards".[39] However, they also leave some room for creative forms of interpretation. Though grounds such as "manifest disregard of the law" or "arbitrary and capricious decision of the case" are not included into the list,[40] they may gain influence in an indirect manner, namely by penetrating the notion of public policy.[41]

After all, the NYC system suffers from two major deficiencies: Firstly, it leaves the question of whether there exists a ground for the refusal of recognition and enforcement (Article V NYC) to "the competent authority where the recognition and enforcement is sought", i.e. a domestic authority. Secondly, it

---

37   Kleinheisterkamp (n 35) para 26.
38   (a) The parties to the arbitration agreement were under some incapacity, or the arbitration agreement is not valid. (b) The opposing party did not have a proper opportunity to present its case. (c) The scope of the arbitration agreement was not respected. (d) The composition of the arbitral authority or arbitral procedure was not in accordance with the arbitration agreement, or, failing such agreement, was not in accordance with the law of the country where the arbitration took place. (e) The award has not become binding, or been set aside or suspended by a competent authority of the country where the award was made.
39   Kleinheisterkamp (n 35) para 24.
40   See, with special regard to US practice, Larry W. Thomas, *Enforcement of International Arbitration Awards in the United States* (April 2013) sub IV. (with further references), available at: <www.lwthomas.com/articles/> accessed 20 November 2021.
41   See s 2.3. (c) (bb).

does not harmonize national court procedures, which may result in a situation where the enforcement of arbitral awards may become hostage to domestic court practices.[42]

2.3.2   Enforcement in the Case of Annulment – International Law
           Options in a Situation of Shared Responsibility
One of the most controversial questions is whether a foreign arbitral award may be enforced after having been annulled in the country where the award was made (Article V [1] [e] NYC). On the one hand, the "territorial approach" suggests that the courts at the place of arbitration have primary jurisdiction over awards issued within their jurisdiction; on the other hand, the "delocalized approach" argues that according to the English version of Article V [1] [e] NYC enforcement of the award "may" be refused – but must not be refused – if it has been annulled in the country of origin.[43] Accordingly, state practice differs considerably in that respect: Whereas, e.g. French courts more or less systematically disregard any foreign setting aside decision,[44] e.g. US, English and German courts seem to allow enforcement only if the annulment decision was taken by the foreign authority in manifest disregard of the law.[45]

The *Hilmarton* case[46] was groundbreaking for the territorial approach. In this case, the French *Cour de cassation* held that recognizing the annulment decision was contrary to the public policy of France. Though the award was made in Switzerland, the Court considered it an international award, which was not integrated into the Swiss legal order and, therefore, despite its setting aside, continued to exist. The *Cour* concluded that pursuant to Article VII NYC French domestic rules pertaining to the recognition and enforcement of foreign awards in international arbitration could be applied. Ever since, awards being annulled in the country of origin may be enforced in France, if the annulment occurred for reasons not recognised by French arbitration law.[47] The French position hence is that an international award is independent from the legal system of the country of origin.

---

42   Mistelis (n 1) 84.

43   For the pros and cons of both theories see Christoph Liebscher, art V, in: Wolff (n 33) mn 381–391.

44   See Patricia Nacimiento, 'Recognition and Enforcement of Annulled Arbitral Awards' (2009) *SchiedsVZ* 272, at 273, with special regard to the landmark decision of the French Cour de Cassation, Judgment of 9.10.1984, YCA vol. XI (1986), 484ff.

45   Kleinheisterkamp (n 35), para 34 (with further references).

46   Cour de cassation, 23 March 1994, Bulletin 1994 I N°104 79, *Société Hilmarton Ltd. v Société Omnium de traitement et de valorisation* (OTV).

47   Kröll, in: Bungenberg and others (n 1) mn 39 (1495).

In the notorious *Chromalloy* case[48] a US federal court chose to enforce an arbitral award, which – for dubious reasons – was set aside by a court in the *forum* state (Egypt). The US court pointed out that it was entitled but not required by Article V (1) (e) NYC to refuse to enforce. It also referred to Article VII NYC according to which a foreign arbitral award can be enforced under any more favourable regime that may exist under domestic law of the state where enforcement is sought. As the Egyptian court in this case seemed to have blatantly repudiated Egypt's obligation not to appeal an arbitral award, some authors considered this decision to be rather exceptional than representative for US practice.[49]

In the case of *Yukos Capital v Rosneft*, the Arbitrazh Court of Moscow had set aside an arbitral award rendered in Russia.[50] Nonetheless, the Amsterdam Court of Appeal finally granted Yukos leave to enforce the award in the Netherlands.[51] The Court argued that, as the judgment of the Arbitrazh Court had violated the principle of due process, the recognition of such judgment would conflict with the Dutch public order.[52] Referring to various reports on the situation in Russia, the Dutch Court found that Rosneft were closely interwoven with the Russian state and that the Russian judiciary lacked independence and impartiality.[53] An English court found in the same case that "there is no principle of *ex nihilo nil fit* in English law" such as to prevent the English court from giving effect to the awards in the circumstances given.[54]

The question remains whether a State, by ignoring the setting aside decision by a "competent authority of the country in which, under the law of which, that award was made" (Article V [1] [e] NYC) violates international law. Though the English text of Article V (1) (e) NYC ("may") seem to grant some discretion, this is not confirmed by other authentic versions of the document.[55] Where

---

48 US District Court for the District of Columbia, 31 July 1996, *Chromalloy Aeroservices v Arab Republic of Egypt*, 939 F. Supp. 907 (1996).

49 See *Neuhaus* (n 29) 35–39.

50 Arbitrazh Court of Moscow, 18 May 2007, Cases A40-4577/07-8-46 and others Upheld by the Federal Arbitrazh Court of the Moscow Region, 26 July 2007, Case KT-A40/6775-07.

51 Amsterdam Court of Appeal, 28 April 2009, Case 200.005.269/01, *Yukos Capital S.A.R.L. v OAO Rosneft*.

52 However, the nullification of a foreign arbitral award by a foreign judiciary is not very likely to interfere with a specific international public order policy of the Netherlands.

53 Critically on that, Albert Jan van den Berg, 'Enforcement of Arbitral Awards Annulled in Russia: Case Comment on Court of Appeal of Amsterdam' (29 April 2009), (2010) 27 J Int Arb 179; Liebscher (n 43) mn 388.

54 High Court of Justice (Commercial Court), 3 July 2014, [2014] EWHC 2188 (Comm), *Yukos Capital S.a.r.L. v OJSC Oil Company Rosneft*.

55 See van den Berg (n 53) 186. This author points to the fact that the French version reads "seront refusés" (shall be refused), offering no leeway for a residual discretionary power.

the official languages of the treaty produce different texts, all of those must be reconciled, because they are equally authoritative; where this is not possible, other rules on interpretation have to be applied in order to achieve reconciliation as far as possible (Article 33 VCLT).

It is true that the enforcement of an award annulled in the state of origin does not violate the latter's sovereignty rights, because enforcement has no legal impact on the decision of annulment as such. However, enforcement under such circumstances renders the decision of annulment null and void. This form of de facto devaluation seems to frustrate the *intention of competence sharing* respectively of *shared responsibility* between the authorities of the country of origin of the award on the one hand and the authorities of the country of enforcement on the other hand reflected by Article V NYC. This, at least, may conflict with the *comity among nations*,[56] which as a principle of courtesy (not law) calls upon states to show deference for the laws, judicial decisions, and institutions of another state. Ignorance of comity respectively the commitment of an "*unfriendly act*" can be assumed in all cases where the decision to annul the award meets the "international standard annulment" test and is not merely based on domestic law concerns ("local standard annulment").[57] Yet, there is more to it: ignoring annulment decisions arbitrarily or systematically constitutes a violation of the state of origin's treaty rights under Article V (1) (e) NYC, because the devaluation of the jurisdiction of the courts of another state, party to the NYC, undermines the object and purpose (Article 31 [1] VCLT) of this provision and thus conflicts with the obligation to interpret and apply the NYC *in good faith*.[58]

However, the problem is more complex: On the one hand, enforcement in spite of annulment can constitute an interference with the state of origin's treaty rights under Article V (1) (e) NYC. On the other hand, the state of origin itself might have violated its obligation by not adhering strictly to the limited number of grounds for annulment provided for by the NYC. Under such circumstances, *enforcement must be limited to exceptional cases*, where the decision of annulment itself clearly constitutes an *abuse of treaty rights*. That is exactly why, according to contemporary state practice, cases like the ones mentioned are relatively few in number,[59] and regularly associated with exceptional

---

56   See Liebscher (n 43) mn 386, with further reference.
57   cf Liebscher (n 43) mn 382.
58   The principle of good faith is also a general principle (art 38 [1] [c] ICJ Statute). See s 2.3. (c) (bb).
59   Francisco González de Cossío lists ten cases that have analyzed the possibility of enforcing an annulled award, out of which eight were successful. See ibid, Enforcement of

circumstances. Commenting on this, there seems to exist an *atypical form of "countermeasure"* aiming at the nullification of "default annulations" in cases where annulment appears to be an abuse of treaty rights.

2.3.3   Defenses to Enforcement (Selected Issues)
2.3.3.1   *Non-arbitrability and Freedom from External Interference*
According to Article V (2) (a) NYC enforcement may be denied, if the subject matter is not arbitrable under domestic law. This happens quite rarely. One example relating to general international law issues is *Libyan American Oil Co. (LIAMCO) v Socialist People's Libyan Arab Jamahirya*, where a US District Court declined to recognize and enforce the arbitral award.[60] The District Court argued that it would have been compelled to rule on the validity of the Libyan nationalization law, had that question been brought before this Court initially. This, however, would have been in contradiction with the classic US act-of-state-doctrine. According to the US Supreme Court in *Underhill* (1897) "[e]very sovereign state is bound to respect the independence of every other sovereign state, and the courts of one country will not sit in judgment on the acts of the government of another, done within its own territory."[61] However, in its ground-breaking *Sabbatino* ruling (1964) the US Supreme Court has also stated that the doctrine is not required by international law but rather seeks to promote international comity by maintaining the proper separation of powers between the political and the judicial branches of the US government.[62]

Though most of the European States have not included the act-of-state-doctrine into their domestic law, they also adhere to the international law principle that one state shall not sit in judgment on the acts of the government of another. This follows from the sovereignty rights of the state concerned comprising the protection of a sovereign State's *domaine réservé*, i.e. freedom from external interference and intervention. According to Article 2 (7) UN Charter, sovereign States are protected against the United Nations' or other States' interventions in matters which are essentially within their domestic jurisdiction.[63]

Annulled Awards: Towards a Better Analytical Approach, 2013, at 2–3. Available at: <www.gdca.com.mx> accessed 20 November 2021.

60   US District Court for the District of Columbia, 18 January 1980, *Libyan American Oil Co. (LIAMCO) v Socialist People's Libyan Arab Jamahirya*, 482 F. Supp. 1175 (1980).

61   US Supreme Court, *Underhill v Hernandez*, 168 US 250 252 (1897).

62   Fausto de Quatros/John H. Dingfelder Stone, 'Act of State Doctrine' (March 2013) in *Max Planck Encyclopedia* (n 30) para 6, referring to US Supreme Court, in *Sabbatino* (1964).

63   See Samantha Besson, 'Sovereignty' in *Max Planck Encyclopedia* (n 30) (April 2011) para 122.

However, in some legal systems domestic courts are even obligated to refuse recognition with regard to internationally wrongful acts of other states, requiring prior examination of such acts.[64] International law does not prohibit any form of sitting in judgment and even obligates states not to recognize certain acts. The essential question hence is: under what circumstances a domestic judgment on another state's nationalization must be considered wrongful under international law. It seems convincing that a state, though it has the right to nationalize within its own territory, has no right to revoke its commitment to arbitrate by treating the dispute about the nationalization *ex post* as non-arbitrable.[65] Accordingly, "sitting in judgment" appears illegal under international law only where a court judges on foreign legislation without any proper justification or in an inappropriate manner – whereas the latter may appear more as a matter of comity rather than law. There is no violation of international law, if jurisdiction with regard to the recognition and enforcement of foreign arbitral awards is entrusted to domestic courts and if their dealing with foreign legislation appears preliminary to administer this task.

2.3.3.2   Public Policy Defence – Does a Flawed Interpretation Violate International Law?

The most difficult issue is to determine under what circumstances the authorities of the state of enforcement can decline to recognize and enforce a foreign arbitral award for public policy reasons.[66] Though the public policy exception being enshrined in Article V (2) (b) NYC must be interpreted restrictively[67] – i.e.

---

64   Eg, in Germany the constitutional principle of "friendliness towards international law" (*Völkerrechtsfreundlichkeit*) under certain circumstances may demand from the domestic courts even to defend international law against internationally wrongful acts of other states including denial of recognition within the German territory. See Bundesverfassungsgericht (Federal Constitutional Court), 26 October 2004, BVerfGE vol. 112, 1, at 26. At the same time, German courts are obligated under the same principle to show respect for the structures and contents of foreign legal orders. See BVerfG, 2 BvR 2259/04, 6 July 2005, EuGRZ 2005, 409 ff, also <www.Bundesverfassungsgericht.de> para 24.

65   David Quinke, 'Article V' in Wolff (n 33) para 454.

66   See, comprehensively, Troy L. Harris, 'The "Public Policy" Exception to Enforcement of International Arbitration Awards Under the New York Convention' (2007) 24 Journal of International Arbitration 9–24.

67   See for the Travaux préparatoires *de Sydow* (Chairman of Working Party No. 3), UN ECOSOC, 12 September 1958, E/Conf.26/SR 17, 3: "As regards paragraph 2 (b) of article IV, the Working Party felt that the provision allowing refusal of enforcement on grounds of public policy should not be given a broad scope of application. It therefore agreed to the deletion of references to the subject matter of the award and to fundamental principles of the law".

a refusal to enforce conforms to the NYC only if there is a clear contradiction to the essential values of the *forum* state[68] – it appears to be quite obvious that the clause offers a breakthrough opportunity for the realization of any kinds of political purposes. E.g. Russian courts seem to use the public policy caveat quite extensively and disparately.[69] Arguments such as the imminent danger of insolvency of the debtor, or the economic situation of a certain region were reported to be presented as public policy grounds.[70] Systematic abuses of Article V (2) (b) NYC also became known with respect to India.[71] Even if most states apply Article V (2) (b) NYC restrictively,[72] the need for more precise criteria on "public policy" has become apparent.

In 2004 the International Law Association Committee on International Commercial Arbitration issued a report on the range and meaning of the term of "public policy". In its report, the Committee recommends that "[t]he finality of international commercial arbitration should be respected save in exceptional circumstances" such as in the case of a violation of the public policy of a state. However, public policy should be understood to be "part of the public policy of a state which, if violated, would prevent a party from invoking a foreign law or foreign judgment or foreign award."[73]

Adopting this definition, the Supreme Court of Mauritius has contributed to the further clarification of Article V (2) (b) NYC. In the case of *Cruz City 1 Mauritius Holdings v Unitech Limited & ANOR* (2014) it found that

---

68   Kleinheisterkamp (n 35) para 32.

69   See Dimitry Marenkov, 'Zur Anerkennung und Vollstreckung von ausländischen Schiedssprüchen in Russland' (2011) *SchiedsVZ* 136ff, at 138–139, 147. According to this author contractual penalties were regarded by some courts as being incompatible with Russian public policy, whilst other courts came to the opposite conclusion (with further references). According to Boris Karabelnikov and Dominik Pellew, 'Enforcement of International Arbitral Awards in Russia – Still A Mixed Picture' (2008) 19 ICC International Court of Arbitration Bulletin 68, Russian authorities had refused to enforce awards by more than 50 percent.

70   See Anton G Maurer, 'Begründet die völkerrechtswidrige Verweigerung der Vollstreckung eines ausländischen Schiedsspruchs einen Schadensersatzanspruch des Schiedsklägers?' (2011) *SchiedsVZ* 75ff, at 76 (with further reference).

71   See Maurer (n 70) 77.

72   For the latest developments see Inae Yang, 'A Comparative Review on Substantive Public Policy in International Commercial Arbitration' (2015) 70 Dispute Resolution Journal 49–83.

73   Final Report on Public Policy as a Bar to Enforcement of International Arbitration Awards (2004) Transnational Dispute Management (TDM) 1, available at: <www.transnational -dispute-management.com> accessed 20 November 2021.

it is the public policy in the international context that will matter and not the public policy that would normally apply when challenging a domestic award [and] the respondent has to show with precision and clarity in what way and to what extent enforcement of the award would have an adverse bearing on a particular international public policy of this country.[74]

Hence, the alleged prejudice of public policy must be of a general character, which applies regardless of a particular award. Even though this standard of international public policy is commonly used today, some authors find it not to be imposed by Article V (2) (b) NYC.[75] According to this position, each state continues to enjoy the freedom to define its public policy as long as there is no uniform standard.[76] Additionally, the principle of comity among states is considered to have led to a more generous standard for foreign awards in comparison with domestic awards.[77]

However, the interpretation and application by domestic authorities of Article V (2) (b) NYC is not unlimited. According to Article 31 (1) VCLT "[a] treaty shall be interpreted in good faith in accordance with the ordinary meaning to be given to the terms of the treaty in their context and in the light of its object and purpose." Even if there exists a comity of tolerance with regard to the particularities of foreign legal orders, which may determine what is required by the principle of good faith,[78] practices on grounds of a clear misinterpretation of certain treaty provisions or systematic ignorance of their object and purpose may amount to a violation of Article 31 (1) VCLT and the general international law *principle of good faith* including the stricter doctrine of "*no abuse of rights*".[79] Matching with this doctrine, it is widely acknowledged today that the definition of public policy by the competent state must neither devaluate the latter's ratification of the Convention, nor shall public policy concerns

---

74 Supreme Court of Mauritius, Judgment of 28 March 2014, 2014 SCJ 100 <https://www
    .marc.mu/media/2923/cruz-city-1-mauritius-holdings-v-unitech-limited-2014-scj-100
    .pdf> accessed 20 November 2021. The Court also referred to the French law (arts 1520.5,
    1522 al. 2, 1524 al. 1 du Code de procédure civile) which apparently has inspired its
    interpretation.

75 Reinmar Wolff, 'Article V' in Wolff (n 33) paras 496–498. According to Wolff a number of
    concepts are being discussed under the notion of "international public policy".

76 cf Wolff (n 75) para 521.

77 cf Wolff (n 75) para 511.

78 See Jörn Axel Kämmerer, 'Comity' in *Max Planck Encyclopedia* (n 30) (December
    2006) para 8.

79 Markus Kotzur, 'Good Faith' in *Max Planck Encyclopedia* (n 30) (January 2009) para 17.

become the rule.[80] On the other hand, it should be noted that, although the object and purpose of the NYC is to promote investment, this must not be conflated with a general preference for the interests of the investor over those of other parties concerned.[81]

2.3.3.3 Foreign Proceedings – Balancing Swift Enforcement and Competence for Annulment as a Matter of "Shared Responsibility"

According to Article V (1) (e) NYC an application for recognition and enforcement may be dismissed if the award "has not become binding" yet. Principally, an award becomes binding as soon as it is made (cf. Article III NYC). In contrast to the 1927 Geneva Convention Article V (1) (e) NYC uses the term "binding", not "final". Accordingly, e.g. German practice tends to treat arbitral awards as binding, even if an appeal in the other state is still pending; the reason being that the latter can only achieve nullification but no "révision au fond".[82] According to US law and practice an award is considered to be binding under the Convention when there are no arbitral appeals available, not when all judicial appeals have been exhausted in the country in which the award was made.[83]

In the case of IPCO (Nigeria) v Nigerian National Petroleum (2015) the English Court of Appeal was to decide whether enforcement could be adjourned pending the outcome of setting aside proceedings in the seat state of the arbitration (Article VI NYC).[84] Unfortunately, the proceedings in Nigeria had already lasted for approximately ten years and were expected to continue for ten more years. The English Court of Appeal carefully tried to balance both positions: On the one hand, the NYC seeks to foster international trade by ensuring a swift enforcement of awards and "a degree of isolation from the vagaries of local legal systems". On the other hand, pending proceedings in the country of origin of the award should not necessarily be pre-empted by rapid enforcement of the award in another jurisdiction. Respecting this, the English Court of Appeal made the outcome dependent on the circumstances of the individual case and named a couple of criteria to be relevant.[85] It came to the conclusion

---

80   cf Wolff (n 75) paras 499–505.
81   cf McLachlan (n 6) 371.
82   See Wolff (n 75) paras 561–562; Heiko Plaßmeier, 'Vollstreckung nicht "endgültiger" Schiedssprüche – Zugleich eine Anmerkung zum Beschluss des BayObLG vom 22. November 2002' (2004) SchiedsVZ 234ff.
83   Thomas (n 40) sub II.B.5 (with further references).
84   Court of Appeal, Judgment of 10 November 2015, IPCO (Nigeria) Ltd. v Nigerian National Petroleum Corporation, [2015] All England Reporter (D) 103 (Nov).
85   Eg whether the application before the court in the country of origin was brought bona fide, whether there is a realistic prospect of success and what extent the delay might take

that after certain conditions were fulfilled, IPCO would have the permission to enforce the award, notwithstanding the on-going proceedings in Nigeria.

At first view, granting leave for enforcement seems perfectly in line with the NYC: according to Article V (1) (e) NYC enforcement of the award may be refused only if the award "has [already] been set aside or suspended" in the country of origin.[86] In all other cases, the award remains binding even though an action to set it aside is pending in the country of origin.[87] Yet the Convention also suggests a certain form of competence sharing (*shared responsibility*) amongst both states. Competence entrusted by the Convention to the authorities of the other state can be "pre-empted by rapid enforcement of the award in another jurisdiction". This can amount to a violation of Article V NYC, – whilst non-enforcement can amount to a violation of Article III NYC obligating the states parties to enforce awards once they are binding. Thus, there exists an antagonism between both norms, which must be handled not only in accordance with "soft law" (comity among nations) but also in accordance with the international law principle of good faith.[88] It follows from this that the court of the state of enforcement must duly consider the competencies of both sides and carefully balance all interests concerned– as has been done by the English court in *IPCO*. This court, late but not too late, sent a signal of pre-emption to any state, the courts of which by the preposterous length of their setting aside proceedings may try to undermine effective enforcement under the NYC.

2.3.3.4   *Procedural Barriers to Enforcement – Does the Rule of* Forum Non Conveniens *Violate Article III NYC?*

The New York Convention leaves to the States, where enforcement is sought, the establishment of the rules of procedure enabling recognition and enforcement of foreign arbitral awards (procedure of the *lex fori*[89]). Domestic procedural

---

The Court also referred to the criteria named by the US Court of Appeals for the Second Circuit in *Europcar Italia S.p.A. v Maiellano Tours*, 156 F.3d 319 (1998).

86   Accordingly, art 53[1], 2nd sentence ICSID provides that the terms of the award must be complied with, "except to the extent that enforcement shall have been stayed". Stay of enforcement is the only exception to the obligation to comply promptly with an award. See Inna Uchkunova and Oleg Temnikov, 'Enforcement of Awards Under the ICSID Convention – What Solutions to the problem of State Immunity?' (2014) 29 ICSID Review 187ff, at 197, referring to *Sempra v Argentina*. Also Kröll (n 1) mn 53 (1499), respecting ICSID: "The mere pendency of an annulment ... procedure does not entitle the State authorities to stay enforcement."

87   See Liebscher (n 43) mn 357.

88   See 2.3. (c) (bb).

89   Kleinheisterkamp (n 35) para 24.

law, however, may provide for all kinds of legal barriers, unless foreign awards will not be treated less favourably than domestic awards (Article III NYC). It can thus require that the court, by which enforcement is sought, must have jurisdiction according to domestic law. E.g. in the United States. the defendant, due to the requirements of the Due Process Clause, should have "certain minimum contacts" with the forum.[90]

According to the rule of *forum non conveniens* a US federal district court, though it has jurisdiction (!), may find that a more appropriate forum exists to enforce the award and dismiss transnational litigation in favour of a foreign court.[91] The *forum non conveniens* doctrine is held by the US Supreme Court to be "procedural rather than substantive".[92] A court may even dismiss on *forum non conveniens* grounds before deciding on jurisdiction,[93] at least in cases in which it is less burdensome for the court.[94] However, an action to confirm and enforce a NYC arbitral award cannot be dismissed on the mere fact that the defendants has no assets in the United States, as they may own property there in the future.[95]

E.g. in *Monegasque de Reassurances S.A.M. v NAK Naftogaz of Ukraine* (2002) the US Court of Appeals for the Second Circuit dismissed an action to confirm and enforce a NYC arbitration award on the ground of *forum non conveniens*.[96] This case dealt with Gazprom (Russia) blaming Naftogaz (Ukraine) of having skimmed more gas than conceded during transport. The US court when examining whether Ukraine were to be considered the more adequate forum for

---

90 See US Supreme Court, *Int'l Shoe Co. v Washington* 326 US 310 (1945) at 316,: Pursuant to the Due Process Clause of the Fourteenth Amendment, *in personam* jurisdiction may be asserted over a non-resident so long as the defendant has "certain minimum contacts with [the forum] such that the maintenance of the suit does not offend traditional notions of fair play and substantial justice." In order not to frustrate the object and purpose of the NYC, "quasi *in rem*" jurisdiction of the court over the defendant will be sufficient. See US Court of Appeals for the Third Circuit, *Telcordia Tech Inc v Telkom Sa Ltd* 458 F. 3d 172, 178–179 (2006)..

91 US Supreme Court, *Piper Aircraft Co v Reyno*, 454 US 235 (1981). See also (groundbreaking): US Supreme Court, *Gulf Oil Corp v Gilbert*, 330 US 501, 507 (1947).

92 US Supreme Court, *American Dredging Company v Miller*, 510 US 443, 453 (1994).

93 US Supreme Court, *Sinochem International Co Ltd v Malaysia International Shipping Corporation*, 549 US 422 (2007).

94 Christopher A. Whytock, 'U.S. Supreme Court Decides Forum Non Conveniens Case' (5 November 2007)11(10) *ASIL Insights*.

95 US Court of Appeals for the D.C. Circuit, Judgment of 17 July 2005, *TMR Energy Ltd v State Property Fund of Ukraine*, 411 F.3d 296, 304.

96 US Court of Appeals for the Second Circuit, 15 November 2002, *In re Arbitration Between Monegasque De Reassurances S.A.M. v Nak Naftogaz of Ukraine* 311 F.3d 488 (2002). For a discussion of this case see *Neuhaus* (n 29) 31ff.

enforcement, had also to answer the question of whether "general corruption in the body politic of that nation" could preclude the assumption of adequacy. Although this objection was repudiated in the specific case, because the creditor of the award had engaged voluntarily in business with Naftogaz, it was not rejected as such. Hence, the case serves as an example for the fact that even procedural law can become an instrument to sit in judgment on the constitutional and political condition of another state.

Again, the manner by which the courts of the state of enforcement exercise their jurisdiction with regard to foreign states can amount to a neglect of comity, or even to a violation of the international law principle of good faith.[97] With special regard to the rule of *forum non conveniens* it should also be noted that this rule does not play a neutral role but rather applies more severely to foreign arbitral awards than to domestic awards.[98] Consequently, foreign arbitral awards are imposed substantially more onerous conditions than are imposed on the enforcement of domestic arbitral awards. Applying the rule of *forum non conveniens* to foreign arbitral awards seems not only incompatible with Article III NYC[99] but also with the object and purpose of the enforcement regime of the NYC.

2.4   *ICSID Convention*

2.4.1   The Enforcement Mechanism

The Convention of the Settlement of Investment Disputes Between States and Nationals of Other States (ICSID Convention) of 1965,[100] which has been ratified by 152 states,[101] specifically relates to investment disputes between foreign (private) investors and host countries where the investment is made. Most BITs and some international treaties (e.g., Article 1120 NAFTA and Article 26 [4] of the Energy Charter) contain clauses offering access to ICSID. Special rules apply with regard to disputes between a contracting state and a non-contracting state such as Russia, Poland, India, Thailand, Mexico, Bolivia, Ecuador, or Venezuela. According to the so-called "ICSID Additional Facility

---

97   See s 2.3. (c) (bb).

98   Neuhaus (n 29) 34.

99   See also Maxi Scherer, art III, in Wolff (n 33) 193ff, para 22. Scherer argues that the *forum non conveniens* doctrine is not procedural in nature but substantive. Applying the doctrine to recognition and enforcement actions, thus would violate the limitation contained in art III that the substantive requirements of the NYC are set forth exclusively in the Articles of the NYC, namely art V.

100   Comprehensively, Schreuer and others, *ICSID Convention* (n 8).

101   See ICSID, ICSID documents, list of Member States, available at: <https://icsid.worldb ank.org> accessed 20 November 2021.

Rules" (AFR), the NYC regime remains applicable to awards made under these rules.[102] Wherever AFR apply, awards remain subject to review by the domestic courts of the host state (Article 3 AFR), whilst the ICSID Convention aims at excluding any objections against enforcement under domestic law.

The ICSID Convention has introduced a much more developed standard with respect to the recognition and enforcement of arbitral awards. Article 53 (1) ICSID as the fundamental rule of the ICSID system states that

> [t]he award shall be binding on the parties and shall not be subject to any appeal or to any other remedy except those provided for in this Convention.

This contrasts clearly to the NYC, where an equivalent rule is missing. Article 53(1) ICSID ("shall not be subject to any appeal or to any other remedy…") together with Article 26 ICSID (exclusion of any other remedy) and Article 27 ICSID (renouncement by the home state of its right to grant diplomatic protection) is often understood to underline the character of the ICSID mechanism as a "self-contained regime".[103] However, the question of whether international investment law constitutes a particular "system" is highly controversial, as some authors cannot see a complete set of rules, which would allow international investment law to remain independent from general international law.[104] This is also confirmed by the practice of arbitration under ICSID, which in many instances refers to international law.[105]

The main obligations of the parties follow from Articles 53 and 54 ICSID. Article 53 (1) ICSID reads in its relevant part (second sentence):

---

102 As the AFR do not contain any provisions on recognition and enforcement, awards remain subject to the treaties applicable. According to arts 19 and 20 (3) AFR arbitration proceedings shall be held only in states that are parties to the NYC. Schreuer and others (n 8) art 54, mn 13 (1120–1121).

103 With regard to art 44 ICSID Convention, Christoph Schreuer, 'International Centre for Settlement of Investment Disputes (ICSID)' in Max Planck Encyclopedia (n 30) (May 2013) para 43.

104 Denying international investment law the character of a self-contained regime Bruno Simma and Dirk Pulkowski, 'International Investment Agreements and the General Body of Rules of Public International Law' in Bungenberg and others (n 1) 361ff (n 1– 17). Also McLachlan (n 6) 369, referring to the ILC Fragmentation Report. See also s 4.3. (b).

105 Simma and Pulkowski (n 104), n 6ff, mention, eg, the rules on interpretation and state responsibility.

[e]ach party shall abide by and comply with the terms of the award except to the extent that enforcement shall have been stayed.

Article 54 (1) ICSID relates to enforcement[106]:

> Each Contracting State shall recognize an award rendered pursuant to this Convention as binding and enforce the pecuniary obligations imposed by that award within its territories as if it were a final judgment of a court in that State.

According to the wording of this provision, the obligation to enforce an arbitral award concerns pecuniary obligations only. The obligation to comply with the award under Article 53(1) ICSID is not subject to the successful investor's recourse to the enforcement mechanism of Article 54 ICSID, as Article 54 ICSID cannot be interpreted to weaken the obligation under Article 53 ICSID.[107]

2.4.2 Stay of Enforcement and Annulment of the Award

The ICSID Convention provides for some possibilities of halting enforcement. According to Articles 50 and 51 ICSID disputes on the meaning or scope of an award as well as the discovery of new facts could serve as grounds for a temporary stay of enforcement.[108] However, an ICSID Arbitral Tribunal and not a domestic court will decide on such requests. Although a stay of enforcement is not specifically mentioned in Article 54 ICSID, it is considered "clear" that an award that is subject to a stay of enforcement and hence does not carry an obligation of compliance is not subject to enforcement.[109]

Like the NYC, Article 52 ICSID lists the grounds for annulment exhaustively, namely un-proper constitution of the Tribunal, manifest excess of powers by the Tribunal, corruption on the part of a member of the Tribunal, serious departure from a fundamental rule of procedure, and failure to give reasons for the award. E.g. if a Tribunal *fails to apply such rules of international law* as may be applicable (Article 42 [1] ICSID), this failure may amount to an excess

---

106   There are very few cases, in which investors have availed themselves of the ICSID enforcement mechanism. See Inna Uchkunova and Oleg Temnikov (n 87) at 200, naming nine cases.

107   See Uchkunova and Temnikov (n 87) 197.

108   For further details see Inna Uchkunova, 'Much Ado about Nothing - Conditional Stay of Enforcement in Annulment Proceedings under the ICSID Convention' (2014) 30 Arbitration International 283–356.

109   Schreuer and others (n 8) art 52, mn 578–579 (1063–1064), art 54, mn 38–39, 1127, referring to *MINE v Guinea*.

of power allowing for annulment (Article 52[1] [b] ICSID)[110] and, eventually, a stay of enforcement (Article 52 [5] ICSID). However, the ICSID Convention differs essentially from the NYC in as much as it does not entitle domestic authorities to refuse to enforce for public policy reasons (cf. Article V [2] NYC). Additionally, there is a time limit of 120 days for the plea for annulment, and it will be dealt with by an ICSID *ad hoc* Committee (Article 52 [2], [3] ICSID). Arrangements like this are part of a general strategy to exclude within the ICSID system any intervention by domestic courts and to establish a denationalized system of recognition and enforcement.

2.4.3   Defences to Enforcement
2.4.3.1   *Principle of Equal Treatment of Foreign Arbitral Awards and Domestic Judgments*

The ICSID Convention demands from the states to recognize the award as binding and to enforce it "as if it were a final judgment of a court in that State" (Article 54 [1] ICSID). In addition, the Convention prescribes that "execution of the award shall be governed by the laws concerning the execution of judgments" in force in the State where execution is sought (Article 54 [3] ICSID). On the first view, these provisions seem to facilitate enforcement and execution[111] and so suggest "true finality".[112] Accordingly, Article 54 (1) ICSID is considered to be the most far-reaching provision that was ever achieved by international agreement.[113]

However, putting both judgments and awards on an equal footing is exactly what creates opportunities for challenging the enforcement and execution of ICSID "default awards" in national courts: As far as binding domestic judgments may be challenged (e.g. because of newly discovered evidence, false testimony, blatant mistakes, etc.) foreign awards may be challenged, too. E.g. in US court

---

110   Schreuer and others (n 8) art 52, mn 250–270 (975–977), referring to *Amco v Indonesia, Klöckner v Cameroon*, etc.

111   Comprehensively on whether both terms stand for different or identical concepts, Schreuer and others (n 8) art 54, mn 64–71, 1134–1136. Some authors, with respect to art 54 (3) ICSID, argue that enforceability is governed by the Convention, whilst execution is governed by domestic law. See Uchkunova and Temnikov (n 87) at 192/193. Other authors opine that "enforcement" will be used to describe the first phase of the enforcement process, while for the second phase after the award being turned into an executory title the term "execution" will be employed. See Kröll (n 1) mn 6, 1485.

112   Significantly on finality, *Maritime International Nominees Establishment (MINE) v Guinea*, ICSID Case No ARB784/4, Decision (14 December 1989) para 4.02. See also Edward Baldwin and others, 'Limits to Enforcement of ICSID Awards' (2006) 23 Journal of International Arbitration 1ff (at 9).

113   See Tosten Lörcher, 'ICSID-Schiedsgerichtsbarkeit' (2005) *SchiedsVZ* 11, 20.

proceedings a decision can be declared invalid, because it is "offensive to the Due Process Clause of the Fourteenth Amendment", even though relief from a final judgment is only appropriate for exceptional circumstances.[114] Similarly, French law,[115] German law[116] and many others offer some chances to reconsider a final judgment. Despite the fact that there are only a few cases where this strategy was actually applied to foreign awards, some authors derive from these examples that national courts have not fully accepted "a deferential role" in the enforcement of ICSID awards.[117] The only limit to this challenge can be taken from Article 53 (1) ICSID, according to which the reopening of proceedings must not amount to any form of appeal.

2.4.3.2   General International Law Principles

General principles of international law[118] such as the international law doctrines of "denial of justice",[119] "abuse of rights", "unfair and inequitable treatment" or "good faith" can be used (or abused) in order to refuse to recognize, enforce or execute a foreign arbitral award.[120] The same applies with regard to countermeasures[121] or necessity being claimed by a state in order to halt enforcement. In such cases, the question of jurisdiction has to be distinguished from the question of the law that is applicable.[122] The initial question in such cases will be whether the tribunal has jurisdiction to decide on the validity of an international law defence. Article 42 ICSID gives a specific answer to that by requiring the tribunals, in the absence of explicit choice, to apply host state law and "such rules of international law as may be applicable".[123] With these contents Article 42 ICSID represents a specific emanation of the general rule

---

114   Baldwin and others (n 112) at 12.
115   See, with regard to art 595 of the French Code of Civil Procedure, Baldwin and others (n 112) 13.
116   §§ 578–591 of the German Code of Civil Procedure (Reopening of Proceedings). For an English version see <www.gesetze-im-internet.de/englisch_zpo/index.html> accessed 20 November 2021.
117   Baldwin and others (n 112) 5–8, with references.
118   See art 38 (1) (c) of the ICJ Statute.
119   See, comprehensively, Jan Paulsson, *Denial of Justice in International Law* (CUP 2005). With special regard to arbitration, *Mondev International Ltd v United States of America*, ICSID Case No ARB(AF)/99/2 (11 October 2002) paras 126ff.
120   Baldwin and others (n 112) 18–21.
121   See s 4.3.
122   McLachlan (n 6) 370.
123   Art 1131 (1) NAFTA similarly provides that "a Tribunal established under this section shall decide the issues in dispute in accordance with this Agreement and applicable rules of international law."

being enshrined in the Vienna Convention on the Law of Treaties: according to Article 31(3)(c) VCLT international treaties (e.g., the NYC) have to be interpreted in light of "any relevant rules of international law applicable in the relations between the parties". However, this provision applies only where the treaty rule is unclear or open-textured.[124] Under such circumstances, tribunals have competence to consider, e.g. human rights as long as they are related to an alleged breach of an investment treaty.[125]

The second question will be on whether a certain rule of general international law is "*applicable*". The specific treaty itself may provide an answer to that. E.g. Article 1105 (1) NAFTA explicitly grants minimum standard treatment "in accordance with international law".[126] Lacking such explicit references, it remains to be determined in every single case, whether the ICSID Convention in conjunction with the pertinent BIT leaves some room for invoking general international law. The same results from the fact that the ICSID Convention in most regards provides for the more specific rules (*speciality rule*). It follows from this that, generally, international law must be introduced into the analysis of a claim under an investment treaty through the medium of treaty interpretation.[127] However, general international law is to be given unfettered priority where peremptory norms[128] will be at stake.

General international law was invoked, e.g. by Argentina in the wake of a severe economic and financial crisis. This state tried to defer enforcement by claiming a stay of enforcement in annulment proceedings, respectively refused to enforce by referring to a "*state of necessity*".[129] According to Article 25 ILC Articles on State Responsibility[130] "necessity" demands from a

---

124   August Reinisch, 'Investment Agreements and General International Law' in Bungenberg and others (n 22) referring to ILC Study Group.

125   cf Balcerzak (n 18) 224. The author suggests that a distinction between wide and narrow clauses on jurisdiction would be decisive (at 220–226).

126   Respecting the reference to a minimum standard this wording has been held to comprise only manifest disregards of customary international law. See Karamanian (n 11) 444, referring to *Glamis Gold Ltd v United States*.

127   cf McLachlan (n 6) 371. Also see s 2.1.

128   cf art 53 VCLT. Eg prohibitions relating to the use of force, genocide, slavery, or torture.

129   See on necessity ICJ, 25 September 1997, *Case Concerning the Gabčíkovo-Nagymaros Project (Hungary v Slovakia)*, ICJ Reports 1997, 7, paras 49ff. An overview on cases brought against Argentina as well as on doctrinal comments is given by Christina Binder, 'Circumstances Precluding Wrongfulness' in Bungenberg and others (n 1), 442–480, n. 13. See also August Reinisch, 'Necessity in International Investment Arbitration – An Unnecessary Split of Opinions in Recent ICSID Cases? Comments on CMS v. Argentina and LG & E v. Argentina' (2007) 8 JWIT 191–214.

130   See s 4.1. (a) (with reference).

state to show that there exists a "grave and imminent peril" and that ignoring its international law obligations would be "the only way" to safeguard its essential interest. However, Article 52 ICSID (grounds for annulment) does not provide explicitly for anything like necessity. Argentina then tried to integrate necessity into Article 52 (1) (b) or (e) ICSID, but regularly failed.[131] In some cases it failed to show a continuous existence of necessity, in other cases certain rules of the pertinent BIT were held to be more specific than the customary law principle of necessity. After all, the relationship between the ICSID Convention and the principle of necessity remained somewhat open. On the one hand, there is some case for the assumption that the general principle of necessity cannot be invoked to undermine the specific regime of annulment, as provided by the ICSID Convention. On the other hand, some ICSID Committees in the *Argentina* cases at least accepted to consider whether Argentina's non-compliance could be justified by a state of necessity.[132] This conforms to the fact that necessity applies to all international treaties including the ICSID Convention. Similar questions have been discussed with regard to "force majeure" (Article 23 ILC Articles on State Responsibility).[133]

Another question is whether a state party to the ICSID Convention can invoke that there is a *"fundamental change of circumstances"* which was not foreseen by the parties (Article 62 Vienna Convention on the Law of Treaties). Article 62 VCLT relates to the consent of the parties to be fully bound by the treaty, i.e. to fulfill all obligations still to be performed. The negative wording of Article 62 VCLT[134] clearly indicates that the plea of fundamental change can be applied only in exceptional cases.[135] As the ICJ has clarified in the *Gabčíkovo-Nagymaros* case,[136] the changed circumstances must be of such a nature that their effect would radically transform the extent of the obligations still to be performed. Additionally, the existence of the circumstances at the time of the conclusion of the treaty must have constituted an essential basis for the consent of the parties. Last but not least, Article 62 VCLT cannot be invoked, if

---

131   See, eg *CMS Gas Transmission Company v Argentine Republic*, ICSID Case No ARB/01/8 (25 September 2007). For a survey see, eg McLachlan (n 6) 385–391, referring to *CMS, Enron, Sempra* and *LG & E.*

132   Binder (n 129) n 14– 16, speaks of "fundamentally different decisions" respectively "divergent approaches" of the Committees.

133   Binder (n 129) n 29– 43, with special regard to *Autopista Concesionada de Venezuela, CA (Aucoven) v Venezuela,* ICSID Case No ARB/00/5 (23 September 2003).

134   The change of circumstances "may not be invoked as a ground for terminating or withdrawing from the treaty unless ...."

135   ICJ in *Gabčíkovo-Nagymaros Project* (n 125) para 104.

136   ICJ (n 135).

the treaty itself accommodates for change. Regarding these requirements, it is very unlikely that a state could use Article 62 VCLT in order to escape from being bound by the ICSID Convention. Rather, a BIT may be attacked on such grounds. Should any plea of fundamental change be substantial at all, it could be argued that with regard to Article 62 VCLT the legal basis for arbitration had ceased to exist from the beginning (withdrawing from the treaty), bearing the consequence that annulment (Article 52 ICSID) would become possible. However, Article 62 VCLT is not a basis for terminating or withdrawing from a single obligation such as the obligation to recognize and enforce ICSID awards.

2.4.4 Compensation for Illegal Interference with Enforcement – the Award as an "Investment"?

In the case of *SAIPEM S.p.A. v The People's Republic of Bangladesh* (2009) an ICSID Arbitral Tribunal (deciding on the basis of the NYC and the pertinent BIT) found that the unlawful disruption of ICC Arbitration by a state (or its agents, resp. domestic courts) can be considered an expropriation and, accordingly, obligate that state to pay compensation.[137] Although this case deals with the consequences of a disruption by state courts of arbitration proceedings between two private parties, its basic deliberations also apply to interferences with enforcement. It serves as an example not only with regard to expropriation but also with regard to other forms of state interference, which might amount to a violation of the fair and equitable treatment standard or constitute denial of justice, resp. in the case of the NYC full protection and security, which then may trigger investment protection.[138] As concerns *SAIPEM*, the matter could become an ICSID case only, because the relevant construction works, which constituted the object of the original ICC arbitration, were considered to be part of an "entire operation" and thus qualified as "investment" in the sense of Article 25 ICSID. Some other Tribunals, e.g. in the case of *ATA v Jordan* (2010)[139] and *White Industries v India* (2011),[140] decided similarly, but

---

137   ICSID Case No ARB/05/07, Decision on Jurisdiction of 30 June 2009. See in particular para 132: "the Tribunal considers that there is no reason why a judicial act could not result in an expropriation". For a commentary to this case see Anton G. Maurer, 'Begründet die völkerrechtswidrige Verweigerung der Vollstreckung eines ausländischen Schiedsspruchs einen Schadensersatzanspruch des Schiedsklägers? – Die "Durchsetzung" multilateraler völkerrechtlicher Verträge durch private Parteien' (2011) *SchiedsVZ* 75–80.

138   Mistelis (n 1) at 86.

139   *ATA Construction, Industrial and Trading Co v Hashemite Kingdom of Jordan,* ICSID Case No ARB/08/2 (18 May 2010).

140   UNCITRAL, 30 November 2011, *White Industries Australia Ltd v The Republic of India.*

there is no consistent practice.[141] The *White Industries* case seems particularly important to our issue, as it deals with a protracted set aside application impeding enforcement.[142]

It is true that all relevant cases remain silent as to whether an arbitral award in itself qualifies as a claim to money, respectively as an investment.[143] However, there seems to be a recent trend in arbitral Tribunals to assume that awards "represent a continuation or transformation of the original investment".[144] Some authors find that the question of whether a violation of the NYC can be alleged before an investment tribunal depends on whether the latter's jurisdiction is based either on a narrow or broad scope of consent.[145] On the one hand, there is some concern about stretching the notion of "investment", as this might provide for an additional instance in the enforcement process.[146] As non-compliance with the obligations under a multilateral international treaty on recognition and enforcement (e.g., NYC) simultaneously brings in a breach of the investor (treaty-based) obligations, a tension between both instruments to the detriment of the multilateral instrument may arise.[147] Thereafter, the pertinent BIT may even modify the obligations of the Member States under the NYC, and the investment arbitration tribunal will be conceded the power to evaluate the compliance of the host state with the Convention.[148] On the other hand, exactly this can be deemed necessary in cases where essential principles of investment protection were infringed.[149]

---

141   For an overview, see Mistelis (n 1). See also Leonila Guglya, 'International Review of Decisions concerning Recognition and Enforcement' (2011) *CzechYIL* 93–121, with special regard to *Western NIS Enterprise Fund v Ukraine, Romak v Uzbekistan, Kaliningrad Region v Lithuania and GEA Group Aktiengesellschaft v Ukraine* (with references).

142   cf the *IPCO* case under the NYC, see s 2.3. (c) (cc).

143   See Mistelis (n 1) 77.

144   UNCITRAL, *White Industries* (n 140), at 7.6.8. See also Mistelis (n 1) 82, with further references.

145   Berk Demirkol, 'Enforcement of International Commercial Arbitration Agreements and Awards in Investment Treaty Arbitration' (2015) 30 ICSID Review 56, at 66–67, 76–77.

146   Explicitly so PCA Case No. AA280, 26 September 2009, *Romak SA (Switzerland) v The Republic of Uzbekistan*, para 186: "Second, the mechanical application of the categories [of investments] found in Article 1(2) would create, de facto, a new instance of review of State court decisions concerning the enforcement of arbitral awards. ... The refusal or failure of the host State's courts to enforce such an award would therefore arguably provide sufficient grounds for a *de novo* review".

147   See Guglya (n 141) at 108: "Investment Related Instruments versus the New York Convention".

148   See Guglya (n 141) at 110.

149   cf Mistelis (n 1) at 87.

3   Immunity of States as a Legal Barrier to the Execution of Awards

3.1   *The Principle of Immunity*

Measures of enforcement against a state in another state unavoidably interfere with the international law principle of immunity. General international law in this respect remains crucial, because the states, by acceding to multilateral treaties like the NYC or ICSID Convention, have not fully consented to waive their immunity, particularly not with regard to execution. As was rightly observed, "[t]he success of the award's enforcement will at all times depend on the creditor's ability to overcome the State's defence of sovereign immunity."[150]

The principle of immunity belongs to the most fundamental principles of public international law establishing as a rule that legal persons of equal standing – such as sovereign states – cannot be amenable to the jurisdiction of one of each, unless they have agreed so by express consent (*"par in parem non habet iurisdictionem"*).[151] With this essential meaning, the principle of immunity has become part of customary international law. However, there always remained confusion on various details including the question of whether immunity must be understood absolutely, or rather restrictively. Although the UN General Assembly adopted the (Draft) UN Convention on Jurisdictional Immunities of States and Their Property,[152] this instrument, due to a lack in the number of ratifications, never became binding.[153] In contrast, the Council of

---

150   Uchkunova (n 108).

151   As early as medieval times the principle of *"par in parem non habet imperium"* was recognized with respect to the sovereign princes (Bartolus de Sassoferrato, *Tractatus repressaliarum* (1354)). The principle in its absolute form was classically paraphrased by the US Supreme Court, 11 US 116 (1812), in the case of the *Schooner Exchange v McFaddon*. See, for more recent times, 'State Immunity from Execution of Judicial Decisions and Arbitral Awards' (various contributions) (1979) NYIL 3–289. Also Andreas Bjorklund, 'State Immunity and the Enforcement of Investor-State Arbitral Awards' in Christina Binder and others (eds), *International Investment Law for the Twenty-first Century, Essays in Honour of Christoph Schreuer* (OUP 2009) 302ff; Alexis Blane, 'Sovereign Immunity as a Bar To The Execution of International Arbitral Awards' (2009) 41 NYU J Intl L & Politics 453ff.

152   United Nations Convention on Jurisdictional Immunities of States and Their Property, adopted by the General Assembly of the United Nations on 2 December 2004. See UN General Assembly Resolution A/59/38 (2004) of 2 December 2004 (annex), available at: <http://legal.un.org> accessed 20 November 2021. For further details see Christian Tams and Roger O'Keefe (eds), *The United Nations Convention on Jurisdictional Immunities of States and Their Property. A Commentary* (OUP 2013); David P. Stewart, 'Current Development: The UN Convention on Jurisdictional Immunities of States and Their Property' (2005) 99 AJIL 194ff; Burkhard Heß, 'The International Law Commission's Draft Convention on Jurisdictional Immunities of States and Their Property' (1993) 4 EJIL 269ff.

153   In accordance with its arts 28 and 33, the Convention had been open for signature from 17 January 2005 until 17 January 2007. No more than 28 states signed during that period.

Europe succeeded in the establishment of the European Convention on State Immunity[154] – yet with no more than eight ratifications up to date.[155] Despite all that, both texts are serving today as main sources of recognition for the identification of more specific rules on immunity that may be deemed customary international law. Whether a certain provision of the two Conventions actually reflects customary international law, must nonetheless be determined with respect to every single provision.[156]

The principle of immunity serves as a comprehensive legal barrier obliging every state to prevent its domestic courts from opening proceedings, pronouncing judgment, enforcing or executing such judgment, or doing anything similar, against another state.[157] No state can be brought to a foreign court unless there is specific consent on the jurisdiction of such court. Such consent can be given in advance, e.g. by ratifying an international treaty allowing for the recognition and enforcement of arbitral awards. A similar consequence applies to certain private-law agreements: According to Article 17 UN Convention on State Immunities (also Article 12 European Convention) a state cannot invoke immunity *from jurisdiction* before a court of another state if it "enters into an agreement in writing with a foreign natural or juridical person to submit to arbitration differences relating to a commercial transaction".[158] Such rules concord to the general *volenti non fit iniuria* principle as well as to the general obligation of not acting contrary to one's own preceding behaviour (*venire contra factum proprium*). In addition, the principle is subject to exceptions relating,

---

For the Convention entering into force 30 instruments of ratifications would have been needed (art 30 of the Convention), whereas 20 of those were actually deposited. See UN Treaty Collection (Database) at: <https://treaties.un.org/> accessed 21 November 2021.

154   European Convention on State Immunity of 16 May 1972, CETS (Council of Europe Treaty Series) No. 74. See also Protocol Additional to the Convention of 16 May 1972, CETS No. 74A. Both available at: <www.coe.int/en/web/conventions/full-list/> accessed 20 November 2021.

155   See Council of Europe, Treaty Office, Chart of signatures and ratifications of Treaty 074, available at: <www.coe.int/> accessed 20 November 2021.

156   This approach was also chosen by the International Court of Justice, which in the case of *Germany v Italy* (2012) refused to recognize as a principle of customary international law the so-called tort claims exception rule, even though it conforms to art 12 of the (Draft) UN Convention as well as to art 11 of the European Convention See *Jurisdictional Immunities of the States (Germany v Italy)* [3 February 2012] ICJ, available at: <www.icj-cij .org/> accessed 20 November 2021.

157   cf art 6 (1) of the UN Convention on Jurisdictional Immunities of States and Their Property (n 152).

158   Art 17 pertains to a proceeding which relates to the validity, interpretation or application of the arbitration agreement, the arbitration procedure; or the confirmation or the setting aside of the award.

e.g. to immovable property situated in the state of the forum and other particular categories[159] with regard to which immunity *from jurisdiction* cannot
be invoked (Articles 13–16 UN Convention on State Immunities, Articles 4-10
European Convention). However, none of the exceptions mentioned will justify the use of measures of constraint in the phase of enforcement.[160]

The principle of immunity benefits *the state* including its political subdivi-
sions and state agencies. Whether there exists a *"state agency"*, is to be proven
by a test relating to the ownership of control: Does the State exercise *effective
control*, e.g. over a private corporation?[161] In the affirmative, a private law corporation may be considered a state agency and, consequently, enjoys immunity before the courts of another state.

3.2   The Principle of "Restrictive Immunity"

Despite of the fact that immunity originally applied in an absolute form, the
"principle of restrictive immunity" has become more and more predominant.
According to the more recent conception, immunity only covers *acta iure
imperii* (acts of sovereign authority) and not *acta iure gestionis* (acts of a private
law resp. of a commercial character). This is reflected, e.g. by Article 10 of the
UN Convention on State Immunities and Article 7 of the European Convention
on State Immunity, and may also be considered to constitute a customary
international law principle. In order to distinguish a commercial transaction
from other types of state action the decisive question will be: was the key transaction accomplished on the base of a private law relationship, respectively, can
an individual make such a transaction?[162] In the affirmative, the transaction
constitutes an *actus iure gestionis* and does not qualify for the privilege of
immunity.

3.3   Immunity with Respect to Measures of Constraint

As concerns the range of applicability of the principle of immunity, two spheres
of application must be distinguished from each other: the sphere of jurisdiction on the one hand and the sphere of execution (measures of constraint)

---

159   Further examples are movable or immovable property arising by way of succession, trust
      property and property of a company in the event of its winding up, etc. See also art 12 UN
      Convention, art 11 European Convention relating to the *Foreign Tort Exception Clause*.
160   See s 3.3.
161   See, with further references, Ian Brownlie, *Principles of Public International Law* (7th ed,
      OUP 2008) 341.
162   See, comprehensively, Stephan Wittich, 'The Definition of Commercial Acts/La défini-
      tion des actes commerciaux' in S Breau and others (eds), *State Practice Regarding State
      Immunities/La Pratique des Etats concernant les Immunités des Etats* (Brill 2006) 21–47.

on the other hand. Even if a state by submitting to arbitration waives its sovereign immunity rights as a bar to proceedings, it still enjoys immunity from execution. It is established rule that the consent of a state to the exercise of jurisdiction does not imply consent to the taking of measures of constraint (cf. Article 23 of the European Convention on State Immunity). Accordingly, Article 55 ICSID clarifies that "[n]othing in Article 54 shall be construed as derogating from the law in force in any Contracting State relating to immunity of that State or any foreign State from execution".[163]

The rationale for preserving immunity from execution is that certain state assets may be indispensable for a proper functioning of the state.[164] Nevertheless, one may doubt the necessity of such blanket protection from execution. Article 55 ICSID in particular is considered the weakest link of the chain within the Convention, as it refers to the domestic law of the state where enforcement is sought.[165] The same problem may result indirectly from the equation of ICSID awards with domestic judgments (Article 54 [1] ICSID), because judgments, just like awards, must not be executed in a manner that violates another state's immunity rights.[166] Even though Article 55 ICSID relates to domestic law concerning immunity, customary international law remains decisive, because domestic law often prescribes respect of the rules of immunity in a quite general manner or even refers to international law. Wherever domestic law is not deferential with respect to immunity at all, the international law principle of immunity remains binding.

Even though the NYC does not explicitly address the issue of immunity, a state may invoke its immunity from execution accordingly. With regard to this Convention, immunity issues may be put forward on grounds of Article III (domestic rules on procedure) or Article V (2) (b) (public policy).[167]

Despite the fact that a state can invoke immunity as a procedural bar to enforcement, it nevertheless remains a violation of its material obligations under Article 53 ICSID.[168] The only exception to the obligation is where an ad hoc Committee has stayed the enforcement, pending its decision on a

---

163   Art 55 ICSID only applies to execution, and neither to jurisdiction nor to recognition. See
        Schreuer and others (n 8) art 55, mn 5–6, 1153.
164   Kröll (n 1) mn 54, 1499.
165   See Schreuer and others (n 8) art 55, mn 8, 1154: 'Achilles' heel'.
166   cf Kröll (n 1) mn 55, 1500.
167   Kröll (n 1) mn 56, 1500.
168   See Kröll (n 1) mn 11 (1486, ICSID), 13 (1487, non-ICSID); Schreuer and others (n 8) art 54,
        mn 115, 1150; art 55, mn 7, 1153; Schreuer (n 103) para 70. See also ICSID Case No ARB/84/4,
        Interim Order of 12 August 1988, *MINE v Guinea*, para 25.

requested annulment of the award.[169] The same applies, *mutatis mutandis*, with regard to the NYC.

In contrast to the sphere of jurisdiction, where the restrictive approach to immunity has become predominant, the sphere of execution remains widely subject to the theory of absolute immunity.[170] However, there is also a strong position opining that the restrictive doctrine applied, *mutatis mutandis*, with regard to the enforcement of judgments – given that the prior making of such judgment was in conformity with the principle of state immunity.[171] According to this approach it must be examined what purpose the relevant state property serves or is intended to serve, *i.e.* whether it serves private (commercial) or state purposes. In the latter case, the principle of immunity prohibits any measures of constraint. According to Article 19 UN Convention on State Immunities, no post-judgment measures of constraint (e.g., attachment, arrest or execution) against property of a State may be taken in connection with a proceeding before a court of another State, unless the latter has expressly consented to such measures, or has allocated or earmarked property for the satisfaction of the relevant claim.[172] Additionally, Article 19 (c) of the UN Convention on State Immunities permits post-judgment measures of constraint only if

> it has been established that the property is specifically in use or intended for use by the State for other than government non-commercial purposes and is in the territory of the State of the forum, provided that post-judgment measures of constraint may only be taken against property that has a connection with the entity against which the proceeding was directed.

In this context, the notion of "*property*" is to be understood "broader than ownership or possession", whereas "*entity*" means the State as an independent legal personality, a constituent unit of a federal State, a subdivision of a State, an agency or instrumentality of a State or other entity.[173] Article 19 does not prejudge the question of "*piercing the corporate veil*", i.e. questions relating

---

169 Kröll (n 1) mn 11, 1486.

170 cf art 23 of the European Convention on State Immunity. See also Lörcher (n 113) 20, with further references.

171 Lörcher (n 113).

172 The same applies to pre-judgment measures of constraint, such as attachment or arrest. See art 18 of the UN Convention.

173 See Annex to the UN Convention on Jurisdictional Immunities of States and Their Property, with respect to Article 19.

to a situation where a State entity has deliberately misrepresented its financial position or subsequently reduced its assets to avoid satisfying a claim, or
other related issues.[174] Further exceptions to the rule may apply, e.g. if a state-
controlled company exhibits a near total lack of autonomy.[175]

Article 21 of the UN Convention further specifies the meaning of property
"specifically in use or intended for use by the State for other than government non-commercial purposes" under Article 19 (c) of the UN Convention.
According to Article 21 certain categories of property – such as *diplomatic and
military property* including property intended for use in the performance of
military functions, property of the *central bank*[176] *and the monetary institutions*
of the state as well as property forming part of the *cultural heritage* or of an
exhibition of objects of scientific, cultural or historical interest – enjoy absolute immunity from attachment or seizure. This rule applies even in the event
of a *general* waiver by the state of its immunity from enforcement.[177]

Despite all that, it can in some cases be difficult to discern, whether a certain
asset of a state is actually used or intended to be used for either sovereign or
commercial purposes. As there are no precise rules on the elements of proof,
state practice plays an important role. E.g. the German Constitutional Court in
the *Philippine Embassy* case[178] had to decide whether a judgment against the
Philippines dealing with rent arrears could be executed by seizing at least some
funds held in the Embassy's bank account. Though the Vienna Convention of
Diplomatic Relations explicitly exempts property of a diplomatic mission from
measures of execution, the pertinent provision does not say how to identify

---

174 Annex to the UN Convention (n 173).

175 Uchkunova and Temnikov (n 87) 209, referring to several decisions of the Paris Court
      of Appeals. See also Kröll (n 1) mn 69–70 (1503–1504), referring to French and English
      jurisprudence.

176 State practice, in accordance with art 21 (1) (c) UN Convention on State Immunity, seems to
      mostly exempt central bank accounts from any measures of constraint. See, eg, Malcolm
      D. Evans, *International Law* (3rd edn, 2010) at 364. In contrast, Brownlie (n 161), at 342,
      proposes to apply the immunity principle *ratione materiae* by distinguishing commercial
      transactions from state action with respect to every single central bank transaction.

177 Evans (n 176) at 363. Emphasis added by the author. With regard to Government loans
      of Argentina, Bundesverfassungsgericht (German Federal Constitutional Court), 6
      December 2006, BVerfGE vol 117, 141ff: There is no rule in international law according to
      which a general waiver to state immunity would allow for the seizure of state property
      serving the purposes of a diplomatic mission. See also Kröll (n 1) mn 62, 1502, referring to
      NOGA v. Russia.

178 Bundesverfassungsgericht (Federal Constitutional Court), 13 December 1977, BVerfGE vol.
      46, 342ff.

such sort of property.[179] According to the German *Bundesverfassungsgericht* (Constitutional Court) an embassy's general bank account must be exempt from any form of execution, even if it serves all sorts of purposes. This court argued that inducing an embassy to clarify the present or future purposes of single assets in its bank account would be in violation of the principle of non-intervention in the internal affairs of the state concerned. Without such clarification, however, any measure of execution against an embassy's bank account might impede the functioning of the embassy and thus would violate the principle of *ne impediatur legatio*.[180] Although the Swiss Federal Court has taken a different view,[181] the restrictive position of the German Constitutional Court can be assumed to have become general practice now.[182] It has also been confirmed by the European Court of Human Rights in the *Sedelmayer* case (2009) relating to the refusal of German authorities to execute a foreign award against the Russian Federation.[183] The target in this case was not even the bank account of a diplomatic mission but a financial debt in favour of Russia allegedly serving the aim of financing its mission.[184]

In contrast, the German Constitutional Court held in the *National Iranian Oil Company* case that assets in a bank account held by a foreign legal person in the forum state do not serve any governmental purposes. This applies notwithstanding the fact that such legal person is legally obliged to transfer such assets to the Central Bank of the foreign state in order to cover general budget expenses of that state.[185] It remains, however, uncertain whether a rule, according to which the property of separate entities of the state generally enjoys no immunity from execution, has become part of customary international law.[186]

---

179   Convention of 18 April 1961, UN Treaty Series, vol. 500, 95 art 22 (3) reads: "The premises of the mission, their furnishings and other property thereon and the means of transport of the mission shall be immune from search, requisition, attachment or execution."

180   Bundesverfassungsgericht (Federal Constitutional Court), Judgment of 13 December 1977, BVerfGE vol 46, 342ff (at 394ff).

181   Swiss Federal Court, 24 April 1985, BGE 111 I a 62. According to this judgment, the governmental use of assets of the Central Bank of Libya in a Swiss bank account was to be clarified in order to become exempt from execution.

182   cf Evans (n 176) 362–363.

183   ECtHR, Decision on Admissibility of 10 November 2009, No. 30190/06 and others, *Franz J Sedelmayer v Germany*, relating to *Franz Sedelmayer v The Russian Federation*, SCC, Award of 7 July 1998.

184   Blane (n 151) at 509, reports that, under most national laws, the heads of a diplomatic mission may issue a certificate as to whether certain state property is immune, and suggests that such certifications must be held conclusive. See also Schreuer and others (n 8) art 55, mn 64, 1169–1170, referring to a plenitude of state practice.

185   Bundesverfassungsgericht, 12 April 1983, BVerfGE vol. 64, 1ff (at 42ff).

186   Affirming such rule Evans (n 176) 367.

It is highly disputed *whether there must exist a connection* between the relevant state property and the subject matter of the proceedings (linkage requirement). E.g. Section 1610 (a) (2) of the US Foreign Sovereign Immunities Act requires that the state property to be attached "was used for the commercial activity upon which the claim was based".[187] According to the landmark decision of the US Supreme Court in *Shaffer v Heitner* (1977) due process also requires a constitutionally sufficient relationship among the defendant, the forum, and the litigation, even though due process concerns can be satisfied more easily in an action of execution.[188] However, as concerns the particularities of execution in arbitration cases, US federal courts tend to decide quite disparately.[189]

Similarly, French law[190] as well as Swiss law[191] seem to impose a requirement of a connection between the property and the subject matter of the claim. This approach, even though it respects property of the state but not property of a state agency or such, considerably limits the property to satisfy the judgment, and eventually creates "*a right without remedy*".[192] In contrast, many European states such as Italy and Switzerland, gear the possibility of constraint measures to the commercial respectively non-governmental character of the use and purpose of the relevant object or asset.[193] Article 19 (c) UN Convention on State Immunity chooses a 'halfway' approach by providing that measures of constraint may only be taken "against property that has a connection with the entity against which the proceeding was directed".[194]

---

187   Section 1610 (a) (2) of the US Foreign Sovereign Immunities Act refers to states only, not to state agencies.

188   US Supreme Court, *Shaffer v Heitner* 433 US 186, 204, 210 (1977). See also Neuhaus (n 29) 29.

189   See, eg US Court of Appeals for the Fourth Circuit, Opinion of 6 March 2002, *Base Metal Trading Ltd v OJSC "Novokuznetsky Aluminium Factory"* 283 F.3d 208, 213 (2002): "the presence of property alone will not support jurisdiction". In contrast, US Court of Appeals for the Ninth Circuit, Opinion of 17 January 2002, *Glencore Grain Rotterdam BV v Shivnath Rai Harnarain Co.*, 284 F.3d 1114, 1127 (2002): "Considerable authority supports Glencore Grain's position that it can enforce the award against Shivnath Rai's property in the forum even if that property has no relationship to the underlying controversy between the parties."

190   Evans (n 176) 367, with references to French judgments from the Eighties.

191   Schweizerisches Bundesgericht (Swiss Federal Court), Judgment of 19 June 1980, BGE 106 I a 142, I.L.M. 20 (1981), 151, *Socialist People's Libyan Arab Jamahiriya v LIAMCO*.

192   Evans (n 176) 366–367.

193   See the survey on European jurisprudence given by the Bundesverfassungsgericht (Federal Constitutional Court), Judgment of 13 December 1977, BVerfGE vol. 46, 342ff (392–393).

194   Denying the customary law character of this formula: Tams/O'Keefe (n 152) 327.

Under such circumstances, one cannot really speak of a consistent state practice, respectively of a common *opinio iuris*. However, the absolute theory exempting states from any kind of execution seems to be superceded by a more refined corpus of rules.[195] Today, immunity prevents measures of constraint against property in governmental use or intended for such use, but does not prevent such measures with regard to property that is in use or is intended for non-governmental (commercial) use – given that both can clearly be distinguished. Even though, as most of a state's foreign assets serve public purposes or are allegedly intended to serve such purposes, their attachment will remain difficult, if not impossible.[196]

3.4 *Immunity in Practice – the Yukos Investors Case*

On 18 July 2014, an Arbitral Tribunal sitting in The Hague under the auspices of the Permanent Court of Arbitration (PCA) rendered three arbitral awards in the cases of *Hulley Enterprises Ltd. (Cyprus), Yukos Universal Limited (Isle of Man) and Veteran Petroleum Ltd. (Cyprus) v the Russian Federation*[197] – all of them being shareholders of the former OAO Yukos Oil Company. The Tribunal held unanimously that the Russian Federation breached its international obligations under the Energy Charter Treaty (ECT) by charging Yukos Oil Company with excessive debts, pushing it into insolvency and appropriating its assets. In consequence, Russia was obligated to pay the Group Menatep Ltd. (former owner of YUKOS) ca. USD 50 billion for unlawful expropriation and costs of arbitration by 15 January 2015 – the largest award ever rendered by an arbitral tribunal. As a representative of the three enterprises has put it, "the award is final and binding, and is now enforceable in 150 States under the 1958 New York Convention on the Recognition and Enforcement of Foreign Arbitral Awards".[198]

In clear objection, the Russian Deputy Foreign Minister spoke of a "politically motivated decision". The arbitral tribunal were not competent to decide on the merits at all, because Russia did not ratify the Energy Charter Treaty

---

195   Uchkunova and Temnikov (n 87) 201, opine that almost all national systems (except Russia) have moved to the theory of restrictive immunity with respect to enforcement.

196   According to Tsai-Yu Lin in ICSID practice judicial enforcement proceedings against states have only taken place in five cases. See 'Systemic Reflections on Argentina's Non-Compliance with ICSID Arbitral Awards: A New Role of the Annulment Committee At Enforcement?' (2012) 5 Contemp Asia Arb J 1, 6.

197   PCA Cases Nos AA 226–228, available at: <www.pca-cpa.org> accessed 20 November 2021.

198   Yas Banifatemi, lawyer for GML, quoted after <www.shearman.com/~/media/Files/Yukos/01-Yukos--Shearman--Sterling-Press-release-of-28-July-2014.pdf> accessed 20 November 2021.

but only "temporarily applied this treaty in as much as this did not contradict the Russian Constitution and legislation".[199] The Arbitral Tribunal in its
Interim Award on Jurisdiction had held that Russia by applying the Energy
Charter provisionally until 18 October 2009 was bound to this treaty according to Article 25 of the Vienna Convention of the Law of Treaties.[200] However,
The Hague District Court on 20 April 2016 reversed the PCA tribunal's decision
against Russia, and the proceedings in Dutch courts are still pending.[201]

Facing the fact that GML immediately started to enact enforcement measures in Germany, the United States, the United Kingdom, the Netherlands,
and France,[202] Russia announced that it would take "countermeasures". After
some accounts, attributable to the Russian Federation, were frozen in Belgium
and France, the Russian President signed the new law "on the jurisdictional
immunities of foreign states and their property in the Russian Federation".[203]

Commenting on this, one has to distinguish between legal and illegal measures of enforcement and execution, the result of which depends on the kind of
state property attached.[204] Where execution with regard to the award violates
the sovereign immunity rights of Russia (e.g. seizure of accounts of a Russian
Embassy), proportionate countermeasures may be justified against the states
responsible, not against private individuals.[205] Where execution, in contrast,

---

199   See ITAR-TASS of 12 August 2014 quoting Deputy Foreign Minister Vasily Nebenzya, avail-
      able at: <http://en.itar-tass.com/russia/744558> accessed 20 November 2021.

200   PCA Case AA 227, *Yukos*, Interim Award on Jurisdiction and Admissibility of 30 November
      2009, at 146. Available at: <www.pcacases.com> accessed 20 November 2021.

201   Ben Knowles, Khaled Moyeed and Nefeli Lamprou, 'The US $50 billion Yukos Award
      Overturned – Enforcement Becomes a Game of Russian Roulette' <http://arbitrationb
      log.kluwerarbitration.com/2016/05/13/the-us50-billion-yukos-award-overturned-enfo
      rcement-becomes-a-game-of-russian-roulette/> accessed 20 November 2021. For later
      developments see Chapter 24 supra (Alexander Trunk, Some Remarks on International
      Commercial Arbitration in the Region of the Caucasus and Central Asia (in this book),
      at 422.

202   'Pfändung gegen Pfändung' *Der Spiegel* (20 October 2014) at 78.

203   Федеральный закон от 03 November 2015 № 297-ФЗ, available at: <http://publication.
      pravo.gov.ru/Document/View/0001201511040006> accessed 20 November 2021. The new
      law entered into force by January 2016. Additionally, new criminal charges were brought
      against the former CEO of Yukos, Mikhail Khodorkovsky.

204   In summer of 2015 French authorities had frozen accounts of the Russian state in 40 banks,
      eight or nine real estates and the shares of the Russian VGTRK holding in the TV station
      "Euronews". In contrast, Belgium was blamed by Russia to have frozen, at least tempo-
      rarily, the account of the Russian Embassy as well as accounts of the Russian missions at
      EU and NATO. See Handelsblatt, 19 June 2015 ("Moskau droht «Vergeltungsmaßnahmen»
      an"); 'Enteignungsgesetz in Russland' *Frankfurter Allgemeine Zeitung* (6 November 2015).

205   See s 4.2. See also art 49 (1) Articles on State Responsibility (n 211).

targets commercial firms, e.g. OAO Rosneft or Gazprom, the application of "countermeasures" would amount to a violation of the NYC if the attachment of assets formally owned by such companies were legal.

Rosneft, Gazprom and other companies may be targeted, if they were dominated or effectively controlled by the Russian state at the relevant time. Hence, there must be some evidence for such a company being a state agency, at least in fact.[206] Alternatively, the creditors could argue that a specific company has participated in the state's interference with the rights of the investors. The latter approach finds some support in Article 19 (c) UN Convention on State Immunities according to which measures of constraint may only be taken "against property that has a connection with the entity, against which the proceeding was directed".[207] As Article 19 (c) UN Convention on State Immunities does not exclude *"piercing the corporate veil"*,[208] the property must not be owned formally by the entity concerned (Russian Federation) but merely needs to have a connection with it. As GML suggests, the status of a beneficiary of the fall of Yukos had established such a connection.[209] Even though this interpretation can be considered reasonable with regard to Article 19 (c) UN Convention on State Immunities, the question remains, whether this provision already reflects customary international law. At any rate, GML has to show that a certain company actually and substantially benefitted from Russia's interference with the investors' rights. If GML fails to do so, it only could attach eventual debts owed by such a company to the Russian Federation, given that those debts have emerged in the country of attachment.[210] Time will show whether the rights of investors can be enforced effectively, regardless of the state concerned.

---

206 Some authors opine that the Tribunal itself had given some hints regarding Rosneft. See Julien Fouret and Pierre Daureu, 'Case Comment: Yukos Universal Limited (Isle of Man) v The Russian Federation' (2015) 30 ICSID Review 336, 344.

207 See ss 3.3., 4.3.

208 See s 3.3.

209 Yas Banifatemi, lawyer for GML, announced its intention to target OAO Rosneft and OAO Gazprom because they were beneficiaries of expropriated Yukos assets. See Henry Meyer and Stephan Bierman, 'Yukos – Hunting Rosneft Assets From Venezuela to Vietnam' *Blomberg Business Week* (31 July 2014).

210 Otherwise, domestic courts of the state of enforcement may lack international competence under *lex fori*. cf *Franz J. Sedelmayer v Germany*, Decision on Admissibility No. 30190/06 and others (ECtHR, 10 November 2009) A.3.

4   **Resort to External International Law Mechanisms in the Case of Non-compliance**

4.1   *Options for States and Private Persons to Induce Enforcement*

4.1.1   Responsibility of States for Internationally Wrongful Acts

International law, due to its focus on state sovereignty, notoriously suffers from a lack of adequate enforcement mechanisms. Only few instruments can be used, if a state violates its international law obligations vis-à-vis another state. Such inter-state disputes can occur, if a state does not comply with its obligations resulting from multilateral treaties such as NYC or ICSID, or from bilateral investment treaties (BITs). E.g. a state not complying with its obligations under Article 53 (1), sentence 2, or Article 54 (1) ICSID violates its international law obligations vis-à-vis all other states parties to the pertinent treaty (ICSID). Under such circumstances, the failure to comply with or the denial of recognition resp. enforcement of arbitral awards to the prejudice of foreign citizens or companies constitutes an "*internationally wrongful act*".

According to the Draft Articles on Responsibility of States for Internationally Wrongful Acts (AoR)[211] an "internationally wrongful act" means an action or omission which is attributable to the State indicted, constitutes a breach of an international obligation of that State (Article 2 AoR), and is not justified (Articles 20 et seq. AoR).[212] The characterization of an act as internationally wrongful is governed exclusively by international law and cannot be influenced by domestic law (Article 2 AoR). Whilst Article 2 AoR only gives a general definition of what constitutes an internationally wrongful act, the range of obligation must be determined with regard to more specific regulation applicable to the case concerned.[213]

---

211   The "Draft" Articles were prepared by the International Law Commission and adopted by General Assembly Resolution 56/83 of 12 December 2001. Although no formal adoption by the states has ever taken place hereafter, the Articles were frequently referred to by international courts and, today, can be considered to mostly reflect customary international law. Nevertheless, the customary law character of specific clauses remains subject to contestation. cf James Crawford, 'Articles on Responsibility of States for Internationally Wrongful Acts', *United Nations Audiovisual Library of International Law* (2012), available at: <http://legal.un.org/avl/pdf/ha/rsiwa/rsiwa_e.pdf> accessed 20 November 2021. Also James Crawford and Simon Olleson, 'The Application of the Rules of State Responsibility' in Bungenberg and others (n 1) 411ff, n 28.

212   Circumstances precluding wrongfulness are consent, self-defence, rightful countermeasures, force majeure, distress and necessity (arts 20ff).

213   cf *Gustav F. W. Hamester GmbH & Co. KG v Ghana*, ICSID Case No ARB/07/24, Award (18 June 2010) para 173.

Any internationally wrongful act of a state entails international responsibility (Article 1 AoR). This means that such a state is under an obligation to cease that act if it is ongoing (Article 30 AoR), to offer appropriate assurances and guarantees of non-repetition if circumstances so require (Article 31 AoR) and to make "full reparation" for the injury (Article 31 § 1 AoR). Injury includes any damage, whether material or moral, caused by the internationally wrongful act (Article 31 § 2 AoR). "Full reparation" means to re-establish the situation which existed before the wrongful act was committed (Article 35 AoR), preferably by restitution, otherwise by compensation, and, failing all of that, by satisfaction (Article 34 AoR), including interest when necessary in order to ensure full reparation (Article 38). Whilst the state responsible may not rely on internal law as justification for failure to repair (Article 32 AoR), it may eventually rely on the fact that reparation is materially impossible or involves a burden out of all proportion to the benefit (Article 35 AoR).

However, only an "injured state" is entitled to invoke the responsibility of another state. If the obligation breached is owed to a group of states, as is typical of a multilateral treaty, a single state may only invoke responsibility, if the breach of the obligation specially affects that state (Article 42 [b] [i] AoR). A state can be deemed specifically affected if it is, e.g. home state of an investor being targeted by the internationally wrongful act. In this constellation, it is not the private investor but the home state, which is "injured" under international law, thereby mediating the individual person or enterprise. The home state, then, may dispose of a couple of options.[214]

4.1.2   Non-contingent Measures and Instruments

In the case of non-compliance, a protector state may grant *diplomatic protection*.[215] Even if diplomatic protection has been excluded by mutual consent, namely by a pertinent clause of an international treaty like Article 27 ICSID, the right of the home state to grant diplomatic protection will revive once the other state has failed to comply with the award rendered in a dispute with the

---

214   See, eg, Jorge E. Viñuales and Dolores Bentolila, 'The Use of Alternative (Non-judicial) Means to Enforce Investment Awards' in Laurence Boisson de Chazoumes and others (eds), *Diplomatic and Judicial Means of Dispute Settlement* (2013) 245ff.

215   ILC Draft Articles on Diplomatic Protection, art 1 reads: "diplomatic protection consists of the invocation by a State, through diplomatic action or other means of peaceful settlement, of responsibility of another State for an injury caused by an internationally wrongful act of that State to a natural or legal person that is a national of the former State with a view to the implementation of such responsibility". See Report of the International Law Commission, 58th session (2006) UN Doc A/61/10, 16ff.

investor.[216] The investor must be a citizen of the protecting state or an enterprise permanently and closely linked[217] to that state, and must also be a victim of a violation by the other state either of human rights or of minimum standard rules on the treatment of aliens (e.g. protection against expropriation, access to court). Exceptionally, a mere shareholder of the victim may enjoy diplomatic protection.[218] The problem, however, is that the victim (or shareholder of the victim) must have exhausted all domestic remedies available in the state of investment or provided for by the pertinent treaties. Another problem lies in the fact that a state, though it has the right to exercise diplomatic protection, is under no duty or obligation to do so. Whilst some of the home states may be obliged by domestic law to extend diplomatic protection to their nationals, international law imposes no such obligation.[219] As the ICJ has put it in its *Diallo* judgment, the role of diplomatic protection, particularly in the context of the much more sophisticated and mostly respected law of arbitration, has "somewhat faded".[220]

If, in very rare cases, the home state actually exercises diplomatic protection in favor of its nationals, it may submit the case to an international court, or take countermeasures. Generally, a state may take *legal action* only where such a friendly settlement is consented to, the rule being that no state can bring another state before the court without the latter's consent.[221] E.g. the protector state can bring a case, in its own name, to the International Court of Justice

---

216 Art 27 (1) ICSID at the end. According to its wording, the provision does not apply to situations where a state fails to enforce an award.

217 For further details on that see art 9 of the ILC Draft Articles on Diplomatic Protection (n 215).

218 The decisive test for shareholders being that the latter were not only affected in an interest but violated in their own rights. See *Case Concerning the Barcelona Traction, Light and Power Co. Ltd.*, Judgment [5 February 1970] ICJ Rep 3, paras 55–58. On the doctrine of "protection by substitution" affirming diplomatic protection as last resort if no other remedy is available: *Case Concerning Amadiou Sadio Diallo (Republic of Guinea v DR Congo)*, Judgment (Preliminary Objections) [24 May 2007] ICJ Rep, paras 86–94.

219 *Case Concerning the Barcelona Traction Light and Power Company Limited (Belgium v Spain)* [5 February 1970] ICJ Rep 4, at 44. Also ILC Draft Articles on Diplomatic Protection with Commentaries (n 215), art 2, para 2, 29.

220 *Case Concerning Amadiou Sadio Diallo (Republic of Guinea v DR Congo)*, Judgment (Preliminary Objections) [24 May 2007] ICJ Rep, para 88: "In that context, the role of diplomatic protection somewhat faded, as in practice recourse is only made to it in rare cases where treaty régimes do not exist or have proved inoperative."

221 This follows from the general principle of state sovereignty. See Samantha Besson, 'Sovereignty' in *Max Planck Encyclopedia* (n 30), (April 2011) para 122. See also note 151 with main text.

(Article 64 ICSID).[222] Even if such an option exists, e.g. in the form of Article 64 ICSID, the same problem may reoccur: Though international courts and tribunals can ascertain the existence of a violation, they do not dispose of any means of enforcement of their own.[223]

A state being victim of an internationally wrongful act of another state, or exercising diplomatic protection can resort to *countermeasures*.[224] It may then take either lawful or unlawful action of retaliation ("reprisals") in order to coerce the perpetrator state to abide by its obligations. However, it must be strong and powerful enough to do so.

Only if the behaviour of the perpetrator state amounts to a *"material" breach of a multilateral treaty* such as the NYC or ICSID Convention, may the other parties by unanimous (!) agreement suspend the operation of that treaty or terminate it in the relations between themselves and the defaulting state (Article 60 [2] [a] [i] VCLT). However, throwing out a state by unanimous vote from a multilateral treaty is neither realistic, nor will it improve the situation of investors.

In the case of non-compliance with an ICSID award, there exists a practice of the World Bank to make further loans dependent on the compliance with ICSID obligations.[225] As ICSID is a part of the World Bank Group, disregard by a state of a decision made by an ICSID Tribunal can be considered a disregard of the ICSID Convention system and be treated alike.[226] Losing credibility within the World Bank system represents the most effective sanction for non-compliance.

In contrast, a private investor, in the case of a state finally failing to comply with or to enforce an arbitral award, disposes of two major options.[227] First, an investor (individual person or company) may instigate new proceedings before an ICSID arbitral tribunal claiming that failure to abide by and comply with the terms of an award constitutes a breach of investors rights ("award

---

222 See s 4.3. (a).

223 Even judgments of the Court of Justice of the European Union, though they shall be enforceable according to arts 280, 299 TFEU, cannot be enforced against states (art 299 TFEU).

224 See s 4.2.

225 See Worldbank, Operational Policy 7.40 concerning Disputes over Defaults on External Debt of July 2001 (revised March 2012), available at: <www.worldbank.org> accessed 20 November 2021. See also Lörcher (n 113) 20; Schreuer (n 103) para 66; Tsai-Yu Lin (n 196), 2 and 19.

226 Doubting on that Baldwin (n 112), 22.

227 In doctrine, some further instruments such as, eg "post-award interest" or "assignment", were suggested. See Uchkunova and Temnikov (n 87) 205, 207.

as investment").[228] Secondly, an investor may approach a human rights system. E.g. an investor can bring a Contracting State to the European Convention on Human Rights to the European Court of Human Rights (Article 34 ECHR) by claiming that this state, by not enforcing a binding award, has violated the right to property respectively the right to fair trial.[229]

4.2   *Countermeasures in Particular*

"Countermeasures" under certain conditions constitute a legitimate means of coercion in inter-state-relations. They may consist of a variety of measures or omissions, which are deemed to put a burden on the perpetrator state that might induce it to comply with its obligations according to international law. They can be lawful in and of themselves but also include *unlawful* action of retaliation ("reprisals"). Generally, countermeasures require the existence of an internationally wrongful act with regard to which an injured state may invoke responsibility.[230] As their purpose is not to punish a State but rather to induce it to comply with its obligations under international law, the measure must be reversible.[231] Additionally, countermeasures may only be taken after due notice and on the precondition that the wrongful act has neither ceased nor been compensated by then (Articles 52, 53 AoR). They must be *proportionate* (Article 51 AoR). The taking of countermeasures is prohibited if they may affect the obligation to refrain from the threat or use of force, as embodied in the UN Charter, fundamental human rights, international humanitarian law, obligations under peremptory norms of general international law or obligations to respect the inviolability of diplomatic or consular staff and objects (Article 50 AoR).

Countermeasures may serve as a "sword" but also as a "shield".[232] On the one hand, the home state of an investor may use countermeasures in order to induce a perpetrator state to comply with its treaty obligations towards the investor. On the other hand, countermeasures under certain circumstances can justify the refusal to recognize and enforce a foreign arbitral award or to abide by and comply with the terms of the award.[233] However, this is not a

---

228   See s 2.4. (d).
229   See s 4.3. (b).
230   See s 4.1. (a).
231   cf ICJ in *Gabčíkovo-Nagymaros Project* (n 125) para 87.
232   cf art 22 ("shield") and arts 49ff ("sword") of the ILC Articles on State Responsibility.
233   See Binder (n 129) n 44– 58, with special regard to three ICSID cases brought against Mexico.

proper basis to deny enforcement vis-à-vis a private investor.[234] As Article 22 ILC Articles on State Responsibility clarifies, "the wrongfulness of an act of a state not in conformity with an international obligation *towards another State* is precluded", if that act constitutes a lawful countermeasure. An obligation towards an investor, however, is not an "obligation towards another state".[235] Last but not least, there is broad consensus today that the individual must not be abused as a buffer for his or her home state. Though it is accepted that indirect or collateral effects cannot be entirely avoided, countermeasures must not target private persons mainly or respectively directly or in an un-proportionate manner.[236] This is also confirmed by arbitral practice: In cases where investors enjoy direct rights, they appear to be third parties who must not be deprived of their rights for alleged breaches of treaty obligations by their home state.[237] At any rate, targeting private investors in order to react to a state's failure would constitute a disproportionate and, thus, a non-legitimate countermeasure.

4.3   *Enforcement through Judgments of International Courts*

4.3.1   International Court of Justice – Article 64 of the ICSID Convention

At first view the International Court of Justice (ICJ) does not seem to be a relevant court with regard to our issue. It can only be approached by states and some UN bodies but not by private investors (Articles 34, 35, 65 ICJ Statute). Additionally, its jurisdiction is linked to matters relating to the Charter of the United Nations. Up to date there only exists one ICJ inter-state case on arbitration, i.e. the *Case Concerning the Arbitral Award Made by the King of Spain on 23 December 1906*[238] regarding the determination of the frontier between Honduras and Nicaragua.

---

234   See Martins Paparinskis, 'Investment Arbitration and the Law of Countermeasures', Conference Paper of 27 June 2008 (Society of International Economic Law) <www.ssrn .com> accessed 20 November 2021; ibid (2009) 79 BYIL 264–352.

235   Paparinskis (n 234) suggests a third-party right.

236   cf UN Legislative Series, Book 25: *Materials on the Responsibilities of States For Internationally Wrongful Acts*, ST/LEG/SER B/25, 2012, Commentary on art 49, 309, at 310, para 5. Available at: <legal.un.org/legislativeseries> accessed 20 November 2021. See also Binder (n 129) n 78.

237   *Corn Products International (CPI) v Mexico*, ICSID Case No ARB (AF)/04/01 (15 January 2008) para 176; *Cargill Incorporated v Mexico*, ICSID Case No ARB (AF)/05/2 (18 September 2009) para 429.

238   In 1960, the ICJ held that this Award was valid and binding and that Nicaragua was under an obligation to give effect to it. ICJ, *Case Concerning the Arbitral Award Made by the King of Spain On 23 December 1906* (18 November 1960). Available at: <www.icj-cij.org/> accessed 20 November 2021.

Yet, the competence of the ICJ can also be established by special reference in international treaties (Article 36 ICJ Statute). E.g. Article 64 ICSID reads:

> Any dispute arising between Contracting States concerning the interpretation or application of this Convention which is not settled by negotiation shall be referred to the International Court of Justice by the application of any party to such dispute, unless the States concerned agree to another method of settlement.

Consequently, a dispute dealing with "the interpretation or application" of the ICSID Convention can be brought to the ICJ by one of the state parties without any need to induce the other state party to subject itself to the jurisdiction of the ICJ. In such *special reference cases* the jurisdiction of the ICJ has been recognized by the contracting states of the relevant treaty in advance and must not be sought once the dispute has already become acute. However, no contracting party has ever invoked Article 64 ICSID thus far.

The reason for this lies in the vagaries of the UN mechanism. As a rule, each Member State to the UN undertakes to comply with the judgments of the ICJ (Article 94 [1] UN Charter) including the obligation to ensure that its domestic authorities will put the teeth into such judgments. If a state fails to do so, the other party may have recourse to the Security Council, "which may, if it deems necessary, make recommendations or decide upon measures to be taken to give effect to the judgment" (Article 94 [2] UN Charter). As this wording reveals, the Security Council, when enforcing judgments of the ICJ, remains free to take a political decision. What is more: the question of whether and how a judgment of the ICJ should be implemented is a "substantive" (non-procedural) matter, bearing the consequence that Article 27 (3) UN Charter applies. Accordingly, each of the five permanent members of the Security Council (United States, Russia, China, France, and the United Kingdom) may enact a veto against any recommendation or decision to be taken under Article 94 (2) UN Charter. E.g. in the case of *Military and Paramilitary Activities in and Against Nicaragua* the United States refused to comply with the judgment of the ICJ of 27 June 1986.[239] A Security Council Resolution drafted under Chapter 6 of the UN Charter, which urgently called for "full and immediate compliance with the judgment of the ICJ of 27 June 1986",[240] was vetoed by the United

---

239   ICJ Judgment on the merits, available at: <www.icj-cij.org/> accessed 20 November 2021.
240   Draft Resolution by five non-permanent members of the SC, S/18428 (28 October 1986) available at: <www.un.org/ga/search/view_doc.asp?symbol=S/18428> accessed 20 November 2021.

States.[241] As a result, Article 94 (2) of the UN Charter providing for enforcement by the Security Council was totally neutralized – and will be so in many other instances including Article 64 ICSID Convention cases.

4.3.2	European Court of Human Rights: Enforcement-Related Issues and Convention Rights
4.3.2.1	*Unlawful Disruption of Arbitration as a Violation of the ECHR*
4.3.2.1.1	The Right to Property

The comprehensive right to property leads a peripheral existence in international human rights law. It is neither included in the human rights catalogue of the UN Covenant on Civil and Political Rights, nor can it be considered customary international law. The necessity to grant protection against *expropriation* reflects a minimum standard regarding the treatment of aliens by a state rather than a genuine human right.[242] Only a few human rights systems grant a comprehensive right to property. E.g. Article 1 (1) of the Protocol (No. 1) Additional to the European Convention on Human Rights (AP)[243] guarantees every natural or legal person the peaceful enjoyment of his or her possessions (Sentence 1), including protection against expropriation (Sentence 2). A similar provision exists in the American human rights system.[244] Even if an arbitral tribunal may find that the pertinent BIT grants to the investor a more specific level of protection compared to the more general protection offered by human rights instruments,[245] this cannot deprive the European Court of Human Rights of its jurisdiction relating to the Convention rights.

---

241 Provisional Verbatim Record of the 2718th Meeting, S/PV.2718 of 28 October 1986, at 51, available at: <www.un.org/ga/search/view_doc.asp?symbol=S/PV.2718> accessed 20 November 2021. The United States did not abstain from voting as being dictated by UN Charter, art 27 (3).

242 International law permits States to expropriate foreign property, if it is in the public interest or for a public purpose, accomplished in a non-discriminatory fashion, and in conformity with due process, whereas the final legality criterion of compensation remains more controversial. According to the classical Hull formula (US State Secretary Hull, 1938) compensation must be "prompt, adequate and effective". Many BITs and other international investment agreements have further specified these requirements. See Ursula Kriebaum and August Reinisch, 'Property, Right to, International Protection' in *Max Planck Encyclopedia* (n 30) (July 2009) paras 19, 24ff Also UN General Assembly Resolution 1803 (XVII) of 14 December 1962.

243 According to art 5 AP all rights guaranteed by the Protocol are given the status of a fullfledged Convention right.

244 American Convention on Human Rights, art 21.

245 See, eg, *Spyridon Roussalis v Romania,* ICSID Case No ARB/06/1 (7 December 2011) para 312.

In the case of *Stran Greek Refineries* (1994)[246] the European Court of Human Rights had to decide whether legislative interference with (domestic) arbitration constituted a violation of the right to property according to Article 1 AP. The relevant award was final and binding; it neither required any further enforcement measure, nor lay any appeal against it, nor was there any ground for annulment. It was only under these circumstances that the Court considered a debt (or claim) not to be a mere expectation[247] but a true "possession" within the meaning of Article 1 AP.[248] It also accepted that there was an interference with the applicants' property right under the first sentence of the first paragraph of Article 1 AP,[249] because Greek law had declared the arbitration award void and unenforceable. Finally, the Greek Government did not succeed in convincing the Court of having struck a fair balance between the protection of the right of property and the requirements of public interest.[250] Not only did the Court conclude that there had been a violation of Article 1 AP, but it also considered it necessary, in accordance with Article 50 ECHR, to accord to the complainants "just satisfaction" by granting them exactly the same sum as was determined by the arbitral award.[251]

As the ECtHR clarified in its later *Regent Company* (2008)[252] and *Kin-Stib* (2010)[253] judgments, the considerations on property in *Stran* also apply in cases dealing with enforcement. It has been argued against this jurisprudence that, e.g. NYC awards could not be expropriated at all, as they can be enforced

---

246   *Stran Greek Refineries and Stratis Andreadis v Greece*, No 13427/87 (ECtHR, 9 December 1994) paras 61–75.

247   "Legitimate expectations", under certain conditions, can be protected by art 1 AP. See Hans-Joachim Cremer, 'Eigentumsschutz' in Oliver Dörr and others (eds), EMRK/GG, *Konkordanzkommentar* (vol II, 2nd edn 2013) ch 22, para 43.

248   *Jasiūnienė*, No 41510/98, ECHR (6 March 2003) para 44: "the Court reiterates that a »claim« can constitute a «possession» within the meaning of Article 1 of Protocol No. 1 to the Convention if it is sufficiently established to be enforceable." See also Cremer (n 247), para 43 (with further court practice).

249   See, in contrast, the case of *Saipem* SpA *v Bangladesh*, see s 2.4. (d), where a similar interference was held to constitute an expropriation.

250   ECHR (n 246) para 74.

251   ibid paras 81–83.

252   *Regent Company v Ukraine*, No 773/03 (ECtHR, 3 April 2008) para 61.

253   *Kin-Stib and Majkić v Serbia*, No 12312/05 (ECtHR, 20 April 2010) para 85: "the Serbian authorities have thus clearly not taken the necessary measures to fully enforce the arbitration award in question and have not provided any convincing reasons for that failure. Accordingly, there has been a violation of Article 1 of Protocol No. 1."

in multiple jurisdictions.[254] However, this objection is only true for cases where property actually exists in more than one country. What is more, the ECtHR did not speak of expropriation (second sentence), but deliberately applied the first sentence of the first paragraph of Article 1 AP. There can be no doubt that an unfounded frustration of enforcement in a specific Convention state, even if new enforcement proceedings in other countries could be commenced, may amount to a violation of the right to peacefully enjoy one's possessions.

4.3.2.1.2   Right to Fair Trial and Access to Court

The ECtHR acknowledged in the same *Stran* case that arbitral awards can give rise to an issue under Article 6 ECHR. It noted

> that the applicants' right under the arbitration award was »pecuniary« in nature, as had been their claim for damages allowed by the arbitration court. Their right to recover the sums awarded by the arbitration court was therefore a "civil right" within the meaning of Article 6 (art. 6), whatever the nature, under Greek law, of the contract between the applicants and the Greek State (...). It follows that the outcome of the proceedings brought in the ordinary courts by the State to have the arbitration award set aside was decisive for a "civil right".[255]

The principle of the rule of law and the notion of fair trial enshrined in Article 6 ECHR preclude any interference with the administration of justice designed to influence the judicial determination of the dispute.[256] It makes no difference whether the state concerned interferes with the award by repealing its legal basis or by refusing to enforce it.

Furthermore, Article 6 (1) ECHR protects individuals from overlong proceedings. The reasonableness of the length of proceedings is to be determined with reference to the criteria laid down in the Court's case-law and in the light of all circumstances of the case.[257] In *Regent Company v Ukraine*, a case dealing with the failure of national authorities to enforce a final IAA arbitration award, the Court stated clearly "that the continued non-enforcement of the judgment debt at issue constituted a violation of Article 6 § 1 of the Convention".[258]

---

254   Yaraslau Kryvoi, 'Can an Arbitration Award Be Expropriated? Introductory Note to European Court of Human Rights: Kin-Stib & Majkić v. Serbia' (2010) 49 ILM 1181, with references to ICSID case practice.
255   ECtHR (n 246) para 40.
256   ibid para 49.
257   ibid para 55.
258   *Regent Company*, No 773/03 (ECtHR, 3 April 2008) para 60.

4.3.2.2   ECtHR – a New Instance of Review of Arbitral Awards?

Even though the cases mentioned relate to awards made in the context of domestic and international commercial arbitration, not in the context of investment disputes, the considerations of the Court taken in general can also be applied to investment cases. However, this jurisprudence may induce some concerns on the introduction of an additional instance in post-award enforcement processes, which reminds us of similar concerns relating to the *SAIPEM v Bangladesh* case.[259] In *SAIPEM* and similar decisions, this concern has been raised by the stretching of the notion of "investment" in order to found enforcement-related investment claims before a new arbitral tribunal. Concerning the ECHR, the question arises, whether the character of the ICSID Convention as the more specific or possibly "contained" regime would oppose the option of bringing ICSID award cases to the ECtHR.

According to Article 26 ICSID the "consent of the parties to arbitration under this Convention shall ... be deemed consent to such arbitration to the exclusion of any other remedy." Will that prohibit private persons from approaching the ECtHR? This certainly depends on the range of the notion of "arbitration" in Article 26 ICSID. Considering the fact that Articles 53 and 54 ICSID belong to Chapter 4 on "Arbitration", it seems logical to assume that recognition and enforcement are governed exclusively by the rules of the ICSID Convention. On the other hand, section 1 of the ICSID Convention on the "Request for Arbitration" is clearly distinguished from section 6 on "Recognition and Enforcement of the Award". Apparently, section 1, despite its title, relates to "arbitration proceedings" only. This conforms to the fact that arbitration proceedings are distinct from enforcement proceedings. The purpose of Article 26 ICSID is to channel the parties of an investment dispute, once it has arisen, into the ICSID mechanism to the exclusion of any other remedy. Yet, the purpose is not to bar such parties from instruments outside of the ICSID Convention in cases where the ICSID system itself does not provide for any remedy – such as in the case that a state tenaciously refuses to fulfill its obligations under Articles 53 and 54 ICSID.

Article 53 (1) ICSID must also be considered. According to its first sentence, "[t]he award ... shall not be subject to any appeal or to any other remedy except those provided for in this Convention." This provision excludes any other remedy dealing with the examination of the legality of the award – which, indeed, would contradict the aim of swift enforcement and interfere with the "pro-enforcement bias" of the ICSID Convention. In contrast, the aim of

---

259   See s 2.4. (d).

approaching the ECtHR is essentially different, as the complainant claims that non-compliance by a state with Article 53 (1) ICSID, second sentence ("Each party shall abide by and comply with the terms of the award"), or Article 54 (1) ICSID ("Each Contracting State shall ... enforce the pecuniary obligations imposed by that award within its territories as if it were a final judgment of a court in that State"), violates his or her human rights under the ECHR. Consequently, submitting an individual complaint to the ECtHR serves a purpose, which is prescribed to be achieved by the ICSID Convention but cannot be achieved by the instruments provided for in this Convention. Article 64 ICSID is no alternative, as it only entitles states to approach the ICJ, not private persons. One cannot assume that this provision, without explicit suggestion, intended to narrow down all privates to the vagaries of diplomatic protection in conjunction with the means provided for by Article 64 ICSID.[260]

After all, the ICSID regime does not preclude remedies, by which the complainant seeks to react to the failure by a state to fulfill its enforcement-related obligations under the ICSID Convention. Moreover, it would be contradictory (*venire contra factum proprium*), if a state, by invoking Articles 26 or 53 (1) ICSID, were allowed to oppose ECtHR proceedings, whilst itself failing to fulfill its own obligations under Articles 53 and 54 ICSID. The same, all the more, applies with regard to the NYC, which neither contains any explicit rules on the exclusion of any other remedies, nor claims to be a self-contained regime.

4.3.2.3 *Enforcement of Decisions of the European Court of Human Rights*
4.3.2.3.1 The Enforcement Mechanism
According to Article 46 (1) ECHR the Contracting Parties undertake to abide by the final judgment of the Court in any case to which they are parties. However, all final judgments of the Court will be transmitted to the Committee of Ministers (CoM) in order to supervise their execution (Article 46 [2] ECHR). Whilst the Court cannot annul any domestic decisions or laws, some judgments contain precise suggestions on implementation, particularly if they qualify as "pilot judgments". According to Rule 61 of the Rules [of Procedure] of the Court,[261] the Court shall in its pilot judgment "identify both the nature

---

260 In this case, the ICSID Convention would be interpreted in a way as to withdraw all rights to individual complaint (eg art 34 ECHR) without substituting private persons by a more specific instrument of the same kind. Such interpretation does not conform to common practice in international treaty law (cf art 35 [2] [b] ECHR), explicitly excluding other remedies. It would also conflict with the object and purpose of the ECHR.

261 Rules of Court of 1 June 2015, available at: <www.echr.coe.int/Documents/Rules_Co urt_ENG.pdf> accessed 20 November 2021.

of the structural or systemic problem or other dysfunction as established as well as the type of remedial measures which the Contracting Party concerned is required to take at the domestic level".

In principle, the State party concerned remains free to choose the means necessary to comply with the judgment. Yet, the CoM shall examine whether any just satisfaction awarded by the Court has been paid and whether measures have been taken to neutralize the violation in the specific case – i.e. individual measures (e.g. enforcement of an arbitral award), and to prevent new violations – i.e. general measures (e.g. changes of law or practice).[262]

Meanwhile, one can speak of a sophisticated system of "standard supervision" or "enhanced supervision" (Twin-Track Supervision System), which results in a final resolution once the problem is settled. As a last resort, the CoM, by 2/3 vote, may refer the matter again to the ECtHR (Infringement Proceedings).[263] Additionally, the CoM publishes the results of its supervision in the form of Annual Reports,[264] which may bear on the perpetrator state a certain blame-and-shame effect.

4.3.2.3.2   Enforcing the *Yukos* Judgment of the ECtHR

The case of *OAO Neftyanaya Kompaniya YUKOS v Russia* (2011)[265] could be held admissible by the ECtHR only because it was introduced by Yukos in its own name, whilst parallel proceedings at the PCA Tribunal were initiated by three shareholders acting as investors.[266] Accordingly, both matters were not "substantially the same" within the meaning of Article 35 (2) (b) ECHR. Concerning the merits, the Court found that Russia had violated Article 6 ECHR (fair trial) as well as Article 1 AP (protection of property) but had not violated Article 18 ECHR (misuse of legal proceeding in order to destroy YUKOS).

As a consequence, the ECtHR in its subsequent Judgment on just satisfaction of July 2014[267] held that firstly, Russia is to pay "the applicant company's shareholders as they stood at the time of the company's liquidation", or their

---

262   Rule 6 of the Rules of the Committee of Ministers for the supervision of the execution of judgments and of the terms of friendly settlements of 10 May 2006, available at: <https://wcd.coe.int/> accessed 20 November 2021.

263   Rule 11 of the Rules of the Committee of Ministers for the supervision of the execution of judgments and of the terms of friendly settlements (n 262).

264   Available at: <www.coe.int/t/dghl/monitoring/execution/Documents/Publications_en.asp> accessed 20 November 2021.

265   *OAO Neftyanaya Kompaniya YUKOS v Russia*, No 14902/04 (ECtHR (Chamber), 20 September 2011).

266   See see s 3.4.

267   *OAO Neftyanaya Kompaniya YUKOS v Russia*, No 14902/04 (ECtHR, 31 July 2014).

successors, ca. EUR 1.87 billion for pecuniary damage. Secondly, Russia is to produce, in co-operation with the Committee of Ministers, within six months a comprehensive plan with binding time frame for distribution. Thirdly, Russia is to pay EUR 300,000 for costs and expenses. The ECtHR dismissed YUKOS' claim for just satisfaction for non-pecuniary damage.

Ever since both judgments (on the merits and on just satisfaction) in the *Yukos* case were made, Russia is under "enhanced supervision". On 15 May 2013 Russia submitted to the Committee of Ministers an action plan concerning the enforcement of the ECtHR judgment on the merits of 2011.[268] However, this plan mainly related to the improvement of the supervision of the national bailiff, whereas Russia did not submit any planning with respect to the distribution of the just satisfaction awarded for pecuniary damage.[269] Ministerial statements relating to the fact that the implementation of the judgment would be in contradiction with the Constitution of the Russian Federation cannot serve as an excuse, as a party may not invoke the provisions of its internal law as justification for its failure to fulfil obligations under an international treaty (Article 27 Vienna Convention on the Law of Treaties). Nonetheless, Russia seems determined not to comply with the judgment on just satisfaction.

The result could be that the successors of Yukos dispose of an ECtHR judgment that cannot be enforced unless Russia cooperates with the C.o.E. Committee of Ministers, whilst the former investors of Yukos dispose of a PCA arbitral award, which can be enforced in a plenitude of third countries.[270] If that were to happen, the investors of the victim would enjoy a better position than the victim themselves.

5   Reflections

The impacts of public international law on the enforcement of foreign arbitral awards are multifaceted in theory – and disparate, if not unpredictable in arbitral practice. Customarily, international law principles have been perceived as a threat to the specific enforcement mechanisms where they were invoked as defenses to recognition and enforcement or respectively execution.[271]

---

268   Council of Europe, Committee of Ministers, Doc DH-DD(2013)565 of 22 May 2013.
269   Council of Europe, Committee of Ministers, Doc. CM/Del/Dec(2015)1236/15 of 24 September 2015. The CoM decided to resume consideration of this case at the latest at their DH meeting in March 2016.
270   See s 3.4.
271   See ss 2.4. (c) (bb) and III.3.

However, it can also be considered a correction of course from an investment-biased culture to a more balanced approach including legitimate public policy concerns. The future will not lie in the continuation of disregard of public policy concerns but in the taming of this shrew. Whilst the ICSID Convention system with regard to its organizational and procedural particularities (e.g. ICSID Committees instead of national courts) is more or less prepared (but not accustomed) to take this challenge, the New York Convention system seems much more critical. However, its intrinsic mechanism of "shared responsibility" (competence-sharing amongst the courts of different countries),[272] the international law obligation to interpret international treaties in good faith,[273] the option of considering a foreign arbitral award exceptionally as "investment"[274] and the possibility of approaching a human rights court,[275] in the case of non-enforceability, allow for a proper handling of international law impacts.

The prospect of achieving a "systemic integration" of arbitration law and practice by applying the same general principles of international law either based on Article 31 VCLT or more specific provisions (e.g. Article 42 [1] ICSID), has not come true. Even though most arbitral tribunals routinely consider earlier decisions, the problem of inconsistency remains with regard to the consideration of general international law as with regard to any other aspect. It is correct that according to doctrine an arbitral tribunal, first, needs to have jurisdiction and, secondly, must have a specific competence for applying international law. Yet it is misleading: As the pertinent treaties on the recognition and enforcement of foreign arbitral awards are themselves "creatures of international law",[276] they have to be interpreted and applied in concordance with the rules of international law. According to Article 31 (3) (c) VCLT or any special emanation of it, a tribunal must consider general international law "applicable in the relations between the parties", unless the relevant treaty would provide for a more specific solution. E.g. customary international law *is regularly applicable* in the relations between the parties, unless one of the parties exceptionally has acted as a "persistent objector" to the custom concerned. It is worth mentioning in this context that sticking to the text of an international treaty tends, predominantly, to serve the interests of the states that are parties to an international treaty, whereas considering customary international law has the potential to empower courts and tribunals.

---

272   See ss 2.3. (b) and 11.3. (c) (cc).
273   See ss 2.3. (c) (bb), (cc) and (dd).
274   See s 2.4. (d).
275   See s 4.3. (b).
276   McLachlan (n 6) 399.

Enforcement under the New York Convention is essentially based on *competence-sharing* between the authorities of the state, where the award was made or may be annulled on the one side, and the authorities of the state of recognition and enforcement on the other side. If either of the parties does not perform its competences properly, swift enforcement as the main purpose of the whole system cannot be achieved. As the study has shown, there exists a variety of situations confronting authorities of the state of enforcement with the question of whether authorities of the other state have failed to perform that state's international treaty obligations. Sitting in judgment on another state does not only imply concerns relating to the *comity among nations*; rather it can undermine the intention of shared-responsibility of the NYC and, thus, violate international law. On the other hand, the other state party by systematically misinterpreting the public policy caveat may violate the international law *principle of good faith*. The practice of eventually enforcing awards in spite of their annulment in the state of origin attests to the fact that an atypical sort of countermeasure has become common in order to restore the functioning of the system of shared responsibility once one of the parties is failing to comply with its obligations.

Within the ICSID Convention system the denial of considering such rules of international law as may be applicable (Article 42 [1] ICSID) can amount to an excess of power allowing for an annulment of the award (Article 52 [1] [b] ICSID) and, eventually, a stay of enforcement (Article 52 [5] ICSID). This has certainly contributed to an increase in the consideration of general international law by ICSID Tribunals and Committees. However, the Argentine cases have also shown that the ICSID Committees produced disparate outcomes regarding the question of whether and how the international law defense of "necessity" could be employed. Where a Committee was minded to consider necessity, Argentina failed to show the existence of the elements of a status of necessity. It follows from this experience that arbitral bodies are not the right place to decide, ultimately, on international law issues that by their very nature include public resp. constitutional law concerns.

As there is growing consensus on the position that human rights law can have an impact on arbitration agreements, arbitral proceedings, and awards, the old wisdom that international arbitration and human rights were two separate and unrelated spheres no longer seems tenable.[277] However, a state cannot invoke human rights as if they were its own rights, but only in an indirect

---

277   Massimo V Benedettelli, 'Human Rights as a Litigation Tool in International Arbitration: Reflecting on the ECHR Experience' (2015) 31 Arbitration International 631–659.

manner. Where it refers to the human rights of its nationals, it actually relates to public policy concerns or its right to exercise diplomatic protection. In contrast, private investors can invoke human rights directly – in accordance with the rules on treaty interpretation and application. It should also be noted that the function of human rights in the context of arbitration proceedings is somewhat different from its role in the context of recognition and enforcement. Nonetheless, the expanding jurisprudence, in particular of the European Court of Human Rights,[278] regarding the recognition and enforcement of commercial arbitration awards, demonstrates a growing "symbiotic relationship" between public international law and international commercial arbitration rights.[279] Neither the New York Convention, nor the ICSID Convention can be regarded as "self-contained" in the sense that they would be opposed to carrying out individual complaint proceedings before the European Court on Human Rights.[280] The precondition, however, is that the aim of such proceedings will not be to review the award but rather to claim that a state, by not enforcing an award, respectively not complying with an award, has violated the European Convention on Human Rights. ECHR rights such as, in particular, the right to the peaceful enjoyment of property and the right to fair trial may function here as *carrier rights*. A parallel strategy can be seen in the recent moves to claim compensation before an ICSID Tribunal by arguing that the failure of enforcement with respect to an arbitral award, in conjunction with other elements of the investment, constitutes a breach by the respondent state of investor's rights.[281] Though it would be unrealistic to expect the ECtHR to satisfy all human rights concerns,[282] it can contribute to a more systematic and balanced integration of such rights into international arbitration law.

The international law principle of immunity continues to undermine the effectivity of any enforcement regime with regard to foreign arbitral awards. Even though a more restrictive approach has become common practice, the decisive question will always be whether a specific piece of state property is per se exempt from execution or serves state purposes. The effectivity of enforcement is further weakened by certain forms of state practice such

---

278 See s 4.3. (b).

279 Stephen Fietta and James Upcher, 'Public International Law, Investment Treaties and Commercial Arbitration: An Emerging System of Complementarity?' (2013) 29 Arbitration International 187–222.

280 See s 4.3. (b) (cc).

281 See s 2.4. (d).

282 Cf Ursula Kriebaum, 'Is the European Court of Human Rights an Alternative to Investor-State Arbitration?' in Dupuy and others, *Human Rights in International Investment Law and Arbitration* (OUP 2009) 219–245.

as the acceptance of mere declarations on the public purpose of property, or the necessity of a connection between the property and the claim or, at least, between the property and the entity against which the proceeding was directed. "Piercing the corporate veil" may compensate these limitations to some extent. However, it has become apparent that in a time of increasing business and investment activities international law needs reform.[283] If the principle of immunity protects state property in order to conserve the material basis for the performance of public functions by a foreign state, property used for public purposes must not be totally exempt from execution but could be limited to a right to offer alternative sorts of property in exchange. However, it will be very unlikely that the states, as the creators of international law, will ever consent to such change. After all, approaching an external human rights system even in the case of immunity-based blockages of execution remains as the last resort.

283   Also Blane (n 151) 505: "excess of caution" in favor of the states.

CHAPTER 27

International Commercial Arbitration and Economic Sanctions

Andrey Kotelnikov

1 Introduction

Over the decades prior to 2014, civil procedure and international commercial arbitration experts from Russia and the Commonwealth of Independent States rarely concerned themselves with the subject of economic sanctions. This peculiar political instrument interested Russian legal scholars primarily as a phenomenon of public international law.[1] However, following the events in Ukraine since 2013–2014, the United States[2] and the European Union[3] adopted various restrictive measures targeting economic relations with Russia. In turn, this has led to the introduction of countermeasures by the Russian Federation.[4] As a result, more and more actors in international trade are finding themselves in a position where the continued existence of such restrictive measures is capable – actually or potentially – of influencing their rights and obligations arising out of commercial contracts, as well as the resolution of their disputes with trade partners. Thus, it becomes necessary to explore the specific set of legal issues that sanctions give rise to, in light of the experience of other countries dealing with similar situations.

It is logical to expect that when a dispute arises between private parties, restrictive measures of this kind might influence the functioning of the mechanism of international commercial arbitration, as well as the rights and obligations of parties and arbitral institutions. This influence may come in many

---

1 See, eg, Iqor Lukashuk, *Mezhdunarodnoe pravo: osobennaja chast'* [International Law: Particular Institutions] (Wolters Kluwer 2005) 407.

2 For the review of the measures in question, see The US Department of State, 'Ukraine and Russia Sanctions' <www.state.gov/ukraine-and-russia-sanctions/> accessed 20 November 2021.

3 For the review of the measures in question, see EU Restrictive Measures Factsheet (29 April 2014) <www.consilium.europa.eu/uedocs/cms_data/docs/pressdata/EN/foraff/135804.pdf> accessed 20 November 2021.

4 Decree of the President of Russian Federation of 6 August 2014 No 560 "On the application of certain special economic measures to ensure the security of the Russian Federation".

© KONINKLIJKE BRILL NV, LEIDEN, 2023 | DOI:10.1163/9789004357839_029

forms. For example, the resolution of a dispute in a foreign arbitral institution may depend on obtaining a licence from this country's respective authorities so that a party from a sanctions list could legitimately transfer the money to pay an administrative fee. Individuals named on a sanctions list would be unable to enter the territory of a foreign State to testify as witnesses before the arbitrators (which, however, would not preclude the tribunal from holding one or two hearings in another country for this particular purpose). The list of potential hurdles can be fairly long.

International commercial arbitration is a legal process of a jurisdictional nature carried out by private individuals, the arbitrators. When they resolve disputes, the arbitrators must take into account the parallel existence of several applicable laws at once. These include the substantive law applicable to commercial relations between the contracting parties, the procedural law that applies to the resolution of a dispute in arbitration (*lex arbitri*), and the laws of countries where the winning party might seek enforcement of an arbitral award. When these competing legal systems take the opposite views on the validity and legitimacy of a certain commercial transaction, the tribunal's task becomes even more complex. One should also bear in mind that resolution of disputes in international arbitration by definition has an international (or transnational) character, and arbiters are not bound by the provisions of national law to the same extent as judges.

The classic debate between the jurisdictional (procedural) and autonomous theories of arbitration[5] becomes very pertinent in a situation where the arbitrators have to make a choice between application and non-application of mandatory rules of national law, particularly where such rules are closely intertwined with international politics. From the vantage point of the autonomous theory and the delocalisation theory,[6] it is logical to insist that such national regulations must not be directly binding for the tribunal, even when the seat of arbitration is in a country that adopts and enforces economic sanctions. On the one hand, arbitrators should be free to deviate from such rules if, as a matter of law or legal policy, there is a good reason to do so. On the other hand, arbitrators and the administrative personnel of arbitral institutions are merely

---

5   See Lazar Lunts and Nataliya Marysheva, *Kurs mezhdunarodnogo chastnogo prava: Tom 3* [International Private Law: Volume 3] (Juridicheskaja Literatura 1976) 218–219; Vladimir Yarkov (ed), *Arbitrazhnyj process: uchebnik* [Commercial Court Procedure: Textbook] (4th edn, Ifotropik Media 2010) 615; Andrey Kotelnikov, *Pravovaja priroda arbitrazhnogo soglashenija i posledstvija ego zakljuchenija* [The Legal Nature of an Arbitration Agreement and Its Effects] (PhD thesis, The Urals State Law Academy 2008) 56, 79.

6   Kotelnikov (n 5) 62–63.

private individuals who in that capacity must comply with all laws of the State of their residence. It would not be prudent to ignore this "personal" dimension because the legislation on sanctions often imposes significant administrative and criminal penalties for non-compliance.

This chapter will consider several aspects of the influence that economic sanctions exert upon international commercial arbitration, and will address the following issues in turn:

1)   The essence and types of economic sanctions, and the significance of various classifications for their effect on international commercial arbitration.

2)   The influence of sanctions on the contractual relations between the parties in international trade, where the resulting disputes end up in front of international arbitral tribunals. The two most important aspects here are the invalidity of the contract, whether in full or in part, and the impossibility of performance (*force majeure*).

3)   The effect of sanctions on setting aside and enforcement of arbitral awards. There are two most interesting issues here. First, what is the effect of sanctions on objective arbitrability, i.e. the subject matter which the parties can refer to arbitration? Second, should one interpret sanctions as an element of public policy – which serves as a ground to refuse recognition and enforcement of an arbitral award under Article v of the New York Convention of 1958?

2   The Definition and the Diversity of Economic Sanctions

Legal doctrinal sources, both in Russia and elsewhere, suggest that there are many approaches to the definition of the acts and actions which must be called "sanctions" *stricto sensu* and the similar phenomena that ought to be designated by some other term. Thus, va Vasilenko included within the definition of "sanctions" all measures of legitimate coercive character, whether adopted by individual States or by international organizations, and whether involving the use of armed forces or not. This definition would include, among other things: retorsion, reprisal, self-defence, coercive measures of international organizations, and so on.[7] GI Kurdyukov and MV Keschner, after a

---

7   Volodimir Vasilenko, *Mezhdunarodno-pravovye sankcii* [Sanctions in International Law] (Vishha shkola 1983) 68.

detailed analysis of various theoretical approaches,[8] conclude that only the measures that fall within the framework of the collective security system, mainly those envisioned in the UN Charter's provisions on collective security, should properly be called sanctions. Unilateral measures by individual States are not sanctions; such measures are lacking legitimacy because the principle of sovereign equality militates against unilateral imposition of sanctions by one State against another.[9]

Scholarly writings from outside Russia rarely draw such a clear distinction. For example, one article points out that a broad spectrum of possible economic sanctions is available to the UN, as well as to the European Union and individual States.[10] B. Early in his study of the economic effects of unilateral US trade restrictions against various States takes it as his starting point that the term "sanctions" will be most suitable to refer to these measures.[11] Foreign authors actively discuss, for example, why, according to the empirical data, unilateral sanctions adopted by one State produce the desired effect more often than multilateral sanctions adopted within the framework of international organizations.[12] Both Russian[13] and foreign[14] media consistently use the term "sanctions" when they cover the adoption of the United States, European Union and Russian unilateral restrictive measures in connection with the events in Ukraine. In an everyday parlance in both the Russian and English languages, the word "sanctions" has the same broad meaning.

---

8   For more details see Gennadiy Kurdyukov and Mariya Keschner, 'Sootnoshenie otvetst-vennosti i sankcij v mezhdunarodnom prave: doktrinal'nye podhody' [The Correlation Between Responsibility and Sanctions in International Law: the Doctrinal Approaches] (2014) No 9 Zhurnal rossijskogo prava [The Journal of Russian Law] 103.

9   ibid 111.

10   Elliot Geisinger and others, 'The Impact of International Trade Sanctions on Contractual Obligations and on International Commercial Obligations' (2012) 4 International Business Law Journal 405.

11   Bryan Early, 'Alliances and Trade with Sanctioned States: A Study of US Economic Sanctions, 1950–2000' (2012) 56 (3) Journal of Conflict Resolution 547.

12   Some researchers dispute the accuracy of this premise. See, eg, Navin Bapat and T Clifton Morgan, 'Multilateral versus Unilateral Sanctions Reconsidered: A Test Ssing New Data' (2009) 53 (4) International Studies Quarterly 1075.

13   See, eg, Ivan Tkachev and Sergey Kanashevich, 'Sovet Evrosojuza odobril vvedenie sek-toral'nyh sankcij protiv Rossii' [The European Council Endorsed the Introduction of Sectoral Sanctions against Russia] (RBC, 31 July 2014) <www.rbc.ru/politics/31/07/2014/5704200f9a7947б0d3d40639> accessed 20 November 2021.

14   See, eg, Kevin Rawlinson, 'Ukraine Crisis: Russia Warns of Reaction to Fresh EU Economic Sanctions' (The Guardian, 6 September 2014) <www.theguardian.com/world/2014/sep/06/russia-eu-economic-sanctions-ukraine> accessed 20 November 2021.

Thus, even while recognising the validity of the terminological distinction between "sanctions" in the strict sense (adopted primarily within the UN) and other international legal measures of coercion of similar character, it must be borne in mind that this difference currently seems obvious only for a small number of lawyers and legal scholars. Therefore, consciously taking no position in this debate, it seems appropriate – for the sake of simplicity if nothing else – to continue using the expression "economic sanctions" in this article as a generic term. At the same time, to the extent that this distinction goes beyond mere terminology, it appears to be very significant to the present author, as will be explained below.

In essence, economic sanctions, despite their effect on the private law sphere and the relations between private individuals and commercial companies, are an instrument of public policy, and in many respects, they are an issue of public international law. Their types are numerous. The most radical measure in the existing "arsenal" is the embargo, i.e. the prohibition of trade with certain States. The embargo may be total, that is, extend to any export-import transactions with the target country, or partial/sectoral when the restriction relates to certain goods or their categories, such as goods that serve military purposes and the dual-purpose goods, i.e. the ones that have both military and civil uses. The boycott is a ban on imports of any goods or services from the target State. Like the embargo, the boycott may be total or partial. Still milder measures include, in particular, making certain commercial or financial transactions subject to prior permission or reporting, the arrest (freezing) of assets held by the named persons on the territory of the host State. The partial restrictions may relate to economic transactions with certain named individuals or entities.[15]

Sanctions usually reflect the political desire to induce a foreign State to perform, or to stop performing, some action or actions. Specific objectives of their introduction can be very diverse: from forcing a State to cease some specific human rights violations on its territory to overthrowing a political regime. The latter appears to be the most common motive. According to one study, in about every third case (80 out of 204 instances examined by the authors), the sanctions' goal was to change the political regime in the target country.[16]

It is not uncommon to explain economic sanctions as an intermediate measure between words and military action[17] which is particularly useful

---

15   Geisinger and others (n 10) 406.
16   Gary Hufbauer and others, *Economic Sanctions Reconsidered* (3rd edn, Peterson Institute 2007) 67.
17   Jonathan Marcus, 'Do Economic Sanctions Work?' (*BBC*, 26 July 2010) <www.bbc.co.uk/news/world-middle-east-10742109> accessed 20 November 2021.

when verbal condemnation is incapable of producing the desired effect, but the use of military force is impossible or inadequate. The mechanism of most categories of economic sanctions is indirect: their primary object, as a rule, is not the elite who take key decisions in the target State. Instead, the targets are the members of the armed forces, the middle class, the workers of the agricultural sector, or the country's population in general.[18] As the UN Secretary General Kofi Annan noted in his report,

> when robust and comprehensive economic sanctions are directed against authoritarian regimes, a different problem is encountered. Then it is usually the people who suffer, not the political elites whose behaviour triggered the sanctions in the first place. Indeed, those in power, perversely, often benefit from such sanctions by their ability to control and profit from the black market activity and by exploiting them as a pretext for eliminating domestic sources of political opposition.[19]

There is no doubt that economic sanctions could lead to very adverse social consequences in the State against which they are directed, including a devastating impact on public health, social care and other vital institutions.[20]

Although there is a recorded history of the use of economic sanctions (especially unilateral sanctions) against other countries since ancient times, their popularity peaked in the 20th century. According to one empirical study, from 1945 to 2005 there were 1412 cases of their use, or threats of use, in the world, with the greatest number recorded in 1990–2000.[21] At the end of 20th century, the so-called comprehensive sanctions were the most popular, well-known examples of which include the UN total embargo against Iraq, Kuwait and Libya. In the subsequent period, when their destructive nature and the extent of damage they caused to the economy and social well-being of the population became better understood, preference shifted to more narrowly

---

18   Jonathan Kirshner, 'The Microfoundations of Economic Sanctions' (1997) 6 (3) Security Studies 32.

19   'We the Peoples: The Role of the United Nations in the Twenty-first Century. Report of the Secretary-General', A/54/2000, (English version, 27 March 2000) para 231 <https://digitallibrary.un.org/record/410974?ln=en#record-files-collapse-header> accessed 20 November 2021.

20   Susan Allen, David Lektzian, 'Economic Sanctions: A Blunt Instrument?' (2013) 50(1) Journal of Peace Research 121.

21   T Clifton Morgan, Navin Bapat and Yoshiharu Kobayashi, 'Threat and Imposition of Economic Sanctions 1945–2005: Updating the TIES Dataset' (2014) 31 (5) Conflict Management and Peace Science 541.

targeted sanctions, with their effect limited to designated persons or sectors of the economy.[22]

It is important to distinguish between sanctions imposed by the UN Security Council decisions and all other types of economic sanctions. According to Article 41 of the UN Charter,

> The Security Council may decide what measures not involving the use of armed force are to be employed to give effect to its decisions, and it may call upon the Members of the United Nations to apply such measures. These may include complete or partial interruption of economic relations and of rail, sea, air, postal, telegraphic, radio, and other means of communication, and the severance of diplomatic relations.

Article 25 of the UN Charter states that the members of the United Nations agree to accept the decisions of the Security Council and to carry them out. Therefore, the implementation of Security Council decisions is an international legal obligation for every United Nations Member State.

In comparison with these UN sanctions, the use of restrictive economic measures by States unilaterally, as well as their use by the Member States of an international organization against third States, produces no legally binding obligation for the target State. In the Final Report of the International Law Association (New Delhi, 2002), the regime of sanctions under the UN Charter is on the list of international obligations the violation of which can amount to a violation of public policy under Article v of the New York Convention of 1958.[23] The report does not mention any other similar measures – perhaps because their status under the New York Convention is a much more complex and controversial issue.

The attempts of a State targeted by UN sanctions to neutralise their effect through their domestic law seem to be quite controversial. For example, the 1990 Iraqi law "On the protection of property rights and interests of Iraq in the country and abroad" stipulated that foreign companies and individuals who fail to comply with their contractual obligations because of the UN sanctions must pay an appropriate compensation. Although the domestic courts of Iraq

---

22   'Follow-up to the Outcome of the Millennium Summit. The Report of the UN Secretary General', A 59/565, (English version, 2 December 2004) para 79–80 <https://digitallibrary .un.org/record/536113?ln=en#record-files-collapse-header> accessed 20 November 2021.

23   Pierre Mayer and Audley Sheppard, 'Final ILA Report on Public Policy as a Bar to Enforcement of International Arbitration Awards' (2003) 19(2) Arbitration International 249.

would enforce this rule, in international commercial arbitration the tribunals would probably refuse to give it effect, as this would be obviously inconsistent with the international public order.[24]

With economic sanctions adopted in the framework of a regional international organization, or by a single State, the identification of subjects legally bound to comply with them may present some challenges. By their nature sanctions are territorial, that is, their provisions are binding only on natural and legal persons who, for one reason or another, are under the jurisdiction of the State enacting the sanctions. Despite the understandable political desire to improve the effectiveness of sanctions by expanding the number of subjects who must comply with them, such an extension should have its limits. For example, the restrictions imposed by the European Union Regulation №833/2014 of 31 July 2014,[25] apply as follows:

(1)   within the territory of the European Union;
(2)   on board any aircraft or any vessel under the jurisdiction of a Member State;
(3)   to any person inside or outside the territory of the Union who is a national of a Member State;
(4)   to any legal person, entity or body, inside or outside the territory of the Union, which is incorporated or constituted under the law of a Member State;
(5)   to any legal person, entity or body in respect of any business done in whole or in part within the European Union.[26]

Thus, other persons not listed in the Regulation as detailed above have no obligation to adhere to the restrictions it imposes. To the extent that the introduction of such restrictions is within the competence of the enacting State, they form a part of its domestic law, and in a dispute where this law is applicable, a court or a tribunal must apply them directly.

In the past, there were more controversial situations where the applicability of measures as detailed in the respective State enactment was open to serious doubts. One such situation arose in the *Sensor* case in 1982 in the Netherlands. The Dutch company Sensor, through its affiliated company (also registered in the Netherlands but a subsidiary of the US corporation), agreed to deliver to a French company seismographic equipment for later use in the construction of

---

24   Hans van Houtte, 'Trade Sanctions and Arbitration' (1997) 25 International Business Law 166.
25   Council Regulation (EU) No 833/2014 of 31 July 2014 concerning restrictive measures in view of Russia's actions destabilising the situation in Ukraine (as amended).
26   ibid art 13.

pipelines in the USSR. The same year, the United States imposed an embargo on exports to the USSR of all oil and gas equipment using components or technologies with a US place of origin. The restriction applied to the supply of equipment to the Soviet Union from third countries; the persons for whom the observance of the embargo was mandatory included subsidiaries of US corporations; the prohibition applied equally to the transfer of equipment to other companies or individuals who planned to pass it on subsequently to the Soviet side.[27] The Dutch company refused to deliver the goods referring to the United States embargo as a *force majeure* event. The French buyer applied to the court in the Netherlands requesting an order for specific performance. The Dutch court decided that the laws of the Netherlands apply to the contract. The judge noted that even in such a situation, the US embargo could in principle be considered a *force majeure* event. However, in the decided case, the court did not give such weight to the embargo as it held that the United States had no jurisdiction to impose extraterritorial sanctions binding on European companies.[28]

Another example of an unsuccessful attempt to produce economic sanctions with an extraterritorial effect was the Cuban Liberty and Democratic Solidarity (Libertad) Act of 1996 (also known as the Helms-Burton Act), enacted in the United States in 1996. The controversial Title III of this Act established a new cause of action in the US federal courts. Namely, US citizens whose property was confiscated by the previous Cuban government without compensation received the right to lodge a claim against persons engaged in "unlawful trafficking" of such assets. These "traffickers" could include companies from countries which retained normal trade relations with Cuba – which included, at that time, many countries of Western Europe, Mexico, and Canada. For the trading companies, the probability of acquiring such property in the course of the normal commercial transactions was very high, as, in the early 1960s, the regime of Fidel Castro made a significant number of confiscations. In the United States, those foreign companies engaged in trade with Cuba could face liability in the amount equal to the value of the respective property, and if they continued their "unlawful trafficking", in the amount equal to its triple value plus interest.[29] These provisions of the Helms-Burton Act caused a widespread

---

27   'Note: Extraterritorial Subsidiary Jurisdiction' (1987) 50(3) Law and Contemporary Problems 71.

28   President District Court, The Hague. 17, September 1982, (1982) 22 International Legal Materials 66.

29   S 302 of the Act; Andreas Lowenfeld, 'Congress and Cuba: The Helms-Burton Act' (1996) 90 (3) The American Journal of International Law 419; Vaughan Lowe, 'Helms-Burton and EC Regulation 2271/96' (1997) 56 The Cambridge Law Journal 248.

negative reaction in the international community. The European Union in the Regulation №2271/96 of 22 November 1996 declared the judicial decision and arbitral awards based on the Helms-Burton Act and similar extraterritorial acts unenforceable in the territory of its Member States. This Regulation has also made it illegal for businesses and individuals to comply with such laws (including through compliance with requests of foreign courts) and established the possibility of "reverse" recovery, through the courts in the EU Member States, of losses incurred in the United States under the provisions of the Helms-Burton Act and similar laws. The United Kingdom has introduced in its territory a criminal liability for violation of the requirements of EU Regulation №2271/96.[30] The validity and applicability of such measures by the European Union and the United Kingdom, aimed at neutralising the effect of unilateral extraterritorial US sanctions, up to the present time have not generated much debate. In UN Resolution №68/8 of 29 October 2013, the General Assembly expressed its concern with UN Member States adopting acts such as the Helms-Burton Act the extraterritorial effects of which affect the sovereignty of other States, the legitimate interests of foreign citizens and organizations, freedom of trade, and navigation.[31]

In March 2014 the UK Foreign and Commonwealth Office (FCO) held an informal consultation on the possible introduction of a new and unusual type of sanctions - so-called "contract sanctions". Their mechanism would involve the following. The UK courts (and the judicial authorities of other participating countries, if they were to join the United Kingdom in this initiative) when hearing disputes between foreign entities would be required to deny enforcement of contracts which require the performance of actions prohibited by a relevant sanctions instrument. For example, when the European Union introduced restrictions on the supply of arms to Russia, such restrictions remained non-binding for legal entities from third countries, such as China. However, the choice of London as the place of dispute resolution is quite popular in international trade. Accordingly, if an English court would hear a dispute between Russian and Chinese companies about the supply of arms to Russia, under the "contract sanctions" regime, it would have to take into account the existence of EU sanctions. As a result, the English court could not, among other things, order a Chinese company to deliver the goods under the contract. From a legal

---

30   Extraterritorial US Legislation (Sanctions against Cuba, Iran and Libya) (Protection of Trading Interests) Order 1996, SI 1996/3171.

31   'Necessity of Ending the Economic, Commercial and Financial Embargo Imposed by the United States of America against Cuba', Resolution A/RES/68/8 (English version) <www .un.org/en/ga/search/view_doc.asp?symbol=A/RES/68/8> accessed 20 November 2021.

point of view, such a rule would have an element of extraterritoriality, but it would not entail any direct obligations for the foreign companies. Therefore, the mechanism would not be open to the same criticism as the US extraterritorial measures. However, this approach would jeopardise the status of London as a dispute resolution venue and a financial centre and would affect the interests of the English legal profession and financial institutions. After receiving some negative responses, the FCO decided not to proceed with the "contract sanctions".[32]

3   The Impact of Sanctions on Contractual Relations

Since it is domestic law that determines the consequences of economic sanctions, their impact on contractual relations will also be different in every specific jurisdiction. Two major effects that economic sanctions can have on the parties' contractual relations are the invalidity of the contract and the impossibility of its performance. For the occurrence of each of these effects, a certain range of circumstances must be in place.

3.1   *Invalidity of the Contract*
For the contract to be annulled on this ground, first, the parties should have entered into the contract before the enactment of sanctions. Second, sanctions should be legally applicable to the contract.

National legislation in many countries specifies that a contradiction to the law is a sufficient basis to render the contract null and void. For example, in Switzerland, the contract may be declared invalid under Article 20 (1) of the Code of Obligations, which stipulates that a contract shall be void if its terms are impossible, unlawful or immoral. This effect occurs, for example, if the contract provides for the supply of goods prohibited by the act imposing sanctions, or the transfer of money to the person from the relevant "black list". In this case, the contract will only be invalid when the statutory enactment expressly states that transactions which contravene its requirements will be void, or when the object and purpose of such a prohibition require such an effect as the nullity of the contract.[33]

---

32   FCO Consultation Document, 'Contract Sanctions: A Consultation. March 2014' <www
       .dropbox.com/s/hxudbtorzqybdpf/Contract%20sanctions%20consultation%20docum
       ent%5B1%5D.pdf> accessed 20 November 2021; 'UK Government dDecides not to Proceed
       with "Contract Sanctions"' (*Lexology*, 15 August 2014) <www.lexology.com/library/detail
       .aspx?g=0aefa386-3f4d-4f19-aadb-3ff55dde8184> accessed 20 November 2021.
33   Geisinger (n 10) 410.

In the United States, the courts will refuse to enforce a contract concluded in breach of the law. As in Switzerland, not every contradiction to the law will be considered a sufficient ground to do so. The court always has a possibility in its sole discretion to provide judicial protection to the contract which, despite a formal violation of the law, does not expressly provide for the commission of prohibited actions. In *Bassidji v Simon Soul Sun Goe*[34] the Court of Appeals for the Ninth Circuit held as follows:

> ... whatever flexibility may otherwise exist with regard to the enforcement of "illegal" contracts, courts will not order a party to a contract to perform an act that is in direct violation of a positive law directive, even if that party has agreed, for consideration, to perform that act.[35]

In Russia, Article 168(1) of the Civil Code makes transactions violating the requirements of a law or other legal acts voidable, which means that they become invalid only if and when a court declares them to be null and void. However, according to Part 2 of the same article, a transaction that violates the requirements of a law or other legal acts and thus infringes upon public interests or the rights and legitimate interests of third parties is void. This rule is subject to a caveat that even in a latter case the law may directly specify that such a transaction is voidable or provide for other consequences of the violation of the law other than the invalidity of the transaction.

Today in Russia there is no published case law on the question of whether a transaction made, for example, in violation of the above-mentioned Presidential Decree №560 of 6 August 2014 "On the application of certain special economic measures to ensure the security of the Russian Federation", would be voidable or void. The resolution of this issue will depend on the position of the respective court as to whether the contract which violates said Presidential Decree would also infringe on public interests.

The notion of "public interest", in turn, requires additional interpretation. Some authors believe that the expression "public interest" in Article 168 Civil Code includes the interests of the Russian Federation, its regional governments, municipalities, and the interests of an indefinite number of persons.[36] Other

---

34   *Massoud Bassidji v Simon Soul Sun GOE*. (15 June 2005) United States Court of Appeals, Ninth Circuit, 413 F.3d 928.

35   ibid 936; Geisinger (n 10) 414.

36   Nataliya Ageshkina and others, 'Kommentarij k Grazhdanskomu kodeksu Rossijskoj Federacii. Chast' pervaja ot 30 nojabrja 1994 g. N 51-FZ (postatejnyj)' [Commentary to the Civil Code of the Russian Federation. Part One of 30 November 1994 N 51-FZ (clause by clause)] (Prepared for Consultant Plus, 2014) Commentary to Article 168.

researchers point out that not every concern of a public authority is properly a public interest. For example, when a statute or another legal act aims to cater to the needs of a particular business community and not those of society as a whole, one cannot equate the government's interest in the enforcement of such regulation with the public interest.[37]

Paragraph 75 of the Resolution of the Plenum of the Supreme Court of the Russian Federation Plenum of 23 June 2015 №25 "On the application by the courts of some provisions of Section I of Part i of the Civil Code of the Russian Federation" contains the following statement. In Articles 166 and 168 of the Civil Code, the notion of "public interest" includes, in particular, the interests of an indefinite number of people, matters related to public safety and public health, as well as defence, security, and protection of the environment. Transactions which contravene an express prohibition of the law are null and void because they infringe on the public interest. This rule applies, for example, to a pledge or an assignment of claims which are inextricably linked with the creditor's personality (Article 336(1), Article 383 Civil Code), and insurance of illegal interests (Article 928 Civil Code). In itself, a discrepancy between the contract and the rules of law, or a violation of the rights of a public authority, does not mean that there is an infringement of the public interest.

There is no doubt that the conclusion of a contract in breach of the Presidential Decree mentioned above should render the contract invalid. As a matter of principle, it seems more logical to consider such a contract voidable so that the court in each case would have an opportunity to assess all the circumstances of the case, the motives of the parties, the information available at the moment when the parties signed the agreement, and so on. This position, in turn, would have to be based on a narrow interpretation of the concept of "public interest" in Article 168(2) of the Civil Code which would exclude Russia's foreign policy interests. Given the wording of the above position by the Supreme Court, it seems more likely that a Russian court would consider such a contract to be void and not voidable. In arbitral proceedings where the

---

37   Evgeniy Sukhanov, 'O chastnyh i publichnyh interesah v razvitii korporativnogo prava' ['On Private and Public Interests in Corporate Development'] (2013) 1 Journal of Russian Law 5; Andrej Stepanchenko, 'Inostrannye investicii i torgovaja politika chlenov VTO v ramkah Soglashenija po investicionnym meram, svjazannym s torgovlej' in Viktor Perevalov (ed) *Pravo Vsemirnoj torgovoj organizacii: vlijanie na jekonomiku i zakonodatel'stvo gosudarstv Evropejsko-Aziatskogo regiona* ['Foreign Investment and Trade Policies of WTO Members under the Agreement on Investment Measures Related to Trade' in Viktor Perevalov (ed) *The Law of the World Trade Organization: The Impact on the Economy and Legislation of the European-Asian Region*] (Statut 2014).

substantive law of the Russian governs the merits of a dispute the tribunal, of course, will have more freedom in the interpretation of these provisions.

A prerequisite for the application of the rules on the invalidity of contracts discussed above is the determination of the substantive law applicable to the rights and obligations of the parties. The substantive law of the Russian Federation will apply where the choice of law clause in the contract so provides,[38] or where the conflict of law rules lead to the application the Russian substantive law. In this case, it is almost certain that the provisions of Presidential Decree №560 of 6 August 2014 and Article 168 of the Civil Code will apply to such contract. Similarly, it will be evident that the validity of this contract cannot be determined, for example, by the provisions of Article 20 (1) of the Swiss Code of Obligations or the contract law of any US state.

However, the impact of economic sanctions enacted before the conclusion of the contract but not forming a part of the applicable law is not as straightforward. Theoretically, if there is a sufficient connection between the object of the contract and the parties' obligations, and the country which adopted the economic sanctions, the court or the arbitral tribunal may also conclude that a contract is invalid and refuse to enforce it.

In the English case *Regazzoni v Sethia*[39] the contract between the parties was for the sale and delivery of jute bags from India to Italy for their subsequent resale in South Africa. The parties knew at the time of contracting that the export of jute to South Africa was illegal under the Indian laws; English law governed the contractual relationship. The seller refused to perform the contract, and the buyer sought damages. The House of Lords decided that the contract was unenforceable, and the buyer could not recover damages where the agreement was contrary to the law of a friendly and foreign State. This conclusion had its roots in considerations of public policy and international comity. As Viscount Simonds pointed out in his speech in the House of Lords, an English court will not entertain a suit by a foreign State to enforce its laws of a penal, revenue or political character. It is, however, nothing else than comity to refuse as a matter of public policy to enforce, or to award damages for the breach of, a contract which involves the violation of foreign law on foreign soil.[40]

---

38 According to art 1210 of the Russian Civil Code, the parties to the contract may, in the contract itself or after its conclusion, select by agreement between themselves the law that is applicable to their rights and obligations under this contract.

39 *Regazzoni v KC Sethia (1944) Ltd.* (1957) 3 WLR 752, (1958) AC 301 at 318–319.

40 ibid.

Professor Hans van Houtte argues that arbitral tribunals can directly apply economic sanctions which do not form a part of the proper law of the contract under three conditions. First, the sanctions have to consider themselves applicable to the case under the wording of the relevant legal instrument. Second, there must be a sufficient jurisdictional link between the economic sanctions and the transaction. Finally, arbitrators should only take sanctions into account if they deem it appropriate after consideration of all the elements of the case.[41]

It is hard to dispute that restrictive measures originating in a decision of the UN Security Council must be applied to contracts, even if the government of the target country attempts to neutralise their effect through its domestic law – as Iraq did in 1990.[42] In this case, one could argue that given the hierarchy of the law, the UN sanctions constitute a part of Iraqi law as international peremptory norms, and compliance with them remains an international legal obligation of Iraq despite the adoption of conflicting domestic legislation.

The possibility that noncompliance with other types of economic sanctions, i.e. those which are not based on the UN Charter and do not form a part of the proper law of the contract might also lead to the invalidity of the contract is quite controversial. An international arbitral tribunal is likely to view the arguments on the applicability of such sanctions with some scepticism. For example, in *Götaverken* the contract for the supply of three oil tankers between the Swedish seller and the Libyan buyer was governed by Swedish law. The buyer refused to accept the delivery citing the Libyan boycott extending to all commercial relations with Israel. The arbitral tribunal considered these restrictive measures to be irrelevant for the resolution of the dispute, except to the extent that the contract itself provided for their applicability. The only mention of these sanctions in the agreement was the seller's obligation to provide a certificate confirming that the construction of the ships did not involve the use of materials and equipment manufactured in Israel. The seller provided such a certificate, so the buyer had no grounds for refusal to perform the contract.[43]

---

41   Hans van Houtte (n 24) 168.

42   The 1990 Iraqi law 'On the protection of property rights and interests of Iraq in the country and abroad'.

43   *Shipyard, AB Götaverken (Sweden) v Libyan General Maritime Transport Organization (GMTO) (Libya), General National Maritime Transport Company (GMTC) (successor First Defendant) (Libya)* Award in Case Nos. 2977, 2978 and 3033 in 1978, ICC Award No 2977 (1981) Yearbook Commercial Arbitration, 133.

3.2   *Impossibility of Contractual Performance*

Ascertaining the impossibility to perform the contract also requires that two main conditions must be in place: the sanctions must have entered into force after the conclusion of the contract, and their introduction must indeed constitute an obstacle to its proper performance.

According to Article 119 of the Swiss Code of Obligations, an obligation is discharged where its performance has become impossible by circumstances for which the debtor cannot be made responsible. The adoption of acts by public authorities that prohibit actions forming part of the debtor's obligations under the contract, as a rule, falls under this definition of a supervening impossibility. At the same time, there is a condition for the application of this rule, namely that the debtor did not and could not foresee the events which would make it impossible to perform its obligations under the contract. In one of the cases decided in 1985 by the Federal Tribunal, a Swiss company agreed to build and deliver the atomic installation "Mini 8067" to Pakistan. Subsequently, the Federal Office of Energy imposed a ban on the delivery of a similar installation "8062 Micro", and the seller did not perform its obligation on the ground that it has become impossible to do so under Article 119 of the Code. The Federal Tribunal rejected this argument and pointed out that the debtor was responsible for the legal impossibility of performance where he knew or should have known, having investigated the matter with due diligence at the time of conclusion of the contract, that the circumstances preventing the proper performance could arise. In the present case, the adoption of such a ban was foreseeable for the debtor. The provisions of the law give the Federal Office of Energy the right to impose such a ban at any time. Exporters of nuclear technology must always expect that the Federal Council may, due to unforeseen political events in the world, introduce some restrictions in the energy industry.[44]

Similarly, Article 416 of the Russian Civil Code provides that the subsequent impossibility of performance shall terminate the obligation where it is due to circumstances for which none of the parties is responsible. A specific ground for the termination of obligations is laid down in Article 417 of the Civil Code. This Article stipulates that where the performance of an obligation becomes impossible in whole or in part as a result of an act by a State or a local authority, the obligation is terminated in whole or in relevant part. Given that the termination under Article 417 of the Civil Code entails the possibility for the contracting parties to recover the resulting damages from the relevant public authority, it is logical to apply this ground only to acts of the Russian Federation,

---

44   Geisinger (n 10) 416.

its regional government authorities and local authorities. Therefore, in cases where the impossibility of performance is due to the enactment of a restrictive measure by a foreign State, obligations of the parties shall terminate according to Article 416 of the Civil Code (if applicable under rules of private international law) and not Article 417.

In the United States, the Uniform Commercial Code (UCC) establishes in § 2-615:

> Delay in delivery or non-delivery in whole or in part by a seller ... is not a breach of his duty under a contract for sale if performance as agreed has been made impracticable by the occurrence of a contingency the non-occurrence of which was a basic assumption on which the contract was made or by compliance in good faith with any applicable foreign or domestic governmental regulation or order whether or not it later proves to be invalid.

These provisions of the Uniform Commercial Code have been accepted in judicial practice and are known as "commercial impracticability". For example, in *Harriscom Svenska v Harris Corp.*,[45] the court applied this doctrine to excuse non-performance of an obligation, even when the relevant government regulation was not formalised in the form of a binding legal act, but constituted merely a recommendation. In this case, it was a recommendation not to supply military equipment to Iran.[46]

It is noteworthy that, for the establishment of the impossibility of contractual performance, it does not matter whether the economic sanctions in question are a part of the proper law of the contract. Indeed, to declare the contract void, it is necessary to understand whether compliance with a government prohibition was legally binding on the parties. Conversely, to determine whether it was impossible to perform the contract, it is more important to understand how significant the practical effect of this prohibition was on the contractual performance. For example, a contract between two Russian companies governed by Russian law may require the parties to carry out some activity in the territory of China. If later the Chinese Government enacts a regulation expressly prohibiting such activity, there can be no doubt that it will have become legally impossible to perform the obligations (Article 416 Russian Civil Code).

---

45   *Harriscom Svenska, AB v Harris Corp.*, 3 F.3d 576 (2d Cir. 1993).
46   Geisinger (n 10) 418–419.

There have been reported cases in Russia and elsewhere where a reference to economic sanctions was regarded only as an excuse and not a genuine reason for non-fulfilment of the contractual duties. Thus, in a decision of the Commercial (Arbitrazh) Court of the Sverdlovsk region of 3 April 2015 the parties entered into a contract for the sale of pink salmon which the defendant did not perform. As a reason for non-fulfilment of contractual obligations, he referred to Presidential Decree №560 of 6 August 2014 "On the application of certain special economic measures to ensure the security of the Russian Federation" and the subsequent Decree of the Russian Government. These legal instruments listed the agricultural products, raw materials and foodstuffs prohibited for import into the territory of the Russian Federation. The consequence of these Russian countermeasures was a significant increase in the price of the fish which the defendant undertook to deliver to the plaintiff. These circumstances were purportedly *force majeure* (unforeseeable and insurmountable) since without making the performance of the contract is impossible as such, they significantly increased the cost of purchase of the goods from the manufacturer. The Court rejected this argument, pointing out that according to Article 2 (1) of the Civil Code, business activities are carried out independently, at one's own risk, and aim at systematically deriving a profit. Therefore, having entered into a contract with the plaintiff for the supply of frozen fish, the defendant, not being the manufacturer of the product, accepted all possible risks, including that of an increase of the costs.[47]

In the ICC case 1782/1973,[48] a German and a Yugoslav company signed a contract for the supply and maintenance of trucks in three Arab countries. After these countries introduced sanctions against Israel, it became impossible for the defendant's employees who were Israeli citizens to obtain visas to carry out services under the contract. The respondent submitted that these circumstances amount to *force majeure* and make the performance of the contract impossible. The tribunal rejected this argument, pointing out that it does not explain the 26-month delay in fulfilling the obligations under the contract. As a company, the respondent also had the right to hire nationals of other countries to perform the work.

---

47   The decision of the Commercial Court of Sverdlovsk region of 3 April 2014 in case No A60-825/2015.

48   ICC award in case No 1782/1973, JDI 1975, 923–924.

4   Challenge and Enforcement of Arbitral Awards

State courts' control of the decisions of international commercial arbitration is limited and carried out strictly within limits provided for by the national law.[49] Article V of the 1958 New York Convention defines the grounds to refuse enforcement of foreign arbitration awards which, therefore, are uniform across all Contracting States of the Convention. The grounds for challenging an award in the courts of countries of the seat of arbitration, on the opposite, are exclusively within the competence of every individual domestic legislature. To date, there are no international treaties that would govern the grounds for setting aside arbitral awards in the country of their making.

At the same time, the UNCITRAL Model Law on International Commercial Arbitration is an example of successful harmonisation of national laws across different countries. It serves as a model for the national statutory regulation of international commercial arbitration in more than 80 States.[50] Article 34 of the Model Law listing the grounds for setting aside an award is identical to Article V of the New York Convention. In non-Model Law countries, the list of grounds for challenging an award may differ. However, even in such jurisdictions (which include, among others, England and Scotland), the main ideas behind these grounds, if not their wording, has significant similarities to those established in the New York Convention.

In those countries where the law permits the review of an award on the merits in some form, the court may verify the correctness of the tribunal's approach to the validity or invalidity of the contract, the presence or absence of *force majeure* (see the discussion above). For example, section 69 of the English Arbitration Act of 1996 provides that, unless the parties agree otherwise, a party to arbitral proceedings may (upon notice to the other parties and the tribunal) appeal to the court on a question of law arising out of an award made in the proceedings. The court will grant the leave to appeal under this section if several conditions are present. First, the determination of the question must substantially affect the rights of one or more of the parties. Second, the question must be one which the tribunal was asked to determine. Third, according to the findings of fact in the award, the decision of the tribunal on

---

49   Sergey Kurochkin, *Gosudarstvennye sudy v tretejskom razbiratel'stve i mezhdunarodnom kommercheskom arbitrazhe* [State Courts in Domestic and International Commercial Arbitration] (Wolters Kluwer, 2008) 7.

50   UNCITRAL Model Law on International Commercial Arbitration (1985), with amendments as adopted in 2006 <https://uncitral.un.org/en/texts/arbitration/modellaw/commercial_arbitration/status> accessed 20 November 2021.

the question must be obviously wrong, or it must be of general public importance, and the decision must be at least open to serious doubt. Finally, the court should be satisfied that despite the agreement of the parties to resolve the matter by arbitration, it is just and proper in all the circumstances for the court to determine the question.[51] This situation is a specific feature of the English Arbitration Act; the UNCITRAL Model Law excludes the possibility to appeal the award on such grounds.

In most countries, courts can consider economic sanctions from the standpoint of their impact on the arbitrability of the dispute and their interpretation as matters of public policy, i.e. as grounds for setting aside or refusing recognition and enforcement of an arbitral award. Courts can review the issues relating to both arbitrability and public policy at the place where the award was made, and in any of the countries where the winning party may seek its recognition and enforcement. Article v of the New York Convention and Article 34 of the UNCITRAL Model Law allow the court to scrutinise both of these grounds on its initiative, without the need for the parties to raise the issue and provide relevant evidence.

4.1   *Arbitrability of the Dispute*

Legal literature traditionally defines the arbitrability of a dispute as the possibility of its referral to arbitration in principle. According to Article v (2) of the New York Convention of 1958, the recognition and enforcement of an arbitral award may be refused if the competent authority in the country where recognition and enforcement is sought finds that the dispute is not capable of settlement by arbitration under the law of that country. Article 34 of the UNCITRAL Model Law on International Commercial Arbitration contains a similar provision: an arbitral award may be set aside by the court specified in Article 6, if the court finds that the subject-matter of the dispute is not capable of settlement by arbitration under the laws of that State. Some authors distinguish between objective arbitrability (in the meaning indicated above, also known as arbitrability *ratione materiae*), and subjective arbitrability which determines the ability of certain categories of persons to enter into arbitration agreements (arbitrability *ratione personae*).[52] Such authors treat the impact of economic

---

51   For more details, see Bruce Harris, Rowan Planterose and Jonathan Tecks, *The Arbitration Act 1996: A Commentary* (5th edn, Wiley-Blackwell 2014) 357–74.

52   Philippe Fouchard, Emmanuel Gallard and Berthold Goldman, *On International Commercial Arbitration* (Kluwer Law International 1999) 313.

sanctions on the possibility of the referral of a dispute to arbitration as a separate issue covered by the rules on objective arbitrability.[53]

The argument that the imposition of sanctions by a State entails non-arbitrability of connected disputes proceeds as follows. The arbitrators, being merely private individuals, have no authority to hear and determine matters of public law. Issues relating to public policy should be resolved only by national or international courts where the decision-making can take into account not only the technical wording of the law but also the political and legal motives behind the government regulation. Moreover, in international arbitration, arbitrators do not "belong" to any particular national legal order. They must comply solely with the procedural law on arbitration in the country of the arbitral seat; they might be citizens of other States or stateless persons which makes them even less fit to resolve disputes of public legal significance. The argument is essentially the same as the one used to exclude from the scope of international commercial arbitration disputes concerning antitrust regulation, patents, and legislation on the securities market.

Nevertheless, already in 1999, famous French authors called this logic outdated.[54] Indeed, if the tribunal simply resolves a dispute between the two parties of a commercial transaction, it is hard to see how the application of legal rules of whatever kind to this private controversy could have an adverse impact on public law and policy. If the remedy against the losing party in arbitration were solely the obligation to pay a sum of money, such a result would be perfectly consistent with the spirit of the arbitration agreement between the parties who from the very beginning agreed to refer their dispute to international arbitration. Even if the tribunal employs an interpretation of rules of public law different from that which the court might adopt, it does not change the situation. By entering into an arbitration agreement, the parties accept that the interpretation of the substantive law by the tribunal will be final. This interpretation, regardless of its correctness on the merits, cannot be verified by the national court (except in countries where the law provides mechanisms similar to section 69 of the English Arbitration Act mentioned above).

One can think of at least two possible arguments justifying the monopoly of State courts in the interpretation and application of the public law rules concerning economic sanctions. First, the losing party may attempt to recover the

---

53   ibid 358–359.
54   ibid 358.

sums it lost in the arbitration as damages from the State authority that adopted the economic sanctions, if they caused the non-performance or improper performance of the contract. However, the arbitral award will not be binding nor will it be *res judicata* for the relevant State authority. Therefore, all factual and legal aspects of the case will have to be reviewed again by a competent court. Also, particularly if the decision on the adoption of economic sanctions was in some way inconsistent with law, recovery of damages from a public authority is not something out of the ordinary. Such a mechanism already exists, in particular, under Article 417 of the Civil Code of Russian Federation. Second, in theory, the arbitration tribunal might order the losing party to perform some actions expressly deemed illegal under an act imposing the sanctions. However, this award will not have an immediate effect. For its implementation, the winning party will need to obtain an enforcement order from an appropriate State court. The competent judge will then be able to assess whether such a performance would be consistent with the law and may refuse the enforcement on the grounds of public policy related to the remedy, rather than to the original arbitrability of a dispute between the parties. If the sanctions in question were not UN Security Council based measures, the decision would remain enforceable in third countries that chose not to accede to the sanctions regime. In the latter fact, again, it is hard to see a convincing argument against the arbitrability of the dispute.

This argument was accepted by Italian courts in the famous case *Société Fincantieri Cantieri*. In that case, three Italian companies and the Iraqi Ministry of Defense entered into three contracts for the supply of warships. The contractual performance became impossible when in 1990 the UN Security Council Resolution established an embargo on shipments to Iraq. The contracts contained an arbitration clause, but the Italian companies filed a lawsuit in a State court in Italy arguing that because of the imposition of international sanctions on Iraq, the dispute became non-arbitrable. The trial court rejected this argument, but the Genoa Court of Appeal reversed the decision and held that the dispute could not be subject to arbitration according to Article 806 of the Italian Code of Civil Procedure. This article states that parties may refer disputes arising between them to arbitrators, except such disputes which may not be the subject of a settlement. The Court pointed out that the UN and the European Union sanctions no longer allow the parties to dispose of their rights under the contract freely, and the submission of the dispute to arbitration can lead to a result expressly prohibited by international sanctions. The Court examined the case on the merits and ruled in favour of the Italian plaintiffs. Subsequently, the Court of Appeal in Paris refused to enforce this decision in

France and criticised it, holding that the dispute was subject to arbitration, and the Italian court had no jurisdiction to hear it.[55]

A related case came before the ICC tribunal in Geneva (Switzerland) in 1994. A Syrian citizen put forward a claim against two Italian companies, demanding the payment of an agency fee for the conclusion of contracts for the supply of military equipment to Iraq. The respondents argued that the dispute had become non-arbitrable because of the introduction of the embargo on Iraq. The interim award by a sole arbitrator rejected this argument and confirmed the tribunal's jurisdiction to hear the case. The arbitrator pointed out that he did not doubt the fact that the rules of national and international law, the existence of which the respondents indicated, can be regarded as a part of the international public order. However, the application of such rules by an arbitral tribunal and the arbitrability of the claim are two different things. The mere fact that the arbitrator will be required to apply those or other public law rules in resolving the case does not mean that the dispute becomes non-arbitrable. An arbitrator is under an obligation to follow the requirements of the international ordre public but is not required, for this reason alone, to decline jurisdiction to hear the dispute.[56] The respondents challenged the interim award, but the Swiss Federal Tribunal agreed with the views of the sole arbitrator.[57]

4.2   *Public Policy*

According to Article V of the New York Convention of 1958, recognition and enforcement of an arbitral award may be refused if the competent authority in the country where recognition and enforcement is sought finds that ... the recognition or enforcement of the award would be contrary to the public policy of that country. Article 34 (2) of the UNCITRAL Model Law on International Commercial Arbitration contains a similar provision: an arbitral award may be set aside by the court specified in Article 6 if the award is in conflict with the public policy of this State.

---

55   'Legal Department du Ministère de la Justice de la République d'Irak v Société Fincantieri Cantieri Navali Italiani, Société Finmeccanica et Société Armamenti E Aerospazio' 05/05404 (Cour d'Appel de Paris, 15 June 2006). For more details, see Ivan Philippov and Yaraslau Kryvoi, 'Russia's Mistral Deal under International Sanctions Will the Dispute be Arbitrable?' (LexisPSL Arbitration, 3 October 2014) <www.lexisnexis.com/uk/lexispsl/arbitration/document/406209/5D8R-6JP1-DXP5-44G8-00000-00/Russia_s_Mistral_deal _under_international_sanctions_will_the_dispute_be_arbitrable_#> accessed 20 November 2021.

56   Partial Award in Case No. 6719, JDI 1994, 1071–1081.

57   *Fincantieri Cantieri Navali Italiani SpA et OTO Melara Spa v ATF* (Switzerland, 23 June 1992) Tribunal Fédéral.

The public policy exception is like an "emergency brake" which State courts may use when faced with an award which is unacceptable for some reason, in the absence of other grounds to refuse recognition and enforcement, or to set it aside at the seat of arbitration. Despite the broad wording of this exception, most experts agree that in the New York Convention of 1958, as well as in domestic arbitration law, one should interpret it with caution. Public policy must not be confused with public law because it defines only the most basic, core values of the legal system.[58]

If an arbitral award contradicts a prohibition imposed by an economic sanctions instrument, the State court will have to face a question whether it should equate the interests of the State's foreign policy and the "public policy" as defined in Article v of the New York Convention of 1958. Several court decisions from the United States provide some guidance on the various aspects of correlation between the two concepts.

According to the rule in the famous case *Parsons & Whittemore Overseas Co.*, the notion of "public policy" must be interpreted restrictively and the enforcement of a foreign arbitral award may be refused on this ground only when it would violate the most basic concepts of morality and justice in the enforcing State. In that case, the award debtor relied on a severance of diplomatic relations between the United States and Egypt in connection with the Arab-Israeli armed conflict. According to the defendant, he had to withdraw from the contract for reasons of solidarity with his country's policy. The Court of Appeal rejected these objections, pointing out in particular that the national policy of the United States and "public policy" under Article v of the New York Convention of 1958 are different categories which must not be confused with each other.[59]

Ministry of Defense of the Islamic Republic of Iran v Gould, Inc. was one of the rare occasions when the US court refused the recognition and enforcement of an arbitral award on grounds of public policy. In that case, the Iran Ministry of War and an American contractor signed a contract for the supply of military equipment. The Iranian side handed over to the contractor communication

---

58   Vladimir Yarkov, 'Proizvodstvo po delam o priznanii i privedenii v ispolnenie reshenij inostrannyh sudov i inostrannyh arbitrazhnyh reshenij' (kratkij kommentarij k glave 31 APK)' [Proceedings Concerning the Recognition and Enforcement of Foreign Judgments and Foreign Arbitral Awards (a brief comment to Chapter 31 of the Code of Commercial Procedure)] (2003) 5 Arbitrazhnyj i grazhdanskij process [Arbitration and Civil Procedure] 6.

59   *Parsons & Whittemore Overseas Co. v Societe General de l'Industrie du Papier (RAKTA)*, 508 F.2d 969, 977 (2d Cir 1974).

equipment necessary for the proper performance of the contract. When after the introduction of sanctions against Iran the performance of the contract became impossible, the parties submitted the dispute to arbitration. Among other things, the resulting award stipulated that the contractor had to return the equipment to Iran. However, it was the military radio equipment which the contractor under the then current US law could not export to the State that "repeatedly provided support for acts of international terrorism." For this reason, the United States District Court refused the enforcement of this part of the award, adding that "if these restrictions are lifted within a reasonable time after this Order is entered, then the defendants must return or make available the equipment as directed by the Award."[60] Iran appealed the decision, but on appeal, the parties settled the case. In this situation, indeed, it would be hard to imagine that the act expressly prohibited by law would have received the support of courts in the United States.[61]

In a sense, the 2011 decision of the Court of Appeal for the Ninth Circuit in *Ministry of Defense of Iran v Cubic Defense Systems* takes an intermediate position between the two situations above. In this case, the Iraqi Ministry of Defense and the US company entered into a contract in 1977 for the supply of military navigation systems. In 1979, in connection with the 1979 Iranian Revolution, the US sanctions had been imposed against Iran, prohibiting the export of equipment to Iran. The next installment of sanctions also made all payments for the benefit of citizens and companies from Iran subject to the authorisation by the relevant US public authority. The arbitral tribunal held the hearings in Tehran, and in 1997 made a final award ordering the contractor to pay a sum of money as damages. The United States District Court took a long time to consider the Ministry's application for recognition and enforcement of the arbitral award (there were several related proceedings concerning the same dispute). Then the judgment was appealed, and the case culminated in the Court of Appeal decision in 2011. Relying on the familiar rule in *Parsons & Whittemore Overseas Co.*, the appeal court stated that the considerations of foreign policy, which includes sanctions against Iran, are not identical to public policy, and agreed with the district court's confirmation of the ICC award. Regarding restrictions on the payment of money in favour of the Iranian Government, the court pointed out that the confirmation of a foreign arbitral award is not the same as payment in cash. The US Treasury Department's Office of Foreign Assets Control has the right to issue a license for the actual

---

60   *Ministry of Defense of the Islamic Republic of Iran v Gould Inc.* 887 F.2d 1357; certiorari denied, 110 S.Ct. 1319.
61   Geisinger (n 10) 429–430.

transfer of funds.[62] Until it does so, or until the United States lifts the sanctions against Iran, one solution could be that the money would remain in a special 'blocked' account which neither of the parties will be able to access.[63]

The commentators welcomed this decision taking it as yet another confirmation that the US courts are committed to a narrow interpretation of the public policy exception in Article v of the New York Convention.[64] However, one cannot help but notice that the actual transfer of funds in favour of the claimant – which, of course, is the main goal for any disputant in arbitration – never ensued. In 2013, the District Court for the Southern District of California attached the Cubic's award debt in favour of the third parties with claims against Iran. It happened in *Ministry of Defense of Iran v Cubic Defense Systems and Jenny Rubin et al.*, on an application of several US citizens who had previously obtained court decisions for the compensation of damage caused to them by acts of terrorism. The defendant in those previous cases was the Islamic Republic of Iran as a State which provided support to terrorism. In the absence of other assets in the United States belonging to Iran, the court found it possible to attach this debt. The money which Cubic Defense Systems owed to Iran under the terms of the arbitral award accounted for only a small percentage of the total debt of Iran to US citizens – victims of terrorism. Although Iran's assets in the United States would otherwise have been immune from execution, since the courts established the fact of the financing of terrorism by Iran, they lost their claim to sovereign immunity.[65]

Thus, although on the face of it, the public policy exception was deemed inapplicable in this case and the US economic sanctions did not amount to a sufficient ground for refusing recognition and enforcement of an arbitral award, the outcome the dispute seems perfectly compatible with the US foreign policy considerations. The money of a US corporation that supplied military equipment to Iran was used to compensate the damage that American citizens suffered from terrorism. The winning party in the arbitration, the

---

62   *Ministry of Def. & Support for the Armed Forces of the Islamic Republic of Iran v Cubic Def. Sys., Inc.*, 665 F.3d 1091 (9th Cir 2011).

63   Aybek Akhmedov, *'Pirrova pobeda Irana'* [Pyrrhic Victory for Iran] (Russian Arbitration Association, 3 June 2014) <https://arbitration.ru/press-centr/news/pirrova-pobeda -irana/> accessed 20 November 2021.

64   Grant Hanessian (ed), ICDR Awards and Commentaries, Volume 1 (Juris Publishing 2012) 480–484.

65   *Ministry of Def. & Support for Armed Forces of Islamic Republic of Iran v Cubic Def. Sys., Inc.*, 984 F.Supp. 2d 1070 (SD Cal 2013), aff'd sub nom. *Ministry of Def. & Support for the Armed Forces of the Islamic Republic of Iran v Frym*, 814 F.3d 1053 (9th Cir 2016).

Islamic Republic of Iran, spent more than a decade before the US courts but obtained no payment.

5   Conclusion

As shown above, economic sanctions do have a major impact on the functioning of the mechanism of international commercial arbitration. Despite the fact that they are a product of foreign policy decisions and altogether a phenomenon of a different order compared to commercial disputes, their impact on private interests is hard to overlook. Legal issues that arise in such interactions are often complex and require careful analysis in every case.

There is no doubt that sanctions adopted by the UN Security Council resolutions under the UN Charter have greater weight than national laws. Attempts to neutralise such resolutions through the adoption of domestic legislation are unlikely to look persuasive for arbitral tribunals that will take into account the rules of international public order. The validity of a reference to UN Security Council-based restrictive measures as a circumstance entailing the invalidity of the contract, the impossibility of contractual performance or the need to refuse recognition and enforcement of an arbitral award on the grounds of public policy, as a rule, will be straightforward for the decision-maker. However, sanctions adopted by individual States or groups of States present more complex questions. International arbitral tribunals should find out whether they are part of the proper law of the contract; whether any legitimate countermeasures exist in the target State and third countries; whether they conform with the conventional understanding of the limits of the extraterritorial jurisdiction where the sanctions instrument makes such an attempt.

Based on the existing practice and doctrine, any impact of sanctions on the arbitrability of disputes seems unlikely. However, it is possible to use them as a reason for refusing recognition and enforcement of arbitral awards (or setting an award aside at the seat of arbitration) on the grounds of public policy. Such a refusal may be justified, first and foremost, when the award requires the losing party to perform an action expressly prohibited by the economic sanctions legislation. The mere fact of the existence of sanctions and their consideration by an arbitral tribunal is insufficient to invoke the public policy exception.

Parties to commercial agreements must also bear in mind that even a court decision to recognize and enforce an arbitral award, in the atmosphere of high foreign policy tension, does not in itself guarantee the receipt of the award debt. As illustrated by the *Cubic Defense Systems* case discussed above, where full-scale economic sanctions coexist with an ongoing political confrontation, a result functionally equivalent to a denial of recognition and enforcement of an arbitral award may emerge through some alternative legal mechanism.

Conclusions

Alexander Trunk, Marina Trunk-Fedorova, and Azar Aliyev

The region of the Caucasus and Central Asia is politically, economically and legally very diverse. However, the common legacy of the Soviet Union (and even the Russian Empire) is still present, with a considerable influence even on today's societies and legal regulation. Russian legal approaches to topics such as international trade continue to influence or at least serve as a major model of reference in the legal systems of all countries of the region – even if political relations with Russia are strained.

The region of the Caucasus and Central Asia is characterized – politically and legally – by three basic approaches: 1) national resurrection with a strong focus on national identity and national interests, including an "all vectors" policy, 2) in one case (Georgia), a strong orientation towards the West, including the European Union, 3) in the majority of countries, participation in different Eurasian regional structures with Russia as the most influential participant.[1] This is also reflected in the approach to international trade. The "national approach", while present in all countries of the region, has led some countries to a certain self-isolation, others to cooperation with different international partners. The "Western" direction is illustrated, in particular, by regional trade agreements (including Association Agreements) of several countries of the region with the European Union. The most important structure for "Eurasian" cooperation is today the Eurasian Economic Union (EAEU), which was founded in 2015 and comprises several countries of the region plus Belarus as another former USSR republic.

The consequence of these differing approaches is a web of structures, which are related to each other and sometimes in conflict. For example, Armenia is on the one side a member of the EAEU, on the other side it has concluded with the European Union an Enhanced Partnership Agreement, and its domestic legislation oscillates between traditional, Russia-oriented approaches and autonomous reform including suggestions from "the West". A common element of the economy of some countries is their role as an exporter of natural resources including energy, which has led to some specific regulation.

---

1 The growing economic influence of China in this region has not been specifically addressed in this volume and has, in any case in the legal field, not reached a level comparable with Russia.

© KONINKLIJKE BRILL NV, LEIDEN, 2023 | DOI:10.1163/9789004357839_030

The purpose of the research project underlying this book was, consequently, not to discover exclusive legal characteristics of the Caucasus and Central Asian region, but to gain information on legal structures and discussions in this region. Some structures of political and legal cooperation in the Eurasian region are specific (in particular the CIS and the EAEU), but most legal issues discussed in this book are of a general character, yet deserve a closer look on how they function in the Eurasian (Caucasus and Central Asian) region.

The research done within the underlying project has produced a broad range of results and insights. Some of them will be put forward on a subjective basis in these conclusions. For details and additional research results the contributions in this book should be consulted.

Among the topics of *public international law* (relating to international trade) one aspect has been recurring several times: the relationship between global and regional cooperation or between different groups of regional cooperation among themselves. A highly relevant finding (by Karsten Nowrot) is that membership even in several advanced RTAs is not excluded, although it requires particular endeavours of negotiation. If this finding had been taken into account by political decision-makers in 2013, the Ukraine conflict (which is outside the scope of this book), might have been avoided. In any case, this finding could be an element for solving this conflict in the future.

Another general topic of international economic law is the legal position of international treaties, such as the World Trade Organization (WTO) treaties or regional treaties, in the national legal systems. This topic is addressed in the book from different perspectives, Kazakhstan and Russia. In Kazakhstan, the Constitutional Council of Kazakhstan affirmed the constitutionality of the EAEU treaty, but has significantly limited the effect of the Treaty in case of conflict with the legislation of Kazakhstan by giving EAEU Court judgments only an ad hoc effect. As the EAEU Treaty itself excludes that the EAEU Court declares national legislation inapplicable, one can hardly speak of the EAEU as a "supranational" organization. However, Russian courts are shown to give high value to decisions of the EAEU court and even admit a direct application of WTO law (which is linked to the EAEU) in some cases. EAEU law may thus have quite different effects in the EAEU member states.

Very instructive are, furthermore, for example, the detailed comparative findings in the book on practical difficulties to apply the WTO SPS and TBT Agreements in the region. The current COVID 19-pandemic illustrates the practical relevance of this topic. Highly topical are also the contributions contained in the book about the relationship between international trade law and environmental law. It is shown that environmental protection considerations are growingly entering trade regulation as well, but generally this issue is rarely brought to dispute settlement, and there is an evident lack of enforcement. Practically very instructive is also the analysis in the book of the practice in Russia concerning the common Customs Code of the EAEU.

In the part of the book devoted to *private law* the comparative notes on sales law and international sales law (or international contract law) in the Caucasus and Central Asian region should be noted, which show the particular approaches in Georgia and Azerbaijan in these fields. Contributions by staff members of UNCITRAL illustrate the necessity to make international uniform law texts better known in the region.

The *dispute settlement* part of this book illustrates the practical relevance of solving possible "conflicts of jurisdiction" between different systems of dispute settlement (e.g. WTO and RTAS). It is shown that this is less a question of legal dogmatics than of value-based drafting of treaties or procedural agreements between parties. The procedural part of the book elucidates several other topics. For example, valuable insights into the EAEU Court are given, documenting a lively discussion how to make the Court more effective. Some other contributions highlight linkages between public international law and international civil procedure, e.g. as to public policy in international commercial arbitration and as to economic sanctions in international commercial arbitration.

The above-mentioned examples from among the many thoughtful contributions of the book are hoped to illustrate the comparative and analytical approach of this study. Aspects of public international law and private law are treated as joint elements of solving problems in the field of international trade, taking the region of the Caucasus and Central Asia as an example. Country-specific reports should encourage further comparative research, and the comparative reports as well as the general studies on specific aspects of international trade law are meant as a starting-point for future studies.

Index